Breaking Out Of Beerport

A Memoir

Al Scheid

ISBN: 0692255249
ISBN 13: 9780692255247
Library of Congress Control Number: 2014912628
CreateSpace Independent Publishing Platform
North Charleston, South Carolina

Dedication

To my wife, Shirley, who, without complaint, put up with a husband tied to a computer for too many months—and then had the patience to proofread the work. I will be eternally grateful for her loving support.

Thank you, darling.

Shirley Scheid, 2012

FOREWORD

We can change everything about ourselves—
the way we dress, the language we speak, even our facial features.
But we're stuck with our genes.

On that premise, Al Scheid's story begins.

Born of working poor parents in a blue—no, make that black—collar coal mining town on the Ohio/West Virginia border, this is an inspiring story of a young man's journey from a downtrodden provincial village to the Gold Coast of California and beyond.

Not just another vanity "me" book, this is a colorfully written account of the first twenty-seven years of the author's life. But it's more than that. It is a lesson in history, a primer in psychology, and a study of culture. It is about *self-improvement* and *self-realization* long before these new-age terms were invented. Such terms were not in the lexicon of this less-pretentious earlier generation of Americans.

Al's odyssey begins in the early 1930s. The nation's economy and spirits had sunk into what became known as the Great Depression. Though the whole nation suffered, it was particularly pronounced in Bridgeport, a village that was poor even in good times.

History and geography conspired to mold this town that lay along the Ohio River into the "Gateway to the West." Bridgeport had been the "last chance" stop for western-bound pioneers, and as such, gambling parlors, houses of pleasure, and its many saloons flourished. That's when the locals nicknamed the town "Beerport."

Then there were the coal mines and steel mills from which ash and fine black soot raised high in the air and slowly settled back down upon the town and its people. It was a place where the buildings turned brown and the lungs turned black.

The industrial pollution restricted visibility, but worse yet, it seemed to dim the vision and stifle the optimism of those who called Beerport home. These Americans accepted their plight without anger, protest, or a sense of entitlement. They lived difficult lives but didn't seem to notice or mind. They envied neither those who were better off nor the well to do. In fact, achievers were discouraged and socially castigated as braggarts, phonies and show-offs. Most puzzling, these people not only accepted their condition; they seemed to embrace it. There existed a profound unwillingness, almost an inability, to leave Beerport.

This, then, was not a fertile ground for the motivated or ambitious. Yet this book is not about a young man with an insatiable ambition. No. Not there. Not in that town. Rather, it is about a young man who discovered, almost accidentally, that he was better than he thought and smarter than he supposed. With growing confidence, Al began to believe in himself and recognized that the town city limits were more than geographical borders; they were limits to his life. Now, determined to succeed, he had to break out of Beerport.

Thus Al's path to success did not come via strategic planning, sage advice, or expert counsel. Bridgeport was a town devoid of mentors and role models. His success came through happenstance and hard knocks. But with each step up, he found he was another step further away from his town and his friends.

Could he smooth out his rough edges enough to compete with the educated elite? Could he join the highly successful and fit in with the well-heeled? Could he shake the coal dust from his shoes? And how could he possibly break out of Beerport without breaking hearts—his and that of his only true love. Love complicated life.

This unembellished true-life story keeps building with each page. Just when you think you've heard it all, along comes another chapter filled with unexpected twists, new relationships, more surprises, and yes, more life lessons.

Breaking out of Beerport isn't a "how-to" success story. You will, however, be entertained and educated. But mostly, you will come away with hope. Bad times, bad environs, and even some bad behavior don't always result in bad endings.

Though it may be true in life that you can't control the hand you've been dealt, it is equally true that sometimes you can reshuffle the deck, draw a few new cards, and walk away a winner.

Stuart Orbach
Public relations executive and writer
August, 2014

PREFACE

It is as easy to dream a book as it is hard to write one.
—Honore de Balzac, novelist (1799–1850)

Writing a book is a horrible, exhausting struggle,
like a long bout with some painful illness.
One would never undertake such a thing if one
were not driven on by some demon whom
one can neither resist nor understand.
—George Orwell, novelist (1903–1950)

Why did I write this book? In 1986, my oldest daughter and I visited my hometown. I drove her around, showing her places I had lived while describing local characters and things that happened during my life there. After a few hours she said that what she really wanted to know was how I managed to get from this run-down little town to graduate school at Harvard. Then she added, "I love hearing the bits of your early life that you've told me. Why don't you write the whole story for your kids?"

Her question made me think: could I really describe how it happened? The thought of relating my odyssey stewed in my brain for years, but I saw myself as too busy to write a book. Finally, I began writing a chronology of events.

Soon I realized that I was embarked on a voyage of self-discovery. Describing the events was often disturbing. Admitting mistakes was easy – there were so many. Exposing my inner thoughts and emotions was quite difficult, but a story without that part is lifeless.

Real names are used for most of the characters. Where a pseudonym is used, it is because the real name could not be recalled, not to protect anyone.

As in all recitations of a life, some things are left out. First, not all events are interesting. Second, unnecessary digressions should be avoided to keep the story moving along.

I made a pledge to myself to tell the truth to the best of my memory, backed up by research whenever possible. If there was a compelling reason not to tell something the way it actually happened, the event has been left out rather than told in an untrue way. These omissions did not change the story in any significant way.

With most of my days devoted to business, personal affairs, travel, and an irrational urge to lower my golf handicap, the writing stretched out for several years; I'm embarrassed to say how many. However, like every difficult task, if one stays focused and keeps working, the drip eventually wears away the rock. One day in late 2013, I wrote those wonderful words: The End. Then the painful chore of editing began.

So, how did I recall so many incidents and people? Having a strong autobiographical memory is formally called hyperthymesia syndrome.[1] I have a degree of this trait, albeit at a much lower level than the people who are noted for this syndrome. I mention this because a reader may be tempted to believe that some of the events are fictional; they are not. The people all existed, and the dialogue is approximately what was said. I know this to be true because I was there.

The story ahead is told as truthfully as I could make it and written as well as my talents permit. It is my hope that reading my journey might supply some inspiration to young people faced with life problems that often seem insurmountable. Older readers may enjoy revisiting things as they were, many years ago.

Mr. Carson, the butler in the popular 2011- ? TV series *Downton Abbey,* said, "The business of life is the acquisition of memories and, in the end, that's all there is." He summed up the purpose of a memoir quite well.

It is up to you to judge if the time spent writing this book was well invested. As I write this, I am eighty-two and in good health, but there is a dim light glowing at the end of my tunnel – the end can't be far away. Keep in mind that I gave up a lot of golf to write the story of how a lucky boy broke out of a town called Beerport - so many years ago.

---

1 The most noted of these is Mary Lou Henner, a well-known American actress. For further information, use a search engine and look up hyperthymesia syndrome or superior autobiographical memory. It is notable that 2013 research has shown that the people who have this trait have no better ability to recall yesterday's shopping list than the average person.

ACKNOWLEDGEMENTS

As an amateur author I had some trepidation about publishing a book. But, with encouragement from my wife and others, I kept slogging and eventually the job was done.

I must thank Jim Novack, a professional writer, who never did my writing for me, but guided me away from many blind alleys. He was compensated, but he went beyond his assignment in many good ways.

To find out if the book would hold interest, I decided to create a panel of readers. Most of the readers knew little about my life prior to reading this book. The idea was to select people who were book readers, not friends rooting for my success. The women and men on the panel range in age from twenty-one to over seventy. To my surprise nearly all of the feedback I received was positive. They all found the book to be easy reading. I believe the opinions were honest and a few changes were prompted by their comments.

I will make no effort to allocate bits of help and advice to certain individuals, with one exception - Stuart Orbach - who helped me arrive at the final title (it was more his idea than mine). I thank these individuals from the bottom of my heart for their time, patience and opinions.

In alphabetical order, the members of the panel of critics are:

Marcia Basque
Jerry Cassaday
John Crary
Laura Finklestein
Renee Gollnick
Lee Hanson
Gordon Kanofsky
Brahm Levin
Mary Longo
Nevena Orbach
Stuart Orbach
Siena Pugnale
Robert (Ed) Sherer
John Tacha

CHAPTER 1

One cannot be a good historian of the outward, visible world without giving some thought to the hidden, private life of ordinary people; and on the other hand, one cannot be a good historian of this inner life without taking into account outward events where these are relevant.

—Victor Hugo, French writer (1802–1885)

The years between 1800 and 1825 were distinguished, so far as our domestic development was concerned, by the growth of the Western pioneer Democracy in power and self-consciousness.

—Herbert Croly, founder The New Republic (1869-1930)

BEERPORT

A village has to earn a nickname like Beerport. The village of Bridgeport had a colorful existence for over two hundred years before it was tamed. Its culture was foreordained by its geography.

In 1773, Colonel Ebenezer Zane laid out a village on the bank of the east channel opposite a large island. He named it Wheeling and the island Wheeling Island. Soon oxen powered ferries carried travelers across the two channels formed by the Island. Thus was the main migration route into Ohio and beyond established. A trail, a river, and an island had combined to create the basis for two population concentrations.

In 1803, a few months before Ohio became the seventeenth state, a Colonel Zane laid out the village of Canton on the Ohio ferry landing site. Three years later, the state of Virginia built a covered toll bridge from Wheeling Island over the west channel to Ohio and Canton was renamed Bridgeport. The Wheeling Suspension Bridge was completed over the east channel of the River in 1849 (still in operation). It was, for three years, the longest suspension bridge in the world.

Bridgeport became a trading center and the last settlement in which to have a "sin fling" before beginning the long, trek west. A wide street (later named Lincoln Avenue), ran along the top of the riverbank, and was lined with eating establishments, flophouses, stables and saloons. Men came to the saloons, day and night, seeking liquor, gambling, and female companionship, all of which were readily available. Compared to the more civilized culture of the eastern cities, the river people were coarse and crude.

Personalities Develop

Just as human personality is developed in childhood, so were the characters of Bridgeport and Wheeling created in their youth. Bridgeport was a prizefighter of a village where tough people made a living in whatever way they chose, with little regard for rules or laws. The local police kept a modicum of order, but inasmuch as they shared in the profits of illegal activities, they were not inclined to be fussy about law enforcement. It was not a pretty place.

COAL, THE KING; STEEL, THE QUEEN

In the latter part of the 18th century, outcroppings of coal were found within sight of the river. Mines were laboriously dug by hand and mule power brought coal to the surface. Wagons and river barges hauled the coal to wherever it was needed. When steamboats began to ply the Ohio and railroads were built, the demand for coal rose dramatically.

The Civil War began in 1861 and created a huge demand for the paraphernalia of war. The demand for iron and steel skyrocketed; factories and mills soon lined the river. More labor was needed, but few farm boys adapted to the claustrophobic conditions of the mines.

The coal companies recruited labor in Europe. Thousands of miners came from the coal regions of Belgium, Alsace-Lorraine, Wales, England, Russia, Poland, et al. They traveled to an unknown land, seeking a better life far away from oppressive, warring, Europe. In ancient Sparta boys were raised from birth to become soldiers. Just as the generations before them, they were trained to take their turn at fighting and dying. Their women understood and supported them. It was much the same with coal mining families. They were proud men who believed they were a breed apart from those who lacked the courage to venture into the bowels of the Earth. Both my maternal and paternal ancestors were among the coal mining immigrants of the mid to late 19th century.

As industry developed, Wheeling became a banking and commercial center. Bridgeport supplied the area with saloons and gambling. Illegal and immoral activities thrived in this town into the mid-20th century.

In 1914, six years before the nation adopted Prohibition, West Virginia voters made the sale and consumption of alcoholic beverages illegal. That event solidified the Bridgeport culture. West Virginia citizens came across the river in droves for booze and everything that goes with it. The town was nicknamed Beerport. In the period from 1917 to the 1950s, WW I, Prohibition, the prosperity of the twenties, the Great Depression, WWII, and postwar recovery came in quick succession. These events reinforced the tough personality of Beerport. Everyone said the town should be cleaned up. But, like the weather, no one did anything to change it. The system worked too well the way it was

CHAPTER 2

We can change everything about ourselves—
the way we dress, the language we speak,
even our facial features.
But we're stuck with our genes.
—A. Scheid, entrepreneur (1932–living)

Those who cannot remember the past
are condemned to repeat it.
—George Santayana, philosopher (1863–1952)

AN EVOLVING SOCIETY

The immigrants of the Upper Ohio Valley were mostly Middle European, with a smattering from Eastern Europe and the Middle East. The new generations tended to follow the occupations of their parents. The immigrant mind-set did not encourage education beyond age fourteen or so.

Fathers expected their daughters to learn to keep house and marry working husbands by seventeen or soon thereafter. Boys were expected to marry by their early twenties and start families, repeating the cycle.

The wealth level of the working class was, in many ways, a self-fulfilling prophecy. Young people who aspired to higher education were seen as trying to appear better than their family and friends. The desired societal norm was for everyone to be relatively equal in wealth and education - that is, equally poor and equally ignorant.

Wheeling/Bridgeport Environment

Open-hearth and blast furnaces, which converted iron ore and scrap iron to steel worked around the clock and calendar. Their flames lit up the night sky as they spewed smoke and acrid fumes into the air.

This fallout turned buildings (and lungs) darker than their intended colors. When necks were wiped, handkerchiefs came away with blackened sweat; coughing up dark phlegm was so common that it elicited no comment.

Up the river, at Pittsburgh and beyond, mills and factories dumped dirty water used oil and acids into the Ohio. Creeks carried raw sewage from hundreds of villages into the river. This pollution colored the river an ugly dark brown. Catfish and carp, the only species of fish that survived in the river, were eaten only by a few, mostly black, families.

Tree-covered high hills rose steeply from the river and creek basins. When the warmth and showers of spring arrived, the tree leaves became a fresh light green, but they were soon darkened as soot settled during the hot and humid summers. The first frosts temporarily turned leaves into a montage of autumn colors. After leaf drop, the forests were wreathed in their funeral colors and the hills were black. When anointed with fresh snow, all turned white for a day or two before the ever-present fallout created shades of gray.

As the dry summer arrived, Little Wheeling Creek began turning an ugly orange, known as copperas water. This color was created by sulfites, iron oxides, and other compounds from the coal mines. As watershed volume dropped, sewage volume remained the same and the stream gave off an acrid smell. The local name for Little Wheeling Creek was Shit Crick. The rains of winter returned the creek to a more normal color.

Adding to the "idyllic" setting were trains that traveled the banks of Little Wheeling Creek and the river. Each day steam engines, puffing out black smoke and fine ash, pulled long lines of empty cars to the mines. The same engines returned, pulling trains of fully loaded coal cars to river barges.

The Burning Hill

A few miles west of Bridgeport, a hill rose nearly three hundred feet and covered many acres. This mound was created by piling up the tailings from the mines. The massive weight of the hill created enough heat for spontaneous combustion to ignite trapped gases and coal particles. In summer, sun heat gave an assist and flames turned the night sky a fiery red.

Hundreds of families lived within walking distance of this miasma of gasses. The residents became accustomed to the odor of sulfur and the heavy chest feeling caused by the foul air. Wheezing, sneezing, and frequent nose blowing were part of normal life. It was often said that we awakened to the sounds of the birds coughing.

East of the tall hills, east of Wheeling, was where the well-to-do people lived. Mansions lined Route 40 and filled the neighborhood. Wheeling and Ogleby Parks, owned by the city, were there. The Wheeling Country Club was located between the parks.

Such was the scene in our neck of the woods near the end of the Great Depression. There were many better places to live, but this was where my ancestors settled.

View over Bridgeport, Ohio and across Ohio River to Wheeling Island

Aldolphine and Alexis Jonard, my great grandparents, circa 1915

Alexis Jonard family, my grandfather, Alfred, is taller boy on left, circa 1897

My mother and her brothers, L to R, Lawrence, Isabelle, Alex and Alfred Jonard in front, circa 1917

Chapter 3

We are able to find everything in our memory,
which is like a dispensary or chemical
laboratory in which chance steers our hand
sometimes to a soothing drug and
sometimes to a dangerous poison.
—Marcel Proust, French novelist (1871–1922)

From the smallest to the largest, all structures are
begun by building a foundation, and a weak foundation
creates a weak structure. So it is with a human life.
—A. Scheid, entrepreneur (1932–living)

My Parents

George Edward Scheid, Jr., and Isabelle Adolphine Jonard were married on August 22, 1927. She was nineteen and a high school graduate; he was twenty-four and had quit school after the ninth grade. Isabelle's parents, Alfred and Annie Jonard, were not just unhappy with this marriage—they hated it.

The Jonards felt superior to the Scheids. Tiltonsville, where they lived, was an upscale coal town compared to Boydsville, home of the

Scheids. Alfred Jonard had left the mines and struggled with his own small business. It was a distinction with little difference.

About 8 p.m. on Sunday evening, February 7, 1932, Isabelle gave birth to a boy she named Alfred George to honor both grandfathers. I have never cared for Alfred. Only my parents, grandparents, some teachers, and a few smart-ass buddies ever called me by that name.

Mom decided to deliver her child in the Wheeling Hospital, making West Virginia my state of birth. Ohio was, and is, a prosperous, well-organized state, famous as the birthplace of eight presidents, the Wright Brothers, Ohio State University, and many other fine institutions of higher learning. West Virginia was, and is, a poor state. It is known mainly for hillbilly music, mountain men, welfare rolls, bootleg whiskey and Senator Jay Rockefeller - a wealthy New York carpetbagger who bought various high political offices for himself. Another West Virginia Senator, Robert Byrd (deceased) was a Ku Klux Klan member who should have considered it a compliment to be called second rate. Whenever possible, I have always named Ohio as my home state.

One of my uncles said that Mom hadn't planned to have children and that I was an accident. I gave no reply but thought snidely; *At least my parents were married when the accident happened.* This was a claim the uncle couldn't honestly make for his first born.

Health problems were my constant companions during childhood. Apparently, I regurgitated milk within a few minutes after feeding. Breast-feeding didn't work for Mom, so they tried various formulas before finally hitting on one that stayed down.

At about six months, I went into convulsions and began to turn blue. One of my grandfather's sisters gave mouth-to-mouth resuscitation and saved my day. After several similar episodes, epilepsy was discussed. But the "fits" just stopped.

Religion was never part of my parents' culture, but concerns that I might not survive babyhood motivated a baptism. To ensure my safe entry into heaven, I was baptized in a Presbyterian church on Wheeling Island. I have no idea why a Presbyterian church was chosen.

The Great Depression

Times were not tough during the 1930s; they were dreadful. When I was born, Dad was working as a laborer in a steel mill. Work in the mills was an on and off affair; men were often told at the end of their shifts not to show up the next day. Dad managed to attend an evening trade school to become an electrician and he was hired by a small electrical contracting firm in Wheeling.

Mom worked as a sales clerk at the largest department store in Wheeling. During the Depression most businesses didn't hire married women, but Mom lied and said she was single. Her supervisor eventually discovered the truth but turned a blind eye rather than lose a competent employee.

The Scheid Grandparents

George Edward Scheid, Sr., and Elizabeth "Lizzie" Mary Lampkins were married in 1900. Neither of them attended more than a couple of years of grammar school. They were plainspoken people and lived simply.

Starting at age two, I was dropped off weekdays at their apartment. It was a small second-floor walk-up, but their front porch had a swing and a wonderful view of Wheeling Island. This was the only place the George Scheids ever lived that had an indoor toilet and a hot/cold water bathtub. Compared to the coal villages, this was high-style living.

The centerpiece of the kitchen was a cast iron, coal-burning cook stove. At about age three, I put both hands on the side of the hot stove. The burn treatment of the day was wet baking soda spread on the burn area and wrapped loosely with gauze. Water was sprinkled on as needed to keep the baking soda damp. It worked like a charm and the scars on my fingers and palms were gone in a few years.

In warm weather, a river has its own signature perfume. The sumac trees, the types of weeds on the banks, the mud at the river's edge, and probably the pollution, gave the Ohio a heavy, damp scent. The view and the odor are locked in my memory.

Large riverboats, many of them rear wheelers, pushed barges up and downstream. Grandpa told me that some of the boats went to all the way to New Orleans, wherever that was.

My grandparents taught me simple card games like Old Maid and Go Fish. When I was seven they taught me a low brow gambling game called euchre. Mom was not pleased.

FM radio did not exist and AM was still in its infancy. Radio broadcasts were live and suffered many imperfections, but we loved them. The majority of the programming on WWVA was hillbilly music. The opening of a program went something like this: "Hello to all you folks out there in radio land. Welcome to WWVA, your five-thousand-watt station, out of the hills of West Virginia." [2] The announcer would then introduce entertainers like Big Slim McAuliffe, Shug Fisher, Singing Bill Jones, Doc Williams, Wilma Lee, Stony Cooper, and many others.

Big Slim was my favorite, because he often sang a song called "Ole Shep," about a dog that had to be shot. It was a long, slow song that ended with; "If dogs have a heaven, there's one thing I know, Ole Shep has a beaut-ee-ful home." The song made me sad, but I sang along with Slim, imagining that someday I would have a loyal, lovable dog like Shep.

---

2 Later in the 1940s, WWVA was moved to 1170 on the AM dial and became a fifty-thousand-watt station, which it still is at the time of this writing.

Most of the commercials were for over the counter medicines. These remedies promised to cure most everything, from gout to insomnia. Religious items, such as a picture of Jesus that glowed in the dark, were also peddled. I can hear it now; "Imagine, folks, you will hang this picture on your bedroom wall and when you wake up during the night, you'll see our Savior, looking down and blessing you." I ragged Grandpa into buying one, and he hung it in their bedroom. We marveled at its glow. They were not the least bit religious - they hung it just to please me.

Grandpa Scheid

Grandpa was about five feet seven or eight. He had a full head of white hair and a small potbelly. He wore black shoes that laced up over his ankles. He always wore a tie, coat, wide suspenders, and a felt hat. His pants and coat were often mismatched because the coats and pants didn't wear out simultaneously. No one discarded wearable clothing.

His coffee was poured, very hot, into a large cup and sugar and canned milk were stirred in. Then he tilted the cup, spilling some of the steaming brew into the saucer. He picked up the saucer; pinkie finger extended, blew on the coffee, then slurped it—and not quietly. He had a large white mustache, the bottom of which was always coffee stained.

Around 1931, Grandpa was hit by a car and never fully recovered from the back injury he sustained. My Jonard grandfather said he was drunk when the car hit him, which was quite likely true. I always suspected that Grandpa Jonard, who was Belgian by birth, disliked Grandpa Scheid mainly because he was of German descent. The First World War was not far in the past.

For the last decade of his life, Grandpa was a numbers writer. Gambling was illegal in Ohio and West Virginia so, of course, it flourished in Bridgeport. The working man's bet was a dime or a quarter. He picked three numbers which were written on a pad and the bettor received a carbon copy. The winning numbers arrived by phone about five o'clock each day.

Supposedly, the winning numbers were determined by rolling special dice. I have always believed that the guys running the racket did a quick survey of the betting slip copies and picked the number combinations that appeared the least often — thus assuring the lowest payout. [3]

When I was about six, Dad took me into the Carlton Bar to visit Grandpa. Grandpa said if I could give him three numbers; he would bet a dime on them for me. I gave him three, four, and eight. The next evening, Dad announced that I had won and gave me a five dollar bill. Mom was neither pleased nor amused. She now knew I had been in the Carlton and had been introduced to the numbers racket. That's a big day for a first grader.

I don't know if I actually won or Grandpa was just giving me $5. I never saw the money again; it probably went into the family budget. At age fifteen, I actually won at the numbers with three, four, and eight. To this day, these are my presumed lucky numbers.

Grandpa Departs

One day in 1940, Dad got word that Grandpa was ill and took me with him when he rushed to his side. The doctor was there, and his diagnosis was indigestion. Later that day, he died of a heart attack. Doctors made house calls, but inaccurate diagnoses were common.

---

3 Gambling on the numbers was essentially the same racket as state lotteries became many years later. The difference is that the government now gets the money. In some ways, playing the numbers was more moral than the lotteries. There was no advertising, a bettor had to seek a writer, and since it was illegal and not advertised, most people didn't participate. The state lotteries are advertised and publicized to people who can't afford to lose even small amounts. Let's leave it with the observation that the greed of modern government is equal to or exceeds the greed of the gangsters of earlier days.

Grandpa's funeral service was held in the front room of the house we shared with Dad's brother and family. Dad held me up to the coffin and had me touch Grandpa's cold hand. I was shocked that it was not the soft warm hand that I knew so well. As I touched his face, I understood that I'd never see him again. It made me sad, but I didn't cry. I wasn't being brave; I was simply stunned into silence. Even when I watched his casket lowered into the grave, I had no tears, just a lonely, empty feeling. Some sorrow is just too deep for tears.

Few coal miners lived until seventy in those days, so Grandpa had a full run. Old George was buried in Linwood Cemetery, within sight of the burning slag pile that he had helped build.

Grandma Scheid

Elizabeth May Lampkins Scheid was born in 1881, and died in 1952. The Lampkins family always lived in poverty, good times and bad. In the common vernacular, they were thought of as white trash; sad to say, but the truth.

Grandma self-treated her ailments with non-prescription medicines. Lumbago (sore back), grip (flu or cold), liver malfunctions (real or imagined), headaches and other maladies—were all treated from an ever-changing cornucopia of nostrums. An assortment of shoe boxes served as her medicine and instrument cabinets.

She also practiced unusual folk medicine. For instance, she believed that an earache could be cured by stuffing a marble-sized ball of hair from the head of a black man into the affected ear. I never asked how she acquired the raw material for this miracle cure and, thank God, I never had an earache.

Her pet theory was that people with money could buy their health, but poor people had to make do with what they could come by cheaply. She believed that doctors prescribed effective medicines to cure rich people, but they wouldn't share this knowledge with poor people—just because they were poor. Grandma disliked and envied people who had even modest wealth. If Grandma's philosophical thoughts had been analyzed, I believe she would have qualified as a card-carrying Communist.

In the Lampkins family tradition, she avoided work like the plague, but she loved to go shopping. She wore tightly laced corsets under her flowered dresses when we "went to town." In the hot, humid days of summer, the powder and rouge she layered on her face clotted and ran with perspiration; winter was only a little better. The only value to these trips was the acquisition of the latest miracle cure she'd heard about on the radio.

These excursions were exciting for me. The streetcar went over the Bridgeport Bridge, across the Island, and then on to the Steel Bridge, from which we could see the Suspension Bridge with its graceful cables. Upon arrival, we walked through Woolworth's, J. C. Penney, and several other nickel-and-dime stores. We usually had lunch at the Walgreens Drugstore.

After she became a widow in 1940, Grandma lived alternately with us and her son John and his family. When her welcome was worn out with one daughter-in-law, she moved in with the other. She didn't drink, swore just a little, and was a loving person. She was a good soul, but had no friends and lived a dull, uninteresting life.

Grandma felt inferior to nearly everyone and was baffled by the world around her. She was a coal miner's daughter, a coal miner's wife, and had never traveled more than a few miles from Bridgeport. By her standards, anyone who finished high school was well educated and only the children of unimaginably rich families went to college. It never occurred to her that anyone in her family would get a college degree.

CHAPTER 4

Happiness ain't a thing in itself—it's only a contrast with something that ain't pleasant. And so, as soon as the novelty is over and the force of the contrast dulled, it ain't happiness any longer, and you have to get something fresh.

—Samuel Clemens (Mark Twain), novelist (1835–1910)

We learn a lot from mistakes
but that's not a good reason to keep making them.

—Anonymous

BIRDS AND OTHER THINGS

One of Mom's aunts raised canaries. The aunt's house was a breeding farm for these small yellow creatures and each new egg was a celebrated event. It was well-known that miners took canaries into the mines to test the air. My great-aunt had no interest in this utilitarian use of birds. Canary song was her passion.

An accomplished singer was often caged with a poor one. The theory was that the mute would imitate the vocalist, not vice versa. There was little evidence that this system worked and I believe it was superstitious behavior.

Older houses were heated with small fireplaces called grates; one in each room. To keep the fire from dying out overnight, ashes were heaped over glowing coals—a process called "banking." The plan was to keep the coal smoldering (and giving off acrid fumes) until morning, when it was stirred up and reignited. By morning the rooms had an acrid smell and were only a few degrees above the outside temperature. This was not a desirable avian environment.

None of the birds lasted long - the scene was oft repeated. One morning Mom would take off the cage cover and there would be a yellow-feathered corpse lying on its side, wings folded like a fallen angel. Sending a canary to our house was tantamount to a death sentence even though Mom tried hard to keep the little buggers alive. Shortly after the latest fatality, her aunt forgave her and a new victim arrived.

Mom said they died because they were left alone all day. Perhaps they did die of loneliness, not the cold, noxious air, but I doubt it.

When the aunt passed away, the family canary-keeping habit died with her. In a short time, no one in the family had a canary and no one seemed to miss them.

A Comment Sidebar—Conveniences and Inconveniences

Most homes shared party lines with three to seven other users. When you picked up the phone there would often be an ongoing conversation. You were supposed to hang up and try again later. However, many people, including operators, stayed on and listened. Private lines were expensive and having one was considered showing off. There were few secrets in small towns before telephones, and there were practically none after party lines became common.

In warm weather, perishable food was kept in an icebox. Ours was about five feet high and made of hardwood. An upper compartment held a twenty-five-pound block of ice. Vents permitted chilled air to circulate into the other compartments.

Open trucks, carrying ice covered with burlap sacks and canvas, arrived on a regular schedule. The hundred pound ice blocks were partially sawed into twenty-five-pound segments so the ice man could chip off the right size. Kids followed the truck, picking up ice chips and sucking on them. During the winter the same truck had delivered coal, so there was always a residual of coal dust on the truck bed. Coal dust was part of our lives—and digestive tracts.

During cold weather, only well-off people bought ice. Everyone else used various types of window boxes with movable shutters and vents. Regulating how much cold air was let in required skillful use of these imperfect devices. As spring arrived we often had food frozen in the morning which was spoiled by sudden heat in the afternoon. But, not buying ice saved twenty-five to fifty cents each week.

Most women were stay-at-home wives and mothers and few families had a car, so home delivery was common. Quart-size glass bottles of milk were delivered by a milkman early each morning and he picked up empty bottles for recycling. The bread man rang a bell as he drove slowly through neighborhoods. White bread and soft rolls with sugary icing, were popular as were cream puffs and other high calorie treats. Healthy eating was not an issue. If you liked it, you ate it; if not; you didn't. Fat, skinny, or perfect, it was assumed you were what your nature intended.

Beat-up trucks stacked high with seasonal fruits and vegetables also came to the neighborhoods. The Fuller Brush Company men followed pre-planned visit routes and there were tinkers who fixed cookware and sharpened knives. Vacuum cleaners, life insurance, magazines, newspapers, and encyclopedias were all sold door to door. One could argue that "lonely housewife" was a misnomer.

As mentioned, personal hygiene was at a lower standard then. Few people took a bath every day. Those without bathtubs bathed in round galvanized steel tubs into which boiling water was poured and cold water added. You jumped in, and washed quickly. This was a painful chore in the winter, which partially explains why daily bathing was not the norm. We never lived in a place with a shower. My first shower was taken in the boys' locker room when I was about eleven.

HARD TIMES [4]

For a while we lived in a house in the west end of Brookside, about a quarter of a mile up a creek hollow from National Road. The house was heated by a potbellied coal stove in the kitchen and grates in the other three rooms. [5] About a quarter of a mile up the canyon, there was a small hand-worked coal mine. On Sundays Dad would put me into his old clunker and drive to the mine. While I held the sacks open, he shoveled in coal that had spilled when trucks were loaded. The coal was in small pieces called "slack." Because it burned quickly compared to the more expensive large lumps, we often had to sack coal by flashlight on weekday evenings. This grade of coal sold for about fifteen cents a sack, but we got ours free by—not quite—stealing it.

Most kids began school in the first grade; kindergarten was unknown. Though I wouldn't be six until February, Mom put me in the first grade in September, 1937. Since I was big for my age and knew the alphabet, Mom thought she could get away with it. After two weeks I was sent home with a note pinned to my coat. I was a reject.

There have been books written about the deprivations of the 1930s, but reading history and living it are vastly different. Although

4 From birth until age nineteen, I lived in eleven separate locations, one of them twice. These places were all within three miles of downtown Bridgeport. Lack of money to pay the rent was often the motivation for moving.

5 Point of interest: This house was still occupied in 2012, but deeply disliked by the neighbors because it was painted a ghastly pink.

young, I have vivid memories of how the Depression affected family and friends. These people were discouraged, insecure, and downright afraid of the future. They counted every penny, sometimes not knowing how they would buy food the next week. It was a time of pessimism, broken spirits and little hope.

Children don't learn much about life when they live in warm, comfy homes and Christmas brings piles of presents. Your understanding of poverty deepened when you needed shoes and didn't get them.

The Depression was expected to end someday, but it went on and on, even worsening in 1937. The gifts kids received were things they needed, not what they wanted. One learned to be grateful for simple things.

The war in Europe was the medicine that cured the Depression, not government programs dreamed up by bureaucrats. By 1939-40, the United States was supplying food and arms to England and this industrial activity spread into the Ohio Valley. By then my parents had steady work, and while we were still poor, there was a whiff of optimism in the air.

CHAPTER 5

Life is a tragedy for those who feel
and a comedy for those who think.
—Horatio Walpole, politician, writer (1717-1797)

A reader lives a thousand lives before he dies,
The man who never reads lives only one.
—George R.R Martin, fiction writer (1948-living)

MOVE TO BENCH STREET

In 1938, we began sharing a small house with my father's brother, John, and his family. Uncle John, Aunt Eleanor, and my cousins Robert and Joan lived on one side of the house; Dad, Mom, and I got the smaller side. Our entrance was from the front porch into the living room, which became my parent's bedroom. Next was a sitting room in which Grandma and I slept. Behind that was a small room which was used as our kitchen. The only bathroom had doors from each side and was shared by all eight of us. It was a crowded, uncomfortable living arrangement.

Mom cooked on a dangerous contraption called a kerosene stove. A one-gallon glass container was filled with kerosene and turned upside down into a receptacle high enough above the stovetop that gravity fed fuel to the burners. Each burner had a valve that controlled how fast the kerosene flowed into it. The burners had to be lit carefully with a match.

Bridgeport was heavily Catholic, and the Bench Street neighborhood was even more so. Most of the neighbors were of Middle European ancestry, with the Polish being in the majority. This ethnic mix was a handicap for a boy who wasn't Catholic and had a German last name. Some Catholic parents forbade their children to mix with "heathens," which meant anyone who wasn't Catholic.

School at Last

That fall, I was enrolled in the first grade at the West End Grade School. Kids in those days walked to school and carried their lunches. My commute was not the old cliché of "through the snow, winter, and summer, uphill both ways," but it was a mile hike each way, downhill and uphill, and was good exercise for a frail six-year-old.

The first and second grades were in one room and the third and fourth grades were in the room next door. Each room had one teacher. The fifth and sixth grades were on the second floor with separate teachers. The sharper students were moved to the part of the room nearest the more advanced grade. This meant that a bright third grader could participate in some fourth-grade work. Advancing me to the next grade was never considered—I was a dull student.

When one considers the results achieved with one teacher handling thirty students at two grade levels, compared to the amount of money per student spent seventy years later, it was a fabulously successful system.

Prior to beginning school, I had learned little beyond reciting the letters of the alphabet and counting to a hundred—pretty dumb stuff for age six. I was put in a seat on the side of the room, furthest from the second grade. But my skills developed and by spring, I was reading well enough to be moved next to the second grade side.

Mrs. Waddell was the school principal, chief disciplinarian, and sixth grade teacher. She was an overweight, corset-wearing woman with a stern face. She enjoyed meting out corporal punishment with a paddle. The threat by a teacher, "Do you want me to take you to see the principal?" shaped up even the most unruly boys. [6]

My Pal Wendell

At about age five, I met Wendell Lyle. We became best friends and were classmates when we entered the first grade at the West End Grade School.

When we were about eight, his family moved to Kirkwood, over a mile away. One of us would walk to the other's side of the valley for a day of exploring the woods, wrestling, and imagining things—just being boys. Soon I was the one who did the walking because the Bench Street kids resented a Kirkwood Protestant kid coming into their Catholic space. The territorial imperative begins early in male mammals.

Wendell was always small for his age and took a lot of guff from bigger kids. He brought some of this on himself because he had a fast, biting tongue and used four-letter words liberally. We shared this problem, and I was often equally at fault. We never did wise up enough to change our speech habits.

For the sixth grade, I convinced Mom to transfer me to the Kirkwood School so I could escape Mrs. Waddell and be in the same class with Wendell. Mom was aware that I feared Mrs. Waddell, and she liked it that Wendell and I behaved like brothers - so the transfer happened.

---

6 Corporal punishment was common practice in those days. Teachers were permitted to use a paddle to strike the behinds of misbehaving students all the way through high school. I have not seen scientific evidence that this practice was detrimental to the education of the students of those days. Corporal punishment of misbehaving students was stopped after the 1950s for political reasons, not well-founded research (opinion of the author).

From then on, through high school and beyond, Wendell and I were pals. We were seen together so often that it was often assumed we were brothers even though we didn't look a bit alike. We didn't realize that we both used the same verbal phrases and were both seen as smart-ass brats.

Wendell wanted to play sports but his size was a problem. He wouldn't give up on football, and went out for the team as a sophomore. He was fast and wanted to be a pass receiving halfback. But, he never got above 135 pounds and couldn't effectively defend himself. Finally, in our junior year, he caught a pass, took a hard hit, and his collarbone was broken. That was the end of his football career.

Wendell worked hard at pitching, and I, of course, was his catcher. His big moment came during the American Legion League playoffs when we were seventeen. He had a no-hitter going at the top of the last inning, and the game was tied with two outs. He gave up two walks and then threw a low fastball as the forward runner was trying to steal third. I caught the ball off balance and threw it over the third baseman's head—a stupid mistake on my part. The runner scored. We failed to get a run in the bottom of the ninth, so Wendell had the dubious distinction of pitching a no-hitter, and losing it, one to nothing.

The local newspaper carried a story about it. I felt terrible and apologized every way I knew how, but to no avail. He was hurt and I understood why; his best friend had thrown away his moment of glory. He refused to take solace in the fact that he had a unique no-hitter that the local fans would talk about for years.

Health Problems

About age six, I began having frequent nosebleeds if I exerted myself, sneezed hard or got a bump on the nose. Doc Harris coached Mom and me to put ice on the back of my neck and squeeze my nose. If I sat quietly the bleeding would normally stop in half an hour or so.

The nosebleeds were added to my respiratory problems as reasons to restrict my freedom. If a week or two went by without an incident, everyone relaxed a bit and allowed me out of the house to play. This enforced inactivity was the reason I was overweight by the sixth grade.

One winter Saturday, when I was about nine, a nosebleed started early in the morning. None of the usual remedies worked. When Mom shoved toilet paper up my nose it worked like a dam. The blood flowed backward into my throat, forcing me to swallow it. I vomited up the blood and that scared the hell out of everyone. Doc Harris didn't make it to the house until evening. Upon examination he said that if he couldn't stop the bleeding quickly, I had to be taken to the hospital for a transfusion. The doc had one thing to try. He took a long strip of gauze bandage, smeared it with Vaseline, and used blunt scissors to push it up my nose. He called this "packing the nose." It was unpleasant and I cried loudly, but it worked.

Two days later the doc slowly pulled the blood-soaked gauze from my nose. He told me that when other methods failed, I could do this little packing job myself by using the eraser end of a pencil to push Vaseline-coated gauze up my nostrils. About a year later, after another packing incident, I decided to give it a try. With Mom's encouragement, I pushed the gauze strip up my nose with a pencil, hating every second of it. It worked.

From then, all through school, I used the pencil, gauze and Vaseline method to stop nose bleeds. I kept the three items in my school locker, carried a set in my gym bag, and the coach put a set in the team's first-aid kit. Some people, even coaches, were grossed out when they saw me pushing gauze up my nose with a pencil. To me, it was just business as usual. By age fifteen or sixteen, the problem became much less severe and the packing incidents much less frequent.

Tonsillitis caused many absences from school. My tonsils should have been removed, but the surgery had to be done when there was no infection. When the infection was arrested, lack of money got in the way. Also, it was believed that if a recurring problem didn't kill you, your body adjusted and you got past it. With the arrival of antibiotics after the war, there was little motivation to spend money for a tonsillectomy, and I never had one.

Only a few vaccines had been developed, so nearly every child my age went through what were known as "childhood diseases." I had whooping cough, chicken pox, measles, influenza, strep throat, and, finally, mumps.

My parents permitted me unlimited use of our radio and, by accident; I fell into a love of classical music. On weekends there were broadcasts of live concerts from Carnegie Hall, the Philadelphia and New York Philharmonics, and other well-known orchestras and venues. They were on my personal schedule and I did my best to avoid missing these programs. As a teenager, my friends thought I was screwy for buying "long hair" recordings. That was not the only reason for that belief.

My Playground

The hillside behind the Bench Street was a steep climb of over a hundred yards to the top. Cow paths crisscrossed through the trees and connected multiple grassy meadows.

A rock outcropping on the point of the hill had a natural chair shape. From this high point, kids took advantage of the prevailing wind from the west and launched kites. The Bench Street kids got into kite flying in the spring but soon tired of it—everyone but me, that is. I had a reliable kite and a large reel to hold the string. Several times each week, I crawled through the barbed wire fence and hiked up to my stone chair. It was wonderful watching the kite soar higher and higher, straining to support the weight of the string.

A Sentimental Visit

During my many visits to Bridgeport as an adult I always intended to visit my old kite flying haunt, but it never happened. Finally, in the summer of 2009, my friend Charlie Wilson and I drove up Old Cadiz Road and found our way out to the stone seat.

About sixty years had passed, but the spot was almost exactly as I had described it to him. At that time, Charlie was a member of the U.S. House of Representatives and interested in local history.

Pets

My first dog, a female fox terrier mix, arrived one day. I named her Mitzi. With the exception of hunting breeds, no one ever bought a dog - you found a dog or a dog found you. Leashes were rarely used. Dogs roamed free. They came, they were loved, and they left in whatever way chance dictated - car collisions, distemper or whatever. Mitzi entered dog heaven after an automobile event.

After Mitzi's demise, a mostly beagle puppy named Biff came along. He could have been the model for Snoopy. He followed me everywhere, and dozed at my feet while I read or listened to the radio. After a long illness, he died of distemper. Watching him die so slowly was painful and my enthusiasm for dog ownership plunged. I never lived with a dog again until I was married.

The First Gun

A Daisy Air Rifle, was a gift for my eighth birthday. I was allowed to set cans on the hillside behind the house and shoot at them through an open window. Dad gave me strict rules on how to handle the gun before, during, and after shooting. After some lessons, I was able to hit a can consistently at over twenty feet.

I was allowed to take my Daisy up the hill. Sparrows and starlings were on my permitted kill list and robins and songbirds were forbidden. I stalked sparrows like a cat and proudly brought home a few kills, but I never got a starling - they flew away when a gun was pointed at them.

Grandma Arrives

After Grandpa Scheid died, Grandma moved into the Bench Street house with us. Though Grandma was functionally illiterate, she was responsible for developing my reading skills. She decided that I should help her read the newspaper every day. We had an old dictionary and she encouraged me to look up words we didn't understand. It was slow going, but with practice, I gained some proficiency.

Small-town newspapers cover mostly local trivia, so I became interested in local events. To spark my interest, Grandma gave me background information on the local news; she was a good storyteller. She particularly liked the obituaries and would often recite gossip about the deceased. She also told me about divorces, petty crimes, drunken brawls, and much more. She didn't trust the mayor, the city council, or the city officials. As I learned over the years, she was mostly correct—being uneducated didn't make her politically stupid.

Grandma had a box filled with dime novels, mostly cowboy adventures that Grandpa had read. She let me read them after I promised not to tell Mom. I caught the book bug and was an advanced reader by the third grade. Reading for her was the bond between us. I don't think she cared about the news all that much. It just made her feel good that I took the time to read to her.

I loved movies and had been to the Saturday afternoon triple-headers at the Family Theater, the only screen in Bridgeport. Occasionally, I attended real movies with Mom and sat through them without being fidgety. Dad rarely went to movies because they conflicted with his beer drinking and social life. I pleaded to see *Gone with the Wind*, but Mom said it was too adult for me. I finally won out when one of her friends told her it was okay for me. The movie captivated me, as did the book when I read it. It's embarrassing to admit it, but I read *Gone with the Wind* three times before high school graduation and once after. Rhett Butler was my hero and I was in love with Scarlett O'Hara.

By 1939, the European war was in the news every day and I followed the events avidly. My knowledge of the war was met with mixed emotions by my parents. While they were pleased that I could read well, Mom and Dad were embarrassed when their son shared his views with adults. A child who knew too much was considered to be a smart-ass brat, not a smart child. Children were to be "seen, not heard." Eventually I learned to hide most of what I read from everyone.

By late 1940 it was apparent that the country was almost certainly going to send an army to Europe in a repeat of 1918. Kate Smith, the most famous singer in the country, had a popular radio show. One evening, in 1938, she introduced *God Bless America,* a song by Irving Berlin, who had written many patriotic songs during WWI. Her timing was perfect. Within a few weeks, it was being sung in schools, on radio and at gatherings of all kinds. By the time we entered the war, GBA had become our second national anthem.

Isabelle Scheid with new son, Alfred, circa March, 1932

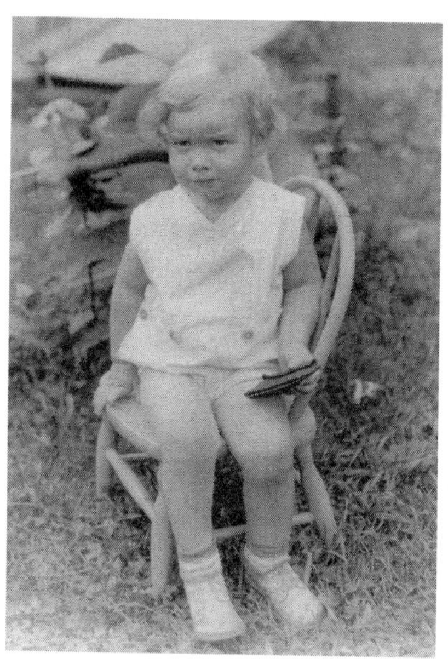

A scowling Al holding photographer's wallet, summer, 1933

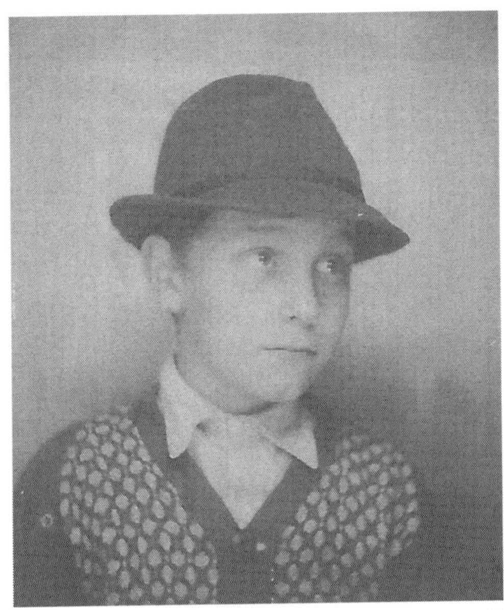

A sickly, shy Al, about seven, circa 1939

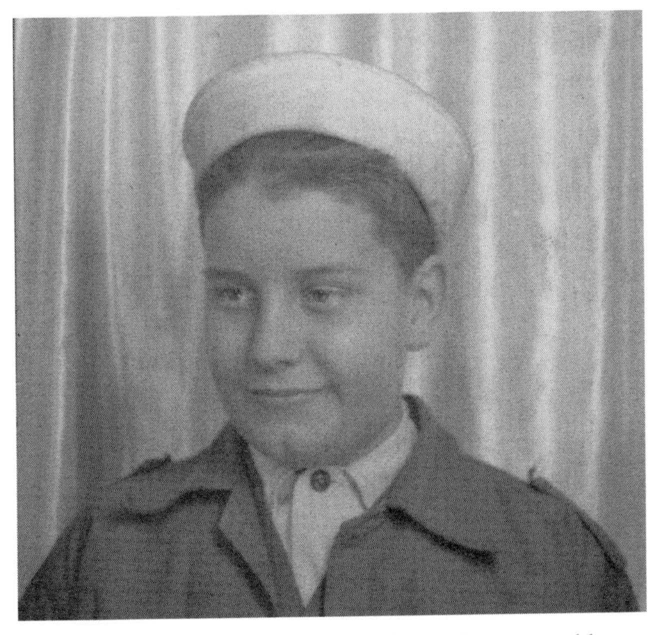

Fat, reclusive boy named Al – about age 11

Street car, on Lincoln Ave., in front of Carlton Saloon before remodeling, circa 1939

CHAPTER 6

It is the man who has done nothing
who is sure nothing can be done.
—Anonymous

Not everything that is faced can be changed,
but nothing can be changed until it is faced.
—James A. Baldwin, writer (1924–1987)

THE NEW BUSINESS

In the summer of 1941, Dad and Mom had decided to start Scheid Electric in a rented storefront at 300 Main Street, directly across the street from the Bridgeport City Building. The plan was for Dad to be self-employed as an electrical contractor and Mom would handle the store, selling radios, washing machines, and refrigerators. Dad had been working steadily and had had a short but profitable stint running a poker game. Savings from that income, along with Mom's earnings, had created the small nest egg they needed to start the business.

Most women still washed clothes on a washboard in a galvanized steel tub and rinsed them in another tub. After wringing out as much water as possible by hand, they hung them outside on clotheslines to dry, winter and summer. Every family wanted a new electric washing machine, a radio, and an electric refrigerator. With the economy picking up, some working people could afford these appliances. It was ironic that Mom and Dad were opening a store to sell appliances they had never owned and couldn't yet afford.

The store was prepared for opening on weekends and evenings by Dad and Mom with some help from friends. Dad built a seven-foot partition separating the front and back of the store. Behind the partition there was a cast-iron potbelly stove, the only source of heat in the store. Dad put a large fan on the floor behind the stove, aimed it above the partition and created his own form of convection heating. It worked remarkably well.

Nearly everyone on the Jonard side of the family, except Mom, suffered from acrophobia (fear of heights). She had been hanging wallpaper since she was a teenager. Dad had no fear of heights and wanted to make sure his nearly twelve year old son didn't succumb to this phobia. He sent me up a ladder to paint the metal ceiling where it came six inches down the walls. It was a fourteen-foot ceiling, but with Dad's instructions and encouragement, I thought the job was fun. My Jonard grandparents cringed when they observed me at the top of the ladder - I enjoyed their discomfort.

Dad had obtained the Bridgeport franchise for Philco radios, Blackstone washing machines, and General Electric refrigerators. With these brands, success was assured. A bank loan financed the inventory, and Scheid Electric opened in the early autumn of 1941. Sales were strong from the beginning. It appeared that after years of hand-to-mouth living, the Scheids were on their way to prosperity.

World War II

On the afternoon of Sunday, December 7, 1941, I was listening to a classical music broadcast when it was suddenly interrupted. In tones just short of panic, the announcer said that Pearl Harbor in Hawaii had been attacked by the Japanese. I had never heard of

Pearl Harbor and knew only that Hawaii was a tropical island more or less on the other side of the world. But, I was keenly aware of what bombing meant. I ran excitedly in all directions to share the news. There was disbelief, there was confusion, and then there was a lot of anger.

The residents of Bench Street understood the implications of the attack. People spontaneously came out into the street. The women were crying, the men were swearing about "dirty Japs," and everyone was apprehensive.

Within days President Roosevelt made his famous speech declaring war on Japan, and then Germany declared war on the United States. The question was: what will life be like in wartime? We were soon to find out. The Christmas of 1941 was a sad one for all of America.

The Business Problem

Almost overnight, the government was embarked on aggressive actions to get the nation on a war footing. The population was doing the same thing - in a different way. People immediately bought the things they knew would be scarce. This included cars, appliances, canned meat, tires, and nylon hosiery - just about anything that wouldn't spoil.

As a countermeasure, the government instituted what was called "the freeze." This meant that, until further notice, all items on a gigantic list had to stay where they were. The idea was to prevent hoarding and give the government time to decide which items should be rationed and which would be confiscated for the war effort.

Scheid Electric had sold nearly its entire inventory before Christmas and had orders for appliances to be delivered in January. The freeze meant that electrical appliance inventory could not be delivered and Dad's store was put out of business. Timing is everything in business - as it is in life.

The store had gone from a budding success in late 1941 to a business failure in January of 1942. For a few months, Mom and Dad had thought they were on their way to a prosperous life. Now that was over and their meager savings were gone. All they had after the freeze was a lease on a store front.

The New Business

Mom came up with an idea. A deal was worked out with a wholesale dry cleaning plant in Wheeling; the store would become a dry cleaning drop-off /pickup location.

A new sign was put over the front doors, and Spic & Span Dry Cleaners was born. Scheid Electrical Contracting and Repairs was painted on one of the glass windows. It was an eclectic mix of businesses, but the local citizens understood.

The owner of the dry cleaning plant, a Mr. Lewis, was Jewish and had red hair. I had never knowingly met a Jew before. When I asked what being Jewish meant, Mom or Dad answered, "It's just his religion." The explanation didn't satisfy my curiosity.

After a visit to the library, I knew more about Jewish history and customs than anyone in the family. This knowledge was shared only with Wendell, who didn't give a damn. I wanted to know if Mr. Lewis was an Orthodox Jew but was afraid to ask. Once the stories about Germany's pogroms for the Jews began appearing in magazines and papers, I didn't dare ask him any questions.

As soon as the war got under way, there was a shortage of clothing. Mom bought a used Singer sewing machine and placed it in front of one of the large windows that looked out over the street. The machine was not electrically powered, so she used both feet to rock a treadle.

Mom had learned to sew and knit as a child. For the rest of the war, and a few years afterward, she made and repaired women's clothing. Women bought fabrics and patterns, and then brought them to Mom who made dresses, skirts, and blouses of much higher quality than could be found in stores. This created a steady stream of customers requiring her to work long hours. The seamstress and dry cleaning businesses complemented each other nicely.

Dad hired a young man named Cyril Beech, who was what we would now call a techie. Very few people at that time had any knowledge of what made a radio tick, so a man who could breathe new life into an old Philco was considered a magician Cyril became my friend and taught me a little about radios. He helped me put together a crude crystal set, and it worked. There was often static, but it picked up KDKA and WWVA, the fifty-thousand watt stations in Pittsburgh and Wheeling.

Cyril also shared some technical magazine articles with me. One of the stories was about a new invention that looked like a radio but had a small screen on the front, on which people would be shown talking and moving, like a movie. The new invention was called television. When I told friends about it, they said it was comic book stuff. Cyril said that television would be available after the war. I believed him, but I quit talking about it. The army needed young men like Cyril, and in a couple of months he was drafted.

To add to the family income, Dad tried selling Independence Day fireworks from a stand he put up in front of the store.[7] He stocked Roman candles, torpedoes, firecrackers, and every other exploding thing he could find. For over a week before the Fourth of July, Mom lived in fear that some careless cigarette smoker would cause a massive explosion. This profitable venture lasted only one year because the printing shop next door convinced the city council that it was too hazardous to sell fireworks in front of commercial businesses. They were right, of course, but Dad held a grudge against the printers from then on.

7 The government permitted limited manufacture of fireworks during the war as a civilian morale booster.

In December 1942, Dad began selling Christmas trees in front of the store. The trees came all the way from Washington State, kept fresh with snow packed among them. They were good quality Douglas firs, from four to eight feet tall. The trees were on consignment, which meant he paid only for the trees that were sold. The topper was that payment wasn't due until after Christmas, when a man came around and counted the unsold trees. Dad taught me how to show trees and quote prices. I was paid a few quarters for my efforts.

Since we had first pick, our house always had a perfectly shaped tree—a tradition kept until we stopped selling Christmas trees years later. Mom was an artist at tree trimming.

Mom began expecting me to help in the dry cleaning business. One of my jobs was to search dirty clothing for lipsticks, lighters, matches, and other junk that people left in pockets. Men carried handkerchiefs in those days and pulling soiled ones out of pockets was a yucky job. I hated chores related to the dry cleaning business and did everything I could to avoid them. As I got older, I solicited jobs shoveling coal into neighbor's basements, hauling out ashes, cutting lawns ... anything to avoid the dry cleaning business.

Move to Main Street

It was decided that we needed to live closer to the store. The building at 300 Main Street had a printing shop and the Scheid businesses, side-by-side on the ground floor. Just above the stores were two apartments, and above those, on the third floor, were two smaller apartments. We moved into the third-floor apartment above our store. It was at the top of two long flights totaling over forty stairs. It was heated by coal-fired grates, and the bathroom was exceptionally small.

This apartment was notable for its view. The living room, which doubled as my parents' bedroom, had three large windows looking out over Main Street and into the second floor windows of the City Building. We could see into Evans Monument Works windows on the corner of Council Street where there was always a nice display of tombstones to brighten our day. Next to Evans was the Family Movie Theater. The next storefront was Gonot's Saloon, which was the lowest class bar in town. A boy could be amused for hours watching the goings on in all of these places, especially the City Building.

In winter, the apartment was always cool by today's standards, so warm clothes were worn indoors. Bricks were heated in the oven, wrapped in towels, and put into the foot of beds before retiring. The grates were banked at night. In the coldest weather, Mom would run up the stairs from the store a couple of times each day and add a little coal to keep the fires going until evening. If the fires burned out, cold air came down the chimneys and the rooms quickly matched the outside temperature. Lugging coal up the stairs was assigned to me as an after-school chore so I was in favor of using as little coal as possible.

Airplanes, Puzzles, and Music

Colds, sore throats, and flu dominated my winters. During one illness, Grandma Jonard gave me a model airplane kit. Mom got me started using single-edged razor blades to cut the balsa wood parts. Gluing the parts together was challenging. Mom was always good with her hands and she trained me. That first effort intrigued me so much that I began working hard at creating some good-looking planes.

The propellers were "powered" by rubber bands inside the plane, which were wound up by turning the propellers clockwise. Rubber bands didn't supply enough power for real flight. If the finished plane was properly balanced, it flew only about fifteen feet before crashing. Model planes never made damage-free landings. I became adept at making repairs.

I was reluctant to fly my creations because I couldn't bear watching them get broken. It took a long time for Wendell to talk me into launching one of my models out of our third-floor window. It was a foolish idea since we had no idea how far it would go before the inevitable crash. There were cars going by on Main Street and people walking on the sidewalks. Only a miracle could have avoided a bad ending.

To our surprise, the damned thing flew really well. It followed a descending flight path all the way across Main Street and was going toward Council Street, beside the City Building, over hundred feet away from us. We watched in horror as it crashed onto the hood of a parked police car. It hit so hard that we could hear the impact.

We ran downstairs and walked slowly across the street, trying to look nonchalant. A miracle had taken place; no one saw or heard the crash. Our luck held, and no one noticed us picking up the plane. The scratches on the car hood were quite noticeable. We hauled ass down Council Street to the creek bank and had a tension-releasing laugh as we wound up the propeller and flew the evidence of our crime out into the creek. We had gotten away with the caper, but I lost a great plane.

In time my best model airplanes were suspended from the ceiling of my little bedroom, gathering dust as I pursued other interests. They were chucked into the trash when we moved again and that hobby ended.

Mom loved jigsaw puzzles, and she got me hooked on them, particularly in the winter. Once we were habituated into this time-wasting hobby, we always had an unfinished puzzle somewhere in our living space. We worked on it for a few minutes every time we walked by, sometimes taking weeks to finish a corny landscape scene or dog picture.

During one of my many winter colds, Mom bought me a cheap harmonica, assuming I would tire of it in an hour or so. In fact, I learned by to play a few simple tunes on it. At the next gift-giving holiday, I received a much better one with improved musical tones. I played what I had learned for the next few years, not losing interest until sports took over most of my free time.

THE LIBRARY

The other good news about the apartment's location was its proximity to the Bridgeport Public Library, a few hundred feet west. [8] The library became my home away from home. At first, the librarian tried to make me stick to the shelves with titles intended for kids my age, but after she learned that I could read well and respected the quiet rules, she gave in on that issue.

Over the next few years, a succession of librarians and I had verbal contracts. As long as I behaved myself, I had the freedom to explore the stacks. By the time I was thirteen, they paid no attention to what I read. A county bookmobile arrived every week, dropping off new books and taking away those for which demand had dried up. The librarians often tipped me off when something new arrived that they thought would interest me. I always returned books on time because I knew they had no love for people who were delinquent. I also didn't like paying late return fines.

When I had finished Mark Twain's major works, the ladies guided me to Jack London. These two writers began forming my young views of life and the world. I fantasized about being with Huck and Tom on the Mississippi and with White Fang in the Klondike. Before

8 Bridgeport carried the term "mixed use" to an illogical extreme. Within the length of a city block we had a bank, the lowest class bar in town, a gas station, a grocery store, a movie house, a tombstone manufacturer, the City Building/jail, a dry cleaner, a print shop, a welding shop, the library, the unemployment office, and the Ohio State Liquor Store—the last three side by side. This strange potpourri attracted an unusual array of people past our Spic & Span Cleaners.

finishing high school, I had read every book London wrote, even the usually overlooked *Martin Eden.*

The librarian was pleased when I started reading James Fennimore Cooper, and she discussed *The Last of the Mohicans* and *The Pioneers* with me (Natty Bumppo became a new hero). With her encouragement, I read the original *Bambi* by Felix Salten and all or part of other obscure books she recommended.

Acting as my guides, the librarians recommended *Ivanhoe, Treasure Island, Gulliver's Travels, Moby Dick, Robinson Crusoe,* and many other adventure stories. I was enthralled by *Moby Dick.* I imagined wandering lower Manhattan as Ishmael did at the beginning of his whale tale. I became so enthralled with this story that I went straight into *White Jacket* and other Melville writings.

Discovering Hemingway was a major event for me. He became my favorite writer and I read all his books and short stories. Hemingway was still alive and led a fascinating life. His writings about the relationships of men and women intrigued me. At about age fourteen, I read parts of *For Whom the Bell Tolls* over and over, finally figuring out why the earth moved for Maria. Robert Jordan joined my list of heroes for the way he blew up bridges and faced death head-on when his time came.

These books made me feel that someday I had to be in an army and live adventures like Hemingway and his heroes. His bullfight stories were enthralling and my interest in bullfighting never died. In the 1960s and 1970s I spent time in Spain, traveling from bullfight to bullfight and visiting Spanish Civil War sites.

Reading led me into the misty worlds of war, death, history, geography, love, and sex, sparking interests well beyond my age. None of the adults with whom I had contact read real literature, and all the boys I knew were obsessed with comic books. Other than the librarians, there was no one with whom to discuss my reading. When I did bring up a book or story, adults thought I was showing off, which was undoubtedly sometimes true.

Each month I watched for the *National Geographic* magazine to arrive at the library. I stared at the pictures and read it cover to cover. The wonderful places to which it took its readers were mind-boggling. It was the first magazine to which I ever subscribed.

My play buddies often questioned why I read real books and magazines instead of *Superman, Batman, Captain Marvel, Dick Tracy,* and other comic books. So as not to appear to be a bookworm (a derogatory title in my neighborhood), I read their comic books even though they bored me to tears. How could the imaginary deeds of Superman, Batman, and the others compete with the real-life heroics of the characters in the books I read? They were truly childish stuff. As I got into my late teens, my reading went far afield, with Mickey Spillane, Frank Yerby, and other pop authors of the time, plus all the popular magazines: *Time, Life,* and so on.

Cold weather and my early health issues encouraged a solitary life. The more I read, the less I liked my surroundings, which motivated me to be alone and read more. It was a reinforcing circle and a happy accident in some ways. I look back with wonderment at how lucky I was to read so much when so young. I would have read (and learned) much less if I had been healthier.

Health Improvement

Even though I overweight and not physically as active as other boys my age, I began riding an old bike I had been given. The exercise undoubtedly helped me get rid of some fat and increased my desire to get out and about.

The strenuous work of carrying coal up to the third floor and ashes down every day also helped me develop strength. Dropping coal on the stairs was considered bad form by our neighbors and a sin by Mom. When a spill happened, I had to clean it up, with no delay. Carrying ashes down the stairs was even more precarious. Coal and ashes were the bane of my existence during the several winters we lived in that apartment building.

CHAPTER 7

Prohibition is an awful flop, we like it.
It cannot stop what it's meant to stop, we like it.
It's left a trail of graft and slime,
It didn't prohibit worth a dime.
It filled our land with vice and crime,
Nevertheless, we're for it.
—Franklin P. Adams, columnist, writer 1881-1960

A pioneer destroys things and calls it civilization.
—Charles Marion Russell, American artist (1864-1926)

1920S THROUGH 1940S

Prohibition was born in 1920 with the passing of the Volstead Act and died in late 1933, when the Twenty-First Amendment was approved by the states. The voters had bought, as the saying was, "a pig in a poke" when they voted for Prohibition. Volstead is probably the worst law passed in the history of the country. It had hundreds of unintended social, economic, and political consequences, all of them bad. It created a new criminal class and made politicians even more corrupt than before. All in all, it fit nicely into Bridgeport's historic business model.

In Bridgeport very little changed during Prohibition. The bars and saloons were just hidden from direct sight by "front" businesses, like restaurants and newsstands. When Prohibition ended, the saloons came out of hiding. The town was still the watering hole for people on both sides of the river.

After the lessons of Prohibition, the politicians became more adept at corruption. The working class suffered unemployment during the Depression; the crooks and politicians thrived. Village and county politics were cut and dried. The men in control of the county Democrat party decided which candidate the party would support in the primary elections. Being the Democrat nominee almost assured election.

Dad often drove older voters to the polls – an effective way to get out the vote. He said it was good for business for him to be seen as an active Democrat.

Except for my best friend's father I doubt I ever met a Republican as long as I lived in Bridgeport. It was a great shock to my family when it turned out that I had conservative beliefs and valiantly defended them. They believed I did this to get attention, not because I was sincere. In fact, my beliefs were arrived at by reading history and the news.

Public drunkenness was an accepted fact, day and night. The mills and mines worked three shifts every day, including weekends. One man's morning was another man's evening. The bars were supposed to close at 1 a.m. Most of them opened again at 6 or 7 a.m. The truth was that the closing time law was lightly enforced and the bar owners had agreements among themselves about business hours. As long as the police were properly bribed, they looked the other way.

The card games went on and on, uninterrupted by curfews or laws. The horse betting joint opened about two hours before the first race on the East Coast and closed after the last race in California. However, the bookies would take a bet, day or night.

Gambling on baseball games was done in the Pastime Billiard Room, where they had a ticker tape clicking all day. As the games progressed, scores were continuously posted on a chalkboard. One could bet before the first pitch, while games were in progress, or the day before game day. You could wager on things like picking a player who would hit a home run that day, how many strikeouts there would be in a game, and other esoteric events. Pastime was always closed on Sundays as a nod of respect to the religious people of the town. Sunday games were wagered before Sunday and paid off on Monday. Patrons of horse racing and card playing ignored the Sabbath. Many a man placed a bet or played a hand shortly after leaving church.

The Bridgeport police were well-known for being tough, and they didn't lack for opportunities to build their reputations. They carried revolvers and nightsticks, but their favorite weapon was the blackjack, sometimes called a sap. These weapons were made of leather and were about nine inches long, with a flexible handle and a loop that fit around the wrist. Lead weights were sewn into the leather at the business end of the weapon. It was swung something like a flexible hammer, which accelerated the weight at the end. This weapon was also commonly used by the gangsters. A blow from a blackjack could easily, and often did, break an arm. A blow to the head usually resulted in a concussion and sometimes a fractured skull.

The Bridgeport Volunteer Fire Department

The fire department garage and office was on Council Street, behind the City Building. The fire chief was Joe Hores (pronounced horse), a short man with a fat belly, who was a plumber by trade. He and his family lived in an apartment half a block from the City Building. Joe was ready for action day or night. Joe's main interest in life was the fire department, and he worked as a plumber primarily to support this habit. He was reliable, knowledgeable, and a fine example for other firemen to follow. Joe trained his men hard, and he was often the first man into a burning building. All respected Joe, and his authority was never questioned.

Dad's entry into the fire department was almost automatic because of friendships going back many years. When we moved into the apartment above the store, his involvement became intense. Since he could put on his boots and coat, run down the stairs, cross the street, and enter the firehouse garage in three minutes, Chief Joe arranged for him to be one of the fire truck drivers. Being a fire truck driver was prestigious, and Dad took it seriously.

Council Street was one block long, starting at Main Street and dead-ending at the bank overlooking Little Wheeling Creek. At this dead end was a large open area that, among other things, was used for the firemen's training exercises. It was also the scene of summer water fights between nearby volunteer fire departments. These events drew large crowds that were expected to be generous when the hat was passed.

Two men held the hose nozzle between them, with their backs to the opposition. It was the job of these two men to block the water from the opponent's hose so the captain could aim their stream at the other team. The last man crouched behind the captain and moved the hose, as the captain directed.

The contest began with both teams pointing their hoses into the air. When a whistle was blown, they lowered the nozzles, and directed the water at the opposition. The idea was for the teams to move towards each other, using the water stream to knock down their opponents. When most of a team had been knocked off their feet a whistle was blown, ending the match. The contests were short, lasting from a few seconds to at most a couple of minutes. Then another match began.

After the scores were tallied, the men adjourned to the fire-house to consume copious quantities of cold beer and settle bets. Bridgeport never let a chance to gamble or drink slip by.

I stopped by the firehouse frequently. I swept the floor, ran out for cigarettes and snacks, and in general helped out in any way I could. They repaid me by ignoring my presence and letting me eavesdrop on their jokes and gossip. It was quite educational.

In the tradition of volunteer fire departments, it was expected that the firemen would raise most of their operating budgets. The best events were what they called "feeds." The annual turtle soup feed was big and the one I liked the best. The spaghetti and meat-balls and the ham and lima bean suppers were excellent as well. It was considered a civic duty to attend these events and the price was low because most of the food and beer was donated. A large paper cup of beer for a nickel also helped bring in the crowd.

Chief Joe was lionized as an expert turtle soup chef—and he was. He made it from scratch—starting with live turtles. I watched the butchering of turtles a number of times, and it was a gory af-fair. The edible parts were cut to size and the rest was carried to the creek and dumped down the bank.

It was customary for fire trucks to go to neighboring villages to participate in parades. Gasoline was rationed, but Memorial Day, Independence Day and a few other celebrations were considered es-sential as civilian morale boosters. Since I was sort of a firehouse mascot, Chief Joe often let me go along on the truck and ride in the parades. This was a great honor. Joe told me to be quiet, stay out of the way, and try to be invisible, lest other firemen would want to get their sons on the truck. It was a thrill to ride on top of the hoses while the truck slowly cruised down the main street of small towns, clang-ing its bell and occasionally sounding its siren. I became a well-trav-eled kid, going to Cadiz, St. Clairsville, Steubenville, Fly, Shadyside, Flushing, Bellaire, and other far-off mysterious places—all within a twenty-mile radius of Bridgeport. Ours was not a cosmopolitan world.

City Building Activities

Bridgeport had no leash law. Dogs and cats roaming around the neighborhoods were part of the environment. When there was a complaint, the stray dogs in that neighborhood were rounded up and put in cages in an old building next to the fire house. If someone wanted a pet, he could pick one from the inventory and take it home, no charge. Hunting dog breeds were nearly always adopted, but most animals met a darker fate.

The end of Council Street was the execution site for unwanted animals. The police put up to three animals at a time in a box connected by a hose to the exhaust pipe of a police car. The animals died of carbon monoxide poisoning when the engine was started. After execution, the bodies were pushed over the edge of the bank so they could roll down into the creek. These executions were usually witnessed by the local boys.

Bridgeport had another anomaly. Every day at exactly 5 p.m., someone, normally the police chief, set off an electric whistle that rose to an ear-splitting shriek and then slowly dropped to silence. This device, called the fire whistle, was so loud that it could be heard well over a mile away. The whistle was tested every day to make certain it would work when a fire call was needed. Without comment, all the people in the downtown neighborhoods put their fingers into their ears every afternoon at 5 p.m. sharp. Then, as the whistle died down, we removed our fingers and continued life. This was simply part of living in Bridgeport.

The sidewalk in front of the City Building was a congregation area for paperboys and the kids who lived nearby. Every afternoon, bundles of newspapers were heaved out of a truck and onto the sidewalk for the newsboys to pick up and deliver. It was customary for the paperboys to arrive early. They would play with yo-yos, trade baseball cards, get into fights, and generally create a nuisance for the adults.

Mom could see all this activity from her seat at her sewing machine. She disapproved of the behavior, but it was the custom and therefore continued. When we first opened the store, I was forbidden to hang out in front of the City Building. That rule died the first summer.

We local boys learned to pass, kick, and catch a football on brick-paved Council Street. Future high school football players honed their early skills there, along with developing the ability to suck up the pain when a knee, or sometimes a head, hit the bricks. Council Street football was played in front of the mayor's office, the firehouse, and the police car parking lot. There were always men sitting outside the firehouse cheering on the players. Young boys were expected to do what boys do, and the men liked watching the mayhem.

The Eagles Club

An "aerie" is the nest of an eagle, and Bridgeport was the location of Aerie 995 of the Fraternal Order of Eagles (FOE). The Eagles Club was much like the Moose, Elk, Foresters, and other fraternal organizations that thrived during the 20th century. Despite its location in a small town, the Bridgeport Eagles had the most impressive building and largest membership for sixty miles around. The club had social nights every Thursday and Saturday, featuring live bands, dancing, and cheap drinks. Admission was limited to members and their guests. Social nights were one of the attractions that made many wives willing to let their men join the club. There was also a Women's Auxiliary which Mom joined.

The Bridgeport Eagles had another attraction that insured its financial success: slot machines. Through the use of judicious payments to law enforcement, the club was able to have a room in the basement that contained about a dozen nickel, dime, and quarter slots. It was common for the mayor, members of the city council, the justice of the peace and other authorities, plus their wives, to put coins in the slots and pull the levers. Some of the profits from the slot machines supported local charitable causes, thus promoting a positive image for the club.

Beginning when I was about ten, Mom let me put nickels in a slot or pull a lever, never both. I believe she felt that as long as I did only one of the required actions, I was not really gambling.

CHAPTER 8

The essence of being human is that one does not seek perfection, that one is willing to commit sins for the sake of loyalty, that one does not pursue asceticism to the point where it makes friendly intercourse impossible and that one is prepared in the end to be defeated and broken up by life, which is the inevitable price of fastening one's love upon another human individual. Sainthood is a thing human beings must avoid. Most people genuinely do not wish to be saints. And it is probable that those who aspire to sainthood have never felt much temptation to be human beings.

—George Orwell, novelist (1903–1950)

On the whole human beings want to be good,
but not too good and not quite all the time.

—The same George Orwell

DOWNTOWN BRIDGEPORT

Bridgeport was not a quiet place. The steel wheels of streetcars screeched as they made turns and the conductors clanged their bells, warning pedestrians out of the way. A steady stream of cars also moved through the village.

From about age eleven, I was free to roam around the downtown area. Because of Mom's business, my deceased grandfather's popularity, and Dad's activities, nearly every downtown regular and business owner knew me. It was a great place to develop street smarts.

Bridgeport claimed nearly five thousand residents in the 1940s, but it probably never reached that number. However, on Friday and Saturday nights, as the bars filled up, the population exceeded five thousand by a handsome margin. The downtown area of Bridgeport had twenty-three licensed bars, all of them busy. There were also roadhouses (aka taverns) on each main route out of town, all within easy driving distance. That calculates to about one drinking establishment for every two hundred citizens, including children. This must have been some sort of record for small mid-western towns.

In addition, there were two banks, a hardware store, a newsstand, a butcher shop, two gas stations, two grocery stores, two pool halls, several restaurants, a tombstone engraver, a small hotel that rented rooms by the hour, and last but not least, a busy mortuary. One could borrow money, gamble, get drunk, dine, buy sex, die, be embalmed and get a custom tombstone all within a three-block area. It was said that a few men managed to accomplish all of these things in one twenty-four hour period.

The gangster and grifter classes bought their peace from the police and operated without fear. There were multiple card rooms tucked away in semisecret places and there was a horse race betting parlor on the second floor, above the largest saloon. In addition to illegal baseball betting, the Pastime Billiard Room permitted gambling on pool games.

The gambling businesses didn't mind if a man had a flask of whiskey in his pocket and took a swig now and then. If he wanted to get swacked while gambling, it was his business. No one was prevented from being a fool.

To top off the fun, when the bars in Bridgeport closed, the after-hours joints in Wheeling had been open since midnight. The theory in Wheeling was that since it was not legal to sell booze at all, it didn't matter if it was sold in the middle of the night—and to anyone, of any age.

The drinking age in West Virginia was eighteen for low alcohol (3.2 percent) beer in licensed bars. Boys who looked eighteen were welcomed into the late-night joints if they behaved well. Girls were judged by their development. If they were cute and looked past jail-bait age (eighteen), no one asked questions. Hookers were welcome as long as they paid the bar owner his share.

The righteous citizens of West Virginia were asleep by midnight and the cops were well compensated ignoring the night life. Everyone got what they wanted and it all worked smoothly. God was in his heaven and all was right with the world.

Local Characters

Bridgeport attracted an eclectic mix of people who didn't work in the mills or mines. Some were professional gamblers, some had unusual jobs, and others were just characters who managed to get by one way or another. Nearly all the men drank heavily, had fun their own way, and didn't worry much about the consequences. They assumed they would have short life spans, but whatever time they had was theirs to spend freely.

Another thing one noticed was men with missing fingers, limbs or eyes. Many men came home from WWI missing something. Only twenty-three years later amputees were returning from WWII. In addition, men were injured in the mills and mines. Effective prostheses had not yet been developed, so the amputees learned to overcome their handicaps any way they could. Men with such mutilations were so common that they were part of the scenery. Living in the middle of the village gave me familiarity with the town characters.

Hot Bun Thornton ran a poker game in the back of the American Restaurant. He was called Hot Bun because he weighed over three hundred pounds and liked pastries. His poker games ran as long as there were players, usually all night on Fridays and Saturdays. Hot Bun's younger, and less obese, brother, Little Hot Bun, ran errands for the card players. There had to be a continuous supply of tobacco, food, and alcohol. Hot Bun became ill and disappeared from the scene not long after the war ended. He was a nice man who once tipped me fifty cents to fetch some cigarettes because he didn't want to walk two doors to the newsstand.

Hooknose Martin had a nose that left no doubt as to how he got his nickname. He worked in the steel mills and did odd jobs when he was laid off. Everyone in town knew Hooknose. He and Dad grew up together and they partnered in a poker game that didn't turn out very well (more about that later). After a life spent consuming booze and cigarettes to great excess, Hooknose died in the late forties.

John Gilhooly was a friend of my grandfather's. He looked like he had just stepped out of an old silent movie. He always wore a white shirt, a black suit, a dark tie, tan spats (stylish shoe covers) over black shoes, and a black bowler hat. He lived in a room at the only hotel in Bridgeport.

John was the secretary of the Eagles Club in the late thirties. It was a paying job but it didn't require all his time. He hung out in the New Carlton Saloon in the afternoons and at the Eagles' bar in the evening. John had his hand in local politics and was a behind-the-scenes advisor to several mayors. He knew everything that was happening in the town—a clue that he was involved in the rackets. He was as Irish as the mayor of Dublin and proud of it.

Dr. Boerngen was the father of Evajean, a classmate of mine. No one seemed to know what kind of doctor he was, but he called himself doctor, so it was assumed that he was one.

When there was a community activity, he would be there as a mechanical man. He covered his face with silver makeup, wore a tuxedo with white gloves, and kept a blank, expressionless stare. He made mechanical movements and stared past anyone who spoke to him, but he would raise his arm and do other movements upon request. The act would have been interesting, but he was not very good at it, often swaying a bit—maybe he had to be a little drunk to do the gig.

At a school open house, Dr. Boerngen put out a display of snakes, lizards, frogs, and other small animals preserved in jars of formaldehyde. That would have been bad enough, but several human fetuses in jars were also part of his show. Some parents were shocked, and complaints were made. This was the forties, and fetus was a word not even taught in high school. Adults who saw the display either thought they were fakes or called them unborn babies. Evajean told me they were real and called them by the correct name. The display was covered with a sheet less than an hour after it opened.

Ludwig "Lud" Hoge was the truant officer, county constable, and head of security at school events. He also drove the school bus to away games and was the full-time secretary of the Eagles Club (having succeeded John Gilhooly). This multiplicity of positions sounds unbelievable, but he got all the jobs done and no one complained.

Lud wore a uniform of his own design. It was dark green and displayed all the appropriate insignias and badges. He drove a 1930s vintage Indian Motorcycle that sputtered and backfired but always got him where he wanted to go.

Lud had a handicap; he stuttered badly, and I do mean b-b-badly. A story went around that Dad swore was true. One day a passing motorist saw Lud in uniform and pulled over to ask for directions. Lud gave him a friendly but stuttered greeting. The man then stuttered when he asked for help. Lud thought he was mocking him and became angry. Before the poor guy could stutter out an explanation, Lud directed the man to follow him to the jail.

Just outside the jail, the police chief spoke to the man, discovered he was a stutterer, and the problem was worked out. Lud apologized, and in short order, the two of them were on the way to being friends. No one knew if Lud ever gave the poor man the directions he needed.

On Mothers' Day each year, the Eagles Club gave a lunch for members and their families. The main speaker at the event was always the club secretary, Ludwig Hoge, and every year he gave the same speech. It was repeated nearly word for word so he could keep stuttering to a minimum. But one word eluded poor Lud, and it always brought muffled laughter, which he blithely ignored. When he said "mother," it came out "mudder." Given the occasion, the word had to be used many times. He never improved; it was mudder for the eight or so years I attended the lunch.

Lud's mudder problem was well known, and for a few weeks after the holiday, everyone used mudder, humorously, in everyday conversation: "How's your mudder" or "Say hello to your mudder for me." Kind, courteous, and hardworking, Lud was the most beloved man in town.

Dad and Lud were good friends, and he became something of an adopted uncle to me when I was a teenager. He also chased me down a couple of times in his capacity as a truant officer, but he always gave me a break. I liked Lud a lot.

Herb Hadley, a.k.a. Pincushion, was the most interesting of all the town characters; a book could have been written about him. No one ever knew where he came from. He just arrived one day and was around for about eight years. During that time, he disappeared from time to time for a few months and then came back. He never said where he'd been. Herb minded his own business, got drunk only occasionally, and did that peaceably and alone. Herb worked around the downtown stores, washing windows, mopping floors, and doing any other job offered. He set no price for his labor, simply taking whatever payment was handed to him and mumbling a thank-you.

He carried everything he owned in one beaten-up suitcase, out of which he lived. He was handy with tools, so the police chief made him the janitor, fix-it man, and food server for the jail. This was an unpleasant task since most of the inmates were drunks who did all the things drunks do when they sleep it off. Herb's reward for this work was a few dollars a week, the same meals prisoners received, and permission to sleep on one of the flat wooden bunks in whichever jail cell was unoccupied. He slept directly on the wood with one blanket and no mattress.

When the jail was full, he slept in a wheelbarrow next to the cells. He lay on his back with his legs stretched out along the handles of the wheelbarrow, a blanket over him and a piece of rolled up clothing as a pillow. Herb didn't demand or need much comfort. He lived his life as fate delivered it.

When he wasn't otherwise occupied, Herb sat on a bench in front of the City Building, where we neighborhood kids and the newspaper boys congregated. Occasionally, if we coaxed him hard enough, he'd send me across the street to get a needle, thread, and a couple of buttons from Mom's sewing kit. Then he would sew buttons on his arm, chest, or ear and leave them in place for the rest of the day.

If adults asked him to do it and promised the right amount, usually a dollar, he would push a hatpin through his cheek on one side, then out the other. Except for a tiny drop, there was never any blood. He could also touch his elbows behind his back, wrap his ankles around his neck, and do all sorts of strange bending and stretching no one had ever seen.

Herb was a big hit at the Wheeling Christmas parade one year. The local icehouse made a hollow block of ice, open at one end and just large enough for a man to wiggle into. Herb was the man inside the ice block that rode through the parade on the bed of a flatbed truck. They sealed the open end with a slab of ice so everyone wondered how he could breathe. He claimed he was able to breathe the air from the melting ice, which made no sense, but no one questioned it.

Wearing long pants but no shirt, Herb was in the ice for about an hour. I ran ahead to be at the end of the parade when they broke the ice. He was shivering uncontrollably, but after a few minutes wrapped in a blanket, he was smiling and waving to the people he knew.

The Firemen's Experiment

While sitting around the firehouse one summer afternoon, Herb offhandedly mentioned that he had once been buried alive. This stimulated some discussion, and he was pressed for details. Some of the men believed him, and some didn't. Gambling appetites were whetted. Within a short time, the burial site was agreed upon. Herb had to stay buried for three hours. After the terms were set, odds were negotiated and bets were made. Chief Joe held the wager money.

Herb was to get 25 percent of the money that changed hands. I have no idea what the arrangement was if he died. I assume the winners would have sprung for some cheap flowers on his grave. Vows of secrecy were frequently essential for every volunteer fireman, and such a vow was taken for this event—no one outside the fireman fraternity was to know about it.

The following Saturday morning, a group of men with picks, shovels, and a couple of cases of beer met behind an old building near the creek to the west of town.

Everything had to be the way Herb wanted it. The hole was to be four feet deep and wide enough for him to lie down on his back, stretched out on boards. More boards were to be placed directly over him and covered with burlap sacks. After Herb was under the boards and sacks, they had to wait quietly—not a word spoken—for exactly twenty minutes before they shoveled in the dirt. Further, they could not compact the dirt by jumping on it.

The he-can't-do-it group promised Herb that if he yelled when the dirt began hitting the blanket covering the boards, they'd stop shoveling. This was a failed scare tactic. Herb didn't ask for it, but a rope, going through the dirt to the surface, was put into his hand so he could pull it if he wanted to be dug up. The he-can't-do-it bettors believed he would pull the rope before all the dirt was filled in.

All went as planned, and Chief Joe marked the time when the last shovel of dirt was put in place. The men sat around on old packing crates, playing cards, smoking, and drinking beer.

When the time was up, they started digging. When they got to the burlap-covered boards, they started yelling at Herb to give them a sign, but there was not a sound and the rope didn't move. Some assumed he had suffocated, and remorse was beginning to set in. When they pulled off the burlap and boards, there was Herb, lying with his hands at his side, looking a bit gray—and very dead.

Panic began to set in, and there was shouting about how to get him out of the hole. Should a doctor be called? Herb let them fry in their own grease for about a minute and then suddenly raised one arm straight up, scaring the hell out of them. Then, he sat up, shook his head a few times, and asked, "What time is it?"

They helped him out of his grave and asked if he was all right. His reply: "I'm fine. I had a nice nap and now I'm hungry." Everyone went back to the fire station for food, beer, and bet payments. Herb was looked at in a different way after that; he was no longer just an odd-job pincushion bum—he was a mystic.

Obviously, this stunt would never be done now. If the man died, the participants would most likely be prosecuted for manslaughter. In those less complicated times that issue never surfaced. The men who knew Herb, Dad among them, figured that if Herb said he could do it, he'd probably done it before. The doubters were mostly men from outside the downtown area, and they didn't know Herb as we did. Herb made more money than he could have in days at his usual occupations.

I wasn't there, but I know this incident happened. After swearing us to secrecy, Dad told the complete story to Mom and me the next day. Within a week, the son of a fireman told me about Herb's burial and I pretended to be surprised. Later, I told Dad the boy knew about it. Dad said he would never trust the boy's father again; the ironic inconsistency of this statement never occurred to him.

Years later, I read about individuals who could put themselves into a trance, control their breathing and pulse, and appear to be dead. I believe that Herb was a lot smarter than we all knew. He may have lived in India and learned all this.

Moving On

Late in the summer of '47 or '48, after he completed some odd job at Mom's store, Herb said, "Mrs. Scheid, I want to thank you for the decent way you've always treated me. You are one of the few people around here who treat me like I'm human, and your son has never made fun of me like some of the other kids. I just want to thank you for being so kind to me."

Mom accepted his statements gracefully and Herb left. He never showed emotion and didn't have personal conversations, so Mom felt this was a unique event and told me about it. She added, "Don't mention it to Herb; it might embarrass him."

A few days later, I noticed Herb was not on his bench in front of the jail. I roamed around the City Building asking about Herb, but no one had seen him. Mom felt the chat she had with him was his way of saying good-bye. The folks around the City Building expected him to show up in the spring. But that was the end of Herb Hadley in Bridgeport - he was never heard from again.

Herb was a strange, gentle man who didn't fit in anywhere and he was a bum by the standards of the day. Nevertheless, he had a sort of unkempt dignity in that he did not beg or complain and worked for everything he received. I learned an important life lesson from Herb: it's okay to be alone and live within yourself, and you don't have to bow to anyone to get by. In many ways, Herb stood taller than the big wheels of the village. He lived life on his terms and people talked about him for a long time. Note that he is being written about seventy years later.

The Top of the Heap—Big Bill Lias

A Wheeling born-and-raised gangster named Big Bill Lias was the top dog in the rackets. It was believed that he ran the mob in the Wheeling market area and reported to higher-ups in Pittsburgh or New York. The Lias gang controlled gambling and prostitution in Wheeling and Bridgeport. He also owned Wheeling Downs, the half-mile horse racing track on Wheeling Island. Most everyone believed it was the most dishonest horse racing venue in America, but this didn't seem to keep the crowds away.

Bill was usually seen in the backseat of a black limousine driven by a cigar-chomping, rough-looking guy in a suit. Bill always wore a black suit and hat, winter and summer. Since the police were well paid, he had no fear of the law.

The New Carlton Bar, where Grandpa carried on his numbers business, was one of Bill's regular stops. Dad told me that Old George had known Bill since he was a young punk. Grandpa always knew what was going on behind the scenes in the village, so I suspect he passed useful information on to Bill.

It might be said that Big Bill was rather placid for a crime boss. He served several short jail sentences and was suspected of a couple of murders. But the gamblers played by Bill's rules, and he didn't rock the boat unless someone got out of line.

About 1950, Frank Lausche became governor of Ohio. One of his vows to the voters was to clean up illegal gambling. Within a few months, the horse betting and card joints in Bridgeport were out of business. Private clubs hung on to their slot machines for a while longer, but they too were eventually closed down. Prostitution and bootleg whiskey continued to thrive in Wheeling into the fifties and early sixties, until reform politicians finally clamped down and drinking laws were liberalized.

Big Bill Lias died in the fifties.

300 Main St., we lived in upper right and lower left apartments; Spic & Span Dry Cleaners was in the store front on the right – store closed, 1952, picture taken about 1980

Mom and Dad with Tippy, in front of Spic & Span store, circa 1942

Tippy and Al at entrance to Spic & Span store, circa 1942

Bridgeport Fraternal Order of Eagles, Aerie 995, N. Lincoln Ave., circa 1945

My father, George E. Scheid, President of Eagles Club,

300+ pound Big Bill Lias, the gangster, racketeer, who ran gambling in Bridgeport

CHAPTER 9

The art of being wise is
the art of knowing what to overlook.
—William James, philosopher (1842–1910)

An error doesn't become a mistake until you refuse to correct it.
—Orlando A. Battista, chemist, author (1917–1995)

MY FATHER

George Edward Scheid, Jr., was born on January 28, 1902 and grew up mostly in Boydsville. The family lived just above the poverty line. Dad and his brother, John, lived a sort of Huckleberry Finn existence, playing and exploring in and around the Little Wheeling Creek and the surrounding woods. They were shoeless in the summer and poorly clothed in the winter.[9] Dad quit school after the eighth grade and did whatever work he could find after that.

He was about five feet seven and 150 pounds. His everyday diet was rich in fatty meat, potatoes, and high-sodium canned vegetables.

9 It was still common in the 1940s for country kids to go barefoot all summer, wearing shoes only for church and special occasions. Only with the onset of cold weather were shoes worn regularly.

Given their diets and lifestyles, it's amazing how many of Dad's generation lived into their seventies.

Dad began smoking cigarettes when he was about thirteen and smoked at least a pack a day for the rest of his life. Adults who were heavy smokers often had a complexion with a yellowish overtone and Dad was no exception. Men drank beer every day and whiskey when they could afford it—or someone else was buying.

Due to lack of care, Dad had terrible teeth. He just let them rot away. Because of the expense, no one saw a dentist until it was absolutely necessary. Injected painkillers were not in common use until after WWII and fear of pain was a major reason people avoided dentists. Even after painkillers were available, they were expensive and considered frivolous - real men didn't take pain shots.

By the time he was about forty-two, Dad had no upper front teeth, only the ugly remains of tooth roots and his lower teeth were stained dark brown. The family doctor told him that the decay was ruining his health. Finally, he was hospitalized and what was left of his teeth were removed by an oral surgeon. The first time I saw him with false teeth, he looked like a new man. In a short time his physical health improved noticeably.

Dad's Mishaps

During the First World War Dad worked in a metal stamping works. His job was to place a flat, piece of steel on a die, then push a lever which caused another die to drop down on to the metal, thus stamping out a food plate for the army. Stamping machines were known to double hit on occasion, so it was a bad idea to reach in for the stamped plate too quickly. He made this mistake and the three middle fingers of his right hand were crushed beyond repair; his thumb and little finger were not touched.

As he told the story, a tourniquet was tightened around his forearm and what was left of the fingers was wrapped in bandages. He was told to hold his hand above his heart and a fellow worker was assigned to go with him on a streetcar to the hospital. A doctor anesthetized him with ether, cut off the crushed parts of his fingers, and then sewed them up. After the ether wore off, he used streetcars to get to Boydsville where he walked half a mile home from the streetcar stop.

He was left with just enough of his right index finger to be able to pull a gun trigger. His other two fingers had only short stubs. Dad overcame this handicap in good form. He fired guns, used tools, and dealt cards right-handed well enough to run poker games. I never heard him complain about losing his fingers; he just moved on with life.

A couple of years after this accident, he was working nights as a gas station attendant. For self-protection, he carried a .32-caliber automatic pistol. As he was leaving for work one evening, his mother picked up the gun, and as she was handing it to him, it fired. The bullet took off the end of Grandma's right index finger, then entered Dad's lower abdomen. The surgeon searched his intestines for holes, sewed them up, and let nature take its course. Had he missed one hole, Dad would have died of peritonitis. He had a high fever for a few days and then recovered. The bullet lodged near his lower spine, where it still resided when he died.

Dad hunted small game with a single shot, 12 gauge shotgun. His attitude was that if you couldn't make a kill with one shot, you should let the animal escape. He was a good shot, and his favorite game, wild rabbit, was a common dinner for our family.

Not long after he and Mom were married, Dad was shot again, this time while rabbit hunting. Just as he was passing a bush that hid him from his hunting partners, a rabbit ran by. He put his gun up to his shoulder to shoot, and at that moment, another hunter fired. The pellets hit his head and right shoulder. His gunstock protected his neck. But about twenty lead pellets entered his scalp, arm, and right cheek. The doctor was able to extract most of them. One pellet lodged below his right cheekbone, where it could be seen as a dark spot. He never had it removed, saying it was a constant reminder to be more careful about picking hunting partners.

The Poker Caper

About 1939, Dad tried his hand at running his own poker game in partnership with his boyhood chum, Hooknose Martin. Big Bill Lias considered gambling in Bridgeport to be his exclusive business. Dad and Hooknose knew this, but their game was intended just for men they knew, and it was not a high stakes game. They reasoned that Big Bill wouldn't pay any attention. Wrong! Late one night, Dad gave the dealer's chair over to Hooknose and went to fetch drinks and sandwiches. While he was gone, two masked men barged in, robbed everyone, and gave Hooknose a bang on the head with a handgun. After telling the players the game was closed permanently, they left quietly.

A few minutes later Dad arrived and took Hooknose to the hospital for stitches. Word spread fast and the George Scheid-Hooknose Martin poker game was finished.

To make certain the message was clear, a Lias man told Grandpa that the gunmen had waited for Dad to leave before they went in. Someone had to take the hit and Dad was spared because Big Bill liked his father. Somehow they knew that Grandpa was not aware of his son's game, so he wasn't blamed for this misstep. Big Bill could afford to be magnanimous

Labors of Love

When Dad joined the Eagles, he quickly became an active member. An active member was often selected for a simple post, enabling him to demonstrate his ongoing devotion to the club. If that went well, he advanced to higher responsibilities through annual elections.

After years of advances, Dad became worthy president, the top job in an Aerie. The Eagles Club was his first love, and his home away from home, for all of his adult life.

Dad's involvement with the fire department and devotion to the Eagles consumed most of his time and energy. Both of these organizations involved constant socializing and drinking. They also consumed most of the money he made. When there were time conflicts, the organizations always came first. This was good for him but not so good for his wife and son.

Dad must have had a large liver. His ability to consume beer all day and still perform duties was legendary among his peers. He could pace his drinking so that he didn't guzzle, but the beer in front of him never got warm. Consuming a case of beer over the course of a day and evening was not unusual for him. Having done my share of boozing, I am amazed that he was able to function as he did, week after week.

It would have been wonderful to have an educated, successful father as a role model, but that's not the way it was. Dad was a man of his time and place, doing pretty much what came naturally. I did not then, nor have I ever, blamed him for being as he was - it would be like blaming a dog for barking. Nor have I ever felt disadvantaged by the way I grew up. Quite the contrary, there are long-term benefits to experiencing hardships when young. My role models were in the books I read. My book heroes prevailed in life and even in death. I wanted to be like them, not the men I knew.

My Mother

Isabelle Adolphine Jonard was born on October 8, 1908. She was barely five feet tall but could accomplish enormous amounts of work in a day. She did many jobs during her life and her employers always seemed to sense that they could trust her with any amount of money or responsibility.

Not many coal mine town girls graduated from high school in 1926, but Mom did - thanks to her mother. But since she had to help keep house for her father and brothers, she didn't participate in school activities. The Alfred Jonard household was filled with conflict and rancor - dominated by a strict father who supported a headstrong, spoiled, and cruel firstborn boy. Mom didn't adjust to her station in life calmly. She resented having to care for her brothers.

Mom's oldest brother, Alex, was an example of the saying that everyone grows old but not everyone grows up. He behaved as a spoiled brat and bully all his life. When Mom didn't serve him as he wanted, he shoved her around verbally, emotionally, and, when he could get away with it, physically. He became more threatening after Mom was divorced. At age twenty, I put an end to his physical threats one Sunday afternoon at a family gathering when I dared him to fight me. Sadly, he backed down, ungracefully, in front of everyone. Like most bullies, Uncle Alex had the courage of a domestic rabbit.

Mom had an aunt named Georgia who was my grandmother's sister. She was the "character," "misfit," or whatever of the extended family. Aunt Georgie, as we called her, smoked cigarettes, drank beer and whiskey, and was divorced. Her speech was sprinkled with profanities adopted while she worked in a factory before, during, and after WWII. She visited us often and was a buddy to me. After swearing me to secrecy at age thirteen, she spent the next few years of visits telling me her versions of the Jonard family stories and secrets. She and Grandpa Jonard didn't like each other.

Because it made me feel grown-up to be part of her conspiratorial style, I listened carefully and never broke my secrecy vow. It was mostly from Georgie that I learned about my mother's upbringing, several family out-of-wedlock pregnancies, a few arrests, and other family dirt. Georgie always had a few beers during our secret-sharing chats. After I turned fifteen, she'd pour me a glass of beer—sometimes two.

She often played cards with my high school buddies and me. We all loved her dirty jokes and humorous profanity. She always made sure everything was cleaned up - with beer bottles in the outside trash can and the cards put away—before Mom came home. She didn't want to be accused of leading us astray, which she most certainly did.

Mom was kind and thoughtful and always willing to help someone in need. At the beginning of WWII, she formed a Wednesday evening knitting group and named it The Community Club. The purpose of the club was for Mom to teach women to knit well enough to make gloves, sweaters, socks, and scarves for the men in the army. The government sent her knitting instructions and skeins of army-brown yarn, and her group sent back finished goods—gobs of it.

A black woman came in the store one day and asked Mom to teach her and some of her friends to knit for the army. They formed a group of black women who met every Tuesday to learn knitting skills. There were a few white women who sniveled about having a separate group of "Negroes" in the Community Club. Mom ignored them, and the problem went away. Most white women thought Mom was doing a wonderful thing, getting more sweaters made for the army. She taught knitting two evenings each week throughout the war. As a little plus, the women became loyal dry cleaning and clothing alteration customers. Not all good deeds are punished.

The Marriage and Family Dynamics

According to Aunt Georgie, my parents had marital problems from the beginning but always managed to make up and move on. The unplanned arrival of a child in the bottom of the Depression was a bummer. Being broke and having a new baby strained the best of marriages.

Some of my earliest memories are of my parents having loud arguments. The name-calling and shouting never stopped. They abused each other as a style of daily living. There was no end to the subjects they could fight about. Once I was old enough to exert some independence they argued over my freedom, one accusing the other of being too strict or too lenient. In the end, I generally got to do what I wanted because the argument ended with no resolution

Occasionally, when Dad got home late or skipped work for a day, Mom would threaten to take me and leave. He would beg for another chance, which she always gave him. For a short time, he would go to work on time and cut down on the drinking and late hours, but he soon lapsed back into his normal lifestyle. It's in the nature of a dog to bark.

Early on, I learned to keep a low profile, appear to be obedient, and then do as I wanted. Forgiveness was easy to get, so why bother asking permission and cause a fight? That pattern seemed to please them both, and by the time I was twelve, they simply left me alone. My efforts were spent avoiding adult complaints about my behavior - teachers, police, and the like. As I developed interests of my own, I spent less and less time with them. This worked well for all three of us.

During WWII, there was heavy demand for Dad's expertise as a licensed electrician, and he was offered many electrical repair jobs. But, there was often a shortage of materials due to wartime rationing. He took this problem philosophically: no materials, no work, and nothing he could do about it, right?

There were ads in the papers for electricians in the steel mills and factories. Mom prodded him to take a job, but his attitude was that he had worked in the mills and he was not going to take a step backward. He saw himself as a self-employed electrical contractor.

Finally they reached an accommodation that avoided divorce. They continued to argue, but the volume was turned down and there were times of peace. After she closed the store Mom either stayed home or met him at the Eagles Club. Dad worked as much as he wanted and did his thing with the Eagles and fire department. Essentially, Mom became what the Alcoholics Anonymous people call an enabler.

The good news of this was that I was relatively free to do whatever I wanted. This worked out well, as I didn't mind being alone with my books, hobbies, and radio—or roaming around town. The bad news was that we had no sense of family. I resented the lack of attention until I was old enough to have an evening life of my own.

The Eagles became their activity center. The Thursday Family Night was a bit of a misnomer. Kids under sixteen were not allowed in the social room those nights, so what did they mean by family? It meant adult drinking and dancing, with kids out of the way.

Until I was nearly fourteen, the normal Thursday and Saturday for the Scheid family was for me to be dropped off at the Village Theater. Thursday was the end of a movie run, and a new feature started on Friday. When the movies were over, I'd walk the half mile through downtown to the Eagles.

The route took me past the New Carlton, the Lincoln Bar and Grill, Pop's Poolroom, the Candy Kitchen, Harding and Burley Restaurant, and a few minor beer joints, with a mortuary and a bank mixed in. Being in no hurry, I sometimes stood in the shadows or across the street and watched the people going from joint to joint.

I didn't yet know exactly what a hooker or prostitute was, but I had read enough by age thirteen that I grasped why certain ladies wore flashy dresses and strolled in and out of the bars alone. A boy can learn a lot just by watching and listening to people.

Occasionally, a cop would ask me, "Why aren't you home where you belong?"

My quick reply was, "I'm meeting my parents at the Eagles," which satisfied them and, after telling me to get a move on, they ignored me.

The routine was for me to go downstairs when I arrived at the Eagles and ring the buzzer at the door. The doorman opened the peep hole and I told him to let my parents know I was there. Then I went back upstairs and sat in the lobby lounge to read whatever I'd brought with me. Eventually, I fell asleep on a sofa.

There were members who didn't approve of my sleeping in the lobby. Several times when they thought I was asleep, I heard people gossiping that it was a shame the way George and Isabelle left their boy in the lobby so late at night.

The sofa was not like sleeping in a bed, but I got enough sleep on Thursday nights to go to school on Fridays. The problem was homework, which never got done. They seemed oblivious to that subject, but I never complained about not having to do homework.

Somehow they thought it was safe for me to go to the movies and then walk to the Eagles, alone in the dark but considered it dangerous for me to be at home alone. That wasn't great logic. When I was nearly fourteen, I finally convinced them it was safe for me to be at home alone after a movie.

Now I had nearly as many options as an adult. When it was cold, I could go to a movie and then run across the street into a warm apartment. Or I could stay home, reading, listening to the radio, working on model airplanes, or whatever. The roaming around town option was still used in good weather. With me safe at home, they felt free to visit the after-hours clubs in Wheeling on Saturday nights. On Sunday mornings, after one of those nights, I wasn't allowed to play the radio and had to make my breakfast quietly.

The town had a 9 p.m. curfew for kids under sixteen, but it was selectively enforced. The police were accustomed to seeing me out and about, and every shopkeeper knew who I was. Mom gave each cop free dry cleaning of a uniform each month and a discount for the rest of their needs. They showed their appreciation in many ways. Once I was picked up by a new cop who wouldn't buy my story about being on my way to the Eagles Club. The first cop we saw at the City Building explained the situation to the new cop drove me to the Eagles. I enjoyed having a cop as a chauffeur.

Mea Culpa

Let me state clearly that the reader should not conclude that I was an abused child. In my mind, I was not. Not everything was to my liking and there was too much drama, but I didn't feel deprived or abused. I was never beaten, as some of my friends were, and I never went hungry.

In the 21st century, my parent's behavior, as a package, might well be considered child abuse. But in the 1940s people tended to mind their own business. The good side about my childhood was that I learned self-reliance. Going to the movies on my own, wandering around town after dark, and being at home alone gave me the confidence that I could run my life quite well. Children of my generation were not catered to and mollycoddled. That questionable cultural model came into style many years later.

The Hobo Incident

When the trains crossed streets, they blocked traffic. We boys watched hobos run to catch trains and admired the way they caught the ladders, threw their bundles on board, and easily heaved themselves on board.

A railroad flagman was stationed at the Lincoln Avenue crossing to make certain cars and pedestrians stayed a safe distance from moving trains. One summer evening, I was waiting with a few other pedestrians for a slow-moving train to pass. A hobo was hanging on the side of an approaching railcar; it was obvious that he intended to jump off just past the crossing. He had a bag in one hand, with the other hand hanging on to the ladder he had just climbed down. As he jumped, his coat caught on something and he was flung under the railcar. The wheels ran over both of his legs, just below the knees. He began screaming, "Help me, help me!" as he thrashed about, flinging his arms.

The flagman ran to him, followed by a few other bystanders and me. The sight was ghastly. The flagman yelled, "Grab the phone in the shack and call the police." Then he pulled the hobo away from the rails and used his and the hobo's belts as tourniquets on the leg stumps. The hobo screamed for a few more seconds, then stopped. The train had passed, all was quiet, and the man lay still.

Several people vomited, but I didn't. Apparently, my intimate acquaintance with gallons of nose blood had hardened me to the sight of bleeding. The flagman shooed us away as the police and an ambulance arrived. I knew the cop and asked if the hobo was still alive. He said, "No, Al, he's dead. Now, you get the hell out of here."

A minute later, while walking away, I started shaking as I realized that I had just watched a man die—then I had to fight vomiting. I walked around a while, trying to decide if I should tell Mom and Dad, thus admitting I had been wandering around town again. I decided against it. The next day, Mom told me about the accident and added, "Oh, that would be an awful thing to see."

Later A cop told Dad I had been there when it happened. Dad cornered me and asked, "Are you all right about this?" he asked. I assured him I was fine. He said, "That's good, but don't tell your mother you were there." We never spoke of the incident again.

For a while I had occasional dreams in which the hobo's bloody stumps stood out much larger than in real life. I told Wendell and a couple other kids what I had seen, but only Wendell believed me.

FISHING

A teenage friend taught me how to catch catfish in the river and creek using fishing worms or raw shrimp as bait. The old rod Dad gave me to use was stiff and the reel was rickety, but with practice, I learned to "thumb" the reel and was able to cast the bait. Fishing for catfish became one of my favorite summer hobbies.

One day at the river, a friendly black man told me I should use chicken guts for bait. He put some chicken intestines on my hooks and showed me where to cast. I caught two eating-size catfish in a few minutes and at least one with each new cast. I was sold on the new bait.

From then on, I stopped by the chicken slaughterhouse on my way to the river and bought a handful of guts for a nickel. With this new bait, filling a stringer with catfish was easy. My fellow fisherman also told me, "Yawl don't cut chicken guts with your knife; you uses a piece of broke glass. Guts has germs that'll ruin your knife and they might make you sick too." He helped me find a piece of glass with a sharp edge, which I wrapped in a rag and kept in my tackle box.

When I had a full stringer of ten or so fish, I'd take them to a black family whose son went to my school. White people wouldn't eat fish from the river, so it was either throw them back, where they'd probably die, or walk over a half mile and give them away. I had a self-created superstition that if I wasted the fish, my fishing luck would change for the worse. Sometimes my fishing friend would take my catch to save me the walk to the black part of town.

Roller Skating

When I was eight, I got steel wheel street skates as a gift. They had clamps you tightened on the soles of your shoes with a skate key. Skating on the cement sidewalks of the town was my favorite activity until the wheels wore down.

After a lot of nagging, Mom took me to the wood floor roller rink on Wheeling Island one Sunday. The wooden wheeled skates they rented still had to be clamped to your street shoes, but the skating was smooth compared to steel wheels on cement. I loved it and begged to go back. That Christmas, my big present was a pair of used shoe skates with wood wheels. It was a real *WOW!*

Within a year, I had persuaded Mom and Dad to let me take the streetcar to the rink on Saturday afternoons. It became my obsession to skate in the evenings. By thirteen, I was going on some Thursday and Saturday evenings and skipping the Saturday afternoon kid time. All my coal hauling earnings were spent on skating.

I learned by watching others take lessons, sort of a "monkey see, monkey do" school. Once I learned to free turn (turning 180 degrees on one skate), first on my right leg, then the left, other maneuvers were easy to learn. By age fourteen, I was skating with girls. One girl lived near the rink, took lessons, and was an excellent skater. She wanted to practice dancing and I wanted to learn more, so we skated together for hours. We entered a couple of competitions but never won anything.

My Bridgeport pals had no interest in the roller rink, and none of them learned to skate even moderately well. For a dollar a month, I stored my skates at the rink so the guys wouldn't see me carrying them. Over time, I developed a group of friends who lived in Wheeling or on the Island.

The roller rink was where I could be a different person than I was in Bridgeport—it let me live in two different worlds. Until dancing and other interests took over my evenings, roller skating was an important and secret part of my life.

The Farm

Just before WWII began, Grandpa bought a thirty-eight-acre farm about ten miles from Bridgeport. He and Grandma lived there for a while before they sold it to their son Alex and his wife, Gertrude. For the next few summers, I stayed a few weeks each year at this farm and, later on, at a larger farm Uncle Alex bought. It was a relief to be away from the constant bickering at home.

Because of my problematic health, Mom had tried to restrict my activities. On the farm, I was expected to hoe corn, pitch hay, milk cows, and do a myriad of other chores. This meant getting outdoor exercise, which I believe improved my health. It certainly toughened me up compared to sitting around reading, making model airplanes, and doing puzzles. Uncle Alex was a stern taskmaster. He expected his kids to work hard and treated me the same. I was a little afraid of him, but if you did your work without complaint, he left you alone.

Aunt Gertrude was a wonderful woman and the best cook in the family. She seemed to understand everything about kids. She often took my two younger cousins and me wild berry picking. The family ate some of the berries fresh, but most were "put up" in glass jars for use over the winter. Putting up means cooking fruits, vegetables, and even meat in quart or pint glass jars designed for the purpose. During the war, Aunt Gertrude's family ate better food than families with much more money.

In a couple of years, Uncle Alex moved his family to a 120-acre farm a few miles from the first one. By then, I was able to drive a tractor and handle the reins of a two-horse team. Since two of my male cousins were older and bigger, they pitched hay onto the wagon while I drove, pulling the wagon forward from stack to stack. When we got to the barn, it was my job to climb up into the loft and spread hay to the back of the loft. Since the Jonards were all acrophobic, they couldn't climb into the loft.

The family had a saddle horse that we were allowed to ride on Sunday afternoons. On days when the workhorses had a day off, we rode them bareback because their bodies were too broad for the only available saddle. Workhorses are walkers by nature, but a thick stick applied to their rumps encouraged them to trot a short distance. By the end of my farm experiences, I was able to ride into the woods to find lost cows and herd them home.

One of the few things I hated was the outhouse we used as a toilet. It smelled awful and gagged me at first. The system was to run in, lock the door, and get your business done as quickly as possible. No one read on the toilet in an outhouse, and no one ever really became accustomed to the terrible smell.

CHAPTER 10

Creativity represents a miraculous coming together of the uninhibited energy of the child with its apparent opposite and enemy—the sense of order imposed on the disciplined adult intelligence
—Norman Podhoretz, author, editor (1930–living)

They told me to take a streetcar named Desire
and then transfer to one called Cemeteries
and ride six blocks and get off at - Elysian Fields!
—Tennessee Williams, playwright (1911-1983)

STREETCARS

Streetcars were slow, reliable, and picturesque. The streetcar system created a useful geographic dimension because the stops were numbered. The Scheid store on Main Street was at stop 2, the footbridge across the creek to Kirkwood was at stop 6 and the Bridgeport school athletic field was at stop 12, and so on to stop 32. To identify where you lived, you simply told someone your stop number.

Streetcar seats had sturdy woven split bamboo coverings that gave off an odor I still recall. The backs of the seats could be pushed forward and backward so passengers could always face in the direction of travel. Young brats often moved the seat backs so we could sit facing each other and foot fight. This annoyed the conductors immensely because they couldn't see what mischief was going on. Some conductors tried threats to make kids face forward, but that rarely worked. There was no rule on how the seats faced, and we knew it. The workday of a conductor was not an easy one.

Diesel-powered buses replaced the streetcars about 1948 and there was nothing picturesque about them and the black diesel exhaust contributed to the air pollution. I missed the smell of the bamboo seats and the charm of streetcars.

The Machine Gun

At about age eleven, a couple of pals and I discovered how to cut the tips off of phosphorous matches, hit them with a hammer and get a loud bang, nearly like a rifle shot. One day a boy had a couple of .22-caliber copper casings. We put a few match tips into the casing and squeezed the end closed with pliers. Then we put the casing on the streetcar rail, hid and watched. When the streetcar rolled over the casing, there was a loud crack—just like a .22 rifle shot. The conductor got out, looked at the front wheel, shook his head, and went back to his job.

It came to me that if we put about dozen of these loaded casings in a row; it would sound like a machine gun when the wheels ran over them.

It was easy to find .22 casings at the dump and one of my pals pilfered a box of matches from his family pantry. We selected a spot at stop 6, just after a bend in the road. One kid went about fifty yards up the road as a lookout. When he gave the signal, it meant that the streetcar was just short of the bend and it was time for us to place our casings and scramble out of sight. The caper worked way beyond our highest expectations.

It did indeed rat-a-tat-a-tat like a machine gun. It scared the bejesus out of the conductor and the passengers. The conductor jumped out of the car, spotted the .22 casings flattened on the rail, and knew what had happened. He was the same conductor on whom we had practiced the day before. It hadn't occurred to us that the same man worked the same shift all week. We stayed hidden and the streetcar drove away toward Bridgeport and another thing we hadn't planned on—the police station.

We were at the small playground below the stop 6 footbridge when the cops arrived. By that age, every boy I knew was an accomplished liar. The cops asked if we had heard multiple shot sounds earlier. With wide-eyed looks, we said, "Yeah, we did. What was that?" They were suspicious, but after a few more questions, they decided to knock on some doors and find a witness.

We went down to the creek and had a meeting during which we swore on all that's holy that we would never tell anyone what we had done, and we didn't—well, not for a few years.

We had enough common sense to make that the last machine gun gig. However, Ron and I couldn't resist passing the idea on to some eleven-year-old boys when we were about sixteen. We figured the statute of limitations had run out for us. The boys did it and got caught. Their parents had to come to the police station to get them, and they received heavy punishments at home.

We felt sorry for them, but a prank like that screamed to be repeated. Our parents were called, but nothing came of it. Ron's father thought it was funny and Mom smiled as she scolded me.

Biking, Exploring, and Guns

By ten, most boys were allowed to ride bikes on neighborhood streets but not on National Road. Of course, this rule was observed mostly in its breach. Helmets had not yet been invented, and there were a few bad accidents. After passing a biking test with Dad driving behind me all the way to stop 12 and back, I was allowed to ride on National Road.

A couple of older boys let me join them for bike explorations. We planned our forays like terrorists, leaving our home territory casually and then pedaling like crazy to make sure we'd get back early enough to avoid a scolding. We explored the Island and local neighborhoods for hours. Within a year I had the freedom to bike as far as I liked, as long as I got home at an appointed time.

We looked forward to hearing the fire siren. If we happened to be near the City Building we rushed there and found out where the fire was. Because we could use alleys and paths the fire engine couldn't, we often got to the fire first. A good fire made for an exciting day.

For my twelfth birthday, Dad gave me my first real gun. It was a Stevens Arms Company "over and under"—that is, a .22-caliber rifle barrel over a .410 bore shotgun.

We took the gun into the woods where I was taught how to handle it correctly. I shot tin cans, and Dad rolled some small boulders down a hill to give me a shot at a moving target. I did well enough to merit his confidence, which was a big thing for me.

The big day came that fall, when I got to take my gun on a rabbit hunt. Dad's hunting pals went along with this because I had hunted with the group for a couple of years while carrying my BB gun.

I was so nervous that I missed my first shot by ten feet. The second was a little closer. On my third chance I nailed the bunny. Dad and his pals were nearly as excited as I was. Beginner's luck is great fun.

Over the years, I learned to hunt and shoot well and continued to use my old .410 long after my friends used 12 or 16-gauge shotguns. It was a matter of pride to me that I could hit rabbits and squirrels with a single-shot, small gauge shotgun. That gun was my most treasured possession and I wouldn't let friends see it unless Dad was present, that being the promise I had made.

I loved going into the woods alone and sitting quietly under a tree, breathing in the aromas of autumn and enjoying the woodsy sounds. I had learned the places where the squirrels lived; the trick was to stand or sit patiently, letting them come to you. When that didn't work, the reward was quiet time to think and reflect in a pleasant environment—not a bad result either way.

Hunting rabbits required walking through fields of harvest stubble and brushy woods to flush them out. It was poor sportsmanship to shoot a rabbit that sat still. A sportsman barked like a dog and shot the animal when it ran. We ate the game we brought home, so we had no guilt about killing it. Shooting game and not eating it was considered wasteful and an insult to hunting. It was okay to give game away when you had a really good day, but I rarely did that. We ate everything I brought home.

Grandpa Jonard

About age ten, I finally began to know my maternal grandfather. Grandma convinced Mom that I was old enough to ride the streetcar the ten miles or so to Tiltonsville and work some Saturdays at Grandpa's grocery store. I hated missing roller skating, but the idea of earning some spending money and being able to show I could work made it easier.

Over the next year, I spent a number of Saturdays sacking potatoes, carrying out groceries for customers, and stocking shelves in the little grocery store. Grandpa saw life as a serious business, but I was sometimes able to tease a smile out of him. He understood my home situation and asked none too subtle questions. While talking to Grandma within my hearing, he was outspoken in his criticism of my father. He didn't approve of heavy drinking. He drank only a few beers now and then and a little whiskey on holidays.

On most visits I stayed overnight on Saturdays. After dinner on Saturday, we sat in the living room. Grandpa added up the charge books from the grocery store, Grandma knitted or crocheted, and I read a book. We all listened to the radio. It was not exciting but quite peaceful. Neither of them were readers, so they paid no attention to what I read.

Grandpa had a limited education and no interest in books. He considered reading novels an affectation of educated people. It bothered him that I knew so much about the war and had opinions about politics. I overheard him say to Mom, "Isabelle, do you have any idea what Alfred is reading? You have to control that boy. He just knows too much for his age and talks too much about it."

Adults did all they could to discourage children from thinking for themselves. We were expected to listen, never questioning, never arguing, but slavishly believing whatever adults told us. One of my uncles had a tantrum because I voiced an opinion on a trivial matter I'd read about. There was fear that kids were trying to be smarter and speak better English than the adults. By the age of thirteen, I'd learned to keep my thoughts to myself and was successful at this most, but not all, of the time.

Eventually, my cousins caught on to my Saturday visits and wanted their turns to work in the store and sleep over. Also, I had wearied of Grandpa's constant negative remarks about my father, so my visits stopped.

Grandma Jonard

Grandma Jonard was very influential in the lives of her grandchildren. I listened to what she had to say because there was wisdom in her thoughts. I have been quoting her sayings, homilies, and old wives' tales all my life. She had a response for just about every circumstance. I have always believed that she made up many of her sayings, even though she often gave attribution to others. Here are a few of them:

- When you forget something and have to go back for it: "What you don't have in your head, you have to have in your feet."
- When you are criticized unfairly: "The most clubs fall under the best apple tree."
- When you are habitually tardy: "You run fast but you start late."
- When something is not good but is what it is: "You can't make a silk purse out of a sow's ear."
- When a kid fell down and didn't know whether to cry or not: "Don't holler before you're hurt."
- When someone who is normally slovenly dresses up: "Is he/she going to a wedding or a funeral?"
- When it rained really hard: "It's raining pitchforks and hammer handles."
- When children are listening: "Little pitchers have large handles [ears]."
- On bragging: "He's not blowing his own horn; he's a brass band."
- And my favorite: "Nothing good happens after midnight."

Of course, there were the sayings everybody used: "Don't buy a pig in a poke," "Monkey see, monkey do," and many, many more. Grandma spoke in tribal code, and her grandchildren learned it.

Grandma never drank alcohol but didn't condemn those who did. But, she didn't speak to Grandpa for a day or two after he had consumed what she considered too much whiskey on a holiday. It was her way to keep him under control, which she did with a firm hand and a quick wit. Grandpa was no match for her in any way.

From middle age, Grandma had false teeth. This was common for her generation, whose diet included too much sugar and practically no teeth brushing. By their late forties or early fifties, many women had their teeth pulled and were fitted with dentures. Grandma had daily trouble with her false teeth hurting her gums and didn't wear them much of the time.

Grandma understood that I was a loner, and she knew this even before I realized it. Regarding being alone, she gave me one of her homilies: “When you decide to be alone, make sure you’re in good company.” This meant don’t be alone just because you’re feeling sorry for yourself. You should enjoy being alone.

Years later, when asked why I sometimes hiked, hunted, skied and played golf alone; I modified her homily to “I was alone so I could be in good company.” It was a smart-ass statement—but, it was usually true. It’s my observation that people who can’t stand being alone have other problems. That’s one loner’s opinion.

Grandma understood kids. My cousins and I were afraid of Grandpa, but we really worried about getting caught by Grandma if we did something wrong. He would yell at us and make threats, rarely carried out. She did not shout or spank; she just made you feel that you were a failure. You had let her down and were disgraced in her eyes. She did this by saying only a few words, but her communication was clear.

Something I never figured out is why she was such a fine grandmother but her own children were messed up in so many ways. Could Grandpa have been the problem? Maybe she learned on her children and applied the lessons to my generation. I dare not hazard a guess—she may be watching. In any case, she enforced discipline with just the right look or a few well-chosen words. She had a rare skill.

One time when Grandma was in her eighties, my girlfriend mentioned that she jogged most mornings and then asked my grandma, “When you were young, did you run for exercise?”

Grandma said, “Yes, when I was playing games, but never after I was seventeen.”

The girlfriend asked, “Why seventeen?”

Grandma’s reply: “Well, I remember very well the last time I ran. I was with my fiancé, the day before we were married, and we ran to catch a streetcar. You see, in my day, after you were married, you had to behave like a lady—and ladies don't run." The implication was clear, succinct, and to the point. The girlfriend changed the subject.

What Grandma didn't explain was that she washed clothes on a washboard; hung them on an outdoor clothesline higher than her head, winter and summer; carried coal to the stove to cook; cleaned her house; then walked to her mother's home to help with the housekeeping there. Later, when her husband had a grocery store, she stocked shelves and waited on customers while still keeping house. Still later, while living on a farm, she milked cows at dawn, made butter in a hand-operated churn, mended clothes, did the laundry, and cooked. Her life was actually not unusual for an uneducated girl from a coal mining family, and she didn't feel she was experiencing anything other than a normal life. She didn't jog or do yoga, but she got plenty of exercise.

Grandma was keenly aware of the troubles in my parents' marriage and was not shy about her concern for me. I never did figure out who her source of information was, but she always knew things that surprised me. She knew about the Eagles Club, Dad's drinking and his poor work habits. She was aware that Mom enabled this lifestyle by sharing the money she made, and joining Dad for late nights out and about.

Grandma instigated buying a house in Kirkwood so they could rent half of it to my parents and we'd have a better place to live. It was she who taught me to play canasta, then invited me to play with her and Grandpa to bring us closer together.

She had no knowledge of what kind of books I read as a teenager. If she had, she wouldn't have approved of many of them. We had sort of a "don't ask, don't lie" agreement about books—she didn't ask, and I didn't have to lie.

CHAPTER 11

Who can explain it, who can tell you why,
fools give you reasons, wise men never try.
—Rodgers & Hammerstein, in South Pacific

What is needed, rather than running away
or controlling or suppressing or any other resistance,
is understanding fear; that means, watch it, learn about it,
come directly into contact with it.
We are to learn about fear, not how to escape from it.
—Jiddu Krishnamurti, writer, philosopher (1895–1986)

THE ARRIVAL OF MACHO

Until junior high my main social activity had been roller skating so I was not "one of the boys." Entry into the athletic cliques was not easy. Most athletic boys began being active in sports from age six or eight. I was way behind the curve.

Years of government war propaganda had promoted tough-mindedness and grit. In the newsreels, shown just prior to movies, we saw flamethrowers torching the Japanese, piles of bodies after a battle, and the dead on the beaches of the Pacific islands. The populace was hardened by this exposure. Things that would have shocked people in 1940 were considered ordinary by 1943.

All of this created a culture that put great store in physical strength, macho behavior and all-around tough manhood. Physical courage was the most important trait a young man could demonstrate. Ours was not a gentle touchy-feely culture by 1945–46. The war was over, but as a popular song lyric said, "The memories linger on ..." And they did.

With no professional teams in the area, high school sports had deep interest and large attendance. It became fashionable for every town to have a group called the "boosters," that supported high school teams with extra money for whatever the coach said he needed. And, the coach had to produce winning teams if he wanted to keep his job.

If a boy wanted to play, it was made clear that he had to live with these conditions or sit on the bench, or maybe be told he wasn't tough enough for the sport. Playing while injured was a demonstration of courage. If a player complained of pain in a leg, a coach would say, "That's a long way from your heart - it won't kill you." Malingering was, in the coaches' minds, a mental defect that could be cured by assigning extra laps and push-ups.

In this macho environment, "real" boys were expected to fight at the drop of a hat; it was cowardly to take an insult or a slur without a reply.

Mothers didn't support this culture—they just lived with it. They soothed their injured son, put on some bandages and expected it to happen again. It was an environment loaded with testosterone. This may be why the Ohio Valley produced so many great athletes [10] along with an army of successful coaches. At the same time, the

10 Among others: Phil Niekro, Baseball Hall of Fame and John Havlicek, Basketball Hall of Fame - Major League Baseball players Joe Niekro, John Blatnik and Bill Mazaroski, NFL players Bill Jobko and Lou Groza, Olympic gold medal wrestler Bobby Douglas - and many noted college athletes.

area produced no outstanding golfers, tennis stars, chess players, or scientists I've ever heard about.

This was the culture when I decided to pursue sports in junior high, and I wasn't prepared for it—not even close. I was overweight and seen by the other boys as a reclusive bookworm. I looked like a soft touch, and there was usually someone around looking for an easy victory. I was pushed around, which I didn't like but did nothing about. That changed in a surprising way.

The First Beating

I reasoned that watching the best basketball players might help me learn about the game. Mom's brother Alfred (a.k.a. "Peanut") was staying with us for a few days and helped me convince Mom to let me go to a game alone. After all, I was twelve and walked to the junior high next to the high school every day. At the game I sat alone and no one bothered me.

My route home was via the footbridge over Wheeling Creek. Near the bridge something hit me from behind and I went down on my chest. It was a second before I realized that a boy was hitting me with his fists. I managed to squirm around and started kicking while on my back and yelling, "Get off of me!"

This discouraged the attacker, and he moved away, saying, "This will teach you to stay out of our place—you don't belong here." One of my eyes was hurting, and I felt blood running down my cheek. Of course, my nose was bleeding hard. While holding my handkerchief to my nose, I trotted across the bridge and hastened home.

When I arrived at the apartment Mom was upset as she wiped my face and I worked on stopping the nosebleed. I looked in the mirror and was frightened at how bad I looked. I had a swollen eye, scratches on my face and a lot of blood on my clothes. Uncle Al decided I had to learn to defend myself.

Within a few days, he and his brother Lawrence (nicknamed "Red") were giving me fighting lessons. Uncle Red had trained as a boxer, which was one of the reasons he quit high school.

Uncle Red stopped by often over the next couple of weeks to train me with boxing gloves. Over time he convinced me that if I fought back hard, my opponent would back off. Uncle Red's theory was that you had to attack, not just to defend yourself. He said that a defender becomes a punching bag. His take-home lesson was simple: when you are trapped into fights, hit first, hit hard and aim for his nose. He said, "The fight goes out of a bully real fast when his nose is broken—so break it! And once you're in control, don't back off—no mercy. Throw as many punches as you can throw at his head. If he goes down, get on top and pound on him until he begs you to quit." This was all new to me, and I wasn't sure I could do it - but it made sense.

He emphasized that I should never start a fight but should always finish it, win or lose. He said, "Even if you lose, if you damage the other kid enough, he won't want to fight you again." He followed with, "If the other guy is a bigger guy than you, or if there's more than one of them get a club and use it." His last lesson: "Once you start running from fights and everyone knows you'll run, you'll be picked on and will have to keep running the rest of your life—so don't start now." This was a great lesson that I found to be absolutely true. Facing trouble goes far beyond physical fighting.

A week or so later a boy pushed me hard from behind for no reason. I dropped my books and almost fell. He then taunted me while his two friends laughed. I suspected he was the guy who jumped on me after the basketball game. I was scared, but I walked up to him with my head down submissively. When I got close enough, I hit him with my right fist, square in the nose. He grabbed his face with both hands and bent over; I threw as many punches as I could at both sides of his head. In a few seconds he was on his knees, a crying mess, and his buddies were pulling me away.

No one was taunting as I picked up my books and walked away. My hands hurt from the punches, I was shivering and there were a few tears. He had never thrown a punch and my nose wasn't bleeding. It was a great victory. He never came near me again and moved away soon after.

That evening, I called Uncle Red and recounted the incident. He greeted the news with laughter and congratulations. A few days later, he came by and gave me more specific instructions about street fighting, which included kicking. He showed me that a shinbone kick works about as well if the nose is not within range.

When I did get in a fight, my nose would usually bleed, which I expected, so it didn't scare me. But, it scared the hell out of the other kid - they didn't want my blood on them. My handicap became somewhat of an asset.

The important thing was that my peers learned that I didn't put up with being pushed around, so the bully boys left me alone. This did a lot for my self-esteem and helped me immensely in sports.

It was a while before I figured out that the beating after the basketball game had been a blessing. At age twelve, I had learned a lesson some boys never learned.

CHAPTER 12

No one imagines that a symphony is supposed to improve as it goes along, or that the whole object of playing music is to reach the finale. The point of music is discovered in every moment of playing and listening to it. It is the same, I feel, with the greater part of our lives, and if we are unduly absorbed in improving them we may forget altogether to live them.

—Alan Watts, philosopher, writer (1915–1973)

When you meet temptation and the urge is very strong,
give a little whistle, give a little whistle
and always let your conscience be your guide.

—Jiminy Cricket, from Disney movie *Pinocchio*

MUSICAL EDUCATION

Music appreciation was taught by Elvira Varns. Miss Varns discovered that I loved classical music, which made me one of her pets. She knew that Wendell and I liked to sing and decided to test us for pitch. Wendell wanted to do it, so I went along. She tested us with a pitch pipe and a piano. We were flattered when she said both of us had perfect pitch. She convinced us to come in after school and sing with a couple other students. After doing it few times, we quit showing up, but she remained friendly. I think she understood that wannabe football players don't sing in groups.

My singing urge was satisfied by singing at Wendell's house with him and his mother, Kitty. Singing was a common form of recreation before TV was available. Wendell and I learned the words to dozens of popular songs by singing with artists on the radio and recordings.

The War Grinds On and So Does Life

From the beginning of 1942 until V-J Day (victory over Japan) in August 1945, the world was in chaos. But for kids around my age, it was an exciting time. War news was in the papers, magazines, on the radio, and on Movietone News, shown before every movie. Towards the end, we saw gory newsreels of Mussolini and his mistress hanging upside down in a Milan gas station after being beaten to death by a mob.

The battles were like serialized thrillers. We followed the Battle of Stalingrad, which lasted over a year and was as bloody it gets. The goal was to keep everyone fighting mad and working hard. Anyone who complained about rationing, except humorously, was immediately criticized. The general attitude was, "We're all in this together until the murdering Nazis and the dirty Japs are beaten. As the paper reader in my group, I was usually the one who announced when local boys were killed or wounded. Unfortunately, this was a frequent occurrence.

Cars got no more than fifteen miles per gallon, and car owners were issued enough ration stamps to buy about five gallons per week. Dad was in a business category that was allocated about ten gallons per week. If he had jobs far away, he could apply to the ration board and get a few extra stamps.

Tires were of poor quality. When treads were worn down a new tread was glued and heat sealed to the running surface. All of this motivated some people to put their cars up on blocks and not drive at all. Then they sold their gas and tire ration stamps at handsome prices.

Civilian car production stopped. The assembly lines were converted to building military vehicles and tanks. By the end of the war, the cars still in service were run-down clunkers belching blue smoke. By late 1945, a few new cars were spotted driving through town, and when one parked, it had the allure of a visitor from Mars. As word spread, people gathered around the vehicle and touched it.

Free Transportation

Due to gas rationing, it was considered patriotic to share rides, so drivers usually picked up clean looking strangers. Servicemen in uniform got a ride with the first driver that saw them.

Successful hitchhiking was an art form. Hitching on a straight, open road was not good because drivers didn't like to wear their brakes, stopping and starting. Just beyond a crossroads or at a traffic light, where the hitchhiker could make eye contact (smiling helped), was better. Ragged, dirty-looking hitchhikers of any age were not successful. Two clean-looking young men could get rides. Boys in clean baseball uniforms got picked up easily.

An experienced hitchhiker went through a quick survey of a car, starting with the license plate because the letters signified if the car was local or from far away. Before getting in, we asked, "How far are you going?" This gave a few extra seconds to size up the driver.

We were taught to never get into cars with three men unless we knew them. Destinations that would leave you in a bad place for the next ride were passed up, as were rides in broken-down old cars. Immediately upon opening the door, you sized the driver up again for any bad signs. If anything was out of sorts, you said no thanks and closed the door. There's always another ride, but you have only one life.

A friendly driver once told me he carried a gun. He took it out from under the seat, which scared me. When he saw my reaction, he handed it to me in the correct way. I took it, admired it, checked to see if it was loaded (it was), and handed it back - correctly. He said, "I was held up by a hitchhiker a while back. My job requires me to drive a lot, and I like having company, but I only pick up clean-looking young men like you. I could see you were no threat."

Every man I knew had at least one bad story about hitchhiking, including my Dad, who had been robbed by two guys. But in my years on the road, with hundreds of rides, I had only one bad experience – more about that later.

Hitchhiking was not seen as appropriate for females of any age. A cop who spotted a female hitchhiker automatically saw her to be a prostitute. If she was very young, he assumed she was stupid or a runaway. Females usually asked for rides in parking lots, gas stations, and bars, face-to-face with the driver. Female hitching was risky behavior.

The War Ends

The landing in Normandy, on June 6, 1944, was wildly celebrated, but a few days later, lists of the wounded, missing, and dead were in the papers. A blue star in a window meant that someone was in the armed forces and a gold star meant that a soldier had been killed. In a small town one death had a large impact and there were a lot of gold stars.

Tuesday, May 8, 1945 was VE Day (Victory in Europe Day) and there was, literally, dancing in the streets. The celebration lasted through the next weekend, even though everyone was aware that the war with Japan might drag on for years. But very soon the euphoria gave way to the dread of more years of war. Many men were being sent home from Europe for a short home leave, then off to the Pacific.

Then in early August, the atomic bombs were dropped on Hiroshima and Nagasaki. Saturday, August, 11 V-J Day was declared. The end of war surprised us nearly as much as the bombing of Pearl Harbor. The streets were crowded and the bars stayed open all night. It was a let-loose celebration everywhere in the country. It was hard to believe that the largest, bloodiest war in human history had ended so abruptly.

Several hundred thousand Japanese had died when the atom bombs exploded, and quite honestly, we thought the news was terrific. Americans would have applauded if every citizen of Japan had been killed. It was a vicious war and we were in no mood to be forgiving. It couldn't have been imagined then that in twenty years I would be negotiating business deals with Japanese businessmen. Such is the way the world spins.

Return to Normalcy

It was time for the country to start a normal life. People below the age of twenty had no idea what "normal" meant. The Great Depression had begun in 1930. In late 1945 and through 1946, an avalanche of men headed back into civilian life. Factories were converting to peacetime production. There was concern that the country would go into another Depression. Or was an economic boom about to begin? In the meantime, Wendell and I were doing business as usual.

Two Young Businessmen

Carts had not yet entered the game of golf, and it was déclassé for country-club members to carry their own golf bags. They hired poor kids, bums, and drunks as caddies. Wendell had heard that some caddies earned as much as $3 for a four hour round and this sparked our interest. One Saturday morning in the early spring of 1945, we risked being accosted by the Wheeling kids and hitchhiked to the Wheeling Country Club.

Luckily, there was a shortage of caddies. The caddy master gave us rudimentary instructions: mainly, don't speak unless spoken to; always say, "Thank you, sir"; and don't swear. In addition: "Keep your eyes on the ball; finding balls is the reason they tip you." We made our first round in the same foursome, carrying one bag each.

The fee for carrying one bag was $1.25 and most golfers gave caddies a $0.25 tip. The way to make $3 to $4 was to carry two bags, something new caddies were not permitted to do. It was no wonder they had difficulty attracting enough caddies.

We were hungry when we finished the round, and a caddy directed us to a screen door at the back of the clubhouse. We knocked, and a black man wearing a chef's hat showed up. He said, "Baloney sandwich with white bread for ten cents. Y'all don't like it, go somewheres else." I asked if we could get some mustard or mayonnaise. He said, "You wants it, you takes it like I said. I ain't got time for you now." We ordered two. When he had two dimes in his hand, he handed over the sandwiches. We thanked him. Each one had a generously thick cut of large bologna that was fresh, cold and tasted great.

The next day, he voluntarily slapped some mayonnaise on the bread for us. When I offered him a nickel for the favor, he looked down at me with a hint of a smile and said, "Get the hell out of here."

There were a few caddies he wouldn't serve because they had called him *nigger*, a word we didn't hear often in Ohio. West Virginia had segregated schools, so the Wheeling boys saw race differently than we did. There were no black caddies.

Golf balls were scarce because they were made of rubber. A fellow caddy told us that he'd found a couple of nearly new Titleist balls and sold them for a dollar each at the Ogleby Park public course, which was only two miles farther up the road. That perked up our interest. We, especially I, were somewhat skilled at figuring out ways to make a buck. We decided to spend Sunday afternoon visiting the woodsy places on the golf course. Many women played on Sundays and hit balls into the trees. They didn't fancy going into the muddy woods - they just sent in the caddies who were mostly lazy.

We didn't hit the jackpot, but we did find four balls, which made a hitchhike to Ogleby worthwhile. While we were ball searching, I said to Wendell, "You know, the trick is to find only very good Titleist balls."

Typical of Wendell, he replied, "Scheid, you're f*****g brilliant!"

I said, "Wendell, where can we find new golf balls the easy way?"

"In a store, asshole," he replied. (Those were his two favorite swear words).

"No," I said, "we can find them in members' golf bags." He got the point at once, and our "zipping" strategy was invented.

Zipping worked like this: when a golfer wasn't paying attention, we looked in the bag compartment where he kept spare balls. We arranged the best balls on top, so the compartment could be zipped open and balls taken out without having to look. At the end of a round, while we were carrying the bags to the storage room, we would reach in, take a ball or two and then zipped the compartment closed. We took no more than two balls so, hopefully, the golfer wouldn't notice the loss the next time he played.

On our first trip to Ogleby, we asked around and learned what golfers were willing to pay for used balls. We were doing market research but didn't know it. Next we decided to buy balls from the caddies who found balls but were too lazy to hitchhike to Ogleby. That was most of them. Every weekend afternoon, we approached caddies after they finished their rounds and bought whatever they had to sell. We still caddied every weekend morning for a few bucks, but the wholesale buying and zipping of balls were much more profitable endeavors.

One afternoon over our bologna sandwiches, we came up with another scheme we called "tramping." When a ball was hit into the woods, the caddy was the first person going in to look for it. If we found it, we tramped it into the ground and pushed dead leaves over it. We carried a pencil stub and a piece of paper to write down information that would lead us back to the balls.

On a typical day, we arrived early; we wanted to be finished by noon. After our round, we bought balls found or stolen balls from caddies (we weren't the only thieves, just the most organized). Then we went into the woods to harvest the balls we had tramped and look for others. By early afternoon, we usually had a bag of a dozen to fifteen balls. Some were good and some not so good, but they could all be sold at a profit.

When we got to Ogleby, we split up. One of us sold to golfers who were leaving and the other went after the people arriving in the parking lot. Our business day was done in an hour. After a couple of weekends we had regular customers who looked for us. We had organized a profitable enterprise.

On a good day, we made combined caddy fees of at least $3.00 and had ball sales, net of what we paid caddies, of about $9 to $12, for a total of about $12 to $15 for the day and around $25 for the weekend. At that time the minimum wage was $0.40 per hour. That wasn't bad for a couple of stupid thirteen-year-olds from the crummy town across the river.

We split everything fifty-fifty and swore an oath that we wouldn't tell anyone about our systems. We didn't want to get arrested, we didn't want more kids coming from Ohio, and we didn't want friends borrowing from us. And, we sure as hell didn't want our parents asking how we came by so much money. If anyone asked about our caddying, we said that we made about $1.50 for the day. Wendell tended to spend his cash quickly on pinball machines and such. I fattened the savings account that Mom had helped me open with $1 when I was ten. It was my secret money since no one ever asked to see my carefully hidden savings account book.

Not long after VE Day, a few new golf balls began to be available. By August, used ball prices were dropping. Then we came up with a new idea.

In the afternoons some caddies played poker in the basement of the caddy shack. The games were not organized; they just happened or they didn't. I had read about marked cards, and we did some experimenting. We decided to organize a regular game.

Wendell's father, Ralph, had taught us to play poker, using matchsticks as money. We took one of Ralph's decks and shaded in the white part of the corners of the aces with a soft pencil. The shading could only be noticed if you were looking for it. We figured that if we both played in the same game, one of us should win. If one of us had two aces, the other would try to bid up the hand, hoping our opponents would go along. If one of the other guys had aces, we would fold unless we had a strong hand. We also worked out signals about having three of a kind.

The poker cheating system worked so well the first weekend that we lost interest in caddying and ball selling. Our new plan was to sleep in and arrive late morning, as the first rounds were ending. One of us would start the poker game. The other one would join later so we didn't look like we were partners. The stakes were mostly dimes and quarters, but in three or four hours we walked away with at least $10 each day.

All went well for a few weeks, until one of the older caddies figured out that we were working as a team. He made a scene that involved the caddy master, who hadn't noticed that we had been sneaking into the basement just for poker. He kicked us out and said if we came back, he'd call the police. Our profitable times at Wheeling Country Club came to a sudden end.

We said good-bye to our bologna sandwich man and a few friends before hitchhiking home. It had been a great run. We made good money and learned at least one lesson: nothing good lasts forever.

We kept our secrecy pledge until we were out of high school, when we finally told a couple of our best buddies about our golf ball business. We never told about cheating at cards because we didn't want them to distrust us. When we played poker with them, we didn't need marked cards - our signal system was more than enough.

Most of the money we made at the country club was not honestly earned, and we knew it. We discussed the dishonesty of it and justified it to ourselves very simply. We needed money and we took it from rich, stupid or lazy people. But the truth is that we knew there was no real justification for stealing as we did and it pains me to admit to it.

Sports

Due to nosebleeds and illnesses I was not prepared physically or mentally for competition against kids that had played sports from a young age. At the time, there were no Little Leagues, Pop Warner Football, or that sort of thing. Boys just got together and played on their own.

Deep inside, I wanted to play football and baseball, especially football. Like most mothers, mine was very anti football, and she received major reinforcement from her parents, who hated the game. Spring was coming, baseball was starting, and I was feeling stronger, so I signed up.

I decided that catcher was the best position for me because practically no one wanted the position and there would be less competition. The coach was looking for volunteers foolish enough to go behind the plate.

Pitchers and catchers started their season on the basketball court in early March. After the first few pitches thrown to me, it was clear that I needed a lot of training. I missed pitches and got hit in the body, arms - all over ... I took low pitches on the legs and one in the groin. The coach said I was probably not cut out for this position, but he wouldn't quit on someone who'd keep trying. So I kept trying.

That was another important lesson. Coaches tend to help those kids who show some determination.

The coach put a catcher's mask on me. He had me keep my arms at my side while he threw balls into the mask so I'd get used to the impact. Then he threw easy pitches while instructing me on catching technique. In a week, I was able to catch most balls within my reach. Soon he started making me go for pitches that hit the floor in front of me, off to the side, and high. By the time we went outside to practice a month later, I was able to catch the slower pitchers during batting practice. Since I had never really been into athletics of any kind, this was a confidence booster.

When I told Dad I was catching, he took me to buy a glove. I'll never forget that he paid $25 for my catcher's mitt. That was a lot of money for him. The glove he bought was the best one available at the time. I wrote my name all over and in the glove so I could prove it was mine.

The catcher's mitt and my shotgun were the most important gifts I ever received from Dad. Despite our lack of time together and my anger at him for the way he treated Mom I wanted his approval. So I worked hard at catching. I still have the gun and the glove.

For no particular reason, hitting a baseball came to me naturally. I was able to hit a slow pitch, and at that age, most pitchers threw the ball slowly. By the end of the season, hitting was the strongest part of my game.

There is much I could write about my early athletic adventures, but let's just say that I made progress. Once a kid has developed some ability in one sport, it is easier to excel at another sport.

The Poolroom

At twelve or thirteen, depending on their size, boys were permitted to play at Pop's pool room, but no gambling was allowed. It cost a dime per game of eight-ball. I didn't like the place because it was too juvenile, with kids yelling, banging cue sticks, and otherwise misbehaving. Wendell, a few other friends, and I played many games and developed a reasonable aptitude for the game.

The Pastime Billiard Room was *the* poolroom in Bridgeport. There was a rule that a boy had to be at least sixteen to come into the Pastime, but I was seeking entry at barely fifteen. The Pastime had baseball and prizefight betting as well as gambling on pool games. I wanted in because none of my friends could get in. It was a prestige thing on the way to manhood.

A young man, whose father was a fireman, was home on leave from the army. He hung around the firehouse so I got to know him. He knew Manuel Thomas, son of the Pastime owner. As a favor to the vet, Manuel let me sit on one of the high chairs in the back and watch the vet play pool. The condition was that I would sit quietly and not speak to anyone. Cops never came in because of the gambling. However, if a cop did wander in, it was my duty to slide out of my chair and go out the back door. Having that privilege for a few visits led me to push the envelope and sneak in through the back door on my own, just to watch the men play. I began fetching sandwiches for players. After a while, Manuel and his brother, George, sort of let me hang around like a stray cat—a cat, who ran errands for their customers.

One cold day, I wandered in to get warm and see what was going on. There were no players around, and Manuel asked me to play a rack with him so he could practice. I played quietly for an hour and acquitted myself well enough to impress him. After that, he let me rent a table and practice when business was slow. He even gave me some pointers on shooting. After a few weeks, he let me play with others, but not for money. That prohibition passed into history in a month or so, but I never flaunted it.

I played with GG (pronounced Gee Gee) George. He was in his late twenties, slightly retarded, and had a minor speech impediment.

He was a stocky, six-foot man who was as gentle as a kitten—that is, unless he didn't understand something and became frustrated. Then he would get angry. If you patiently explained some rule he had forgotten or stopped him from making a mistake, he was grateful and said thanks.

We played eight-ball and he would have lost every time had I not made sure he won about a third of the time. My friendship with GG was one key to my getting into Pastime at fifteen.

After a while the Thomas boys let me play eight-ball for quarters—even half a dollar – as long as the money was kept out of sight. Causing them no trouble was my way of keeping them happy. Who would believe I learned to keep my comments to myself and developed some decent manners in a poolroom? The Pastime was my main hangout for the rest of my life in Bridgeport, and it supplied me with much of my spending money.

Victory Parade on Main St. - end of WWII. In front of store, boy with white sailor hat is me, next to Dad in white shirt. Grandpa Jonard in front of entrance, suit and white hat, various relatives in doorway, August 1945

Al - high school sophomore in 1948, age sixteen

Wendell and Al on Main Street, in front of the chicken slaughter house, circa 1949

Al at American Legion All Star game dinner, voted MVP, late summer, 1949

CHAPTER 13

The way we imagine ourselves to appear to another person is an essential element in our conception of ourselves. In other words, I am not what I think I am, and I am not what you think I am. I am what I think you think I am.

—Robert Bierstedt, sociologist, teacher (1913–1998)

Love is the triumph of imagination over intelligence.

—H. L. Mencken, journalist, essayist (1880–1956)

HIGH SCHOOL

In high school years, most of us experience the first real dramas of our lives. Voices change, mammary glands develop and puberty arrives. We discover many things about ourselves and others, and we don't like some of what we find. Some young people go through these years easily. Are they the lucky ones? Or do those who have difficult experiences become stronger because of them? I guess it all depends on how each individual handles his or her trials and tribulations. We all get one shot at growing up, never to be repeated.

Many of my fellow travelers through the teenage years hated high school. I was not one of them. I disliked only homework—and managed to avoid most of it. It was the period in my life during which

I played sports, learned to shoot pool, roller-skated, hunted small game, read many books, had close friends, learned independence – and discovered love. What more important discovery is there in life?

My Blessing, My Curse

I had noticed Virginia Lee Davis the first time when I was about ten and saw her playing hopscotch. She had a friendly face and laughed a lot. She was a skinny girl then. On one of my first days as a freshman, I saw and remembered her. She had grown into an attractive girl. After I saw Wendell talking to her, I asked who she was. He said she was his cousin on his father's side.

By trading around with other students Wendell and I had managed to get lockers next to each other. One day his cousin stopped by to say hello, and he introduced her to me as Jake Davis. I blurted out a lame hello.

A few days later she stopped to chat and began asking questions. I stumbled around but soon became comfortable with her. I learned she was a junior, active in several clubs, detested gym class, and liked to watch sports. Her unusual nickname had been hung on her by an uncle who thought she was going to be a tomboy.

Later on, Wendell told me she was born on January, 18, 1931, making her almost exactly a year older than Wendell, January 28, 1932 and me, February 7. Jake would graduate in 1948 at seventeen, two years ahead of us. She was a popular junior, and we were clumsy freshmen boys. There was not much synergy there.

It was easy to learn about Jake because everyone beyond the freshman class knew her. She was a straight-A student and none of the other girls could match her combination of speed and accuracy in typing and shorthand. Perfectly behaved and possessed of a sly, charming sense of humor, teachers loved her. She was a star.

Wendell said her father wouldn't permit her to go on dates, which was unusual for a girl in her junior year. It was easy to see his point; Jake was no tomboy. In fact, she was one of the two or three best-looking girls in the school. She wasn't "cute." She had the bearing of a young woman rather than a teenager. She dressed in the fashions of the day: bobby socks, pleated skirts, sweaters, and saddle shoes. But, there were no animals on her sweaters.

Her soft blue eyes, light brown hair and impish smile made her the kind of girl boys stared at but feared approaching. If this description makes her sound almost perfect, it's because we boys saw her as close to that. Despite all this, she was modest, friendly, and adored by the other girls. No one ever said a bad word about Jake.

We began waving to each other and having short conversations when we passed in the halls. Wendell spotted this budding friendship and accused me of having a crush on her, which I vigorously denied. He was, of course, absolutely correct. By the end of the school year the crush was large, growing—and one-sided. I knew she was too old for me, and I tried not to be attracted to her. In this, I was a complete failure.

FOOTBALL

Even though I was a sickly overweight kid, football had always appealed to me. I did everything possible to attend high school games from the sixth grade on and played touch football with kids my age. Wendell and I spent hours throwing and catching passes. As a freshman I went out for the team.

August 20 was always the first day of football practice. The weather was usually hot and humid, and we suffered through a tough grind of practices, twice a day. The coaches worked us to exhaustion, but by the time school started most of us were past the pain.

I wanted to be in the backfield, but with my lack of speed, that was not in the cards ... yet. Centers had to learn all the plays so the ball would be passed to the correct man. Centers also played linebacker on defense, my favorite part of the game. For hours, I practiced passing the ball through my legs and into the backfield for a punt or run. I also memorized the plays for every position.

During the war, many boys had quit school at seventeen and joined the armed forces. After discharge they were encouraged to finish high school by being permitted to play sports until their twentieth birthdays. These young men had been toughened physically and psychologically by the demands of military service. Normal sixteen to eighteen year old boys were no match for them.

The veterans were not a large percentage of the players, but they were a major influence on the attitudes of younger guys. They had become men early in their lives. They treated us like younger brothers, telling us war stories and teaching us many things, some of which would have shocked our parents.

Coach John McClain and his first assistant had been army officers. The camaraderie between them and the ex-GI players set a fine example. We learned to put the team first and never let down on the job. The vets gave the younger boys no breaks when it came to blocking and tackling. Scrimmages were all full speed. These were life lessons that came in handy just a few years later, when the young men of my generation did military time for the Korean War.

Football was recognized as a way for boys to work off aggression, and the coaches encouraged rough play. An army vet named Buck DeLuca took a liking to me. He told me that what a player lacked in skill, he could make up with enthusiasm, conditioning, and fearless physical contact. "Hit 'em hard," he said, "and you'll get respect." He gave me extra practice, making me block him one-on-one. I usually ended up on my back. He helped me up, and we did it again - and again.

Even though I was eating like a horse, fat turned to muscle and my running speed improved. A fit fourteen-year-old weighing 145 pounds would be considered small twenty years later but was above average in 1946. Consequently, I played in varsity team practices.

My nosebleeds were a frequent nuisance and the coaches were freaked out about my pencil and gauze treatment. But, after they understood the technique, it became a joke. Face masks were unknown then. Broken noses and knocked-out teeth were seen as normal. After a few bleeding incidents, an assistant coach put what was then called a nose guard on my helmet. This device reduced my nose bleeding incidents to nearly zero. It would be nearly two decades before face protection was introduced into football.

Bridgeport had a fine team that year, losing only two games to much larger schools. Nearly all of the first-team players were graduating, so everyone knew the team would have to be rebuilt the next year.

High School and Grades

A counselor talked me into taking algebra. English and a course called Education and Guidance were required. I signed on for mechanical drawing and art because they were considered easy. I did no homework and pulled a D in algebra. From then on, I wasn't considered college material and academic prep courses were never mentioned. Course selection, done in collaboration with Wendell, was governed by homework avoidance.

Most parents, including Wendell's and mine, assumed their kids would finish high school and go to work in a factory or a trade. Paying for college was not even vaguely in their plans. Mom signed my course selection form with no questions about the subjects. Dad never looked at my report cards, and Mom just glanced to see if my grades were passing, which they barely were. She had a sliding scale for my grades. A was not expected, B was terrific, C was okay, D elicited a frown, and an F brought freedom restrictions and demands for homework. This system suited me, and I carefully avoided the F grade.

If there was a parent-teacher association, my family never heard of it. Parents were not encouraged to contact teachers. Education was left to the educators. Deportment was another matter. The school believed in strict discipline, and parents fully supported this attitude. Most male teachers, and a few female, had wooden paddles that were used, mostly on boys, who disobeyed some rule. As many as five hits on the buttocks were meted out, in front of the class to inflict embarrassment and as a warning to others.

Bill Logan watched over a study hall and was an assistant football coach. He took particular pleasure in corporal punishment and had a paddle about two feet long with holes drilled in it to reduce wind resistance. In the world of thirty years later, he would have been arrested for assault, but in the forties, parents and the school administration approved of his punishment.

Boys were allowed to be poorly educated, have fistfights, swear, smoke, and misbehave outside of school, but lying, talking back, and being impolite to any adult were nearly capital offenses. My interests in sports, reading, skating, and radio listening kept me out of trouble, and I was rarely disciplined. Mom was busy, and Dad had his outside interests, so I could mess up with impunity as long as my deportment got high grades.

My jobs on Saturday mornings and after school, when there was no sports practice, were working at Mom's dry cleaning business and carrying in coal for us and a few neighbors. Mom's store was open every day but Sunday. Mom closed the store no earlier than six, and Dad drank beer and traded bullshit at the Eagles or the fire department until then. We lived organized and predictable lives.

Another Move

In my freshman year, we moved from the apartment above the store to Kirkwood, sharing the house Grandpa Jonard had bought. They lived on one side of the house, and we lived on the other. They had the real kitchen and ours was on the bottom floor, next to a cellar that housed the heating furnace. This was my grandparents' attempt to help Mom and Dad resolve some of their marital problems. It was a naive, wasted effort.

Dad bought a used prewar electric refrigerator and put it in the cellar next to the kitchen. It replaced the old icebox that they had used since before I was born. The kitchen was also the dining room. At street entry level, there was a living room, one bedroom, and a small alcove. I slept in the alcove, on the same daybed I had used since leaving a crib.

The house was across the street from the middle school, which was adjacent to the high school. My commute time was a six-minute walk or a three-minute run. Wendell lived even closer, on the other side of the schools. With this close proximity, it was preordained that we would often be tardy.

BASEBALL

After the rigors of football, I was stronger than the previous year. My hitting was above average, and my catching improved. I volunteered (begged, in fact) to catch batting practice. I enjoyed catching immensely.

The last few games of the season, the coach put a couple of reserve team players, including me, on the bench as a reward for extra effort. There was no thought that I would play.

Our team had a big lead in the eighth inning. With two outs, the coach put me in to pinch-hit. His plan was to let the reserve catcher work the ninth inning after I had struck out. Lucky me—I hit a hard line drive for a stand up double. The next batter got a long single, and I scored. As a reward, the coach let me catch the last inning, which I did with no errors. It was my only appearance in a varsity game that season. Wendell told our friends that I had a perfect season: one at bat, one hit, one run scored, and one inning as a catcher with no errors—a short, but perfect season.

TIME FOR WORK

During the war, Americans had invested billions of dollars in war bonds. Now they were cashing in the bonds and embarking on a buying spree.

Electrical wiring that hadn't been repaired for years needed fixing, and a few new homes were being built. Dad was offered more electrical work than he could handle, whether he liked it or not. Restarting Scheid Electric was never discussed. It appeared Dad no longer had the ambition for it.

Mom decided it was time for me to begin learning the basic skills of an electrician. We gave it a try, but Dad couldn't get started early, and at lunchtime he had to stop by the Eagles. By the time he got around to work, it was after noon and I wanted to go play baseball at three. After a few weeks, Mom and Dad had a monumental argument about him not working enough. The next day, he left the house early without waking me. That was the end of the work-with-Dad program, which suited me just fine.

While trying to work with Dad, I received the only bit of life philosophy he ever gave me. We were rewiring a house for a Baptist preacher who overheard Dad swearing. The preacher said, "George, you may not take the Lord's name in vain in my home. This is the house of the Lord."

Dad looked at him and said, "Go to hell, preacher. What I say is my business. Any more of that bullshit and you and the Lord will have to finish this job on your own." The preacher looked to heaven and walked away without a word.

After the preacher left, Dad turned to me and said, "Son, don't ever trust a man who doesn't smoke, drink, chew tobacco, or swear—and then spends his time telling other people how to behave. A man like that is hiding sins that are worse than mine." My experiences in life have demonstrated to me that Dad's point was well taken.

The parental fighting continued, and I hated hearing it. I called Grandma and got myself invited to work on Uncle Alex's farm. Everyone treated me well, but it was just not as it had been. My oldest cousin had gone into the army, and the other cousins had local interests I didn't fit into. My farm days were over.

Chapter 14

Dancing in all its forms cannot be excluded from the curriculum of all noble education; dancing with the feet, with ideas, with words, and, need I add that one must also be able to dance with the heart.
—Friedrich Nietzsche, philosopher (1844–1900)

Dancing is a perpendicular expression of a horizontal desire.
—George Bernard Shaw, author, playwright (1856-1950)

Pas de Deux

Our little town had only one parent-approved teenage hangout. It was Shaheen's Ice Cream store, owned by a Syrian immigrant named Jimmy Shaheen. If you spent enough time there, you eventually ran into everyone. It was there that I talked to Jake a few times during the summer. During one of these short chats, I found that she and her friends were attending the city-sponsored dances in Bellaire, a small town about four miles down the river. She suggested that I come to a Friday dance. I was honest and said I didn't know how to dance. She said, "Show up and we'll teach you." I didn't go.

Spending evening time at Shaheen's cut into my skating and pool playing time, so I settled for accidental Jake sightings. I knew she was out of my league, but I liked watching her. Wendell accused me of staring at her, but I denied it.

Learning to dance was a big thing for boys. Girls danced with each other, and an older sister usually taught boys. An only child was in a bind on that score. I had been dancing on skates for several years, which was much more difficult, but it didn't have the physical closeness of real dancing.

One evening at Shaheen's, I met a girl named Mitzi Paul (I did not tell her that my first dog was named Mitzi). She had moved to Bridgeport late in the previous school year and had few friends. She asked if I could dance. When I said no she invited me to her apartment for lessons. Before I had a chance to chicken out, I said that sounded like fun, and the next evening I was there.

Mitzi's mother, Mrs. Paul, and a female partner had bought the Lincoln Bar & Grill. While eavesdropping on my mom's phone conversations (a constant sin of mine), I had heard about the lady bar owners. The gist of the gossip was, "respectable women don't own bars." Mitzi and her mother lived in an apartment just above the Lincoln. I had an educated hunch that Mom wouldn't approve of me going to Mitzi's apartment, so I didn't mention it.

Two nights each week for the next month, while Mom thought I was hanging out safely in the poolroom or at Shaheen's, I was at Mitzi's apartment taking dance lessons. She had the latest records and a new phonograph that changed them automatically. Mitzi was a patient teacher and I was a willing student. Slow dancing came easily. Soon we were speeding up the tempo and getting into swing (then called the Jitterbug). Each session lasted about two hours, after which she made terrific toasted cheese sandwiches.

Her mother made at least one unannounced visit each evening. She was obviously protective of her daughter. Our evenings together were quite innocent. The truth is that if Mitzi had even hinted at kissing, she would have scared me off.

Just about everyone eventually came to Mom's store, including Mrs. Paul. When she came in, she went on and on about how cute it was that Mitzi was teaching me to dance, because she had always wanted a brother. She complimented Mom on her nice, polite boy.

Mom was suspicious about Mitzi's motivation to teach dancing to a younger boy. Mitzi was a year ahead of me in school and a year older; maybe she was leading me astray. Mom was protective of me in strange ways.

Mom made it clear that she didn't approve and it was easier to give up the dance lessons than argue. Thanks to Mitzi, I became a decent slow dancer, could do a reasonable waltz, and, in a clumsy way, could Jitterbug a little. But I was still too shy to venture into the regular summer dances.

Back to School

Selecting classes was always a major discussion between Wendell and me. Jake pushed us to take typing, telling us it was easy and it would enable us to get office jobs when we graduated. Since the class was all girls, plus one overweight classmate named Rollo, we decided to take it if we could get a couple of other guys to go along.

When Paul Florence, Jim Irwin, Wendell, and I walked into typing class the first day of school, the teacher nearly fainted. She didn't want four football players. It mattered not because Paul and Jim quit in two days, and Wendell lasted only until the end of the week. After that, I was there alone with a room full of girls and Rollo, who was assumed to be gay. For a while I took a lot of razzing from teammates about dating Rollo, but when I forcefully told them to f**k off, the joke soon died.

I stuck it out because of Jake and a certain amount of stubbornness. When football season ended, Jake met me in the typing room after school and coached me. I tried much harder for her than the teacher, and my skills improved. I passed with a B, and typing turned out to be one of the most valuable subjects I ever studied. I also had the satisfaction that Jake said she was proud of me for putting up with the crap from teammates without getting into a fight.

The First Dance

Jake asked if Wendell and I were going to the first Friday night school dance and she remarked that she'd heard about my lessons with Mitzi. I was taken aback that she knew but pleased that she showed a little interest in me. In my mind, I was too everything for her: too young, too ugly, and too stupid. I said I'd come to the dance … and then wondered how I'd make myself do it.

There was no way I could go alone, and Wendell was not a possibility. Two football teammates said they would go if we all went together. Then Wendell opted in. We met in front of the school and walk in together.

We arrived half an hour late so we could hide in the crowd. We were wallflowers, standing in a corner, wondering what to do next, when Jake walked over to us. After some friendly chatter, she asked Wendell to dance. But he stared at his feet and stuttered a refusal. She turned to me and said something like, "Come on now, Scheid. Show me what Mitzi taught you."

All at once, in one sentence, she had given away my secrets, I had taken dance lessons and with whom. I didn't know how to say no, so we danced to a slow ballad. As Mitzi had taught me, I took the lead and she followed beautifully. She was in my arms and I was deliriously happy. But, I was having difficulty controlling my breathing, and I realized she noticed. Jake said, "Mitzi must have given you a lot of lessons. You dance very well." I was thrilled! When the dance ended, I thanked her and had enough courage to ask if we could dance again. She said, "Only if you ask me."

My pals congratulated me for having the nerve to dance, and they wanted to know about my time with Mitzi, whom they considered a hot number. I lied, telling them there were only two lessons and her mother was always home. Wendell was ticked off that I hadn't told him about my "dance dates." I said I was sorry and would never do it again, and he accepted my apology. We always shared our secrets, and I felt badly that I'd let him down.

A few songs later, I swallowed hard, approached Jake and we danced. It was delightful. During the evening, we danced four times for a total of about twelve minutes, which raced by like twelve seconds. I also danced with Mitzi, who got very close, putting her arm tightly around my neck and embarrassing me. But I liked it. By the end of the evening, I had a sense of accomplishment, having danced with two older girls and a couple of my classmates. It was a big leap for a clumsy sophomore. Skating had initiated me to being close to girls, and all I needed was a little push to begin dancing. I learned that the fears of social things were usually exaggerated, and if you could muster the courage to "just f*****g do it," things tended to work out.

By the end of the school year, I liked dancing ballroom more than skate dancing. When a couple dances on skates, synchronization is essential. Falls were often painful and injuries happened. That's why skate dancing was done mostly with repeat partners whose skills you knew and trusted. Dancing with smooth leather soles presented little chance of a broken elbow if someone made a mistake.

A Disappointment

Our excellent head football coach from the year before had been hired away by a larger school. Unfortunately, his replacement had an uninspiring personality and openly predicted a losing season. We players understood that you don't give up before the season begins so we had no respect for him.

My strength had improved, and I was able to do things I hadn't dreamed of the year before and I became the punter and extra point kicker on the reserve team. Mr. Hughes, the reserve coach, put me at fullback in the first practice game. My main play was to take a direct pass from center, put my head down, and plow straight into the line for a couple of yards. Using my catcher's throwing technique, it was easy to connect with short passes.

Mr. Hughes recommended that I get some playing time at fullback in a real game, but the head coach kept me at center. I would be stuck at center as long as he was our coach.

High school football was an important part of the local culture, and the police and townspeople helped the coaches enforce the 9 p.m. curfew imposed on players. During the season, we had games on Friday or Saturday nights, which meant Thursdays were open for skating, which ended at ten. It was easy to be recognized on a bus, so I jogged the darkest streets to get home. I took the risk for love of skating - and beating the system. After graduation my favorite assistant coach told me that he was aware of my curfew violation but had ignored the infraction because he knew skating was important to me. It pays to have friends.

The players, the fans and the student body were relieved when the season ended. To general delight, the word came out that the head coach would not be rehired for the next year. The good news was that I won my letter, which meant I could wear a letter sweater.

Winning a football letter as a sophomore was an accomplishment I was proud of. Mom sewed the large blue Bridgeport B on a front pocket of a button-up sweater. Letter sweaters had some informal rules. If you wore it too often, it was considered showing off, but twice each week was modest enough. If you were going steady with a girl, she wore your letter sweater part of the time. I didn't wear mine often—it made me feel self-conscious. Jake was the only girl I would have wanted to wear it, and that was out of the question.

Classes

It was my second year in art class, and the boy who had been helping the teacher build sets for plays had graduated. I had taken a semester of wood shop in junior high, helped build things on the farm and knew how to use a saw and hammer. I volunteered for the job. Miss Mary Jane Woods was receptive and gave me a try. Building stage sets became an important activity for me through the rest of high school.

After I got my driver's license, Miss Woods often had me drive her car to the local hardware store or to Wheeling for supplies. With her support, I was able to take four years of art, despite my limited skills. I did learn to draw a few crude cartoons.

English classes interested me to the extent that they were about reading books. I never learned sentence diagramming, seeing it as a silly waste of time. History class was just interesting reading and listening. Algebra, geometry, or languages were out of the question. Homework was a dirty word. The academically inclined kids actually studied; the rest of us just killed time. We could not have defined the word "ambition."

Sadie Hawkins Day

The annual Sadie Hawkins Day dance in late November, had become a tradition in nearly every high school and college in the country. The event got its name from a popular newspaper cartoon series drawn by a cartoonist named Al Capp. It was called *Li'l Abner.* In the Appalachian village of Dogpatch, there was a woman named Sadie Hawkins who was single, well past marriageable age, and alarmingly ugly. No man would come near her. With a double-barrel shotgun in hand, Sadie's father forced all the single men of Dogpatch to line up one morning each year at dawn. When he fired the shotgun, the men ran and tried to hide. Two minutes later, he fired the other barrel and all the single girls in Dogpatch joined in the annual man-catching event. If a girl caught a man, he was dragged to Marryin' Sam, the preacher, who performed a marriage ceremony on the spot. If the men could avoid being caught until sundown, they were free for another year.

A handsome young man named Li'l Abner was pursued every year by Daisy Mae, a curvaceous, barefoot girl wearing a low cut blouse and very short black skirt. Abner wore bib overalls with one suspender, a checkered shirt and large clumsy shoes called clodhoppers. Each year Li'l Abner somehow managed to evade Daisy Mae. Even though he professed his love for her, he just wasn't ready for marriage. Al Capp had no idea what he was starting when he came up with the cartoon series.

Everyone dressed like the cartoon characters, and girls dragged boys to the dance floor. Boys liked this arrangement because it took the pressure off them to initiate contact with the girls, and the girls liked it because they could decide with whom to dance.

After resisting for a while, Wendell came along, bitching all the way that he wouldn't stay long. He turned out to be one of the more popular boys. It was a week before he found out that I had solicited girls to go after him. It was an easy task; the girls thought he was cute and understood that he was just shy.

It was the last Sadie Hawkins dance for the seniors, so nearly all of them showed up. My classmate Pat Gatchell claimed me and we danced. Mitzi and a few other girls also invited me, and I was wondering if Jake would ask me. Soon Pat asked me again and she got really close. At that age, girls were much more aggressive than boys.

When Jake got to me about halfway through the evening, she said that she had to ask boys in her class first since it was their last Sadie Hawkins Day. I understood and was happy that we danced a couple of times. During the last one, I held her close and she cooperated. I had the breathing problem again.

As the evening was ending, Jake said, "Hey, you and Pat looked like perfect partners," clearly implying that we should be a couple. She also said that she hoped I would begin doing better in school. She was treating me like a young brother, but that wasn't the relationship I wanted.

Consumer Education

Before long it was time for us to select courses for the spring. An argument erupted when Wendell and I couldn't agree. I voted for public speaking, which I figured had no homework. Wendell was terrified of standing in front of a class and talking.

Jake had taken public speaking and said students didn't ridicule each other because everyone was in the same boat. Wendell still refused and wouldn't discuss it. Since he had dropped out of typing in the fall, I felt free to take the class without him. It was a decision I never regretted as the class prepared me for things that happened a few years later.

All of Jake's requirements for graduation were completed. She suggested that the three of us take the consumer education class together. I would have taken anything to be in the same classroom with her.

We got there early on the first day and secured three chairs in a row at a table by the windows. Jake took the middle chair and it stayed that way. Consumer education became my favorite class. We participated in the discussions but also had fun passing notes and laughing. We had no interest in the size of food cans or how to select vegetables, but we learned that stuff because we were having fun. Jake got her usual A, and Wendell and I each got a B. We agreed that we'd been marked down due to our casual, sometimes sarcastic attitudes. It was the most enjoyable class I took in high school, and I did learn quite a bit about how to buy consumer products.

Even though they were first cousins, Jake and Wendell had never been close, but they bonded after this class. It was also during that class that I discovered the obvious: I loved Jake as much as a teenage boy can love a girl.

Chapter 15

Perfect behavior is born of complete indifference.
—Francois de la Rochefoucauld, philosopher (1613--1678)

Depression is rage spread thin.
—George Santayana, philosopher (1863–1952)

Things Brighten for Dad

Over the years, Dad had advanced through elected offices of the Eagles until he finally became president. It was an honor, but the responsibilities took even more of his time. Mom was an officer in the Women's Auxiliary and attended many events with him. They argued off and on during the day, then shut it off and went to the Eagles together most evenings. Since I put a high value on freedom, their system worked fine for me.

Surprisingly, things improved for the George Scheid family that year. As busy as Dad was as president of the Eagles, he was working as an electrician in a more organized way. He usually got home around midnight but didn't drink as much. Mom's explanation was that as President, he was expected to be sober and cutting down on his drinking made him feel better in the mornings. The heavy drinking fire department had taken a backseat in his life.

Another reason for reducing his alcohol intake was that he was politicking for a paying job with the Eagles' statewide organization. Mom told me she was confident he would get the job if he kept making a good impression on the right people. Whatever the reason, as booze intake dropped, his life improved and the bickering with Mom was reduced.

He wanted to be prepared for the new job, so he needed a more reliable car than the unreliable old clunker he'd been driving. He had some good luck. He bought a car that had been up on blocks in a garage for five years. When the owner came home from war, he bought a new car and sold the outdated Studebaker to Dad. It was a gem of a car, with low mileage and not a blemish on it.

Things were looking up for me as well. For several years, Dad had sold Christmas trees in front of the store and I had assisted him. This year, he let me take over the business completely. He had always hated the job and was happy to give up a chunk of the profit to avoid it. We agreed that I would get 35 percent of the profits and a free hand to run the business. My plan was to keep the business open until 8 p.m. on several Fridays and Saturdays before Christmas because most men got paid on Friday. Dad had always refused to work evenings because he wanted to be at the Eagles.

Another strategy occurred to me. We had all the names of customers from previous years, and it was easy to get their phone numbers. Just after Thanksgiving, I began calling these people and telling them we would pick out a nice tree, same size as their last one, and set it aside for them. Most of them thought it was a good idea and agreed to it. I called again when the trees arrived and when they showed nearly all of them bought my selection or some other tree.

A local radio station played Christmas music almost nonstop. To create a more convivial holiday spirit, I ran an extension cord out the front door to power an old radio we had. From then on, the Scheid tree business had Christmas music playing all afternoon and into the evenings. It created a warm and friendly atmosphere in which to sell trees.

Sales went so well that Mom agreed to call in an order for more trees which arrived a week before Christmas. I phoned the no-shows from the first round of calls and told them about the new delivery. By Christmas Eve, tree sales had almost doubled any previous year. Mom and Dad were happy with the success, and my share of the profits was almost a $100. To put this in perspective, that much money would buy a serviceable used car in 1947.

When his presidential term was completed at the end of 1947, Dad got the job he wanted. The new job paid a modest monthly salary and all expenses. His duties entailed visiting Eagles' clubs in several counties and advising them on various things. Dad was happy, and we were happy for him. Since the job was part-time, he could continue to work as an electrician.

Mom and Dad bought an old run-down upstairs-downstairs duplex on Main Street, less than half a mile west of the store. It was the first property they had ever owned. Grandpa Jonard loaned them half of the $1,000 down payment, and the bank loaned the balance of the $3,000 purchase price. Living in the same house with my grandparents had been a strain for both families, which probably motivated Grandpa to make the loan.

A nice old couple rented the second-floor apartment, which helped pay the mortgage. The ground floor had two bedrooms, a bath, and a kitchen with a small cellar behind it. For the first time, I got a room of my own, with a separate door into the bathroom. It was a tiny room with a built-in bed under the only window, but it was mine and all my personal belongings were stuffed into it.

Girls Become Interesting

As a dance evening was ending, Pat asked if I would walk her home. When we got to her front porch, it was natural to kiss good night—several times. I had kissed a girl outside the skating rink, but it was a giggling nervous kiss, not a real hugging kiss. It was different with Pat. She put some real feeling into it. It was obvious she'd had some previous experience, and I was, of course, a willing student. The kissing ended when her mother clicked on the porch light.

A few days later, she asked me to visit with her while she was babysitting at her aunt and uncle's apartment. She said her aunt had a record player with good records, and we could practice some dancing. When I showed up, Pat was alone and her baby cousin was asleep. She wanted to learn to waltz. She was a majorette in the school band, had done acrobatics, and was well coordinated. In no time, she was waltzing well, so we went to faster stuff, then some slow Sinatra ballads.

The necking (that's what we called hugging and kissing) had just begun in earnest when her aunt and uncle came home, but we had a torrid twenty minutes. We walked to her house and did more hugging and kissing on the porch until the light blinked on. I had lived through my first real date and had a lot of physical contact with one of the best-looking girls in the school. It was an important evening for me.

During the war years, romantic ballads had become extremely popular and the style stayed on. The music was soft and easy, and the lyrics were, more often than not, suggestive in sexy ways. I believe these ballads, sung the way they were, had more to do with the liberalization of sexual mores than any other social activity of the time. Mothers who had been raised with strict rules regarding behavior with boys permitted their teenage daughters the freedom to dance close, kiss, and fool around in ways that would have shocked their mothers. The romantic music just set the scene and fired the emotions; the hormones took it from there. Romantic ballads also did a lot to loosen public opinions about sexual behavior.

Over the next couple of weeks, Pat asked me to babysit with her a couple of more times. Each one was the same, dance, then to the sofa and hot necking. She hinted about wearing my letter sweater. I liked Pat and enjoyed our time together, but feared anything that looked like going steady. She asked if I was afraid to show interest in a girl in front of Wendell and the other guys. I lied and said that had nothing to do with it. My attitude put a damper on the evening and I left early, with no good-bye kiss. In just a couple of weeks, my first little romantic dalliance had ended.

I didn't tell Wendell about the dates with Pat, which was stupid. I should have known the word would get around. Wendell was soon grilling me. I told him half the truth. He said, "You were there all evening with no one home and never even kissed her? I don't believe you. You're a lying sonuvabitch. This pisses me off." I understood his anger, and after making him swear on his mother's life that he would keep it secret, I told him the truth. His response was, "See, I knew it all along!" That was Wendell.

Not long after that, Jake stopped by my locker and said, "Hey, Scheid, I heard you and Pat are dating and you've become a dance teacher." I was mortified and stammered.

She said it was common knowledge and not to worry. "You're sixteen now—your parents don't care if you go on dates, do they?" she asked.

I assured her that my parents couldn't care less. "I just helped Pat learn to waltz better," I said defensively.

Her response was, "Well, like I said, you two are a great-looking couple."

It sort of stung me as I admitted to myself that Jake was the reason I wanted the evenings with Pat kept secret. Now she knew about it and thought it was wonderful. It occurred to me that she didn't care what I did. She was a senior and in a few weeks would leave all this kid stuff behind. From then on, we would meet only by chance. I had to get her out of my mind.

AN UNEXPECTED OPPORTUNITY

Baseball season eventually arrived. After our high school team was finished with the field each afternoon, the semipro team sponsored by the Eagles Club took over the field to practice. The Eagles' manager, whom everyone called Brownie, usually stood around watching us practice for a while before they took over the field.

After our last game, he called me aside for a talk. He proposed that I catch batting practice for his team in return for coaching. I agreed immediately but said I planned to play in the American Legion League that summer. That was fine with him. He just needed a batting practice catcher as long as I was willing to do it.

He asked my name, and I said, "I'm Al Scheid, George Scheid's son," assuming he knew Dad. He said, "Okay, Al, we got a deal." It turned out that Brownie was a miner during the day, lived in Lansing, didn't drink, was not a member of the Eagles, and didn't know who Dad was. He had been a catcher, missed baseball, and managing a team was his way of staying involved with the game.

After a couple of weeks, I alerted Brownie that it was time for me to start practice with the American Legion team. He said, "Al, I have something for you to think about. With the American Legion team, you'll be catching young pitchers who don't throw hard and can't control a curveball. If you stay with us, you'll be working with grown men who throw hard and have good curveballs. It will improve your catching a lot. And I'll give you the hitting and catching coaching you need to improve."

The starting catcher was one of the team's best hitters, but he was in his mid-thirties and had some leg problems. It was clear to me that Brownie wanted me to do nearly all the pregame and hitting practice catching so he could save his catcher's legs for the games. I would be doing the dog work, but in the bargain, I would learn from an expert. At the end of practice, I accepted his proposal.

After we shook hands on the deal, he added that he'd give me a team uniform and I could sit with the players during games. The uniform was the frosting on my cake. When I thanked him, I asked why he was giving me this break. He said, "You're not afraid of work and have a good attitude. And for your age, you're the best backstop I've seen in many years. I guess you remind me of myself when I was sixteen." That was the most complimentary thing anyone had ever said to me.

When the season began, I found he was right. Working with mature pitchers took me to a new level, and his coaching dramatically improved my hitting. I loved it.

School Winds Down

Jake, Wendell, and I had a great time telling jokes and exchanging school gossip every day. We were always happy to see each other, and we saw humor in everything; they even laughed at my clumsy imitations of a couple of the male teachers. I knew school would not be as much fun after Jake graduated and dreaded losing her company.

Wendell and I enjoyed suggesting the most dorky, unlikely senior guys as Jake's prom date. She was nice to the boys in her class, but she felt it was time for them to grow up. But, she didn't want to be a stay-at-home girl on prom night, so she finally invited a guy who was out of school and not even a Bridgeport graduate.

Jim Furich was about twenty and new in the area. He was dark-haired and handsome, and he drove a bright red Indian Motorcycle. It was rumored that his father was a successful businessman and that he worked in the family business. Worse yet, he was a nice guy and friendly with everyone. Wendell liked him and shared the thought that he might become Jake's steady boyfriend—maybe even her husband. I hated those possibilities.

After the prom, Wendell told me that Jake was dating Jim. This reinforced my determination to forget her when school ended. Besides, a problem had developed in my life that bothered me a great deal.

Driving

When I got my learner's permit Dad gave me driving instructions on nearby country roads. At that time, all cars had three speeds forward and manual gear shifting. I had driven a tractor and understood how to use a clutch, but a tractor isn't a car. When I let the clutch out too fast, Dad got shouting angry with me, which was not like him. He sat in the passenger seat and let me drive the narrow roads slowly. He kept one hand on the steering wheel and the other near the hand brake. He appeared nervous, was short of patience, and angered easily. When we stopped and he took over, he said I had learned enough. That was it. He pronounced me ready for my driving test.

With no parallel parking practice or much time behind the wheel, I didn't feel ready for the test. Craig George, a good friend, gave me some lessons in his father's car. After a couple of parking and left turn lessons with Craig, we decided I could pass the test.

When the driving part of the test was finished, Dad was waiting at the curb. The examiner said, "George, he answered all the questions right but didn't do very well with parking. I'm going to pass him if you promise you'll take him out and teach him to park better." Dad agreed, but he never did it.

A day later, he gave me the keys and told me to take the car out alone and practice. His instructions: "Be careful and bring it back with no marks on it." I drove around the neighborhood in Kirkwood, uphill, downhill, starting, stopping, parking, and making left turns. It was a confidence-building solo mission for an hour.

Dad's Illness

Dad hadn't come to a single game during football season after saying he would see them all, and he never came to a baseball game either. He was focused on his Eagles job so the broken promises didn't bother me much. But I noticed. What did bother me was that he had recently begun showing more anger towards me for trivial reasons. He often wanted to know where I had been the night before and never liked my answers. My whereabouts had not interested him when I was fourteen, so why the questions now at sixteen? Also, he often didn't recall things we had talked about a day earlier. It was all mystifying to me, so I asked Mom about it. Her reply was, "Well, the new job is difficult and he's distracted. Just stay away from him for a while and don't borrow the car." I thought maybe the car was the issue, so I quit asking for it.

One day Mom told me that she and Dad had visited a doctor in Wheeling and he had to go into a hospital for a while. I began asking questions. She said it was very complicated and she'd explain it all later. The next day, Dad checked into the hospital and Mom told me he'd be there for over a week. When I asked about visiting him, she said she'd let me know when I could go. She also said I had to go with her the next day for a blood test. When I asked why, I got the usual answer: "I'll explain later." I was suspicious that something important was being kept away from me.

A few days later, she told me that my blood test was fine and so was hers. This raised more questions than it answered. By then, I had figured out that Dad had some disease and we had been tested to find out if we were infected. When I asked that question, she admitted there was a disease involved but refused to tell me about it, saying, "He'll be fine soon. Let's leave it at that." When Mom decided to clam up, wild horses couldn't pull anything out of her.

A few days later, I drove Mom to the hospital to see Dad. He had a high fever and had lost weight. He recognized me but was not lucid beyond telling me to be a good boy. Then he looked away. He didn't want to talk, and the nurse said he should try to sleep.

After two weeks, we brought him home. He was weak and shaky and had to be helped into the house. In a week, he was able to walk steadily, but he wasn't allowed to drive or drink alcohol.

I drove him to the Eagles most evenings so he could socialize for a couple of hours. After I dropped him off, I was allowed to use the car until time to pick him up Most of the time I parked the car and went to the poolroom.

The doctor told Mom that Dad's memory would be a problem for a while—and it was. He lost track of conversations and often sat for a couple of minutes, staring at nothing. The doctor also said that Dad should not work with electricity because of the danger of a major shock. The Eagles Club agreed to continue paying him, which helped Mom as she tried to keep up with the medical bills. I asked questions, but Mom put me off, one way or another.

After a few weeks, he began having temper tantrums over nothing and swearing more than usual. These events would pass quickly, but we never knew when he would fly into a rage. He had begun to drink a few beers, and we thought this might be the cause of his behavior.

Mom began working Thursday, Friday, and Saturday nights as a waitress in the Eagles social room. We needed the money, and since Dad was there every evening, she could keep track of his beer consumption. I overheard conversations that convinced me she was going to have difficulty making the house, car, and hospital payments. Things were looking grim. As kids do, I was able to put most of this out of my mind and continue a normal life. I never asked for money, and none was offered. I got by using my meager pool winnings, but I knew our family was struggling. I got an idea that I thought would solve our immediate financial problems.

Chapter 16

Out of the night that covers me,
Black as the Pit from pole to pole,
I thank whatever gods may be
For my unconquerable soul.

In the fell clutch of circumstance
I have not winced nor cried aloud.
Under the bludgeoning of chance
My head is bloody, but unbowed.

Beyond this place of wrath and tears
Looms but the Horror of the shade,
And yet the menace of the years
Finds, and shall find, me unafraid.

It matters not how strait the gate,
How charged with punishments the scroll.
I am the master of my fate:
I am the captain of my soul.

—Invictus, William Henley, poet (1849–1903)

Dad's Problems

The men with whom I was practicing baseball were telling me how much I was improving. It was possible to play ball and work, but it was not possible to work full time and go to school. After ten years of school and constant reading, I felt that a strong, healthy sixteen-year-old could find a decent full-time job. I knew several boys who had quit school at sixteen. I figured that if I worked, we could keep the house, the car and pay the other bills. And, I could still be involved in baseball after work and on weekends. I had hopes for baseball, and I wanted to stay with it. The more I thought about the plan, the more I liked it.

When I shared the idea with Mom, she was appalled that I would even consider quitting school. We had a long argument. I was accustomed to doing what I wanted to do and wouldn't give in. Without telling me, she called the matriarch of the family. I talked back to a coach once in a while, but doing that with Grandma was not possible.

She got me on the phone and angrily said, "Alfred, your idea of quitting school is out of the question! All of my grandchildren are going to graduate from high school - there will be no exceptions. Do you understand me?" When Annie Jonard spoke, people listened – in her mind a law had been passed. As far as money was concerned, her stern advice was, "Quit baseball and get a job. When school starts in September, work after school and on weekends. You can play baseball after you graduate—or never." This was good advice, but the school year was almost over, we needed money, and I wanted to find a way to continue baseball.

Dad couldn't drive. He asked me to drive him to Marietta, Ohio, on a Saturday morning for an Eagles meeting. I had never driven more than ten or twelve miles away from home and this trip was nearly ninety miles each way. Route 7 was a twisty highway, mostly hacked into cliffs along the Ohio River. Driving south we were on the side of the road next to the hillsides. The sheer drop into the river on the other side didn't register with me. It was an easy trip.

The plan was for me to drop Dad at the meeting, have some lunch on my own, and then sit in the car and read, until the meeting ended. When we arrived he talked with some men, and then told me that he had a ride home and preferred that I drive back in daylight.

Very little road maintenance had been done during the war. Route 7 was composed of asphalt patches and potholes. There were meant to be guard rails on the river side of the road, but long stretches of them had slipped down the slope, putting the road close to the edge of the cliff. This was scary, but I was able to cruise along dodging potholes at about fifty miles per hour.

About halfway home, the right front tire blew out, pulling the car toward the cliff overlooking the river. I had never observed a blowout, much less had one while driving. It took me completely by surprise. The car veered hard to the right. I hung on, struggling to turn the wheels away from the cliff (steering in those days was mechanical, not power assisted). At the same time, I hit the brakes. The car stopped. It had spun to the right, off the road and into the grass-covered muddy border a few feet from the edge of the cliff. I had damn near gone over the side and it frightened me out of my wits! After recovering my composure, my main concern became the car. It was the best car Dad had ever owned. Had I wrecked it?

Still shaking, I got out and examined the situation, trying to figure out how to jack the car up on the mud so I could put on the spare. In a few minutes, a Highway Patrol car pulled up. I explained what had happened as best I could while trying, not quite successfully, to stop shaking. They got boards out of their car to put under the jack. They said it was better for me to change the tire on my own to gain experience and to calm me down. They were right. In twenty minutes, the tire was in place and I was calm enough to drive.

The officers pointed out that if the blowout had happened a hundred feet back down the road where there was no grassy margin, the car most likely would have ended up in the river. They gave me their cards and said if my father called, they'd tell him I had done a sterling job of averting a disaster. They were great guys. I drove home carefully and slept until Mom got home. I was exhausted.

When Dad got home late that night, I was asleep. The next morning, I explained the mud-spattered car and gave him the officers' cards. I expected a temper tantrum, but there was none. He listened, looked at the car, and said he was glad I handled it well. He asked me to wash the car and get the spare fixed. That was all. It occurred to me that he didn't understand exactly what had happened.

The Big Event

The next Friday, Mom told me she had spoken to Dad's doctor and a decision had been made. Dad had to be hospitalized again for treatment, and it was all arranged. I assumed he would be going back into the Martins Ferry Hospital.

When I arrived at the store on Saturday, Mom was pacing around nervously. I asked her what the problem was.

She replied, "They're picking up your father this morning and taking him to the hospital."

"Who are 'they'?" I asked.

"The people from the hospital in Columbus."

"What are you talking about?"

"Alfred, I signed the papers to have your father committed to the state mental hospital in Columbus."

"Why?" I asked in growing panic.

"Because he needs to be there!" she said as she started to cry.

While this conversation was going on, an official-looking car pulled up in front of the store. Two uniformed men got out, came into the store and announced, "Mrs. Scheid, we looked for him at the Eagles building, but he wasn't there."

Looking past them, I saw Dad walking up Council Street from the firehouse. I didn't know what to do, but I sensed these men might harm him. I walked outside to go to Dad just as Mom pointed and said, "That's him." The cops came out the door behind me. About the same time, Dad saw the uniforms and the car. He quickly turned to his right, down Main Street, and one of the officers shouted to him to stop.

I went into a panic. My only experience with police officers was observing the Bridgeport police and their brutal treatment of arrestees. I told the officers I'd catch up with Dad and bring him back, but they weren't buying it. Meanwhile, Dad was trotting down Main Street toward Lincoln Avenue.

Mom jumped in and said, "Let him do it. George will listen to him. You'll never find him once he gets to Lincoln. There are a hundred places to hide."

One officer said, "Okay, go," and I took off, running down the street on our side so I could cross the street and cut Dad off before he reached Lincoln Avenue. I wanted to protect him from these men.

Dad seemed to be aware of what was happening. He saw me when I was even with him. He stopped, waved, and then turned around and began walking slowly back toward the City Building. I stayed on my side because I didn't want him to start running again. When he got to the Family Theater, he crossed over to my side, and I met him at the curb.

As he approached, he said, "Alfred, I have to go with these men."

I said, "Yes, Dad, I know." We walked the last few yards together, and he began crying as he surrendered. The men gently put handcuffs on him and guided him to the car.

Mom was yelling, "You don't need handcuffs!" The officers tried to explain that it was required by regulations. She argued that handcuffs had never been mentioned to her.

Dad was sobbing and shouting, "Isabelle, I'm sorry! I'm sorry. Please forgive me—I couldn't help it! I couldn't help it!" As the car pulled away, I rushed into the back room of the store and cried - for a long time.

After one attempt at consoling me, Mom left me alone. I had only a vague understanding of what had happened. I only knew that the doctors had decided that my father was crazy and he had been sent to an insane asylum by his wife—my mother—and that I would never see him again. It was a tragedy for me. I wanted to be alone. I ran home and locked the door. I offered no support to Mom. She had to struggle through the day on her own. I was not a brave boy.

Just as the events of that day are crystal clear to me so many years later, so is the memory of my feelings of despair. We had been through many family traumas before, but none like this. My first thoughts were about what people would think. I lay on my bed the rest of the day, dwelling on the meaning of what had happened. Finally, I fell into a deep sleep. Mom came home, got organized, and went to work at the Eagles without waking me.

I woke up, sleepwalked through some food and a couple of beers, and went back to bed. I wasn't fully conscious again until early Sunday morning.

Mom wanted to visit her parents, but I didn't want to drive her there and put up with their comments about Dad. She called them, and they picked her up. I stayed in my room and never saw them. I called Brownie, told him I was too sick to come to the game, and then spent the day in bed reading and napping. Mom came home and we had a silent dinner. [11] There was nothing to talk about. I went to my room and closed the door.

---

11 In the Midwest of those days, the evening meal was called supper and what is now called lunch was called dinner. To eliminate confusion, the author decided to use the more modern words.

Mom had to open the store on Monday and deal with real life, but I didn't. I stayed home with cornflakes, milk, and a book. I skipped afternoon baseball practice, which made me feel guilty, not better. Mom brought food home, and we spoke very little. After dinner, she tried to comfort me by saying, "It had to be done; there was no other way. It will all work out." I admired her courage for going out to face the world of curious people. I was of no use to her or myself.

The next day, I ran out of reading to escape into, so I went to the library. I brought home several books, then caught a bus to Wheeling and saw an afternoon movie, skipping school and baseball again.

The next morning the phone awakened me. It was Mom calling to tell me the school had called. She said I had to go there.

Lud Hoge showed up on his motorcycle while I was sitting on the porch reading. He was well aware of Dad's problem. I sat behind him on the old motorcycle, and it sputtered us both to school in time for lunch. I said I had missed school because of a cold, and the excuse wasn't questioned. No one mentioned Dad's event, not even Wendell, and the school year would be over in a few days.

On Saturday, Wendell called and convinced me that things would be better if I got out and about. I couldn't bear the thought of going to the poolroom and risk being asked questions. And I knew I wouldn't be able to concentrate on shooting pool anyway. That night I went skating, and predictably, no one there asked anything about my family disgrace. I dance-skated with a couple of Wheeling girls and lost myself in the moment. It was a great escape, and I came home feeling better.

Wendell came by on Sunday morning. We talked about Dad and what embarrassment his departure had been. Wendell patted my shoulder and said something like, "Hey, buddy, you're tough. You can handle this. You'll be okay in a few days. All you need to make you feel better is to go to the game, catch some pitches, and take batting practice. Nobody's going to ask questions, and I'll go with you."

He was right. After the game, we went to his house and played cards with his father. Wendell had helped me just by being there. I knew he would always be on my side for everything. That's what brothers are supposed to do.

Years later, I realized that I had gone through a period of deep depression and really needed help to work my way through it. No help arrived, but as people do when they have to, I muddled through. At the time, I believed people would look upon me as the son of a man who had lost his mind. My imagination had run wild. Worse, I promised myself I would hit the first son of a bitch who made some smart-ass comment and told Wendell to pass the word around. It was probably not necessary, but he did as I asked and nothing happened.

I had assumed that all my friends knew about Dad being in a mental hospital. It was a bout of paranoia that took a long time to get over. The truth was that if friends and schoolmates knew my father was carted off to a mental institution, and most didn't, it was not a big event in their lives – it was history. It took me a while to figure this out.

Some of the books I'd read had insane characters. The first I recalled was Mrs. Rochester in *Jane Eyre*, who was hidden in the attic for years. Captain Ahab and Mr. Hyde, the bad side of Dr. Jekyll, also came to mind. But these were all more extreme cases than Dad's appeared to be.

I also understood that most people believed that mental illness was passed down from generation to generation. I was genuinely fearful that his problem might have been passed on to me. I concluded that I had to find out more about his illness.

One evening I told Mom I wanted the truth—all of it. I was tired of being treated like a child. That's all it took. She explained that she had felt it was better to shelter children, even mature sixteen-year-olds, from ugly truths. I shouted that if I'd been living a sheltered childhood, that might have been true. But that wasn't the case. I had been anything but sheltered, and at age sixteen, I knew as much about life as many adults around me. Mom and I had never had a conversation like this. She mopped up a few tears, but she understood my distress.

She told me that several months before; blood tests had shown that Dad had a disease called syphilis, which had affected his brain. He'd probably been infected many years earlier, maybe even before they were married. The disease had been latent and then suddenly flared up. While looking at me quizzically to see if I knew what the word meant, she said he most likely got the disease from a prostitute. In reply to her unasked question, I said I knew what the word meant but didn't add that I knew a number of synonyms as well.

She went on to explain that Dad's first stay in the hospital was for a treatment that caused him to get a high fever, which would cure the disease. But he didn't recover as he should have. The doctor felt he was getting worse and would become a danger to himself and us if he wasn't put into a supervised environment. With the help of the doctor, she'd managed to have him committed to the state mental institution. I asked questions about his chance of recovery. She said she had told me everything she knew; there was nothing else. By then, she was crying and wanted to end the conversation.

She finished by saying, "Alfred, I want you to swear to me that you'll never tell anyone about your father's disease. If people know about it, they may believe that one of us has it." She hadn't told her parents or brothers, not even her best friend. They all believed Dad had a nervous breakdown, probably caused by drinking too much for too long. It was agreed. I swore I would stick to the nervous breakdown story. I was as fearful of reactions as she was. I shared the secret with no one for nearly forty years, and unbelievably, Mom and I never, ever discussed it again. The first time most of my children will know about Dad's problem will be when they read this book.

Another thing Mom didn't know was that I was aware of the implications of the disease because it had been mentioned in books I'd read. I knew that famous classical composers like Beethoven, Mozart, and Schumann had contracted the disease, as had well-known kings and politicians. But I didn't have knowledge of syphilis from a medical standpoint.

To be assured of privacy, I went to the library in Wheeling. Within a few hours, I had read the history of the disease and about using mercury as a cure, often with disastrous results. There was also information about inducing fever, which helps the body kill the syphilis bacteria. The treatment was to inject an infected person with a mild strain of malaria. The problem was that a fever as high as 107 degrees was needed for effectiveness and a fever that high can cause brain damage. I concluded that this must have been what happened to Dad.

I also found an article that said antibiotics had been used to cure infected soldiers in WWII. Antibiotics were considered miracle drugs that killed just about any germ. Why hadn't Dad's doctors used it? Regrettably, I never did talk to the doctor. I just locked the whole event in a compartment of my mind and never looked at it.

I never told Mom I'd been to the library and looked things up. I did ask her to call the Columbus hospital and ask about Dad's progress. She said she would, but I could tell she just didn't want to think about the problem.

My research had a long-lasting effect on me. Reading about the suffering of men infected with syphilis scared me, and I gave it a lot of thought. This information, along with navy classes about the seriousness of other venereal diseases, persuaded me to never even consider being with a prostitute. And I never have been, despite having many opportunities. In short, I was given aversion therapy in the extreme.

Slowly I came back to life. Pool, work, and baseball were my therapies. Was the paranoia overcome and put behind me quickly? The answer is emphatically no. It would haunt me for years, affecting my behavior and thinking. However, as Grandma was fond of saying, "If something bad doesn't kill you, it'll make you stronger."

CHAPTER 17

It is the nature of the human species to reject what is true but unpleasant and to embrace what is obviously false, but comforting.
—H.L. Mencken, journalist, essayist (1888–1956)

Our language has wisely sensed the two sides of being alone. It has created the word loneliness to express the pain of being alone. And it has created the word solitude to express the glory of being alone.
—Paul Tillich, theologian, philosopher (1886–1965)

MAKING MONEY

After Dad was taken to the hospital in Columbus, the Eagles quit paying him. I had to find a job. One day I was sitting in the Pastime looking at want ads. A guy noticed what I was reading and told me about a help wanted sign he'd just seen. It was at the new Meadowcrest Dairy store at the corner of Route 250 and Lincoln Avenue, just two blocks away. I was there in five minutes.

A middle-aged overweight woman named Agnes was the store manager. Her family owned and operated the business. She said she needed a strong young man to unload cases of milk and large metal cans of ice cream arriving fresh from the dairy every morning. The job was for about two hours starting at eight in the morning, seven days a week, and paid seventy-five cents per hour. This left my days free for baseball and further job hunting. The job began the next morning.

After a few days, Agnes suggested I learn how to dip ice cream cones and make milk shakes. On Sunday, she put me to work behind the counter to replace a no-show employee. It went well, but I had to leave just after midday to make it to my baseball game. Agnes accepted my explanation that skipping a Sunday game was something I couldn't do. The next week, she offered me a full-time job working behind the counter after I had unloaded the morning truck.

Leaning over the freezer dipping hard ice cream into cones for hours is hard work, even for someone in good shape. Agnes said her family set the freezer temperature extra low because they believed customers wanted very cold ice cream that melted more slowly. It was a dumb theory that only slowed down service. There was a passing parade of teenagers who worked a day or two before getting a sore wrist and quitting. I understood their problem because my right wrist hurt for the first few days and I was accustomed to throwing a baseball thousands of times each week. In no time, I was the senior employee except for one fat and lazy eighteen-year-old boy.

It was a low-paying pain-in-the-ass job but better than nothing; even crappy jobs were hard to find. Agnes and I eventually became friendly in a limited way.

With my long work hours, I had little time to spend money, and I gave Mom some cash each week. But I wanted to make a change. Football would start in late August, and an idea had surfaced that might make it possible for me to make money at Pastime.

Learning Pool

For some time, I had been shooting pool with GG and a few other guys I could beat and picking up some pocket change. However, I was constantly making foolish mistakes on positioning the cue ball. I was primarily a shot maker. A shot maker is at a disadvantage to a player who can control the cue ball. I knew my weakness.

Jimmy Raies lived with his family in an apartment on the other side of the dead-end alley next to our store, over Mitchell's Grocery. He had graduated the year before Jake, and played pool for a living.

Jim's father, a Syrian Christian immigrant with a thick accent, paid me to haul coal up into their coal storage bin several times each year. Once, out of curiosity, I asked him why he didn't have his son carry in the coal. Mr. Raies said, "I don't want my son doing black man's work." When I asked why he had no objection to paying a white boy to hoist buckets of coal up a twelve-foot wall to his house, he said, "If your parents want their son doing the work of black men, that's none of my business." Fair enough. His prejudice was not uncommon.

There were some very good pool players who hung out at the Pastime, but none of them could beat Jim at nine-ball. A good player might be hot and win a few games, but eventually Jim would take his money. I had watched him play many times, trying to learn by observing. The bridge I used (the way the cue stick slides through the fingers of the forward hand) had been copied directly from Jim. He was aware of my admiration and would sometimes tell me what he was thinking when he was practicing - things like where he intended the cue ball to stop after a shot and how he would make it happen.

I approached Jim about helping me become a position pool player, explaining that I needed to make some money now that Dad was gone. He knew about Dad and was sympathetic. He agreed to give me some lessons if I demonstrated that I was a decent shot maker. He said, "Al, I'll do this to help you and Isabelle, but keep your mouth shut about it. I don't want pool bums asking me to teach them." I promised that pool lessons would be our secret. I passed Jim's shot making test.

That same day, I gave Agnes a week's notice. She was disappointed but not surprised. She thanked me for hanging in with her for so many weeks and said I was the best ice cream dipper she'd ever had. I thanked her for the compliment, and we parted on friendly terms.

Jim liked to practice in midmorning, when only men placing bets on baseball were around the Pastime. That was perfect for me as I had baseball practice or a game nearly every late afternoon. We always split the hourly table fee.

Playing "position" is making the cue ball stop where you want it to stop. A fine player can make shot after shot, nearly always leaving the cue ball in a good position for the next shot. Jim peppered me with questions about how and where I planned to leave the cue ball. He moved around in front of my line of sight, toyed with a white handkerchief, and did other annoying things so I would learn to ignore distractions. After two hours, we had lunch, during which he continued giving me tips about how to win at pool.

We played a game called "banks," which meant that the object ball had to bounce off the side of the table at least once before falling into the called pocket. It was damned difficult but fantastic practice.

Jim had solid nerves and didn't suffer from what was called "buck fever." When it was his turn to shoot, he walked around the table looking at every angle, made a decision, and took the shot. If he missed, he never showed a sign of anger or frustration. He lectured me on making every shot as important as any other. If it was for the win, or just to stay in the game, every shot had to be taken seriously. A lesson he repeated was, "You can't let yourself get sloppy on easy shots."

Accomplished players sometimes missed a shot on purpose as a matter of strategy, and there were right and wrong ways to do this. The most common miss on purpose was when you had an almost impossible shot. The trick was not to make the miss obvious. This was a difficult thing to do, but we practiced the deceptions repeatedly.

He coached me on playing deliberately, at my own pace, not being rushed or slowed down by opponents. He said, "Keep the speed of play you like best and keep your nerves under control. Put the pressure on the other guy; don't let him put it on you. Don't talk to him; ignore him. You can be friends after you beat him." Ours became an apprentice and master relationship. It was interesting that many of the mental things he was teaching were the same as I was being taught about being a catcher.

In two weeks my ability to position the cue ball had improved dramatically. Jim still won all the games we played, but the scores were getting closer. Just like any sport, playing well comes down to staying cool under pressure and keeping your head in the game.

I began playing for higher stakes with selected opponents, and I nearly always came out even or ahead. Jim warned me to stay away from players I couldn't beat at least three out of five games. He wanted me to become accustomed to winning. Still, sometimes I took on better players, did well under pressure, and lost only a little … but I lost. Jim advised not getting under intense pressure until after I had built my confidence up.

He also passed on another useful philosophy: "If you want to practice, practice. If you want to play with friends with no bets, that's okay too, but never play for money just to play. When there's money on the table, always—no exceptions—play to win. If there's only one game available and that game is not one you think you can win, don't play. Discipline yourself and stay in control. Play to win or be a spectator." This advice works for everything, including business.

With Mom and me both working jobs outside the store, our finances had improved. Mom refused to take money from me during the school year, saying she was meeting all obligations and that she would rather I use what I made to cover school expenses and clothing. She never asked how much I earned or spent and took little notice of my activities. She knew I hung out at Pastime but had no clue that I made a little cash there. In fact, I had accumulated over $200 in my savings account, a princely sum in the days when most people we knew had never seen a one-hundred-dollar bill.

As for clothing, I had always gotten hand-me-downs from older cousins, and Mom altered those to fit me. She also made winter shirts for me that my friends admired. Since our dry cleaning and laundry was done for cost, my clothes, even jeans, were always well pressed and clean. Friend's mothers and others often complimented me on being well dressed. The thanks belonged to Mom.

From that summer on, I never took money from Mom again—ever. She told Grandma about me making my own money. Grandma called and said, "See, you can go to school and work at the same time—and shoveling coal will make you strong." She would have had a heart attack if she knew the facts about my earnings.

The Drawer Phone

One day not long after Dad's departure, Mom told me we were going to get a separate private phone line at the store. All we had to do was make a few phone calls every afternoon and it would be paid for, plus $15 per week. She instructed me to be at the store the next day to meet the man who was going to tell us all about it.

A chubby black man wearing a suit and tie showed up exactly on time. He smiled as he took off his hat and said, "Mrs. Scheid and Alfred, just call me Joe." He left out his last name. The deal was this: every afternoon, about five minutes after five (just as the fire whistle wound down), the phone would ring and one of us would answer, "Hello." There would be no conversation. A male voice (never female, he emphasized) would ask, "Is [code name—e.g., Larry] there?" Our reply was to be, "This is Larry." The voice would give us the three winning number groups of the day for the numbers racket—for instance, three-four-eight, five-six-one, and six-eight-nine—which we were to write down carefully. Accuracy was paramount. Then our job was to call about ten phone numbers immediately. When a called phone was answered, we'd say, "Is Larry there?" If the person on the phone said, "This is Larry," we repeated the winning numbers slowly and clearly - and hung up. He wouldn't repeat them back. Sometimes the voice might say, "I'll get Larry for you," which was okay. If they said something like, "Who's Larry" or "Larry's not here," we were to hang up and call the number again in five minutes. If Larry was still not available, we were to report the event to Joe. Joe made the point that after the last call, we had to tear up the paper with the numbers on it and flush it down the toilet. Under no circumstances were we to use the phone to make a personal call or to give out the number to anyone. The phone was to be stored in a desk drawer. He ran us through a playacting routine until we got it right.

He also said, "Once in a while, I gets busy and I'll call you with the new code name instead of coming in on Friday. You'll recognize my voice. Ifen that phone rings and it ain't five after five, jes pick it up and listen. If no one says anything or if someone talks and it ain't me, hang it up. I am the only man who gives out the new code name. There ain't nobody else ever gonna call you on that phone, never—'ceptin' the man who gives you the numbers and me."

With that, he gave Mom a suit to be dry-cleaned and a few white shirts, saying, "I likes light starch. Can you do that for me, Mrs. Scheid?" Mom assured him it would be done as he liked. He thanked her, tipped his hat, and left.

Joe was a mystery man. He drove a dark, late-model Chevrolet. In warm weather, he wore a light tan suit; when it was cool, he wore a dark-colored suit. And, he always wore a matching fedora hat. I had never seen a black man that dressed up. I wanted to know more about him but never asked a question.

Joe was meticulously polite, always calling us Mrs. Scheid and Alfred. He slipped by any questions, making it clear that our conversations would be limited to something to do with business or the weather.

Every Friday, he gave Mom the fifteen-dollar fee and a new code name that started the next day. When Mom gave him the phone bill each month, he looked at it, handed it back, took out a wad of cash and peeled off the payment, always rounding up to the nearest dollar.

Mom offered him the dry cleaning discount she gave to a few notable citizens and he politely declined. He graciously accepted homemade holiday cookies but didn't buy a Christmas tree, even though I offered him the friend's discount. I figured he was a bachelor.

I did the calls about a third of the time, and after a few months, I began to recognize one of the voices that answered. It was a bartender who was willing to serve beer to a few of us underage guys at small bar called Winky's. One evening I called him the code name of the week instead of his real name, just to see how he would react. He reacted all right! He took me by the arm into the back room and told me that he recognized my voice too. But if the wrong person heard us use the code name, we'd both be in trouble. He ended with, "Are you trying to get us killed?" I apologized profusely. He wasn't seriously angry, just irritated by a stupid act. It was a dumb kid move, and I never did anything like that again.

A couple of weeks later, I went back to Winky's and used his real name when he set down my beer. He smiled and called me Al. Nothing else was ever said. We had a secret and we kept it. He was a good guy who just didn't want to rock the boat—or get beaten up.

CHAPTER 18

That sorrow which is the harbinger of joy is
preferable to the joy which is followed by sadness.
—Saadi Shirazi, Persian poet (c. 1213–1291)

If you can make a woman laugh,
you can make her do anything.
—Marilyn Monroe, actress (1926-1962)

If a relationship has to be kept secret,
You shouldn't be in it.
—Anonymous

SHE REAPPEARS

For over a month, I had been working hard at pool for at least two hours every morning and was involved with baseball Sundays and at least three afternoons. Evenings and Saturdays I maneuvered to get into pool games I could win. Pool gambling was producing a cash flow of about $8 to $10 during a bad week and more when I got lucky. Slowly but surely, my skills were improving.

Football practice was about to begin, and my freedom would be restricted. I needed a break. I had seen Jake only a couple of times over the summer and we never had a real conversation. I screwed up my courage and decided to attend the Saturday evening, city-sponsored, dance in Bellaire. The Bellaire dances were the best. The lights were kept low, and two slowly turning mirrored balls hung from the ceiling, reflecting several spotlights and filling the room with bright spots. This created the "starlight effect" exactly like the skating rink did for couples skating. For our day and place, it was as close as one could get to sexy and romantic. I knew Jake and Marie went to these dances and hoped they'd be there.

If they didn't show up, my plan was to size up a nearby poolroom for a game. I was about to leave when Jake and Marie walked in. I hid in the crowd and considered sneaking out. That option died when I saw Marie point toward me. Jake waved, and they motioned for me to join them. As I arrived, a new song was starting, and Jake said, "Hi, Scheid, let's dance while you tell me what you've been up to." In a few seconds, I realized how much I had missed her and wondered how soon she'd be out of reach for a friendly dance. She didn't ask questions, and I said nothing. We stayed on the floor for another song and talked a bit. She said she'd had a dull, uninteresting summer but liked her new job in the Bridgeport bank. I liked the dull summer part.

When I danced with Marie, we joked and laughed. She was still going steady with Lindy Potter, the Bridgeport graduate she had been dating for over two years. I got up my courage and asked if Jake and Jim Furich were going steady. She gave me a coy smile and said, "Why don't you ask her?" I ignored the question. As the number ended, she volunteered, "He calls her often, but they have only gone out a couple of times. He's not her type, and she doesn't like motorcycles." I breathed a sigh of relief, which I suspected Marie noticed.

I had hitchhiked, so the girls gave me a ride back to Bridgeport, where I bought the ice cream at Shaheen's. They laughed at the stories of my misadventures in baseball and as an ice cream dipper/ milk shake maker. My Pastime activities were left out. My summer had been more interesting than theirs. After they left, I wondered when I'd see Jake again. I knew I'd be better off if I didn't see her, but I still wanted to. I realized that I was as hooked on her like an alcoholic is hooked on booze.

When I got to the store on Monday, Mom told me that Jake had called and left a phone number. I called her, and in a light and friendly way, she said, "Hey, Scheid, if you don't have anything else to do, how about we have something to eat in Wheeling and go to a movie tomorrow night? I'm buying."

I was taken aback and only mumbled, "Hmm, okay, sounds great. Where shall I meet you?"

She said, "I finish work at five and we can catch the bus in front of your favorite poolroom."

I replied, "Can we make it five twenty?"

"Sure, I'll be there," she said

The next day, as soon as the numbers racket phone calls were finished, I jogged the three blocks to the bus stop. I stood next to the Pastime windows, not in front of them so the men inside wouldn't see us together. I watched her walk down the front stairs of the bank and across the street. She walked beautifully and the medium height heels showed off her legs. A bus stopped just as she arrived, and we jumped on.

After dinner, we had time before the movie started, so we walked down Main Street and into the small park overlooking the river. We chatted about nothing in particular, and she called me Scheid, as she always did. I told her I'd like her to quit calling me Scheid because that's what football coaches call me. After a lot of joking about made-up nicknames, she said she wanted to call me Alf, and that it would be a special name only she would use. I was thrilled. No one had ever called me Alf. I liked it a lot.

I had used the name Gin for her in my mind because Jake was not feminine enough. I told her and she liked it. Now we had private names for each other. It was deeply exciting.

It was a warm, balmy evening. The familiar river aroma was in the air, mixed with the smell of the flowers and trees in the park. It was all soothing and romantic. As we strolled and talked, the only sound was the low buzz of a few boats going by. We stopped under some trees, alone and unseen. She held my hand as we looked over the river. Talking stopped and I could smell her perfume. It was heaven. I don't know how it happened, but suddenly my arms were around her and we were kissing … and kissing … and kissing. Finally, we came up for air. She said, "Alf, I've wanted to do that for such a long time."

I said, "Me too," or something equally unimaginative. We sat on a bench under a tree and resumed kissing. I couldn't get enough. It was the most marvelous thing I had ever experienced. I had kissed a few girls by then, but I had never had a feeling like this. It was soon past movie time. We just sat, held hands, and kissed now and again, giving each other pleasure.

Finally, we walked back up Main Street. We giggled, laughed, looked at each other and walked hand in hand. We decided to walk across the suspension bridge to the Island and on to Bridgeport. I thought about us being seen together and starting gossip, but I didn't care. I was in love.

It crossed my mind that she might think things over the next day and wish none of this had happened. Under the darkness of the trees on the Island, I asked, "Will you regret all of this tomorrow?"

She stopped walking as she held my face in her hands, and looked straight into my eyes. "I promise you, I will not forget tonight, Alf—ever." Then she kissed me. I was elated beyond words. As I held her close I knew my life would never be the same. Neither of us had said the magic words: "I love you." It had crossed my mind, but I lacked the courage.

A breeze came up and she was getting cold, so we caught a bus. We held hands, looking at each other almost in a trance. She said, softly, "Alf, let's not tell anyone about this evening, okay?" I agreed without a thought, keeping secrets came easily to me. After a long look into her eyes and a short kiss, I got off in Bridgeport and she continued on to her stop. I watched the bus until it was out of sight.

Ignoring the poolroom, I went for a walk. I needed to think. I was confused and uncertain. This was all new to me. How would I relate to Gin after this? Should I call her at her office the next day? Would we keep everything secret? How could that work? What if our friends found out? What about Mom? Should I tell her anything? No, that was a bad idea; she'd ask too many questions.

By the time I arrived home, I was tired and went straight to bed, grateful that Mom had not yet arrived. I knew she'd recognize that I was a different person and ask questions I wouldn't want to answer. My last thought before sleep was how happy I was that Gin cared for me … and that I could hold her and kiss her again soon - I hoped.

The next afternoon, I was looking up Gin's phone number just as she called. "Alf, want to come to my house and play cards for a while?" she asked.

"What time?" I asked.

"We'll be finished washing dishes by six thirty - how about then?" I had another date—hooray!

When I arrived, she introduced me to her mom and dad. I had met them briefly at Wendell's house a year earlier. Roy was cool, nodding and not offering to shake hands. Her mother was friendly and warm. Her father left. Gin explained that he was going to his regular card game at Soup Kidney's beer joint, a block down the hill on Route 40. The evening passed with record playing and talking. When I left, we had a short hug and kiss on the porch. She said, "Call me tomorrow. I'll be home just before six."

It seemed like a week, but the next afternoon arrived, and I called as scheduled. She said she couldn't talk then but wanted to see me the next evening. She suggested we meet in a small sandwich shop on the Island at five thirty. This sounded mysterious, and I felt a discomfort in my gut.

She was there when I arrived, sitting at a small table in a corner with a coffee cup in front of her. I knew instantly that something was wrong. She began slowly, telling me how important Tuesday evening had been for her and how much she enjoyed our time together at her house. I knew the "but" was coming, and it did. She said, "Alf, I really care for you, and I think you care for me." I assured her I did. "You're starting your junior year, and you need to be free to date girls who are in school with you. There will be dances, parties, and the prom next spring. You shouldn't be tied to a girl who's out of school. If you pass up all of that to be with me, I know you'll eventually resent it. I'll still be here when you graduate." With that, she paused. I didn't want to stay in this brightly lit room.

Two hours later, we had walked the length of the Island, had not eaten dinner, and were both emotionally exhausted. At first, I thought she just wanted my assurance that I didn't mind missing out on some social stuff at school, which I didn't. Her mind was made up. She wanted us to go back to the way we were before our romantic evening. She wanted to be friends, have fun when we ran into each other, dance when we were at the same venue, and continue caring for each other. She wanted to turn the clock back, pretending Tuesday hadn't happened. There would be no outward sign of affection that people would notice; no hand holding, no hugging, and no kissing. I wasn't crushed; I was devastated. The clock couldn't turn back for me; Tuesday had happened. Something important had been given to me only a few days earlier, and now the girl I loved was taking it all back.

She reiterated that she meant every word she had said that night and would miss me terribly. That didn't satisfy me. I wanted to be with her, not any other girl. However, I was smart enough to know that arguing and getting angry would get me nowhere. It was time for us to go our separate ways.

I walked her to a bus stop, and we parted with a brief hug. I turned my back and walked away, promising myself I would avoid her for the rest of my life. I couldn't resist glancing up at the bus window, and she was there, looking at me and crying. The sight brought tears to my eyes.

As I walked home, I couldn't escape the irony that I was being treated like Ilsa in *Casablanca* when Rick tells her that if she doesn't get on the plane, she'll regret it: *"Maybe not today, maybe not tomorrow, but soon - and for the rest of your life."* He was sending her away for her own good, as I was being sent away for mine.

It angered me that someone else was planning my life for my own good. Other book characters came to mind, but there was nothing to be gained by romanticizing my dilemma. Plain and simple, she just didn't want to take a chance on me. She didn't want to be seen as a cradle robber, going steady with a kid who was a junior in high school. My mind cycled from a belly-wrenching realization that she was gone for good, to anger at what she had done to me, and then back again. She had disappointed and hurt me.

After some food at home, I tried sleeping but couldn't. I felt the same depression coming on that I had felt when Dad was taken away. I knew I didn't have the luxury of checking out of life for days as I had done then. Things were happening. I had to deal with football, school, and making money. Mom knew nothing about my short romance, and our relationship was not such that I could share my feelings with her. I slugged down two beers and fell into a deep sleep. The next morning, I kept to my schedule, determined not to let Jake (that was her name again) upset my life completely.

The last game of the season was on Sunday, and I had to be there regardless of how I felt. About the sixth inning, a foul tip hit our catcher on his right middle finger, splitting the nail and bending the joint backward. He was in excruciating pain and had to be taken to the hospital.

Legally, I couldn't play, but Brownie said, "Hey, it's the last game of the season; we're out of the running for everything. I'll give the umpire a phony name and you finish the game." I caught the rest of the game as Albert Smith - Brownie had no imagination about names. I had no errors. I got a hit my second time at bat and scored a run. No one ever picked up on the fact that, technically, I had lost my eligibility for high school sports.

FOOTBALL

Bridgeport had hired a new coach named James Wade. His claim to fame was that he had played on the same team with All-American Charlie "Choo Choo" Justice at the University of North Carolina. He was tall, slender, and blue-eyed and combed his blond hair into a stylish pompadour. The female teachers and older girls swooned over him. The local men began calling him "pretty boy" and speculating on whether or not he dyed his hair; the truth was never established. The players were impressed with his credentials, but after his predecessor, we would have happily welcomed a circus clown.

Wade preached hard hitting, rough football. He believed in dominating opponents with physical force and promised we'd be in better physical shape than any team we played. He scheduled practice mornings and afternoons every day but Sunday until school started. I decided to give him what he asked for. Football is a great place to put pent-up anger to good use

My aggressiveness didn't go over well with some of my teammates. There were a couple of near fights when I was accused of unnecessary roughness. The coaches complimented me and I saw their approval as my ticket to playing fullback.

Being used as a positive example just pissed off more guys, and my popularity plunged. Wendell talked to me. "What the hell has gotten into you? Are you trying to hurt someone? You're gonna make the team anyway. Cut it back before they all go after you." It didn't happen often, but this time Wendell was right. The problem was that I got angry easily and sometimes lost control. Finally, a senior player I liked threw a punch at me after a particularly hard block. The coaches broke up the fight and we both had to run laps after practice. It pretty much ended our friendship, but I didn't blame him.

One of the important plays for the fullback was a power play, up the middle with no faking. In practice games, the defensive team could see that play coming and react to it. Instead of having just a tackle or linebacker to run into, other players were converging on me. The coaches saw this but said nothing. They liked the physical contact.

I was convincing myself that being popular wasn't important, but it did make sense to throttle back. Wendell did some public relations for me, and by the first game of the season, the problem was behind me. No one cared how hard we hit an opponent in a game.

We had a number of injuries. Wendell's collarbone was broken, Craig George (my driving instructor) suffered a broken leg, and there were others. With two games left in the season I came down with the flu and my season was over. I made no effort to get out of bed for picture day, so I wasn't even in the yearbook as a player. My letter was earned easily, but all in all, it was a lousy football season for everyone.

It was about this time that I began having headaches. At first, they were just an annoyance, but after a while, the pain didn't respond to aspirin, the only painkiller we used in those days. The pain in my forehead would show up for a day or two, then go away. I learned to live with what Doc Harris called migraine headaches.

SCHOOL

My enthusiasm for life was low. Music and dancing cheered me up, but nothing else did. Skating was too much bother, and I rarely went. I hated the cold, cloudy weather and my pool playing was poor. Life wasn't much fun.

My attitude was bad and I managed to irritate teachers very effectively. I saw humor where teachers felt it didn't fit and I didn't do homework. The teachers didn't like me, and I was determined not to care. The exception was Miss Woods. When we worked together I told her jokes I picked up at the poolroom and she loved them.

My school problems came to a head when I came back after another bout with flu and I began dozing off in classes. With football over, I was no longer immune to being punished and was getting more than my share of detention hours. I sat in the back reading novels inside a large history textbook.

In early December, a male substitute teacher kept me back after a class. He berated me for not turning in that day's homework, my attitude, and for dozing off. I said I had been out with the flu and was still not well. He rejected the excuse and began telling me what he expected from students. I kept trying to leave for my next class. He shouted for me to stand still. He said he wouldn't let me leave the room until he was finished. I dared him to stop me and used some forbidden words for emphasis. The teacher from the room next door was standing just outside in the hall. She moved into the doorway just as my swear words were spoken. She got between us, took my arm, and walked me down the hall to the principal's office. The sub teacher was still yelling at me as we left.

Mr. Orville Edmundson, our principal, was "Mister" to everybody. He had been nicknamed "Tubby" when he played football for Bridgeport High and that's what everyone called him—behind his back. He wore a suit and tie at all times, even to games. He addressed teachers as Miss, Missus, or Mister and students with their full first names. The altercation concerned me because it was my first serious disciplinary problem and I didn't want Mom to find out about it. If I got a suspension it would kill her. I was guilty of swearing, talking back to a teacher and God knows what he might add to the list. The things I had going for me was that the teacher was a substitute and there were witnesses that he had been shouting at me. As I stood in the hall, Tubby got the story from my rescuer.

He opened our meeting in a somber tone, "The language you used requires punishment." As he looked through my folder he said, "Alfred, if you could just bring the attitude you have in sports to your schoolwork, you'd be an A student. Why can't you do that?"

"I don't know, Mr. Edmundson," was all I could muster.

He added, "Mrs. Shelhamer [the study hall teacher] tells me she's caught you hiding novels behind your history book."

I muttered, "I've already read the history book, and I get good grades in history."

He looked at the folder, "Hmm, you are doing well in history. Do you mean you've read the entire world history textbook?"

"Yes, I read it during the first two weeks of the class," I said with some pride.

"So why don't you work like that with English and other courses?" he said, a bit disbelieving.

"I do read the books assigned in English, but grammar bores me. I read a lot."

He asked me to name some of the books I'd read. He stopped me after about a dozen titles, sort of smirked, and asked, "Oh, really? What can you tell me about *Moby Dick*?"

It sounded like he didn't believe I had actually read the book, so I showed off a little. I named the author, quoted Ismael's opening line, and gave a general outline of the story. He seemed impressed. He asked about *Brave New World,* and I described that book. He cleared his throat, and said, "I see you have study hall this period. Go there now and come back here when the next bell rings."

After the next class change, I sat in the same chair. He showed up in twenty minutes. We went through a few more books, and it came out that he too was a Jack London and Hemingway admirer. It was kind of fun to show off my reading accomplishments since no one had asked before.

He complimented me by saying, "Your grammar is good and you have an above average vocabulary, which shows the value of the reading you've done."

He looked straight at me and said, "I understand your father has been ill for some time." That made me uncomfortable, so I decided to stare at my feet and not reply. The ploy worked. After a short, pregnant silence, he terminated the interview with, "I want you to come back here first thing tomorrow morning."

Wendell and I speculated later about what Tubby's sentence might be. A gob of detention hours and maybe a couple of swats with a paddle was our best guess.

The next morning, I was in his office before first bell. "I have a plan for you," he began. "Mrs. Shelhamer and I have decided you can read in study hall and any other free time as long as you follow a few strict rules. Do you want to hear about it?"

"Yes, of course," I replied.

"Okay, here they are: you will always sit at the table to her left, facing her. There will be no exceptions. You will not take bathroom breaks during study hall. You must select the books you read from a list Mrs. Shelhamer will give you. If you want to read something not on the list, she must approve it. And, there will be no more roaming in the halls. Those are the rules.

"As punishment for your swearing and arguing with a teacher, you must go to detention hall after school for an hour each of the next ten school days. In addition, you must apologize to the substitute teacher. I decided to spare you the humiliation of giving you whacks on your behind. If you misbehave again, the punishment will be much more severe."

Even though I felt making me apologize wasn't fair, I agreed to it. He asked his secretary to tell Mrs. Shelhamer to come in. Upon her arrival he went through the rules again as she nodded agreement. Then he said, "Alfred, this is an unusual accommodation and we expect your deportment to improve. I hope you appreciate what we're doing for you."

I said something like, "Thank you, Mr. Edmundson. I'll stick to the rules and I do appreciate that you're giving me a break."

He concluded by saying, "This arrangement is between the three of us, and I expect you to keep it to yourself, Alfred. Do you understand?" I said that I did. "If you talk about it you will be punished for breaking your word. Do you understand?"

"Yes, I do. I won't even tell my mother." Not telling Mom was easy.

Mrs. Shelhamer added, "I hope this new program will make you a better student, Alfred. Your reading accomplishments are impressive and we don't want to discourage you from that. But you do have to work on your behavior and homework."

I had come out like Br'er Rabbit in the Uncle Remus story—Mr. Edmundson had thrown me into briar patch of reading as punishment. I resisted the temptation to share this irony. By that age, I had learned that when you've just been lucky, you shouldn't tempt fate with mockery.

During the class change break, I choked out a minimum apology to the temp teacher and he gave me a grudging, "Thank you," but no handshake. He was gone at the end of the week. I suspect Tubby knew he was as guilty as I was, because we never saw him again.

Tubby was an intelligent and intuitive man. He stepped outside the box to do something imaginative. I didn't read any more hours than usual, but Mrs. Shelhamer guided me into better reading. She also began discussing some of the books with me, which deepened my understanding of them. We became friends, and the arrangement between us lasted until I finished school. When I was a senior, she ordered *Lady Chatterley's Lover* for me, which was not then on approved high school reading lists.

For the rest of my school career I stayed out of trouble because I felt an obligation to Mrs. Shelhamer and Tubby. Maybe Tubby spoke to my teachers, maybe not. In any case, they seemed more patient with me, and my attitude improved. It was a chicken and egg sort of thing. In addition, the passage of time since the twin shocks of Dad's illness and the Jake incident helped my psyche. But self-analysis is something seventeen year old boys don't do often or well. Suffice it to say that I was more at peace with myself. The headaches didn't go away, but they came less frequently.

A Visit with Dad

When Mom asked the hospital if I could visit Dad, they felt I should wait for a while. Then football season came along and I had no time. Finally, I received permission to visit him.

One Saturday Jim Reddy borrowed his father's car and drove me to the hospital in Columbus. While Jim waited in the car, I found the main office and was given an ID card and a map showing the path to the visitors' center. After going past a few buildings, I saw Dad walking toward me carrying a broom and dustpan as if going to or coming from work.

He wasn't sure it was me until he recognized my voice. He gave me a full hug, which we hadn't done since I was about six. His first words were, "Alfred, let's get in out of the cold. I'll show you where I live." He took me to a nearby building and opened a door with a key on a chain he had fastened to his belt. There was a row of open-to-the-ceiling cubicles on each side of a middle aisle. Most of the doors were closed, and I saw no one. His cubicle, just inside the door, had a single bunk, a small dresser, a few shelves, and a chair. He began by telling me that his job was to sweep floors and empty trash cans. He also did leather crafts.

He said, "Alfred, most of the men are locked in their buildings and some of them aren't safe to be near. There are a lot of crazy people here. I have my own key. I can come and go as I please, and I'm feeling much better. I'll be getting out soon."

He wanted to know about school, football, and whatever I'd been doing. I did my best to fill him in. My pass said I had to return to the office in an hour, so it was not a long visit. When I said I had to go, he gave me a wallet he'd made and walked me to the back of the main building. We hugged and said a short good-bye. As he turned to go, I could see the tears running down his face. I mopped my own tears, took a deep breath, and went into the building to return the pass.

The officer at the desk asked where I'd been. "With my father," I said.

He looked at me strangely and said, "You never showed up at the visitors' center, and neither did he. Both of you were supposed to sign in at the visitors' center."

I was nonplussed. I didn't want to get Dad in trouble, but the cat was out of the bag. I said, "Well, we just ran into each other when he was on his way to meet me."

"Well, where was he when you left?"

"In his room and he's fine," I lied. The guard gave me a suspicious look and shook his head. I had no idea what had gone wrong, but it appeared to me that Dad wouldn't be coming home soon.

Chapter 19

To become a spectator of one's own life
is to escape the suffering of life.
—Oscar Wilde, playwright (1854–1900)

Success is getting and achieving what you want.
Happiness is wanting and being content with what you get.
—Bernard Meltzer, talk radio host (1916–1998)

Picking up the Pieces

Over the months after Dad had been taken away, Mom and I had slipped into a routine. We lived separate lives. We were normally in a rush in the morning, and we had different interests all day. Several days each week I handled the five o'clock phone calls and swept the store or some other chore. She worked at the Eagles three or four evenings a week and came home late. We rarely had a disagreement, and I knew things would be harmonious between us as long as I stayed out of trouble.

On her evenings off, Mom hung out with her girlfriends. One of them, Jeanie, was a real character. She was bright, happy, and had a lovely face. She was born with one leg that was shorter than the other, which required her to use one crutch. She swore like a coal miner, drank more than her share, and gave her opinions freely. It was Jeanie who first observed that Mom and I lived like roommates, not mother and son. She was very much like Aunt Georgie and I liked her. Jeanie was sort of Mom's Wendell. She was always trying to fix Mom up with dates, but Mom wasn't ready for a man in her life.

While I was tending the Christmas tree business, Mom and I were both at the store all day and chatted more than normal. One afternoon, she suddenly said, "I filed for a divorce over a month ago. It was in the legal notices in the newspaper, but apparently you didn't see it. I should have told you, but the time never seemed right."

The only surprise was that she hadn't started the divorce sooner, which I proceeded to tell her.

"I didn't know how you'd react. Do you mean the divorce is okay with you?"

I said, "Mom, you should've done it years ago. The only person who will be less surprised than me is Dad." Mom was concerned about what people would think about divorcing him while he was in a mental hospital. I said, "Mom, if you don't divorce him, they'll say you're crazy too," and we both laughed.

Then she asked how I'd feel if she was seen with another man. I said, "Mom, you have a life to live; what you do is your business." We never discussed the issue again, and before Christmas she went to dinner with a man Jeanie had introduced.

Like many women of her generation, Mom had never learned to drive. I persuaded her to keep the car until after Christmas so I could use it to deliver Christmas trees. I believed we would make more money if we offered free delivery for the higher-priced ones. That light had come on when I was calling customers and women said they had to wait until their husbands had time to pick up a tree. When I added free delivery, the sales rate went up dramatically. We made $2 to $4 on each tree, and gas was about twenty cents per gallon; the arithmetic was easy.

Women took the bus into town for shopping. If she bought a tree, I'd drive her home with the tree tied on top of the car. Most of them gave me a quarter or half a dollar as a tip. We got a second tree delivery about ten days before Christmas, even though we had nearly doubled the first delivery. With the phone calls and delivery, it was a stellar year for tree sales. We had a great Christmas.

Now that I was over sixteen, I was permitted to be at the Eagles Thursday and Saturday social evenings as long as I was with a parent. Clearly, this rule assumed the teenager would sit with their parents, which couldn't happen when Mom was working. Lud Hoge, told her I could be there as long as I sat with her friends. If Mom asked me to show up, I did. When she got her midevening break, she loved to take off her apron and dance with me. She was pleased that I could dance better than most of the men. Mom's attitude motivated me to behave well. I lived in fear of doing anything that might embarrass her.

The car and the house were sold in January. The same third-floor apartment above the store, where we had lived in 1942-3, was available. It was smaller than the house, farther from school and I had to go back to carrying coal up and ashes back, two flights.

The move brought back memories of flying model planes from the windows, doing picture puzzles, boxing lessons with Uncle Red, and many other events. Overall, we were pleased with the cheaper living costs.

School

With the new arrangement at school and the passage of time, I became a happier young man and was leading a calmer life. Mrs. Shelhamer asked me to read Lewis Carroll's *Alice's Adventures in Wonderland* and *Through the Looking Glass*. She said, "You can't be a well-read person without reading these classics."

After I finished them, we had a discussion. She said, "Through the characters and events, Carroll was describing subtle things about

real people, not just writing a children's story. Keep that in mind."
Her words were true. Who has not met someone who believes that a word means whatever they want it to mean, as Humpty Dumpty did? And who has not met a Mad Hatter and a Cheshire Cat?

Carroll's real name was Charles Dodgson. I looked up Dodgson and read some of his other works. The last stanza of his poem *Solitude* pleased me so much that I copied it and put it in my hunting coat to reread while sitting peacefully, waiting for squirrels.

I'd give all wealth that years have piled,
The slow result of Life's decay,
To be once more a little child,
for one bright summer-day.

One afternoon at our weekly meeting, Mrs. Shelhamer put Poe on my reading list. I was pleased to recite most of *The Raven* for her, having learned it for English class. She was surprised and complimentary, so I showed off by reciting most of Robert Service's *The Cremation of Sam McGee,* imperfectly but a good effort. I was not a fan of poetry or poets, especially the mushy ones. But Robert Service was different. He wrote about real people. She had never read Robert Service, but gave him a try, and unlike most women, she liked his style. We had become book buddies.

A few years later, I realized that reading for Mrs. Shelhamer was the best thing that ever happened to me in school. Tubby and she had forced me to get at least some education.

Dancing and the Prom

Mrs. Paul had sold her interest in the Lincoln Bar to her partner, Daisy, and was now working as a waitress in Wheeling. Now she couldn't run up the stairs and check on us. When Mitzi invited me to visit, I said yes. She was seriously dating a guy from Martins Ferry on weekends, so we became dancing and petting partners on certain weekday evenings. There was a lot of heavy breathing but no real romance. Mitzi helped keep Jake off my mind. They were very different girls, but feminine physical contact had become important to me, and Mitzi filled that need.

From time to time, I saw Jake, but we avoided eye contact. I often surreptitiously glanced at her at Shaheen's, hoping she didn't notice. She was often out of my mind for days at a time, but when she popped up, the hurt was still there. I had touched the "love stove," been burned, and didn't want to repeat the experience.

The prom motivated a working-class family to buy a seventeen-year-old boy his first business suit, dress shoes, white shirt, and tie. Some families couldn't afford this, and their boys skipped the prom. This meant that there were more girls than boys looking for dates.

I wanted to go, but digging into my savings for a suit I would probably outgrow in a year had no appeal. Mom said she would pay half, which was generous of her, but I had pledged not to take money from her. I decided to skip the whole thing.

During a rambling conversation at lunch one day, I shared my decision with classmate Jim Irwin. He said, "Hell, I'm getting a new suit for the prom, why don't you wear the one I got last Christmas? It should fit." Since his dad was an executive with Wheeling Steel, getting another suit was no big deal for Jim – his father gave him a car when he turned sixteen.

I tried on the suit. It was a bit snug, but I borrowed it. He also loaned me a tie that matched. When I went to buy a dress shirt, I got carried away and bought a stylish tan gabardine topcoat with a zip-out lining. Now I needed a date.

I heard that Pat didn't have a date yet, so I asked her to the prom. I was reluctant to start things up with her, but I knew she'd be a lot of fun. I was not disappointed.

We partnered with Jim and his date and went in his father's new car. So Jim was supplying my suit, tie, and transportation. He was a good friend indeed. We had a great evening of dancing, a late supper in a Wheeling restaurant, and some necking in the car. We made it to her house by 1 a.m., and her father feigned some anger, even though he expected it.

Baseball

It was announced that Jim Duff, an assistant football coach, was going to coach baseball. Everyone was disappointed. He ran disorganized practices and added no team spirit. He just went through the motions.

Duff was aware that I had hung out with the semipro team the previous summer. He made no attempt to coach me. After school practice ended each day, I caught batting practice, and took my turns at bat with the Eagles. Two days each week, I had to rush to the store for the numbers phone calls and was late for practice but Brownie was okay with that.

Our high school team was dispirited. Brownie gave me a pep talk: "Ignore the situation, play your best, and don't pay attention to the other players. If they make errors, they're not your errors. You've done your job as long as you catch well and get hits." This was easy to say, not so easy to do - but I did it. It was a relief when the high school season ended.

Mom Gains Her Freedom

The court date came up for my parents' divorce, and I had to testify (no-fault divorce had not yet been invented). Mom's lawyer told me what I should say. Just like in the movies, I was called and sworn in. Her lawyer asked questions, and I gave the answers he'd taught me. The judge thanked me. Then he instructed the clerk to prepare the final papers and, just like that, my parents' marriage was over.

On the way home, Mom made no attempt to hide her elation. That night, "Mom's girls," as I called her group, went out to celebrate. They drank too much but had a great time. Mom had celebrated the end of that part of her life.

Summer Baseball

The Martins Ferry American Legion team manager graciously invited me to join his team even though I'd backed out the previous year. Wendell did a great job in his tryout and we were both on the team. At seventeen, it was the last year either of us could play American Legion Baseball.

Brownie had been right about my practicing with older players the previous season. My batting average for the season was over .400, with a couple of home runs. We won our division and went to the playoffs, where we lost in the second round. I won the MVP award and was selected for the league all-star team. Wendell pitched well and won most of his games. It was a successful summer for the Bridgeport boys.

Summer Work

The mills had been laying men off, and the area was having one of its frequent mini-recessions. Prospects for summer jobs were bleak. Then a break came my way.

Mitchell's Grocery was across the alley from Mom's store. Mitchell had to compete against the A&P, which had lower prices. To make up for this, Mitchell offered free grocery delivery on Fridays and Saturdays if the order exceeded some dollar minimum. This service was well known and widely used.

One Saturday morning, I was sitting at the bottom of the stairs that led up to our apartment, reading the help wanted ads. I heard shouting in front of Mitchell's store. The delivery truck helper was quitting and calling the truck driver a sonuvabitch, among other things. An idea popped into my head. I walked across the alley, entered the store, and found Mitchell in the back room. An employee brought him the news as I stood there. I volunteered to fill in for the assistant. He scratched his head and said, "Well, Al, okay. That would be great, but only for today. I need someone who will stay on the job for a while, and I know you have other things you do." That was it. I had a day's work and maybe a chance for a summer job. Mitchell explained the situation to Ken Kilgore, the driver, and we began filling the truck with bags of groceries. Kilgore worked quietly, head down, giving me instructions in a low, even voice.

Kilgore was a smallish wiry guy a two years out of high school. He was the kind of nondescript kid you seldom noticed. It was well known that he treated his helpers badly, chastising them for mistakes. No one worked with him very long. Apparently it was easier for Mitchell to keep hiring new helpers than to find a driver who knew the delivery routes.

Customers called in their orders. The driver, his helper, and a clerk ran around the store with the orders in hand, picking items off shelves and putting them in bags. The orders had to be filled correctly, down to the last item. We muddled through the day with no real friction.

Mitchell was a short, roly-poly Syrian immigrant with an affable demeanor. He was certainly aware of my family circumstances. As he paid me, he asked, "How did it go today?"

I said, "Everything went fine. It's hard work, but I'm used to that. If you want me to do the job, tell me now and I'll quit looking for something else."

He thought for a while before he said, "I've watched you haul coal for Bob Raies since you were much smaller, so I know you can work hard. But can you get along with my driver?"

“I don’t know,” I replied honestly. “But if he gets too nasty, we’ll just have to work it out.” What I really meant was that I wouldn’t let a kid his size bully me under any circumstances.

Mitchell must have sensed that because he said, “Okay, be here on Friday when we open at eight and we’ll give it a try.”

Friday went all right, but we had our head-on collision on Saturday morning. During the first delivery run, a bag tore open. We carried extra bags for this eventuality, and I began to re-bag the groceries. He said, “If you’d packed the stuff the way you should have, that wouldn’t have happened. You gotta listen to me and do things right.”

I thought about letting it go but just couldn’t. I said, “First of all, asshole, you put that order in the truck. Second, if you want to have this out now, it suits me. I’ll knock the shit out of you and then quit.”

As I said this, I climbed down from the truck. We stood there for a few seconds before he said, “Hey, don’t get so excited. I’m responsible for the deliveries, and I have to make sure things get done.”

I said, “Kilgore, I’ll do what you ask me to do, but if you treat me like you’ve treated other guys, we’re gonna have a problem. I don’t take shit like that from anyone, especially a skinny dumbass like you.”

Without replying, he grabbed some bags for the delivery we were making. I picked up the rest, and we walked to the customer’s door. Very little was said the rest of the day. The few times he raised his voice or complained, I listened carefully and then said, “I got it. There’s no need to repeat it.” By the next week, I knew the store inventory well enough to assemble orders more efficiently, and we worked together without incident. Deliveries went quickly, and he actually became a bit friendly when we took a short lunch break. Mitchell remarked that I got along with Kilgore better than anyone he’d ever had in the job. I didn’t tell him how we kept an uneasy peace.

I wasn't making enough money and politely asked Mitchell for more hours. When employees took vacations, he used me to work behind the counter, fetching items for customers. When Kilgore took a vacation, I drove the truck with a teenage helper and discovered what a miserable job it really was. As a helper, I had been shielded from the housewife complaints. By Saturday night of that week, I was reminded of something I had read about walking a mile in a man's shoes before you judge him.

I made a little money and learned something about the grocery business, but I hated the job. I was looking for something better, but nothing came along; it was a bad summer for student work. With my pool winnings and my usual coal shoveling, I managed to get by without using my savings.

Dad Returns

Mom heard that Dad had been released from the hospital. Inasmuch as they were no longer married, she hadn't been notified.

A day or two later in Wheeling, I saw a man walking on the opposite side of the street who reminded me of Dad. I ran a few yards for a better look, and sure enough, it was him, hands in pockets and head down, not looking left or right. It was reminiscent of the day he was taken away. I was in a quandary. Would it upset him if I crossed over? Why hadn't he contacted me? I decided to leave him alone.

When I told Mom about the incident, she said she'd found out that he was out of the hospital only on a trial basis and was supposed to live with Grandma. Grandma was living in a small second-floor apartment, on the opposite side of Main Street, a block west of Mom's store.

The next day I saw him sitting in front of Grandma's apartment. I crossed the street and walked up to him. He was surprised and obviously nervous as I spoke to him. Without looking at me, he invited me up to the apartment. When we walked in, he said, "Look who's here," to Grandma, who also seemed uncomfortable. Grandma said I looked good and that she was going to the grocery store.

I asked Dad when he'd arrived home. "I got here a few days ago, Alfred. I was going to call you, but I didn't know if you'd want to see me." That did it. Tears welled up, and I needed my handkerchief. This upset him, and he began walking in small circles, holding his head and muttering, "I knew I should have gone somewhere else. I don't belong in Bridgeport anymore."

I hugged him and said, "That's okay, Dad. Don't forget that all your friends are here and you belong with them. Have you been to the Eagles?"

"No," he replied, "I don't want to ruin things for Isabelle. She works there and has made a new life for herself. I'm going away somewhere."

It was clear that he was in no condition to go anywhere on his own. *Maybe he shouldn't have been released,* I thought.

We sat for a long time, saying nothing as he held his head and looked at the floor. Finally, he said, "Your grandmother will be back in a minute, and I can't let her see me like this. I have to wash my face."

As I left, I said, "Don't forget to call me."

Grandma was waiting on the sidewalk. "How is he?" she asked.

I said, "Fine. I think as soon as he sees his friends at the Eagles, he'll be a lot better."

She responded, "That club was most of his problem. They all drink too goddamn much. I want him to spend time with Johnny, he'll straighten him out." Uncle John was a kind man, but a recovering alcoholic. He was dominated by his wife, who was also a recovering alcoholic. Uncle John wasn't going to be of any help to Dad.

Mom cried when I told her what had happened. We decided she should talk to Lud Hoge and they met that evening.

The next morning she told me that Lud had a plan. He said he'd see Dad and welcome him home. Then he would arrange for some of his Eagle brothers to spend some time with him and welcome him home.

My first question was, "Where the hell have his friends been the past two weeks, anyway?"

Mom said, "You know those guys. They need someone to tell them what to do. Lud will handle it." She had faith that Lud could and would handle every situation well. She was right - he generally did.

Two of Dad's best buddies picked him up and took him to the club. They arranged for a slow parade of friends to wander casually into the social room. In a short time an impromptu welcome-back party was on. Mom wasn't working that night, so Dad stayed, had dinner. Lud said he had to help Dad up the stairs to the apartment. Over a year with no booze had lowered his alcohol capacity.

Lud told me to stay in contact with Dad, because it was going to take time for him to adjust to being back. I went to Grandma's place several times in the next few days, but Dad was never there. She said he spent most of his time with friends in Wheeling and had said that he might move there. After that, Mom and I decided that when he wanted to make contact, he would.

An Anniversary

The summer had flown by quickly, football practice was starting soon, and I needed a break from grocery deliveries. When I gave notice, Mitchell was cordial and told me he'd give me a good reference. It was the end of my worst job yet.

I ran into Marie at a downtown bus stop. I hadn't spoken to her in nearly a year. She was all smiles and took my hand, saying, "Al, where have you been? I saw you delivering groceries once and went by you on a bus a couple of times. What have you done all summer?" I was trapped. We swapped summer activity news. She told me, confidentially, that she and Lindy were going to announce their engagement soon.

I said, "I promise to keep this news off the radio and out of the papers, cross my heart."

She laughed at my typical smart-ass remark. "That's why I miss you," she said as she gently poked my chest.

Then she got really confidential, pulling me away from waiting passengers. "We have to discuss something," she began. "Jake is hurt that you have avoided her for the past year. She knows it's her fault that you're angry, but she hasn't forgotten you."

I said, "Marie, you know I don't want to see her, talk to her, or talk about her. There's nothing for us to discuss on the subject."

She looked straight into my eyes and said, "You both care for each other. She wants to talk to you, but won't call because she promised she wouldn't. As a friend to both of you, I beg you - please call her."

I felt trapped and looked down the street, hoping her bus would arrive. "Marie, I'm not going to call her. The decision for us not to see each other was hers, not mine. We're both better off this way."

While giving me the older, wiser woman look, she said, "I know you don't mean that and I've just got to get you two together. Jake and I tell each other everything, and I can see how you feel about her. You can't hide it. Please call her." Thankfully, her bus arrived. She gave me a kiss on the cheek and said, "Think it over and call me if you want to talk more about it." Then she was gone.

I went into the Pastime and sat for a while, watching pool and thinking. I couldn't play. There was no way I could concentrate after the visit with Marie. I called Wendell and told him we should visit Carl, our bartender pal at the Lincoln Bar.

Wendell replied, "Good idea. He's probably lonely. I'll be there in half an hour."

Carl Duncan needs some explanation. During a school game, a high foul ball was hit above our opponent's bench. Brownie had taught me to go after all foul balls aggressively. I threw off my mask and went after it, pushing opposition players out of the way and stumbling over their bench. As I was falling backward, I reached up—the ball hit my glove and it stuck. It was what was called a "circus catch." It brought applause from the small group of spectators.

After the game, Carl came to our bench, shook my hand vigorously, and congratulated me on the catch. He said, "Hey, I just found out you're George Scheid's son. Since he isn't here, I'm proud of you for him." He said he had known my grandfather, and then asked if I drank beer.

I answered, "You kidding? I'm a Bridgeport boy!"

He invited me to visit him in the Lincoln Bar. "Just go to the back booth, close to the bar. We can bullshit and the beer is on me." That's how I met Carl Duncan, and we became lifelong friends.

Sometime later, when I introduced Wendell to Carl, he asked, "Are you Ralph Lyle's son? He and I buddied up for some bar-hopping nights before he went on the water wagon. Tell him I said hello."

Carl was a handsome, friendly, intelligent man who had avoided all successful endeavors, but he had hundreds of friends. He had played baseball in Bridgeport in the thirties and was successful enough to be invited into a stronger league in Akron. But, after his army stint, baseball didn't pan out for him. He became a bartender, a lousy husband, and his own best customer. After a divorce, he moved back to Bridgeport and reinserted himself into the downtown culture.

Daisy hired him because his personality and jokes attracted customers. She was aware that he slowly sipped whiskey while working. Drinking was part of Carl's shtick, but I never saw him staggering drunk - and I rarely saw him cold sober. The Lincoln attracted the best clientele in town largely because it had the most popular bartender.

Daisy didn't mind Carl's drinking on the job because he was more amusing when tipsy. He was also good company when she wanted to get a little drunk after she closed up. It was common knowledge that after one of their late drinking sessions, Carl usually stayed overnight in her apartment. Theirs was a happy symbiosis.

The pay phone in the Lincoln was at the back end of the bar. If the phone rang, Carl answered it. He was always willing to take a message for customers or call them to the phone. Also, if so instructed, he would say they weren't there. He also ran tabs for his clients, expecting full payment on payday—plus a reasonable tip.

When I showed up and had my first beer with Carl, I was seventeen but had been drinking beer at Winky's and a few other places for nearly a year. Carl thought I was eighteen.

Carl had strong feelings about age, military service, and being treated like a man. Veterans believed that if you are old enough to fight and die for your country, you are old enough to drink. This view was shared by every man I knew, whether parent, policeman, or judge. Only a few women and a few men who hadn't served seemed to feel differently.

The last booth in the back held six men comfortably. There was an unspoken rule that no one but regulars ever sat there unless they were invited by Carl. Wendell and I spent many hours in that booth talking with and learning from Carl and his regulars—nearly all of whom were vets.

These men were kindly hardworking guys, escaping the humdrum of their lives for a couple of hours of camaraderie. My entry into this society happened after Carl and I began discussing Robert Service poems, Jack London, Hemingway, and a few others. Reading was Carl's daytime habit. Even bartenders read books before mind-numbing TV arrived on the scene. He and I were literature soul mates.

Carl and his friends made certain Wendell and I never got really drunk—a three-beer limit was imposed. Once football season was over, they gave me a hall pass as long as I could walk a straight line to the men's room.

Carl liked young guys who could discuss ideas sensibly. He persuaded me to read Dale Carnegie. "Al, you have a gift for gab. You can tell a joke, you can talk to anyone, and you're smart enough to learn. Follow the advice of Dale Carnegie and you'll do well. I did and look what it did for me!" Sometimes it was hard to know when to take him seriously.

I bought and read *How to Win Friends and Influence People* and *Public Speaking for Success.* I found them well written with a heavy smattering of common sense, and clear explanations of the obvious.

With my encouragement Wendell took a crack at *How to Win Friends.* About halfway through it, he quit, saying, "Scheid, why do you mess with bullshit like this? It ain't gonna do you no good. We were born poor and we're gonna stay that way, no matter what you read." Unfortunately, Wendell was reflecting the prevailing wisdom of the boys our age—and their parents.

I asked him, "How can anyone as smart as you be so stupid?"

"I practice a lot!" he responded. Wendell could often be an impossible pain in the ass. But he was the best of my best friends.

CHAPTER 20

It is what you read when you don't have to that determines what you will be when you can't help it.

—Oscar Wilde, playwright (1854–1900)

Man will do many things to get himself loved, he will do all things to get himself envied.

—- Mark Twain

TAKING STOCK

Reading the Carnegie books brought me to the realization that planning your life was preferable to just letting it happen. I hadn't yet read Socrates but had picked up his statement: "The unexamined life is not worth living." How could anyone argue with that? It would have been great to know a successful adult from whom I could seek guidance, but, except when I was a caddy, I'd never met a successful man.

My world was populated with uneducated people who worked to buy food and clothing, pay their rent, and settle up their bar tabs. People like us didn't set goals. We lived day to day, beer to beer, game to game, and we went fishing or hunting on days off. The only long-term goal was to retire and squeak by on Social Security.

When you live in an environment where a bartender is your source of wisdom, you learn ethics in a poolroom, and men who have no goals try to set your goals for you, how could you expect to meet anyone who could discuss a book? Even a young dummy like me understood that he was living in an intellectual desert.

Putting young people down was a common amusement for men who knew they were stuck in dead-end jobs for life. Uncle Red, the ex-boxer and career coal miner, asked me, "Al, do you think all that reading will make you amount to anything? Get back to Earth, Boy. Put the books away and learn a trade." Whenever Grandpa Jonard was present, he reinforced Uncle Red's opinions. Their attitude was that my reading was a useless affectation and an attempt to appear superior to others - especially them.

Smart-ass kid that I was I knew that they lacked the knowledge to even ask the right questions to make their point. Years later, I considered thanking them for their "encouragement" because their smarmy remarks actually motivated me to "amount to something." The urge to prove someone wrong can be a powerful motivator. Deep down, I wanted them to envy me someday.

A Painful Appraisal

Baseball season was over, I had quit my job and football practice had not yet begun. I had some daylight time to myself. Following Mr. Carnegie's advice, I decided to take stock. Seated in the library with a pad and pencil I attempted to make an honest appraisal. I thought and wrote.

After a two hour session, I concluded the obvious: I had been an idiot to take only those classes with no homework. A number of my classmates were headed for college, but that door was closed for me. And it was too late to fix that mistake. I couldn't bring myself to take algebra as a senior when it was considered a freshman or sophomore class. What if I couldn't make a passing grade?

Football and baseball were my only accomplishments in school. I didn't consider my reading hobby a school thing. That was just my way of escaping reality.

The coach had told a few of us that small colleges often offered scholarships to outstanding players. He said the scout for Shepherd College in West Virginia would be at one of our games about midseason. The coach told me, "You have the talent; just play hard and show it." It was vague advice but the best I had.

And there was also baseball, which I considered my best sport. But few colleges gave scholarships for baseball. Promising players went into professional baseball straight from high school and worked their way up through the minor leagues. They often started where I was, in the semipro leagues.

With this all between my ears, I determined that I had to focus on football even more than I had in the past. Regardless of the outcome, I should then work really hard at baseball in the spring. This was not a great plan, but it was comforting that I had come to grips with the fact that sports might be my only way out of being poor.

I dreaded living like everyone I knew for the rest of my life. My vision was not to live in one of those big houses out on Wheeling Pike. That never occurred to me as even a vague possibility. I just wanted a good job or business that would permit me to have a family, own a small house and a nice car, and be able to take a vacation once a year, maybe to Florida. The other thought bouncing around in my brain was that I had to get out of Bridgeport and go somewhere that offered more opportunity. I had read about California in *Life, Time,* and other magazines. Things were booming there, and the thought of living in a warm climate appealed to me.

The time in the library was a mind-clearing exercise. A few days later, during one of our infrequent dinners together, I told Mom I wanted to leave Bridgeport as soon as I was out of school. Much to my surprise, she said, "Alfred, you're right. There is no future here.

I've seen your attitudes change as you've grown up. Your grandma and I agreed a long time ago that all that reading would put ideas in your head. This comes as no surprise to me."

It was a great load off my mind that Mom was not upset. I made her promise she wouldn't tell anyone about our discussion. I didn't want Grandma giving me advice about where to go and what to do, nor did I want the men in the family throwing cold water on my idea. I just wanted to let the concept cook in my imagination until I came up with a plan. One way or another, I was leaving the town after graduation. That decision was made. Now I had to save some money.

I had read that the unconscious (or if you prefer, the subconscious) mind is always at work. In a day or so, I had gone from uncomfortable confusion and indecision to the calming feeling of having made a commitment to myself. My thought was that poverty could be lived with for some period in a life, but to look forward to a life of poverty was grounds for suicide.

DÉJÀ VU

Marie called the store and left a message with Mom for me to call her at work. It had to be something to do with Jake. When I called, her first words were, "You know why I called, don't you?"

"You want to take me to dinner and a movie, right?" I replied.

After a laugh, she said, "I get what you're referring to; she told me all about it. I called to tell you that Jake and I will be at the Bellaire Civic dance this Saturday, and I would like you to show up." Before I had time to collect my thoughts, she added, "You don't even have to dance with her. Just listen to what she has to say. Will you please do this as a favor … to me? I promise I'll never bring her name up to you again if you'll do this one little thing."

I felt crowded and said, "Marie, I'm already doing something else Saturday."

She snapped, "Al, everyone knows you shoot pool Saturday evenings. You don't have to be at the dance early. Just show up before nine. It won't take long."

I said hesitantly, "I'll think it over. If I'm not there by nine, you'll know I'm not coming. Thanks for calling, Marie. I know you mean well."

She thanked me and said, "You won't regret showing up. I'm sure of it."

The message was intriguing and disturbing. I had learned the phrase déjà vu and spoke it out loud. It had been a year, almost to the day, since Jake and Al became Gin and Alf for a three-day romance. Jake was my Cheshire Cat. She appeared and disappeared, and now—if I chose to let her—she'd reappear again. To continue the metaphor, I was Humpty Dumpty and had taken a great fall - and I didn't feel put back together. Now I could be as mad as a hatter and go to the dance—or not.

There was actually nothing to think over, although I pretended there was—for about three minutes. The combination of inner excitement and curiosity couldn't be ignored. Suddenly, Saturday seemed a month away, and it was Thursday.

Having decided to look more grown-up, I had recently spent some savings on new shoes, pants and shirts. I wore my best and showed up at the dance before nine, when the crowd was largest. I wanted to see if Jake was dancing with certain guys I knew had an eye for her, and sure enough, she was dancing with one of them. It was well known that Marie had a steady boyfriend, so she was a wallflower. I sneaked up on her and said, "Let's dance." She greeted me happily as we danced away to a slow ballad.

"I knew you'd show up," she said. "Jake said you wouldn't, but I just knew you would. And you look really nice." At the end of the number, we walked over to their usual spot, coming up behind Jake. Marie touched her shoulder and said, "Jake, there's someone I want you to meet." As she turned around, Marie said, "Hey, you two dance," which we did.

I put my arm around her, and we danced so smoothly that it was as if we had never been apart. The steps came without thought; I was on autopilot. The scent of her hair was intoxicating, and I breathed it in deeply. I closed my eyes and reveled in the delight of feeling her close. We said nothing during the number. When it was over, she said, "Let's go outside."

As we strolled on the sidewalk, she said, "Alf, I've missed you, and I'm sorry I treated you so badly. I want us to be together—if that's what you want. Did you miss me at all?"

I was honest and answered, "Yes, I missed you a lot, but I'm not sure I can get back the trust. You hurt me … but I still missed you and …"

She stopped me. "I've been rehearsing this. Please let me say it all." As we walked, she said, "If you can forgive me, I would like us to spend time together, but I don't want to ruin your fun in school. I meant it when I said that a year ago. I think there is a way for us to see each other while you enjoy your senior year." We sat on a bench and she laid out he plan.

"It's like this. We agree to see each other on certain nights, and the rest of the time you're free to go to parties and take dates to school events. I promise I won't be jealous. I'll come to football games, but you can ignore me and be with your teammates after the game. In other words, I'll settle for us being together three nights each week, and I won't go out with anyone the other nights. Being apart for a year gave me time to figure things out. When you graduate, things will be different."

The plan was appealing, but I couldn't believe it would work. She would be jealous; I knew she would. I asked, "Will you go to the prom with me?"

"Alf, the prom is a long time from now, but I think it's better if you take a classmate. How do you feel about the rest of my idea? Do you see that I'm trying to work things out for us to be together?" I said I understood and that I'd think about it. We sat quietly for a while. I was genuinely concerned that it would fail and I'd be tossed aside again. I was still in school, and she was out in the world now, meeting men who were in their twenties and looking for wives.

When I explained all of that to her, she replied, "I know I hurt you and you have reasons not to trust me but please try. Let's spend an evening together after you've had some time to think things over. Now, kiss me. It's almost ten, and the crowd will be coming out." I did as she asked, and we kissed many times. Before we got up I looked into those wonderful blue eyes and I knew I was hooked again.

Marie was waiting near the door and saw us walking hand in hand and smiling. Marie said, "Come on, Al, I've got Lindy's car and I have to pick him up when he's finished playing for a wedding. I can drop you two off wherever you want." I thanked her and said I was going to the poolroom two blocks away and would take a bus back to Bridgeport - which wasn't true. I needed thinking time. After they left, I caught a bus to Bridgeport and went straight to the Lincoln where I drank beer until the crowd thinned out and I could talk to Carl.

Young people in love are impulsive and prone to take risks but not given to deep thought. A smart guy would have thought Gin's plan over for a few days and rejected it. A cautious girl would not even have proposed the concept. There were just too many ways for things to go wrong. My only precaution was to have a late night beer-sipping chat with my bartender-psychiatrist. It wasn't much help.

Carl had met Gin when she was in the Lincoln with a date a few weeks earlier. He had no idea that I was close to her and couldn't hide his amazement. "Al, she's a beautiful girl. What do you have to lose? She's offering you what most guys would die for. She'll be going steady and you can still be with other girls. Take her offer, man. Don't be an idiot."

I was not comforted and kicked myself for discussing the situation with him. The beer made me sleep soundly, but the problem, as problems usually are, was still with me in the morning. I called her on Sunday and made a date.

Gin met me at the Pastime bus stop after work on Tuesday, and we went to dinner in Wheeling. We were both a little standoffish and uncomfortable as she carried the conversation by telling me about her promotion to a new job at the bank. We started walking toward the same park where we had kissed and hugged so intensely a year before. This was becoming a reenactment event, and it made me a little queasy. She didn't know the word déjà vu, so I explained it. She agreed that it was creepy, and we laughed about it. "What the hell, Alf. Let's sit on the same bench. Maybe we can make it work this time." We did just that, and in a few minutes, it was as though a whole year had not intervened.

This time we walked to Bridgeport, talking about our new dating plan all the way. The more we talked, the more I liked it. The part I liked was that I would see Gin several times each week. Until that evening, I hadn't really understood the depth of pain I had endured for a year. I needed time to get to know her better. She was much more willing to throw caution to the wind than I was.

We agreed not to hide the fact that we were dating but also not to advertise it. When people asked about us, we would stick to the story that we saw each other when we wanted to and didn't when one of us had other plans—sort of friends, not lovers. If I wanted to go to any event that required a date, I could arrange one. But, I would tell her in advance. We knew Wendell would figure things out, so I would extract the usual vow of secrecy and explain everything to him.

On our first date under our new arrangement, we spent most of the time talking about my run-in with the substitute teacher and my agreement with Tubby and Mrs. Shelhamer. Gin thought it was wonderful and decided she should read some of the books I was reading —then we could talk about them. I liked that idea and got her started on *For Whom the Bell Tolls*. We were off to a good start, and I was happier than I had ever been thus far in my young life.

My plan to leave Bridgeport somehow didn't register with me as a contradiction. Or, maybe I was playing Scarlett O'Hara: "I'll think about that tomorrow ... After all, tomorrow is another day." Or was I developing the ability to hold and believe two conflicting thoughts at the same time—the lie-to-yourself syndrome that Orwell called doublethink.

School Moves On

When football got under way, I had renewed energy and enthusiasm for the game. At the physical exam, I found I was an inch taller and my playing weight was now over 170 pounds. Twelve practice sessions per week shaped us up. We ran faster, hit harder, and had much better team spirit than the previous year. The local paper picked us as one of the teams that could have an unbeaten season.

When I spoke to Coach Wade about my newfound interest in college, he was surprised but encouraging. He said that Ohio Valley boys were looked at closely by colleges because an emphasis on fundamentals was traditional in our conferences. When I asked about my grade problems, he said, "First, they will make allowances for grade problems. Second, we both know you're a f**k-off in classes. My bet is that you can get passing grades in college, and I'll pass that on to the scout. Now, just play your ass off and get noticed."

Over the next few weeks, I worked hard on acceleration and improved my ten yard sprint time considerably. I was never going to be a speedster, but acceleration was the key to playing fullback.

Our first game was against our archrival, Martins Ferry, just a couple of miles up the river. They had a reputation for doing what it takes to win, rules be damned. At the beginning of the game, their biggest tackle tried to intimidate our two smallest linemen with out-and-out physical threats. The first plays they called ran directly over those two guys. They fought back halfheartedly. The weakness in the line meant that the other linebacker and I were faced with two or three blockers coming at us ahead of the ball carrier. On offense, our disheartened linemen didn't block aggressively. We couldn't get our game going. We lost without scoring. It was a disgraceful performance.

After the game I met Gin at Shaheen's with Wendell. I gulped down a milk shake that Wendell had bought me. I had more bruises than ever before. It had been a rough game, and I had played every minute of it. Gin and I walked around town for a while before she took a bus home. I was depressed.

She improved my mood by saying, "Alf, you played really well. Everyone saw that." The coach had said the same thing after the game to several of us who had hung in all the way. Playing well was some solace, but we still lost in an embarrassing way. My last season was off to a terrible start.

We won the next two games, but several of our best players suffered injuries. As a result, we lost the following three games, the last of which turned out to be my final game. On an off tackle slant to the right, just as I thought I had broken into a clear field, a defensive halfback dove under my left leg. His shoulder hit the inside of my right knee while my cleats were solidly in the ground. A coach told me he could see my knee bending sideways when the player's shoulder collided with it. The pain was excruciating, and the swelling began immediately. I was barely able to hobble into the locker room with a man on each side.

I knew it was a bad injury before the doctor said a word. He splinted the knee and sent me off to the hospital for X-rays. There were no broken bones. The nurses elevated the leg and put ice packs on it. Mom and Gin showed up and tried unsuccessfully to cheer me up. The only good news was that I hadn't mentioned anything about a scholarship to Gin or Mom and there was certainly no reason to tell them now.

The doctor called my injury water on the knee and said the swelling would go down in a few weeks. Mom called a cab and we went home. I took codeine for the pain, and it brought on a fitful sleep.

The next morning, the knee was so swollen that it wouldn't fit into my pants leg and I couldn't put any weight on it. I had to wear gym shorts, wrap the knee with a wide elastic bandage, and elevate it on pillows. Mom put ice packs on it.

Coach Wade came by to see me. He volunteered that since the scout hadn't seen me play there was no chance for a scholarship. It was as I expected. I realized that going to college was not a possibility. Football had been my only hope, and now that dream was over.

Being cooped up alone all day deepened my melancholy, and two all-day headaches limited my reading. Staring at the ceiling and daydreaming took up most of my awake time.

The injury caused a nearly two-week absence from school. Teachers sent my text books and assignments via visiting classmates and Wendell showed up often. Gin wanted to avoid running into my school friends, so she visited only during her lunch hour, while school was in session.

At the end of the first week, Lud Hoge stopped by. As the truant officer, he had to submit a report on me. He told me to walk across the room, which I did with my crutches.

As he was leaving, he told me to work at learning to use crutches and to show up at school on Monday. Lud had no patience with malingering. I realized he would hound me until I went back to school.

I skipped Monday and he showed up on Tuesday morning. He waited until I dressed and downed a glass of milk, and then he took me to school on his motorcycle. It was not a comfortable ride for my knee. "I-f-f you c-c-c-can't get a ride h-h-h-home, I'll take you a-a-a-after school," were his last words as he putted away. I struggled into the school over an hour late. Ready or not, I was back in school.

Each morning, I started down Main Street on crutches with a mile hike to school but never went more than a few blocks before someone picked me up and delivered me. People were very caring—and it helped to be recognized.

A Reading Event

At the beginning of my incarceration, Mrs. Shelhamer had called to say she would be willing to keep books going back and forth to me, using classmates as messengers. Reading helped keep me out of a complete depression.

I had read about the Kinsey Report in a magazine and was curious to read the original. The correct title was *Sexual Behavior in the Human Male.* I would never have brought the book up to Mrs. Shelhamer face-to-face, but during a phone chat, I found the courage to ask if she would get a copy for me. I assumed she would give me a quick no. She said in a calm voice, "I'll think about it and let you know."

When I returned to school on crutches, looking a little gaunt and definitely not a happy young man, she welcomed me warmly. I took my usual seat in the library. She came to me and whispered, "You asked for a book over the phone. Do you still want it, and are you sure it's all right with your mother if you read it?"

I said, "Mom lets me read anything I want. You can call her if you like." Mrs. Shelhamer thought a moment and then laid down a book with a brown paper dust cover on it, no title showing.

"Thank you for getting it for me," I whispered.

She whispered back, "You are not to tell anyone I got it for you, and you can't share it. I have to return it in two weeks—understand?" I gave a reassuring nod.

As I looked at it lying on the table, it occurred to me that there was no better way to draw attention to a book than to put it in a plain brown wrapper. I took it home and read it. It was a scientific presentation with nothing arousing about it. It was, however, very enlightening about many things not covered in the novels I had read. It seemed to me that everyone my age should read it. I probably received the best scientific sex education of any boy in the Ohio Valley that year, but Mom never knew it. A week later, I returned it with colored flowers and Bugs Bunny faces drawn all over the plain brown wrapper, a product of my time in art class. Mrs. Shelhamer smiled at the cover and asked, "Learn anything?"

My reply was, "Uh, yeah, quite a bit, about many things. It was very enlightening. Thanks, Mrs. Shelhamer." And with that, she took the book, walked away, and we never discussed the Kinsey Report again.

Things had gone well between Gin and me for weeks. I spent an evening at her house every week, playing cards, listening to records, and laughing. Her mother was nice, and her father was rarely home. When he was around, he was his usual gruff self, listening to the radio and hardly speaking to me. Gin explained, "That's just his way. Don't let it bother you."

We had exchanged vows of love, and our actions supported this emotion. When alone we were physically affectionate and intimately touching but had not, as was said, gone all the way. In public, we did nothing more than hold hands.

Gin insisted that I attend the Sadie Hawkins Day dance, even if I could only slow dance because of my knee. "You can't miss your last one and cheat all those girls. You gotta go." She knew how to massage a guy's ego. I agreed to go only if I left the dance early and we met at my house for a while before Mom came home. We had slipped into a routine of going to my place about once each week while Mom was working. Mom didn't care since ostensibly we were just cooking dinner—sort of playing house.

Since her mother did everything for her, Gin couldn't fry an egg. Sandwich making was the limit to her culinary talents. We had a lot of fun with our klutzy performances in the kitchen. We made tasteless meatloaf, flat muffins, and assorted other failures, which we ate anyway. When we wanted a predictable meal, I cooked one of the recipes Mom, Aunt Gertrude, or Grandma had taught me. We enjoyed our time alone and the future beyond a week was never discussed. We were just marking time until I was out of school.

The Beginning of the End

The class of 1950 had been active at raising money since our freshman year and had accumulated a large treasury. The event planning committee, of which I was a member, came up with the idea of sponsoring a Saturday night dance before Christmas. Coach-teacher Albert "Big Al" Blatnik and a couple of other single teachers were recruited to be chaperones. We figured the single ones wouldn't be so strict.

The dance was scheduled into the Eagles' Club main ballroom, with a small band, punch, and food. There was a lot of buzz about the dance, and we assumed everyone would show up.

After some coaxing, Gin agreed to go with me—a major concession from her. As planned, the chaperones and the committee arrived early. It was a cold, windy night with snow flurries, and the forecast was for worse to come. At seven, the band began to play and we danced a while, but no one but the chaperones, the committee members, and their dates showed up. About forty-five minutes past start time, Big Al made a deal with the band to quit early for less than full pay by letting them take the food.

Big Al said he and his date were going to the Hilltop restaurant out beyond Ogleby Park. He said to me, "Come with us. It's the Christmas season, and it's too damned early to go home."

The Hilltop was a lively roadhouse that had a band on Saturdays. The four of us had a great time. Al swore us to secrecy because teachers just didn't drink with students, even though the legal beer drinking age in West Virginia was eighteen (I was a few weeks short of that age). I was flattered that he trusted me to keep the secret.

Gin's standard drink was whiskey and Coca-Cola, known as a coke-hi. I stuck to beer because I knew how much I could handle. I had never seen Gin tipsy, but the fun of the evening took over and she had one or two more than she should have. When we arrived at her door, it was after midnight and she was unsteady. Her mother was up, having just helped her husband into bed because he had come home drunk. She was upset that Gin had been drinking.

Unfortunately, she told Roy about it in the morning. Drunk that he was, he didn't want his daughter getting tipsy. When he questioned her, she lied and said she was with Marie and some other girls. She said she had just made a mistake, had learned her lesson, and swore she'd never do it again. In a few days, Roy cooled down and the event blew over.

One evening in early January we took the bus to stop 10 after an early movie. A light snow was falling and it was a picturesque winter evening. The normal thing would have been for me to go into the house and warm up before heading home, but she stopped at the bottom of the porch stairs and turned to me. She had tears in her eyes, which shocked me. What was there to cry about?

She said, "Alf, you can't come into the house … and I can't see you anymore. Please don't ask questions; just accept it—we have to break up."

I felt I had just been punched in the gut. I asked, "Why? What happened?"

"I can't tell you. It is just that way," she said, dabbing tears from her eyes.

I insisted she explain things to me. We had been together all evening, but nothing had been said. "What have I done? Is there someone else?"

She refused to answer and said, "Please don't call me. It's nothing you did wrong, and there's no one else. We just have to break up, and I can't tell you why." With that, she started up the stairs.

My frustration turned to anger and I shouted, "Yeah, it's the same old crap about my being in school, right? You're embarrassed to be seen with me! You want a guy you can marry, right?"

"No, none of that," she said, continuing into the house. I turned and started down the walk to the street, swearing to myself and wanting to hit something.

At the end of the walkway, I decided to go back, knock on the door, and demand an honest explanation. How could she throw me away like this? As I neared the porch stairs, I heard loud shouting coming from inside the house. It was her father screaming: "Why would you go out with that son of a bitch! I told you I never want him here again, and if I see you with him, I'll kill him before I throw you out!"

While crying, Gin screamed back, "I told you, it's over! We broke up … and I'll never see him again." Then I heard her bedroom door slam and a shouting match between her father and mother began. Since they were both yelling at the same time, I couldn't get what they were saying, but it bordered on violence. I left, confused, hurt, and determined to find out what this was all about.

Home was over a mile away through ankle-deep snow. But I decided to walk because tears were flowing. My stomach hurt, and I felt like vomiting. I was a wreck! I kept my head down and my coat collar up so no one would recognize me and offer a ride. The most important person in my life had just rejected me, and her father hated me. Why did he hate me? What had I done to mess things up? All I could think of was that my life was ruined. I hid out in an alley a block from home, got somewhat normalized, then trudged on.

It was a relief that Mom wasn't home. One look in the mirror told me I had to shape up or face deep questioning. I had a couple of beers while staring at the wall, then went to bed and had a night of tossing and turning. The next morning, I tried to be normal, but Mom sensed something was wrong. She asked if I was feeling okay. I lied and said that I might have a cold coming on. Then I worked out a scheme that might get me to the bottom of my problem.

Without telling Wendell, I went to see his mother, Kitty. There was no way to be coy. I just up and asked if she had any idea why Roy Davis didn't like me. She caught on immediately and made me tell her what had happened. She was sympathetic, but her only comment was, "Well, that's Roy; he was probably drunk and just lost his temper. He's an idiot—we all know that." She promised to see what she could find out.

The next day, Kitty told me what she had learned from Gin's mother. There were two problems, both related to my father. First, Roy had lost money in the poker game that Dad and his pal Hooknose had run. Roy considered himself a fine card player, so if he lost, the game must be crooked. Based on that evidence, he decided Dad was a crook. This was a decade-old grudge, but people in our culture often kept grudges for a lifetime.

Then there was the more important reason. It was well known that Dad had been taken away to a state mental institution. Based on this, Roy had concluded that insanity ran in the Scheid family. These were the reasons Roy had wanted Gin to stop seeing me long before the drinking incident. But he had given in to her mother and left us alone.

Then one of Roy's buddies had mentioned that he'd seen Gin and me dancing at the Eagles on a Saturday evening before Christmas. Roy figured out that was the same Saturday night Gin had come home a little intoxicated. That was the last straw for Roy. He knew Gin had been with me that night and decided I was leading his daughter into wicked ways. This gave him the ammunition he needed to get rid of me. He told his friends at Soup's bar that he was going to forbid his daughter to see the drunken son of the insane George Scheid. Once committed to this, his pride would never let him back down.

During a temper tantrum, he told Gin that she couldn't live under his roof if she continued to date me. She was afraid of him, so she gave in and agreed to dump me. She decided to tell me in person but couldn't bring herself to do it until the end of the evening. Roy had seen us walking to the house and attacked her the moment she stepped in the door.

Gin's mother said that if Gin was forced out of the house, she would go with her. That's when their fight began. Roy drank more and slept on the sofa. Now Jake and her mother weren't speaking to Roy, and that's where it stood.

I told Kitty that I understood how Roy didn't want his daughter involved with the son of a man who might suffer from congenital insanity. His response was foolish but understandable. The other things were just bullshit.

I asked Kitty to speak to Gin and tell her that I understood the problem. She said she'd get back to me. Kitty went on to say that both Gin and her mother were afraid of Roy, especially when he was drunk, which he was several times each week.

I realized that since Gin was willing to give me up, maybe her commitment wasn't as strong as I had believed. I called Marie, and she wasn't encouraging, "Al, I was wrong to help you two get back together. We thought with your Dad out of the hospital, her father wouldn't be a problem. Jake is confused and wants to leave things as they are for now. I don't think you should call her. She needs time to work things out in her own mind. She's not going to do anything now." I thanked Marie for being honest and hung up. It was over—again!

My mind was on a merry-go-round of being more angry than hurt and then more hurt than angry. I loved her and missed her, but

I was tired of the drama. She hadn't been honest with me and had given me up without a fight. She had to know I would find out the truth, one way or another. Why hadn't she just told me?

School

As a result of reading Carnegie and taking stock of my life at the beginning of the school year, I had signed up for science, public speaking, English literature, art (of course), and a civics class—not hard academic courses but the best I could do with no math background. Tubby saw me in the hall and said, "No one should take art for four years unless he wants to be an artist." It was his parting shot—he approved all my selections.

It was my second time in public speaking class, and this time I got much more out of it. Miss Varns, the music teacher, was a real improvement over her predecessor. She encouraged us to use imagination in our presentations and not just do stultified recitations from notes held in shaky hands. She let us pick our own subjects and even let us recite famous speeches. As a result, over the course of the semester, I memorized and gave Lincoln's Gettysburg address, Mark Antony's funeral oration from Shakespeare's play, and most of Cyrano de Bergerac's "thrust home" scene. The way she handled us, it bordered on an acting class, which was probably a good way to teach public speaking to teenagers. Miss Varns justified her methodology by saying that the best public speakers were actually acting. A few years later, I learned how correct she was.

Christmas

Even without a car to deliver trees, we had a great year for tree sales, nearly matching the previous year. We had developed a franchise, though we didn't know that word. Mom insisted I keep all the profits from the business, saying that I would need extra money for the rest of my senior year. With this injection, my savings account was in great shape.

Being on my feet, lifting trees, and constantly walking up and down the five stairs from street level into the store and the two long flights to the apartment were all great therapy for my knee.

We had many visitors over the holiday season, Mom's friends and mine, with some beer drinking. We were completely accustomed to Dad's absence, and his name never came up.

CHAPTER 21

Education is an admirable thing,
but it is well to remember from time to time
that nothing worth knowing can be taught.
—Oscar Wilde, playwright (1854–1900)

Being deeply loved by someone
gives you strength,
while deeply loving someone
gives you courage.
—Lao Tzu, Chinese philosopher (604 bc--531 bc)

BIRTHDAYS

In January/February, 1950, Wendell, Paul, and I turned eighteen. We had to register with Selective Service and become eligible to be drafted into the armed forces. We were draft bait, but felt safe because we had no idea the Korean War was just over the horizon.

My pals, who had always said they couldn't wait to graduate, were now having grave second thoughts. Getting a weekly allowance, playing sports, and having summers free would suddenly be taken away. We would soon be relieved of the burdens of school and forced to find full-time jobs. Reality was setting in.

Jim Reddy, the fourth of our tight group, had been working since graduation two years earlier. By our standards, he had a good job as a common laborer, shoveling asphalt for road repairs. He came home dirty and tired every afternoon, complaining how hard the work was. In our society, having a job was important, but being happy with the job was not.

Of the four of us, I was the only one who had earned his own money during school and the only one who actually wanted school to end. I saw staying put in Bridgeport as being a life sentence to be a laboring man. With Jake out of my life, I was motivated to strike out into the world.

Pool playing was a dependable sideline income for me, but it never crossed my mind that I could make a living at the game. First, I knew I was not, and never would be, good enough to compete in large cities where the big money was. Jim had taken me to the largest poolroom in Steubenville, and I had observed how good the best players were and the high stakes they played for. Second, I was aware of the kinds of men who played pool for serious money. They were untrustworthy across the board. Given half an opportunity, they would, and did, cheat at anything they did. It appeared I had to find a job, like everyone else.

Everybody Smoked

Smoking became an issue when I turned eighteen. Nearly every man I knew smoked, as did many women. I had promised Mom I wouldn't begin until I was at least eighteen and it had been an easy promise to keep because of sports. All of my friends began smoking soon after turning sixteen. I was a holdout.

Shooting pool and smoking cigarettes went together. It was part of "the look" to take a drag on a cigarette, slowly exhale while surveying the table, and casually lay the cigarette in an ashtray before bending over the table to make a shot (placing a cigarette on a pool table at the Pastime was grounds for excommunication). Smoking cigarettes was just too cool for a young shooter to pass up, and I succumbed. For a long time, I smoked sparingly, only when playing pool or drinking beer. Saturdays, when I was at a pool table for six or more hours straight, I smoked about ten cigarettes.

My Cheshire Cat Reappears

On January 18th I ignored Jake's nineteenth birthday. A card from her, with no message, arrived on my birthday. I toyed with calling her office and thanking her, but what would I say? I could say something like, "Sorry my Dad's crazy and yours is a stupid drunk?" I decided that ignoring her card sent the message that our relationship was over.

Bill McConaughey, a heavy-drinking ex-GI and Bridgeport graduate, was well known for getting into fights just for the hell of it. He and I often played pool, and he always lost a few bucks, but he never complained. In addition to pool, we both liked to tell jokes and bullshit about politics. We had become good friends. Bill was about four years older than Jake and had watched her grow up. Because I was still in school, he was surprised Jake had been my girlfriend.

On the Friday night after my birthday, he took me to the newest and best bar in Wheeling, called the Cork n' Bottle. The purpose was to celebrate my draft registration and birthday. Any excuse for drinking was a good one for Bill.

After returning from the men's room, Bill asked, "Have you seen Jake lately?" I said no and he grinned. "Well, walk to the men's room and you'll see her sitting at the corner of the bar with some guy." My heart rate increased, and a lump rose up in my throat. I said I had no interest in seeing her. Bill said, "Go ahead, asshole; you know you're going to do it. I'll have another beer waiting when you get back."

On the way to the men's room I glanced at the bar. It was Jake all right, sitting with a guy wearing a felt hat. When I returned, I said I wanted to leave and gulped my beer to make the point. We walked to another bar. I refused to talk about Jake, and Bill didn't push the issue.

The phone woke me up the next morning. "Happy birthday, Alf," Jake said. "Did you get the card I sent?" I verified that the card had been received. There was an uncomfortable silence for a few seconds before she said, "You didn't even say hello at the Cork n' Bottle last night."

I said, "Jake, there was no reason to say hello—you know that. And I didn't know you saw me."

She quickly replied, "So I'm Jake again? Are you going to wish me a happy birthday, or did you forget I had one?"

This game was not pleasing me, so I said, "Happy birthday, Virginia. I don't know why you called; we have nothing to talk about." I assumed that would end the conversation, even though I wasn't sure I wanted it to end.

She said, "Do you want to know why Virginia called? Just ask Gin and she'll tell you [she had a clever way with words]. If you hang up Alf will never know."

"Okay, Gin, why did Virginia call? Please tell me. I have a giant hangover and can't stand the suspense."

"She wanted to tell Alf she loves him, but now I'm not sure she should do that."

"Alf is still listening," I said, going along with her game.

In a sort of choking voice she said, "Alf, I love you, I miss you, and I want us to be together. How do you feel about me?" She paused, waiting for a reply.

"Gin knows how Alf feels, but the problems never go away. Alf has decided he wants to stop the pain."

She said, "How about tonight? Will your mother leave for work, as usual?"

As my heart leapt, I said, "Of course."

She said, "I'll be at your place at six. I know how to solve our problem, and I'll tell you then. I love you." She hung up.

I was in a state of shock. I went back to bed and took many deep breaths. For the first time in weeks, I felt some happiness.

In the afternoon, I got into a game with some real pigeons. By five, I was up over $20. I should have let my luck run and kept playing, but I had to get ready for my dinner guest. Flush with my winnings, I stopped at Mitchell's for steaks and potatoes, which I hid in the hallway to avoid Mom's questions. After having played controlled pool all afternoon, I was amazed to notice my hands were shaking.

She arrived right on time, and I had the potatoes in the oven. We were hungry for each other and were in a tight embrace before I could close the door. We overcame our lack of intimate experience and learned things together – at last we knew our love was real. Over an hour later, we had the steaks, potatoes and beer, and we agreed that we'd never had a better dinner.

She caught me up on events. After speaking with Kitty, she felt confident that I would be willing to go back with her if she moved out. She had decided to find a place to live and then call me. Her mother begged her to stay. She believed Gin had the right to date whomever she pleased. They decided that Gin would go back with me but they'd keep it secret from Roy. If he found out, her mother was quite willing to move out and get a divorce. She was completely fed up with Roy's drinking and card playing. They also didn't believe he'd harm them. I didn't share their confidence about that.

The plan was that I would never come near their house. They figured Roy wouldn't find out about us for a long time, maybe never. He went nowhere but his job, Soup's Bar, and his fishing camp at

Piedmont Lake. They felt certain that none of his friends would tell him if they saw us together.

Gin's attitude was that as long as it worked, we should do it. If Roy found out, we'd worry about that then. Well, here was the Scarlett O'Hara syndrome all over again, only now with three players. I was so happy to be back with her that I would have agreed to an even more outrageous plan.

One loose end was the man she had been with at the Cork n' Bottle. She said his name was Jack Donahie and the reason she was with him that night was to tell him that their dating was over. She had explained our on-and-off relationship and made it clear that she wanted to be with me.

Running into Bill and me had been an unforeseen event that prompted her to call me right away rather than have Kitty talk to me. She said that dating Jack was actually what convinced her that we should be together. She said, "I missed you even more when I was with him." I was pleased, flattered, and wanted to believe everything she said. I explained that I needed time to establish new trust. She promised she'd prove her love.

The next morning, I told Mom as much as she needed to know about Gin and me. She liked Gin and was happy for us, but she was concerned about the father

Life Goes On

Baseball practice began in the gym. Coach Wade had changed since football season. He had a lot less enthusiasm and was not much better than the coach he replaced. The rumor was that he was looking for a job outside of coaching.

One day Wade unexpectedly told me that standing up for hours shooting pool would keep my knee from healing and I had to quit pool to be on his team. At first, I thought he was joking, but he left no doubt that he was serious. I didn't think my pool playing was his business.

After practice, I walked over to see Brownie, whose team was just taking over the field. With no preliminaries, I told him what Wade had said and asked if he would take me on his team. Brownie took off his hat, scratched his head, and said, "Well, Al, I'd sure like to have you, but I don't want a run-in with your coach. Why don't you try it his way? You can live without pool for a while." It was obvious he didn't want to be seen as taking a player away from the high school team.

I said, "Okay, I understand, but I may quit anyway. Wade has a shitty attitude, and the team is not motivated. And what I do with my evenings and Saturdays is my business as long as I don't break training rules."

Brownie allowed that he understood. "Why don't you keep me up to date as things go along?" That was it. My guess was that if Wade caught me playing pool, he would throw me off the team and that would be fine with me.

That Saturday, Wade came into Pastime and took a seat near the table where I was in a nine-ball game. I said hello, and he nodded.

At the end of the game, my opponent paid up and quit. I called for a rack, intending to practice for a while, and Wade said, "Well, you got a pretty good stick." That was the language spoken only by pool players. *Either he knows something about the game or he just picked up the phrase,* I thought.

He said, "Does your mother know you play for money? Does she like her son hanging out in a poolroom?" The way he spoke those remarks made me realize I didn't like him.

I said, "My mother is of no concern to you, but for what it's worth, she knows where I am and has no problem with how I spend my time."

"You have a smart-ass attitude, don't you?" he said with a sneer. "Where I come from, kids don't talk to adults that way." His southern accent irritated me and I didn't like his curly blond hair.

"Well, Mr. Wade, you could move back to the South where the people are more to your liking," I suggested as politely as possible.

As he left, he said loudly, "I don't want to hear about you being in here again," and he was out the door.

Wendell had been playing on a table across the room and observed the exchange. "What was that all about?" he asked.

I said, "It was about me quitting high school baseball, which I'll do on Monday."

Wendell was incredulous. "Who the hell does Wade think he is. F**k him, he can't tell us what to do with our free time. I'll quit too."

We went for a walk, and I persuaded Wendell to cool down. I told him I'd just go into semipro ball early, and it was better for me anyway. But he should stay on the school team and finish the season. We both knew that other than pickup games, it was doubtful he could play ball after high school. He finally agreed.

On Monday, I took my uniform to school and turned it in to the assistant coach without speaking to Wade. Mr. Hughes was not surprised since he was aware of the conflict, but he said, "Al, are sure you want to do this?" I thanked him for all he'd done for me in sports and assured him that I had reached my decision carefully.

As it worked out, Wade hadn't thrown me off the team, I'd quit. It was a distinction without much of a difference, but I liked it better this way. Had I gone to practice, Wade and I most likely would have had a confrontation that would have hurt me with Tubby. It was a weight off my shoulders. On the Eagles team, I would have several more weeks of practice before playing in games, and not running bases for a while longer would help my knee. I called Brownie, and he said to wait a week before showing up at his practices. He didn't want to risk losing use of the practice field.

Wade had a players' meeting where he said I had put my selfish interests ahead of the team, adding, "He wants to shoot pool because he's pretending to be a man when he's just a snot-nosed kid, too big for his britches. He needs a father to take a belt to him." I ignored this provocation but vowed I'd take no more crap from him.

A Dad Sighting

While in Wheeling, I ran into Dad again. He was much more lucid than the last time we talked. He invited me to see where he lived. It was a second-floor walk-up, just two blocks from the Twenty-Third Street red-light district. Some underwear hanging on a line showed that a woman lived there, but I asked no questions.

He said he was doing some electrical jobs and was looking for steady work. We chatted about my knee injury until he began looking nervous. I thanked him for the visit and left. We'd had nearly an hour together, and it was nice to hear he was looking for a job. I wondered who the woman was, but decided not to mention that part to Mom.

War on the Horizon

The smell of another war was in the air. The Cold War with the Soviet Union was in full swing, and there was talk that we needed a larger army. We didn't know that Korea would be the place, but we knew something was brewing.

Gin and I were getting along really well. As agreed, I took dates to a couple of senior parties. It was there in front of me, so I did a little necking, but it was not like being with Gin.

The date for the yearbook pictures, sneaked up on me before I got around to buying a suit for the prom. Jim Irwin was generous again and loaned me the same suit and tie. So I wore borrowed clothes in my graduation picture.

With the prom coming up, I bought my first suit, the only one I owned for the next four years. It was dark gray worsted wool, bought at the best men's clothing store in Wheeling. I paid about $50 for it, which was full price in 1950.

Sidebar

This appears to be a good time to put some economics in perspective. In 1950 you could buy a well-made men's suit for $45, dress shoes for $5, shirts for $4, denim jeans for $3, a full-length woman's cashmere coat for $50, women's nylon stockings for less than a dollar, a new Ford car for less than $1,300, and gas was $0.18 per gallon. When it came to food, coffee was $0.43 per pound, sugar was $0.52 for a five-pound bag, mayonnaise was $0.62 per quart, pork and beans were $0.15 per can, bacon was $0.66 per pound, sirloin steak was $0.77 per pound, and tomatoes were $0.15 per can. A new washing machine, including an electric "wringer," cost about $70. The average income in the United States was about $4,000 per year for men, less for women, and lower than that in our area. There's been a lot of inflation since the 1950s.

School Winds Down

Gin wouldn't consider going to the senior prom. Carolyn Lewis was a sweet, intelligent, classy girl who was going on to college. She agreed to be my prom date, and we had a good time, despite a Wendell problem.

Wendell managed to get a date. He took a pocket flask and sipped on it in the men's room. He made it to the after-prom party at a Wheeling restaurant, where he passed out at the table. We found a place for him to sleep in a back booth and put his date into a cab. She wasn't a happy camper. When the party broke up, I loaded Wendell into a cab with Carolyn and me. After dropping Carolyn off, I took Wendell home and helped him onto the living room sofa without waking his parents. He would pay the price in the morning when Kitty and Ralph found him sleeping in his new suit. Nights like this were a pattern of life for us.

Just after the prom, Pat Dudley, a classmate, asked me to be her partner for a dance contest in Wheeling. Gin encouraged me to do it. Pat and I were both decent dancers, and who knows, we might win something. That would be a hoot. We performed well but didn't win a prize.

A few days after the contest, Pat Dudley's mother called Mom and told her that Pat had come down with the mumps. A few days later, I woke up in the middle of the night with a fever and pain in my neck. I had the mumps. Since a vaccine was developed, mumps has become almost unknown, but in the 1950s, it was a dangerous disease, especially for boys. Bed rest was necessary while mumps ran its course.

Somehow Gin didn't contract the disease, which was a miracle since we kissed constantly, right up to the day my fever began. The other strange thing was that I had never kissed my dance partner, not even once. Apparently, Gin had natural immunity and I had bad luck.

Friends and classmates came to visit. All visitors, except Pat Dudley, who was now immune, had to stay at least six feet away and touch nothing I'd touched. Having the mumps was not just painful; it was frightfully boring.

School Days End

By graduation day, I had recovered enough to participate in the ceremony. Grandma and Grandpa attended, but Dad didn't show up. I knew he wouldn't risk running into Mom and her parents.

We all came back to the apartment after it was over. Grandma loved Gin instantly. We climbed out the back window and took pictures on the roof behind the apartment—in cap and gown, of course.

It had convinced Gin that I would much rather be with her that night than with Wendell and other classmates. We met them later in a Wheeling joint, filled with graduation celebrants from many schools. Eventually, we all got maudlin about getting drafted and killed in the war we expected soon. Gin, bless her, convinced us to go home.

With mumps and graduation over, it was time to find paying work that didn't conflict with baseball, pool, and time with Gin. I felt confident that I could find a full-time job that accommodated all my activities. Leaving town receded into the deeper recesses of my mind. I couldn't leave Gin - at least not immediately.

Now that I had graduated there was nothing to hide we let our relationship be known. A bad scene with Roy was our only concern. Being out in the open was a relief for both of us.

A Little Religion

Gin gave me a new surprise when she asked me to go to church. Her parents didn't attend church, but Gin had been going for years with Marie and had joined the Presbyterian Church in Kirkwood. I agreed to give it a shot, though I had a low level of enthusiasm for religion. I did like the organ music. I sang hymns along with the congregation and tried not to fidget during the sermons. I endured the preaching for the sake of love.

The first Sunday, I saw a couple of my regular coal-hauling customers and some other people I knew. Many of them were surprised to see us holding hands as we walked in. After the service, a number of people came to us to say hello. They just had to get a closer look.

Great Atlantic & Pacific Tea Company

The week after graduation, I went to many of the nearby mills and factories, filling out job applications wherever possible. There were hundreds of new graduates looking for work, and prospects were not encouraging.

A couple of years earlier, the Great Atlantic & Pacific Tea Company (A&P) had opened a self-service market across Bridge Street from the Pastime. The store was an instant success.

One afternoon, a Pastime patron told me that a man had been fired from the A&P that morning. I walked across the street to check it out. The assistant manager, Mr. Kowalski, was a man I'd seen at the Lincoln several times. I explained that I had delivered groceries for Mitchell's, shoveled coal, sold Christmas trees, scooped ice cream, and worked on a farm.

He said, "Well, it sounds like you are used to hard work." I looked straight at him, just as Mr. Carnegie instructed, and said, "Yes, sir, and I'll do whatever job you have available." He gave no reply, but I sensed he liked my positive approach.

He said, "The job is unloading boxcars on the siding out back, stocking shelves, mopping floors, and whatever else I tell you to do. Are you still interested?" I said firmly that I could do all those things. He was pleased with my completed application and told me to show up the next morning at eight. "The pay is forty dollars per week for forty-five hours, and you'll get half an hour for lunch. Wear a white shirt, a plain tie, clean leather shoes, not sneakers; blue jeans are okay if they're clean. See you tomorrow," he mumbled, as he walked away. *Not a friendly guy*, I thought.

The next morning, Kowalski gave me his rules: "Employees are not allowed to eat on the job; there is no smoking and no long breaks in the men's room. I don't like conversations that aren't about the job, and I don't put up with complaining or back talk. Get here on time, do your job well, and then you'll have no problems."

In the boxcar, I met a guy a couple of years older than I. Once we were acquainted, Jimmy clued me in to the scene. He said that Kowalski looked for reasons to criticize employees and had a nasty temper.

Jimmy said that when there was a problem, Kowalski went looking for someone to blame. We were on the bottom of the totem pole, so we would get more than our share of blame.

Jimmy's warning: "When a customer puts a can of beans with the canned tomatoes, he will always accuse us of doing a sloppy job of stocking the shelves." He said my predecessor was fired because he had objected to being blamed for something he didn't do. Kowalski called his defense "talking back" and fired him on the spot.

Jimmy was married with two young kids and lived with constant fear of losing his miserable job. *What a way to exist,* I thought.

Because I defended myself, in a Dale Carnegie sort of way, Kowalski figured out early on that I wouldn't put up with being jumped on for no reason. I quit using "sir" when he was bitching about something. I had been yelled at by football coaches who made a fine art out of ass chewing. Kowalski was an amateur compared to an angry coach. Kowalski was a mean little man who was infected with the small man complex.

A few days after I started at the A&P, Lud Hoge called Mom and said that Dad wanted to see me. We met in a beer bar in Wheeling. After we settled with our beers in a quiet booth in the rear, he gave me a gold Bulova watch as a graduation present. It was not an expensive watch, but I knew he couldn't afford any watch at all. Tears came to my eyes quickly as I tried to thank him. He got up and went to the men's room. Any sort of emotional scene distressed Dad and put him into a confused state.

When he returned, we had the first emotional discussion we'd ever had. He said he was sorry for all the pain he had caused Mom and me and how much he regretted all the mistakes he'd made. I assured him that I understood what his problem had been and I harbored no bad feelings toward him. He was my father, and I wanted a relationship with him.

We spoke about my gun, the catcher's mitt he had bought for me and the hunting and fishing times we had enjoyed. He retold the story of my first rabbit kill and a Piedmont Lake fishing trip where we caught so many crappies that we gave half of them away. It was a catharsis for both of us and way overdue. At times, it was a difficult visit, but I felt better when it was over - and I'm sure he did too.

From then on, there was an unspoken understanding that what had transpired within our little family was in the past and there was no need to blame anyone. We lived with the way things were. I knew he wouldn't call me and risk Mom answering. He was not ready to talk to her yet. I gave him the phone numbers at Pastime and the Lincoln so he could leave messages for me.

War Arrives

On June 25, 1950, the North Korean army crossed the 38th parallel and invaded South Korea. The anticipated war had begun. This event changed how we looked at the future. No plan could be made without considering the consequences of being drafted. Some young couples married and tried for children as quickly as possible so the man could avoid being called up. Some young men suddenly developed a hunger for higher education and started college so they could get a four year deferment. Those of us who didn't consider ourselves college or marriage material were left to be "selected" by the Selective Service Administration. We were aware of what the term "cannon fodder" meant and knew that could be our fate.

I looked into joining the Naval Reserve, which had a base in Wheeling. Wendell and Jim were talking about joining the air force, and Paul's doctor told him he would be 4-F because of a poorly healed arm fracture. Waiting to be drafted meant going into the army infantry, a prospect none of us liked.

My friend, bartender, philosopher, and ex-GI, Carl, told me I should join the air force, the navy, or one of the reserve units. He said it was better to drown in an ocean than in a foxhole. He had been in combat in Europe during WWII, and knew what he was talking about.

Waiting for Wendell or the other guys to make up their minds was useless. I went alone and joined the Naval Reserve. The physical was cursory, and I passed easily.

I tried to get Wendell to join, but he was afraid the reserve units would be called up first. Korea was not a naval war, and I didn't believe inexperienced reservists would be called early on. I was issued a uniform and began attending monthly meetings, learning to march and handle a rifle. The rest of it was mostly movies teaching us about ships. I found the meetings interesting, and being paid a few bucks each month softened the pain.

The Gangster Connection Ends

Not long after I began working at the A&P, Joe arrived one Friday when Mom was alone in the store. He paid for his dry cleaning, the phone bill, and the fifteen-dollar fee. But instead of giving Mom the new code name, he said, "I'm sorry; Mrs. Scheid, but we can't do the phone call business no more. Just go ahead and have the phone taken out." When she asked why, he smiled and said, "Ma'am, you ain't done nothin' wrong; you and Alfred done a fine job. You made things easy for me." Then he laid a new twenty-dollar bill on the counter and said, "It's been really nice knowing you and Alfred. Good luck to you." He tipped his hat and left. We never heard from Joe again. When Mom explained the event, I asked questions, but she insisted that Joe had given no reason for terminating the relationship. But she had a guess about why it happened.

The Eagles Club had used Lias gang slot machines for years, and Dad, as president of the club, had dealt with the gang. When he'd gotten sick his wife and son needed money. In their own way, the Eagles took care of their own. They had arranged the phone job for us with the Lias guys. Mom's guess was that once I had finished high school and was working, they felt we'd been helped enough. Or could it have been that the gamblers had a system of changing phone people regularly? We never knew the reason we lost the job.

I never told anyone about the number calling arrangement, and I suspect Mom never did either. We agreed that it was not something anyone needed to know and we were experienced secret keepers.

We were aware that we had been participating in an illegal operation, but we never discussed the legal issue or gave it deep thought. Numbers betting was an open secret, and there had to be some way to get the winning numbers passed around. We were just a cog in a large wheel. Besides, bottom line, we needed the money.

Virginia Lee Davis (aka Jake and Gin) age 17, high school graduation, 1948

The fullback in uniform, Bridgeport football field, autumn 1949

High school graduation - wearing borrowed suit and tie, June, 1950

My grandmother, Annie Burdess Jonard, philosopher and disciplinarian, about age 65-71.

My best buddy, Wendell Lyle, high school graduation, 1950

A 1950 graduate with his mother, on roof outside back window of third floor apartment

CHAPTER 22

The moment you have in your heart this extraordinary thing
called love and feel the depth, the delight, the ecstasy of it
you will discover that for you the world is transformed.
—Jiddu Krishnamurti, author, philosopher (1895–1986)

Love is a many splendored thing,
It's the April rose that only blooms in the early spring,
Love is nature's way of giving, a reason to be living,
The golden crown that makes a man a king …

Yes, true love's a many splendored thing.
—Sammy Fain, songwriter (1902–1989)
—Paul Webster, songwriter (1907–1984)

THAT SUMMER TOGETHER

Life was good for Gin and me. We saw each other at least four evenings each week. A couple of nights were reserved for her to wash her hair, shop, and gossip with her girlfriends while I was with my pals or shooting pool. It was a comfortable arrangement. Her workday finished at 5 p.m. After dinner at home, she took a bus back to meet me. We spent evenings going to movies, walking on the Island, having a beer at one of our watering holes and hanging out in the apartment.

Often Marie and Lindy would invite us to take drives out in the country with them. The four of us were good at harmonizing, and we sang for hours. These were enjoyable evenings.

The dance band, in which Lindy played, performed in the open-sided pavilion in Wheeling Park on Saturday evenings all summer. It was a nice venue, regardless of weather. During summer showers, we watched the rain falling outside as we danced or sipped beer and listened to the band. They played the music we liked, mostly the love ballads of the time. It was all so romantic. These dances were our favorites.

Gin was an excellent dancer and taught me steps she knew. I taught her to polka, which I had learned at Polish parties after baseball games. In a short time, we could turn both ways, and by the end of summer, we often went dancing at the Polish bars a few miles from Bridgeport

Wendell and other dateless pals often showed up at the pavilion to hang out and drink beer. The draft dominated many conversations because the war was heating up. Reddy wanted to join the air force and Wendell was weakening. The naval reserve had stopped taking in new sign-ups. I had joined just in time.

Baseball and an Incident

My temper containment had improved dramatically since my early days in sports, and I now got involved in only the normal confrontations that happen during spirited competition. However, one incident turned out to be important. We were playing the best team in the league, and we had a one-run lead in the ninth inning. The opposing first baseman, named Kenny, was near the end of his career. He had lost some of his speed on the base paths, but he was one of the best hitters in the league.

Kenny was on second, and the batter hit a line drive into left center field, which our center fielder scooped up and threw home. Kenny had rounded third, and a close play at the plate was on the way. The throw was on line but short, so I went in front of the plate to take it on a hop. Out of the corner of my eye, I saw Kenny running from third - just as I got the ball. A catcher is trained to leap backward in this circumstance, using his body to block the base path and trying to make the tag as the runner slides by. Kenny decided not to slide. He and I reached the same place at the same time, a few feet toward third base from home plate. His foot hit my shoulder, which sent him flying headfirst over home without touching it. Both of us scrambled to recover. His goal was to touch home, and mine was to tag him with the ball before he touched it. I was able to roll over and dive toward the plate with the ball in my right hand. Again Kenny and I arrived at the same place at the same time. It's complicated to relate the dynamics, but suffice it to say that I tagged him out with the ball in my bare hand… on his face. He was out!

It all happened so fast that I wasn't aware that it might look like I tagged his face on purpose. Players came out of the opposing team's dugout and our guys rushed into the fray, with the umpire in the middle, trying to prevent a gang fight. As I got on my feet, I was hit and swung back, ducking low as the fists flew. Fans were cursing and yelling as Brownie pushed in and dragged me away from the mob.

In the middle of all of this confusion, Kenny got to his feet and yelled as loudly as he could, "Stop! Break it up! It's okay—it was an accident." Everyone stopped as he stood in the middle with blood running down his chin, still yelling: "Go back to the benches; let's play ball!" And that's what happened. He had been called out, and he agreed with the call. He taught some young men a lesson in sportsmanship that day.

After two more outs the game ended and we won. Kenny was heading toward the parking lot with a towel held to his mouth. I caught up to him and said, "I'd like to talk to you, Kenny." He stopped, put his hand on my shoulder, and guided me behind the backstop. "I didn't tag you in the face on purpose and I'm sorry you got hurt - believe me."

He said, "What's your name?" I told him. "Well, Al, I know you didn't do it on purpose—it was a hell of a play. There is nothing to apologize for. Now, I have to go get some stitches." As he shook my hand, he said, "We'll play against each other again. Let's put this behind us, okay?" I agreed as we shook hands again.

Brownie had observed us and walked over. "Al, you did the right thing by telling him you were sorry. His manager knew it was an accident. He apologized to me for his team trying to make a fight out of it. We all hate losing, but someone has to."

A few weeks later, the two teams played again. When Kenny came to the plate, he looked back at me and said, "Al, if I'm on second and our batter gets a hit, you can bet your ass I'm gonna slide into home."

I said, "I'll be here waiting for you, Kenny."

We both laughed as the umpire told us to play ball. We talked several times after that, on and off the field, and became friendly. He liked young guys who played all out to win.

Baseball wound down at the end of August, and I ended up with a batting average well over .300, with a couple of home runs. My knee had healed, but I was definitely a step slower running to first. I could handle my game behind the plate and Brownie liked the way I called pitches. Unfortunately, our team missed the playoffs in both the twilight and Sunday leagues.

It was discouraging, and I didn't see it improving the next year. Pitching was our problem. Teams with more established histories attracted the best pitchers. As I told Gin, "My batting average would be higher if I could hit against our own pitchers." Also, my performance as a catcher would have been better if I had worked with pitchers who kept the ball nearer the strike zone. Catching is much more difficult if you are constantly jumping left and right to stop wild pitches. As the season ended, I knew I had to switch teams if I was going to have any success in the sport.

The Buddies Leave

Reddy's father had word from an inside source that Jim's draft notice was coming soon. That news and hatred of his job motivated him to join the air force. Wendell was working for his carpenter father. He was out late every night and had to be dragged out of bed in the morning. He had a messed up life, feared the draft, and wanted a change. After a few beers one Saturday, he and Reddy went to the air force recruiting office and enlisted for four years.

Their last week at home, they drank with anyone they could talk into joining them. They were my best buds, so I had to join in. A large party was put together for the night before they left. It was a relief when they were gone.

A Job Change

After just a few days, I had decided that Kowalski was a psycho. He assigned dirty jobs early in the day and then complained if you used a second clean apron. If you kept the soiled apron, he bitched about looking dirty. And he complained if you unloaded a boxcar without an apron. Was there something about the grocery business that attracted nasty people?

With the war ramping up and young men leaving, there were more available factory jobs. Mom took a phone call from the Wheeling Steel plant in Yorkville. I was invited for an interview. I made an appointment.

The personnel man was friendly and said he had rarely seen an application by an eighteen year old that showed so much work experience. I thanked him, called him sir, and said he could depend on me to do a good job if he hired me. My Dale Carnegie manners were in play all the way.

He offered me a full-time job on a labor crew beginning the following Monday. The pay was $1.25 per hour, which was a nice raise from the $0.94 per hour I had been earning at A&P. He told me to report for the afternoon shift, from three in the afternoon until eleven in at night. The bad news was that I would have no free evenings Monday through Friday. The good news was that I was out of the A&P.

There was a large sign at the city limit: *Yorkville, Home of Ductalite Steel.* Each day, hundreds of coils of unfinished sheet steel were trucked into the factory to be processed. The premier thing to see was the immense mills that rolled and stretched a rough coil into one continuous sheet of steel, hundreds of feet long. The steel would sometimes tear, throwing pieces flying through the air. When this happened, the first man to see it yelled "duck" as he hit an emergency stop. Everyone ducked under low shelters designed for protection.

The steel heated up as it was stretched and was cooled by a steady spray of palm oil. The oil ran off the steel and down into a sort of cavern, where it ran into sumps. From the sumps, it was pumped out for reclamation. A greasy smell and bluish smoke enveloped the entire area.

As the oil cooled, it coagulated into a thick, gooey consistency. It hung down from the ceiling of the cavern, like stalactites, and built up on the floor, several inches thick. Once a week, the roller mills were shut down to permit removal of this goo. The cleaning job was always given to three strong, agile young men. Experience had shown that young men could avoid falling, and if they did fall, they probably wouldn't get hurt. I was picked to be on a team.

It was necessary to carry a high pressure water hose down ladders. Once into the cavern, we walked half-crouched, with feet wide apart. The hoses shot water through the nozzles at such high velocity that it took one man to bear most of the weight and the other to direct the stream that loosened the semisolid oil. The third man used a shovel to assist the oil blobs on their way. At the end of the shift, we were exhausted. I caught this duty every Friday.

Another day, a new man and I were assigned the job of chiseling out a four-inch-deep, four-inch-wide channel in a concrete floor so a new gas line could be installed. From where we started, it was about three hundred feet to the terminus of the channel. A foreman gave us about ten minutes of instruction before letting us take turns using a pneumatic jackhammer. It was not difficult once you figured out that all you had to do was guide the machine as it jumped up and down and chiseled the channel. The noise was the worst part of the job, and by the end of the shift, we both had trouble hearing normally. We weren't given earplugs and didn't know enough to ask for them.

On our way to the time clock, a man introduced himself as a United Steel Workers Union shop steward. We knew the steward was "the man" for the USW.

He said, "You guys need some wising up—you work too hard." I guess we looked back stupidly because he continued: "Men need work. If you two show-off kids do eighty feet of channel on this shift, the job will be done in only one more shift. That means you'll go on to another job a union man should have. Slow down. Spend an hour of your shift in the bathroom and stop to sharpen the cutting bits about twice as often as they need it. I'll be watching you." The concept of working slowly to make more jobs was something that I would observe many times during my manual labor career.

The next day as we were finishing the job, the steward came by and told us we were still working too fast. We said we'd try to do better, and he seemed satisfied. We were being educated.

And so it went, day after day, on the labor gang. We did the low-skilled dirty jobs. Some of the men claimed they were not physically capable of certain jobs. When they complained, they were reassigned easier jobs. It didn't take a lot of deep thought to conclude that the strongest men were stuck with the hardest jobs. I thought about talking to the foreman, but I decided to do the jobs assigned and not complain. I was happy to have a job and didn't need any complications.

CHAPTER 23

What lies behind us and what lies before us
are small matters compared to what lies within us.
And, when we bring what is within us out into the world
miracles happen.
—Ralph Waldo Emerson, writer, poet (1803–188)

The journey of a thousand miles begins beneath one's feet.
—Lao Tzu, Chinese philosopher (604–531 BC)

THE LAST MOVE

The second-floor apartment above the printing shop next to our store became available. It had an additional small room, a nicer bathroom and carrying coal up only one flight of stairs was a major attraction. After living in so many places, Mom was tired of moving and intended to remain in this apartment indefinitely. She made curtains, bought new towels and we painted the kitchen. We were not on easy street, but we could finally afford to live a little better. She was dating a man and wanted the apartment to look nice for him and her friends. It was nice for me too since Gin spent some time there. The Isabelle and Al team was getting its act together.

THE AIR FORCE CAPER

The naval reserve announced that it was not taking more volunteers for active duty. My escape hatch from the draft was suddenly gone. A rumor went around that the air force was taking only a few more men. I went to the recruiting office and found it was true. Gin and I discussed the problem. If I got my draft notice in the mail, I was a goner. We decided that even though the air force was for four years, I wasn't likely to come home in a casket. Also, when drafted, there was no limit to your term of service. I decided to join the Air Force.

I filled out papers and went through an interview. The sergeant asked if I could leave on short notice of two or three days. Knowing I could always refuse, I agreed to it. A few days later, I passed a simple physical.

A couple of weeks rolled by before the call came. I had to leave the following afternoon or risk not getting in. When I called Gin, she left work for the day and met me at the apartment. We were in a quandary of indecision. It was one thing to talk about being apart for a long time, but quite another to know I would be gone in twenty-four hours. Instead of moping around, we called friends to meet us that evening. Gin's boss gave her the next day off. At least we could spend the morning together and say goodbye at the air force bus.

The call to Wheeling Steel was easy. They were so accustomed to men leaving for military service that it was routine business.

I made a quick visit to Pastime to say my good-byes and tell the Thomas boys to keep my favorite cue stick until I came back. They said it would be kept in the closet until I used it the next time. It was a touching gesture.

At the Lincoln party, Carl and Bill McConaughey agreed that I had made the right decision. They had both been drafted into the infantry and felt that was to be avoided at all costs. An extra year or so in the service was worth it to avoid foxholes and mud. Soon it got late and everyone was a little drunk.

I walked Gin to the cabstand for her ride home and went back to the party. Daisy was closing, so the group decided to go to an after-hours joint in Wheeling. Everyone headed to the bus stop in front of the Pastime and I hung back to say good-bye to Carl. When I came out the door, the last bus was pulling up and everyone was yelling at me to run. I raced across Lincoln Avenue, across the A&P parking lot, and leaped the wall that separated the lot from the sidewalk. The arch of my right foot landed on the edge of the sidewalk, and I fell forward into the street. I knew I was hurt, but drunks don't feel much pain.

My friends saw the accident and ran to me as the bus left. As they helped me up, I discovered I couldn't stand because my ankle hurt. They sat me down on the wall under a streetlight, and we looked at the ankle. It was swollen and bent. A local taxi was nearby, so a couple of the guys took me home and helped me up the stairs. Mom had just gotten home and was aghast when she saw me.

She put ice on the ankle and gave me aspirin. I was awake all night. In the morning, we took a cab to the Martins Ferry Hospital. After X-rays and an examination, it was determined I had a broken ankle and stretched ligaments. That was the end of my air force enlistment.

The swelling made a cast impossible. The doctor wrapped it loosely with elastic bandages and told me to ice it constantly. He told me to come back in three days so a cast could be put on.

Codeine made me gaga and was addictive, but I took it anyway. It didn't help much. I was home alone all day except for short visits from Mom to bring lunch and fill my ice bag. Gin came by after work. I had messed things up with a stupid act, and I was suffering self-directed anger.

Ever the optimists, we decided there were some bright spots in to the incident. First, I was still home and wouldn't be drafted with a broken ankle. Second, maybe by the time I was healed, the navy would take me. And, I was still on the air force eligible list. Last, since I had quit Wheeling Steel to join the military, I might be able to get my job back.

The doctor had a different view. He said I wouldn't be able to pass the physical for the armed forces for a long time, maybe never. He pointed out that it was a bad break and might not heal well. He thought this would please me, but he didn't realize that he was telling me I was out of baseball. That's all I needed. In one stupid moment, I had made myself into a cripple who couldn't work, play ball, or join the military. I was immediately and deeply depressed. My headaches returned.

Ten days after the accident, I was able to hobble on crutches, slowly and painfully, down to the Pastime and the Lincoln. It was difficult to shoot pool because I had to stand on my left leg only, but I practiced. Time passed slowly.

Wheeling Steel returned my call. There was going to be a layoff and being rehired was not likely. Then an idea came to me. The State of Ohio Employment Office was just a few hundred feet up Main Street from our store. Why not apply for unemployment?

Over three weeks had passed, and I was able to get along with one crutch, so I limped up to the employment office, filled out the forms, and got in line. When it was my turn, the woman at the counter and I recognized each other - she was a dry cleaning customer. It didn't help. She said I wasn't eligible for unemployment compensation because I was injured and couldn't work.

On my way back home, it occurred to me that I could work, just not as a laborer. I could be a clerk in a store and could do office work since I knew how to type. The next morning, I got in line for the same woman. She didn't agree with my argument, but at my urging, she took me to see her supervisor, who was also a dry cleaning customer. I impressed upon him that I had diversified experience, knew how to type, and could do work other than mill labor. He asked, "Are you willing to go out and look for office or clerk work, and will you promise to go for an interview if we call you?"

"Yes, sir, I'll do all that," I said firmly, using my best look-'em-in-the-eye Carnegie method.

"Okay, we'll give you the benefits and you'll come in here every week to see your counselor, right?"

"Yes sir. Thank you, sir," I replied. Mom and Gin thought I had pulled off a miracle. It was only necessary for me to show up each week, hand in a list of places I had looked for work and pick up a check for $20. Persistence had paid off.

Taking buses to factories and hobbling around was good exercise for my ankle, and it kept improving. In a short time I was in a walking cast and able to shoot pool. With pool winnings and the unemployment check I could get by.

The Christmas tree business came on stream and business was good and the profit matched the previous year. Just as working had helped my knee heal a year earlier, the same regimen helped my ankle recovery. It was a great Christmas.

A Trade to Learn

In early January Wendell's father called me. It was not about Wendell—as far as he knew, Wendell was fine. Ralph wanted me to come to his house; he had something to discuss. I was there in half an hour.

Ralph said, "Al, have you ever thought about learning the carpenter trade?" I hadn't. He continued. "If you want to learn the trade, Pug and I will take you on as an apprentice. It will pay a dollar twenty-five an hour to start and work will be steady. If you learn fast, there will be raises. Are you interested?"

The proposal took me by such surprise. I was at a loss for words - an unusual circumstance for me. I asked, "Do you really need an apprentice, Ralph, or are you just trying to help me out?"

He replied, "When Wendell wasn't too hung over, he earned his keep. I don't see any reason you can't do better than that. You've always been willing to work, and we need another man. The offer is not just to help you, but we thought of you first."

Ralph was a man who spoke his mind, so there was no reason for a long discussion. I asked if I would get off early enough for baseball when the season began. He said, "We start early and quit before four; that should work for you."

When I told Gin the story, she smiled and said, "I knew about this. Kitty called me and asked if I thought you'd take the job, and I said you most likely would. You will, won't you?" We agreed that it was a good idea—having a trade beat working in a mill or factory.

Ralph had a bad temper and profanity was a large part of his speech, but he was a kind man at heart. I had known him since I was a child and felt we could get along. He had been a drunk, but he hadn't had a drink for over ten years.

His brother, Pug, had been a heavy drinker before going into the Navy Seabees during the war. When Pug came home, he no longer drank or swore. The rumor was that Pug had taken an oath that if he got off one particular island alive, he would stop drinking and swearing for the rest of his life. All I know is that he never swore or drank and it wasn't a religious thing. The Lyles were drinkers, not churchgoers.

I began work as a nail pounder, lumber carrier, ditch digger, and any other job they needed done. It was hard work, and my ankle was swollen at the end of every day. Every morning, I taped it. Using it actually helped the healing and, in a few weeks, my little limp was gone.

Ralph and Pug shared the business, and their Uncle Walter Lyle worked as a crewmember. Walter was a binge drinker. One day, he'd tell Ralph he was going to drink over the weekend and wouldn't show up until Wednesday. They went along with Walter as long as he gave notice of his intention to go on a binge.

Pug became my main carpentry coach. After about three months, they gave me a raise. I had been accepted as a contributor to the business.

During the winter, I had called Kenny, and he arranged for me to get a tryout with his team. Their first team catcher was almost Kenny's age and not up to playing every game. The tryout went well, and I got on the team. It was a step up.

As the season progressed, my batting average held over .300, with a few extra base hits. Behind the plate I had a few throwing errors. But, with a hot bat, you get playing time, so I was starting every other game and was often used as a pinch hitter. My confidence had never been higher, but there was no doubt that the knee and ankle injuries had slowed me down. The stretching exercises a physical therapist taught me helped.

To make things even better, Gin and I were happy with each other. My plate was full and time passed by quickly. Things were too good to stay that way.

CHAPTER 24

Baseball is ninety percent mental.
The other half is physical.

The future ain't what it used to be.
—Both by Yogi Berra, catcher, philosopher (1926–living)

Sometimes you win,
Sometimes you lose,
And, sometimes it rains.
—Old baseball saying—source unknown

A MAJOR BLOW

One Saturday evening in July, before meeting Gin's usual bus, I stopped in the Lincoln and ran into my team manager. He was alone in a booth, working on what I guessed to be about his fifth beer. He said there was something he had wanted to tell me for a while. Then, he proceeded to talk in an almost continuous stream, "Al, you're a good catcher. You handle pitchers well, and your hitting is strong. But your throwing isn't good enough to make it in the pros, and you've had too many leg injuries. Squatting behind a plate wears out even good legs, and you've got a weak one. You're just good enough to make it to something like the Texas League and hang on for a few years. Then you'll come back here, work in a steel mill, and play semipro ball till your legs are completely gone. Al, you're too damn smart to be wasting your life trying to make it in baseball."

It was as if he had hit me with a bat. I probed with questions, and he gave me examples. He knew the game, so I took it all to heart. The conversation took less than twenty minutes, but it changed my life. I was upset when I met Gin's bus.

What made it worse was that deep inside, I knew he was right. My throwing to bases was not the best, but it had been getting better as I got bigger. My ankle was not yet one hundred percent, but the knee was pain-free. I had lost a step to first base. It was true, my right leg had taken a beating, and I was only nineteen. He wasn't throwing me a curve.

I related the conversation to Gin, and said that I should probably quit baseball. Her attitude was that I should get some other opinions. She said, "Alf, think it over for a while and don't do anything hasty. After the first pitch tomorrow, you'll be back to normal." We dropped the subject and went to a movie. That night was one of little sleep and much pondering.

Paul was living 130 miles away in a city called Mansfield with his brother Gene. They had told me it was easy to find jobs there. A large tire factory and steel mills were working day and night.

Delfred "Ollie" Oliver had been in Gin's high school class and frequently in trouble. It was not unusual then for judges to let young boys off a sentence if they joined the army and that's what Ollie did. He was stationed in Japan when the war started and was sent to Korea immediately. He'd seen combat, was wounded, and got a discharge. He was unemployed and looking for something to do.

I had seen Ollie in fistfights since I was in the eighth grade. He was a tough cookie, and I knew he'd stand with me if things got rough. He would be a wonderful guy with whom to leave home.

I called Ollie, and explained about jobs in Mansfield. He liked the idea. I promised I'd make a decision in a few days. I was pretending the draft didn't exist. It was just too hard to think about it.

Ironically, I had a great game on Sunday, with three hits and I threw a runner out at second. The manager and I shook hands at the end of the game but had no conversation.

The things he'd told me had a strange, unexpected effect on me. It was as if a weight had been lifted—I felt free. The realization came to me that I wasn't good enough. I had clung to baseball as a hope and nothing more. With that starry-eyed dream gone, I could move on. Even distasteful decisions are sometimes liberating, and important ones often happen suddenly. Maybe it was time to put my failures behind me and start fresh in another town.

A Firm Decision

That evening, I told Gin that I wasn't good enough to make it. Despite my youth, I had learned that truth is often imperfect and fragmentary, but decisions must be made. Reading good books, learning the underside of Bridgeport, and having hours of discussions with a philosophical bartender, a pool shark, and a street fighter had helped me develop some street smarts. In addition, Gin understood that real success in any sport was a long shot.

Then I told Gin about going to Mansfield. At first, she said I was just overreacting and leaving would be the end of us. But she calmed down and heard me out. I explained that, except for her, there was nothing in Bridgeport for me once baseball was gone. I loved her and wanted to marry her, but I saw no way I could ever offer her a decent life in this place. It went on and on. She didn't want me to go but finally agreed it might be the best thing.

She understood that I had to find a future somewhere, somehow, and, buried deep in my being was the belief that I could succeed at something. I was short on confidence, but at the same time, I wanted to be tested. It would be easy for us to settle down to mundane lives with no future and regret it later.

If she had said firmly that it was over between us if I left for Mansfield, I wouldn't have gone. My deepest concern was that she would start dating that guy Jack or someone. But she assured me that she was completely committed. I couldn't imagine life without her and the thought of her being with another man made my stomach hurt. But I had to see the other side of the mountain.

When I told Mom I was quitting baseball and going to Mansfield, she wasn't surprised. Her first question was, "What about Virginia?" After that was explained, she said, "I knew this day was coming. You told me years ago that you were leaving after graduation, and I think it's a good idea. I'll be lonely without you, but you need to find your own way." It was so easy; I couldn't believe it.

She asked how I was fixed for money. I lied and told her I had plenty. The truth was that I had been spending faster than I earned. My social life with Gin had cut down my pool shooting time, and the expenses of my broken ankle had been paid out of savings.

Now I had to face Ralph. I was concerned about being seen as ungrateful for the opportunity he and Pug had given me.

Quitting the Job

On Monday, Ralph picked me up on our usual corner. Five minutes into the trip he said, "You look like your dog died. What's eating you?" I had rehearsed my speech and launched into it. At the end I added, "Jake agrees with me."

When he parked, he said, "Al, I'm sorry to see you go, but you're smart to get out of here. This place is played out. I wish Kitty and I had moved when we had the chance after the war. I just hope you and Jake stick together; you make a good couple." He got out of the car quickly and went to work.

Later in the day I said I'd like to make the next day my last. At the end of the next day he gave me my last check, and we shook hands. Walter came forward with a handshake and some Lyle advice: "Don't drink too much … or too little."

When I looked at the check, I saw that Ralph had added $20 on to my earned pay. It was very kind and thoughtful of him.

When I turned in my uniform, the manager was unhappy that I wasn't finishing the season. I reminded him that he was the guy who told me I had no future in baseball. He got the point and wished me luck, saying, "That's the last time I'm gonna talk to a player when I'm half drunk." We laughed and went our separate ways.

When I spoke to Dad on the phone, he was supportive of my decision, and I promised that I'd see him the first time I came home for a visit.

Saturday night with Gin began at the apartment after Mom went to work—a last intimate moment. After that, we met friends and bar-hopped until Gin caught the last bus home. We weren't as sad as we thought we'd be. We had faith in each other.

On to Mansfield

On Sunday morning, Mom gave me a bag of sandwiches and a good-bye kiss. There were a few tears, but she held up well.

After an emotional good-bye call with Gin, I went to the corner where Route 250 started up the hill from Bridgeport. Ollie was there, overflowing with optimism despite his hangover. We got our first ride quickly.

We had just over $80 between us. We needed to find jobs in a couple of days and get paychecks in a week or two. Only the young have that kind of blind optimism. The 130-mile trip was completed in less than four hours.

We found Gene Florence's apartment easily. The plan was for us to stay there for a few nights until we made other arrangements. It was a tiny place, but Gene and his wife Marcy welcomed us. Ollie and I took turns sleeping on the floor and sofa while Paul had a rollaway to himself. I will never forget Gene and Marcy's generosity. They put up with a lot of inconvenience for a couple of young guys they barely knew.

First thing Monday morning, Ollie and I went to the tire company and put in our applications. They told us they were not hiring for a while. But since the demand for tires was strong, we had high hopes we'd get called.

Over the next few days, we took bus trips to other factories. None were encouraging. There had been an influx of boys like us. Then, Ollie got a call from Mansfield Tire and went to work as a laborer the next day. His time in Korea had put him in the front of the line, as it should have. Now all three of us had jobs and it was time to find a place to live.

The next day, the personnel guy at Empire Steel looked at my application and interviewed me. He asked questions about the jobs I'd done, gave me a typing test, and told me to come back the next day.

The next morning, his first question was, "Does heat bother you?" I said no. I asked about the typing test and what had happened to that potential job. He said something like, "You want work now, and I have a job for you. I'll give you first crack at a shipping clerk's job when it opens up." That afternoon I became a laborer on an open hearth furnace.

Empire Steel

By 1951, the open hearth was becoming an obsolete steel-making system. The open hearth is basically a pool of molten iron heated to well over two thousand degrees Fahrenheit to produce steel.

There were six of us on the team. We wore asbestos jackets and pants over our work clothes and asbestos hoods that had a dark glass window to see through. Every so often, a man from the lab would direct two of us to heave on a large lever, which lifted a steel door and exposed the front of the hearth. Even though we stood to the side of the opening, the heat hit like a physical thing. The lab worker had a ladle with a long handle with which he scooped a sample of the white-hot molten metal and took it away.

When he returned, he would instruct us to measure out a pile of one or more granular chemicals kept in small stalls. Then the fun began. Two men held the door open, and the rest of us walked in a circle, each picking up a shovel full of the chemical, walking to the opening, heaving the material through the door, and walking away as quickly as possible. This process was repeated until all the chemicals had been shoveled in.

Between "charges" of new molten iron, we had little to do. During downtime, we got as far away as possible and took off the hoods so we could sweat freely. The men on this job were called, appropriately, the "sweat gang." Half the men on the gang were black, and one of them had worked this job for years.

A New Job

After two weeks on the sweat gang I got word to come in the next morning to meet the head of the shipping department. He asked questions about my education. I emphasized my reading accomplishments, and as luck would have it, he was an avid reader. I had the job after ten minutes of book chat.

The job required filling in the blanks on shipping orders and bills of lading on the four to midnight shift. There was one catch. Because so many numbers and symbols were used, the key placements were different from a standard typewriter. They knew the strange keyboard required extra training. They told me I had to arrive early to practice typing.

For a week, I came in two hours early each day for typing practice and training. The man I was replacing and I stayed an hour late every night to check paperwork and fix my mistakes. So I worked nearly an eleven-hour shift and was paid for eight. The pay of $1.25 per hour was way below my expectations, but better than no job.

At the end of the week, my two trainers decided I was ready to be alone on the job. The man who supervised truck loading was experienced. Thanks to his help, I got through the first week without making any major mistakes.

Mansfield Tire & Rubber was considered the best employer in Mansfield. The company wasn't hiring, but I had a plan. Every weekday morning, I went to the tire company employment office. Howard, the man in charge of personnel, told me I was wasting my time. Since I had nothing else to do until my shift at Empire, I brought a book and sat there, quiet but in sight. About lunchtime, I would buy a sandwich, catch a bus and, after a couple of transfers, arrive at Empire Steel.

After a couple of weeks of this routine, Howard became somewhat friendly and complimented me on my perseverance. I figured he couldn't he pass me over and call someone else if I came in every day.

One day he asked if I could go to work the next morning at seven o'clock. I said, "Yes, sir." The next morning, I became *the* white guy on the "black gang." The name was not about skin color, it was about the job. We unloaded fifty-pound bags of carbon black (nearly pure carbon) from boxcars and delivered them to the rubber mixing machines.[12]

When I went to work at Empire I told them I had found a better job that started the next morning but I'd still work the four till midnight shift until they replaced me. They weren't happy, but they knew the job could be done in seven hours, so it was no problem if I arrived a little late.

12 Artificial rubber was not yet perfected. Rubber came from rubber trees and it is not naturally black; it is various shades of gray. Carbon black was blended into the rubber to make it a consistent black color.

For the next few weeks, I experienced the glory of sixteen-hour work days. The good news was that with two jobs and no nightlife, I saved some meaningful money.

Once they discovered that I actually worked and was not just some lazy white boy, the men on the black gang became friendly. One of the older guys told me I was only the second white man he had ever seen in his ten years on the job. It was hard physical labor but easier than the sweat gang.

Just as a day was beginning and I still looked white, a man in street clothes walked up. He asked what the hell I was doing there. I told him Howard had given me the job, and he stomped off. Within fifteen minutes, he came back with a man wearing a tie and white shirt. It turned out the man who had gruffly questioned me was a union steward and the man in the white shirt man was a company executive.

I answered the same questions again, and the white shirt man told me to follow him to the employment office. I figured that was the end of my tenure at the tire company. When we arrived, he motioned me to wait, as he went into Howard's office, leaving the door open. He asked Howard what the hell he was thinking putting a white boy on the black gang. He said to put me in a job somewhere else and do it today.

As he left, I thanked him for not laying me off. He said it was not my fault and that Howard should have known better. As he walked out, I kept my eyes on the floor, fearing what Howard might do. He told me to take a seat.

After lunch, Howard told me he made the mistake because I was so insistent on getting a job. In other words, it was partly my fault. He said the black gang was reserved for black men and I wouldn't have been happy there anyway. He was right about that. We got in his car and went to the shipping department building, where he introduced me to the foreman. I finished the day learning to stack tires in boxcars.

The Shipping Department

The shipping building had many open doors, and the boxcars and truck trailers we loaded were outside. We worked in pairs stacking tires on four wheel dollies which we pushed to the shipping docks. Then, we loaded the tires into the trucks or boxcars.

My buddy, Stan, was a strong young guy with a wife and a young baby. We handled mostly heavy truck tires going to the army. He taught me how to lift in unison by counting "one, two, lift - heave." In a couple of days, we quit counting and just used eye contact to time the lift. Stan was a nice guy.

Within a month the temperature was below freezing every day. But the physical labor kept us warm most of the time. Including incentive pay based on the number and types of tires loaded, I was earning over a dollar an hour more than at Empire Steel.

The only fly in the ointment was John, the union shop steward. He was an overweight man with a nasty personality who used his union position to bully the foreman into giving him cushy jobs. Mostly, he filled inner tube orders, which required no heavy lifting. [13]

John resented me from day one because he had not been consulted when I had been moved into the shipping department. He did all he could to make things unpleasant for Stan and me. He told the foreman that we took extra breaks and made other childish attempts to get us in trouble. Stan couldn't afford to lose his job and was afraid of John.

I developed a deep dislike for the fat jerk. Finally, I had a verbal confrontation with him after something he told the foreman caused me to get a warning. During this discussion, which was witnessed by other workers, I promised John a beating if he kept harassing us. He continued the campaign but was careful about getting caught.

13 Tires in those days had rubber tubes inside them to hold air. Tubeless tires had not yet been invented.

A Home Away From Home

Ollie found a furnished one bedroom apartment with a small kitchen. It was the top half of an upstairs-downstairs duplex on a nice tree-lined street. The landlady, about sixty-five and widowed, lived alone downstairs. At our interview she served tea and told us how she expected us to behave. She said it was against her better judgment to rent to three young men, but she liked our manners and would give us a try—week to week. We moved in immediately. Gene and Marcy had been real troopers to help us out, but it was time to let them have some privacy.

Welcome Visitors

Gin had bought a car and gotten her license. She told her parents she was tired of bus riding, but the real reason for the car was so she could drive to Mansfield. She hatched a plan with two girls that Paul and Ollie knew. The three of them would drive to Mansfield for a weekend. Gin's mother didn't like it. In 1951, nice girls didn't drive to other cities, stay in hotels and visit boys. But it was less outrageous if there were three girls. Her father was told that the three of them were going to Pittsburgh for a weekend of shopping and movies.

The girls stayed at a hotel, and everything was on the up-and-up. I didn't realize how much I had missed Gin until I saw her. Our friends understood when we drove off on our own for a while. We all had a great weekend, but it just reminded me how much I missed home. It was a painful farewell when they left.

Risky Transportation

Paul borrowed money from his brother and bought a used car. Now we could visit Bridgeport without hitchhiking or a long bus trip. We took turns staying sober on Sunday evenings so that one could drive while the other two slept. The driver didn't get enough sleep, and the other two had hangovers and stiff necks; it all balanced out.

With one bedroom, we had to rotate sleeping two in the bed and one on the sofa in the living room. Paul argued that since he came to Mansfield first, he should get the sofa and be able to sleep alone all the time. It was typical Paul logic.

Finally, after too many beers one Friday night, Paul commandeered the sofa and it was not his turn. I pulled him off and took his place. This started a wrestling match. Paul was not a good wrestler, and I got him pinned down. Ollie intervened by pulling me off by the neck, and I resisted. Finally, he pulled hard and punched me in the process. No surprise, I hit him back.

Suddenly Ollie and I were in a wrestling/hitting match. An end table was knocked over, a lamp was broken, and the whole scene made a lot of noise. Paul yelled at us to stop because the landlady was knocking at the door and insisting on coming in.

She was visibly angry and gave us hell. She considered Paul and me to be wayward boys—and we were. But she had seen Ollie as a mature army veteran who would keep us in line. She said she would speak to us after the next day. We shook hands, had another beer, and called it a night. I got the sofa.

The next morning, we apologized and paid her for the broken lamp, so she let us stay. After the meeting, we made a pact. From then on, fights would be taken into the rear alley. It never occurred to us to have a pact not to fight - it was just too much a part of our culture.

There were no residual ill feelings between Ollie and me, and we put the incident behind us. Ollie predicted that one of us was going to have it out with Paul eventually. He was simply too selfish to share an apartment.

We went to Bridgeport for the Christmas weekend. It was wonderful, and while there, we decided to return for New Year's Eve. Jim

Reddy was home on leave so he, a school friend named Joe, and I went with Paul to the Hilltop Restaurant to have a few beers and make reservations. Paul got noticeably drunk. We tried to persuade him to let one of us drive, but he wouldn't hear of it. He slurred, "It's my car, and I'm driving." Coming down the hill into Wheeling, he was going too fast and we all yelled at him to slow down. He just laughed and drove faster. It was Paul being Paul, a synonym for acting stupid.

The car went into a skid on a turn. It hit the hill and a telephone pole at the same time. The car rolled over and ended up sliding down the road on its top. Seat belts had not yet been invented, so Reddy was tossed out of the car, and Joe and I were jumbled with the backseat. We extricated ourselves and looked each other over. Reddy had badly scraped knees and hands, and Joe had a sharp pain in his abdomen. My head had gone through a side window, and I was bleeding down my back. Paul had held on to the steering wheel so tightly that it was bent, but he didn't have a scratch.

Someone from a nearby house yelled to us that the police had been called. While we were waiting, we talked about Paul's stubbornness. We were all pissed off at him and made no secret of it. He ignored us. Finally, he said with a giggle, "Well, guys, I guess I'm going to have to get a heavier car." We couldn't believe he said that and told him he was full of shit. But he insisted that if the car had been heavier, it would have made the turn. This put me into a rage, and I hit him once. Just as this happened, a police car and an ambulance arrived. We agreed to settle the matter later.

Joe had to stay overnight in the hospital, and Reddy was bandaged up like a mummy. The doctor pulled a six-inch long shard of glass from under my scalp and stitched me up. Reddy's father arrived and took us home.

The next day, Reddy and I went to the junkyard to see the car. It was totaled. The back door containing the window my head went through was twisted backward. I was lucky to be alive.

On the bus to Mansfield, Ollie made peace between Paul and me, as he always did. Ollie bought a car the next week with money he managed to borrow from the company credit union. So we had wheels to go home for New Year's Eve.

Paul and I got over things well enough to go in the group to the Hilltop nightclub on New Year's Eve. He got drunk and managed to get himself into a fight just after midnight. Ollie and I jumped in and attempted to rescue him from getting beaten up by several Wheeling guys. He was in the wrong, and we knew it. We tried to make amends by saying we'd take him home immediately. But the Wheeling guys didn't like us being there in the first place, so they didn't want a peaceful ending. Punches were thrown, chairs knocked over, and several guys who had nothing to do with the argument got involved—we were outnumbered and losing.

Gin overheard the bartender calling the police and shouted, "The police are coming!" There was a stampede out the side door and we made it to the car. Ollie used his head and drove away from town, and then down a narrow side road, where we parked with lights out for half an hour. We finally got the girls home about two in the morning. No one called it a fun New Year's Eve. We'd had another close call and bad evening for which we could thank Paul.

A day later, we had to get back to Mansfield for work. I lost the toss, limited myself to two beers, and drove Ollie's car. Paul jumped into the backseat and went to sleep. It was cold, snowing, and windy.

About halfway there, I stopped to relieve myself by the side of the road. Paul swore at me for letting in the cold. I was not in a mood to hear his complaints, so I opened the back door and gave him a little more of it. He threatened to beat the shit out of me and I told him to get out of the car. Ollie halfheartedly tried to stop it, but too much water had passed over the dam. We squared off just a few yards into a field. The only light was from the headlights of passing cars. We both stumbled around and threw poorly aimed punches, but enough contact was made to do some damage. The whole exercise was a perfectly bad idea.

Ollie yelled at us to get back into the car before the Highway Patrol showed up and put all of us in jail. He finally broke it up by hitting both of us from behind. The fight probably lasted two minutes. Young men do foolish things for stupid reasons.

When we got home, we found that, for once, Paul had gotten the worst of things. He had some cuts on his back from the debris on the ground and a bad-looking eye. I had managed to stay on my feet most of the time but had a badly bruised nose, scraped knuckles, and other miscellaneous marks. Ollie did first aid on Paul's back, and I cleaned myself up. We got a couple of hours' sleep (I got the sofa because I drove).

The next day one of my hands was sore, and heaving tires all day was a painful experience. That evening, Paul and I shook hands and agreed to chalk the whole thing up to fatigue and too much beer, but we remained cool to each other.

Paul and I got along better after the fight. Young men in our day were accustomed to seeing fights and fighting, and it was not unusual for a dust-up to clear the air and give both sides a new start. We had been classmates since the sixth grade, went to movies, fished together, fought on the same side, slept in the same bed, and were more like cousins than friends. I had always had some sympathy for Paul because he was not very bright. But my patience with him was all used up.

Ollie was the most mature of the three of us, and we respected him because of his army service. We hadn't killed anyone, and Ollie had killed at least one North Korean that he knew about. Also Ollie could have beaten the hell out of either of us. He was two years older, had martial arts training, and had always been a scrapper. His army experience had made him wiser and more understanding, but it had also made him tough, inside and out.

The Time Came

With my twentieth birthday arriving in February, it was clear that my time for the draft was coming soon. Ollie reminded me that it being better to drown in an ocean rather than a foxhole. He told me about the horrendous winter he had spent in the combat zone in Korea. And, I had learned that the naval reserve was taking volunteers again.

I called Gin and told her I had decided to volunteer for two years of active duty. She agreed that this was the best way out for us.

I had transferred my naval reserve status to the base in Mansfield. I went to the armory and signed the forms. A week later, I rode a bus to Columbus and took a physical. My ankle raised a question, but the doctor passed me with a written comment. He said, "When you are examined at boot camp, they may send you home, but if I don't pass you, you'll still be subject to the draft." I thanked him for that insight.

We decided to celebrate that Saturday night at a roadhouse a short distance out of town. It was a dive, but they had a band and there were girls for dancing. By late evening, both Ollie and Paul were drunk. When we got to the car, both of them piled in and were asleep in seconds. I decided that my celebration night was ending too early and wanted to dance some more. I locked them in the car with the windows cracked open and went back into the bar.

As I walked in, people were going out the back door and down some stairs to watch a fight. I followed the crowd. As I got near the door, a short, stocky guy told me not to go down the stairs. I pulled his hand off my shoulder and walked past him. The next thing I knew someone was beating on me and I lost consciousness. When I came to, I was gasping for breath and a man was holding my head and wiping my face with a handkerchief. He told me a guy had jumped me from behind and beat the hell out of me after I hit the ground. He said they were ready to call an ambulance when I revived.

He got me on my feet and helped me up to the men's room where I looked in the mirror. It was not a pretty sight. I had a swollen eye, cut lips, and bruises on the sides of my head. The man said he and another guy had to pull the attacker off me. He didn't know the assailant, but he heard his last name was Couch.

I went to the car and woke up my pals. Paul was passed out, but Ollie rallied and wanted to go back into the bar and beat someone up. I told him the bad guy had left and, since my sight was compromised, it would be better if he drove home.

Soap, water, ice, aspirin, and help from Ollie got me patched up. The next morning, I looked much worse than I had ever looked after a fight—and my body hurt. Sunday was a day of recovery, with a few beers to lessen the pain. It had been a stupid move for me to go back into a bar alone. We had always agreed to stay together in strange places. Another tough lesson learned.

Ollie and Paul both remembered meeting my assailant and were sure they would recognize him. They didn't intend to let this sneak attack go unpunished, and I wanted to put some marks on the little bastard myself.

We went back to the same bar Sunday evening, looking for our man. The bartender admitted that he knew Bob Couch, but he didn't know where he lived. Through several other conversations we learned that he lived in a nearby town. One girl told us that he knew we would be looking for him and he was staying out of sight.

We kept trying, even looking him up in local phone books, to no avail. Truth be known, it was good that we never found him. He had friends who would not like outsiders coming after him and it could have become a messy affair. A young man's wounds heal quickly, and by the time I left for Mansfield, I had only a little blue near one eye as a reminder of the attack.

It was beginning to occur to me that I was having entirely too many altercations and should clean up my act. One of Gin's concerns about me was that I had a penchant for getting into scrapes like this. She blamed it on the company I kept and my temper. Of course, she was right on both counts.

My orders arrived, to report for induction just over two weeks later. Mansfield Tire treated men going into the service quite well. The company gave me nearly a week's pay as a good-bye gift, along with the promise of a job when I returned. On my last day, everyone wished me luck, except John, the shop steward. He told some coworkers I was lucky he never punched me out. I couldn't swallow that insult.

The foreman told me I could leave early. I decided to keep a promise I'd made to myself a few weeks earlier and went looking for John. It was a snap decision. I just decided I couldn't leave without settling things. I kept my work gloves on so my knuckles were protected.

I found him between the rows of inner tube boxes, stacked six feet high. As soon as he saw me, he knew what was up. I walked up to him and said something like, "Okay, you fat-assed bastard, now is the time to punch me out like you said you would." He said I could go f**k myself as he reached an arm in my direction. I grabbed the arm and pulled him toward me with my left hand, using my right to punch him hard in the stomach. When he bent forward from the first punch, I hit him along the side of the head. He fell backward into a row of inner tube boxes, which then fell on him. He was shouting that he would have me arrested. Standing over him, I told him that if he called the police, my buddies would give him a real beating. It was obvious he wasn't going to get up, so I started throwing inner-tube boxes on top of him. In a few seconds, he was covered three deep with the boxes. He was whimpering but not yelling. I was breathing heavily and just stood there for a moment, wondering if I really would be arrested.

When I looked up I saw Stan and two other guys watching. They gave me a thumbs-up and walked to the time clock. I had done what each of them would have liked to have done. When I caught up with them, they told me to get the hell out before the foreman showed up. No one went to help John dig himself out of the boxes.

This sounds cruel, but here was a man who used his union power to bully men and to get advantages for himself. He expected to have his ass kissed by coworkers or he would make life miserable for them. Well, this time he got his comeuppance and I made my coworkers happy. Right or wrong, I felt good about the deed. Looking back after all these years, I still feel no remorse.

My adventure in Mansfield had been a good experience. I learned a lot. The main lesson was that I could fend for myself in the outside world. And the physical labor had kept me physically strong for the rigors of boot camp.

Another Parting

The time passed quickly. Gin had to work weekdays, but we spent every possible moment together. We had seen each other on weekends about twice each month while I was living in Mansfield, but now it would be eleven weeks before I would be home again. Then, after boot camp, who knew where I would be sent or for how long; it was an uncertain time. Young love is full of hope and we chose not to dwell on the future.

Many of our friends expected us to get married before I left, but we had lived through WWII and knew lengthy separations brings about changes in people. Last-minute marriages often became divorces when the men came home. We declared to each other that we'd stick together. My worst fear was not being hurt or killed; it was that Gin would not be there for me when I returned. The thought haunted me.

I called Dad and met him at the Eagles. He was proud that I volunteered and that I had had the courage to move to Mansfield. He said he wished he had left when he was young. I believed him. His had not been a happy life. He was about fifty but seemed a lot older.

Mom was dating a man who was an ex-marine who saw action in the Pacific. He was wounded twice, and was discharged as a master sergeant. He gave me some advice. He said, "Al, you have nothing to offer the navy. You have no experience and not much education. You will probably end up with some shit assignment they give to expendable guys like us. Take my advice: don't plan for the future and don't think about coming home. The military is not a safe place. Give up all hope and assume you will be killed. If you survive, it's a gift. But don't expect to and it will make everything easier."

This fatalistic approach made sense to me, and I adopted the concept as best as I could. If you have no hope, you have nothing to lose, and if you have nothing to lose, there is no point in being afraid—just take things as they come. Taking life as it happens got me through some difficult times in the navy and later in life.

Finally, on the evening of March 16, 1952, the sergeant drove Mom, Gin, and me to Pittsburgh, where I caught a train to Baltimore. It was an emotional drive. Small talk stopped after a few minutes, and the only sound in the car was Gin softly crying from time to time. It was a relief to get to the train station. I was both fearful and confident.

Gin and I had long kisses outside the gate. Then I was on my way and didn't look back. The last thing I heard was the sergeant shouting the last words I ever heard from him: "Don't forget what I told you!" I didn't.

The navy paid for a sleeper car, but I couldn't sleep. As I watched the lights of small towns roll by in the darkness, it came to me that I would never be the same, regardless of what happened. A great adventure was beginning.

Gin and Al in Mom's apartment, Christmastime, 1951

Gin and Al, at Ogleby Park swimming pool, summer, 1950

Bridge St. (bridge on far left), Pastime Billiard Room on ground floor, entrances on right

Lincoln Ave., looking towards Main St. - L to R, Carlton Saloon (white front), Bridgeport National Bank, the Candy Kitchen, then Dick's Tavern, (toughest bar) circa 1951

Two tough guys, Ollie Oliver and Al, Mansfield, Ohio, 1951

Al the ukulele player, with ever-present book in Mansfield apartment, 1951

Paul Florence's Ford the morning after the big crash, December 30, 1951. Al was sitting next to the twisted door when it hit the telephone pole. Glass cut on head only injury – achy body for many days - very lucky

CHAPTER 25

We shall not cease from exploration,
and the end of all our exploring will be
to arrive where we started and
know the place for the first time.
—T. S. Eliot, poet, essayist (1888–1965)

Every man's got to figure to get beat sometime.
—Joe Louis, world heavyweight champ (1914–1981)

WELCOME TO THE NAVY

When I got off the train, I saw several buses marked U.S. Navy—Bainbridge. My bus was soon full of quiet young men who recognized, as I did, that this was our last look at the outside world for many weeks. It was an empty feeling.

An SP (navy shore police) told us to find our service number on our orders and commit it to memory. "Anyone who forgets his ID number will be subject to discipline!" he shouted. Ollie had warned me to be prepared for this, and I had already committed mine to memory. It is said that a serviceman never forgets his ID. Believe it. He may forget his birthdate ... but never his ID.

As the bus drove onto the base, we saw hundreds of men moving slowly in single file lines that went into a building and out the other side, then across a street and into another building, like ants, one following another. They were naked except for towels around their waists, and it was a cool, cloudy, day.

We were debussed and directed into a barracks building, which turned out to have a broken heating system. Each of us was given a blanket but no pillows, towels, or sheets.

There was hot water and a few bars of soap in the head (navy for toilet).

A junior petty officer appeared and assured us that towels and sheets would arrive soon. He also said that we were to be clean-shaven every day, no exceptions. We fell into ranks and were marched to chow. The sheets and towels never arrived. We slept in our clothes and shoes. It was cold and no one slept well. At six the next morning we were marched to chow and back.

Since nearly all of us were reservists and somewhat familiar with navy efficiency, we were not surprised at our treatment—just pissed off. We milled around the barracks all day, bullshitting, cursing the navy and waiting for the next chow call.

For two days, it was cold during daylight and colder after dark. We slept fully clothed and shivering. Out of fear we shaved every morning but didn't shower. Our orders had instructed us to bring no spare clothing, so we were becoming a smelly group.

On the third morning, we were marched to a building to take the standard tests given to all recruits. My veteran friends had warned me that these tests were important. There were four sections covering math, reading comprehension, clerical skills, and logical reasoning.

I was doing fine until there was a pause before passing out the clerical section. During the delay, I put my head down to rest and dozed off. Someone put the test next to my head and gave me a shake. I was groggy and had difficulty getting oriented. As a result, time was called before I finished the test. I knew I had messed up, and that woke me up for the last test.

The next day, we were rousted out and told to double-time to the mess hall for a fast breakfast. It was haircut time. The barbers used electric shavers to cut each man's hair to the scalp in about a minute. We were now "skinheads." In a few weeks, we would become experts at judging how long a recruit had been in boot camp by his hair length.[14]

Back at the barracks, each man was given two small towels and a white cotton bag (ditty bag) with drawstrings. We were instructed to put our shaving gear, valuables and orders in the ditty bag and keep it with us. Each of us was given a cardboard box into which we put our smelly civilian clothes for shipment home. Now that everyone was naked, lines formed up for the showers. One towel was for drying off, the other to cover up as best we could.

As we walked single file and barefoot to another building, it became apparent that we were now one of the lines of semi naked men we had observed upon arrival. It was an overcast day of about fifty degrees, and given our state of undress and newly hairless scalps, we were cold. Some men decided to hell with modesty and put their towels over their shoulders. The idea began catch on. The petty officer in charge considered this a breach of navy etiquette. He shouted at the offenders to wrap their towels back around their waists.

It took nearly an hour for my part of the line to make it to the building entrance, where a petty officer shouted, "Listen up! If you talk, you go back to the end of the line." There was no talking, no

14 Cutting the hair to the scalp was supposedly to eliminate lice, but with modern chemistry, there were other ways to do that. Shaving heads was actually meant to reduce every recruit to the same level and to make it clear that the navy had complete control of you. The goal was to make men earn back their dignity, gain confidence, and become proud to be in the navy. It was tough, but it worked!

whispering, not even animated glances. A sailor at a desk with a checklist said "Service number" to each man as he entered. Any man who couldn't recall his number was sent to the back of the line—a severe punishment under the circumstances.

The physical exam was done in full view of everyone in the room. As the doctors poked private parts of bodies and looked in embarrassing places, a few boys were fighting back tears. There was no sympathy, and they were told to knock it off: "You're a sailor now. Stop the sniveling."

When I got to a doctor I mentioned my broken ankle and that the doctor in Columbus almost didn't pass me. The doc looked at the ankle carefully and said, "I'm going to note this in your record. If it gives you trouble, go to sick call and tell them to look at your physical record." The ankle was actually feeling fine.

As we walked up to a line painted on the floor, two corpsmen hit both shoulders simultaneously with injections. We stepped forward two paces for the next pair and so on. About six shots were administered in less than a minute. Extra corpsmen were standing by to catch anyone who fainted. The two I saw pass out got up quickly after their cheeks were lightly slapped.

We finally entered the clothing issue building and were given new white T-shirts and underwear that we put on quickly. Each man was issued a large, white canvas, sea bag. We received three different uniforms, blankets, lace-up leggings, T-shirts, and marching, gym and dress shoes. After putting on blue denim work clothes, we hoisted the heavy sea bags on to our shoulders and had a long march to a barracks building.[15]

15 Bainbridge was the navy's largest navy training base. It is in the state of Maryland, at the north end of Chesapeake Bay, next to the Susquehanna River. Thousands of recruits were trained there during WWII and the Korean War.

A New Family

My assignment was to Company Forty-Two of Battalion Forty-Two. A chief petty officer (CPO) was in charge of the company. He picked certain men to be recruit petty officers; they would be the leaders of the company. The leadership group consisted of a recruit chief petty officer (RCPO) and a small group of first class recruit petty officers acting as platoon leaders and staff officers. I wasn't considered for any leadership position and never expected to be.

The first day, we were marched in formation onto the grinder (drill field) and sworn in. After that formality, a senior officer gave us a short "Welcome to the navy" speech that was basically, "Do as you are told and you'll do just fine—don't obey orders and you will be punished." We now belonged to the navy, body and soul.

The chief explained that we would be in formation in fifteen minutes after revellie. We were to shave and shower the night before, so all we had to do in the morning was dress, make our bunks, and police the barracks (clean up cigarette butts and so forth). If anything was not "shipshape," the responsible recruit would receive demerits while the rest of the company stood at attention. The company had a time slot for breakfast, so every minute we were late was a minute that we didn't have for eating. Even these simple tasks were too much for a few of the men. These were the men selected to clean toilets and stand late night watches. [16]

Each barracks had a laundry room with large waist-high sinks and hot water. We were required to wash our own clothes using hand-held brushes and white bar soap. It was impossible to make white hats, T-shirts, and underwear bright white with the old-fashioned

16 Watches were not for security; they were for training. On board ship, at least one-third of the sailors are on duty 24-7. In boot camp, watches were stood at parade rest, at doors, by garbage cans, by clotheslines, and other useless places. The idea is for the men to learn to stay awake and observant at night. In boot camp, watches are also used as punishments and lack of them as rewards.

Ivory soap we were issued, but with enough effort, you could come close.

The first week set the routine. We were up at dawn to do calisthenics before chow, followed by marching and rifle drills. After that came classes, lunch, and then more marching. All those months spent throwing tires around had kept me in good shape, but there were guys who fell behind in everything.

One afternoon after duty, I was called into the chief's office. He informed me that my mother had called the base and left word that my grandmother Scheid had passed away and the funeral had been that day. I was given permission to go to the phone center and call home.

When I got hold of Mom, she said she didn't call earlier because she assumed I wouldn't be allowed to leave the base. She was wrong, but it was too late then. I took a walk after chow that night and reminisced about Grandma, our Wheeling shopping adventures and sharing the newspapers. The rigors of boot left little time for thinking about anything beyond the task at hand, so my mourning period for her was short. Grandma didn't have a very interesting or rewarding life, and for that I was truly sorry.

The Illness

Men were coming down with sore throats and fevers. I joined the group after about two weeks. The first time I went to sick call, they sprayed my throat with something that smelled like Methylate and I promptly threw up. Yuck! I decided not to return to sick call again unless I was at death's door.

A couple of mornings later, my fever had gone higher, so I went to sick call. A corpsman took my temperature and gave me a serious look. He sent me back to the barracks to pack my sea bag so I could be picked up for the hospital. Within an hour, I joined two other men in the back of a pickup truck. It was drizzling, and we got soaked. When we arrived at the hospital, my face was burning hot and I felt faint. I was a sick puppy.

After checking in, I was directed to a door down a hall. The last thing I recall was being confused and light-headed—then the lights went out. I woke up in a hospital bed with an aching throat and an ice bag on my head. A nurse told me it had been over twenty-four hours since I fainted on my way to see a doctor. She also said that my mother had been called and assured I would recover (how could they be so sure?).

After two days, my temperature returned to normal, but I was too unsteady to walk to the head without assistance. In a day the sore throat went away as I received regular injections and pills. This was the sickest I had ever been.

A doctor explained: "You have pneumonia in both lungs, but you're in good health otherwise and you'll get well soon. You'll be in here for a couple of weeks, and you must be fully recovered before you go back to training." The first five days, I slept at least twelve hours every night, plus a mandatory nap in the afternoon.

After that I was encouraged to go outside for short walks. The sun was shining, the food was passable, and I felt better each day. Recovery from an illness can be a soft, warm experience under the right conditions. If Gin had been there, it would have been perfect. The mail caught up with me, and I had letters from Mom and Gin. It was nice to be taken care of by the navy and loved by the two women in my life.

The hospital library was just so-so, but I went there every morning to read the newspapers and stay abreast of the war. One morning I saw a story about a congressional investigation of Bainbridge. The navy had rushed to get the best men into boot camp before they could be recruited into some other service. The article said there were more men arriving than the base could process. It told about men living in their civvies for days because of a shortage of uniforms. Lastly, it covered the mini-epidemic of flu and pneumonia. I brought the paper back to the ward for the patients and staff to read and we all had a good laugh.

The ambulatory patients were assigned chores such as mopping the ward floors. The psychology worked, and a few days later, I told the doctor I felt strong enough to return to training. I was discharged from the hospital about sixteen days after checking in. I would soon discover that I wasn't as ready for duty as I thought.

The Casual Company

My new assignment was with Company 270 of Battalion Forty-Three. I had hoped I would be assigned to a company that had already completed a few weeks of training—kind of picking up where I left off. The navy didn't see it that way. This was a casual company that was just beginning training, thus extending my boot camp time by nearly a month.

A casual company is made up mostly of men who lost their original companies for various reasons. Many had been sick, some needed remedial education and some had psychological issues. A few new recruits rounded out the group. The day after my arrival, the company reached its full strength and training began.

Chief Stanley Kapinski introduced himself as a Chief Bosun. He said we would salute him, address him as "sir," and no one was to call him "Skee" (in the navy men with Polish last names were often called Skee). He told us we were a bunch of misfits, but he intended to turn us into sailors. He made it clear that he would put up with no malingering—none. He was a WWII veteran and had heard all the excuses and all the bullshit. He said, "Work hard for me and you'll be fine; mess up and you will suffer." Lastly, he made it clear that his training companies won flags (commendations) for marching, rifle drills and fire training—lots of them. It would be an embarrassment for him if we were not an outstanding company, and he didn't intend to be embarrassed. He left the severity of the punishment he would mete out to the imagination, but there was no doubt that he meant business.

The next two days, we did marching and rifle drills all afternoon, and most of the guys did them badly. My energy level was low and I was dog-tired at the end of the day.

Since we were such a mixed bag, there was a lot of joking about being a skinhead or a "vet," who had several weeks of hair growth. My month of hair growth made me a vet.

The First Trouble

Our recruit bosun's mate (BM) was a skinhead named Tom Smith. The BM had the job of making sure everyone got up on time, policed up the quarters and other trivial details; otherwise, he was just a member of the Second Platoon. Smith took himself seriously and exceeded his authority at every opportunity. He was always on alert to catch someone missing a detail. I didn't like him from the first look.

About the third day, I was struggling with my legging laces when the chief called formation. Smith saw me bent over my shoes. Without warning, he grabbed me by the hair, pulled hard, and yelled at me to stand up. Reflexively, I hit him as hard as I could in the middle of his stomach. He stumbled backward, and as he backpedaled with his arms flailing, he grabbed two bunks. The bunks slid, noisily knocking into others as he went flat on his ass. I was on my feet, set for him to come for me, which he fully intended to do. But the chief had witnessed the whole thing and called, "Attention!" We both stood at attention. He was angry. He said, "Okay, you guys wanna fight, you'll do it—my way. We'll go to the ring at sixteen thirty. Now go straighten out those bunks and fall in." We did as ordered.

The word that a fight was scheduled was passed around quickly and several guys said they hoped I'd kick the crap out of Smith. The fight was something I was not eager to do, but I resigned myself to it happening.

When we got back to the barracks in the afternoon, the chief told Smith and me to put on our gym shoes. He announced that there would be a fight in ten minutes and anyone who wanted to watch could follow us to the athletic building. The whole company joined in.

The gym supervisor told us to strip to our waists, roll up our pants above our knees, and climb up into the ring. He wrapped our hands, laced boxing gloves on us, and shoved rubber mouthpieces into our mouths. There was no head protection.

He recited the normal boxing rules, with one exception: the bell would ring only once. The rule was to fight until one man stayed down for a count of ten, one of us quit fighting and walked into a corner, or the supervisor stopped the fight. He sent us to opposite corners.

Fighting where I came from was street fighting, which included wrestling and punching while on the ground. The typical fight ended when one guy got on top, using the other man's head as a punching bag until someone pulled the winner off.

At sixteen, I had sparred at a gym in Wheeling and had lost two three-round matches before I decided boxing wasn't for me. I had also attended one evening of professional matches in Wheeling. I knew boxing took skill and it was not my forte.

I was a bit shorter than Smith. No matter—I had to make the best of it. The bell rang and we sparred around before he landed a couple of good punches. It was obvious that he knew something about boxing and trying to outbox him wouldn't work. I attacked, throwing punches and trying to get inside his reach. This took him by surprise, and I landed a few good blows to his head. Then he came back at me with punch combinations. Suddenly, I was out of the ropes on the edge of the ring, a couple of shipmates holding me so I wouldn't fall to the floor. They yelled at me to climb back in. I had been taught that you fight until someone wins, and I didn't feel beat, so I got back in the ring. I was determined to make him know that he was in a real fight. My nose wasn't bleeding, and as long as that didn't happen, I could hang in.

After a few minutes of ineffective punching, we were both winded and just making weak motions at fighting. I knew that as soon as someone could breathe well enough, there would be another attack. I hyperventilated as I would have after sliding into third on a triple. Having gotten my wind, I went for it first, hoping to catch him by surprise. We had an exchange of punches, and I got in a solid right to his face. I pressed the attack. Then he caught me coming in with a right on my left cheekbone. The fight was over. They could have counted to fifty over me.

I woke up on my back with the supervisor patting my cheeks and looking into my eyes. He asked some questions to ascertain if my mind was working, and my answers satisfied him. He helped me up, took off my gloves, and gave me some ice in a towel to put on my cheek. When I climbed out of the ring, a lot of "attaboys" and "great fight" things were said. Most of the guys were patting my back and shaking my hand. The winner was ignored. He was not a popular guy.

My nose didn't bleed; at least that weakness wasn't exposed. Most importantly, I had lost while fighting, not by quitting. A group walked with me back to the barracks. They had wanted me to beat the hell out of Smith and I was sorry I had disappointed them.

Someone told me later that the fight had gone on for about twelve minutes. It seemed longer than a fight I once had after football practice and that one lasted nearly twice that long.

When the company assembled for chow, I sneaked out the back door. I wanted to be alone. New recruits weren't supposed to go to the gedunk (combination junk food and general store) on weekdays, but I went anyway. I didn't feel like eating but knew that if I didn't, I'd be tired the next morning. A vanilla milk shake and Twinkies sounded good, and I got some candy for later. Just as I got back to the barracks, I threw up the milk shake and Twinkies. After lights out, the candy bars became my late supper.

The next morning after chow, the chief told me to go to his office. *He knows I skipped chow last night,* I thought, *and now I'm in deep shit.* Smith was in the office, standing at attention. The chief made us shake hands and explained that he had used our altercation to make a point—that those men who got into fights would be made to finish them. He dismissed Smith and ordered me to stay.

The chief said he was making me a first class petty officer (FCPO) and First Platoon leader, replacing the current First Platoon leader.

This took me completely by surprise, and I asked, "May I know why, sir?"

He said, "You stood up to Smith, and the men liked that. The man you're replacing is afraid of him. And I've noticed that you know how to execute marching commands. Now, listen up. I expect you to improve the First Platoon's marching. You can drill them until midnight, but I want to see improvement by Saturday, when the company competes in marching drills."

This was not a "Do you want the job?" kind of thing; it was an assignment. The chief added, "I told Smith that you just came off three weeks in the hospital and that I suspected he'd get his ass kicked next time he f****d with you. Don't make me wrong!" The chief knew his psychology, but Smith and I became somewhat friendly and never had another disagreement.

He called in Dave Keene, the recruit chief petty officer (RCPO), and explained to us, "A marine sergeant friend of mine will be here later. He's an experienced drill instructor [DI] and will teach you about training men to march. I expect you to learn fast. I want a lot of improvement by Friday afternoon." Then he said, "Dismissed."

A few minutes later, the chief called an assembly on the quarterdeck and announced the change of assignments. He told the men there would be major improvement in their marching by the end of the week or we would be punished. His words made an impression on me. If I could keep the job as a FCPO, I wouldn't have to stand late watches. That was a real motivator.

Keene and I had been friendly from the first day. He was a mature college graduate from New Hampshire. He was smart but had less experience with marching and life than I did. He said he was pleased I had been promoted.

The marine DI took Keene, the Second Platoon leader, and me to the grinder, where he gave us drill lessons. The Second Platoon leader couldn't remember the commands, and the sergeant wasn't happy with him. He sent him back to the barracks, saying, "I don't think you'll learn the commands fast enough to give the men what they need." The sergeant kept up the drills with Keene and me marching.

Two hours later, he took us aside like friends. "Skee wants to have another company like his last one. [17] You two can shape these men up if you have the determination to do it, and here's how you do it." He spent half an hour giving us advice on what to do beyond drilling.

The sergeant said that we had to single out the worst marchers, drill them until they responded, and make examples of them. "If the worst men learn the rest will shape up," he advised. "Show no mercy and you'll get results—show weakness and you'll fail. Lazy, uncooperative recruits will pay attention and work hard only after they are completely convinced they have no other option." He added, "Win

17 We had not known that the chief had the reputation as the best recruit trainer on the base. His previous company had won every award possible. Consequently, the chief had gotten a commendation from the commanding officer.

their minds and their bodies will follow." That's a lesson I've never forgotten.

The company had about fifteen men who could not, or would not, execute rifle or marching commands.[18] Even worse, they sniggered when they made dumb mistakes, which showed they were not serious about learning.

The next day Keene kept everyone out on the grinder after the 1630 quitting time, and we marched them around. It took about ten minutes to verify who the laggards were. He put the fifteen idiots into formation and turned them over to me while he did rifle drills with the rest. I explained that we were going to march until they showed major improvement. After a few minutes, I could see they weren't trying. One, named Busby, slouched and gave me a disgusted look. I said, "Busby doesn't believe me." I told him to fall out and hold his rifle above his head with one hand. While he held that pose, the rest of us marched around him. In two minutes, he was sagging, and I called a halt in front of him. I asked, "Is your arm tired, Busby?"

He moaned, "I can't hold it up any longer!"

I said, "Okay, switch arms." We marched around a while, and then I halted the group in front of him. "Do you want to rejoin the group, Busby?"

He said, "Yes, I'd like to rejoin the group."

I said, "Okay, fall in." Then I asked, "Does anyone else want to hold a rifle over his head?" There were no takers. "Well, Busby screwed up, so he's going to drill now and the rest of us have to keep him company." In other words, Busby's mistakes had caused them to drill longer, thus creating social pressure. The Marine DI had told us about the rifle-over-the-head punishment, and it worked like a charm.

---

18 18 The 1903 bolt-action Springfield army rifles we were issued weighed about nine pounds and were longer than present-day rifles. Taking one of them through the "manual of arms" was a tiring upper-body workout.

The next morning, I marched the fifteen problem men for an hour after chow while the rest of the company scrubbed the barracks decks. They showed some real improvement.

There were men who resisted the discipline and physical training. A few refused to wash clothes and shower, but standing extra watches brought most of them around. Punishment hadn't worked to change two of the worst malingerers. One told Keene that he was going to hurt himself to get a discharge. Keene took him to the chief, who had the man picked up and taken to sick bay with his sea bag packed. The other guy refused to dress the next morning. The chief called the MPs, and he was gone by the time we came back from chow. The instant rumor was that they had both been sent for examinations that could lead to what was called a psycho discharge—or they could get time in the brig (jail).

The chief called an assembly and told us, "You all know that two boys have left the company. I call them boys because they're not men. Men face up to their responsibilities. Men don't run home to Mama. These two boys are getting psycho exams, and they'll try to convince the doctors they should get medical discharges. When the docs ask me about them, I'll tell the truth: they are cowardly malingerers. They may get dishonorable discharges, and if they do, their family and friends will know they are weaklings and cowards. If anyone else wants a psycho examination, put your hand up … NOW!" No hands went up. He paused nearly a full minute to let his words sink in before he said, "Dismissed." It was an effective talk, and some shaky guys tried harder after that.

The next day, the chief gave Keene late chow passes for the whole company. Keene did rifle drills with one platoon while I marched the other one, then we traded. The grinder lights came on, and we kept it up. We were just as hungry as the guys were, but we were determined to starve them into learning. During a two-minute break, Busby asked if he could speak, and I said, "Go ahead."

He said, "I promise to learn to march better—honest I will. But I'm so hungry I'm going to fall down. Please can we go to chow?"

He looked white and shaky. Keene said, "Okay, give us ten minutes of perfect execution and we'll go to chow." It wasn't perfect, but they tried. About twenty minutes later, when we went to chow, none of the men were speaking to Keene or me. Hunger is a motivator and anticipation of hunger perhaps even more so.

The DI's program was working. The men were on the way to accepting that there was no way out; they had to do it. On Friday morning, they had begun to execute most commands quickly and accurately. The improvement from earlier in the week was dramatic.

After lunch, the chief took my fifteen screw-ups and me onto the grinder and watched while I put them through their paces. When he called a halt, he was smiling and said, "Good job, Scheid, they're improving. Tomorrow we'll see what they do under pressure."

Then he called out the whole company and drilled them himself. He got a positive response; they tried hard. The laggards were executing sharply and on command, better than most of the other guys. The chief was pleased as hell.

That evening, a couple of the guys came to Keene and me. They said they were beginning to like being competent at marching, and they would really try at the competition in the morning.

Like everyone else, I wanted out of boot camp ASAP. But in a strange way, I was sort of enjoying the challenges. Physically and psychologically, I was in a good place.

The Competition

Every Saturday morning, the marching competition took place in a large building that covered an area the size of two football fields. Because it had hardwood floors, boots hitting in unison echoed like thunder. The sound of marching with perfect cadence is impressive.

Each company was put through marching drills called by their chief. While we were marching, the chief gave commands to maneuver the rifles, right and left shoulder, and so on. Following the commands required concentration. Competition between the company chiefs was open and vigorous—we suspected that they had bets with each other.

Flags were awarded for the best performances. The more flags a company won, the fewer painful duties that company was assigned. Those companies that didn't win flags were given extra night watches and the worst cleanup duties. We won our first two flags that Saturday. It was not a big victory, but it was a start. We were smilingly happy, but the chief wasn't. He said his last company won three flags on its second Saturday. He had a plan.

On Monday morning, the chief ordered Keene and me to increase the time spent on marching and rifle drills. We marched between classes and every time we had a break. We also drilled nearly two hours before evening chow. Keene gave the worst watches and duties to the worst performers, and that got their attention. The next Saturday, the company won about five more flags and we were on our way. More important for me, I was learning some important lessons about leadership.

There is more to tell, but each Saturday our company won more flags and lost none. Soon the company was assigned only a few early evening watches, which improved attitudes and motivated the men to try even harder. By our sixth Saturday of competition, we had won every major flag and were singled out for special notice by the base commander.

The march back to the barracks that day was one of pride. Boots hit the ground with one thud, and our cadence caller was so on tempo that heads turned to watch us go by. We had been transformed from an unhappy, sloppy bunch of casual company misfits into a team. We had accomplished something that none of us would have predicted and we were proud of our newfound status. The chief was slow to praise, but before he dismissed us, he said he was proud of us.

Everybody Swims—and Jumps

One morning we marched to an Olympic-sized pool housed in a large building. We carried swim trunks and towels, as each of us was required to pass a swimming test. It was an easy test, but a few men couldn't swim. Those who passed put work blues back on in preparation for the abandon ship drill.

When abandoning ship, men may have to jump off a deck high above the water. This could mean a drop of seventy feet or more. Life vests of those days were filled with balsa wood slats that surrounded your body. The slats came up under your chin so you couldn't look down and see your feet. We had to put one of these contraptions on and climb a ladder to a high platform. One at a time, we were to jump into the pool. The drop was forty feet or so—not as high as a carrier deck but high enough to scare the hell out of most of us.

There were instructors on the platform who assured us that if we did exactly as they told us, we would be safe. We were told to cross our arms under our chins and just step off the platform. If you leaped, it was more likely you would land on your back or face and get hurt.

An instructor kept repeating, "If you don't go when I say 'now,' we'll push you off." The man ahead of me had just barely passed the swimming test. When he got to the edge and heard the word "now," he froze. The two instructors gave him a second chance, and then they lifted him up by the arms and dropped him over the edge. He landed perfectly, came up coughing, and swam out of the way. I slavishly followed orders and stepped off. It was a hard hit on the water, but it was over in a second with no harm.

The chief became friendlier now that the company was shaping up. We were becoming his men, not just a bunch of problem kids. One Saturday he stayed after the parade drill competitions and had chow with the company. Then he invited the recruit petty officers into his office. He told us we were doing our jobs well and asked if we had any questions. Keene asked him to tell us something about his career. That launched the chief into a few sea stories, as yarn spinning is called in the navy.

He had enlisted before WWII and spent his war years in the Pacific. He had two ships sink under him, both torpedoed by Jap subs. He became a chief originally because the chief he worked for was killed. He had seen a lot of action and lost many shipmates. When he got to this part, he said he had to go home. As he left, he said, "There's still time to get in some drills this afternoon." We did two hours of polishing up our routines.

From then on, we admired the chief as a fighting man, not just our teacher and leader. We would have followed him wherever he led us.

Lessons Learned

The company's success was a revelation for me. A culture of success can be built. It was like being on an undefeated team, an experience I had never known. A group of strangers, with the right guidance and motivation, had pulled together and accomplished things way beyond our expectations. We learned that the harder we worked, the better we got. Success breeds success—just as failure begets more failure.

Marching was not all we did. We attended classes on shipboard living, hygiene, venereal diseases, the organization of the navy, and the rules and laws we had to obey. We even loaded and shot a simulated four inch ship's gun. The navy wanted every man prepared to walk on board a ship and be productive immediately. Such an organization amazed a small-town kid like me.

The navy also believed that every man should know how to use a rifle and a .45-caliber semiautomatic pistol. We had our share of city boys, but many of us were from the Midwest and had used guns. Over half of the men qualified with rifles the first day, and a few got a marksman badge, as I did. It was not the intensive weapons training given to marines and the army, but it was real guns and real ammunition. I had gotten little handgun training before, and I qualified by taking the instructions seriously and following them to the letter.

A Surprise Offer

One morning just over halfway through boot, the chief told me to take a bus to an administrative building on the other side of the base. He said it had something to do with the GCT (General Classification Test) given to every recruit. I found the building and was ushered into an office with a lieutenant sitting behind a desk. I snapped to attention and gave a sharp salute. He said, "Uncover [take off your hat] and sit down, Recruit Scheid."

For a few minutes, he asked questions about my education and work experience. Then he asked if I knew why I had done so poorly on one part of the GCT. I said, "Sir, I was still in my dirty civvies and had gotten very little sleep for several nights. I just dozed off and didn't finish one test."

He said, "Just as we thought. There is no way you can do as well as you did on the rest of the tests and so poorly on the clerical part. Follow me."

He led me down the hall into a kind of classroom, sat me at a desk, and handed me the clerical test and a pencil. With no discussion, he said, "You have twenty minutes to complete the test. Start now."

The test was actually pretty easy, and I finished it in time to review most of the questions before he returned and said, "Stop!"

After he graded the test, he asked more questions about my high school education, and I told the truth. I also explained my reading accomplishments. He seemed to be impressed as he asked, "You actually read all those books?" I assured him I had—and many more.

I knew the GCTs were used to decide what recruits did after boot, so I volunteered that since I had experience as a carpenter, I would be a natural for the Seabees after boot was over. He smiled and said, "I think the navy has something better than that for you," offering no further explanation. His last words were, "We'll call you back down here in a few days."

Taking his friendly demeanor as a sign that I had done well, I stood up tall, saluted sharply, did an about-face, and marched out. Officers like open respect from enlisted men, and I gave him a full measure. The chief would have been pleased—so would Mr. Carnegie.

A few days later, the chief sent me to the same office again. He said I was going to be interviewed for the NAVCAD (Naval Air Cadet) program and that he had given the calling officer a positive report on my leadership abilities. He said, "Scheid, you have an opportunity here. Take it seriously." I was apprehensive but excited.

I met with the same lieutenant I'd seen before. He told me to sit down and relax; there was no need for saluting and such because this was an interview. Then he described the NAVCAD program, which was flight training to be a pilot.

After that, he sent me to a neighboring building that I recognized as the same one in which I had taken my physical. Only a few corpsmen and doctors now occupied it. This examination was very thorough, with eye and ear exams and coordination tests. The doctors were encouraging, often saying I was doing well. It took well over an hour.

Back with the lieutenant, I learned that if I signed a five-year commitment, I could leave Bainbridge almost immediately and take a two-week leave before beginning the prescribed courses. After completing those, I would go to flight school, get my wings, and be a naval aviator.

I was taken aback. It had never vaguely occurred to me that I could be a pilot and a U.S. Navy officer. The lieutenant told me I had a week to make up my mind. There would be an additional interview, but he was confident that I would be accepted. He gave me a brochure, which I read as I bussed back to the barracks.

I lay awake late, thinking of what it would be like to be a pilot and officer. It was heady stuff. I had seen several WWII movies about flight training at Pensacola with a few guys washing out but most getting their wings. I imagined myself at Pensacola in that slick uniform, having my wings pinned on at graduation. Gin and Mom would be there.

It came to me the next day that all my buddies were enlisted men. Would they be envious and give me the cold shoulder? When we met, would they salute me? How would the guys in the Pastime react if I walked in as an officer? I had Walter Mitty dreams for a few nights.

The chief called me in after 1630, offered me a seat, and was unusually friendly. He told me that the NAVCAD recruiting officer had called. I thanked the chief for the positive report he had given about me. He waved it away, saying, "I support the men who do their jobs well."

He had a list of the GCT scores for everyone in the company. He said mine were good but not, in his opinion, good enough to merit consideration for NAVCAD training. I told him about dozing off on part of the test and about the officer letting me take that part again.

He leaned back in his chair laughing and said, "You lucky son of a bitch. Do you have any idea what the odds are that someone would notice that you messed up one section and then let you take it again?" I could see that he was enjoying the event.

I laughed too, saying, "I was just lucky, Chief. But now I don't know what to do about flight training."

He couldn't understand why I wouldn't jump at it. Over the next few minutes, he pushed me to grab this once-in-a-lifetime opportunity. "Son, this may be a long war, and take it from me that being an officer is a lot better than being a swabbie. As a pilot, you'll get the best the navy has to offer."

I promised I'd consider all he had said, and I meant it. The main thing on my mind was what Gin would think about my signing up for five years, officer or not. I needed to speak to her before I made a decision.

The chief gave me a pass to go to the telephone booths that evening. Gin and I had a long talk. As I suspected, she wouldn't take a position. It was my decision. Without an agreement to get married, I was in limbo. She wasn't eager to leave Bridgeport and follow me to wherever I might be sent. The choice became clear to me. It was NAVCAD or Gin. By the time I got back to the barracks, my decision had been made.

Another Fight

We had only a few watches to stand, everyone was getting enough sleep, and a daily routine had settled in. But young men have high energy and testosterone levels, and they're imaginative at finding ways to irritate each other. The recruit officers had to break up altercations every week.

There were continuing conflicts between a few New York Jews and New Jersey Italians. They rarely missed an opportunity to call each other names or make derogatory comments.

Joe Martinez, our master-at-arms, was an Italian from Jersey City. He had lugged crates of produce around in his father's wholesale fruit and vegetable business. He was about 190 pounds, short, stocky, and had an easygoing personality. He was one of the few who looked at the navy as an escape from a life he hated.

One Sunday afternoon, we were lounging around with nothing to do but smoke, talk, and write letters. Joe pulled me aside to ask about an incident when I had stopped a fight between one of the Jersey Italians and a Jewish kid from New York. Someone told me they had gone to the empty barracks upstairs to fight, so I ran to stop it. They had just begun swinging at the top of the stairs when I jumped in.

I pushed the Italian one way and the Jew in the opposite direction. Suddenly, the Italian was teetering at the point of falling backward down the stairs and I tried to grab his shirt and pull him back. When I grabbed, I missed his shirt and my hand pushed him a little. He fell backwards down half a dozen stairs. I ran down to him and found he was shaken but not really hurt. I said I was sorry and explained what had happened. He said he understood. I went to the head with him while he washed his hands and face and collected himself. He had no fight left in him and agreed to stay away from the other guy. I went to the Jewish kid and got the same agreement.

I had congratulated myself on a mission accomplished and told Keene about the event. I explained all of this to Joe, but he wasn't listening. He accused me of pushing the Italian kid down the stairs. I didn't take him seriously because it was so stupid. He called over the Italian kid, who said I had purposely pushed him down the stairs. Joe said I had to apologize to the kid. I said, "Joe, there is nothing to apologize for. He knows I didn't push him. Just let it go - it's over." Joe got angrier. I was surprised that he was pursuing this since he was a recruit officer and was supposed to help keep order.

Since I wouldn't apologize, he challenged me to fight on the quarterdeck. He had appointed himself the defender of the pride of the New Jersey Italians. Keene told him a fight would get us all in trouble. There was no graceful way out of this confrontation; someone had to back down. Joe wanted an apology for something I hadn't done, and I wasn't about to do that just to satisfy his ego.

I tried walking away, and Joe pushed me from behind. He wanted a fight. Keene knew that if he was present during a fight, he would lose his rank, so he was leaving. I told him he was ratting out on his job, but he left anyway. I was on my own.

Joe wanted an alley fight and he wanted it now. We took off our T-shirts and rolled up our pants above the knees. He threw the first punch, which was a wide miss. As we sparred around, it was obvious that he had done no fighting. He threw mostly roundhouse punches, which were easy to avoid or block. I stayed away from him and tried to punch under his long swings. When we clinched, he didn't try to wrestle me to the floor, where he most likely would have won easily, given his size and strength.

As is normal, there were flurries of punches that winded both of us. Then we both stood there panting until someone had enough wind to start again. I was in much better shape than Joe and could resume sooner than he could, so I kept him short of breath by keeping the breaks short. Soon he was tiring.

I had read about the famous Jack Dempsey fight with Argentinean Luis Firpo. The story was that Dempsey's strategy was to punch the spot just over the heart as often and as hard as possible. Once this area was sensitive, Dempsey faked to the spot and when Firpo dropped his hands to protect it, Dempsey hit him in the head. This came to me in a flash, and I decided to try it. He was throwing wild outside punches, so it wasn't difficult to get under them. It took only a few solid punches into this spot to make him begin to cover it up. In a few minutes, Joe was totally winded, but he wouldn't quit. He wanted to be a hero to his buddies. It was senseless and frustrating. I felt myself getting deeply angry.

In the past, I had gone into a blind rage during a fight, and it happened again. I didn't hate this guy and didn't want to fight him – the situation frustrated me. I began yelling at him and calling him names. I didn't care about anything but hitting him. It was as if I was not in my own body and I was on the verge of tears. It was complete frustration.

Then one of his tired outside right-hand swings hit my left elbow and he bent over, holding one hand with the other. In my rage, I hit him hard on the left side of his head. He went down, and several guys grabbed and held me. The fight was over. I walked outside panting and sweating. I knew I had hit him hard in the head because of the pain in my hand, so I walked back in to find out if he was okay. He was sitting up holding his right hand and groaning. I had visions of being hauled to the brig.

The collision of his right hand with my elbow had dislocated his thumb, and that was why he had suddenly bent over. I didn't give a damn; he asked for it, and he got it. I was still angry!

The fight had lasted about fifteen minutes, and I was exhausted. I had pain spots all over my body, a badly bruised cheekbone, and a swollen right hand. Both winners and losers suffer damages in fights - another good reason to avoid them.

When he got his breath and stood up, Joe asked everyone present to promise not to tell the chief about the fight. They all agreed because they figured the whole company would be punished. Now that it was over, everyone was worried about the repercussions, just as Keene had tried to tell Joe.

His pals helped him get to sick bay. I didn't go, not wanting to be written up for fighting or admit I was hurt. One of the guys got some ice from the mess hall so I could minimize the swelling on my cheek and in my hand.

There were no volunteers for fights like this one, so it was a good bet that I wouldn't be challenged again. I hoped that was the case because I was tired of fighting—really tired. I was also tired of boot camp, tired of conflict, and just wanted peace. I left the barracks, walked into the woodsy area down the hill and cried tears of triumph at winning and tears of fear for what was coming next. I didn't vomit, and my nose bled only a little, a first for me.

Keene and I sat together at chow, and no one came near us. He felt guilty for not helping me avoid the fight, and I didn't let him off the hook. He'd made a big mistake, and I was disappointed in him. I accepted his apology in order to get the thing behind us, but it was never the same between us. My trust in him had evaporated.

My friend Ollie taught me many things, one of which was that winning a street fight is about 10 percent skill and 90 percent getting in a lucky punch or two. A couple of the guys told me later that they knew it was all over when I went into a rage and attacked. A blind rage makes you somewhat impervious to pain - but careless—and one punch can cool that rage quickly. Losing your reasoning and going crazy in a fight is a bad idea. I had been lucky ... again.

Joe quietly returned from sick bay late in the afternoon, a cast on his right hand. To his credit, Keene got us together just before lights out and made us shake hands—left hands, that is. It had been a stupid fight about nothing and hurt us both. I had a lot of self-directed anger for letting myself get sucked into it.

It was strange that I didn't fear fights as much as I had when I was younger. I tried to stay out of them but accepted the inevitable when it couldn't be avoided. Uncle Red had been right when he said that running doesn't work.

My injuries healed fast, and Gin never learned about the boot camp fights. Her knowing would have been a difficult thing for me to handle. I hated looking like a fool in her eyes.

It took the chief about an hour the next day to figure out what had happened. When questioned, Joe said he had fallen down the stairs, but it didn't sell. My cheek was red and swollen, my hand was hurting, and I had difficulty handling my rifle. He called both of us into his office late in the day and said, "I don't give a shit what you were fighting about—don't tell me. I like fighting spirit among my men, but you are both petty officers and you both got hurt. I'm not putting it in my report; we'll pretend it didn't happen. But, if either of you cause trouble again; you'll pay dearly for it. That's a promise. Now, get out of here."

We had dodged a bullet, and I pledged to myself that I'd be a model recruit for the rest of boot camp.

In a couple of days Joe and I were speaking, and by the end of the week, we sat across from each other at chow. The situation was a matter of ethnic honor to him, and he understood why I couldn't back down. That's how most young men in my generation operated. When a fight is over, it's over.

Two Tough Trials

The time came for our company and one other to attend firefighting school. We knew this was serious stuff when we saw two standby ambulances parked next to the area. The instructors explained that our job was to learn how to climb up on the superstructure of a fake ship while dragging large-diameter fire hoses with us. The black smoke would be thick, with visibility near zero, and breathing would be difficult, so putting the fire out quickly was essential.

The high-pressure hoses were heavy and had a mind of their own as to where they would bend. We were taught that as long as we kept a thick spray directed at the fire, it would blow the smoke away from us. If the hose was misdirected, the smoke would come at us and we'd lose visibility. The big risk was that someone on the team would panic and run because it deprived the team of manpower needed to control the thrashing hose. It reminded me of the water fights at the Bridgeport Volunteer Fire Department.

After midday chow, the most difficult drill was set up. Six-man teams had to climb up the mock ship and descend into the chamber below while fighting clouds of black smoke billowing out of the hatch. One of the other company's teams panicked as the smoke engulfed them and two men climbed out of the hatch, leaving the rest below. The instruction crew donned gas masks and got the men out. Several of them suffered smoke inhalation and were taken to the hospital.

This compelled the chief to give us a pep talk on courage, which ended with this: "You're men now, goddammit, act like men—don't quit; don't run!" Then he asked if we wanted him to put on fatigues and lead each team in.

Every one of us yelled something like, "Hell no!" And we went after the task.

Every order was obeyed quickly and completely. We had only one man panic in the smoke, turning and running into a steel post, which knocked him down and out. We put out the fire and then carried him up through the hatch without the instructors' help. He was back in the company the next day with a bandaged head and a wounded ego. We got a high score and had only one minor injury. The chief was ecstatic.

At the end of the day, we were dirty worn-out young men, but our march back to the barracks was one of victory and pride. Our faces were black, our fatigues were stained with sweat and soot, and we had our share of bruises and cuts, but we had performed. The chief called a halt at the barracks and congratulated us on a job well done. He was smiling broadly as we ran for the showers.

The next day, we went to gas training. When we arrived at the small wooden building, the acrid odor of tear gas was in the air. The company was marched into the building and commanded to stand at attention. We were told that we had to sing *Anchors Aweigh* before the door would be opened. The instructor warned us: "Don't rub your eyes. There are fountains outside; when you leave, line up and take turns rinsing your eyes." With that, he put on a gas mask, stood in front of the closed door, and activated a grenade-sized canister. White smoke filled the room in seconds. Some men tried to hold their breath, but most of us sang the words as fast as possible. Coughing prevented us from finishing the song.

When the door opened, we all rushed out, and a few vomited loudly. Predictably, some men wiped their eyes, which extended their pain for hours. Haphazard lines formed up at the water fountains. The recruit officers had to let the men go first, but we pushed each of them out of the way of the next man after five seconds of eye rinsing. After a couple minutes of hell, the officers got their turns.

The chief gave us a "Well done, men," and we marched home.

To Fly, or Not to Fly

The chief sent me back for my next interview for NAVCAD. His only words of advice were, "Don't be an idiot and pass it up."

At the interview, I was asked about my swollen cheek. I said simply that another man and I had an argument. The lieutenant smiled and asked what I had decided. I explained that while I was honored to be offered a chance at NAVCAD, I didn't really want a navy career. He began telling me all the advantages of being a pilot, about the prestige and the other perks. He gave up when I said that my long-term girlfriend and I had discussed it and I wanted to return to civilian life and get married.

He asked if I would be interested in a specialist school. I gave a quick yes. He said there were openings and, if I did well on another test, I would be eligible. The test was short and consisted mostly of matching up letters and numbers in various columns, a sort of visual thing. He asked me to demonstrate my typing, which I did, but poorly. I assured him, "I just need practice," and we moved on.

After grading the test, he said I was qualified for class A yeoman school and was confident I would be accepted if I wanted to go. He told me that yeomen were the men who kept records, typed letters, and did other office work. The school lasted ten weeks and was at Bainbridge. The scuttlebutt (rumor) was that my company was headed for landing craft training. I said I would be delighted to go to yeoman school.

Before leaving, I told him what the chief had said about the odds of my poor test results being noticed. He nodded and explained that a senior officer had heard about recruits being tested when they were tired and hungry and there had been an investigation. My cognitive ability score was too high for me to have scored so low on the clerical part … It just didn't fit. There were quite a few men who scored in a similar way, so it was decided to investigate. I was a part of the sample of men who were interviewed.

Nothing Lasts Forever

Our company of misfits had acquired every marching flag that could be won, along with good scores in all other phases of training. At the graduation ceremony, with hundreds of civilians in the bleachers, the chief received a commendation from the captain. He was as proud as if they had made him a four-star admiral.

When the companies marched in review, we "stepped out smartly," as the saying goes. None of us had ever been part of anything that achieved so much, and it felt great.

That afternoon, the chief called us into formation to announce our assignments. Keene got the battleship he wanted. Half a dozen men were assigned to special training at communications and corpsman schools. Two men were assigned to class A yeoman school. One was a tall, quiet sailor named Rick Hanover; the other was the kid from Beerport. Rick had been in the Second Platoon and I hadn't gotten to know him, but I would soon.

Then we witnessed proof that scuttlebutt is often true. It was announced that most of the men were being sent to landing craft training in Norfolk and the rest to destroyers in the Pacific. Our men had shown they could work as a team with spirit and determination. The chief said these were just the qualities needed on a landing craft. It was a sincere compliment, but no one really wanted to run a boat full of marines up onto a beach while under heavy fire.

The chief's last words to the company were, "Don't forget, from now on, don't any of you address a noncommissioned officer as sir or salute him. Beginning now, you can call me Chief or Skee but never sir—that's over. Now fall out." Everyone stood in line to shake his hand and call him Skee.

The next morning, we were all packed and ready for a fourteen-day leave before going to our new posts. The company was breaking up, and it was a little sad. Even guys who thought they hated each other gave "happy sailing" handshakes.

Keene and I had been through a lot together. I had forgiven him for not backing me up with Joe Martinez; he had just made a dumb mistake. We shook hands and exchanged sincere thanks. We never met again. That's the way military service works.

The chief called the recruit petty officers into his office and thanked us for making him the envy of all of the other training chiefs. He said he was retiring for good after a few weeks of teaching a new group of chiefs how to train recruits.

It was one of the most touching moments I had ever experienced. Here was an old salt that had two ships shot out from under him and his career was over. The chief had shaped up a company of misfits and made them ready for service. It was an honor to have served with him. And he was thanking us? We had tears welling up when the chief said, "Now get the hell out of here and go become real sailors."

As I was leaving the barracks, he was talking to some of the chiefs he was to train and our eyes met for a moment. I waved, and as he waved back, he yelled, "You should've taken NAVCAD—but good luck, Scheid!" There was a lot of navy time ahead, but for now I was extremely eager to get home.

Boot camp was a great experience for every man who finished with his body intact. We learned skills we'd use the rest of our lives. There were some navy sayings we found to be useful. For instance: "Don't be first, don't be last, and don't volunteer for anything." A similar dictum: "Don't volunteer for anything but extra liberty, extra chow, and more pay." And my favorite: "Ten percent never get the word - even for abandon ship."

CHAPTER 26

Parting is such sweet sorrow
that I shall say good night till it be morrow.
—William Shakespeare, playwright (1564–1616)

People change and forget to tell each other.
—Lillian Hellman, American Playwright (1905-1984)

HOME AGAIN

I was in first-class physical condition and felt great. Gin and Mom hadn't seen me in uniform and they almost didn't recognize me when I walked through the train gate in Pittsburgh.

My first evening home we went to the same bench under the trees where we had first kissed. The sounds and smells of the river were as they had been. Memories of that first romantic encounter flooded back upon us. We kissed hugged, talked, and kissed some more. Then we went to the apartment. It was an indescribably wonderful homecoming.

Walking around town alone the next morning, while wearing strange-feeling civilian clothes, the place seemed surreal. It was sort of a Rip Van Winkle syndrome. The same stores were there, the people walking around looked the same, and the good old Pastime was open, but things were somehow different. So much had happened to me since I left that it seemed like years had passed. As Alice said in *Wonderland*, "I can't go back to yesterday, because I was a different person then." It was then that I realized Bridgeport hadn't changed—I had.

In late afternoon I was in the Lincoln having a beer with Carl, and things began to seem familiar again. Carl was a rock. He hadn't changed, and he still called me kid. He said, "You're the best I ever seen you. Your shoulders are big, your complexion is clear, and your posture is terrific. Clean living agrees with you, kid," whereupon he set up another beer. Clean living was not Bridgeport.

He pumped me for stories about basic training, and I told him about fire-fighting school and a few other things. I liked Carl, but he loved to repeat stories, and I didn't want my personal stuff spread around.

Gin and I were together every night. She had ceased to care if her father found out we were together. She said they ignored each other at home. Her mother had told her that Roy knew I was in the navy and that she believed his views had softened, but he was not about to admit it. Still, it was no time for a kerfuffle with him, so we avoided her house, spending our time out and about or in Mom's apartment.

I had weekdays to myself while Gin was at work. I tried hanging out at the Pastime, but I was too rusty to compete for money. Jimmy Raies, my pool coach, had joined the navy months before I did and was on the aircraft carrier *Franklin D. Roosevelt* on the around-the-world cruise. Jim got lucky on that one.

I spent time helping Mom in her store and I passed a few afternoon hours shooting rats at the town dump. Only a Bridgeport kid would shoot rats while on leave. Mom was still working at the Eagles Club three or four nights each week, so we didn't spend much evening time together. She knew that Gin and I wanted alone time anyway. Mom was always considerate, giving us lots of time and space.

A Gift from Dad

Mom and Dad had eased into limited conversations at the Eagles. They were not friendly, just civil, which was good. Their marriage was over, and they had moved on. I called him, and we met at the club.

He gave me a membership card for the Eagles, explaining that there were no dues as long as I was in the navy. I was surprised; joining the club required an application and a formal induction. He said, "Alfred, I have done nothing for you, and I feel really bad about that. I was able to arrange this membership for you. Please take it and use it. There are hundreds of Aeries in the country, and you'll always be welcome at any of them. Just don't ever tell anyone you never went through the formal initiation."

I understood that, as a favor to Dad, his friends had arranged for me to become a member without going through the formalities. It was a touching moment and I said, "Thanks, Dad. I appreciate it, and I'll use it often." He told me he was proud of me.

Dad was in much better shape than the last time I'd seen him. He looked me in the eye rather than directing his gaze past me, and he could hold his thoughts during a conversation. He still smoked heavily and drank every day, but he had a job in a factory and lived with a woman named Blanche. A couple of days later, I met her at a bar that Dad frequented, and she seemed to be a nice woman even though she drank and swore like a man. Over the next few years, I got to know Blanche and always liked her gruff but kindly mannerisms.

Some Realizations

I went to the library and returned to the comfort of reading, which I had done practically none of for months. It was great to browse the stacks, pick up strange titles, read a few pages, and move on until I found something that held my interest for a while. I got involved in the thoughts of Socrates, Plato, and other ancient Greek philosophers, for the first time.

Reading the philosophers got me to thinking about education, and it came to me that I was going to a school that could change my life. Maybe I could even learn enough to do office work instead of factory jobs when I reentered civilian life.

I also realized that I could flunk out of yeoman school because I had never learned to study. I had the sinking feeling in my stomach that I always had when something bad might happen. It was an emotion of helplessness. I knew that going to yeoman school was just as inevitable as fighting Joe had been and that I had to do it - but I dreaded it. A lucky punch was not likely to save me this time. The school was going to be a real test.

My old trick in sports competition was to talk to myself, saying things like, "Get off your ass, Scheid. Put your head down and hit the line. Swing at the fastball; don't hold back. If you lose, you lose, but you gotta try." Brave thoughts like this and a beer always made me feel better. I knew this was false bravery, but it was the only kind of bravery I had. The self-confidence I had built up in boot camp seemed to be eroding. Was I spending too much time brooding over this? Yes! Could I stop? Maybe!

The last Saturday afternoon, while we were lounging on the grass by the pool at Ogleby Park, Gin came up with something that helped me. She suddenly said, "Alf, you've changed. It's taken me a while to figure it out, but the change is there."

"What do you mean?" I asked with some trepidation.

"You're much stronger now," she said.

I answered, "Well, of course. I've been going through intense physical training for months."

A bit exasperated, she said, "That's not what I mean. It's that, well, you are much more calm and assured, more at peace with yourself—strong in that way. You seem more confident, not worried about the future as you've always been. What did the navy do to you?"

I lay back on my towel for a while, laughing internally about the irony of the conversation, before saying, "Well, honey, maybe I'm just growing up and learning to be my own man."

She answered, "There. That's what I mean. You thought over what you were going to say instead of just coming out with something. I like you this way. In fact, I love you." Then she kissed me, something she rarely did in public.

No words could have pleased me more. Her love and respect were what I wanted most. For the first time, I realized that perhaps I really was becoming my own man. The navy had given me a new start. Anticipation of yeoman school was frightening, but I wanted to face it.

The next day, Gin drove me to the train in Pittsburgh. I promised I'd hitchhike home the first weekend I could get off. That made parting much easier. Though still painful, we were becoming accustomed to saying good-bye, and most importantly, I had regained my trust in her.

On the train, it hit me that I hadn't bothered to learn much about yeoman school. As I look back, I think fear made me ignore it as long as possible. With my high school record, how could I be confident that I could make the grade in anything labeled class A? Perhaps it was better this way. Had I known what I was getting into, I might have finked out before I started. [19]

---

19 The word yeoman goes back to feudalism. The title was applied to a reliable man tilling a rich man's land, later to a small farm owner, and finally to a trusted employee. Eventually, the term was applied to a literate sailor who interacted with the captain and handled the paperwork of a ship. A ship's yeoman had knowledge of finances, personnel records, and other confidential information. A yeoman was among the most respected members of a ship's company, and chief yeoman, the top rank attainable, carried high prestige. During a war, the navy needs trained men quickly, and formal schools are developed to add to the existing apprenticeship system.

Yeoman School

With typical military logic, the members of my class had been ordered to report a week before classes were scheduled to begin. In other words, the navy denied us a week of leave so it could pay to feed and house us. In addition, we were restricted to the base.

A sailor at the EM Club (enlisted men's club) gave some advice. He said, "When the bosun's mate arrives to form work parties, don't be at the barracks. Get on a bus and go to the other side of the base, walk around for a while, and then take a bus to another location. Just blend in to the scenery all day."

The next morning, six of us did just as he said. During a bus ride, we spotted the main library and several of us went in. The library became our main hideout for the rest of the week. It was in the library that I ran into Rick Hanover, the man from my company, and we began to get acquainted.

Evening hours were passed in the EM Club, getting to know classmates. Rick and I met Paul Schnoblin, and the three of us became beer buddies. The quality of these men was way above the recruits I had known in boot camp.

Paul, Rick, and I shared a love of reading and beer drinking—a sure formula for friendship. We talked about our favorite authors and books and I loved it. I had never been around guys who were so well read. They were college grads and were genuinely surprised that I had read so much in high school.

Neither of them had kicked around tire factories, steel mills, and poolrooms. They were amused by my stories about those places and asked many questions. Paul had graduated from boot on the same day as Rick and I, but in a different company. Both of them had avoided responsibilities during boot camp.

I shared my concern about getting through the school. They tried to put my mind at ease by telling me I'd do fine if I just didn't let myself fall behind. It was flattering that they hung out with an uneducated factory worker and treated me as an equal. My confidence about being able to handle the work in the school was low, but they helped bring it up a little.

An Important Learning Experience

There were just over two hundred men in our class, broken into four groups. We would all take the same subjects, taught by a staff of chiefs and first class petty officers, each of whom had years of yeoman experience.

School began with a long day of orientation. The head of the school was a chief yeoman who gave a straightforward speech. He emphasized that we were required to be prepared and on time for classes every day. He emphasized that we were lucky to have been selected for one of the most sought-after navy schools. For those of us who were seaman first class, we would be allowed to take the exam for promotion to third class petty officer six months after graduation. He emphasized that we had to be instantly productive in our next job.

The chief said we were going to be given additional training in the Uniform Code of Military Justice (UCMJ), which had gone into effect a year earlier. [20] Most of us would end up working for navy lawyers who were prosecuting or defending sailors accused of crimes. This extra training would extend our time in school by two weeks.

There was an incentive to strive for high grades. The top ten men in the class would be permitted to bid on the available billets (assignments) upon graduation. The top man would have first choice; second man, second choice; and on down. Finally, any man who failed to get passing grades on the first two exams would be assumed to be too lazy or not smart enough for the school and would

20 The UCMJ replaced the legal codes for each of the services; after 1951, one set of laws was applicable to all branches of the military. In 1952, intensive efforts were being made to educate the officers and men about the UCMJ.

be expelled. With that happy ending, he said study materials would be issued immediately. Classes began at 0800 the next morning.

Rick, who had been an honors student in college, had it in mind to be at or near the top of the class. He wanted a chance to get a billet in Norfolk, Virginia, his hometown and a major navy base. He had a serious girlfriend waiting there. Paul had no interest in working hard.

Much to my surprise, Rick invited me to study with him. He said his observation of me in boot camp made him confident that I would work hard. I thanked him for his confidence and promised I'd try to justify it. But there was doubt lurking in the back of my mind.

The first evening, we hunkered down in a study room in a small library a block from our barracks. Rick was a disciplined student and we studied in whatever way he dictated. I had a combination tutor, lesson planner, and disciplinarian. The first three weeks, I passed every test with a ninety or better, just a few points below Rick. My confidence rose dramatically. I began feeling sure I could get through the school as long as I stuck with Rick.

The curriculum was mostly details complicated by more details and overlaid by layers of minutia. We were tested frequently on acronyms, details about departments and command zones, the navy way of filing, filling out documents, keeping personnel records, learning the correct language protocol to be used in memos, and spelling—lots of spelling. It was clear that rote memorizing was the way to succeed in yeoman school - and that was up my alley.

Rick decided that we should plan which weekends we could take off, making sure to be on the base to study on the weekends before important exams.

Traveling on the Thumb

During school, we had twelve weekends, and I spent four of them in Bridgeport, one in Washington, DC, one in Atlantic City, and the rest of them studying. Train and bus schedules didn't work for me to get home and back over a weekend. Hitchhiking in uniform was the answer. On my first trip, I was off the base before five in the afternoon and arrived in Bridgeport about one Saturday morning. This gave me about thirty-six hours at home in exchange for about seventeen hours of travel. Looking back, it seems insane to have made these trips, but I was twenty and in love.

On one trip, I spotted an Eagles Club in Cumberland, Maryland. I asked the driver to let me out. When I showed my membership card, the doorman handed me off to a couple of members who treated me like a son. For the next two hours, I was showered with food, beer, and questions. One of the men drove me many miles to a Pennsylvania Turnpike entrance so I could make up some of the lost time. I always wanted to stop in there again, but the rides just never worked out that way.

Another time, a man who said he was going through Wheeling picked me up in eastern Pennsylvania. It was a lucky break to get a ride all the way home, I thought. After a while, it became obvious the driver was gay and aggressive. He made his proposition on an isolated and hilly piece of Route 40. When I rejected him, he stopped the car and yelled at me to get out. I got out and kicked a large dent into the passenger side door as he sped away. That left me stuck on a lonely road in the dark, in the middle of nowhere.

I sat on my bag and leaned against a tree. I dozed off and was awakened by a car horn. It was two sailors in an old ambulance—yes, an ambulance. The driver asked me for $2 as fare to Washington, Pennsylvania, and told me I could lie on the gurney in the back. He said the vehicle belonged to his father's ambulance service. He sold rides to sailors, priced on how far they went. He used the siren to get through red traffic lights in small towns. Hitching was adventurous and sometimes amusing. How often does one get to take naps in an ambulance?

We had Labor Day off, and the school let us out early on Friday. Rides were plentiful and I was having a beer in the Lincoln by midnight. We had a great Saturday, relaxing at the Ogleby Park pool and then barhopping until late. On Sunday, we went to Piedmont Lake for a picnic with friends. It was a glorious weekend. Monday afternoon I was back on the road with my thumb out.

During the Labor Day visit, Mom told me she was leaving Bridgeport. Her brother Alfred in El Monte, California, had invited her to move there and start a new life. There were no buyers for her business, so she was closing it. The move was planned for October so she would be in California for the winter.

It was sad for us. She had started her business in early 1942 and over the next decade everything had changed. She had no husband, no romantic interests and her only child was gone. There was nothing to keep her in Bridgeport. I admired her for making such a life-changing decision. I knew how difficult that was.

The Fifty-Yard Line

About halfway through yeoman school, there were casualties. One Monday, a couple of guys were missing from my group and the next week two more were gone. These men hadn't made minimum grades.

The library was our home. Except for a couple of poker games, all we did in the barracks was sleep and shower. We never went off base for an evening. My grades were all over ninety, and I began to let myself dream that I could make it into the top ten.

What's an Intelligence Quotient?

Our friendliest teacher was lecturing on something boring when he offhandedly asked if any of us knew our IQs. Only a couple of hands went up. He went on, "All of you had high GCT scores or you wouldn't be here. I'll show you how to calculate your IQ from your GCT score." Though I knew what IQ meant, I had no inkling of mine.

He chalked a formula on the blackboard and explained that by inserting your GCT score for X, you got a number that was your IQ. The teacher said, "I expect that all of you are at least 115. Now, let's get back to work.

At the EM club that evening, Rick, Paul, and I shared our scores. When mine turned out to be the highest, they were not nearly as surprised as I was. Rick said, "You have a great memory and read well – of course you have a high IQ." Paul said he was happy to be over 115; Rick was higher, over 120.

Here I am, over sixty years later, I have told only a few people the score I calculated that day. The reasons for secrecy no longer exist, so here it is: 139.

It would be nice to say that I took all of this in stride, but I didn't. I went from upset to excited and back again. I was upset because I could have gotten good grades in school. I was angry that I hadn't taken academic prep courses and that the school never tested us. While I didn't yet know about bell curves and geometric progressions, I understood that if a score of 160 was considered genius, then 139 was damned good.

Learning my IQ was a life changer. From that day on, whenever I've been struggling through something complicated, I remind myself that most of the people who have figured it out aren't any brighter than I am. However, even then, I knew that having a high IQ is one thing and using it is another thing altogether. Perseverance trumps intelligence most of the time.

This theory was tested when we studied the UCMJ. The goal was for us to learn the forms, phrases, and pleas used by the lawyers as well as the basic laws and rules and interpretations. It was a tough grind. It was all about memorizing. Most of our classmates trudged through it while complaining of boredom. Rick and I learned the stuff.

My big hurdle was typing. In high school, I never did over thirty wpm. The requirement for graduation from yeoman school was forty-five wpm - after error adjustment. It eluded me. I set aside time for practice and Rick coached me. I was a typing klutz. Rick and I joked that I had a ninety-plus grade average and might not graduate because of typing. It wasn't really funny.

Final exams were spread over two days. There wasn't a question or a form that stumped me. I felt good about my performance. Rick said, "When you feel good about an exam, the odds are you did well." I wanted to believe him.

It was taken for granted that everyone would pass typing. They gave us three tries to do forty-five wpm. Rick could type about seventy wpm in his sleep. We came up with a plan. He sat in front of me. When the bell rang, everyone typed the same text for three minutes. When the bell rang again, we had to stop immediately and grade the paper. If we were satisfied, we were to sign it and hand it in. If the score was too low we could try again. The first time I touched Rick's shoulder to signify that I had failed. He passed his paper under his chair, back to me; it was sixty-five wpm. The teacher wouldn't believe that number from me, but I kept the paper. I whispered, "Too good!" The second time, he scored about fifty wpm and I did just over forty-five. We had two winners and we turned them in. The teacher would have been suspicious if Rick had taken three tries so we just made it. Was Rick a friend or what?

As we left the room, the teacher said with a wide smile, "Hey, I'm glad you guys finally managed to get past forty-five."

Outside the room, Rick said, "I think the sonuvabitch knew what we were doing."

That evening, as we tried to drink all the beer the EM Club had, we concluded that the teacher ignored our little game because he didn't want to coach me until I got the minimum score. Paul said, "You guys are full of crap. With your grades they'd ignore your typing score." He was probably right.

When final grades were posted, the top ten were all in a narrow range, calculated to two decimal places. Rick was first, which was no surprise.

A guy I barely knew was second, and just a few hundredths ahead of the fourth finisher was the f****d up kid from Beerport—third in the class. Paul, who spent most weekends on liberty, missed the top ten but did well.

Bidding for billets had been a topic of conversation for weeks, and the top ten guys crowded around the posting board. There were only few land-based billets in the United States. The aircraft carrier *Roosevelt* was "showing the American flag" around the world. There was one billet in California, at Los Alamitos Naval Air Station, Long Beach and I knew my uncle lived not far from Long Beach.

Rick took the only billet in Norfolk. Rick and Paul argued that I would regret it for the rest of my life if I didn't try for the around-the-world cruise, so with some trepidation, I made the *Roosevelt* my first choice. As my second choice, I picked the Los Alamitos and my third was a battleship.

The second highest finisher also bid for the *Roosevelt*, so I got Los Alamitos. I had no idea what a diamond I had accidently mined. I would be going to California about the same time Mom was moving there. I rushed to the library, looked up Los Alamitos. To my delight, I learned that the base was about thirty miles from El Monte. It was a miracle. Christmas had come early for the Scheid family.

I called Mom and told her the news. If there was ever any doubt in her mind about moving to California, it was gone. Gin wasn't as pleased. She had hoped for something closer to home, like the Great Lakes base near Chicago. I never told her about trying for the *Roosevelt.*

This was the most important accomplishment of my life. I had out-studied and out-tested men with college degrees. Class A yeoman school taught me that I could learn any damned thing I wanted to learn—if I just made the effort. All my excuses for learning failures were *gone with the wind.* [21] I had been working at building my

21 Margaret Mitchell is the author of *Gone with the Wind.* Certain words of the lead character, Scarlett O'Hara, and her attitude about putting things off are mentioned a number of times in the text of this book.

physical confidence most of my life. This new type of confidence was much more important.

When the Chief handed me my diploma, I was truly proud. In many ways, it was Rick's victory as much as mine, and I thanked him deeply and sincerely. The only negative that day was that Gin and Mom weren't there.

Written orders had been passed out before graduation, and the class was scattering around the world. That last night, Rick, Paul, and a couple of other classmates and I went into Baltimore and drank too much. The next morning we said our good-byes, never to see each other again. Rick and I exchanged a few letters, but shipmates lose touch. It's the navy way.

The Last Week at Home

This was the kind of time in a life that's never forgotten. It was autumn, Indian summer was upon us, and the colors and smells of the season were everywhere. Gin took vacation for a week. We drove out into the farm country, had a picnic by the lake one day, and visited my grandparents on another. We hiked in Ogleby Park, walked around the Island, and went to local bars, where we could put coins in the jukebox and dance slow and close. Probably because of the movie *Casablanca*, every couple had to have an "our song," and we were no exception. Ours was *Tenderly*, recorded by Nat King Cole, Rosemary Clooney, and others. These few words were our favorite part of the song:

Your arms opened wide
and closed me inside
You took my lips,
you took my love, so tenderly.

I wrestled with what to do about my IQ score. I felt I was holding something important back from Gin and Mom. But, if I told Gin she might see it as bragging, and it brought up uneasy questions about my poor performance in high school. Mom might tell grandma, and it would leak to the rest of the family. I decided to keep it to myself. I could always tell them later. As it turned out, I put it out of my mind so completely that I told no one for many, many years and never did tell Mom or Gin.

Gin knew that I had had the pick of many billets, and she was not fully on board with my explanation that most of the billets had been on ships. I explained that in California at least I was in the States. She was not comfortable with the idea of coming to visit me. She said, "What would people think about a single girl chasing after a man so far away?" We both knew the problem was her parents.

A Silent Soliloquy

For about six months, I had been surrounded by people. There's not much privacy in the military. I needed to think about where I was, where I was going, and how things might work out with Gin. And being trapped in the navy troubled me. It felt like being in prison and my sentence could be extended.

When Gin wanted to do personal errands in Wheeling, I begged off. I put an old blanket under my arm, caught a westbound bus, and got off near Lansing. From there it was about a mile walk into the woods. The smell of drying leaves was in the air. I sat on the blanket with my back leaning against the tree and lit a cigarette. I knew the squirrels would come to investigate.

Closing my eyes and breathing deeply, I let thoughts flow freely. Suddenly, the dumb things I had done in high school began reeling through my mind like a movie. What a failure I had been at everything—even sports. I watched Wendell and me wasting our school years with our smart-ass ideas of refusing to do homework and skipping every class we could. We were so pleased that we got away with so much. The truth was that we got away with nothing.

We had cheated ourselves. Miss Woods had been my enabler, who helped me play at art.

As I sat there watching bits of the same movie repeatedly, my insides hurt. I was experiencing remorse. Tears slipped down my cheeks as I looked at the truth. I had been a phony, an unsuccessful big-deal athlete, and a stupid joke of a kid. And it didn't have to have been that way. I could have gotten good grades, maybe even gone to college. I did better in yeoman school than most of the men who'd gone to college, but their futures were still brighter than mine. Algebraic equations were beyond me, as was any understanding of a foreign language and everything else that educated people learn. The only times I used my brain was when reading novels, learning a few poems, telling jokes, playing cards, and outwitting the school system. My reading had been my way to escape reality, not become educated. Staying ignorant had been a conscious decision.

Of course Gin wouldn't commit to a future with me. Why should she? I had nothing to offer her but a lonely wait of at least another eighteen months—and then what? So I could work at Wheeling Steel or become a carpenter? She knew what that meant. All her life she'd watched her grease monkey father come home dirty after work and drunk after card games. Her mother had a miserable life. Why should she want to follow in those footsteps?

And my Dad, what a winner he was! Why would she want him as a father-in-law? I concluded that if Gin asked me for honest advice, I would tell her to find a man who had a future. How could she not be reaching the same conclusion?

Then I began blaming others. Why didn't my parents or the school make me buckle down and learn? Why didn't they give me tests so I would have known I was smart enough to get good grades? Everyone had let me just stumble along, being stupid.

But it was no good. The rationalizations didn't work. The fault was mine and mine alone. Not even my f****d up friend Wendell deserved part of the blame. I had been much cleverer at avoiding schoolwork than he had. He would've been better off if he hadn't conspired with me.

I wiped the tears away and sat as blank-minded as I could manage. The squirrels had gotten so used to me that they were flitting around in the fallen leaves not thirty feet away. My mind was tired, and the catharsis was over. It was time to head back to town. But I didn't get up.

It came to me that Gin, Wendell, Carl, and a few others had told me that the thing I had going for me was my determination and positive attitude—and that I stood up to tough situations. Well, here I was doing just the opposite, feeling sorry for myself and flagellating my psyche with mistakes of the past.

A self-lecture began. I reminded myself that I had valid reasons to have confidence that I would do all right in life. I had earned my keep from a young age and made my way in Mansfield. Not only had I gotten through boot camp, but I had also become a leader. And I had just graduated from a difficult school, near the top of my class. When I got to my new base, I had to do my job well and keep my eyes open for opportunities. There had to be something worthwhile in my future. I just had to find it.

Most importantly, I had a girl I loved and who loved me. I had so much more than most of the young men I knew. I had no right to sit around crying about past mistakes.

Yes, I'd made a mess of my education, but I wasn't twenty-one yet, and the trials I had faced had given me some confidence. Finally, as I read somewhere, it doesn't pay to worry about the things you can't control. That was it. I had to get control of my life and my future, and I damn well intended to do that.

By the time I boarded the bus, it was late afternoon and I felt better. It had been a cleansing experience. I had faced the demons of regret and renewed my confidence that I could handle life as it happened. And maybe, just maybe, I could find a way to learn something that would help me be more than a working stiff. As the bus rolled through the familiar villages, good thoughts popped up and I looked forward to the evening with Gin.

Time to Wind Down and Leave

Mom and I talked for a while when I got to the store. She knew something was up with me, but she kept her peace. Her only comment was, "You seem much happier now than when you left. Something good happen?"

"Yeah, Mom," I replied. "I sat in the woods and thought things over. I feel much better now about going to California."

"I know you'll miss Virginia, but maybe she'll decide to come to California too," she said, trying to comfort me.

Fat chance of that, I thought, *but who knows?*

Gin and I went to the Lincoln so I could do good-byes with Carl and a few Pastime pals who came across the street for the occasion. I was going to miss Carl.

It was my last night, so Gin and I excused ourselves after a while. We had decided to spend the rest of the evening at the apartment, eating, having a few drinks, listening to music, and making out—our standard formula for a great evening.

Early in my stay, we had discussed getting engaged. She said it was not a good idea because I was going far away and we wouldn't see each other for God knew how long. The truth was that if her father learned we were engaged there would be a family upheaval. Everyone was afraid of what Roy the drunk might do.

We agreed to write three times each week and talk on the phone at least once a month. She said, "Couples had the same problems during WWII and survived; so will we." She reassured me: "Alf, I love you and always will. We'll be together eventually. I just know it will all work out for us."

I answered with little conviction. "Okay, we'll hang in. You know how much I love you. I'll be home on leave in a few months." She was all smiles and reassurances. I did my best, but I didn't share her optimism.

Early the next morning, Gin drove Mom and me to the Pittsburgh airport. Mom was focused on our meeting in California in a few weeks, so she had no tears. Gin cried gently as we swore we'd get through this separation with our love intact. We had our lives ahead of us, and nothing could push us apart.

I boarded a DC-3 for Chicago. It was my first airplane flight. In Chicago, I switched to a TWA Constellation for the eight-hour flight to Los Angeles. The sadness of leaving Gin was replaced somewhat by the thrill of looking at the earth from thousands of feet in the air and the excitement of beginning a new adventure.

As the plane approached LAX, I looked down at a carpet of multicolored lights. Bright searchlights crisscrossed the sky. The scene looked like a movie of the London Blitz, with antiaircraft gun crews trying to spot our plane and shoot it down. [22]

As the Connie touched down, excitement rushed through me. I was on the ground in California. I had dreamed years before that I'd come here someday and the day had finally arrived.

22 From the late forties to the sixties, every opening of a new LA business and every used-car sale felt compelled to have at least one searchlight pointed to the sky. The custom died out eventually. LA is still a beautiful city to fly into at night. The earth is a carpet of lights for the last half hour of the flight.

Al in navy boot camp, circa late March, 1952

Al and shipmate, outside barracks, circa June, 1952

Yeoman School friends, third from left is Rick Hanover, next man is Paul Schnoblin, September, 1952

Yeoman School graduating class. Rick is second man from left in top row – Paul is sixth man from left in 4th row – Al is fifth man from right in fourth row - late September, 1952

CHAPTER 27

Some people follow their dreams,
others hunt them down
and beat them mercilessly into submission.
—Neil Kendall, English lecturer (unknown–living)

To be successful,
you must decide exactly what you want to accomplish,
then resolve to pay the price to get it.
—Bunker Hunt, oil executive, speculator (1926–living)

CALIFORNIA, HERE I AM

When I walked down the stairs from the plane, Uncle Al and Aunt Thelma were there waving to me (this was a long time before covered ramps and airport security). It had been about two years since we had seen each other, and they barely recognized me. I was now taller than Uncle Al. I was delighted that they planned to drive me to Los Alamitos.

Los Angeles was expanding rapidly, and new streets were created almost daily. Uncle Al said that road maps were always months out of date, but he knew the way. After a food stop, he got lost. They finally dropped me at the Los Alamitos Naval Air Station main gate near midnight and left immediately to find their way home. They had gone to a lot of bother for me, and I was grateful.

Getting Started

After a night in a transient barracks I went to the personnel department and handed in my orders. There should have been a letter or wire transmission notifying the base of my arrival date, but they had no record of any kind with my name or ID number on it.

The chief in charge agreed that my hand-carried transfer papers were in order. I said I expected to be in the legal department due to my training on UCMJ and asked if he could assign me there until my files arrived. He said that perhaps I could just wait patiently while he checked with BUPERS (Bureau of Naval Personnel). Meanwhile, I couldn't leave the base, get a bunk assignment, have a job, access my bank account, or get paid.

I asked if I could walk around the base and he was okay with that. But he gave me a hard look and said, "You are not to leave the base." He was a hard-ass, by-the-book, chief with the attitude of a Nazi, the imagination of a flea, and the suspicious nature of a prison guard. He did give me a chow pass. I had used up nearly all my cash at home. I counted my cigarettes and decided rationing was in order.

That afternoon and the next day, I wandered around, exploring every nook and cranny of the base. It was impressive. There was an Olympic-sized swimming pool; a large EM club with several TVs; a golf practice range; a baseball field; a large gymnasium for basketball, badminton, and Ping-Pong; and finally—thank God—a library. It was not a large one, but at least it was a quiet place to read. I ventured into the plane hangars, then to the edge of the field and watched fighters doing simulated carrier landings. There was a relatively current movie every night in a large auditorium. I had adequate creature comforts but no job, no freedom, and no money.

Since I was in a transient barracks, I had no locker and was given a new bunk assignment each day. Every morning I had to repack my sea bag and put it in storage before going to chow. Just before lunch, I visited the personnel office and was told that they hadn't heard anything yet." After that, I went to the library to write letters and read.

After a week of this, I had a nodding relationship with a 3rd class petty officer named Montana. He worked directly for the hard-ass chief. After learning I was a yeoman school grad, he told me that he had gone to the class A school after two years as a yeoman apprentice. Then he invited me to sit with him at lunch.

He was from a poor Mexican family, married with no children, and intended to make the navy his career. He explained that the main mission of Los Alamitos was the care and feeding of the reservists who came in on weekends. He said, "Al, we started calling them nose pickers a couple of years ago and the name has stuck."

"Why nose pickers?" I asked.

He said, "Because they stand around with nothing else to do." It sounded like a good nickname to me.

After lunch, he volunteered to send a wire to Bainbridge and request that a tracer be put on my records. Back in his office, he arranged a permanent bunk and locker assignment for me in the barracks nearest the chow hall. When I asked about pay, he said, "You're screwed until we establish that the orders you brought are not forgeries." The forgery wrinkle hadn't occurred to me.

While unpacking my sea bag into my new locker, I met Ray Helstrom, a friendly guy who bunked nearby. We sat together at chow after which he suggested going to the EM Club for a beer. I explained my order mix-up and said that I had no money. He offered to buy, and when I declined, he handed me $20 and said, "Pay me back when you get paid." We went to the EM club and were pals by the end of the evening. This was the beginning of a long friendship that lasted many years after the navy.

Late one morning, after ten days of hanging around, Montana gave me a happy handshake. My personnel file had arrived from Terminal Island (TI), where it had been waiting for my arrival. He let me look through it. Somehow after I had been handed the orders sending me to Los Alamitos, they had been changed to TI. As far as the navy was concerned, I had been AWOL since the day after I arrived at Los Alamitos.

Montana said I was being considered for Building 16 which, he opined, was the best place on the base to work. He said, "All you have to do is interview with Chief Morrey at 0800 tomorrow. If you click with him and Commander Wilson, you'll be assigned to that office. Your personnel file will be messengered over there immediately."

My curiosity was aroused, and I asked, "Well, if my file was sent to TI and my handheld orders were a mistake, shouldn't I be going to TI?"

He held up his hand to stop me and said, "Scheid, you just got a big break. Don't f**k it up. You'd hate TI; everybody stationed there hates it. Don't blow it by asking too many questions."

He gave me a liberty pass, which entitled me to go off base after work and on days off. He also handed me several papers to take to the bursars' office to straighten out my pay situation. A few minutes later, I had cash in my pocket and back pay added to my savings account. Montana had done well by me and I had to return the favor.

Building 16

Building 16 was just a few buildings away from the base headquarters. I decided to scope out the place. As I walked into the lobby, I could hear the clacking of many typewriters coming from the open doors of a large office. I peeked in and saw at least twenty desks with sailors wearing white T-shirts sitting at most of them. I explored both floors of the building and discovered they were made up of a series of other similar large open offices with desks but no people.

The next morning, I was at the counter at exactly 0800. The chief arrived about 0830. He had a friendly look as he offered me a seat in front of his desk and began peering into my personnel file. Without looking up, he commented, "Your GCT scores and grades from yeoman school are quite impressive. How did you like the school?"

"It was hard work, but I enjoyed it and hope I can put what I learned to good use." He seemed satisfied and began asking all the usual get-acquainted questions. He volunteered that he also went to class A yeoman school after serving as a yeoman during WWII. It was dawning on me that class A yeoman school grads saw themselves as sort of a fraternity.

I showed him the thick loose-leaf binder of the UCMJ and key judicial opinions that I had been issued. He said he'd never seen one before. I offered to loan it to him. Then he launched into a description of the mission of Building 16.

He explained that the building was a beehive of activity with fully staffed offices every weekend, when hundreds of reservists arrived for their monthly meetings with their squadrons. Everyone in Building 16 worked weekends, dealing with the extensive paperwork necessary to keep the reservists organized.

On Mondays and Tuesdays, it was a ghost building, with only two men on duty in case of an emergency. The rest of the week was spent getting paperwork ready for another group of squadrons arriving on Friday.

It sounded interesting, but my interest was in working with lawyers on trials. I said nothing.

He led me to a private office to meet Commander Wilson, the officer in charge of Building 16. I put my hat on as we walked (a sailor, unlike a soldier, never salutes unless he is "covered"). Upon entering, I gave a sharp salute and stood at attention. The commander gave a casual return salute and told me to uncover and take a seat. I sat at attention with my hat in my lap. I wanted the commander to see that I knew the protocol of enlisted man behavior. I could tell he liked it.

After glancing through my personnel file, he looked up and said, "I'm going to be honest with you, Scheid. The enlisted men in this office are almost all reserve volunteers, with little experience or training in anything. They volunteered for active duty to avoid the draft, but maneuvered themselves into what's called the station keeper program. You have to have "connections" to get such a soft deal. Regular navy men don't like the station keeper program, but we're stuck with it."

He went on to explain that station keepers had to do only a four week "learn to march and salute" boot camp in San Diego. "It's not like the boot training you got, Scheid. You did regular boot and went to a real navy school." He opined that nearly all of the men in the office were college graduates, mostly from the University of Southern California. Most were fraternity boys, and he didn't like that about them either.

He said it was hell trying to get these slugs to work. All they wanted to do was play basketball, hit golf balls, lie around the pool, and go to the beach. He had no respect for what he called "California beach boys," who avoided the draft and got easy duty because their families had connections.

When he learned I was from a small town in Ohio and had worked in factories, my image got another big boost. He was from a working-class family in central Pennsylvania. We had common ground.

Finally, I pointed out that I was specially trained for UCMJ work. I also explained that my missing orders had been found at TI, where trials were held, and that my hand-carried orders sending me to Los Alamitos had been rescinded.

He looked up and said, "I'm aware of all that. Now, are you telling me you want to go to TI, Scheid?"

"Well, sir," I replied, "I was expecting to be working with lawyers."

His retort was, "Do you know anything about TI?"

"No, sir, I don't."

He proceeded to explain the place in detail, about the prison, the lack of recreational facilities, the long hours lawyers and their helpers worked, and many other unattractive aspects about a job I would have at TI. Having explored the excellent facilities at Los Alamitos, I grasped his point.

He said, "Scheid, Los Alamitos is known as the country club of the navy. Men would give a testicle to be here. You're one lucky sonuvabitch." I knew he was right about that.

I had learned from experienced sailors that if you kept a senior officer happy, he could make your life easy. In addition, the commander could hold up any request I might make to set things right with my orders. During that delay, he could and probably would make life miserable for me. It was an easy decision.

I said, "Commander, I see your point and I'm happy to be on this base. I'll work hard at whatever assignment I'm given."

He was smiling as he walked me to the door with his hand on my shoulder. "Scheid, your record is outstanding, and you have the training we need. You'll be happy here—welcome aboard." He gave me a strong handshake, and just like that, I had a cushy job and a friendly commanding officer. TI was never mentioned again, and I was never sorry I stayed at Building 16.

Since the chief had been so friendly, I asked how I had been reassigned to this base. In a conspiratorial tone, he said that Montana had tipped him off about the mix-up in my orders and that I was a yeoman school graduate. When my file was found, the personnel chief had called a pal of his at TI and had it sent to him. He called Chief Morrey, and they worked out a deal with some friends in personnel at TI to reassign me to Los Alamitos. Somehow they were going to make everything copasetic with BUPERS. I never learned how they did that.

The chief had a chance to steal a trained man for his office, and he took advantage of it. The navy had trained me for a job I would never do, but what a lucky break it was for me.

The next day I was assigned to head a small department, composed of two men and me. We were to do all the paperwork for reservists going on or off active duty. But, my personal job was to review all forms and memos being sent to BUPERS. This job was critical because two weeks earlier, a senior officer at BUPERS had sent a memo to Commander Wilson, complaining about paperwork mistakes coming out of Building 16. The base commander had been copied and he was not pleased. The letter amounted to a reprimand of the Chief and the Commander. By coincidence, just days after that letter, a yeoman school grad - with high graduation marks - had dropped into their laps. Timing is everything.

When I found mistakes, I was to go to the culprit, get the mistake fixed, and do some training to prevent a recurrence. The chief said he was too busy with administrative work to check every form, and no one else in the office had the training to do it. All I had to do was make sure BUPERS had no further complaints and I would be a hero.

The word in school had been that there is a wrong way, a commonsense way, and the navy way. The navy way wins every time. I was determined to do the job well and stay in favor with the chief and the commander. I began this effort with some trepidation. BUPERS forms were not easy to fill out correctly, and there were constant changes. Fortunately, I had brought my training pamphlets with me.

The existing paperwork snarl was hateful, but I forced myself into it. The office was way behind with filing, and it was often difficult to find folders. When I discussed this with the chief, he assigned a full time WAVE to me for filing duty. Now I had three people to keep organized. [23]

Who Stands Watches?

The chief told me to report for roll call at 1700 in front of the HQ building for my first duty day (in addition to a regular job). About sixty men and WAVES were there. My name wasn't called, so I assumed my paperwork had not yet been processed. I went to the nightly movie while most of the others stood watches on the flight line and around the hangars.

The next day, I told Montana that my paperwork had not yet found its way to the watch lists. He asked slyly, "Do you want to stand night watches on your duty days?"

I answered, "Hmm, no, not really. Why?"

"Who do you think left your name off the duty watch list?"

I got it and said, "You, of course."

Smiling he said, "Yes, that could be the case. Would you *really* like to thank me?"

I nodded and said, "Of course."

Montana grinned. "Then meet me for chow tonight and bring some of that back pay I got for you. We'll take a walk after dinner and discuss it."

We took that short walk, and it cost me $30 to say thanks properly. It was one of the great bargains of my life. I didn't stand a watch on my duty days until someone other than Montana revised the watch list a year later.

23 WAVE is the acronym for Women Accepted for Voluntary Service. It was started during WWII so young women could serve in the active duty navy. They did mostly clerical work, freeing up men for more physically demanding duty. The program was still active during the Korean War.

Mom's Arrival

Mom arrived in California. In a few days, she had a job as a clerk in the jewelry concession in a unique store called Crawford's at Five Points—more about Crawford's later.

By year's end we were both enjoying the absence of cold weather and snow. By our standards, there was no winter in Southern California, just some rainy and chilly days. Mom missed her friends and I missed Gin, but other than that, we both loved our new state.

CHAPTER 28

To accomplish great things,
we must not only act, but also dream;
not only plan, but also believe.
—Anatole France, Nobel Laureate, (1844–1924)

The woods are lovely, dark, and deep,
But I have promises to keep,
And miles to go before I sleep,
And miles to go before I sleep.
—Robert Frost, poet laureate (1874–1963)

FITTING IN

I put my Dale Carnegie lessons to work as best I could and, in a few weeks, was being accepted into the Building 16 crowd. My goal was to make sure the chief and the commander were pleased with my work without looking like an ass kisser. The number of bitchy notices from BUPERS had been reduced from about one or two each week to none for over a month.

My group was operating like a well-oiled machine. Once learned, the paperwork was simple; we just had to stay on top of it. The chief left me alone except for approving memos I wrote to BUPERS to correct old mistakes. Chief Morrey was a nice man who just wanted to live a trouble-free life until his retirement.

The station keepers in Building 16 were generally a friendly bunch. Over time, nearly every man came to me with a question on a regulation or about filling out a form. Knowing the answers or where to find them was a great contact point. My training was being used in a meaningful way.

By the Christmas season, I was drinking beer and swapping jokes at the EM Club with nearly everyone. Paul and Rick had been my first educated friends, but now I was working and socializing with college graduates all day and many evenings. No one seemed to mind that I hadn't been to college, even though a few kidded me about my Ohio Valley accent. By January, I was settled in my job and was becoming comfortable in my new social life.

The chief liked to arrive late and leave early. To get away with this, he needed two key men to trade off opening and closing the office. The chief told me that he had picked me to replace a key man who was leaving. He saw this as an honor bestowed - it was his way of thanking me for doing a good job. Actually it was a pain to be the first in and last out. I was flattered that he showed such confidence in me after such a short tenure.

There were also advantages to the job. I could stay as late as I pleased, typing letters or just reading in peace and quiet. The SPs were advised of my new status, and they never questioned me about going in or out of the building, day or night. It also made it easier for me to carry on a small business that developed.

Cumshaw—A Successful Business

When a reservist went on active duty, he turned in all the uniform items he had been issued. When he got to boot camp he was issued a new sea bag full of clothing. My admissions-discharge group took the uniforms, shoes and all. Most men went on active duty soon after joining the reserves, so their uniforms were mostly new.

The system set up by my predecessor was to put these uniforms into a large storage room next to our office and secure it with a padlock. He had never set up an inventory system, so no one knew how much stuff was in the room or who had turned it in. As the group leader, I had the only key to the padlock.

My original thought had been to create an inventory log and keep track of the stuff we took in. It took about two days for me to figure out that I had been given a navy clothing store with free inventory. My attitude was that there was no inventory system when I took over and no one told me to create one. If I was ever asked about it, I would just play dumb. The ethics were questionable, but it turned out to be a profitable decision.

Cumshaw is essentially anything you can scavenge (or steal) and then trade for favors, money, or other cumshaw. Cumshaw was an active cottage industry at Los Alamitos because the rules were so lax.

Montana was a smaller guy who had difficulty getting uniforms that fit well. I searched the clothing locker and assembled shoes and other items that I judged would fit him. I stowed them in a nearby locker, on which I put my own combination lock. Each time he did a favor for me, I gave him one or two items. He became my fount of base knowledge and I was his source of uniforms. It was the perfect cumshaw for both of us. Mess cooks ruined shoes quickly due to spills and splashes, so I made a deal with several cooks; I traded shoes for back door access to the chow hall any time I wanted in. My best friends and I never went hungry.

The Art of Party Crashing

Grover Simmons was about three years older than I and was fun-loving and gregarious. He had been an Eagle Scout and had the energy and intellect that implies. When we met, we liked each other immediately. He had volunteered for the marines after graduation from Stanford. Somehow he had gotten himself transferred to the navy and assigned to Los Alamitos. It was a real coup because his home was just a few miles away in Santa Ana. His job was teaching basic boot camp classes for the athletes stationed at our base. He had a car and a lust for going places and doing things.

Grover was many times more sophisticated about the world than I was. By his standards, I was a country bumpkin and a bit of human clay that could (and should) be molded. I recognized that he'd taken me on as a project, and I was just smart enough to be grateful for the education. I did have a couple of qualifications. He observed that I could hold my booze, was not afraid of girls, and could dance well. These were the skills that qualified me to be Sancho Panza to his Don Quixote.

In early December, he told me we were going to a party in Long Beach on Friday night and another one on Saturday. I asked, "Whose party?"

He said, "We'll figure that out when we get there. Just wear your suit and tie. We have to look nice."

Various departments of Douglas Aircraft and other large companies began having Christmas parties on Friday and Saturday nights in early December. We would hang around the entrances to the parties, looking for a way in. Grover preferred that we find two girls who would take us in as their dates. He said that he'd been doing this during holiday seasons for years. The only risk was that we'd be asked to leave and would have to go find another party.

An engineering department at Douglas was the sponsor of the first party we found in one of the best hotels. We blended in with the crowd, acted as if we belonged, and strolled in with other arriving guests. Immediately, Grover spotted two attractive young ladies, sidled over, and asked them to dance with us.

When we walked them back to where we'd found them, two men were waiting for us and asked for our IDs. Without hesitation, Grover showed them his navy ID and said we were from Los Alamitos.

One of the men asked, "Did anyone invite you here?"

Grover answered, "No, sir, but Douglas Aircraft delivers planes to our base, and we thought the company wouldn't mind if we had a Christmas drink and a dance. Sailors don't make much money, you know."

The guys were stymied. They didn't really want to throw us out, but we had gone after the girls they wanted.

The girls chimed in, "Come on, let them stay. No one will notice in this crowd."

Grover pulled one of the men aside and assured him we'd walk away. That closed the case. The men said they wouldn't turn us in. We stayed until we had enough booze to feel good, and then we went down the street to another hotel.

This time, we stationed ourselves near the ladies' room in the lobby and followed two average-looking young secretary types to another party. Just before they reached the door, Grover approached them and asked if they would take us into the party with them—or would they rather go to the bar for a drink with us? Grover turned on the charm and in a minute we walked in with them, arm in arm. No one took notice of us, and we stayed, dancing and drinking until the party was breaking up.

After work on Saturday, we showered and dressed up for another night in Long Beach. The parties seemed to have suspicious doormen at every entrance. We managed to get into only one party with the girl-pick-up system and had a dance and a drink before a bouncer told us to leave.

Grover was not going home early on Saturday night, so we walked down Ocean Boulevard to the next hotel. As we got there, about thirty men, all wearing American Legion caps, were marching in single file down the boulevard behind a trombone, a trumpet, and a drum. We fell into line with them. The musicians led the group into a hotel bar overlooking the bay. One of the men asked us, "Aren't you boys a little young for an American Legion convention?"

We pulled out our ID cards and Grover said, "We're on active duty, based at Los Alamitos Air Station. We saw you guys having a good time and just thought we'd join in."

The men said things like, "Terrific, glad to have you, have a drink, come back to the hotel with us and have some chow," and so on.

After a couple of drinks and getting acquainted, the band started up and the group headed back to their hotel, where they marched through the lobby and into their party room. We ate, drank, and met many more legionnaires, all of whom were cordial and kind. Singing began and they were surprised I knew songs from the thirties. We had massive hangovers on Sunday.

A week later, we met two girls who were attending a party with the parents of one of them. The girls were from Riverside and were students at the University of California at Berkeley. One of them took to Grover in a hurry. The other was stuck with the high school graduate, but she was a nice girl and told me a lot about college. She was not a good dancer, so I became the instructor and that helped bridge the educational gap. She liked her booze and was affectionate when we sneaked away onto a balcony for a little necking. Everything went fine, and we stayed to the end of the party. On the way back to the base, Grover told me he had set a date for us to go to Riverside and see the girls before they headed back to school.

The next Saturday we drove to Riverside. We picked up paper cups, ice, orange juice, and vodka before meeting the girls. Mixing these ingredients created a screwdriver, an aptly named new drink at the time. Grover and his girl had decided we'd go to a drive-in movie, drink screwdrivers, and make out. We all had a good time

Grover managed to drive the fifty miles back to the base while I slept all the way. He got practically no sleep. Grover and I had good times together.

Another New Friend

A few days after I began working in Building 16, I met a station keeper named Jim Jackson. He was tall, friendly, always smiling, and one of the most popular men in the office. He had only two years of college and no intention of doing more. Jim also had a wry, sometimes even cruel, sense of humor and liked to drink beer. We were made for each other. My old Ohio jokes were new to him, and we laughed a lot when we were together. Jim was married to a beautiful girl named Aline, who was half-Irish and half Narragansett Indian. Married men were permitted to live off base, so Jim was in a carpool for a seventy+ mile round trip from Burbank every day.

Two men had to be in the office when it was closed on Mondays and Tuesdays. Jim and I did some successful trading of duty day assignments so we could do our required duty days together.

The petty officer who ran the EM Club and I became friendly. After acquainting him with my cumshaw capabilities, we agreed on two twelve can cases of beer as a swap for new shoes, pants, and a jumper (top half of a navy uniform). I delivered the beer into Building 16 after dark and put it into one of my secure lockers.

On our next duty days, Jim came up with the idea of using a CO2 fire extinguisher to chill the beer. We put four cans of beer in an empty wastebasket, aimed the fire extinguisher nozzle into it, and squeezed the handle for a short burst, and then another. In just a couple of seconds, the beers were frozen solid. With experimentation, we learned to put the beer under crumpled paper for a perfect chill.

Because it was illegally obtained and consumed during duty hours, it was great-tasting beer. With the system perfected, we never had another completely sober Monday/Tuesday duty day. It never occurred to us that we could get arrested and do time in the brig for drinking on duty. When Jim and I were together, we always had a great time, but we didn't think very deeply.

Not the Navy I Had Known

Discipline at Los Alamitos was loose. Everyone wore white T-shirts in the office, putting on regulation navy jumpers only when it was chilly and to walk outside. Everyone took more than the allotted hour for lunch. We also had unusual services available.

The classic racket on the base was our "come to your door" bookie, who was also the trash truck driver. As they traveled around the base the driver and his helper picked up money for bets. All one had to do was hand them the money and a note selecting the horse, race, and track. They scribbled receipts, which they gave to the bettors. They stopped their truck at pay phones and called in the bets to the driver's father, who had a bookie operation in LA.

Few of us knew much about horse racing, but betting was the thing to do. We studied the racing form carefully and convinced ourselves we knew what we were doing. We pooled our money and usually made a place bet. We won about a race a week and lost our money slowly but surely. This racket was going when I arrived at Los Alamitos, and it was still going when I left.

Extra Money and Wheels

I told Uncle Al that I intended to find a job for my days off. He was pleased with my ambition and said, "How about painting houses? I just signed a contract to paint over fifty of them. But this is hard work."

"Could it be harder than hand loading tires into boxcars or framing houses?"

He said, "Okay, find a way to get here and you can work for me whenever you want."

A few days later, in the base parking lot, I spotted an old Model A Ford coup for sale. A day and $50 later, I was its proud owner. It had a ragged top and the side windows were missing. It was a mess, but it ran. I drove to El Monte the next Sunday evening, worked two days for Uncle Al and drove back on Tuesday evening. I wore my heavy navy peacoat, a wool cap, and heavy gloves with a wool blanket over my lap; it was cold but invigorating. This routine was repeated for a number of weeks.

The old Ford refused to start one Sunday, and I had to hitchhike to El Monte and back to the base on Tuesday night, arriving on both ends late, hungry, and freezing. A navy friend and I got the damned Ford running well enough to sell it to another sailor for $50.

A few days later, I bought a 1935 Ford coupe. It looked good, but its obsolete mechanical brakes had a tendency to lock. After a near accident at an intersection, Jim Jackson convinced me to sell it.

My next try was a 1941 Cadillac for which I paid $300 at a used-car lot in El Monte. It was a real hit to my savings, but it lasted until a few months after I left the navy.

Night School

One evening, Ray Helstrom took me to Long Beach City College to look into night classes. I signed up for Psychology 1A. It was easy and fun. The other class had a highfalutin name, something like Advanced English Communication. It was really about diction and pronunciation for people with accents. This speech class, and coaching by friends, was how I managed to drop my Ohio Valley accent and slang phrases. When the semester ended, I had achieved an A in each of my first two college courses.

Painting Career Ends

Near quitting time one Tuesday a fat, six-foot-plus man showed up and began yelling at the painter with whom I was working. Uncle Al, who was about five feet eight inches and 150 pounds, arrived on the scene a moment later. The man was shouting, "You sonuvabitch, you're a union man, and here you are working for this f*****g nonunion scab contractor! And who the hell is this guy?" he snarled, pointing at me.

An argument ensued. The union man shouted threats and called names. Uncle Al yelled back an equal number of threats and followed him to his car with me close behind. He invited the man to get out of the car and get the shit kicked out of him. The fat ass drove away. The scene made me feel like I was back in Bridgeport. The day's work was over. In a few minutes, we calmed down and got our gear together. Uncle Al said he'd call and let me know the end result of the dustup. I had a hunch my days as a painter were over.

A couple of days later, Uncle Al phoned that he had to use union painters to finish the tract. I wanted the money, but I was not terribly disappointed. Compared to carpenter work, painting walls and ceilings was boring. Now I had to find another job. Fortunately, one came along easily.

A large, muscular station keeper named Jerry Gresham had been transferred into Building 16. His father had taught him the plastering trade, and he was doing small jobs on his days off. It came out that he had trouble finding a hod carrier for only two days' work each week. While working for the Lyle brothers, I had watched hod carriers. They were well paid because it was such arduous work.

I asked Jerry for the job and he said he needed help the following Monday and Tuesday. He was concerned about a yeoman working that hard but was willing to give me a try. He offered me $3 per hour, about double what Uncle Al had been paying and the highest hourly rate I'd ever earned.

For the next few Mondays and Tuesdays, I was able to add hod carrier to my growing list of job experiences. Jerry was a patient teacher, and by the end of the first day, I had learned to mix and dump the "mud" (wet cement) correctly and in the right places. For the two days, he paid me $50 in cash—no tax deductions. This was great! For working eight days each month, I could make $200. At the time, experienced secretaries and bank tellers were making about $200 per month.

Evening Work

In anticipation of night school ending, I decided to find an evening job. When I mentioned this to the guys during a coffee break one day, a newly arrived transferee said he had an idea for me.

Moe Flantzman, a Jewish kid from San Francisco, had just come to work in Building 16. He had graduated from UCLA and was planning on a career in the advertising business. He was lazy, and the chief was on his ass constantly. On the good side, he had a great sense of humor and was funny. We joked and laughed constantly.

Moe sold *Los Angeles Times* newspaper subscriptions door-to-door. Using a reverse telephone directory, the *Times* sales supervisor created cards with the names and addresses of the residents of a preselected street.

The next evening, I went with Moe during his first few calls and observed him in action. When a resident opened the door, there was Moe in his navy uniform, wearing a phony gold wedding ring and a smile. He greeted them by name, such as, "Good afternoon, Mr. Jones." [24] Immediately, he would explain that he was getting out of

24 It was against navy rules to wear the uniform while working off the base, but the chances of getting caught were minimal. We decided that if a uniformed officer answered the door, we'd just ask directions to a local street and move on. If an officer out of uniform identified himself after the sales pitch began (which happened to Moe once), the plan was simply to run like hell and get out of the neighborhood - which he did.

the navy in a week, and if he could just get twenty subscriptions to the *Times* by then, the paper was going to give him a job in the circulation department. His clincher was, "You only have to sign up for a month and pay two dollars now. The *Times* will bill you for future months, but you can quit the paper in a month. Mr. Jones, you will have helped a Korean War veteran have a job waiting for him. My bride will be happy too; we've only been married a couple of months. I would sure appreciate your help—it's just two dollars."

He sold about one of every four people he pitched. The deal was that the salesmen gave the subscription card to the *Times* man and kept the $2 as a commission.

The first evening I made $6. Moe did much better—and always did. After a few evenings, I was making $6 to $8 for a little over two hours of effort.

Common sense told me that getting caught selling in uniform could be disastrous. There had to be better evening jobs. The *Long Beach Press Telegram* came to the office every day, and I began scanning the help wanted ads.

I answered an ad from Cutco Cutlery, a division of Alcoa Aluminum. The man who answered the phone gave me an address for a meeting in Long Beach at six.

At the meeting he began with, "I'm Charlie, a successful Cutco Cutlery salesman and manager of the Long Beach District. If you give me your full attention, I'll teach you how to make money selling this excellent product, manufactured by Alcoa Aluminum, one of the finest companies in the world." He slowly opened a dark polished wooden box with rows of slots, each holding a knife. They looked great.

Then Charlie did a sales pitch during which he described the uses and high quality of the knives. At the end of his show, he used a long knife to cut a slice of soft white bread in half lengthwise, creating two slices from one. The knife was so sharp that it did this with no effort. He passed out knives and cutting boards and had each of us create two bread slices from one.

Charlie explained that Cutco's primary marketing plan was to sell the knives to young women of marriageable age who were in the process of creating hope chests for their wedding day. The trick was to find girls who would invite their girlfriends to attend a demonstration. If one of the friends bought a set of knives, the sponsor received a knife as a gift and a discount on a full set. If enough friends eventually bought sets, the sponsor could get a set of knives free. The problem was that, except for the two WAVES in the office, I didn't know even one girl.

We had to buy our demonstration kit for cash to become Cutco salesmen. The cost was about $70, a hefty chunk of change at that time. This hurdle eliminated about half the attendees. I decided to take the leap, figuring that I'd give the knives to Mom as a present if things didn't work out.

Alcoa advertised in magazines that single girls read. The ads offered a free gift if a girl would send in her phone number. A few did, and Charlie gave me one of these leads.

The first girl, call her Ellen, agreed to let me come by her house in the evening. I was nervous but figured I could do no worse than being sent away by an irate father. At seven I rang the doorbell of a small, well-kept home in a Long Beach neighborhood. The father came to the door and invited me into the living room, where he introduced me to Ellen and her mother. In a few minutes, I was launched into my first presentation.

I must have muddled through it well enough because her father showed real interest. He said he would buy a starter set for Ellen if she would promise to pay for the rest of a full set from her earnings as a receptionist.

After writing up the order, I explained to Ellen how it was possible to get her full set free by inviting some of her girlfriends to a demonstration. As I was leaving, her father turned to Ellen and said, "Honey, I think you should call your girlfriends. Al's an ambitious young man, and he's selling a good product." He gave me a look that required a reply.

I said, "I'll call Ellen tomorrow and work things out with her." In a few seconds, I was out the door and breathing easily for the first time in an hour. I had made my first sale on my first call and I felt lucky.

When I reported to Charlie, he was pleased and asked me to drop off the check and order form the next day and get more training on how to proceed with Ellen. I smiled all the way back to the base.

At Charlie's insistence, I called Ellen from his house and asked if I could come by, give her some full-color Cutco brochures, and help her organize a meeting. She was cooperative.

The sponsored meeting went well. All four guests were receptive to buying Cutco. Unfortunately, two of them didn't have jobs. The other two bought starter sets and said they would consider holding meetings later.

When we parted, Ellen's father said, "Al, if you weren't in the navy, I'd offer you a job selling for my company. You meet people well and have some ambition. You should be selling something with more potential."

On my drive back to the base, I concluded that he was right. There was no long-term future to this kind of selling. I was negative on selling Cutco after only a week or so of a relatively successful sales effort. When I met with Charlie and told him I was not going to continue, he was flabbergasted. "Al, you got off to a great start. Now isn't the time to quit." Charlie loved selling Cutco and couldn't understand my decision. I gave my demo set of knives to Mom, and she used them for many years. Though overpriced, they were excellent knives.

Flying Lessons

Two pilot lieutenants, both Korea combat vets, moved into an adjoining office, and my little group was assigned to type letters for them. Their assignment was to interview college students who were potential NAVCAD recruits and they often took them flying as part of the program. One day as I was delivering some finished letters, I asked Lieutenant McClure if he would take me flying one day. I was surprised when he said yes.

Two days later both officers, another yeoman named Doug, and I went to the flight line and climbed on board two SNJ trainers. The pilots had decided it would be fun to let the two sailors do some flying (combat vets often came up with risky amusements). The plan was for us to take turns getting behind each other, and then the front plane had to get the following plane off his tail.

After half an hour of showing us how to maneuver the planes, they agreed by radio to go out over the ocean and begin the game. Over the intercom, Lieutenant McClure said, "Scheid, don't worry. I'll have my feet on the rudders and my hand on the stick. If you do something stupid, I'll correct it. Now, he's on your ass. Ditch him." And the fun was on. I used the controls aggressively, left and right, just as he had shown me. After a straight down dive and a sharp pullout to the right, Doug missed the turn and we escaped. McClure shouted, "You did it, good job! He's off our tail. Now circle around and get on his ass."

Once we were behind the other plane, Doug began his maneuvers. As we twisted and turned, we got lower and closer to the shoreline, near Huntington Beach. In an attempt to lose me, he dove toward the town and then pulled up sharply to the left. His plane lost air speed and the prop made a loud roaring sound. Our plane did the same as I followed him into the turn. McClure came on the intercom and said, "Oh, shit. I hope no one picked up our wing numbers. That was too much noise over a town."

The two pilots decided they should take over the controls and get back to the base. They were afraid they'd be reported for the noise—and they were.

The base commander called them in the next morning. Before going, they made Doug and me promise we'd never admit we had the controls for even a minute. They got off with an ass chewing and a warning. But Doug and I had a memorable experience.

Lieutenant McClure took me flying again and did aerobatics, which caused me to vomit. It was not fun cleaning up the plane after we landed, but I had to do it, sick or not. That was my only adventure with aerobatics.

On our last flight, he let me handle the controls, and we buzzed Mom's house in La Puente. I had tipped her off ahead of time, but she was at work and missed the show. A neighbor told her about it.

The lieutenant and I maintained a friendly relationship and he treated me like an equal, despite the difference in rank. After I was discharged, I learned that he was killed in Korea. He was a fun-loving flyboy who never got a scratch while giving close support to ground troops on many missions. Then, after the war ended, he was killed on a routine flight. Death is not fair.

Friends and Events

Grover took me to Corona del Mar Beach for my first dip in the Pacific. As he ran into the water, I followed, diving into a wave behind him. The first thing that hit me, besides the cold water, was the taste. Seawater was a salty shock to a guy who had never been in an ocean. In a short time, Grover had me diving through waves, swimming out to the break, and bodysurfing back to the beach. I loved every minute of it. After that, I went to the beach frequently - with Grover, Ray, and Jim as well as on my own. It would have been easy to become a beach bum in California.

A new station keeper arrived in Building 16. His name was Jerry Cassaday, and he lived in Long Beach. Jerry was twenty-three and already had a master's degree from the Wharton Business School. He was the most educated and well-read man in the building. Because of his willingness to put up with my uneducated questions, Jerry became influential in my life.

My friendships with Ray, Grover, Jerry, and Jim deepened. They each filled a role in my life. Ray was the street-smart guy from Vallejo, a tough navy town; Grover was a born teacher, constantly educating me in various ways; Jerry was my intellectual; and Jim was my new Wendell. He and I became best friends, sharing our thoughts on everything.

I loved visiting Grover's parents, who lived in a modest old bungalow in Santa Ana. His father was a blacksmith and worked full time putting shoes on riding and race horses. His mother made chicken dinners for us, with sweet potato pie for dessert. They were rightfully proud of their son, who had won a scholarship to Stanford and spoke perfect California English, unlike the Oklahoma country accent they had never lost.

Jerry was impressed that I had read Hitler's *Mein Kampf*, which led him to loan me a book of Schopenhauer's philosophy. After I read it and we had discussions, he assigned some Nietzsche and Hegel readings. I had no knowledge of these philosophers, but with Jerry's guidance, I began to understand some of what each of them believed about life. It was a new world to me inasmuch as philosophy had not been part of my past reading. With all this exposure to smart people, my secret desire to go to college was morphing into a life goal. I still felt like a hick in a big city, so I kept this thought to myself.

Exposure to Luxury

Jerry invited me to his family's home in Long Beach for dinner and an overnight stay. He had told me his father was the president of the Lomita Gasoline Company in Long Beach, and that made me nervous. I had met a president of a business only once - as a caddy. The backyard of the Cassaday house extended to the golf course of the Virginia Country Club, where Jerry's father was a member. I had never even been in a beautiful home like this.

Mr. Cassaday offered drinks. Jerry took a scotch and soda, and I said, "Same for me please." Carl had given me scotch and soda once and I didn't like it. To my surprise, I liked it this time. As we went into the dining room for dinner and it occurred to me I wouldn't know which fork to use. Fortunately, it was a weekday and the service was everyday knife, spoon, and fork. A servant brought the food courses to the table one at a time, and each was wonderful. Desert was a baked apple with thick cream sprinkled with cinnamon – it was wonderful. After dinner, we watched the largest TV set I had ever seen - with the best reception.

I thought; *People live like this only in the movies!*

Jerry had told his parents about me, and they asked questions about my upbringing. These were not questions I wanted to answer. I fudged the truth a bit and managed to change the subject. Mr. Cassaday said, "Jerry tells me you are a very smart young man and you should go to college. Have you decided where to go?" I said that I wanted to get a degree in business but money was a problem. Mr. Cassaday said, "If you really want an education, you'll find a way to get it."

I slept in a guest room that was, by my standards, quite large. The bed had crisp snow-white sheets and I had trouble falling asleep—unusual for me.

Early the next morning, when Jerry and I came down, his father was at the table, reading the paper. Mr. Cassaday renewed the conversation regarding my education. He suggested I look into Claremont Men's College, which Jerry's brother was then attending. He explained that the school was founded in 1946 and had not yet built a big reputation, but it was well financed, had an outstanding founder, and scholarships were available. He said he was willing to write to the president of CMC and give me a recommendation. I thanked him and said I would probably take him up on that offer.

During the drive to the base, I told Jerry that he and his father had inspired me about trying to go to college. He said, "Al, that's a very smart decision, and I'll help you as much as I can." From then on, he and Grover seemed to make me their project.

The visit to the Cassaday home popped into my daydreams for weeks. These memories were matched against the way my family lived. I had gotten a small taste of a luxurious lifestyle. I wanted to live like the Cassaday family but dared not dream that I could ever achieve that level.

I had met my first millionaire. I was surprised that he was a pleasant human being who had normal sons and a nice wife. He didn't have the superiority attitude I had observed in so many of the men from whom Wendell and I had stolen golf balls.

I thought of "Toto, I've got a feeling we're not in Kansas anymore." Well, I sure as hell wasn't in Ohio anymore.

Chapter 29

In the book of life, the answers aren't in the back.
—Charlie Brown, cartoon philosopher

In every question and every remark
tossed back and forth between lovers
who have not played out the last fugue,
there is one question and it is this:
"Is there someone new?"
—Edna O'Brien, novelist, poet (1930–living)

Concerns about Gin

Gin's letter writing had slowed down. When I received a letter, I wrote back within two days, but she often didn't reply for a week. I decided it was time for a visit home. Planes came and left the base each day, and their schedules were posted in flight operations. There was one going to Glenview, Illinois, the next Monday. If I could get leave quickly, I could fly to Glenview, hitchhike to Bridgeport—a mere four hundred miles—and be home sometime on Tuesday. That was a lot of bother for a few days at home, but I was dying to see Gin. I decided to arrive without notice and not risk her telling me not to come.

The chief said I had to speak to Commander Wilson about taking leave because we were busy planning for summer training sessions. The commander agreed that I had worked long and hard, and that a short vacation was in order. However, he extracted a promise that I would be back in ten days, missing only one weekend. Good old Montana rushed my papers through the personnel department.

On Monday morning I was waiting by the plane, dressed in a fresh white uniform and carrying a small bag. Our ETA in Glenview was before 6 p.m. central time, which was 7 p.m. in Bridgeport. It would take some luck to get rides once it got dark. I was betting on truck drivers seeing my white uniform.

It was a brand-new plane from Douglas, Long Beach. Except for about ten seats, it was completely empty and there was no padding on the inside of the fuselage to dampen the engine and wind sounds. It was a noisy airplane and a tiring trip, but we arrived on time.

Just about sunset, I was on a strange road with my thumb out. By midnight, I was in Indiana, where I got lucky. A patriotic truck driver picked me up. He let a tired sailor sleep for hours and then bought my breakfast. He let me out near Columbus. By late morning, I had a room in the old Valley Tourist Home in Brookside. The room was clean, cheap and about a mile from downtown Bridgeport.

Gin was surprised and a little uncomfortable with my call, but we agreed to meet after her workday. I hitched into town and spent the afternoon in the Pastime before we met in the Candy Kitchen. We went to a back booth and had a long, affectionate kiss. I realized how much I had missed physical contact with her.

After a few minutes she admitted that she had been dating Jack Donahie for several months. It was a blow but about what I had expected. She had a date with him that night—again, no surprise. The surprise came when she went to the pay phone, called him, and canceled. She said she told him that I had arrived unexpectedly and she wanted to be with me every evening while I was in town.

It had been our longest and most difficult separation. Gin insisted that her feelings were the same. She saw Jack because she had gotten lonely and tired of so much time with her girlfriends. She insisted that there was nothing intimate between them and that he was aware of her commitment to me. "But you could have told me," I moaned.

"I was afraid you'd get angry, go looking for a girl in California, and then I'd lose you." How could I argue with that logic?

We had dinner in Wheeling, went for a drive, and parked so we could kiss and talk privately. "I love you and only you," she whispered. "And I'll be here when you get back." This raised an issue I hadn't really dealt with. Would I ever return to live in Bridgeport? But I said nothing.

Mom's apartment was no longer available, and visitors of the opposite sex were not permitted in the tourist home rooms (midwest prudery again). We were like two homeless people, wandering around and looking for a place for intimacy. Her car was the only option.

Gin took a vacation day, and we drove to Pennsylvania to swim and sun at a resort we used to visit. We lacked the courage to play married and check into a motel, so we had dinner and came home late.

One day my grandparents drove in and joined me for lunch, and it was great to see them. Grandma pecked at me about how lucky I was to have a girl like Virginia. Her advice: "Marry that girl and take her to California with you. If she doesn't like it, you can always move back here." Her advice was heartfelt, but she didn't have the picture in full color.

Gin and I were hardly ever apart during my stay. By the time I left, I had regained confidence that we would be together somehow, someday, somewhere.

I took a train from Wheeling to Chicago, where I transferred to the Grand Canyon Special to Los Angeles. A sleeping car was too expensive, so for three nights and four days I sat in a chair car. I read paperback novels and tried to sleep. The bar car was well stocked, and about half my drinking was paid for by men who chatted about their time in the service. It always paid to travel in uniform. I promised myself that someday I'd make the same trip in a sleeper, getting off here and there to see the sights—one of many personal promises that would never be kept.

FINDING A JOB

Upon my return, it was time to get serious about finding an evening job. I got the want ad sections and stayed after work poring over the hundreds of jobs that were advertised.

One ad intrigued me: it was an evening job as a telephone representative for the RCA Television Service Company. The next morning, I sneaked off to an upstairs office and made the call. A man named Leland Lewis explained that his employment agency was screening applicants for RCA. He invited me to come to his office in Lynwood for an interview.

I filled out a lengthy application. Leland, a plump and pleasant man of about fifty, reviewed the form slowly and carefully. Then, the questions came. He wanted to know about yeoman school, my navy job, and my ambitions. He inquired about the steel mill, tire factory jobs, and baseball. I worked it in that I was a strong believer in the principles espoused by Dale Carnegie, and he liked that. He said, "I want you to go to the drugstore down the block and call me. I need to hear your phone voice."

In a few minutes we were on the phone. After many questions, he said, "Can you come into the RCA office in Lynwood tomorrow afternoon and meet the sales manager?"

The RCA Service Company was in a storefront building on Long Beach Boulevard. Leland was there, and after introducing me to Phil, the sales manager, he left. Phil began by saying, "You're young for this job, but Leland is really high on you because you've always worked and are a Dale Carnegie devotee."

Phil explained that many people who bought RCA TV sets declined to sign up for a service contract. The job was to call these people and persuade them to activate their service contract. He said that people didn't understand that a TV set was an imperfect product; vacuum tubes malfunctioned, the antenna got twisted (in 1953, a metal antenna on the roof received the signals) and picture tubes capriciously stopped working. For these reasons, everyone should have a service contract.

Then he said, "My experience is that the best way to find out if a man can do this job is to give him a minimum of information, then put him on the phone. If you click, you click, and if not we'll know it right away. Are you game to try it?"

He was a man who didn't like futzing around, so I said, "Let's do it."

He clapped his hands as he stood up and said, "Good attitude! Follow me." We went to an office where four men were talking on phones. He took a few cards from a pile, saying, "These are people who didn't buy a service contract." He sat down at a desk, picked up the phone, and dialed. He motioned me to pick up the same line at the next desk so I could listen in.

His approach was friendly but businesslike. It went something like this: "Hi, my name is Phil and I work for RCA Television. Mr. Jones, how is your new TV set working?" If the person said, "Just fine," his reply was, "Well, we want to keep it that way. Do you have any questions about operating the set?" If the person had complaints, he got right into them.

Once Phil had the person engaged in conversation, he asked, "May I call you [insert first name]?" The answer was always yes. Only after he was on first-name basis did Phil get around to the service contract. "Our records show that you didn't accept the service contract RCA offered you when you bought your new TV. My boss would appreciate it if I could tell him why you passed on it." They gave him a reason, usually the cost, which allowed Phil to explain the value of the contract. He asked anything to keep a chat going for at least three minutes, eventually working it into the conversation that a new picture tube cost over a $100 and the original warranty lasted only a year. "Mr. Jones, you have ninety days from the date of purchase of your TV to sign up for a service contract and you're still within that period."

He told me that TV salesmen rarely mentioned the high cost of a picture tube to customers because it might scare them off from buying the TV. The salesmen would rather forego the commission on the service contract than risk losing a TV sale.

Between calls, he told me that if all else failed, he always promised the customer he'd call them back before the ninety-day period ended. The odds were they would have some sort of reception problem by then. Lastly, he pushed them to take down his name and the office phone number in case they had a problem. He kept a log of every call for future reference.

Phil didn't let go of a potential sale. If a person hung up on him, he called back immediately and said, "Sorry, I believe my phone system cut us off." He gave up only if the person got angry, and even then, the card went into his logbook for a call two weeks later. He sincerely believed that everyone who owned a TV should have a service contract.

He called three customers over a twenty minute period and sold two service contracts. As he finished, he turned to me, "Now you see how easy it is, if you use the right approach. You must convince the customer that you're his friend." I knew little about selling, but I realized I was observing a master at work. I was hooked. I wanted the job. I made half a dozen calls and sold three or four.

Phil's final words that night were, "Okay, Al, I know you can do the job and you're hired for a trial. Come in as early as you can tomorrow. You'll have five evenings to show me you can be productive. I'll help you, but success has to come from inside you. If you want it to happen, you'll make it happen."

The next day, I sweet-talked the chief into letting off work early and was at RCA before four. After I filled out employment papers, the receptionist gave me a small stack of customer leads. Phil encouraged me: "Go ahead and get on the phone. Doing the job is the best training. I'll be in and listen after a while." When he showed up an hour later, I was pleased to show him two sales from my first seven calls. He said it was not a high percentage but not bad for a beginner.

The job came easily - it was like putting a baby duck in water. I followed Phil's systems, and he continued coaching me. The key was to be on the phone all the time, breaking only for a snack and nature calls. One difficult thing to accept was getting a hang-up before you could even explain why you were calling. Phil explained, "You can't take the rejection personally or let it influence your next call."

Phil's system was to accept a rejection and, with great sincerity, say, "I'm very sorry I disturbed you at a bad time." Then call back a few days later. Over the next few months, I learned things from Phil that I have used ever since.

Over time, my sales percentage increased. My routine was to get to Lynwood just after five, grab something from a nearby diner, and get on the phone. On my navy days off, I came in early, looked up phone numbers, and grabbed a phone as soon as the day people left and a desk was available.

The other salesmen left at nine, but I often stayed for up to an hour, organizing calls for the next day. By the end of the first month, my commission rate was over $40 per week. The minimum wage was then $.75 per hour, and my RCA earnings were running nearly $3 per hour. This was damn good for a part-time job in a clean office environment.

Most men couldn't take the grind. After two months, I was the senior salesman. Leland brought men in for interviews, so I saw him frequently. One day he invited me for a beer after work. As soon as we sat down, he said, "Al, you've done a fine job at RCA. What are your plans when the war is over?" I admitted I wanted to go to college.

He replied, "When you have a discharge date, come see me. Maybe we can get you a full-time sales job where you can earn some real money and save enough to go to college." I assured him that he was among the first people I would call when that glorious day came.

Mom's Romance

Mom lived in one of six small bungalows behind a large house. A man about her age had one of the other bungalows, and she invited him for dinner during one of my visits. It looked to me that they were having some sort of romantic relationship, but I followed my policy of letting her live her life.

George Pearce was a polite, gentle man who had little education. He made a modest living as an independent gardener. Mom asked what I thought of him. My appraisal was, "Mom, you had a husband named George who couldn't support you. Do you want another one?"

She wasn't pleased with my answer but assured me that she didn't intend to marry this George—once was enough. "But," she said, "This George is not like your father. He goes to work early every day, and he doesn't drink. He's nice to me, and I like his company."

One Monday, about a month later, Mom called me at Building 16. She said, "Everyone is just fine, but I have something important to tell you."

"What is it, Mom? I'm on duty and can't take much time."

"I know you'll be angry, but George and I were married last weekend in Mexico. I didn't call you because my mind was made up and I didn't want you talking me out of it."

I said, "Congratulations to both of you, Mom. George is okay with me. It's your life and you can marry anyone you want to marry."

"I know you think I'm making a mistake because George is just a gardener," she said.

"Well, Mom, time will tell if it was a mistake. It's not for me to judge." I promised to come for a visit soon. She seemed put at ease.

When I got off the phone, I thought, *She just wants someone to look after. She'll end up supporting him, just as she supported Dad. She loves losers.* It was a relief that I hadn't been invited to the wedding.

Pressure to Advance

The chief told me BUPERS had notified him that I had been eligible for the petty officer third class exam since March but I hadn't applied for it. He said it reflected badly on him and BUPERS would soon ask questions (he greatly feared BUPERS). I said it was just an oversight. I would get the forms and apply.

What the chief didn't know was that I had been dreading this day. I was aware that I could have taken the exam in March. When I had gone to personnel to pick up the application, Montana told me that the base had exceeded its compliment of petty officers. If I advanced in rank, I'd be the most junior third-class on the base and would most likely get transferred. I didn't want to exchange this cushy life for destroyer duty, so I didn't apply for the exam. I had played the Scarlett O'Hara game, and tomorrow had finally arrived.

The next day, I went to the personnel office and asked for the exam application. As Montana gave it to me, I asked, "What if I don't pass the test?"

He gave me a strange look and said, "That's risky business, Al. BUPERS will know you flubbed it on purpose ... and so will the chief. You'll probably get transferred anyway, and you'll get a shit job in a place you don't want to be."

When he approved the papers, the chief smiled and said, "Great. You'll get a nice raise."

About three weeks later, I sat for the exam. It was difficult to decide which questions to get wrong. I wanted to fail just enough that I could claim I had a bad day, a hangover, a cold—anything to convince the chief that I hadn't failed on purpose. When the test was completed, I thought, *It's in the laps of the gods; I've done all I can do.* Then I had about three weeks to sweat the results.

A Promise Broken

I had successfully kept my promise to myself that I would stay out of fights. On several occasions, I had put up with some crap I didn't like, just to avoid physical conflict. But nothing lasts forever.

One Friday night, I was sitting at a table at the EM Club with some weekend warrior yeomen when the WAVE in my group came in and took a seat at the bar. We waved to each other. She was a cute girl about my age who did her work quietly and efficiently. She had a civilian boyfriend and never dated sailors.

A little later, a guy at my table said, "Hey, one of our flight line crew guys is making a move on your WAVE." I looked and it was clear he was pressing the issue. After a few minutes, I decided to rescue her.

I walked over and invited her to join us. She was sliding off the bar stool when the flight line guy snapped at me: "I'm talking to this girl. Get the hell out of here!"

I replied, "You don't understand. We work together, and she's coming to my table."

He said, "I don't like assholes interfering when I'm talking to a girl." Mary told him she wanted to leave. He gave me a stare and said, "Okay, ball bearing WAVE (a very derogative name for a yeoman), I'll see you outside when you leave."

Without thinking, I retorted, "Do what you like, nose picker." I knew at once that was a mistake. Mary and I went to the table, where we learned from the guys that the flight crew man was a known troublemaker.

After another beer, we decided it was time to call it a night. As we walked past the flight crew guy, he got up and followed us out the door. Then he ran past us and turned around, saying, "Okay, asshole yeoman, stop and fight." He stood in front of me, calling me names. There was no way out. I moved my shoulders in a fake, just as my uncle had taught me. He responded to the fake, and I hit him hard in the face. He went down, but he began to get up quickly. He was drunk enough that he didn't even feel the blow. I hit him again as he was getting to his feet, but it didn't stop him. The punch throwing and clinching lasted about a minute before the guys I had been sitting with jumped in and broke it up.

When I got back to the barracks, I looked in the mirror and saw that I had a few scratches on my face, a bruise on my cheek and my uniform jumper was torn down the middle to my navel. Overall, I was in good shape, but I wasn't sure who won the fight. I took a shower, dabbed the blood off my face, and hit the sack.

The next morning, the mirror told me that the guy had long fingernails. The scratches on my face and neck were much worse than I had thought and it was obvious I had been in a fight. It didn't matter what I looked like; I had to open the office.

Mary blabbed to a couple of our office mates and word got around.

About midmorning, the chief called me over and asked for details. I said I had been in an argument that escalated to a fight. He wasn't pleased but went along with it because I had come to the rescue of a shipmate. As chiefs do, he liked his people sticking together.

When we went to chow, many questions were asked. I said, "If you want to be helpful, just leave it alone and don't talk about it. I don't want any SP involvement." The damn fools didn't seem to understand that fighting on the base could bring punishment. I wanted to avoid an investigation that might get me restricted to the base and cause me to lose my RCA job.

The weekend ended, Monday and Tuesday were our days off, and by Wednesday there were other things to gossip about. I hoped it would be my last fight. I genuinely didn't want any more. Fortunately, the event passed without a problem. I never saw the flight line guy again and neither did Mary. It is likely the EM Club was put off limits for him.

A Strange Relationship

Except for duty days, we had evenings free, plus all day on Mondays and Tuesdays. The weekend warriors were mostly men, with a sprinkling of WAVES, and it was sometimes a volatile mixture. From Friday afternoon until late Sunday afternoon, everyone was cut loose from spouses and significant others. Friday and Saturday night parties were common. During the summer, Saturday night beach parties were wild and lasted late into the night. Building 16 personnel were usually invited. My pals said it was like social life in college and even better since the girls were more mature and cooperative. I took their word for it and joined in wholeheartedly.

During normal work routine I met an attractive reserve WAVE named Norma. She was about thirty and a yeoman first class, three grades above my seaman first class rank. That evening we happened to be at the same beach party. After a couple of vodkas, we did a slow, hold close dance and became a couple for the evening. We sneaked away from the party and spent the rest of the evening in her car in a nearby parking lot, with me sneaking back for fresh drinks as needed.

After that first encounter, we spent Saturday nights together once each month. Norma made it clear that she wanted to keep our dalliance a secret. A few days in advance of her visit I received an unsigned typed note, telling me where to meet her on Saturday night. There was never a return address. She eventually let it slip that she lived in the San Fernando Valley but nothing more. She said she wasn't committed to anyone, but I suspected she was married. I didn't care enough to find a way to check her personnel file. She was right; we both knew everything we needed to know to keep the affair rolling. I had some guilt, but I knew Gin was seeing Jack Donahie and could only guess where that relationship was going. As I'd heard Grandma say, "What's fair for the goose is fair for the gander."

When Norma and I were together she told me a little about her active duty and college times. We talked about my college ambitions. After dinner, she parked her car in an appropriately private place and we adjourned to the backseat. I understood she was amusing herself with me on what might otherwise be a lonely weekend night. The arrangement suited me, as it would most shallow young men. The other good news was that she insisted on paying the expenses of every other date.

We never had a farewell evening or an opportunity to make any ongoing arrangement. When I got my discharge, I didn't think about which week it was. Her note was forwarded to my new address, but it arrived after our weekend had passed. I had no way to contact her and explain why I was a no-show. She probably asked around and discovered I had been discharged. She could have sent a phone number to my navy address; it would have been forwarded. I hoped that's what she'd do. Apparently, she decided the time had come to end the affair. It would have been easy for her to replace me and my bet was that she did just that.

I was sad about the way it ended. Norma was attractive, well-educated, interesting, and taught me many things. I missed our secret nights. On the other hand, I sort of welcomed an end to the guilt feelings I had because of Gin. Before long, Norma faded into a distant memory of a few interesting evenings with a lovely, mysterious woman.

The Hollywood Canteen

Ray Helstrom and I went to the Hollywood Canteen to see what it had to offer. The Canteen provided free food, entertainment, music, and theater tickets, to servicemen who were far from home.

Not many men our ages liked what was known as longhair music; Ray and I were exceptions. I attended my first Los Angeles philharmonic concert with free tickets from the Canteen. Later we had front-row, center seats to the opera *La Boheme* at the Greek Theater in Griffith Park. It was my first live opera, and it was sung in English. It was a marvelous experience. We went to several other concerts at the Greek and the Hollywood Bowl.

One evening we got to the Canteen early, hoping for some good tickets. I saw Ray talking to a beautiful girl who had just walked in. Soon a few other men joined them and Ray took her hand and bowed slightly, obviously saying good-bye. She gave him a big smile and a semi-curtsy as he backed away.

He walked to me looking like the cat that had caught the canary. He said, "That's Debbie Reynolds and she's in love with me." I took a more careful look at the girl, now surrounded by about ten guys, and sure enough, it was her. It was my first sighting of a real live Hollywood star. *Singing in the Rain*, one of the best musicals ever made, had been out for a while, and Debbie had starred in it with Gene Kelly and Donald O'Connor. I couldn't believe I didn't recognize her from twenty feet, but actors look different in person. Ray had seen her arrive and was the first man to say hello to her. He said she was gracious and chatted as any other girl would. We were impressed that a star at her level would give up an evening just to talk to servicemen. We saw other movie actors during our Hollywood Canteen visits.

Monday, July 27, 1953

The Korean War officially ended on this date with the signing of a treaty. It had lasted three years and thirty-three days. The United States suffered 128,000 casualties, including 36,516 dead. There were also over 8,000 missing in action.

The optimists were projecting discharges in a matter of weeks. Those of us who read the newspapers knew this wasn't going to happen. The government feared that the North Koreans and Chinese would find an excuse to attack if the Allies folded their armies too soon. Then it would all be on again. It was going to wind down slowly.

Autumn in the Los Angeles area is a nice time of year. The ocean is actually warmer than in early summer, and I was hooked on bodysurfing. October came, and I had been in California for a year. I had been totally occupied with working, pursuing a social life. I had also learned to spend money like my California friends and hadn't saved much.

Unexpected Good News

Just before Thanksgiving, Montana called and suggested that I stop by his office and walk to lunch with him. As we walked, he said he had a confidential directive he would show me, but it was top secret. I pledged secrecy. We walked behind a building, and he handed me a Teletype message.

It was from BUPERS to commanding officers of all naval bases and ships, and it was dated nearly a week earlier. In simple terms, it said that all active reserve personnel who had completed a full year of active duty could request a discharge if they were enrolled in an accredited college with a term beginning in less than thirty days or they had immediate full-time civilian employment waiting for them. He was right, it did make me happy. There was a way out of the navy—go find a full-time job.

My first question was, "When will this be released?"

Montana said, "I don't know. The captain has been sitting on it. He's probably concerned about losing all his active reserve personnel." He was right. Building 16 would lose most of its staff quickly if this memo was released. There were civilian jobs available, and many of the men had family connections for work.

On the way back to the office, my mind was running full speed. If I found a full-time job, I could be discharged in a matter of days. The thought of being free to pursue a civilian life was intoxicatingly wonderful.

I called Leland Lewis and told him I could get out of the navy immediately if I had a full-time job waiting for me. Leland said, "Once the war was over, we knew you'd be getting out. Your timing is good. I have a meeting tonight at RCA. When that's over, let's have a beer and talk." I was excited as I hung up. I would take any full-time job - absolutely any job - to get out of the navy. I hadn't realized how much I wanted my freedom until the possibility appeared.

A Big Break

That evening, Leland explained that he had a terrific job possibility for me. The catch was that I wasn't fully qualified. The employer preferred at least two years of college, and the youngest man they had ever hired was twenty-two. I was uneducated and two months too young—so how did this make me a likely candidate?

Leland explained that because he had placed several men with the company and all had done well, he felt he had a lot of credibility with the man in charge. He intended to speak to him and sell him on interviewing me. "He'll be impressed with your work experience, the special navy school, and your record at RCA. I'll tell you about the job only if you agree to fill out a long application and go to an interview." After my eager agreement, he asked, "Have you heard of General Motors Acceptance Corporation? Most people call it GMAC."

I replied, half guessing, "They make car loans, right?"

He went on to explain that the job was as a field representative, contacting people who were behind on their payments. "Sometimes you have to repossess a car. That's the unpleasant part of the job. But you'll also learn about financing the car inventories and get some other great experience."

"Can you tell me how much the job will pay?

He said, "The starting salary will be two hundred and fifty a month, with a possible raise after a trial period.[25] And you'll have a company car. It's a good job and there's a future with GMAC."

"Hey, that's great. I probably won't get to first base, but I'll go anywhere you send me and do my best to get hired. I just hope I won't embarrass you."

Leland's parting response was, "I know you better than you know yourself. You'll do fine, and worst case, an interview like this will be a good experience for you. If you don't land this job, we'll find another one." How lucky was I to have a man like Leland in my corner?

The next morning, I filled out the papers to go on leave for two weeks. Things were winding down for the year, so the chief saw no problem with my taking time off. He wondered aloud why I was taking a leave that brought me back to work just before Christmas, and I mumbled something like, "It's just more convenient for me this way." He shrugged and signed.

When I handed the leave papers to Montana for processing, he laughed and whispered, "Looks like someone is going job hunting. I'll get your papers on the boss's desk right away. By the way, have you gotten any shoes my size lately?" I assured him that I had been gathering up a Christmas package for him.

---

25 In 1953, schoolteachers were paid about $5,000 per year, bank tellers about $3,000 and the minimum wage was less than $1. A new Buick sold for $2,000–$2,200 and a Chevrolet for less. Gasoline was 29 cents per gallon, hamburger was 53 cents per pound, and a steak dinner in a nice restaurant was $2.50, including bread, salad, baked potato, and a vegetable; home-style pie was about 30 cents.

Some of my buddies asked why I was taking leave. I said I just wanted some time off. Jim was suspicious of my answer, but held his peace—until later. Jim was like Wendell in so many ways; he wanted to know everything.

The next morning I was in Leland's office, using a typewriter to fill out an employment application, it was long and thorough. They wanted to know if I had ever missed a payment on a debt, been arrested, or gotten any speeding tickets.

Leland had arranged lunch with the assistant manager of the GMAC office, and he would present the application to him then. I went to a sandwich shop for lunch.

When Leland returned, he was smiling. The GMAC assistant manager, a Mr. Chill, had liked my application and agreed to interview me the next morning. My excitement was soon overcome with dread. Leland came to my rescue with a pep talk. "Al, you've spent hundreds of hours successfully selling RCA contracts on the phone, and you've proven you can learn fast. Just be yourself and let your story unfold with Mr. Chill. If he's happy with you, he'll recommend you be hired, and then you only have to get by a short meeting with the manager. They are both good guys, and they like scrappy young men in the field rep job. Just wear your suit, be neat, be on time, and stay alert. I have confidence in you."

Leland was married but childless. It seemed to me that to some extent, I filled a gap in his life. He had stuck his neck out to get me into RCA, and he was doing it again at GMAC. Above all, I couldn't embarrass him. I had to do well in the interview for that reason, if for no other.

They're Going to Hire Someone

At ten the next morning I appeared at the front counter of the GMAC office. It was a large, deep windowless room with about thirty desks arranged in perfect rows. Behind most of them there was a person talking on a phone, examining papers. Some of the men were in shirtsleeves, but they all wore ties. The women were dressed in conservative skirts with blouses or sweaters. This was a serious business office.

All the way in the back, on the left, a desk and a couple of chairs were situated on a platform a step above floor level. The bespectacled, heavyset, bald man sitting at that desk could see over the entire room. Behind him, at the same level, was a glass-enclosed office. I accurately surmised that the bald man was Mr. Chill and the glass enclosure was the manager's office.

In a blink, I was standing next to the desk, shaking hands with a smiling Mr. Chill. He offered me a seat in a friendly way. "Leland tells me you typed this application yourself in his office," he said, as he looked at me over his glasses.

"Yes, sir, that's correct," I answered.

Looking straight into my eyes, he responded, "I gather this neat typing is something you learned in the navy school you attended?"

"Yes, sir – learned it in yeoman school and while working in a navy office for over a year. As you may know, the navy has forms for everything."

He smilingly allowed that he had been in the army during WWII and the army was the same way. Then he said, "Al, tell me about your job at RCA. Leland said you're the star salesman there."

I gave him a short explanation of the job, covering the general methodology of selling service contracts. He listened intently, making a few notes.

He covered my A & P, factory, and carpenter jobs in order and seemed to be pleased with my answers. From that, he went to, "Were you a good student in high school?"

I hesitated, gathering my thoughts. He said, "Take your time. I understand you're nervous. Just tell the truth as briefly as you can."

This put me at ease, and I launched into a description of my schooling, being very honest that I was not a good student but relating that I had been an avid reader. He asked the names of my favorite books and commented that he had read some of them. I added that I had attended Long Beach City College in the evenings and gotten A grades. Then he took over the conversation.

He described the field representative job, pointing out the hardships of working evenings on the phone, driving all over Southern California to call on clients, and the rush to get accounts current by the end of each month. He emphasized that there was some danger, especially when a car had to be repossessed, pausing to gauge my response. As he went on about the problems of a field rep, half of me was intrigued and the other half wondered why anyone would want the damned job.

Finally, he concluded with, "Al, we normally interview only men with at least two years of college who are at least twenty-two years old. You are a little short on these qualifications. However, Leland is very high on your success at RCA and other work background, and that's why I agreed to an interview. We recognize that young men who began working young, as you did, are mature beyond their years. A proven work ethic is important to us. Also, I must admit to a personal prejudice in favor of men from the factory towns of the Midwest. They seem to deal with life seriously, work hard, and can handle adversity. We see so many young California men who can't control their urge to be at the beach or playing some game. It's often discouraging."

At that point, he asked, "Are your parents alive?"

"Yes sir. My parents were divorced, and my mother worked two jobs to get us by. I did odd jobs like shoveling coal, dipping ice cream, and having my own Christmas tree business. I hitchhiked out of my hometown when I was nineteen and made my way by working in factories. As a response to his mention of danger, I added, "And I've never run from a fight." He looked pleased but didn't respond. I wondered if I had overplayed my hand by mentioning fights.

"Well, Al, I want to think this over. Leland will let you know if you'll be invited to interview with Mr. Warner. He has the final say on hiring field men. Regardless of how this comes out, it was a pleasure to meet a sensible, hardworking young man." We rose and shook hands. As I turned to leave he said, "One last thing—I nearly forgot. Leland told me you could get an honorable discharge quickly. How quickly can that be?"

I looked him in the eyes, just as Mr. Carnegie had instructed, and said, "Mr. Chill, once I give Commander Wilson a letter verifying that I have a job waiting for me, I know he will expedite my discharge. I suspect it will take two days." He thanked me, and I left. The interview had lasted over an hour, and I was emotionally exhausted.

By the time I got to Leland's office, Mr. Chill had called. Leland stood up and shook my hand vigorously. "Al, you hit a home run. Chill loved you. I'll hear from him later today. My instincts tell me you'll be hired. By the way, I'm meeting a new recruit at RCA tonight. I'll see you there."

That evening, Leland told me to go back to GMAC at ten the next morning; Mr. Warner wanted to meet me. He added, "If Mr. Warner likes you, they'll want to call your commanding officer. Now, listen carefully. Do not tell Phil that I sent you to GMAC. RCA is a good account, and I don't want to lose it." I assured him I wouldn't blow his cover.

Even after a few beers, sleep didn't come easily that night, and I was at chow so early that practically no one was there. I walked around after breakfast, rehearsing answers to the questions I believed Mr. Warner would ask. My nerves were jangling as I went to the front desk at GMAC.

Mr. Chill ushered me into the office and introduced me to Mr. Warner, who came around his desk and extended his hand. As I took it, I wondered if he felt me shaking. We sat down at a table as Mr. Warner said, "Well, Mr. Scheid, do you want to work for GMAC?" Calling me mister and being so direct threw me for a loop.

I figured the question was meant to test my composure. It was time to think clearly and hit the curveball he'd just thrown me. As I had learned from Mr. Carnegie, I took a deep breath, and a feeling of calm came over me as I said, "Mr. Warner, my answer is a definite yes; I want the job. It seems to me that the real question is, do you want me?"

He laughed as he said, "You turned the tables nicely, and thinking on your feet is a lot of what this job is about." Mr. Chill smiled and nodded slightly. I had hit the curve.

We chatted about what it was like growing up in a small town and making my way in factory jobs. Finally, he said, "I think we'll take a chance on you, Al. Everything I've seen shows you work hard and are adaptable. You're young and, I suspect, rough around the edges, but all the best men start that way. We would like you to begin training next Monday. Can you be ready by then?"

I said I would be ready and eager to begin then.

Mr. Chill added, "We need to speak to Commander Wilson and your boss at RCA as soon as possible. What would be the best time for me to call them?"

I replied, "I need the rest of today to explain things to them. They have both been very kind to me, and neither of them is aware that I am interviewing for a job and leaving the navy. Would tomorrow morning work for you?"

They both said that would be fine. Then I added, "As you know, I need a letter from you that says I have a job so I can get discharged early. It would be great if I could give that letter to the commander when I speak to him this afternoon. Can that be arranged?"

"Hell yes," said Mr. Warner. "Raymond, you dictate something and I'll sign it."

I left the office half an hour later with a letter I was not looking forward to giving to Commander Wilson. The job offer was contingent on a good reference from the commander. He could keep me in the navy if he wanted to.

The commander and the chief had been good to me. The commander had gotten me out of a bad report once for sleeping in, and he had let me go to Ohio when he needed me in the office. It was difficult to jump ship on short notice, and I thought hard about what to say. The chief was on leave, so at least I didn't have to face him.

I went directly to Building 16 in my civvies, getting a few funny looks from the guys in the office. I just waved, walked to the commander's office, and knocked.

The commander read the letter and looked at me with half a smile—the other half was a smirk. "So this is why you wanted to go on leave? How the hell did you know you could get out early if you had a job? That's practically top secret information on this base."

I told a large but logical lie. "Commander, yeoman school classmates stay in touch. One of my buddies wrote me about the directive the day it came out. I assumed it had been released or would be soon, even though I hadn't heard about it."

"Do you really expect me to believe that bullshit, Scheid?"

"No, sir, I guess not, but it is the truth," I lied again. "Commander, the job at GMAC is a dream come true at my age and educational level. I'll get the job if you give me a good reference when a GMAC management man named Mr. Chill calls you tomorrow morning. A bad reference will kill the offer."

He looked back and forth between the letter and me a number of times before he said, "Okay, I'll give you a good send-off, but in return I want a promise from you. You must swear that you won't tell anyone about the directive. Just take your discharge and leave quietly. This base can't afford to have half its personnel applying for discharges all at once. A stampede could put us out of business.

God knows what the brass hats were thinking when they put out that directive. Will you promise that?"

I quietly replied, "Commander, you've been a fine officer to work for, and I'm very grateful for all you've done for me. I promise I will not discuss it, and you can depend on that. But when I don't show up for work, the men will ask why."

He had a ready answer: "I'll announce that you got a special dispensation for an early discharge for family reasons. It sounds fishy, but that's not your problem. If anyone asks, tell them the same story and say you can't disclose all the details. You got that?"

"Yes, sir," I replied.

He asked when I wanted to get my discharge. I said, "Sir, I'm going from here to personnel to terminate my leave, and I'll ask Montana to type up my papers immediately. If you will sign off on my discharge tomorrow morning, I'll drop it off at the personnel office on my way to the infirmary for my severance physical. If all goes well, my discharge can be effective by the day after tomorrow and I'll officially check out of the base." He nodded with a grunt, which I took for assent.

He added, "I'm going to call the captain and tell him about your promise to keep things confidential. He won't like it, but he'll go along since the directive is in effect and can't be ignored."

As I got up, I realized I couldn't salute him because I wasn't in uniform. He understood and gave me a firm handshake, saying, "Scheid, you've done a good job here. If you keep the same attitude and work habits in your new job, you'll do fine. Now, get the f**k out of here. I have to figure out how I'm going to replace you with one of these lazy short-timers." His good-bye was the finest compliment anyone had ever given me. Perhaps more importantly, I felt I deserved it.

The next morning, everything went as planned. I would be a civilian the next morning. All discharge information is put on a form called a DD-214. It said I was six feet tall, weighed 185 pounds, and was in excellent physical condition. I had grown an inch and added about ten pounds while serving my time.

Good-Bye, RCA

While driving to RCA all I could focus on was how to tell Phil I was resigning. When I walked in, he was about to leave but sat back down at my request.

"Phil," I began, "working here has been a great experience for me. You've been good to me and taught me how to sell on the phone. I want you to know how much I appreciate all you've done for me."

"Well, have you been transferred or do you have what you think is a better job?"

Phil was smart and intuitive. It took only a few minutes to explain about leaving the navy the next morning and having a full-time job waiting. His only question was, "So why didn't you come to me and tell me you needed a full-time job? I would have written a letter for you to get discharged. When do you want to quit?" I knew that the newest recruits were not doing well and that Leland was working hard to find better salesmen, so I volunteered to work evenings for the next two weeks. Phil was appreciative and said he would like to pay me by the hour so I could spend most of my time helping to train the new men. The pay would be the average commissions I had been earning the past two months. It was a generous proposal and I accepted gracefully.

Even after I was settled in at GMAC, I did a few Saturday training sessions when Phil asked me to. All those hours on the phone gave me some of the best sales training I would ever get. In addition, trying to use understandable English had forced me to follow what I'd learned in my speech class. According to my friends, my Wheeling-Pittsburgh accent was no longer noticeable.

Good-Bye, Navy

Since I had promised Commander Wilson that I'd just fade away, a going-away party was out. But word leaked out of the personnel office. By midafternoon, my pals were all asking questions. With a wink, Jim said, "See you at the EM Club after work?" As I nodded yes, I knew then there was no way to keep things quiet and decided to let nature take its course. I called Phil and told him why I had to miss work that night; he understood.

Within a few minutes after the EM Club opened, a group of Building 16 guys and WAVES were hanging out at the bar. Any excuse for a party was a good one, and a discharge was a damned good excuse. When asked how I got a discharge, I simply said I couldn't talk about it except to say that it was an honorable discharge for family reasons. Several of them knew I was an only child, so they assumed I had worked a hardship deal with Commander Wilson, who, as Jim always said, was my navy father.

I brought a package of clothes to the EM Club as a going-away present for the club manager. We shook hands and acknowledged how much we'd miss each other. As long as my pals drank draft beer, a bill never arrived. We put down gallons and I got more than a little drunk.

A couple of guys wanted to go to a bar not far outside the base and continue drinking after the EM Club closed. Sanity prevailed for once, and we just drank beer and sang until the manager shooed us out. I was drunk and knew I'd feel crappy in the morning, but I'd never been happier. My navy adventure was over.

A Fond Farewell

I woke up Thursday morning with a painful hangover, had a long, hot shower, and barely made chow before it closed. After loading my car I drove to the gate for the formality (and pleasure) of showing my discharge papers and surrendering my liberty card.

It was a beautiful day—all sunshine and birds singing. The car was a few yards out of the gate when an idea popped into my head. I pulled over, got out of the car, stood at attention facing the flag flying high above the base, and gave my best salute. The marine guard on gate duty snapped to, returned the salute, and smiled. I think he understood I was saying good-bye to the navy. Then I got into the car and drove away as a civilian.

Why did I do this little exercise? It had suddenly hit me that an important time in my life had just ended. I had come into the navy as a confused, naive nineteen-year-old boy. I had learned some leadership skills, found out I was not stupid, and now, less than two years later, was leaving the navy with a great new job waiting. The salute was my personal good-bye to an institution that had done many good things for me. As I drove away, I felt a wave of nostalgia for the U.S. Navy. It was a feeling I experienced frequently for many years.

Chapter 30

One of the most tragic things I know about human nature
is that all of us tend to put off living.
We are all dreaming of some magical rose garden over the horizon—
instead of enjoying the roses that are blooming
outside our windows today.
—Dale Carnegie, writer, lecturer (1888–1955)

Dost thou love life?
Then do not squander time,
for that's the stuff life is made of.
—Benjamin Franklin, multiple talents (1706–1790)

A New Life Begins

In Long Beach I bought a newspaper and settled into a phone booth. By midafternoon, I had found a clean room in the well-kept home of an elderly couple. The house was a few blocks from Ocean Avenue, in a nice neighborhood. I paid two weeks rent in advance and moved in. I had my own room with some privacy - at last.

After my evening at RCA, I drove to El Monte to see Mom. She cried when I gave her the surprise news. I had seen no need to get her excited and then let her down if my plan failed. Her first question was, "What about Virginia? Have you talked to her? Do you think she'll come to California now?"

I explained that it was all very complicated and we would discuss it after I talked to Gin over the weekend. In fact, I didn't know how to handle the Gin situation. I feared putting the facts into a letter that could easily be misunderstood, and I dreaded telling her on the phone.

The Sunday morning call didn't go well. Gin was upset that I had just gone off on my own and gotten a job without telling her. She said, "I can see you have no intention of coming back here. You like California and have probably found someone else. I knew it would happen." There was no way to explain it to her except to repeat over and over that there was no one else. I pleaded for her to take a vacation and come for a visit.

The conversation ended shortly after she said, "I guess this means we spend another Christmas apart." I had to admit that was the case. My last words were to say that I was writing a letter explaining all the details and would she please read it carefully. We agreed to talk the next Sunday.

I was torn in two by the situation. I wanted to be with her, but I didn't want to fall into the trap of returning to Ohio and getting lost in a factory job. Once I was established at GMAC, we could be married in Ohio and move to an apartment in Long Beach. She'd have no problem getting a job, and we could build a new life. I knew it was not likely this dream would happen, but dreaming was something I had become awfully good at.

On to GMAC

I reported to Mr. Chill on Monday at 9 a.m., wearing a suit and tie with well-shined shoes. He introduced me to Duke Martin, who was to be my trainer. After a twenty-five-year career with GMAC, Duke was training new field reps until his scheduled retirement a year hence. He was a WWII vet and had the kind of big shoulders that reflected weight lifting in a gym. He had a pleasant smile that beamed self-confidence. His handshake was firm as he said, "Al, you'll learn the business, and we'll have some fun while you're doing it. Let's go."

In two minutes, we were on the way to our first contact. His first words were, "Here's a pad and pencil. Take notes on everything we discuss, everything you observe, and questions you have." He talked constantly, explaining details of the job. I did my best to keep up, writing as fast as the motion of the car permitted.

"Don't wear sunglasses when you speak to clients," he instructed. "You want them to see your eyes. Only traffic cops wear sunglasses when talking to people." He also made a point that I should be aware of my surroundings at all times. "Take in everything. Always know where you are and what's happening around you. This is for your own safety. As you get experience, you'll learn to size people up. If you read people well, it makes this job much easier. It's also important to be friendly and keep eye contact. Never forget, your mission is to solve a collection problem, so don't let anyone get you off the subject. You control the conversation." It was all common sense, but I had never heard it before.

When he parked the car, he left a generous space in front of it and he asked if I knew why he did this. I had no idea. He enlightened me. "You may want to leave in a hurry and backing up before pulling out slows you down. Always leave half a car length in front of you, even if it means walking a block or so. And never park facing into a dead-end street; they are traps. Avoid confrontations. You don't get paid extra for physical contact. When you're threatened, and you will be, leave the scene at once and always look back to see if you're being followed." He finished with, "Got all that?" I got it. This wasn't Duke's first rodeo, and it was easy to see he knew the job top to bottom.

As instructed, I stayed about six feet behind him when he began talking with the first client, call her Mrs. Smith. He had reviewed the account papers in the car and remembered all the details. His voice was firm but pleasant, and he had a nonthreatening demeanor.

In a few minutes, he was able to get a check for one payment of the two overdue and a promise of another payment at the end of the next week. He carefully and calmly wrote the promise down on a pad with carbon paper copy. He gave the original and his card to Mrs. Smith. He thanked her and said, "I know you and your husband will be able to get current on your payments and keep your car." With that, he said, "Nice meeting you, Mrs. Smith." Since he had gotten a payment and a promise of another one, it surprised me that he mentioned losing their car.

When we got in the car, I asked why he bothered to write down their agreement. Duke said, "I wanted to make it like a personal contract between Mrs. Smith and me, and I want her to understand that I expect her to keep her promise. My bet is that she'll make her old man pay up."

As we drove on, I asked, "Why did you give her the original, not the copy?" He smiled. "Hey, you're being observant. I gave her the original because it makes her feel more important – a copy is all we need."

Of course, I asked about his parting comment. "Well," he said thoughtfully, "it's been my experience that dropping a subtle message that their car could be repossessed improves the chances that they'll find a way to make the payments. When she speaks to her husband tonight, I'm hoping she'll tell him that I was nice to her, show him our agreement, and tell him they might lose their car if they don't come through. Does that all make sense?" Did it make sense? *Wow,* I thought, *did it ever!* Duke had just given me Bill Collection 101 in a few minutes. Many times each day, he had new and insightful lessons for me.

He took me to the used-car lot of one of our dealers to demonstrate some of the tools of the trade. He opened the trunk and got out two long, thin pieces of steel. They were about two inches wide and twenty-five inches long, with several notches in them. He called them door jimmies. Duke explained that one was designed to open GM cars; the other was for Fords. He slid one of them down between the window glass and the door of a car and maneuvered it for a few seconds. When he lifted up on the tool, there was a click, and voilà, the door was unlocked. He explained the technique, and I did it a few times on different cars. After several tries and coaching, I got it done, but I needed practice.

Next he got out a tow bar and explained it. The tow bar is attached to the car being towed by wrapping heavy-duty bicycle chains around the front bumper. The chains were welded to each end of the bar. The bar was attached to the back bumper of the towing car in a similar way. Since every model had a different bumper, there were many variations to fastening the bar in place. It took some skill to hook up this heavy, unwieldy contraption quickly.

Duke said that nearly half of all repos (repossessions) were done by towing. Sometimes people wouldn't surrender the keys, and often cars were taken without the owner's permission. In other words, he was teaching me to be a car thief. I thought; *would my Bridgeport friends believe this?*

At the end of the tow bar lesson, he added, "Always carry leather gloves and a change of clothing and shoes in the trunk. When you're in a hurry, those bicycle chains can give you some nasty cuts if you use bare hands. You may also be taking a car when it's raining or muddy, so sometimes you'll change into work clothes in your car or a gas station. You'll learn more about this next week."

One of the most interesting tools he showed me was a handheld machine that cut a new key from a blank. He explained that new cars had key numbers. All one had to do was lock in a blank key, then turn a dial to the first number and squeeze the grip once—then repeat this for each number. A series of small pieces were cut from the soft metal key blank. This technique made a key just good enough to use a few times. He warned, "Al, the keys made this way don't always work the first time, and you can't force them because they'll bend. And, sometimes they work in the door but not in the ignition. They often need some delicate adjusting with a small file to make them workable. Don't use one of them if you are in a hurry unless you have tested it first." It was dawning on me that this was a much more complicated job than just collecting late payments. Mr. Chill had glossed over a few details.

Late in the day, Duke said, "Al, you look good in that suit, but getting in and out of cars all day, in all kinds of weather, is hard on clothes. From now on, just wear a white or pastel shirt with a tie, a sport coat or blue blazer, cotton pants, and shoes with rubber soles." I asked why rubber soles, and he replied, "They're quieter, and you can run better in them." I understood what he meant but didn't want to think about it.

On the second day, I spoke to clients with him behind me, wrote the contact reports, and did the driving. The next day he began waiting in the car while I made the contacts. He called these my solo flights. He believed in learning by doing.

Duke explained that I was going to be assigned three or four car dealers to service. It would be my job to follow up on all the delinquent accounts from each of them and deliver any repossessed cars to the dealer. Since they had to pay off the outstanding GMAC loan balance, dealers didn't welcome repos and it was a friction point with the field reps.

Field reps reported to a loan supervisor, who in turn reported to Mr. Chill. Each supervisor dealt with about a dozen dealers and had three or four field reps reporting to him. Mr. Chill had told me I would be the thirteenth field rep in the office and the youngest.

Duke said I would be replacing a man who was let go. "He's a nice fellow, but he just didn't have the balls for the job." Duke didn't sugarcoat anything. "Al, I think you'll be an effective field rep because you have a positive attitude. But it's a tough job, make no mistake about it. About half the men we hire are gone in two years or less. Some don't make it because they have no initiative and need constant hands-on supervision. Some don't like working alone, and some just don't have the guts for the things a field rep runs into. There are many ways to fail, but if you stay organized, learn from the experienced men, and have the courage to face some difficult problems, it's an interesting job."

Duke constantly asked questions like, "What make and color was the car parked in front of the house we just left?" He said, "Al, a person can sleep-walk through their days, or they can be aware of everything that's happening around them. In this job, being a careful observer can pay off big." His goal was to make me aware of everything around me because you never knew what might be important later.

Finding my way around Southern California was a major concern of mine. Where I grew up nothing was over ten miles away. Sometimes Duke and I drove ten miles between stops and often ended the day well over twenty miles from the office. He said geographic knowledge would come as I learned the main thoroughfares. He also gave me lessons on using the Thomas Street Guide every rep carried.

The more information I received, the more complicated the job appeared to be. It was way beyond anything I had done before. Duke sensed my uncertainty and assured me that things would fall into place by the end of the following week. He said the main thing was to focus on getting the problem loans current and all repossessions done by the end of each month. It was a simple concept. Get the money, get a reliable commitment, or take the car.

Back in the office, he had another test for me. He said, "Tell me about every contact we've made. Begin with the first one and describe them all without referring to your notes." With heavy-duty effort, I was able to recall them, almost in order; it took over half an hour. He slapped my shoulder and said, "You did really well. Now I have to report to Mr. Chill."

About twenty minutes later, Mr. Chill said, "Duke tells me you passed everything with flying colors. Congratulations. If you complete the rest of your training as well as the first week, I think you'll have a successful career at GMAC." I replied that Duke was a fine teacher and made learning easy. My first week had gone by quickly.

We went for a beer, and he continued my training by telling me stories of unusual things to watch out for. A few of his stories were weird, some were scary, and some came with a warning. He told me about women who would offer sexual favors for special treatment and warned that once begun, these situations never ended well. Also, once in a while a man would seek revenge on a rep who had repossessed his car. He said, "Be careful how much personal info you let a client know and never socialize with them. The less they know about you, the better. Just keep everything formal and avoid problems."

Duke had heard all the excuses for not paying and had responses. He had dealt with tough guys and knew how to handle them. He was, to my mind, a master psychologist—always a jump ahead of the clients.

We had put in full days, starting at eight in the morning and working until about five in the afternoon, with an extra hour of lecturing over a beer. For me, it was a week of straining to grasp many things fast. I was tired but genuinely felt I had learned my lessons well. As I had discovered all through my young life, an experienced person can teach you a lot, but only if you listen closely and remember.

My next Sunday call with Gin went worse than the one before. She felt that I had made up my mind to live in California and the quick discharge was just an excuse to stay. There was no consoling her, and she didn't want to come to California for a visit. We finished with "I love you" back and forth, but our relationship was getting rocky.

Bad Luck with Bad Buck

On Monday, I learned that Duke had been called up to the big Los Angeles office to hold a series of field rep training sessions. I had been assigned to a man named Buck Gaouette for my second week of training.

Buck was about thirty and my height, with a narrow fat roll over his belt. He had been a field rep for over two years. Within the first few minutes, he told me he was a college graduate, had been an outstanding officer in the army, and was excellent at his job. I listened to what he said and took notes.

He instructed me to stand behind him on house calls so I could learn important lessons. I had already progressed to conducting my own house calls with Duke, but I was more than willing to learn from another experienced man. His approach to clients was the polar opposite of Duke's. Buck was gruff, made lightly veiled threats of repossession, and talked down to clients. Overall, he was discourteous and accusatory. He told me he often repeated the same words several times so they wouldn't forget. It was clear the people didn't like him, but he did scare most of them.

Between calls, he told me stories about his military accomplishments and the awards he'd won. He considered himself a fine leader of men and gave me "One time we were ..." stories to prove it. I pretended to be interested and impressed, but I was growing less and less thrilled with his act.

Over lunch, Buck told me he had read my application and was surprised that I was hired, given my lack of education and experience. He made it clear that he thought I wasn't qualified. He said he'd do his best to train me, but it would be difficult. We were off to a bad start.

After two days of riding around on his calls, with him telling me that most of what Duke taught me was old man bullshit, it was firmly established that Buck and I didn't like each other. According to him, everything I did was wrong and every question I asked was stupid. By the end of the second day, we were barely speaking. It was obvious that he resented having to train me and that he didn't care if I succeeded.

At the end of the third day, I got the word that Mr. Chill wanted me to come into Mr. Warner's office. I had a hunch this was not going to be a happy meeting.

When I sat down, they said they wanted to be honest with me about my training. Mr. Chill read some of the comments that Buck had turned in. The comments were intended to show me as an incompetent. I didn't drive well, I got lost, I talked back to him, I refused to take instructions, and I couldn't use the tools to open a locked car. He also said I had my own opinions about everything. He contradicted everything Duke had said about my training.

They asked me to tell them my side of the story. I decided that I had nothing to lose by coming on strong. After taking a deep breath, I said something like, "To begin with, Buck doesn't think I'm worthy of the same job he has. He can't imagine how an enlisted man, not yet twenty-two, and with no college degree, can be an equal to him. He's an ex-officer, a college graduate and he's damned proud of himself. He bragged about his army accomplishments and treated me like a dumb recruit. He expected me to do everything but salute him."

"Buck also thinks the things Duke taught me are old-fashioned and that his methods are much more effective. I didn't agree with him, and that made him angry. Buck thinks he's always right and won't discuss his opinions. He behaves as if he's still an army officer. He expects people below his rank to agree with everything he says and to take orders with no questions asked. Frankly, I don't think I was the problem. I think Buck was the problem. He tried to make me kiss his ass and treat him like my commanding officer, and I refused to do it. I didn't ass kiss in the navy, and I'm not doing it as a civilian. A man with Buck's superiority complex, wouldn't last a week in my hometown before someone taught him some manners." Then I shut up.

I was angry and didn't attempt to hide it. They looked at each other and said nothing until one of them asked me to go to the lunchroom and wait.

I figured I was fired and promised myself I was going to go find Buck and let him show me just how tough he really was. I hated the lily-livered son of a bitch. He was all bluster and bragging. Being in charge of a bunch of enlisted men he could order around fed his ego but had taught him nothing about leadership. He was an asshole of the first water. I had never been more frustrated and furious. Thankfully, he didn't walk into the lunchroom.

After about twenty minutes I had calmed down somewhat. They called me back into the office, and Mr. Warner said, "Starting tomorrow, you'll report to Don Pevehouse as your supervisor. Don will go in the field with you and observe and coach you part of each day for the next few days. By the middle of next week, you'll be on your own as a field rep, working for Don, or you won't have a job. If Don approves of your efforts, you'll be on probation for ninety days. If that time goes well, you'll have a secure job. Does that work for you?"

Feeling like a man who has just avoided the gallows, I managed to say, "Yes, sir, that's okay with me. I'm confident I can do it."

A cold feeling went up my spine. I was going out into the world of collections and repossessions the next day with a supervisor watching my every move. It was a scary situation, and the confidence I'd built up with Duke had been shattered. I thanked them and promised they wouldn't be sorry they gave me a chance to prove myself. What else could I say?

A few minutes later, Mr. Chill caught up with me in the lunchroom and motioned me to follow him into the parking lot in back. He led me to a shiny blue Chevrolet two-door coupe. It was a thing of beauty, with large chrome bumpers and a sleek look. It had a small backseat, but was really a two passenger coupe. It was an exciting moment. I had never driven a brand new car.

Mr. Chill said, "You'll need these." He handed me the keys and a bag containing an LA Country Thomas Guide, a set of jimmy tools, and a tow bar rig. "You're all set to go to work tomorrow. Do a good job and you'll have a job after next week. Do you have any questions?"

I said, "Mr. Chill, you can count on me. I'll do what it takes, and you won't regret giving me a chance. But I do have one question. Why are you giving me a new car when you may fire me in a few days?"

He looked straight at me and said, "You've had a rough time this week and I thought you could use a little confidence builder." It was a confidence builder all right - and I sure as hell needed one.

I drove my new car to my rooming house, put on casual clothes, and went for a walk. I took in the sea air and let my mind wander into my problems. I had gotten a bad break losing Duke and getting stuck with an asshole like Buck. I wanted to find a way to pay him back. Where I came from grudge keeping was a natural emotion, but Mr. Carnegie would tell me to think positive thoughts. I put Buck aside.

What if this job didn't work out, what would I do? I thought about calling Leland but discarded that idea quickly. I didn't want to upset him. He'd stuck his neck out for me, and if I was a loser, he'd be a loser.

Hunger drove me into a small restaurant. On the way back to the house the cold was invigorating, and my anger eroded. I began taking stock. It was not complicated. I had to succeed or die trying. It was as simple as that; I couldn't live with failing at this job. By the time I was back in my room, I was feeling better.

Being a field rep at GMAC was the pinnacle of all my jobs and success could lead to many good things. I had gotten out of tough spots before and I could do it again.

Failure was not an option. My spirits were up, and I was mentally ready to face the dragon.

CHAPTER 31

If you get up one more time than you fall down, you will make it through.
—Old Chinese proverb

Sex without love is a meaningless experience,
But, as far as meaningless experiences go,
it's pretty damn good.
—Woody Allen, writer, director, actor (1935–living)

THE CHALLENGE

The next morning I was at Don Pevehouse's desk when he arrived. He assured me he'd do his best to help me. He spent the morning standing behind me as we called on delinquent clients and gave me helpful advice after some contacts. He sat next to me and gave me tips while I made phone calls in the afternoon. He said my phone technique was excellent. My RCA phone experience was paying off.

I mentioned my clash with Buck, and he assured me that both Mr. Warner and Mr. Chill realized it had been a mistake to give him a training job. Buck got the assignment because he had a good record for collections and he was available. But they would never use him again for training. I was delighted.

Late on Friday afternoon, Don said, "Mr. Chill and I discussed your progress. I told him that with a little guidance, you could handle the job just fine. You have the ninety-day probation deal now. On Monday, I'm going to introduce you to the dealers assigned to you."

I refocused my efforts to prepare for my first week of my probation. I made phone calls that night until nine. On Saturday, I studied the street guide and then drove around, trying to learn the main arteries. On Sunday, I drove around all day finding the addresses of my open accounts and organizing them into a logical sequence. By evening, I felt well prepared to face the week ahead.

Don and I met with the general managers or owners of two Chevrolet dealers, a Buick dealer, and an Oldsmobile dealer. Don said that my predecessor hadn't been popular with these men because he gave them too much bullshit. It all went well, and they seemed pleased to have a new man on the job.

An Unexpected Event

It was over a week before Christmas, when Mr. Chill and I passed in a hall and he said, "Well, Al, are you all geared up for the party?"

I asked, "What party, Mr. Chill?"

"Oh my, no one told you about the Christmas party? Please accept my apology. It's on Friday night, and I hope you don't have other plans. I assured him that I would squeeze this event into my crowded social calendar.

At five that Friday everyone went from the office to, of all places, the Virginia Country Club, Jerry Cassaday's family club. At the party Don introduced me to everyone I hadn't met in the office. I wasn't very comfortable, and it probably showed. I had never been to a party with so many attractive and well-dressed women. After a couple of bourbons, I perked up.

Just as a slow ballad was beginning, a secretary named Wanda Gephardt asked if I could dance. I said, "Yes, I like dancing." Wanda had good rhythm and was easy to lead.

After two numbers, she took me to her office pals and said, "Hey, this guy can dance!" I danced with a series of girls for the rest of the evening. A few men could dance, but most of them just shuffled their feet vaguely in time with the music, just as they did in Bridgeport. Wallflowers grow everywhere.

When the disk jockey took his break, Mr. Chill took over a piano and began playing carols. Wanda and a few others sang along. I knew the words for every carol and became an enthusiastic participant. It was a fun evening.

As people were leaving, Wanda was a bit wobbly. Mr. Chill spoke to her, and she agreed to leave her car there until the next day. I volunteered to drive her home. When we got there, she asked me in for coffee. El Monte was a tedious thirty-mile drive with many stoplights, and coffee was a good idea.

She told me she was thirty-two, divorced, and had two girls under ten who spent a lot of time with her ex-husband and his wife. She also said it was well known that Buck had almost gotten me fired. She said, "Everyone knows Buck is a jerk. He'll get his comeuppance someday. Just stay away from him, Al."

As I was leaving, we had one long lingering kiss, which I took as sort of a thanks-for-driving-me-home gesture. The kiss also reminded me that for the second year in a row, Gin and I were not together for the holidays.

The timing of the party couldn't have been better. It would have taken months for me to meet all of my fellow employees on a social basis. It was a boost I needed.

Party Animals

The GMAC crowd liked to party. Some parties were planned and some happened spontaneously, mostly TGIF (Thank God it's Friday) parties. Wanda put on a TGIF/BYOL (bring your own liquor) party at her house in January.

The weather was cool, but there was dancing on her patio. During a slow dance, Wanda whispered that her kids were with her ex-husband and she had a suggestion. Her plan was for me to leave with the last partiers, drive around for ten minutes, then come back and spend some time with her. I said I had a long drive to El Monte. But, after a few more drinks, I whispered that I'd circle back for some coffee.

It all happened as planned, except that I didn't leave. The next morning I suffered heavy guilt compounded by a hangover. After a great breakfast, I felt better and promised myself I'd write an especially nice letter to Gin as a sort of a penance.

Staying overnight with a woman was a new experience for me, and I gave it a lot of thought. I wondered if Gin and Jack had found a way to be with each other overnight. The Gin thing was gnawing at me and I didn't need the additional problem of an affair with Wanda. I decided to call off whatever had started between us.

New Friend and New Quarters

Also in January, Jack Cronkite began training as a field rep. Shrapnel wounds in Korea had gotten him a discharge. Jack was a graduate of Washington State, where he was a football lineman. He was a big, tough, happy fellow who liked booze and women. We quickly became friends.

He was renting a room in a home just as I was and he suggested we become roommates. We found a two-bedroom, one-bath furnished apartment with a small kitchen and living room. Our apartment became the scene of a number of GMAC poker games.

My big purchase for the new apartment was a used Smith-Corona typewriter that was nearly as old I was. Now I could write reports in a third of the time handwriting took. That Smith Corona and I got a lot of work done.

THE DEACON

I asked Don to introduce me to a field rep everyone called the Deacon, or Deke. Wanda had told me he was the best repo man in the office. Don said Deke had turned down an office job because he liked the freedom of being in the field. He also worked as little as possible. Management put up with Deke because his delinquencies were caught up and all necessary repossessions were made by the end of each month. Deke knew the job, and I could learn from him.

When we met, he was friendly and said he'd help me as long as I didn't take too much of his time. To start things out, he told me to meet him at five that afternoon at Harvey's Bar in Long Beach. Harvey's was only a few blocks from our new apartment - a happy accident. [26] He said he'd answer questions for a while but had a date later. When Deke arrived, he introduced me to Harvey, the owner and bartender and I immediately had bar credit. GMAC guys were favored customers with Harvey.

Deke explained that repossessing a car without the owner's permission was called "stealing" or "creating a pedestrian." He added, "Al, always have another man with you. You need a lookout and may

26 Harvey's Bar & Grill deserves some explanation. Harvey was one of his own best customers; he was never fully sober. On any given evening, the patrons would range from unshaven men in work clothes to well-dressed men and women, with a few hookers tossed in. Harvey said he didn't permit sex soliciting in his establishment, a rule that was observed in its breach. The food was passable, and the price was right. The only cardinal rule was that you had to pay your bar tab at the end of each month. No one knew why the place was a GMAC hangout—it just was.

need help if you're confronted. If you're alone and get the chance to steal a car you really want, do it. But it's risky. The mildest of men can get deeply pissed off when you take his wheels." He told me about having guns pointed at him, bottles thrown at him, and a number of physical attacks. Hearing these stories was a little frightening, but I was in the game now and there was no backing away.

After too many drinks, Deke canceled whatever date he had and we had dinner. As guys do, we exchanged background information. My coming from a poor family in a coal/steel town pleased him. He laughed about my cumshaw activities in the navy and sympathized with me about the problem with the girl back home.

Deke had never been married, and he lived alone. He came from a poor family in San Pedro, a tough seaport town next to Long Beach. He skipped college and made it clear he didn't like the self-satisfied jerks who thought college was everything. He didn't like fraternity men. I liked his attitude because I had gotten a belly full of the frat bullshit from the USC station keepers. Deke also didn't like Buck; that alone would have made him my friend. After three hours of food, booze, and frank talk, we had a budding friendship.

Deke strongly suggested that I pick two pseudonyms. One name was for use when a repo was the issue and one when only a collection was involved. With two names, I would always know what the issue was if someone called the office and used one of them. I picked Albert Mansfield and Al Carpenter.

I said Duke had told me about the extra clothes. Deke said, "Yeah, sometimes you want to look different. A tie, white shirt, and shined shoes stand out, but you can blend into the background wearing jeans, a T-shirt or sweater, and sneakers."

I asked, "Do you use these disguises often?"

He replied, "Not since last night, when I went knocking on neighborhood doors asking questions about a bastard who moved. I told the neighbors I was his cousin, and it worked. Now I know where he lives and he'll be a pedestrian tomorrow night. Wanna help me?" I said yes immediately. I was delighted to be invited to buddy up with Deke on a repo.

I pointed out my total lack of experience. Deke wiped that aside, saying, "Al, I don't give a shit about experience. I want a partner who will be there when I need him; besides, learning about repos ain't that hard. I trust my people judgment, and you're my kind of guy. We both survived growing up in tough places. Let's give it a try."

Deke was an expert at starting cars by using alligator clips to bridge the ignition lock. He could jimmy a car door, hot-wire the ignition, and drive away in two minutes in daylight and three minutes in the dark.

My assignment was to stay near my car as a lookout, then follow when he drove the repo away. I was on high alert, watching for a light turning on or a neighbor coming out. My first repo experience went smoothly.

Like most people, Deke liked to impart knowledge to a willing student. One thing he shared was, "Be careful with flashlights; the beam goes both ways. You may see them, but they can see where you are too and they may have a gun."

Claremont Men's College (CMC)

By March Jerry and Grover were pushing me to apply to CMC. As an added incentive they pointed out that CMC permitted no fraternities. They were right, that put CMC in an even more favorable light for me. I made a Saturday appointment at CMC and mailed my high school transcript, my resume, and a covering letter to the admissions office.

I arrived early and browsed around Pomona College as well as CMC. There were young men and women walking around everywhere, and I wondered if I could I be one of them someday. I envisioned riding a bike around the village. I determined to do my best to get into this environment.

I met with Miss Ruth Witten, a pleasant woman with a warm smile. She opened the conversation with, "Mr. Frisbie is actually the director of admissions. I'm the registrar, and I'm filling in while he's out of town. We received a very nice letter about you from Mr. Cassaday. He thinks you would fit in at CMC. As you probably know, his son just graduated."

She said, "I read everything you sent in. Tell me why you were such a poor student in high school." I told the truth—all of it—as best I could. She then said, "Your letter states that you did a lot of reading, beginning when you were very young. Tell me about that." We talked about books and authors and I answered more questions. Finally she said, "You've had wider reading experiences than most college seniors, let alone someone with your high school grades." She left the obvious question unasked, but I decided to answer it.

"It may sound strange," I began, "but I didn't think I was smart enough to take academic courses in high school. Where I grew up, most kids go from high school to a steel mill, a coal mine, or a trade. That's what I figured my life would be like. Getting into yeoman school in the navy changed all of that; I found out I could study and pass exams. Now my goal is to get a college degree."

She was fascinated with bill collecting and repossessing cars and asked questions about my GMAC job. Finally, she asked about my life goals. Using my best Carnegie demeanor, I made it simple by saying, "Miss Witten, I want to be successful in business, and I think the best way to achieve that is to get a degree from a fine college like CMC."

She said I wasn't qualified for admission. But if I attended a junior college for a year and demonstrated that I could get good grades, she would help me. She said she'd tell me which courses to take so the credits would transfer to CMC. There it was quite simply: prove myself worthy and I could get into CMC. I couldn't ask for a better break than that?

She recommended Citrus Junior College in Glendora, which wasn't far from CMC. She said, "The classes are small, and I have been impressed that the new director of Citrus is trying to raise the level of teaching. It's a much smaller school than Pasadena JC, and it might be a good fit for a young man with your background. I suggest you get their catalogue and look it over." I said I'd look into it right away.

As I stood up to leave, Miss Witten reached down and picked up a crutch, which she put under one arm. It was only then that I saw that one of her legs was short and thin. She was much the same as Mom's best friend, Jeanie. As she hobbled around her desk and extended her hand, she said, "I really enjoyed meeting you, Al. You have an interesting background, and I hope you come to CMC." The interview had lasted over an hour, and I felt really good about it.

The next week, I sneaked some time off and drove to Citrus JC. Citrus was a few plain stucco buildings next to Glendora High School, but it looked cozy and friendly. I found the administrative offices and picked up the catalogue. The girl behind the counter urged me to sign up early because the classes filled up quickly. I pored over the catalogue for a while, and then I decided to meet with Miss Witten to make certain I took the right subjects.

The Skip Tracer

Our office skip tracer, named Charlie, and his assistant were mystery men to me. It was their job to locate delinquents who had moved and didn't want to be found. These were called "skips." There were many people who skipped from some other part of the country and drove to Southern California, in what amounted to a stolen car. Their files were sent to our office, and it was Charlie's job to find them and repossess the cars. He didn't collect delinquent accounts or work with dealers.

During a chance meeting, I questioned Charlie's assistant over a beer or two and concluded that being a skip tracer was a damned interesting job. They were permitted to pay bribes to get information, and they had generous expense accounts. They could stay in a hotel when it was necessary. They also worked with the police because they were often looking for the same people. It was fascinating.

The assistant liked the work, but his wife was bitching up a storm about his unusual hours. Skip tracing was interesting, but I could see the drawbacks for a married man.

Don had decided that a delinquent client I could not locate was a serial skipper. It was time for the account to be turned over to our skip tracer department, so I prepared a file.

When we met, Charlie instructed me to tell him everything I knew about the skip while he took notes. After I covered the contents of my file and memory, he asked questions, some of which I had already answered. When he declared us finished, I asked why he'd asked some questions twice.

His reply was, "I wanted to see if your answers were the same both times."

"Oh, then you were checking my memory?" I asked.

"Yes, your memory, your attention to detail, and please don't be offended, but your honesty as well."

"I'm not offended, but why would I lie? This skip means nothing to me."

"Reps frequently want to make the story sound better, so they make stuff up, and they often tell it differently the second time."

"Did I pass?" I asked.

He said, "You appear to have an excellent memory, but some liars have excellent memories too."

"Thanks for the compliment on my memory, Charlie, but if you speak to Don, I think he'll verify that I don't alter the facts in my reports. I write things up the way I saw and heard them."

His smiling reply was, "I've already done that, and Don says you work hard, you're getting better at the job every day, and he trusts you. I gotta go now." He stood up and left. I enjoyed the banter with Charlie. I wanted to get to know him better and learn from him.

Repossession Adventures

Every delinquent has a story to tell, and sometimes they are even true. More often, they create a story that they think will convince the collector to go away, at least for a while. About 90 percent of the delinquents were decent people who were down on their luck. Most of them could be dealt with on the phone or during a friendly visit. There were also people, nearly always men, who leaned toward violence or the threat of it. They were resentful about being asked for the money. An experienced collector can usually read the drama in their faces in a few seconds. Most of our time and energy was spent with that small percentage of delinquents who were not nice folks, and a few of those were downright dangerous.

As Duke said, "If you learn to read faces and body language, you'll avoid tons of trouble." There's no reasoning with people who are defiant. They never seem to understand that insulting or attacking the collector only worsens their problem. The trick is to keep their frustration levels low.

A bill collector wants all his delinquent accounts paid up by the end of a month. The longer an account stayed delinquent, the less likely that it would ever be caught up. When people got out of the habit of paying their payments, they often developed a mind-set that they didn't have to pay. After three or four months, they resented someone pushing them. The goal was to collect before they reached that point. Once the collector was convinced that the client couldn't or wouldn't pay, repossession became the only option.

Cars go down in value every month. Once it becomes clear that the payments won't be made, the dealer wants the car back so he can resell it and cut his loss. A field man was taking a physical risk every time he set out to take a car. A repo is a tragedy for the person losing the car and a royal pain in the ass for everyone else involved.

During my time with GMAC, I was involved in repossessing well over sixty cars, most taken without incident. Some cars had to be stolen because the owners refused all cooperation and some were stolen because we considered the owners to be dangerous. No one I knew ever took a car for spite or fun.

Stealing cars takes training, nerve, and willpower. Depriving an owner of the use of his automobile is a major personal insult, especially for men. There are a wide range of circumstances that surround repossessions. While some of the repos described here could have had serious outcomes, in retrospect they are mostly humorous. As Mark Twain wrote, "Humor is tragedy plus time."

Two Lessons Learned

About a month after I was on my own, I walked on to the front porch of a house, hoping to find the client at home. He had hung up on me the night before, so I was expecting a negative reception. When I rang the doorbell, a man wearing a dirty undershirt and baggy pants, with a potbelly overhanging his belt, opened the door. His greeting: "What do you want?" I could smell the whiskey through the screen door. He knew the answer.

I tried to discuss his delinquency, but he said he was too busy to talk to an asshole bill collector and made motions to close the door. I tried to keep the conversation going. Then he said, "Okay, okay, you wanna talk, come on in."

As he pushed the screen door open with his left arm and I began moving forward, I glimpsed his right fist clenching as his arm started moving back. I ducked. His fist hit the screen, and the motion took him off balance. It was a reflex—there was no thought - as my right fist with my full weight behind it struck him in his fat belly.

The air came out of him like a blown-out tire, and he fell backward into his living room. I was shocked and just stood there as the screen door hit my shoulder. He was gasping as I had seen many football players gasp when the wind was knocked out of them.

After a few seconds, I regained some composure, looked around, and ascertained that no one had observed this altercation. The only sound was his gasping, which I knew would end soon. As nonchalantly as I could, I walked back to the car, got in, and drove to the office, where I described the entire incident to Don.

The jerk had already called Don and given his side of the story. He said I had attacked and beaten him up. He said that if Don agreed to leave him alone for a couple of months so he could catch up on his payments, he wouldn't call the cops. Don could tell the guy had been drinking and said, "I'll investigate. Call me in a week; meanwhile, you can keep your car." Don hadn't believed any of the attack bullshit.

When I explained what had gone down, Don laughed. "Well, it's happened to all of us. It would have been better if you hadn't punched him, but you won't lose your job over it. You're allowed to defend yourself!" He went on to say that Mr. Chill didn't want to be bothered with stuff like this. The two of us would handle it quietly and keep it to ourselves.

"Al, it sounds like you hit him hard, so we need time for any bruises to go away. We'll ignore him for about two weeks to see what he does. My bet is he'll do nothing if we leave him alone. He'll think I'm going along with him and he'll get careless. That's when you'll steal his car. Don't contact him in any way, and if he calls, don't talk to him. Once we have his car, we're in control." I was impressed. There was nothing these men hadn't faced before.

We followed Don's plan to the letter. About three weeks later, Deke and I did a midnight steal and the fat gut guy became a pedestrian. The next day he came into the office and made a scene; Don told him to leave or he'd call the police. He came back a day later with the money to bring his payments up to date. Don made him sign a new loan and agree that if he went delinquent again, he'd surrender his car without an argument. After all this, Don gave him the keys, a bag of car junk and told him where it was parked. I never saw the creep again. The fat man and I had taught each other valuable lessons.

Hot Pursuit

Late one night, Deke was upside down in the front seat of a Buick with his chest under the steering wheel and his head under the dashboard, putting clips in place to start the car. The car was parked on a gravel driveway next to the client's darkened house. I was on the sidewalk playing lookout. If the owner came out of the house, my job was to whistle and then jump in my car, driving slowly with lights out. The idea was for me to get the car into a position that Deke could jump in and we could make a fast escape.

Suddenly, Deke heard footsteps on the gravel and whispered loudly, "Al, is that you?"

There was no reply, and Deke was trying to extricate himself when his foot was grabbed and a man yelled, "You're stealing my car—I'll kill you!" Deke kicked hard with both feet, and the guy fell over backward. Deke got to his feet and ran toward the street.

We always assumed we could outrun a pursuer. We also assumed the client wouldn't run far in the dark. This angry man didn't cooperate with either assumption.

Deke was running full speed, but the guy was keeping up with him. I caught up to them with the car lights out. As I neared the man, I hit the horn and flashed the lights. He broke stride and fell. I passed him, slowed to a crawl, and Deke jumped in.

Still panting as he groped for a cigarette, he asked, "Where the hell did that guy come from?"

"I think he came from the house next door or from the backyard. I didn't see him until I saw him chasing you," I said.

Deke wheezed, "We'll steal his f*****g car next time. He said he'd kill me and I don't take that shit. He's going be a f*****g pedestrian." We went into tension-relieving laughter.

We got to Harvey's before closing time and relived the story over a drink. I was concerned about the man's fall. Deke said, "Don't worry about it. Chill's done his share of repos and understands the problems."

The next morning, while we were relating the story to Mr. Chill and Deke's supervisor, the delinquent showed up at the front counter. He had one arm in a sling and both hands were bandaged, but he had no visible head injuries. Mr. Chill told us to leave through the back door.

That afternoon, we heard what happened. Mr. Chill had schmoozed the man for an hour and worked a deal. The client would forget the incident and GMAC would rewrite his loan with reduced payments. We were off the hook, and the man got a new chance to keep his car. It was a rosy ending.

Big Bad Tex

Nearly a year before I started at GMAC, a man called Tex bought the biggest pickup Chevy built at that time. He used it to pull large horse trailers. Tex missed his first payment and every payment thereafter had to be collected in person. After Tex came to the door holding a rifle, the rep wouldn't go back and ask for payments.

When I took over the account, Tex had just gotten sixty days behind in his payments ... again. Don had found out that Tex was also behind on his house and barn rent. These were good reasons to believe he might skip town with the truck, most likely back to Texas.

I drove by Tex's place so I could get the lay of the land for the repo. Tex was easy to recognize. He was over six feet tall and wearing a ten gallon hat, just as he had been described to me. He was putting horses into the van hooked up to the truck. I drove away and came back later, hoping to speak with his wife and get some information.

An old man came to the door and said he was Tex's father. As soon as I said I was from GMAC, he got nasty. I thanked him for his time and walked down the street to a phone booth. The booth had windows of supposedly shatterproof glass. Just as Don answered, the old man began throwing fist-size rocks from only a few feet away. The glass was shattering with each rock. I told Don I was under attack, and he said, "Threaten the old bastard—anything—just get the hell out of there before that crazy Tex comes back!" I jumped out yelling and waving my arms at the old man as if I were going after him. He held up his hands and backed off. It was obvious he was a little crazy and very drunk - or vice versa.

By the time I got to the office, I had a repo plan to test on Don. He didn't like it at first but said he'd go along with it if Deke buddied with me. After I diagrammed the scene and explained the plan, Deke agreed. Tex would be anointed as a pedestrian that very night.

Deke and I drove to the Chevrolet dealer to examine a truck exactly like the one Tex had. I had never driven anything like it. The gears had a compound low variation and it was a tricky move to get it into reverse. After some practice, I drove it around a couple of blocks with Deke, stopping, starting, and shifting the gears. Deke always had a laid-back attitude and said, "Hey Al, you got it. You'll do just fine." It was easy for him to be nonchalant; he wasn't going to be the guy stealing the truck.

Tex's house backed up to a road that bridged over the Los Angeles River. The plan was for me to slide down the slope from the road and approach from the back of the house. I wore a black navy watch sweater and a black knitted navy cap. At Deke's suggestion, my face was blackened with burnt cork. Deke dropped me at the top of the slope near midnight. We assumed Tex and his family would be sleeping. It was a scary moment. I took a deep breath, then the first step. After negotiating the slope, I crept through the weeds to the truck. I had two copies of the key, carefully made from the key number. We assumed one of them would work.

The truck was parked facing the back of the house and the kitchen lights were on. The idea was for me to open the truck door quietly, slide in behind the wheel, then fire up the engine and drive away before Tex knew what was happening. Deke would be parked on the street in case I needed a running escape. We had covered every detail. But, "The best-laid schemes of mice and men oft go astray."

The key worked in the door. As I climbed up into the truck, I could see Tex sitting at the kitchen table drinking beer with his crazy father – not what we had planned. I got the key into the ignition, and it turned just fine. As I was ready to push the starter, I realized it was too dark to see where reverse was on the gearshift. I pushed in the clutch and quietly moved the shift stick around, finally making my best guess which was the reverse position. I fired up the engine, slammed the door shut, hit the accelerator, let out the clutch, and turned on the headlights all in one continuous motion. The truck surged backward. The men jumped up from the table. They knew exactly what was happening.

I had to stop the truck's backward motion, shift to a forward gear, drive past the side of the house, and down the driveway to the street. I hit the brake and shifted into what I hoped was first gear. What I got instead was the lowest and slowest gear the truck had. In this gear, even with the engine racing, the truck couldn't exceed ten miles per hour.

As I passed the house with the engine roaring, Tex came running out the front door. The truck started down his driveway as he grabbed the door handle and tried to pull it open. It was locked. He hung on and hit the window with his fist. The glass broke into a spider web of cracks. There we were, me driving in slow motion and Tex hanging on and yelling threats as the truck got to the street.

Deke drove up behind us with lights flashing and horn blowing. Tex let go, and in the rearview mirror, I could see him stop as Deke drove past him. The chase was over. In a moment, I was able to get the truck into a higher gear, and Deke followed me to a parking lot near Harvey's where we often stashed vehicles.

It was a great victory and required some celebration. At Harvey's, I washed my face and had a scotch with Deke, Jack, and a couple other guys. Deke told the story, with imaginative embellishments. He raised his glass and said, "To Al, for a job well done." Harvey got into the spirit of things and served drinks after he locked the doors.

The next morning, I drove the truck to the dealership, with Jack following in his car. I was looking forward to handing over the keys to a happy dealer. This was to be a victory lap of sorts.

As we approached the dealership, I saw two police cars. I got out and headed toward the office. The manager rushed over and said, "Al, thank God you didn't get here sooner!"

"Why?" I asked.

With eyes wide, he said, "Because that crazy f*****g Tex was going to shoot you! We tried to reach you at your office to keep you away."

Just then, two cops came out the front door of the used-car office with Tex between them in handcuffs. One cop had a rifle in his hand. Tex glared at me as he called me unflattering names. In a few seconds, he was put into a police car and driven away.

By the time Jack and I got to the office, Mr. Chill and Mr. Warner had heard the story. They had me go over the repossession in detail. They were concerned that the story would be in a newspaper. I was told not to talk to a news reporter under any circumstances. GMAC wanted to keep details about repossessing out of the press. After checking with the GMAC lawyer, they had a plan.

An hour later, I gave Mr. Chill a written report. He read it, nodded his approval, and ushered me into the manager's office. After congratulating me, they explained that everyone at the dealership would be told I had been transferred out of the Long Beach office. I would be assigned a different dealer. They made it clear that I was never to stop by the dealership again. These were experienced men, and I took their instructions seriously.

The story appeared in the newspaper, but it wasn't accurate. The dealer was quoted as saying the gun incident was all a misunderstanding and the repo was never mentioned. The two salesmen that Tex had held at gunpoint must have been given a story and stuck to it.

The police and the newspapers never contacted me and the story died. GMAC had kept a lid on the incident. Tex was charged with some minor crime and released on bail.

A few weeks later, Tex jumped bail and left town. That was the last I ever heard of old Tex.

Arrested

One night Jack and I teamed up to steal a car. The client had been hiding the car a few blocks from his house, but Jack had spotted it. The car was facing down a gentle slope. It was an easy repo. All we needed to do was jimmy the lock, hot-wire the ignition, coast down the hill, then start the engine and drive away.

After Jack struggled with the tools for a while, he signaled me. I walked away from my lookout position and held a flashlight to help him. Just as he got the door open, we had lights on us. It turned out a police car had slowly crept down the slope with its engine off and lights out. We were so intent on the jimmy tool we hadn't seen or heard it.

In a few seconds, we were handcuffed and patted down. When we explained who we were, they checked our IDs. When they saw our GMAC cards and the loan papers, they chatted amicably, but they said they still had to take us into the station. After surrendering my money and ID, I followed them, driving Jack's car.

The sergeant on duty recognized Mr. Chill's name. He said, "Well, boys, if you don't want to spend the night in a cell, you better call your boss and get him down here. We'll sign you out to him if he says you're his boys."

Waking Mr. Chill at midnight didn't appeal to us, but neither did spending a night in jail. When showed up, he wasn't a happy camper, but understood the situation. On the sidewalk, Mr. Chill asked, "Well, where are you going now?"

I replied, "We're going back to get that damned car, right, Jack?"

Jack responded, "What else?"

Mr. Chill looked at us and said, "A man with common sense would go home and start fresh tomorrow. But I'm not going to tell you what to do." We knew he was actually pleased. It was what he would have done.

An hour later, with the repo parked nearby, Jack and I toasted the victory in our apartment. The next day Mr. Chill said, "By the way, if you'd gotten arrested the second time, you would have stayed in jail. I don't get up twice in one night."

Jack spoke up, "I told the cops we were going back for the car. They thought it was funny."

A Deadbeat Doc

A doctor, who was three payments behind, was quite clever at hiding his Cadillac, refused to see me and would not take phone calls. Finally, I posed as a patient and saw him. He went ballistic and threatened to call the police. As I left I said, "Doctor, you won't like the medicine I'm prescribing for you." It was time to take his car, but first I had to find it.

One evening Deke and I stopped at a tavern for a drink on our way to a repo job. As we walked in I looked down the bar and there was the doctor, with an attractive woman. He didn't see me. I dragged Deke outside and we found the Cadillac in the lot.

Deke said, "You go back in there and keep him busy. When I have the car out of the lot, I'll come to the door and give you the signal.

I walked back in, took a seat next to the woman, and ordered a drink. After a big sip of my drink, I leaned in front of her and said with a smile, "Dr. Smith, what a surprise to see you. How are you?" He was so surprised that he introduced me to the woman and we exchanged pleasantries.

"How do you know each other?" she asked.

I said, "You might say Dr. Smith is sort of a patient of mine."

He nodded and in a dismissive tone said, "I don't have anything for you now, but early next week, give me a call."

In a minute, Deke gave me the high sign from the doorway. *Gawd, he was fast.* I drank up, told the woman how nice it was to meet her, and then turned to the doc and said, "Doc, don't spend all your money here." He gave me a quizzical look as I added, "You're going to need cab fare." I waited a split second to enjoy the look on his face and then walked quickly out the door.

As I walked to my car, Deke blinked the Caddy's lights from across the street. The doc was yelling at me as I zipped out of the lot. After parking the repo a few miles away, we had a good laugh and went after our primary targets for the night. Sometimes you just get lucky!

Duke's Prediction Comes True

Miss Smyth was a twenty-five year old Long Beach school teacher with a good work history but a spotty payment record. The two payments she had promised me on the phone hadn't arrived, and her next payment was due in a couple of weeks.

It was late afternoon when I parked in front of her car near her apartment building. I was relieved that she hadn't moved. She opened the door with a smile and said, "What can I do for you?" She was quite attractive, was wearing a clingy bathrobe and her hair looked like she'd just taken a shower. As I gave her my card, I asked if she was Miss Barbara Smyth.

"Yes, that's me. Please call me Barbara. You have such a nice phone voice. I wondered what you'd look like."

At her invitation, I entered the apartment and sat in a chair. She sat on the sofa and crossed one shapely leg over the other. She said she was sorry to have fallen so far behind, but if she could just get a little more time, she'd catch up the payments. She asked, "Would you like a drink, Alfred? I was just going to make one for myself."

I declined, saying, "Thanks for the offer, but I have more calls to make." She popped up and went into the kitchen.

I heard ice cubes tinkling as she told me how much she was enjoying some beach time, ending with, "You have a great tan. You must spend a lot of time at the beach."

When she came back to the sofa, her robe was looser and showing a little more than a girl should show to a bill collector. She said, "Aren't you young for such a responsible job? The man who called on me several months ago was much older. Are you married?"

As I said, "No," a memory surfaced about something Duke had told me. Was I about to be offered a romantic interlude in exchange for more time or skipping a payment?

She gave the usual excuses for not paying, then got up and walked toward my chair. While looking straight down into my eyes, she said, "Nice single men like you are hard to meet. I wish we had met in a different way. Do you want that drink now?" There was now no doubt where this was going and my job was worth more to me than a roll in the hay with a pretty schoolteacher.

I stood up and said, "Miss Smyth what I want from you is your car keys."

In a sweet voice, she said, "You aren't going to take my car, are you?"

"Yes, ma'am, that's what I have to do unless you have some money for me."

She purred, "I'd be ever so grateful for a little more time. Isn't there any way I can persuade you?" In a firm voice, I asked for the keys again. She turned, walked into the bedroom, which was just out of sight, and cooed loudly, "You'll have to come in here to get the keys."

That was enough. As I opened the door, I called, "Miss Smyth, this is your last chance—money or the keys." She appeared in the bedroom doorway without her robe and smiled, crooking her finger for me to come to her. I hurried down the stairs. She had a nice body, it was a great show, and it would be fun to tell about it later, but she was obviously a dangerous woman.

As I passed her vehicle, I tried the door and, much to my surprise, it opened. Miss Smythe arrived as I was attaching the tow bar. She was wearing shorts and a sheer blouse with no bra. She was no longer lovey-dovey. "How much money do you need to leave the car here?" she said curtly.

"You're behind two months; I need all of it,"

She offered one payment, and I said, "That's not enough. I need all of it. The tow bar was in place and I said, "Here's the best I can do for you. Come in tomorrow morning with two payments and Mr. Pevehouse will rewrite your loan to make it easier for you."

Switching to being cozy again, she asked, "Will you be there? I'd rather work things out with you, Alfred." Calling me that name was getting on my nerves.

"It's not likely I'll be there, but Mr. Pevehouse will know what to do. If you don't show up before noon, the vehicle is going back to the dealer. It's all up to you." She said she'd show up the next day and handed over the keys.

As I pulled away, I could see her in the rearview mirror, blowing me a kiss and waving. I wished I'd met her in some other way.

I left a memo telling Don that she was not a skip risk and I thought she had learned a lesson. She showed up, and Don rewrote her loan. She told Don, "Please give my thanks to Alfred; he was so nice to me." It was an educational experience for both of us (clients gave me many lessons). I never spoke to her again, but I was sorely tempted on a couple of lonely evenings. It wasn't that easy to meet pretty, educated girls like Barbara—under any circumstances.

CHAPTER 32

If you think nobody cares whether you're alive or dead,
try missing a couple of payments on your car loan.
—Flip Wilson, comedian (1933-1998)

Travel is fatal to prejudice, bigotry and narrow mindedness,
And many of our people need it sorely on these accounts.
Broad, wholesome, charitable views of men and things cannot be acquired by vegetating in one little corner of the earth all one's lifetime.
—Mark Twain author, humorist (1835–1910)

AN UNEXPECTED EVENT

Don shared a story about a used Desoto that Charlie had just stolen. The dealer was in Gary, Indiana, and it was going to be driven back there instead of being sold in Los Angeles. This was unusual but the GMAC office in Gary wanted to make the dealer take the car back.

I asked, "Who drives cars all the way back to the Midwest?"

Don said, "Anyone we can find who wants a free trip to the Chicago area. You wanna do it?"

He meant it as a joke, but it got me thinking. It was the beginning of the month. I could drive the car to Gary and hitchhike to

Bridgeport. After a few days with Gin, I could fly back. I'd never driven across the country and I wanted to see it.

I grabbed the *LA Times* and searched for people wanting a free ride across the country. There were dozens and Chicago was a preferred destination.

I tested the idea on Don. He was surprised but said, "Hey, if Chill will give permission, be my guest. Your accounts are in good shape, and it would be a great experience for you."

I went to Mr. Chill and asked for the time off. He asked, "Why the urge to drive across the country?" I jumped in with both feet and told him about Gin. With a chuckle, he said, "You must really be in love to drive nonstop across the country for such a short visit. But who am I to stand in the way of romance? Tell you what, Al. You've worked hard and you have a week's vacation coming sometime this year. If we call delivering the repo three days of GMAC business, it looks like you have about ten days to make the round trip. When are you leaving?"

I was amazed that he consented so quickly. "Thank you, Mr. Chill. I'll leave as soon as possible." I gave Don the numbers for the Lincoln, Pastime and Reddy's house in case he needed to reach me.

The Auto Club of Southern California prepared well-marked maps and a travel guide that showed it was just over 2,200 miles. Driving time was estimated at just less than forty hours. I figured I'd find someone who was willing to drive straight through, taking turns sleeping in the backseat.

About the fifth call, I spoke to man who was a bartender in LA and wanted to go to Chicago on the cheap. He said he loved to drive and had done this trip before. He added that even though he was a bartender, he didn't drink. That was a comfort. His only request was that we drive through Las Vegas and stop for two hours while he played some blackjack.

We had to arrive at the GMAC office during business hours, so we agreed to leave the next afternoon. If all went as planned, we'd be in Gary in the morning, just over a day and a half later.

Las Vegas was bigger and brighter than I had expected. In less than two hours, Tony lost the $50 he had allocated to his gambling venture and I put about $5 into a slot machine. The next highlight was driving across Hoover Dam which was magnificent.

Tony was an easy man to be with. He told me dozens of jokes. Everything went well until we were in the Arizona desert where the engine began heating up. We managed to get into a gas station. The mechanic discovered that the thermostat was closed and wouldn't open, so no water was circulating through the radiator. Getting a replacement could take days.

Tony asked, "What happens if we just leave the thermostat out?" The mechanic said the only problem was that the engine would then run too cold during cool weather.

I said, "So leave it out. Winter isn't coming anytime soon." He did as directed, and we were on our way—for a while.

A few hours later, the engine began heating up again. This time we were near a larger town when we stopped. The mechanic lifted the hood and had me start the engine. When the engine was revved up, the hose from the radiator to the engine collapsed, allowing practically no water to circulate. It was a simple fix. He installed a new hose and we were on our way again.

A few hours later, the engine heated up once more. This time a different water hose was leaking. It was replaced, and we got going—again. Before the trip was over, we stopped two more times to replace hoses. The engine overheating had damaged every hose needed to keep the car running. Each time we lucked out and found a gas station easily.

On Friday morning, we were in the GMAC office, where Tony and I had an Italian-style good-bye, with hugs and backslapping.

The assistant manager was kind enough to drive me to a main intersection on the edge of town. The jackpot I didn't hit in Vegas came when my first ride took me all the way to Indianapolis. Three more rides and I was sitting in the Lincoln, permitting Carl to buy my beer. Just seeing Carl almost made the trip worthwhile.

Jim Reddy, always the pal you could count on, picked me up and took me home with him. By 1 a.m. I was asleep on his sofa.

Gin nearly dropped the phone the next morning when I told her where I was. She canceled her shopping trip with Marie and picked me up. Our next stop was breakfast in the back booth at the Candy Kitchen. She volunteered to call Jack and tell him she couldn't see him for a week because I was in town. He was crazy in love with her and willing to take any abuse just to stay in the game. I felt sorry for him—and for me too. Gin was not treating either of us fairly and the situation was becoming intolerable.

In the evening we went to our favorite bench by the river, the place where it all began between us. I began by telling her how much I wanted her to come to California to meet my friends and see how I lived and worked. She said, "Alf, I just can't do that. You know that would upset my parents."

My reply was sarcastic. "Do they really think they're protecting your virginity? Are they that stupid? You have to live your life for yourself, not for them."

She replied angrily, "No, they're not that stupid, and you know the problem - people talk." This raised my anger further and nothing was accomplished. We both knew it was all about what her mother's friends would think if their daughter went to California to visit a man without being married.

I nearly shouted, "Gin, these people are hypocrites, just like my uncles and aunts. Half their kids get married because a girl got pregnant, but everyone pretends it didn't happen that way. And, sometimes they're not really sure who the father is. They lie to each other and they lie to themselves. I can't stand the backwardness of this place." She didn't disagree. She knew the closed-minded attitudes of the older generations.

The conversation cooled down, and we had our usual passionate kisses and embraces, declaring our love to each other. However, like always, nothing was resolved. I felt like an idiot for using up my vacation week to make the trip. But it was my own fault; I should have known what would happen.

For the next few days, Gin and I pretended everything was fine and we did the things we always did. Grandma sensed that all was not well and asked me about it. By coincidence, they were going to drive to California soon for a long visit with Mom and her brother. I said I'd know more by the time they arrived.

I got a message to call Don Pevehouse, ASAP. Don explained that there was a repo in Joliet, Illinois that I could drive back to California. The dealer would pay all my expenses, and Mr. Chill had approved the idea. Saving the airfare appealed to me, and nothing was going to change with Gin, no matter how long I stayed. Now I had to find a driving partner.

A Cross-Country Adventure

I had known Bill Glitch (that really was his family name) since childhood. He was a WWII veteran, a Bridgeport High grad, and a patron of every bar in town. He was a gentle soul, and everyone liked him. He had lost his job and was free to do anything.

In explained my plan. He and I would take a plane from Wheeling to Chicago, hitchhike to Joliet, pick up the car, and drive to Mom's house, where he could stay until he found a job. Our mothers were close friends, and I knew Mom would welcome him. A beer later, Bill agreed to go.

Suddenly, it was time for me to travel. We both knew things were not right between us, and we didn't know what to do about it. Gin asked, "When will I see you again?"

My answer was, "The way things are now I don't know. There is a limit to how much trampling my love can take, and we're reaching that limit. I think the answer to your question is in your hands, not mine." It was an uncomfortable parting.

Bill and I flew to Chicago, got lucky with hitchhiking, and made it to the Joliet GMAC office by late afternoon. The car turned out to be a 1947 Hudson, which wasn't a very good car even when it was new. The GMAC guys told me it had been checked out and it would be no problem for a two-thousand-mile trip. If all went well, we'd be at Mom's place in two days.

The first hundred miles were uneventful, and then things began going wrong. We had high winds and rain all night. Just before dawn, the car lights began to dim and the voltmeter showed that the battery was discharging. We stopped at a gas station and waited for it to open. The problem was the voltage regulator, so we had it replaced.

After a couple of hundred miles, the battery was discharging again. This time the battery had to be replaced. Half a day later, we replaced the generator. That night we got stuck in a little town because we had no headlights. After buying another voltage regulator and generator the next day, we mushed on. A saga was developing.

We stopped for dinner and gas on the western outskirts of Flagstaff at an elevation of about seven thousand feet. It began snowing, the temperature dropped, and we had only summer clothes with us. We figured we'd be out of the mountains and in a warmer zone in a couple of hours. About this time, the windshield wipers stopped working. I was able to stay on the road by leaning my head out the window and watching the taillights of the car ahead.

The gauges showed that the battery was discharging again and we were going to lose our lights. We realized that a serious emergency was brewing. There was over an inch of snow on the road, and it was coming down hard. There was no place to stop - we had to stay the course.

Suddenly, there were bright lights shining into the back window. Bill stuck his head out and ascertained that it was a big rig truck following close behind us. Then the big rig began blowing his horn. I was not about to speed up. The big rig decided to pass us.

As the truck passed, his lights made it possible to see a slow right curve coming up. The truck tried to slow down, but his tires slid in the snow. A second later, he went through the railing and disappeared. I pulled off to the right and stopped. We decided Bill would keep the engine running. If it stopped, it probably wouldn't start again. I ran to where the truck went over.

When I got to the edge of the road, I could see the truck about sixty feet below, lying on its right side with its lights still on. I went down the hill, climbed up on the cab, and looked through the window. The driver was struggling to open the door. I was able to get a stance and pull the door open. The driver was in a panic to get out but kept slipping back in. I asked if he was hurt, but he kept repeating, "Get me out of here … I gotta get out of here … It might catch fire." I offered my hand to pull him up and out, but he was too heavy.

Suddenly, another man was next to me on the cab. He said, "Hey, there are four of us. We can handle this. Go back to your car. Your buddy says the lights are going out, and you'll both freeze if you get stuck here." I saw three more men in blue air force topcoats. They repeated, almost in unison, "We'll take care of this. Go back to your car and get the hell out of here." I thanked them, and went back to the car.

Bill told me that the air force guys saw our taillights and stopped to see if we needed help. When Bill told them what had happened, they ran to help. We wondered about the truck driver, but we had our own problems. I was shivering almost uncontrollably.

We started the slow drive down the hill, hoping to reach the village of Parks or even make it to Kingman before the lights were completely gone. In fifteen minutes, we had driven out of the storm and the snow had melted from the windshield. Occasionally, a car would pass and we'd have a few moments to follow its taillights before it sped away.

We reached Kingman late in the evening and drove in to the first gas station we saw. I explained our problem to the owner/mechanic. He said, "You're going in a circle. The voltage regulator messes up the generator and vice versa, then the battery probably gets overcharged. I can't do a thing for you until morning. I'm goin' home now, but you're welcome to pull into the garage and sleep in your car. You'll be warm here." He handed us a blanket and said his name was John.

John came back early with homemade buttered biscuits and a thermos of coffee. He refused payment. He was a WWII vet and had lost both legs to a land mine in France. He walked by lifting his shoulders and swinging his legs, but otherwise didn't seem to be handicapped. He had the kind of courage Hemingway wrote about, and I admired. Moreover, he seemed to be a happy man.

John called a parts shop and had them deliver our third voltage regulator and parts for the generator. Meanwhile, he loaned us his pickup to drive down the road to a diner for lunch. In early afternoon, we paid up and were on our way. We had no windshield wipers, but who expects rain in the desert? It began raining in less than an hour. I could see through the raindrops on the windshield well enough to keep going, but it was a struggle.

We were traveling on the new highway that was being built to replace Route 66. When we came to a curve to the left, we were going too fast to make the turn. The car went diagonally down a sloped ten-foot bank, ending up on the old Route 66. There was no damage other than a lot of mud on the car.

We drove down the old road about a mile, hoping we could find a way back on to the new highway. We reached the place where the two roads intersected, but we were about fifteen feet below the level of the new road. The bank was gently sloped, and I decided that if we could get up enough speed, we could make it up the muddy incline and back on to the new highway. The construction site was deserted because of the rain so there was no one there to stop us. We had to try it.

We found a likely place where the slope was the flattest. There was a construction trailer next to the new highway, just beyond the spot we had in mind. I figured that if we went up the bank diagonally, the car would sideslip some, but with enough speed and the spinning wheels helping, we could make it to the top. I backed down the old road nearly a mile.

We were going over sixty mph when we started up the incline. It was going well except we were side slipping more than expected. We were within a few feet of the top when we realized we were heading towards the construction trailer. The front wheels were on top of the slope and the engine was racing when the right rear of the car hit the uphill edge of the trailer. That small collision seemed to straighten out the car and improve our traction. We made it to the top.

I stopped the car to catch my breath and Bill got out for a look back. He yelled, "Oh my God, Al, there goes the trailer!" I jumped out and looked. Sure enough, the trailer was beginning to slide slowly down the slope. It went all the way to the bottom, stopping at the edge of the old road. It didn't roll over, but it was tilted at a sharp angle.

We stared at each other in shock and dismay; what would we do now? We looked around but didn't see a person or a car in sight. I said, "Bill, get in the car. We're gonna haul ass out of here."

As I accelerated away, Bill looked at me, gave a nervous laugh, and said, "Am I correct that we are not going to tell anyone what we just did?" Then we both burst into laughter. In fifteen minutes my heart rate and respiration were nearly normal.

The electrical system held up all day, and we made real progress before the gauge showed discharge again. With no headlights, we drove the last ten miles or so down Garvey Boulevard (now I-10) to El Monte. Our only light was from the businesses on Garvey and the few cars that passed us. I kept the right wheels on the berm of the road and felt my way along. Our main fear was being hit from behind or that the highway patrol would spot us. Our luck held, and we made it to Mom's house just after dawn on Sunday. The nightmare of the Glitch-Scheid driving adventure was over. I vowed never to drive across the country again. Like most of my vows, it would be broken.

The old Hudson had a dead battery and was covered with mud. The dealer wouldn't be happy, but I had receipts, and all the old generators, voltage regulators, and batteries were in the trunk. On Monday, they sent a tow truck for the car and sold it to a junkyard. The dealer paid for everything without a whimper.

It all turned out fine for me. Mr. Chill and some of the guys belly laughed over coffee in the lunchroom when I told them the details of my cross-country saga. The collision with the construction trailer was left out. The truck going over a cliff and our method of getting back on the new Route 66 were exciting enough.

Bill Glitch—and a Memoriam

I introduced Bill to Leland and, within a week, he had a job as a shipping clerk with Shell Oil in Long Beach. He bought a used car and went to work. After a week on our apartment sofa, he rented a small studio apartment in Belmont Shore. Another Bridgeport expatriate had made his way to California.

When Bill's father died a few years later, he bought a house and moved his mother to Long Beach. It had never occurred to me that Bill was gay until he brought his boyfriend to Thanksgiving dinner. We had never discussed his sexual orientation—not one word.

Many years later, after breaking up with his long-term partner, Bill retired and moved back to Bridgeport, where he could live on his pension and Social Security checks. He finished his days in a small house with a view of the Ohio River; he was never completely sober. Friends came by every afternoon to drink his booze and trade small talk. Whenever I visited our hometown, I always went to Bill's house and had a drink or three with his group, all of whom were straight.

Bill had many friends, and none of them ever guessed he was gay. When he died of heart failure about 2006, there was a large crowd at his funeral, including some gay friends. It was only then that some of the local people began putting the pieces together. A year or so after he died I was in Bridgeport and one of his old drinking buddies asked me if Bill was gay. My eye to eye reply was, "I never asked him and he never told me." And, that was the absolute truth.

CHAPTER 33

Courage is the first of human qualities
because it is the quality that guarantees all the others.

The problems of victory are more agreeable
than those of defeat, but they are no less difficult.
—Both by Winston Churchill (1874–1965)

THINGS FALL INTO PLACE

The Los Angeles Basin was booming as people moved in from other parts of the country, drawn by job availability and the mild climate. Thousands of tract houses were replacing citrus groves. Car sales were also setting records. Unfortunately, many families couldn't afford all the payments they took on. When there was a money problem, the tendency was to pay the mortgage and let the car payments fall behind. GMAC was expanding rapidly.

Don told me that the manager had said that my typed month-end reports were well done and he was happy with my performance. I thought what if I decided to pass on college and stayed with GMAC? It dawned on me that I could have a future at the company. How many guys with so little formal education had a job like this with one of the largest companies in the world?

I was making house calls every Saturday morning and spending the early part of most evenings on the phone. This method yielded excellent results and my accounts were in good shape at month-end. Deke, Jack, and I evolved into a team of two good rookies and a veteran. I began to feel secure.

One day, as I was getting started on phone calls, Mr. Chill pulled up a chair next to me. "Do you plan to spend the evening here?" he asked. I explained that I had found that getting promised payments from clients was more likely if I called and reminded them. He nodded and said, "Al, your trial period ended weeks ago, but you didn't bring it to my attention."

I said, "Mr. Chill, an enlisted man doesn't bring himself to the attention of an officer, even when things are going well."

He said, "I understand. Al, you've worked harder than any rep in the office. Mr. Warner and I are impressed, so you're getting a raise a little early and it's larger than we normally give. You'll notice it in your next paycheck." I was sincerely surprised and very grateful. The raise of $35 per month was much more than I expected.

A Brief Visit to the Past

One evening Jack and two other GMAC reps decided we should visit a poolroom near Harvey's. It had been nearly three years since I had played serious pool.

We played nine-ball one-on-one for a while, and although I made some good shots, my game was inconsistent. Even worse, I found it boring. The guys were surprised at my ability and suggested that I play one of the guys hanging around looking for a game. It was laughable. I had once been one of those hang-around guys. My pals had no idea of the abilities of men who spent nearly every evening playing for money. The local pool bums would have eaten me alive.

When we went back to Harvey's for a nightcap, I treated because I had won a few bucks and didn't want to keep my friends' money. I was relieved to be away from pool. It was years before I played again.

Boys and Girls will be ... Boys and Girls

It hadn't taken long for even an inexperienced young man like me to realize that the office was a hotbed of flirtations. It was reminiscent of my last year in high school, with fickle girls switching boys constantly. The difference was that these people were sexually active.

Women's liberation didn't yet exist, but equality wasn't an issue. Each gender had its roles to play and play them they did. Both single and married girls were happy to have drinks bought by the men who made more money than they did. The simple-minded diversion of hundreds of TV channels and the Internet were many years in the future. People created their own fun. Secret little affairs were a diversion that was pursued with carefree abandon.

No one really cared much what others did, but they loved gossiping. For instance, Wanda told me that all the girls knew Buck was hot for an attractive woman who had an unhappy marriage. She didn't discourage him, but she didn't sleep with him either. She just led him on. He tried to look nonchalant when he sidled up to her table in the lunchroom or sat next to her in a local bar.

Mr. Chill was a regular in the bars, but he never participated in the game. His attitude seemed to be that it was normal for men and women to play around. The restrictive culture of sex had changed during the war, especially in California. Management kept their noses where they belonged as long as the work got done.

Deke warned me that there was some gossip about Wanda and me and suggested we be more discreet. "And," he advised, "Don't get involved with a woman with two kids. She's also too old for you." I appreciated his advice which was spoken like a big brother.

After Deke's warning Wanda and I stayed away from each other at parties except for dancing, which I did with all the girls. We had no business reasons to interact in the office, so we didn't. In a couple of weeks, Deke told me the gossip had moved on to newer subjects. Meanwhile, Wanda and I continued to see each other secretly when the mood struck one of us. She understood I wasn't a candidate to be her next husband.

Buck Again

I was still the youngest man in the office, which was never mentioned by anyone except Buck. He and I hadn't spoken since our training fiasco. Wanda and others told me that among other nasty remarks, he said I was the recipient of favoritism by management. He had personal animus toward me and my success in the job only made it worse.

One day in the lunchroom, just loud enough for me to hear, he used my name and the words "fair-haired boy" in the same sentence. Those were the only words I caught, but I decided to call him on it. As I walked into the group, I said, "Buck, everyone knows we don't like each other, and no one cares. I never mention your name in any way. Please do the same for me." I turned away with my anger bubbling. I didn't want a showdown on GMAC property, but it was obvious he was baiting me. I couldn't just ignore it.

He replied, "I'll say anything I want, when I want to say it."

He didn't get a chance to say more. "Okay, Buck, you want it, you got it! All you have to do is come to me outside the office and we'll finish this. We'll find out how tough a wimpy-ass army officer really is."

To avoid any more of a scene, I turned and walked deliberately out into the parking lot, got in my car, and left. I didn't know if he'd follow me, but I was happy that he didn't. I wasn't looking for a fight, but my pride wouldn't let him get away with insulting me publically.

I learned later that he passed off my confrontation as a juvenile act, but the observers didn't buy it.

Buck did have a point. Mr. Chill had helped me in many ways. Buck had put low expectations about me in the minds of management and it had worked to my advantage. The joke was on him.

Time to Face Facts

Early the next Saturday morning, I was in a quiet phone booth near Mom's house by nine, Ohio time. When Gin answered, I got straight to the point. "Gin, we can't go on like this. It's time for you to come to California. You say you won't like it here, but how do you know? I have used airplanes, trains and hitchhiked thousands of miles to be with you. You haven't walked across the street to come to me. Do you love me or not?"

"You're right, Alf. Marie and I have talked about it many times. Now that you're out of the navy, we have to come to a decision. But I've never been on a plane … and where would I stay? You have to work. When would I see you? My mother won't like me going there alone; people talk. I don't think I can do it." She began to cry softly, but I pressed on.

I took her objections one at a time. "You can stay with Mom and her husband. I'll take time off, we'll go sightseeing and you'll meet my friends. The weather is great; you'll love it. As for flying, it's time you did that." She said she'd think it over and write to me. I drove to the office and tried to get her out of my mind.

That evening I went to a barbecue at Wanda's house. I arrived a bit late and found the party in full swing. The minute he saw me, Don took me aside and said, "It is time for you and Buck to mend your fences. He'd like to apologize to you and asked me to talk with you about it. I strongly suggest that you accept his offer." It occurred to me that Don had bent Buck's arm, but I didn't want to be seen as a grudge keeper, and who cared who promoted the peacemaking?

"So how do we do this?"

Don said, "Go out to the front yard; I'll send him there." He quickly added, "And this is not to have a fight, got it? Don't mess it up. This took some doing!"

I just had time to light a cigarette before Buck came out the door. He had no hesitation as he said, "Al, I've treated you unfairly and I was wrong about you. You've proven yourself and I'm deeply sorry about my past attitudes. Will you accept my apology?"

My reply was to extend my hand as we met eye-to-eye. I said, "Thanks, Buck. Yes, I accept your apology. Life's too short to keep grudges going." He agreed and, after another warm handshake, he suggested we join the crowd.

As we began walking in, I said, "Buck, for what it's worth, you motivated the hell out of me."

He chuckled, "I figured that one out." He ushered me through the door ahead of him while most of the guests stared. He introduced me to his wife, and we chatted about their kids for a few minutes before I went to refill my glass. My Buck problems were over, and it was a weight lifted from my shoulders.

Later, after Buck and his wife left, Wanda told me they'd reconciled. He'd stopped putting the make on the married girl. Resolving our feud was the logical next step for him to clear the decks of his personal problems. No one could be happy living life as Buck had been.

As had become our modus operandi, I left with the crowd and circled back to stay overnight. On Sunday, I went bodysurfing with Grover and some other buddies and had a marvelous day. I had much for which to be thankful. Except for the Gin problem, I was at peace.

I had adjusted to civilian life. I had a new company car, my mother lived not far away, and I had a relationship with a compliant girlfriend and lived in a shabby but comfortable apartment. In addition, I was succeeding in a good job. How much better could life be for a guy from my background? My big problem was that I wasn't saving any money, but I promised myself I'd get on that—soon. My Scarlett O'Hara syndrome was ever active.

Gin Sends a Surprise

A letter from Gin arrived. The first words: "I love you, and you've been right about so many things. I want to visit California." I couldn't believe it. This was a giant game changer.

She wrote that Marie had spent hours commiserating with her and she had a long talk with her mother. Both encouraged her to do it. Her mother said she'd make it right with her father. After all, she was twenty-three, a grown woman, and had a right to live her own life. If friends asked where she was, they would say she was in Virginia Beach with some girlfriends.

Still playing it safe, she wrote, "I'll tell Jack as soon as I hear from you that you still want me to come. I've been horrid to you, so if you've changed your mind, I'll understand." She went on to say that Jack would be upset and might not want to see her again, but she was willing to accept that outcome.

I thought *Fat chance of that—he'll hang on any way he can.*

After a phone call, we agreed she'd stay for two weeks. It would be difficult for me to get time off, but I'd make it happen. I saw Gin's visit as one of the big events in my life, and I wanted it to be perfect in every way.

CHAPTER 34

Schopenhauer refused to conceive of love as either trifling or accidental, but rather understood it to be an immensely powerful force lying unseen within a man's psyche and dramatically shaping the world: The ultimate aim of love affairs is more important than all the other aims in a man's life; and therefore, it is quite worthy of the profound seriousness with which everyone pursues it. What is decided by it is nothing less than the composition of the next generation.

—From *Thoughts of Arthur Schopenhauer* - philosopher (1788–1860)

Life is like a ten-speed bike. Most of us have gears we never use.

—Charles Schulz, cartoonist, Charlie Brown creator (1922-2000)

CALIFORNIA, HERE SHE COMES

Gin's boss gave her Friday off, so she was in Los Angeles by that night. She had two full weeks to see California. The plan was for me to work three short days each week and spend the rest of the time with her. We'd end up in San Francisco, and she'd fly back to Pittsburgh from there.

If there were no terrible accounts on your plate from the previous month, the first two weeks of each month were relatively easy. In the second half of the month the broken promises and repo possibilities surfaced. Jack volunteered to pitch in and help on house calls and Don said he wouldn't call for any inventory checks during Gin's stay.

My grandparents had arrived in California. In a few days they bought a three-bedroom house just east of El Monte. Mom and George were invited to move in with them. The third bedroom was where Gin would stay. I would sleep on the sofa in the living room or in Long Beach, depending on my schedule. Grandpa and Grandma volunteered to take Gin sightseeing. We all wanted Gin to love California.

I took her to Big Bear and Arrowhead lakes and to Long Beach to visit Bill Glitch. He told her he loved California. We spent a Sunday at Malibu Beach with Jim and Aline Jackson and had a barbecue at their house. We visited Chinatown, Olvera Street, and the Rose Bowl. A day was spent touring the sights of Hollywood, Beverly Hills and Santa Monica. We went to the beach at Corona del Mar.

While I was working, my grandparents took her to Knott's Berry Farm and San Juan Capistrano, two of their favorite places. Gin saw so much that she begged for a day just to walk around Pasadena and visit the department stores. We both had a great time, and it was undoubtedly the happiest we had been together. But we didn't have much time alone to sit and talk quietly, or be intimate.

The gods who look out for fools gave me two easy weeks with no client or dealer emergencies. It was so smooth that I was able to drive back to El Monte and sleep there almost every night.

When I told Mom that Gin and I were going to San Francisco two days before her plane left I knew this would be a problem. In the fifties, single couples didn't travel overnight together. The propriety of the day called for a third person as a chaperone and separate hotel rooms. Mom asked, "Are her parents aware that you'll be staying in a hotel for two nights?" I refused to get into the details.

I simply said, "Mom, Gin is twenty-three and I'm twenty-two. Just leave us alone. We know what we're doing, and you might as well accept it." I suspect Mom discussed it with Grandma, because it didn't come up again. Grandma was the wise old bird who hungered to reach her goal line - and that was the wedding. She never asked about hotel rooms and such, most probably because she didn't give a damn.

The truth was that we would be together for three nights because I had told them Gin's plane left on Saturday, not Sunday.

The first night we stayed in a new motel in San Luis Obispo recommended by the Auto Club. I signed us in as Mr. and Mrs., a first for us. It was such a nice place that we could have spent a week there.

After a morning drive to San Francisco, we visited Coit Tower and drove along the Embarcadero before checking into the Sir Francis Drake. Gin was fidgety about the elegance and size of the hotel. She'd never been in one that large before. The possibility of an earthquake came up, but cocktails settled her down.

The next day, we drove across the Golden Gate to the Alta Mira Hotel in Sausalito so we could look back at the city. We had drinks at the Top of the Mark Hopkins and she wouldn't go close to the windows. The size of everything in California was what she seemed to notice most. She said everything was too big. She could have said, "I came, I saw, I was overwhelmed" and been quite accurate.

After these three days together, we agreed that we had never been so much in love. We had come a long way over a five-year span. We knew we had to come to some resolution.

The sensitive things had to surface, and they did. She was aware that I was thinking about college in the fall, and she wanted to know my decision. My reply was, "Are you willing to move to Los Angeles to be with me? That controls my next move."

She said, "If we get married, the wedding has to be at home." There was no argument about that. She understood that I wouldn't move back to Ohio, and she wanted time to think about that. She put everything off whenever possible. She was also infected with the Scarlett O'Hara syndrome.

I wanted to know about Jack. Did she intend to go on seeing him? Finally, on Saturday evening, she agreed to stop seeing Jack and think hard about getting married and moving to California. She was not very convincing. The trip had been tiring for her. She was ready to go home even as she was sad that our time together was ending.

Saying good-bye at the airport was heartrending. As I watched her go up the stairs into the plane, tears came to my eyes. Why couldn't we get it right?

The drive to Long Beach went fast because my mind was chugging on several levels. First, there was Gin. What the hell was going happen with us? Second, and connected to the first, what was I going to do about college—go or not go? I could try night school or just give up on it. I had met a guy in the navy who got his degree in three years. Could that work for me?

Then GMAC and the stack of work I would face on Monday came to mind. The last thing was about Wanda. We had no future together. Should I just break off the relationship?

The GMAC problem was easy. I had to get in the office early on Monday, thank Don for his support, and then work hard, seven days a week, until I had nailed a good month-end report.

Gin was a conundrum. I decided to find out what she thought about California before I drew any conclusions. If she wasn't willing to move, I'd enroll in college for sure. If she leaned toward moving, night school was on the table. By the time I reached these conclusions, I was within a few blocks of the apartment and looking forward to sleep.

A well suntanned Al with his GMAC Chevrolet, summer 1954

George Pearce and Al's mother, Isabelle, not long after their wedding in 1953

Al - just after body surfing at Corona del Mar Beach, summer, 1954

Gin during her California visit, Corona del Mar Beach, summer, 1954

Gin taking a rest while hiking at Lake Arrowhead, near Los Angeles, 1954

Chapter 35

In time, and as one comes to benefit from experience,
one learns that things will turn out
neither as well as one hoped
nor as badly as one feared.
—Jerome S. Bruner, cognitive psychologist (1915–living)

Luck is being in the right place at the right time,
but location and timing are to some extent under our control
—Natash Josefowitz, Lecturer, writer (unknown-living)

A Surprise

When I arrived at the office, Don greeted me with, "I want to hear how things went with your girlfriend, but first we have to talk about something important. He led me out the back door to his car and drove to a coffee shop. "This is super confidential, Al," he began. "I need your promise that what we are about to discuss will go no further." I promised.

He launched into it without preliminaries. "Charlie's assistant quit without notice. He had to leave or lose his marriage. Charlie asked me to find out if you'd be interested in the job. If you turn this down it must be kept secret. He doesn't want the next man he considers to know he was second choice. Well, what do you think?"

Surprises were common at GMAC, but this one was overwhelming. I thought, *Me a skip tracer—why me?*

All Don would say was, "Charlie doesn't want a man who's been plugging along as a field rep for years and is set in his ways. He would rather have a reliable man he can train to do things his way. And, he likes you and your record."

I said, "Let's do this. Give me an hour or so. I need some time to let the idea stew in my head. I'll hand you a note shortly after lunch with yes or no on it and you'll understand."

He said, "That's a good plan. But by two, okay? Charlie will be in about four."

The decision to take the job was easy. I wanted it. The problem was doing it for only a couple of months—if I went to college. I met Leland for lunch. After my explanation, he said, "Al, if you knew for sure you were going to quit and go to college, it would be a difficult decision. But you have that Ohio girl in your head. Being with her and going to college probably doesn't mix. So take the new assignment. Do a bang-up job so they'll be disappointed if you leave and not focus on how long you had the job. No one owes his life to his job. Employers buy your time and labor, and you've been a bargain for them. Don't let potential guilt hold you back from something you really want to do." Leland saw things so clearly when I was befogged.

After lunch, I sat in the car, smoked a cigarette and let my mind wander through the situation. Finally, I wrote YES in big letters on the back of a report form and folded it. At exactly two o'clock, I reached over Don's head and dropped it onto his desk. He glanced at it, swung around, and gave me a smiling thumbs-up. He liked the decision even though it might make his job more difficult.

When Charlie walked into the lunchroom, he silently signaled me to follow him. We drove to a bar, went to a back booth, and ordered beer. Charlie had a well-known penchant for secrecy. It was part of his job, but it was also Charlie's personality.

He explained his operation, methodically and in great detail, with examples to illustrate his points. He was a fine lecturer and I took notes carefully.

When he stopped to sip his beer, I was able to ask, "Why me for this job?"

His reply was, "I want an energetic, smart young guy I can trust who is a proven field rep. Trust is a key ingredient. My intuition and what I've learned about you tell me you fit the job description."

We moved to a better restaurant for dinner, and Charlie gave me his background. He had a degree in criminology, worked a short time as a policeman, was happily married, had two young kids, and was in his mid-thirties. He loved his job and had no interest in going inside to a desk job. He was like Deke in some ways.

After sharing a bottle of wine and some Drambuie after dinner, we were both well oiled. It was nearly ten when we left the restaurant. On the way back to my car, he told me that although the job change was a done deal, we still had to meet with Chill and perhaps Mr. Warner the next morning. Then he added, "Because I didn't want money to be the reason for you to say yes, I didn't tell you that this job will give you a fifty-buck-a-month raise, but now you know." That was a pile of frosting on the cake.

The meeting with Chill and Warner was brief. All they wanted was to hear from each of us was that we felt we could work together. As we were leaving, Mr. Chill grinned and said, "Al, it will be easy for you to help your replacement. I understand you share an apartment." Pevehouse had asked for Jack to move into my job.

It came as a surprise to everyone that I had been selected for the skip tracing job. Now it really did look as if Buck was right and I was a fair-haired boy. Some of the older guys were disappointed that they were not considered, but all congratulated me, even Buck.

Charlie handed me my first assignment immediately after we left Mr. Warner's office. It was two four-inch thick files from the Chicago office. He told me to study them and be prepared to discuss them with him the next morning because we were going after these two. I knew this was a test of sorts, so I went home and spent hours reading every scrap of paper, making notes, and trying to learn all I could about the two skips.

Skip tracing was seen as a mysterious job, and being such a mysterious person, Charlie promoted that view. Skip tracers had a lot of freedom - only results mattered. There were no car dealers to argue with and no month end grinding out of refinancing deals and repos. No one knew how hard Charlie worked, but I found out quickly, when I went to his home. He lived only a couple miles from the office.

Charlie laid out the security precautions that he followed, and they were extensive. He told me to get a separate phone with an unlisted number and use it for skip business only. This was to keep our home phone numbers from getting into the wrong hands. If the business phone was ever compromised, you just got a new one. He added pointedly, "Make it clear to your roommate that he is not to use that phone for anything—ever. I want that line clear unless you are on it. If it's busy, I'll know you are home." Charlie had two company phones. If one was busy, GMAC people could call the other one.

He said that every case would have a phony name so we could refer to it without giving away who the subject really was. He also approved Mansfield and Carpenter as my phony names. He was firm about keeping all personal information about us away from contacts and out of our files. "There's no reason for people we contact to have any personal knowledge —it only increases your risk. If the shit really hits the fan, company info can be subpoenaed, but there is no access to personal information unless it's in a file." It all made sense to me.

For that same reasoning, he said that I should not speak about a case in progress to anyone outside or inside GMAC, with the exception of Chill and Warner. He said, "After we nail a skip, it's okay to talk about it with some of the other reps, but not with outside people. And don't use real names. You never know who it might get to. Some of the guys we take cars from are nasty characters with sympathetic relatives and friends." I heeded his advice in spades and never used real names even when swapping stories with Jack.

Just as I was becoming acquainted with my new job, the other choice of directions in my life surfaced. The new Citrus JC and CMC catalogues of classes had arrived at Mom's house. When I picked them up, I didn't tell her about the new job. I knew she would fret about it being more dangerous than just being a field rep, and in some ways it was.

A Decision Is Made

A letter from Gin arrived. It was full of thanks for making her trip a delight. She had liked what she saw and would give serious consideration to moving, but she needed time. The letter ended with a pledge of undying love and "I began missing you before the plane took off, and it's worse now." Well, I missed her too, but I needed a decision soon.

I decided to sign up for classes at Citrus JC. I could always drop out if I changed my mind. The cooperative Miss Witten helped me navigate my way through the course catalogue. I mentioned that I wanted to spend only three years in college because I was already going on twenty-three. She pointed out that achieving a degree in three years was a formidable mountain to climb and probably not possible. But, with careful planning and attending two summer school sessions, it was possible. The plan was for me to attend Citrus JC for one school year, and if my grades were high enough, I could transfer into CMC. If I couldn't handle a heavy workload, I would not graduate until the spring of 1958. This was not good news; I wanted to finish my degree in June of 1957, when I'd be twenty-five.

Citrus didn't offer every class every semester. I had to figure a way around that. Miss Witten said, "Let's get you started on these classes in September. I don't want to put more pressure on you, but the closer you come to a 4.0 grade point average, the more likely it is that you'll be allowed to carry heavy study loads, and that you can get a scholarship. Call me if you need advice."

The following week, I sneaked a few hours off, drove to Citrus JC, paid some fees, and signed up for the selected classes. Now the question was when or if I should tell Gin. I decided just to let things sit and work like hell on my job.

Skip to My Lou, My Darlin'

Skip tracing is a unique occupation. It is essential to have patience, followed closely by perseverance. Skips often come to believe that if they can stay out of sight long enough, the lender will give up. This is a totally inaccurate theory.

Unlike the average delinquent who is having temporary financial problems, a high percentage of skips are people who have many long overdue debts and are hiding from everyone.

A few skipped to buy time. They told themselves they really intended to catch up on their payments—someday. But once they were on the lam for a few months —and many were on the run for over a year—they figured the value of the car had gone way below what was still owed on it. At that point, they had no intention of paying. They sometimes abandoned the vehicles or sold them to people who would resell them in Mexico. They sometimes rented the car to someone who would drive it until they got caught. The car was almost certainly not insured. There were cases of skips destroying or hiding their cars, then reporting them stolen. Our job was to get the cars before any of these drastic actions had happened.

First, the GMAC office that held the bad loan tried to find the car. Once they knew the delinquent had moved out of their area, they sent the file to the GMAC office near where they thought the skip had landed. The files were usually full of the names, addresses, phone numbers, and even pictures of the skip's relatives and friends. Sometimes there was mail that a field rep had picked up from the skip's last address. This was a violation of post office regulations, but many regulations were ignored in the heat of the chase. We had to be clever enough to sort through the information and come up with useable facts. It wasn't easy, but I had a great coach. Charlie was the sorcerer, and I was his apprentice.

The vast majority of skips we got were people moving to California because the economy was booming. Invariably, they also ran out on their rent and any other time payments they owed back home.

Skips often had other reasons to get lost in the crowd, such as legal offenses. As a result, the police were on the lookout for them, if not actively searching. One of Charlie's accomplishments was that he had established connections with a number of police detectives in the communities of Southern California. He was useful to them because he'd often give them first crack when he located a person of interest. If they got their man, he got the car. In return, the police usually told Charlie where the car was when they arrested one of his skips. If the police impounded the car, the GMAC lawyers took over the job of retrieving it.

Charlie and I met at his house every Friday afternoon to review everything from the previous week, plan our actions for the coming week, and discuss any new cases we'd received. His home office was stacked with folders and pictures of wanted cars were pinned on the walls. His wife was nice but stayed pretty much out of sight when we were working. I never really got to know her.

We stayed in touch constantly. He expected me to call in every morning about eight, and he would call me if he wanted to talk earlier. The same held true in the evening, but if I wasn't home, he'd call Harvey's or a night line in the office. I was likely to be one place or the other. If something important was happening on a case, everything else in our lives took a backseat. Charlie was obsessed with running his quarry to ground and expected me to be the same.

Frequently when we had a tip, I staked out somewhere waiting for a skip to appear. It could be a home, office, factory, barbershop, a mistress, a supermarket - any place we had information that a skip might show up. People are creatures of habit. They may move, but they often return to their favorite habits, hobbies or sports. They often parked their cars a few blocks away or in an alley and walked to their destinations. Some hid their car under fitted car covers. That ruse only made the car stand out, and we always checked out covered cars near a skip's address. Once we laid eyes on the skip, we eventually found the car. Nearly all skips were amateurs, and Charlie was a professional skip finder - we had the advantage.

Hitting a Home Run

On one occasion, an informer told us where a skip's sister lived and said that he often visited her. He had been discharged from the navy a year earlier, and was on the lam immediately. Charlie told me to stake out the house late in the afternoon and wait for him. Assuming he had a job and assuming he was living nearby, he might visit after work. That was too many assumptions, but that's all we had.

After three fruitless afternoons, I decided to try something. I went to a gas station, changed into navy fatigue pants and shirt, and returned to the address. A woman came to the door. I said, "Sorry to bother you, Mrs. Smith, but your brother and I were shipmates. He gave me this address in case I came into Long Beach. My ship just docked this morning. Is he here?"

I could see she was sizing me up as she said, "He doesn't live here and never has."

I said, "Please accept my apologies for bothering you, ma'am, but Bob told me that if I got into Long Beach, to contact you and you'd know where he is. He gave me your phone number, but I lost it. When you hear from him, just tell him that Jeff Carpenter came by looking for him."

I began to turn away, and she said, "Well, I guess it'll be okay to tell you. He's living in Las Vegas, but he's coming here late tomorrow afternoon if you want to stop by then." I thanked her and walked away slowly. This was a possible home run.

Late the next afternoon, in Charlie's personal car (he figured the skip might ID our standard Chevy coupe), we were parked with the house in sight. We were hoping he'd park on the street so we could make an easy steal. We didn't intend to speak to him.

About five, he rolled up, parked, took a bag out of the trunk, and went up the stairs and into the house. While Charlie jimmied the door and put the gears in neutral, I hooked up the tow bar. We were ready to pull out in two minutes. As we pulled away, I looked back and saw the skip run down the stairs to the sidewalk, watching his car leaving. It was my first skip victory. I felt like a fighter pilot making his first kill.

Getting Lucky

We had ascertained that a skip was living in a trailer park in Carson. There were dozens of trailer parks in and around the area. Most of the parks had rate signs by the street and we reasoned that the skip would be in one of the cheapest parks.

By late morning, I had been through a dozen parks looking for the correct Indiana license plate. Just before lunch, I saw an Indiana plate, but it wasn't our subject. *What the hell?* I thought. *I need to get out and stretch my legs anyway.* I was wearing jeans and a T-shirt, so I looked like trailer park material. I knocked on the trailer next to the car.

A fat woman came to the door and gruffly asked what I wanted. I said, "Well, I'm looking for my uncle. I was told he lived in a trailer park on this street, but I forgot which one."

"So why come to my door?" she asked.

I said, "Well, there's a car right there with Indiana plates and my uncle is from Indiana. I just thought I might get lucky."

"What's his name?"

I replied without hesitation, "Bill Campbell, from Indianapolis."

She perked up and said, "Yeah, I know the sonuvabitch. He's married to my cousin. He borrowed money from me, and now I never hear from him. Wanna know where he is?"

Remaining calm, I said, "Yeah, I'd like to see the old rascal. I'll remind him he owes you."

"How much is it worth to you?"

I looked unhappy and said, "All I have is twenty dollars, and I'll give you half." She put her hand out as I fished two fives out of my pocket and reached them toward her, stopping short of giving them to her.

I said, "Tell you what: I'll give you one of the fives, you give me his address, and then I'll give you the other one." She laughed, took the five, and said, "He's in the trailer park next to this one, just a block north, in space number one fifteen."

I put the second five in her hand, thanked her, and walked away thinking, *what an old bitch. She sold out her cousin's husband for a measly ten bucks, and she damn well knew I'm not his nephew; she's just wants to send him some trouble.*

Sure enough, there it was: a year-old Buick with the right license numbers parked at space 115. As I drove past the trailer, I could see people inside. This was not the time to play the hero. I found a phone booth and called Charlie. His wife said he'd be back late in the afternoon. I was sitting in his office when he arrived. When I told him the story, we had a good laugh and a beer.

Just before midnight, we did one pass to reconnoiter the place. There were no lights on in the trailer, and the car was still there. Charlie silently jimmied the Buick's door while I attached the tow bar as quietly as possible. When he finished, he jumped into my car and backed it up. I finished the hookup. Just as I finished the last latch, the lights in the trailer came on. I was on the driver's side of the cars. I ran to the exit, crossing to the passenger side behind the Buick. Charlie slowed down and I jumped in. The skip yelled curses but made no attempt to catch us. Charlie said the guy always knew that someday he would be a pedestrian.

WATTS

We received a file from the Santa Ana office. After study and leg work, we decided the skip was living in what was called "the projects." These were large, government owned, apartment houses. They were run-down but not yet the slums they became later. I wasn't concerned about moving around in the black neighborhoods, but I kept my eyes open in Watts, as Duke had taught me. After a few hours of searching, I pulled into a project that was about six smaller apartment buildings around a circular drive. In the middle was a grassless pocket park that contained a phone booth.

The subject car was sitting in front of a ground-floor apartment. When I knocked, a man came to the door. I asked, "Are you James Brown?" He said he was, and I handed him my card. Then he asked, "Hey, man, how'd you know I was here?"

Ignoring his question, I said, "Mr. Brown, you're four payments behind on your car loan, and you've been hiding from us. I have to repossess your car."

He said, "I can't let you take that car, man. I needs it to get to work. I'll pay all the payments next week." The palaver went on for a few minutes, during which several men gathered behind me and listened. I sensed some intimidation might be on the way, and I considered leaving. Then an idea popped up.

At that time, anyone could call the Los Angeles Police Department and ask for an officer to "keep the peace." I excused myself, walked briskly to the phone booth, consulted my pocket phone book, and called the local precinct. I told the answerer I was about to repossess a car and needed an officer to keep the peace and gave the address. The voice said, "He's on the way." I walked back to Mr. Brown and listened to his bullshit. In a few minutes, a police car arrived.

There were two cops, and one asked for my ID. I also handed him the account record, which showed the skip's license plate numbers. He said, "Okay, take the car, but do it quick. This could get sticky." I backed my car up to Mr. Brown's car, jimmied the door, put the gears in neutral, and hooked up the tow bar. Meanwhile, Mr. Brown took his personal stuff out of the trunk and the officers leaned on their car, saying nothing. The nearby group of men stared silently and mumbled things about the police helping me steal a brother's car, but they made no moves.

Things were tense when I said politely, "Mr. Brown, come into the office tomorrow and we'll see what we can work out for you. If you bring enough money, you can probably get your car back."

He used a polite tone when he said, "You is an asshole for takin' my car, but I knows it's your job. Here's the key." I thanked the police and drove away. The sun was setting, but it was a clear twilight and I was looking forward to the praise Charlie would give me. I also knew he'd tell me it was a dumb, high risk repo.

Every day was a new, exciting one when you worked with Charlie. I liked the job better than anything I'd ever done.

The Decision

It was obvious that Gin didn't want to leave Ohio, but she'd not yet definitely said so. She just wrote around the issue. I pushed for a decision because I had to go, or not go, to college. She finally wrote a long letter explaining what she could have said in a paragraph. She just couldn't see herself living in such a big, busy, complicated place. In addition, she felt I was different. She wrote, "Alf, you don't realize how much you've changed since you left Bridgeport. You don't think the same, you don't act the same, and you don't even talk the same. I'm just a simple high school graduate who's good at office work. I couldn't keep up with you and your educated friends. I just can't do what you want me to do. I love you and want what is best for you, and that is getting your education. I can't stand in the way of that." It sounded final to me, and I couldn't argue with some of her points. Gin was taking herself out of my life.

I'd known she was leaning that way, but it was still a shock to read the finality of it. Lastly, I just couldn't shake the idea that Jack was more important to her decision than she admitted. It would have been easier if she had just said she was in love with him. I was angry and unhappy but determined to move forward. When I put the letter down I had decided that I'd quit GMAC and begin college.

Saying Good-Bye Ain't Easy

It is said that time goes fast when you're having fun, and skip tracing with Charlie was the most fun I'd ever had fully clothed. Sometimes the hours were brutal and futile, but I looked forward to the challenge and excitement of each day.

At the end of our usual morning phone call, I enquired what he had planned for the day. He gave a typical Charlie reply: "Well, I thought I'd take the missus and the kids for a day at the beach, then a nice dinner and a movie. Let's just give the f*****g skips the day off and let them catch their breaths. Why do you ask?"

"Charlie, I need some private time with you to discuss something important. Can we do that sometime today or tomorrow morning?"

He picked up on the seriousness of my voice and said, "Sure, Al, how about four this afternoon at my house?"

I said, "I'll be here," and he hung up. We always skipped polite formalities.

He came to the door with the necks of two beers in one hand and gave one to me. "Is this a two, three, or more beer conversation, Al?"

"I don't know, Charlie, but we'll find out." After a long swig of Bud, I launched into a short monologue, which he didn't interrupt. I explained I had hoped that Gin would move to LA and I'd stay on the job at GMAC. Now that it was certain that she wasn't coming, I felt I had to go to college.

He leaned back, looked out the window, and drained his beer before hopping up and getting two more. He started, "First, Al, forget the guilty conscience bullshit. You've tried harder than anyone I've ever teamed with and you haven't been a burden. Second, you have your own star to follow so just f*****g go do it. I'm sorry your girl jilted you, but you're both young, and she may change her mind." He knocked my socks off with his understanding attitude.

I asked his advice about Chill and Warner and he said, "Tell them right away and then call me. I need to talk to Chill about your replacement, but I'd like you to stay with me as long as you can." Charlie was such a realistic and sensible human being. I had just told him he had to start training a new assistant, and he was helping me. I thanked him and said I'd work until he needed me to step aside for a new man, but I had to be finished up by shortly after Labor Day.

The next day, I called Mr. Chill and made an appointment. He had been my supporter in so many ways, and I didn't want him to be angry with me. When I got to his desk, he said, "From the look on your face, I think we need privacy." He motioned to the small conference room. We sat down, and as is my way, I explained what had happened with my girlfriend and that I had to start school in a few weeks. I finished with, "Mr. Chill, I am deeply grateful for the breaks you, Mr. Warner, and others have given me. And I want you to know how much I appreciate all the personal attention you've given me."

He replied, "Al, I appreciate your forthrightness, and I'm sorry your love life didn't go your way. I hate losing you, but I would never discourage a bright young man from getting an education. I think you'll do well in college, and I congratulate you for having the courage to make this decision. Damned few men can bring themselves to give up a good job to go back to school at twenty-two. Now, have you worked things out with Charlie?" I said that I would work as long as possible or leave when Charlie asked me to.

He said, "I'll speak with Charlie and I'll explain things to Mr. Warner when he comes in tomorrow." *At least I was spared that chore,* I thought.

I took Don into the parking lot and explained my situation. He also understood and wished me luck. "Stay in touch," he said. "I'll miss you, and so will many others." What a great bunch of people I had been privileged to work with at GMAC!

That evening, I told Jack that I had to move near Citrus JC. He groaned about not being able to afford the apartment on his own, but he wished me luck. There was no one else he wanted as a roommate, and the rent was due in a week. He gave notice to the landlord the next day, and by the day after that, he had found weekly rental rooms for both of us in a large Long Beach house.

The Friday after Labor Day, I turned in my car and picked up the used Chevy I'd bought. There were a lot of goodbyes to deal with. I had bonded with quite a few people, and leaving them was more emotional than I had expected.

When I shook hands with Mr. Chill, he said, "Al, if anything happens in your life that makes you quit school, come and see me. There just might be an opening for you at GMAC." That meant a lot to me; I just hoped it wouldn't happen.

Don, Deke, and Jack met at Harvey's. After Don and Deke left, Jack confided in me that he had asked Mr. Chill to let him interview for my job with Charlie. Jack asked if I would intercede on his behalf. My response was that Charlie might resent the interference, but I'd say all the right things if Charlie called me.

After a late visit with Wanda, my time in Long Beach was over. The next morning, I drove to Mom's house. She was surprised when I told her of my decision, and she understood about the Gin situation being hopeless. She was supportive and pleased that I would be moving in with them. The house was an easy ten-mile drive from Citrus.

Not long after I arrived, Grandpa attacked me. "Alfred, you're doing a crazy thing giving up your job with General Motors to go to college. Why would you do such a thing? You have a company car and wear a tie and a white shirt to work. Just do a good job and you'll move up the ladder and you can retire with a pension. And, your mother tells me you're not going to marry Virginia. Do you think college is more important than having a family of your own?"

Grandma joined in. "Alfred, you won't find a better girl than Virginia—ever. You're smart, and you're getting an education every day you go to work. You don't need college. Marry that girl and have a family!"

I attempted to explain. "You don't understand. Virginia refuses to move to California, and I won't go back to Bridgeport. I want a college education, and I intend to get it. My boss at GMAC told me that if I change my mind, he'll hire me back, so I have nothing to lose." In a week, they were living with the stupid decisions their grandson and his girlfriend had made.

Early the next week, Jack called. He had gotten the job with Charlie. He was ecstatic but keenly aware that now he had a bear by the tail. He had sworn off booze and promised everyone he wouldn't walk into Harvey's until his probation period was over.

"Jack, call when you're coming near El Monte, and I'll get Mom to do spare ribs and sauerkraut the way we like it."

He replied, "How about Sunday?" Jack never passed up a home-cooked meal.

After that Sunday dinner, we had the kind of good-bye good friends have, with a hug and bitchy comments. His last words to me: "Stay away from booze and women—that's what killed my grades in college." As I waved good-bye, I had no idea I'd never see him again.

CHAPTER 36

There comes a time in a man's life
when to get where he has to –
if there are no doors or windows –
he walks through a wall.
—Bernard Malamud, novelist (1914–1986)

Things don't go wrong and break your heart
so you can become bitter and give up.
They happen to break you down and build you up
so you can be all that you were intended to be.
—Charles Jones, car salesman, motivator (1927–2008)

A NEW JOB

A pressing problem was finding a job that accommodated school. My savings had been spent on Gin's visit, buying a car, and having good times. My school fees were paid, but I needed books and supplies. I was determined not to ask Mom or my grandparents for money.

Bill Glitch came to visit, and I borrowed $80 from him. He was grateful that I had brought him to California and said the loan had no due date; whenever I could afford to repay it was soon enough.

Crawford's Market at Five Points in El Monte, California, was called "The Biggest Little Country Store" because it claimed to offer everything a family needed. Basically, it was a supermarket in a building so large that many other businesses leased spaces.

The parking lots held hundreds of cars, and it was a busy, buzzing place. [27] Mom worked in an independent jewelry store in the main building. Through Mom's boss, I had met a Crawford son named Lou. Mom suggested I ask Lou for a job.

Lou reviewed my application and was impressed that I had worked at A&P. He gave me a job stocking shelves and assured me that if I did that well, he'd move me into a better situation. After a week he took me to a check stand and told the girl there to train me between customers. In a few days, I had developed enough proficiency to do some checking out of groceries.

One afternoon, Lou assigned me to be the cashier for the candy and tobacco department. To prevent theft, this department was separated from the rest of the store by a wall. Every imaginable kind of candy was displayed, including expensive stuff with high profit margins. Nearly every brand of cigarettes, cigars, snuff, and chewing tobacco were also stocked.

As an incentive for people to come to Crawford's on payday, we cashed paychecks. To control the flow of money, only a couple grocery checkout stands and the one at the tobacco/candy stand were used to cash checks. There was always a supervisor standing at a

27 Crawford's was located where Garvey Boulevard (now the I-10 Freeway), Valley Boulevard, and Mountain View Avenue all crossed. The Crawford family owned and ran the business. There was a barbershop, real estate office, drugstore, shoe repair, ice cream store, bakery, snack bar, pony rides, and more. Special events were held—e.g., Santa arrived by helicopter each year. There was an Easter celebration, a circus set up for a week each summer, and prizes were given for all sorts of events like dance contests. It was Wal-Mart, The Home Depot, and an entertainment center all in one location. In 2012, the location was still market center but does not have the panache that Crawford's had.

convenient kiosk to approve checks and mark them with the code of the day.

On Friday evenings and all day on the weekends, I cashed piles of paychecks and checked out hundreds of small purchases. At each check-cashing stand, the cashier pushed a button when they needed more currency. The job was more like being a bank teller than a checkout clerk.

Checkers who worked my location frequently had a line of customers waiting. Lou noticed that I was getting people checked out fast and came to investigate.

To speed things up, I had begun adding items in my head and entering one or two totals in the cash register for a dozen items. It was not difficult to add up the price of a carton of cigarettes, some chewing tobacco, and a box of candy and then enter one total. When I told him how I was doing it, he smiled and said, "Don't tell anyone about this. If one of the checkers is standing nearby watching, enter each item separately." I asked why. He said, "Al, we have a contract with the Retail Clerks Union, and they don't want more speed; they want us to have more employees to pay dues. If they found out what you were doing, they'd try to make us add another check stand. Just keep on doing what you're doing. Find me when you go on break and we'll talk more."

We met at the coffee counter. He said the union would soon be in touch with me because an employee had tipped them off that I might be working enough hours to be considered full time. He said he would be more careful and not schedule me for over thirty hours per week. He added that some of the cashiers felt that working a checkout stand was a women's job. They didn't like a male college student taking a job away from one of their own. I told Lou about the black gang at the Mansfield Tire, and we both laughed at the parallel. He said the union wanted every department and every concession in the building unionized. The Crawford family was fighting them and contract negotiations were coming up soon. It was a tense situation.

This was not my first dustup with a union. The carpenters' union had been on my case to join when I was an apprentice, and there had been the issue with my uncle's painting contractor business. I was familiar with the United Steel Workers and the United Rubber Workers unions and didn't like most of the shop stewards I'd met, particularly the fat one in Mansfield. Suffice it to say that I was no fan of unions and didn't want to join the Retail Clerks.

After this conversation, I was careful to work slowly when another employee was nearby. I got away with doing it my way.

COLLEGE—THE ADJUSTMENT

The first day at school, I was eager to get started. I was determined to get myself into the study habits Rick had taught me in yeoman school. My confidence was high, but I was also apprehensive about getting close to a 4.0 grade point average.

I got off to a colorful start. At the entrance to the campus, I was accosted by two young men who told me I had to buy a small cap, sort of like a yarmulke. They called it a beanie, and it cost a dollar. They said I had to wear it the first week of school to show that I was a freshman. I gave them the dollar, took the beanie, stuck it in my hip pocket, and moved on. One guy caught up with me and insisted I wear it. When I said I didn't want to, he said, "Then you have to go into the pokey until you put it on." They had a small wood-barred cage into which they put noncompliant freshmen. One boy was already in the enclosure. I should have just worn the damned thing, but it irritated me that teenage boys were telling a vet to wear a silly hat.

One of them took my arm to guide me into the cage. When I pushed him away, he got more insistent. I said, "Look, kid, you can leave me alone or you can get knocked on your ass—which is it?"

It was a tense situation until he said, "You're just a bad sport," and then he walked away. I made no friends with this act, but from then on, the young boys steered clear of me. It had taken me less than two minutes to become one of the crotchety old men on campus.

A tall guy about my age caught up with me and said with a smile, "So you don't want to wear a beanie either?" as he showed his to me. "I came through just behind you and they intended to put me through the same routine until I said I agreed with you. They took my buck and didn't argue. After four years in the air force, I'm not wearing that f*****g beanie for anyone." We shook hands and exchanged names; his was Don Schmidt. It took about a five-minute conversation for us to become friends. Don was studying to be an electronics engineer, so we had no classes together, but he became my best college friend and math tutor.

We were both heading into the administrative office to sign up for our educational assistance under the GI Bill. It paid $110 per month. Because my hitch in the navy was less than two years, I was eligible for only twenty-one months of payments. Schmidt, with four years of air force service, would get monthly checks all four years.

Classes Begin

Classes and homework got going quickly, and by the end of the first week, I knew algebra was going to be my downfall if I didn't get help. Schmidt was a fine math student and came to my rescue. He coached me for the entire course, which was fortunate, as I would have gotten no better than a C without his help.

It was also in my favor that Mr. Bergen taught my algebra class. He was tough on the outside but a real softy when you got to know him. He understood that ex-GIs had been away from school for a long time and needed extra help.

The Spanish teacher was Mrs. French, and you guessed it: she also taught French. She was a small lady who rarely smiled and was strict. Tardiness was punishable by death, or as close as she could get to it: an F for the day. Spanish was like yeoman school, almost all rote memory.

My history teacher was Frank Martinez, an ex-marine who was five years my senior, and had a sharp sense of humor. He was also dean of men so I had a compulsory interview with him. It was the custom then for teachers and students to be called Mister, Missus, or Miss. Every teacher called me Mr. Scheid.

At our first private meeting, Mr. Martinez and I got along splendidly. He said that when we were not interacting as teacher and student, it was okay for us to use first names.

Both world history and English were no problem. My fifth class was a sociology class, where all one had to do was read the textbook, and participate in class.

As Rick had taught me, and Jerry and Grover had reinforced, the trick was not to fall behind in any subject. I worked to a tight time schedule, arriving at school before eight in the morning. If I had no class, I went to the library and studied. When I had an hour or more between classes, the library was my home. I left Crawford's immediately after closing at nine o'clock at night, had a snack, and studied until midnight and sometimes later. Saturday and Sunday mornings were key study times because I worked from early afternoon until closing. It could have been a very dull existence, but I was motivated and enjoying the challenge.

Going to school with a bunch of younger kids had one advantage: only a few of them said anything in class that really impressed a teacher. Telephone selling and face-to-face bill collecting had honed my verbal skills. And compared to facing Warner and Chill in month-end meetings, the give-and-take of a classroom was tame. Schmidt and I agreed that the age and experience advantages we had over the kids made school easier. I needed this advantage and damn well used it.

The discipline of the first six weeks paid off. When the first grades came out, my worst was a B in Spanish. I began putting my Spanish vocabulary on three-by-five cards and rubber banding them to the sun visors in my car. This gave me an extra half-hour of vocabulary and pronunciation practice during the drive to and from school.

The Disappearance

Toward the end of October, a secretary came into a class and handed me a note. The message was from Don Pevehouse. It was marked urgent and instructed me to reverse charges on his private line. I left class and went to a phone booth. When Don answered, he said that he was sitting with an FBI agent who needed to speak to me. The agent wanted to know when and where I had last seen or heard from Jack Cronkite. I said I hadn't seen or spoken to him for over a month. He said it was important for me to come to the GMAC office the next day for an interview.

I asked why. He said, "Jack is missing, and we are trying to find him. I can't tell you more now, but you'll get the whole story tomorrow." I decided to go early and ask questions. I hated missing work, but I was concerned about Jack.

The information from the FBI and individuals at GMAC gave me the complete story. Late afternoon on the previous Friday, Jack had called his girlfriend from Westminster, just east of Long Beach. He said he was working a hot lead and had one more stop to make; he would be at her house in an hour. When he didn't show up, she called Harvey, who said Jack hadn't been around for weeks. Then she called several of his other haunts. No one had seen him. She assumed he had started drinking again and would show up later. When he hadn't arrived or called by Saturday morning, she got anxious and called the landlord where Jack was rooming. He hadn't been there since Friday morning. The girlfriend assumed he was shacked up with some other babe, got angry, and decided to stop looking for him. On Sunday, she relented and called Deke, who in turn called Charlie. Charlie hadn't heard from Jack, and was pissed off at him for dropping out of sight.

It wasn't until Monday morning, when Jack missed his morning call to Charlie, that anyone took his disappearance seriously. Charlie got Mr. Chill involved, and by late morning the FBI was involved. Chill assigned two reps to call all the hospitals and emergency rooms in Los Angeles and Orange counties. The hunt was on.

Everyone assumed that Charlie would have some idea why Jack was in Westminster that Friday afternoon, but he didn't. His best guess was that Jack turned up a lead on one of their cases. Charlie reviewed every case they were working on, but came up with nothing related to Westminster.

If there had been foul play, it was almost certain that it would involve a skip Jack was working on. Charlie said, "Dammit, it's a good bet he found a car and tried to take it on his own. He was eager to show he could perform." Poor Jack … What had he gotten himself into?

During my interview, the agent grilled me about Jack's friends and people he hung out with. He also wanted to hear anything I knew about Jack's personal life—whether he associated with hookers, gambled, messed with drugs, and so forth. I was of no help because, except for drinking and an occasional female liaison, Jack was a straight arrow.

Jack's dirty laundry was in his room, along with his suitcase. His checkbook and some cash were in his dresser, and no money had been withdrawn from his bank account. There was no sign that Jack was skipping out or on a binge. Jack and his car had not been seen since Friday morning and there were no clues as to where he was. This spooked everybody.

Don agreed to keep me posted. As I left the office, a car blinked its lights. I could see it was Wanda. We had dinner before I drove home. She was concerned that there was some skip tracer murderer on the loose, and she asked me to be on the lookout. I assured her I'd look under my bed every night and promised to see her during Christmas vacation.

Jack's parents retained a private detective agency, and an investigator called me. He asked the same questions as the FBI, and he said he might call me again, but he never did. When the year ended, Jack and his car had been gone for over two months and not a trace of him had been found. Don and I agreed he was mostly likely dead, but he was listed as missing. This was disturbing. I really liked Jack.

Gin and I had been keeping up a once-each-week letter exchange. She complimented me on my grades and encouraged me to stay with it. When she heard about Jack's disappearance, she admitted that she had never liked my GMAC job. She felt it was dangerous, and was happy I was out of it. I didn't tell her that Jack was in my old job when he went missing.

Miss Witten approved my course selections for the next semester. She was pleased with my grades and that my goal was a minimum of a 3.5 GPA. For the first time, she used the words "*When* you transfer to CMC," instead of "*If* you transfer." She didn't notice her slip. Or was it a slip? Either way, it was a boost to me.

The Union Rears Its Ugly Head

From the beginning, I knew that working and going to school was going to be a marathon. I kept to my routine: up early, Spanish vocabulary in the car, classes, library time, then to work and more study later. Going to movies, dating, and all social life was out.

Time passed quickly, and when Christmas vacation started, I began working at least forty hours every week. We hoped the union people wouldn't notice, but they did. The union agent came to my check stand as I was being relieved for my break. He joined me for coffee and a smoke and said, "I don't want to make a big fuss. I'm sure you need the money you're making. But we don't like the idea of part-time workers. Guys like you take jobs away from union members, and you don't pay dues so you're getting a free ride. I'd like you to come to my house in Pomona and learn why you should join the union voluntarily." After more palaver, I agreed to meet him at his home in Pomona. He fancied himself a smooth talker, but I read him as having the same mentality as the jerks I had chased for car payments. I didn't like him, not even a little bit.

The agent's two-car garage had been converted into a meeting room and contained folding chairs and a movie projector. I had to watch a propaganda film telling the viewer how downtrodden and mistreated retail workers had been until a man named Joe De Silva took over and led them out of the wilderness. Of course, it neglected to mention anything about the strong-arm tactics that Joe had used to force workers into the union and the fact that the union leaders had large salaries. I was aware of the background of De Silva and his group simply because I had been reading the *LA Times* (then a conservative newspaper) since my arrival in California. Goons had rolled trucks through the front windows of supermarkets, beat people up, and so on. The Retail Clerks had a well-earned reputation as a tough union.

After the movie ended, he added some verbal history about how he had been a checkout clerk before joining Mr. De Silva in his mighty struggle. I said I had to leave, and he gave me some pamphlets to take with me. His parting comment: "You know, you'll either join our union or lose your job."

During the holiday season, I worked up to twelve hours some days due to many absentees caused by a flu bug. Lou told me the agent would probably come at me again after the first of the year.

By the end of December, I had developed a decent level of competence at cashing checks, running the register, and processing multiple items quickly and accurately. When I turned in my cash drawer at the end of each shift, it nearly always balanced perfectly or was plus or minus a few pennies. It was easy to make mistakes with coins so an exact balance every day wasn't expected. One Saturday morning in January, Lou took me aside and said, "Your cash drawer was off over twenty dollars last night. Do you have any idea why?" Friday night had been busy and I had cashed many checks, but nothing extraordinary had happened.

"I'll replace the money if you want me to," I said, "but I don't know what happened." He said that replacing the money wasn't necessary but I had to be more careful. He suspected I had overpaid on a check. It was quite possible, and I decided to count check-cashing money more carefully.

When I came in on Sunday, Lou said I was off just over twenty dollars again on Saturday night. He took me to a private office and said, "Al, I know you're not stealing; I think this is about you joining the union." Then I related the union agent's remark about many ways to skin a cat. He said, "I think that's the answer. We have two women in the cashier's office who are strong union people. They might have been told to send you a message." He checked the records and found that neither of those women had done the counting on my cash drawer. My comment was, "They're not stupid. They know you're aware of their union loyalty, so they took the money before the drawer was counted."

He agreed but added, "Our contract says part-timers can work extra shifts in emergencies, but contract language means nothing to these assholes. Just go back to work and let's see what happens over the next couple of days. I'm going to speak to the agent about this."

That evening I stayed after work and balanced my own drawer in full view of the woman who was standing by to do the job. She said, "Come on, Al, this takes too long. We wanna go home." Lou wandered over, and she said nothing. The drawer was off a few cents by my count, and I handed the balance slip to Lou.

When I picked up my starting drawer the next evening, I was told that they didn't want me to count my own drawer because it made them late closing up. I said nothing as I counted my starting cash. I was checking on them, and they didn't like it.

I had to get home and study for a test that night, so I didn't count my drawer. Sure enough, the next day I was told I was off over $30. It was obvious what they were doing, and they wanted it to be obvious. They wanted me to know that I was going to join the union or lose my job. What a bunch of assholes!

During my break, I found Lou. I began, "You'll think I'm just a stubborn jerk, but I'm not going to be forced to join this union. F**k them. They want us to know what they're doing, and they know you won't accuse the cashier room people of stealing so they could file a grievance against you. So there are only three alternatives. You have to conclude I'm a clumsy thief and should be fired, I join the union, or I quit." He agreed that it was pretty clear, and he was pissed off about it.

He said that he'd tried to talk to the agent and he said, "Why doesn't he just join the union and be done with it? Is it really worth all this hassle?" In short, we were up against a stone wall. They would get what they wanted one way or the other.

Lou and I agreed that I would work that evening and it would be my last shift. At nine, I would count my drawer very slowly, with him watching. We wanted to shove it up their noses as best we could. The cashier office women were livid when I turned in my balanced drawer about half an hour after the store closed. I smiled and wished them a pleasant evening.

Lou offered to be a reference for me and said I had done a great job. He said he admired me for quitting rather than joining the union. He also said there were a couple of employees who were on his hit list. I didn't want anyone thinking I was fired for dishonesty, so he agreed to announce that I quit because of school work.

Mom found out later that a memo had been placed on the employee bulletin board. It said something like: "We are sorry that Al Scheid had to resign from Crawford's due to the time pressure of his studies. We wish him the best of luck." On my behalf she thanked Lou for the note. She was never told the full truth about why I resigned. I was afraid she'd say something to the women in the cashier room and lose her job as well.

She asked for nothing, but I had been giving Mom $10 to $15 each week for food and my room. I felt strongly that I didn't want to take money from my grandparents, even indirectly. I had a beer with Grandpa occasionally and met Schmidt after work at his favorite beer bar in Monrovia a few times, but other than that, I lived like a monk. I had paid Bill the $80 I owed him and had some money in the bank. Now I had to find a new job.

A New Job

I found an ad in the Pasadena paper for a weekend bookkeeping job at Huntington Memorial Hospital. After a short chat about my experience, Mrs. Smith, the head of the bookkeeping department, invited me to for an interview.

Mrs. Smith was a nice, polite woman, but clearly a person-in-charge type. She asked about my experience as a checker at Crawford's. I said I'd left the job because I needed more study time. She took me into another room and sat me down in front of a National Cash Register 5100 bookkeeping machine. I had never seen one before. It had a keyboard just like the NCR cash registers I had been operating. Now I understood her interest in me. She handed me charge slips, and I entered the numbers fast and accurately. She gave me a typing test and told me to stop after a minute. She didn't even grade it for errors.

Back in her office, she said, "I'm curious why you did a job that included repossessing cars." Just like everyone who learned about my

GMAC experience, she was fascinated about taking cars from people. I explained that repossessing was always a last resort. Finally, she said, "Do you mind waiting in the lobby while I call your references?"

When she called me back in, she said, "Mr. Chill recommends you highly, and he would like you to call him. Lou Crawford says hello. Now I'll give you more details about the job." She explained that I would work alone on weekends, entering every transaction that took place in the hospital. All of the accounts had to balance each day. I would be paid for nine hours at $2 per hour, which included an hour for lunch. In addition, there might be some weekday work to fill in for illnesses and vacations. I could expect something like twenty hours on average each week. I agreed to begin working immediately, and training began the next day after school.

My income would be lower, but having weekday nights available for study was a real plus. I had been unemployed for only a few days. California was wonderful that way; anyone who wanted to work could find a job.

The four girls who worked in the bookkeeping department were all pleasant, and two of them were single and attractive. My main trainer was a single girl a few years my senior, and she had a knockout figure. From the first day, she had me pounding away continuously on the NCR machine, and the training went fast. She also worked with me the first weekend, and all went well. After the next weekend, she told Mrs. Smith that I could handle the job alone. I was on my own.

On Saturday, I got all the entries made in good time but couldn't get the accounts to balance. I had made an input error. This meant I had to go back through hundreds of slips, checking each one against the printout. After over two hours of intense effort, I hadn't found my mistake. This was not an easy job. Each slip had to be keyed in as a charge to categories like the drug dispensary, an operating room, physical therapy, and many more. And it all had to be charged to a patient by room number and name. It was boring, and it was easy to make errors.

The same problem occurred on Sunday, and I was embarrassed. I left a note that said I would come in after classes on Monday and work until I fixed the mistake. When I arrived the next afternoon, the girls were unperturbed about the errors, and they laughed about my consternation. They had found my errors in an hour. One of them said that compared to my predecessor, I was a dream at the job. I thought *that's the secret to success. Always make certain to follow a guy who was worse at the job than you are.*

In Control and Better Wheels

For the first time since starting college, I felt in control of my performance. With more evening time to study but still living like a monk, producing high grades just required staying organized.

I found a freshman boy who couldn't get car insurance and needed a ride to Citrus every day. He was my passenger for a $2 a week. He was a nice kid and helped me study Spanish with my three-by-five card system.

A few weeks into this arrangement, my old Chevy wouldn't start one morning. It was a tired car. As the kid's dad drove us to school, he said, "Al, I own the local Nash Metropolitan dealership, and I'll make it easy for you to buy one." I had no idea what a Nash Metropolitan was but said I'd take a look.

The Metropolitan was a two-passenger vehicle about the size of a Volkswagen Bug but a little cheaper. The boy's father was willing to sell the car for $900 and take my old Chevy and $100 as a down payment. I would owe $600 and have a payment of about $30 per month. It was a good deal for me. This man was desperate to avoid driving his son back and forth to school.

The Metro was underpowered, but it got nearly twenty-five miles per gallon. It was easy to park and fun to drive. Mine was tomato red with a white convertible top that was a pain to put up and down. I figured I would drive this car until I finished college.

Girls and School

At the hospital, I met a student nurse named Alyce Mercer. She was physically attractive, had bedroom eyes and was always upbeat. The student nurse residence had a recreation room in the basement, with a jukebox and a Ping-Pong table. If there were several girls present, a boy was allowed to play Ping-Pong, but dancing was prohibited (we ignored that rule).

When she had a weekend day off duty, we went into the basement for an hour of Ping-Pong, or we just went for a walk. It all depended on whether the housemother was in or out for the day.

I liked Alyce, but with the demands of her duties and my study schedule, it was difficult to find times to be together. We spent a few Saturday evenings at the local bars frequented by young nurses and interns. It was a slow, easy relationship with no commitment. It was just what I needed.

Early in the year, I had met Lee Chamberlain, a cute young blonde in my English literature class. Over coffee, I learned she had been valedictorian of her high school graduating class. She was seventeen, which was, to my mind, much too young for me to date. But she had a sharp imaginative mind and was fun to talk to. She had a part-time job writing stories and covering events for the *Glendora Press* newspaper. Her goal was to be an A student at Citrus and win a scholarship to Pomona College for the fall semester of 1956.

Frank Martinez and I had become friendly. He had seen public speaking on my high school transcript and felt I should take it again in a college environment. He introduced me to Joe Olivo, who taught public speaking and coached the debate team. Joe got permission for me to add the class for my second semester, which meant I was taking twenty units when the supposed limit for good students was fifteen and average students took only twelve. Frank and Joe were certain I could handle it, and I took their word for it. The more units and the faster I accumulated them, the better it was for getting into CMC - as long as the grades were at or near the A level.

Joe encouraged imagination. His attitude was that if a speaking idea went awry, laugh it off as a learning experience and move on. One of his early assignments was for each student to stand and tell the class their life story in three minutes. When my turn came, I told them I was born in China to missionary parents and was living there when the Japanese invaded. My father was taken away to prison camp, and my mother and I had to work in Japanese army kitchens for over two years before we were liberated. This is why I could cook Japanese food, loved raw fish, and was fluent in both Mandarin and Japanese. To conclude, I added a maudlin ending. With my head down, I said we never saw my father again and, in seven years, he was declared dead.

Just as I finished, Joe said, "My goodness, I had no idea you had such an interesting background. Do you mind answering a couple of questions?"

"Of course not, but I have one thing to tell you first." I said, "The whole story is a complete fabrication. My real life has not been very interesting, and I just didn't want to put everyone through a dull story."

Everyone in the room was stunned, and there were a few giggles. Before any questions could be asked, the bell rang. The laughing began as they stood up to leave. Joe held me back and said, "Do you mean to tell me that entire story was made up; there was no truth to it at all?"

I replied, "That's right, Mr. Olivo. You said to be imaginative, so I was." We both laughed, and from then on, we were friends. He put me on the debate team.

I didn't have the money for CMC and had no way to get it. In my usual way, I simply gave Miss Witten the truth. I told her I could support myself and pay for books, but the tuition was out of reach for me. She said, "I'm sorry, Al, but considering your high school grade history, I know the scholarship committee won't give full tuition. But you're the kind of student we want. I hope I didn't mislead you about scholarships."

"No, ma'am, you didn't mislead me. I knew from the beginning that I wasn't scholarship material. I'll go to Citrus for another year and then apply for a scholarship. If I keep getting high grades, I can always get into UCLA."

She replied, "Get those grades your second year and you'll get the scholarship you need at CMC. I've been keeping Mr. Frisbie informed about you. You must meet him the next time you're here." We agreed I'd be back at the end of the semester to plot summer school and the next year."

After School Comes Summer

My grandparents had gotten itchy feet again and moved back to Ohio. The house they had lived in with Mom and George was listed for sale. The arrangement had lasted a year and a half, which was about as long as Mom had expected it would. Mom and George couldn't afford to buy a house, so they began looking for a rental. I had to find a place to live on my own. Schmidt and I discussed rooming together.

Gin added a new twist when she woke me up one Saturday morning with a phone call. She knew that school was ending in a few weeks and suggested it would be a great idea if I spent the summer in Bridgeport. The mills and factories were busy, and there would be vacation replacement jobs available. She had been dating Jack again but promised she'd break that off if I would come back there. We agreed that with the whole summer together, perhaps we could work things out. After all, I'd been gone a long time. Her attitude was good news, but going to Ohio upset my plans. I said, "Gin, it was only a few months ago that you said we had no future if I went to college.

She said, "Yes, I know, but I've had time to think things over. I love you and there has to be a way we can be together."

I said, "Gin, but there's a lot to consider. I'll write you with my decision." That was bullshit. I knew before I hung up that I'd go.

I was about to do something really stupid, but I couldn't help myself. Skipping summer school would probably kill my plan to graduate in the spring of '57, but young men in love are not rational critters. Thoughts bounced around in my head about the two weeks we spent together the previous summer and how much in love we were in San Francisco. There were a hundred reasons for not going to Ohio and only one for going. I called her back the next day and said I'd be there as soon as possible after my last school day.

I hated going to Mrs. Smith and resigning after less than five months on the job, but I recalled what Leland had taught me. Well, I'd delivered the goods for the pay I received. I knew Mrs. Smith would be disappointed, maybe even quietly angry. I decided to tell her the truth about why I was leaving.

When the meeting with Mrs. Smith was over, she was dabbing at her eyes with a Kleenex. She understood why I had to go to Ohio for the summer and have one last try with Gin. With a month's notice, she was confident she'd find a good replacement. She promised to keep my reasons for leaving confidential.

I shaded the truth with Alyce, saying that I could make and save more money working in a steel mill and I could see my Ohio family. Regardless of how things turned out in Ohio, I intended to come back in the fall. She was okay with the explanation, and we continued to see each other until I left.

My last chore was to visit Miss Witten at CMC. She was surprised that I had changed my plan but delighted with my second semester grades. We decided on my schedule for the fall term. As I was about to leave, she asked, "You really are coming back at the end of summer for sure, right? Or is there a chance you'll decide to stay in your hometown?" I assured her that I would contact her as soon as I returned, around Labor Day. "Then it's time you met Mr. Frisbie, our director of admissions."

She called him, and he walked in moments later. We shook hands, and he motioned me to sit. "Ruth has been telling me about you for a year. You've become one of her extracurricular projects, and you've done a good job. If you continue to get high grades, we'll be pleased to accept you in the fall, and tuition won't be a problem." I thanked him, and after a few pleasantries, he left.

I thanked Miss Witten for all her help and encouragement. She suggested I buy the textbooks that were assigned to my fall classes and read them during the summer. It was a great idea, and I did just that with two courses.

My grandparents invited me to stay with them for the summer. They had rented a house about seven miles out Route 250 from Bridgeport. The house sat on a two acre plot, and Grandpa was planting a large garden with a variety of vegetables. The snapshots they sent looked great and made me look forward to living in the country again for a while.

A Driving Partner

A guy named Doug replied to my note on the student bulletin board. He was going to spend the summer on Cape Cod. His plan was to drive with me as far as Wheeling and then take a Greyhound bus to Boston.

The size of the Metropolitan greatly limited the amount of luggage we could take. I packed summer and work clothes in a box and sent it to my grandparents. Everything was set for the trip. I was in high spirits and looking forward to seeing Gin.

CHAPTER 37

Happiness is always a by-product.
It is probably a matter of temperament,
and for anything I know may be glandular.
But it is not something that can be demanded from life,
and if you are not happy you had better stop worrying about it and
see what treasures you can pluck from your own brand of
unhappiness.

—William Roberston Davies, novelist, playwright (1913–1995)

Remember, not getting what you want
is sometimes a wonderful stroke of luck.

—The Dalai Lama (1935–living)

THE LAST SUMMER

Loaded up with two full-size men and a fully packed trunk, the Metropolitan's top speed was about sixty-five miles per hour on level ground. A low hill or a headwind slowed us considerably, and we climbed some grades at thirty-five miles per hour. We tried not to let this handicap get us down by repeatedly saying that it gave us more time to appreciate the scenery.

We took turns sleeping by lying in an L shape, with our bodies on the flat place behind the driver's seat and our legs stretched out on the laid-down back of the passenger seat. This cramped position required always lying on our left sides. Sleeping was not easy.

After my two previous cross-country misadventures, I was hoping for a boring trip, and it was ... for a while. All went well until just past Amarillo, when the music programs on the radio began being interrupted with storm warnings. Doug found our location on the map, and it appeared we were heading directly toward the storms. We drove into a truck stop for gas, restrooms, and information. The attendant confirmed we were heading into the storms. He warned us that we were in tornado country and we should stop for a day. Because we were behind schedule we elected to keep going.

An hour later, a strong headwind came up and the Metro was laboring to go fifty mph.

The wind was getting under the convertible top, and I was concerned that it would be ripped off the car. Doug was pulling down on the main strut with both hands, almost doing chin-ups.

Weather news was constant and tornados were being forecast everywhere. Several tornados had been formed south of our location. We decided to turn north as soon as possible and outrun the storm.

Suddenly, Doug pointed to the right (south) and said, "Goddammit, Al, there they are!" And there they were: two twisters, probably miles apart, were stretching vertically from the ground into the leaden sky. Neither of us had seen a tornado before, but there was no mistaking the funnels. They looked to be a long way off—we guessed at least five or six miles. The wind had shifted and was getting stronger, and the sky was getting darker. We knew we had to get the hell out of there.

We passed several people standing near cars and taking tornado pictures. They were crazy; this was no time for snapshots. It was time to haul ass out of there! On the map, Doug found a county road that went north and appeared to be just ahead. When we came to it, I turned and drove as fast as the Metro would carry us. We had no idea where we were going and didn't care. Away anywhere away from the twisters was good enough for us. Then the rain came, pounding the cloth top. The top wasn't designed for such weather, and the rain came in on us from one side and then the other as we followed the winding road and the wind changed directions. After a while, the rain stopped and the sky took on an eerie look, with large thunderheads and lightning a long way off to the east. We were pleased with ourselves for having outrun the storm. Actually, we were two dumb guys who had just gotten lucky.

We came to gas station next to a half filled diner. It was now dark and it had been a tiring day. We asked the man behind the counter about the twisters. He said they had died down and there was nothing to worry about until the next day, when more storms were expected. He directed us back on Route 66. Before dawn, we were chugging along on good old Route 66. The tornado adventure was over. I decided I was jinxed for cross country driving.

From then on, it was the boring trip I had hoped for. We pulled up to the Greyhound station in Wheeling in early evening instead of early morning, as we had planned. I was happy to be in the town I still thought of as home, but I was too tired to stop for a free beer with Carl.

Grandma and Grandpa greeted me happily, and they had my room all ready. I called Gin and explained that I was about to drop from exhaustion and would call her in the morning. After food and a quick bath, I slept nearly twelve hours.

After breakfast, Grandpa showed me around. It was an old house but newly painted white with green trim. It sat in a glen with a large garden in the rear and trees beyond. In front was a lawn with a white birdhouse on a pole. A creek trickled under the short wooden bridge used to enter the property. The place was so picturesque that it looked like a movie set.

I did several hours of textbook reading before driving into Bridgeport to visit my old haunts and meet Gin. We met in Wheeling and walked to our favorite river view bench. Seeing, holding, and kissing Gin was worth every minute of the trip.

BACK IN TOWN AGAIN

The boys who had left in 1950–51 had been discharged, and a few of us decided to get together for a reunion. The word got around, and we ended up with a large group of guys and girls who had known each other since childhood. We began by drinking and laughing in the Candy Kitchen. Later we closed the Lincoln and some of us went on to the after-hours joints in Wheeling. I stayed at Wendell's house. We slept until nearly noon, and Kitty made roast beef and mashed potatoes for us, just as she had when we were teenagers. It was great to be home.

For days I felt I was in a time warp. Nothing had changed in the village, but it didn't feel the same. A few boys hadn't come back from the war. Since childhood, casualties had been part of life. But all of my close buddies were in one piece. We were older, more experienced, and wiser - although that last part was questionable.

Wendell was working for his dad, living at home, and drinking too much. After his discharge, Jim had gone to Ohio State for six weeks, flunked out, and was now living with his parents. Paul and Ollie settled in Mansfield. Ollie had a good job at a finance company. Paul was getting married, and he was, of all things, a carpenter.

As best we could, Gin and I took up where we left off in San Francisco. Not much had changed in some ways, but much had changed in others. I had come to Ohio on a three-month mission. I intended to go back to school in September, and I wanted a decision about the future of Gin and Al. I had made it clear that I wasn't going to continue the in-again-out-again circle we'd been in for over four years. I was optimistic that three months together is what we needed to make things right with us. Or was it wishful thinking?

Gin swore that she told Jack it was likely that we would get our lives together this summer and that he should find another girl. I wanted to believe her, so I did. Jack had said that he'd wait until September and see how things were then. As I had predicted, he wouldn't give up easily. How could he live with this and how could she do this to him time after time? She was a kind, loving person, but the way she treated him bordered on torture. Truth be known, Jack and I were both fools, but humans believe what we want to believe, and we were all too human.

At the first interview, I was hired by the Wheeling Steel factory just up the river from Bridgeport. Better yet, the job was from seven in the morning until three in the afternoon, with weekends off. I looked forward to a simple, pressure-free summer with Gin.

If a young man ever received motivation to avoid factory work, it was me in the summer of 1955. College kids who got summer jobs at Wheeling Steel were not loved by the average union worker, who would have liked his son, brother, or nephew to have the job. Therefore, there was pressure on the foremen to give the dirtiest, nastiest jobs they had to college students.

My assignment was as a hookup man for a crane. The job was to attach a device to stacks of sheet steel, which were then lifted, moved laterally, and lowered on to flatbed trucks. I had to hook up a load, then run, sometimes the length of the building, to guide the load into place and release the hookup. The steel was oily and slippery and accidents happened. The most common mishap was a stack of steel sheets tilting and sliding out of the holding mechanism. When this happened, the steel didn't fall flat; it went sideways, floating and gliding like sheets of paper dropped from a ladder. The steel was thin and sharp, and a man could be cut badly if a sheet hit him just right.

When a spill was imminent, the crane operator usually saw it first. He sounded an alarm, and everyone at floor level ducked behind anything handy that was large and heavy. I saw only one of these events, and it wasn't close enough to threaten me. Crane hook-up was not a sought-after job, but there were worse.

This job ended the second week because of an injury. I had just hooked up a load, given the lift-up signal to the crane man, and stepped away with my back to a wall. The crane operator lifted the load at an angle, and it swung my way, pinning me against the wall, with my right arm in front of my body. The edges of the steel were pressed hard against my bare forearm. The crane man couldn't see me, so he started lifting the load straight up, instead of away from the wall and me. This action made the steel cut into my forearm. I yelled as loudly as I could, and another man heard me. He signaled the crane operator, who stopped everything and pulled the load away from me. My arm was bleeding from rows of thin cuts, from elbow to wrist.

As the infirmary nurse cleaned the cuts, she told me that the acid and dusty oil on the steel could cause an infection. She added that there might be scars. She agreed to keep me on active status if I promised to come in early the next morning to have my bandages changed. If there was no sign of infection, I could continue to work. I went back to my job and received a "sorry about that" apology from the crane operator.

The next day, after my wound was bandaged; I was assigned to drive an old two-ton truck at a construction site. My coworker was another college student. Together we hand loaded the truck with old lumber, bits of concrete, and other detritus normally discarded from a construction project. Then I drove the truck to a dumping point near the river. We unloaded it by hand, after which I drove the truck back. In this fashion, we yo-yoed back and forth all day.

We wore heavy gloves, but the junk was clumsy to handle, and cuts and scratches on our arms occurred almost daily. At least once every day, I promised myself that this would be my last work as a factory laborer. Remembering the union instructions I'd received, we kept a reasonable pace, attracted no attention and the workdays passed uneventfully.

My assistant was twenty. During breaks, we discussed our problems. His family was paying his way at a small college, but he envied me going to school in California. He was right, I was damned lucky.

The Great Surprise

Gin and several of her girlfriends planned a Sunday picnic at Piedmont Lake. We hadn't discussed her home situation and I was taken by surprise when she told me to come to her house to pick her up. "What about your father?" I asked.

She smiled and said, "I've been keeping this as a surprise for you. Mom told him you were here for the summer, and they had a serious talk. He's had a change of heart. You can come to the house anytime." I almost fell over, and, of course, I asked why. She explained, "After my trip to California, he finally realized that I'll move out of the house if he continues trying to control me."

I hadn't seen Mrs. Davis for nearly five years, but when I arrived she acted as if I had been there the day before, saying things like, "Hello Al, beautiful day, isn't it?" There was no apology, no welcoming handshake - no nothing. Just like that, years of past insults were wiped away and her parents were given a full pardon. I picked up the basket and thanked Mrs. Davis for all her trouble.

Our group had all the usual paraphernalia, including a beer keg in a tub of ice; a Beerport necessity. After lunch, half of the guys were fishing and catching nothing, the other half were napping, and the girls were gossiping. Gin said, "Let's go somewhere." I asked where and she said, "Just drive where I tell you. It's an interesting place—you'll see." Within a few minutes, we pulled into a dirt road that ended at a small, crudely built, old house with multiple cars parked outside. Then I guessed it. This was where Roy and his pals pretended to be out in the country, communing with nature, while they drank beer and played cards. I wasn't eager to go in, but she assured me it would be fine.

They could see us through the screen door as we walked up. Roy called a break in the poker game, shook hands with me, and proceeded to introduce us to the men, most of whom I had met before. He said, "Most of you know who Al is. He's going to college in California and working at Wheeling Steel for the summer." After Roy handed me a beer and showed us where food was spread out on a table, the poker game resumed as though we hadn't arrived. I felt we were intruding on their inner sanctum.

I whispered, "Let's get out of here."

We went for a walk in the woods and sat on a log. "Well, isn't this an amazing turn of events?" I said. "All of a sudden, his friends will think that Roy and I are buddies."

She said, "It took a while, but he came to grips with reality. He knows he was wrong about you. He admitted to me that he misjudged you and he's sorry. He doesn't know how to apologize, so he treats the past like it never happened. That's just his way. He knows I'll apologize for him, and I told him you'd go along with it and not ask questions."

I agreed. Words couldn't change the past. It was a complete victory—Roy had capitulated. I had won and it felt good.

A Hot, Wonderful Summer

In a blink, it was July. We'd fallen into the same sort of routine as when I lived there. We were together three or four weekday evenings and every weekend. A couple of Fridays, we drove on to Pennsylvania in late afternoon and got back about two on Saturday morning. Gin said her mother woke up when she came in, but Roy was sleeping off his booze. Neither of them said anything in the morning. My grandparents asked few questions. Grandma still wanted that wedding.

I seldom ran into Roy when I picked up Gin. When I did, he made a polite comment about the weather and nothing more was said. That was enough for me. I didn't trust him and suspected that he kept his peace only because the alternative was too distasteful.

I mentioned to Gin that I had to get the brake shoes replaced on the Metro. The next evening when I arrived at the house, Roy said, "Virginia tells me the brakes on your car are shot. Those small foreign cars aren't built to go down mountains with a heavy load. Drive out to Hundley Ford Saturday morning and we'll take care of that problem." At first, I didn't understand and it must have shown. "You know I work there, don't you?" he continued.

Then I got it. "Yes, of course I know you work at Hundley," I said. "The problem is finding the parts to fix the brakes."

He smiled, saying, "I ordered the parts from Pittsburgh and I'll have everything we need. Can you be there by nine?" I thanked him and promised to be on time. Later Gin told me this was his way of making amends and showing he was over his animosity. She said, "Just go along with him; he wants to be friendly."

When I arrived, Roy was waiting in the repair area. Once the car was up on the lift, he set to work. He had been a mechanic all his life, and it showed. He had no wasted motions as he replaced the brake shoes. The job was done in less than hour.

While he was working, he asked questions about California, things like, "Don't you miss the seasons?" and "Is that smog as bad as I've heard it is?" He was surprised I didn't miss the cold weather. As he finished, he said, "Well, I'd like to see the place someday, and maybe I will." I wondered what he meant by that—probably nothing.

As he washed his hands he said, "Well, Al, I gotta get to the lake before those guys drink all the beer." As we shook hands I thanked him and asked about the charge for the brake job. He said, "This one's from me to you. Just drive this little thing carefully; a truck could run over it." With that, he got into his car and drove away.

I was heartened by the questions he had asked. Had he and Gin discussed her living in California or was he just making conversation? In any case, I was thrilled that he had changed after all the heartache he he'd caused. He was behaving liked a decent man and I was willing to forgive.

Life Settles into a Pleasant Routine

Every day I was home from work before four and helped Grandpa with a chore or two, one of which was harvesting vegetables. We had fresh vegetables, the likes of which I hadn't seen in years. After my quick bath, we had a country meal fit for a king. After supper, I laid on the living room floor with a fan turned on me. It was hot. An hour or so nap prepared me for the evening's activities.

On those evenings when I wasn't with Gin, I met up with the same old buddies, in the same old places. Again, it was a time warp. The same characters were there. Carl was still telling jokes, Wendell was still getting drunk and fighting with his father, and Jim was still bitching about how much he hated working. No one I knew had a job they liked, but we all soldiered on, because we had to.

Lindy and Marie had gotten married, but they did the same things they had always done, with the same people. The Saturday summer dances were still held at Wheeling Park, and Lindy was still playing in the band. When the music stopped at eleven, we all went to one of the same local spaghetti joints.

Friday and Saturday night polka dancing was still going strong at a nightclub in Lansing called Melody Manor. The Rainbow Room, on Route 250 still made good hamburgers, and the jukebox still had slow, romantic music for close dancing. Gin and I played the

Rosemary Clooney rendition of our song, *Tenderly*, several times each evening, and sang it softly as we danced.

The summer was absolute déjà vu. Everything I saw I had seen before and everything I did, I had done before. This repetitive lifestyle gave a safe, comfortable feeling, but I was not naive enough to begin believing I could thrive in this environment. I could put up with a crappy job to be with Gin for the summer, but that was the end of it for me. It was obvious that one thing had changed dramatically and, as Gin had pointed out, that thing was me.

Bridgeport and nearby villages were filled with peeling paint houses. The business signs were fading and the streets were dirty. When you live within this scenery every day, you don't notice it. But as I drove around, my California-conditioned eyes saw a poor decaying area with little hope of improving. The Ohio Valley economy was in a long-term downward trend, with only short intervals of limited prosperity. American-made steel was becoming less and less competitive in world markets. The area was being called the "Rust Belt" for good reason.

I was concerned for my friends and their futures. Wendell was thoroughly unhappy with his life because he understood the economic scene. We talked about what he was going to do. During his four years in the air force, he had worked shifts in a communications center, typing messages. He said, "Can you believe they picked me to type?" I pointed out that his GCT scores were probably high, and that's why he had been picked from the crowd. He had no idea what his scores had been.

We talked about how I had quit a good job to go to college and it wasn't too late for him. I said, "You can do it. You have the GI Bill, and working part time is not that bad. If you start this fall, you can get your degree in three years."

"Nah," he said, "I'd never make it. I'm too damned lazy to study, and I like to drink every night. I'll be a carpenter in this shit hole of a town for the rest of my life." He was resigned to a fate he hated. When he was just drunk enough to dream a little, he was willing to talk about his future. Then, in a few minutes, he would revert to wallowing in self-pity and self-hatred. When he was sober enough to think about his life seriously, he wouldn't discuss it at all.

Regardless of his problems, Wendell was still my old pal and the closest thing to a brother I would ever have. He was supportive of what I was doing and never showed the slightest hint of jealousy. I admired that about him.

Even though I participated I was getting bored by the repetitive banter of my friends. I felt guilty about having these thoughts, but the transition from reading my philosophy textbook to hearing the conversations created a stark contrast. For the past few years, I had been around well-educated people who kept up with world news and read books. I was realizing that the gulf between me and the people with whom I had grown up was widening.

Several friends commented that I had changed my way of speaking. They meant that I had lost most of my Ohio Valley accent. In a way, I was pleased they noticed, but I didn't want to sound like I was showing off. When I asked Carl about it, he said, "Well, they're right—your English has improved a lot—but so what? You're getting an education, and they're not. Don't change anything for these people. Go your own way, and improve yourself." Good ole Carl was right again.

I still stopped in the Pastime and played eight-ball with GG because it would've hurt his feelings if I'd refused. But I didn't have to let him win; he did it on his own. Pool playing had moved out of my life, or vice versa. I tried to get interested again and even practiced a little, but it wasn't the same. My abilities had deteriorated so playing for money was a fool's errand. Jim Raies, my pool guru, had quit playing. After he left the navy, his future wife had made him promise that he would quit pool and get a full-time job. He had become a clothing salesman at the largest men's clothing store in Wheeling. When he and I played a couple of hours one evening, he was concerned that his wife would find out.

Dad and Blanche liked me to come to the Polish Club, near Boydsville, and play euchre. He recruited a friend to be his partner and played against Blanche and me. Blanche and I won most of the time—she was an excellent euchre player. I saw them every week.

Nothing Lasts Forever

Despite certain drawbacks, I was having a nice summer. The work was boring and dirty, but my mind was always on something else, and work time passed quickly. Gin and I were closer than ever—and it showed. Friends and family remarked how perfect we were for each other. Not-so-subtle questions about marriage came up constantly.

One day Grandma handed me a letter from Mom, saying, "Here it is; you read it." It said that things had not been going well with her and George, and she was considering a divorce. She planned to store her belongings and come to Ohio for a while. She would arrive by Greyhound bus a couple of days before Labor Day, just when I planned to return to California.

Grandma said, "I'm not surprised. She and George were having problems when we were there. That was one of the reasons we decided to sell the house and move back here."

I said, "Well, her timing is good. As I move out, she can move in here with you. Grandma, I don't get involved in Mom's personal life; she has to work things out for herself." That ended the conversation. But this brought me face-to-face with planning my return trip. I got off a letter to Don Schmidt about us being roommates. It was already August.

Decision Time

Gin had been doing her best to avoid our problems. I wanted to take her to one of my favorite quiet places on a Saturday morning so we would talk about our future in the peace and quiet of the woods. Before I could bring this up, she and Marie scheduled a picnic on the same day and we went to Piedmont Lake. The guy responsible for the beer didn't bring enough, so I volunteered to make a beer run to a boat dock store. As we got there, a summer thunderstorm hit. We had to use a dirt road to return, and I feared the Metropolitan might get stuck. We stopped in a wooded area to wait out the rain.

Gin suddenly said, "When are we going to talk about you going back to California? I know you're going, but when?" This was not the time or place, but at least the door had been opened.

I said, "I need to get back around Labor Day because I have to find a job and a place to live before school starts. When are you going to join me?" Then the tears began.

So there we were. The temperature in the car was about ninety degrees, the humidity was higher, the rain was coming down hard on the convertible top, and there was thunder and lightning. It was too noisy to talk. As Gin cried, I watched, saying nothing. After a while, the storm began to move away and the rain softened to a light shower.

I began with, "Gin, do you realize how bizarre this scene is? If I were a God-fearing man, I'd think he sent this storm as a message for us to wake up and get our lives together. We love each other, and there's no reason for us to be apart. Even your father has made peace with our situation. Don't you see that everything has fallen into place? All you have to do is decide to take a chance and we can have a great life. I'll be finished with school in less than two years.

If I leave without you agreeing to join me, we're finished. I can't go on this way. I put everything on the line when I came back here. Goddammit, what do you want to do?" She said nothing. Her shoulders moved as she sobbed and shook her head slowly from side to side.

Finally, she said, "We have to get back to the picnic. We can talk about this later."

"When is later?" She shook her head and looked out the window.

We found our group in a shelter near the picnic spot. There was no hiding the fact that something had happened. We were both soaked with sweat, Gin's hair was a mess, and her eyes were red. We offered no explanation. I dove into the lake to cool off. By the time I came out and toweled off, Gin had the car loaded. We said some cursory good-byes and left.

We didn't speak during the drive to her house. She said, "I can't talk now. I need to lie down." I kissed her forehead and left. My wonderful summer had come to an abrupt end.

As I drove, a sad feeling came over me like a shroud. This was it. Her unwillingness to talk explained more than a discussion might have. She was not going to make a decision. I decided to put it out of my mind for a while. There were still a few days left.

Grandpa and I harvested the last of the sweet corn and drank beer while Grandma prepared fried chicken. Dinner was the high point of that day for me.

On the porch enjoying the twilight, Grandma asked why I wasn't going out. Without details, I told her it appeared that Virginia was not moving to California but I was driving back to finish college. She said, "Alfred, if she doesn't love you enough to get married and move to California, let her go. The sooner you do that, the sooner you'll be over the pain and grief. Virginia is a fine girl, but she's not the only fine girl in the world. There will be others." Good old Grandma was a woman of much wisdom.

She and Grandpa had invited everyone for a Jonard family reunion on the Sunday of Labor Day weekend. Mom would be there by then, and all the rest of the family would show up for an afternoon barbecue. She asked me to stay for the event and, of course, I agreed.

On Monday, it was two weeks until Labor Day. I wasn't looking forward to driving the Metro back to California at all—and certainly not alone. Driving through New Mexico, Arizona and the California desert in August would be a living hell. I would have to take the northern route. This would add an extra day, and the Metro would have to climb more mountains. It was a dilemma.

The next day I got an idea. After work, I went to the Wheeling News Register and placed an ad for someone to drive my "nearly new" car to California, leaving out what kind of car it was. Calls began coming in the next day.

Grandma told me one man sounded middle-aged and asked if he had to drive quickly. He was a sixty-year-old widower who was going to Southern California to see his daughter and wanted to sightsee one way and fly back. I called him and discovered he knew Carl. We met at the Lincoln.

He planned to spend nine days on the road and take the northern route. He liked the Metro, even after I told him about the underpowered engine. Since Carl confirmed he was an okay guy, I decided to make a deal with him. He agreed to pay for the gas and arrive at my uncle's house in Temple City no more than nine days after his departure.

With that done, I made plane reservations for just after Labor Day. I would be in California without a car for a week, but I could manage by hitchhiking or renting a clunker from my friendly Metropolitan dealer.

Schmidt had called and told me he was switching from Citrus to UCLA. He wanted to live someplace like Arcadia so he could drive to UCLA and still be close to part-time work at his father's printing business. We agreed he'd find an apartment for us. Hopefully that would solve my housing problem, and with some luck, I'd find a job within a week after arrival.

Another Self Analysis

After work the next day, I took an old blanket into the woods behind my grandparents' place and walked around, smelling the odors of a warm woodsy late summer afternoon. I picked a dry spot and sat down by a brook surrounded with ferns. It was a tranquil setting in which to think.

I made a conscious effort to examine the negatives of my relationship with Gin. Since age fifteen, she had been my paragon of virtue. That was about eight years of ignoring reality. She was not an adventurous person and I was, and the educational gap she had brought up did in fact exist. In addition, she always went back to Jack when I left town. Did that really matter? I had not led a life of celibacy.

Could she adapt to the sheer bigness of Los Angeles? Then there was the reality of building relationships with my friends; she had little in common with any of them. The fact was that so far she had rejected a life with me. She seemed to love the day-after-day sameness of the way she lived. She didn't see the ugliness of the place or the lack of opportunity. If I believed these negatives, why should I keep trying? What was left?

What was left was that I had loved her since I first became aware of love. When we were together, there was no place else I wanted to be. She said that it was the same with her and we were physically compatible. But was that enough to sustain a relationship? Another reality was that my crowded schedule left little time for a wife, especially one who would have none of her friends or family nearby for support.

There were negatives on my side of the ledger too. I'm the one who stayed in California instead of moving back to be with her. Why didn't I try to go to college nearby? Ohio was full of good colleges. Could I finish school, move back to the valley, get a good job, and live happily ever after? Perhaps Pittsburgh might be close enough. An educated young man could get a good job there.

I stopped myself. I needed a conclusion, not a debate. Time had passed, and I had tried. It had been Gin's decision all along. The final truth was that I couldn't live in the Ohio Valley. I had to seek my fortune, and the valley was the wrong place. My contacts, my friends, and my future were in California. I was shoveling against the tide by pursuing Gin, and I was weary of the drama. I needed to finish college. Perhaps things would somehow work out someday, but I couldn't spend any more psychic energy on my quest for Gin. It had to end. Maybe finality would shake her and she'd reconsider. No, that wasn't likely. The clock had simply run out—the game was over, and I had lost.

Back at the house, all-knowing Grandma asked, "Well, did you make up your mind about anything?"

I said, "Yes, Grandma, I did. I'm putting Bridgeport behind me for the last time and going back to school. Virginia will live her life her way, and I'll live mine my way. It's over."

Grandma put her arms around me and said, "Alfred, I think that is the right decision for you, but it's not the right one for Virginia. She'll wake up one day and realize her mistake when it's too late. But, Alfred, remember, you're both still young, and people do change." Since I had changed, I was aware of this truism. That was the last time we discussed Gin. I sensed that Grandma was pissed off at her, and so was I—deeply.

Grandma promised to keep everything about my romance secret until after the family reunion so it wouldn't be embarrassing for Gin to be there. I promised I'd tell Mom the day after the reunion.

That evening, Gin was waiting for me on the porch when I arrived, and little was said. We drove to Wheeling and walked to our bench by the river. With no prelude, I told her I had reconciled myself to her decision not to get married and come to California. I said, "Your decision has become so obvious that there's no point in discussing it." She breathed a sigh of relief; I had done her painful job for her.

She said, "Alf, I'm sorry, deeply sorry, and so grateful that you're not angry."

"Not angry? Who told you that?" I said. "I'm livid! If I didn't love you so much, I'd throw you into the f*****g river. But I do love you." She managed a small smile as I added, "I know you'll never move from this wonderful, lovely place, and I'm dealing with that sad, pathetic fact. I had high hopes this summer, but the summer is over and reality has arrived."

She was mopping tears from her eyes as she said, "Marie says I'm making the mistake of my life. But I can't bring myself to face a new life in a new place. Los Angeles scares me. I don't fit in there for a hundred reasons. I want you to go back and finish your education. You've worked hard, and I've just been a problem. When you left for Mansfield, I knew you wanted something you couldn't find here. You're ambitious, you want a career, and you need a woman who will help you achieve your goals. I'd just hold you back, darling. But I shouldn't call you darling anymore, should I?" Then the tears really came - from both of us. When we recovered, I took her arm and we walked around Wheeling for a while.

We were silent while driving to her house, until she said, "What are we going to do? You don't leave for a week. Am I going to see you?"

With no forethought, I pulled over, stopped, and said, "I have an idea. Let's just act as we have all summer. Love and respect for each other isn't our problem, and there's no reason for us not to see each other while I'm still here. It won't be easy, but let's try it. I just don't want to explain anything to anyone."

She said, "Okay, let's do that. The gossip will begin after you leave, and I'll tell the truth then. And you know I do love you."

I replied, "We can handle it, Gin. I'll call you tomorrow, and we'll decide when to see each other." We had a short, soft kiss on the porch, not close to our usual passion. We were both emotionally drained, and I was feeling dead inside.

I went to the Lincoln and had too much to drink. Carl finally shut me off and sent me home with, "Hey, you gotta work tomorrow, and to do that, you gotta get home alive!" Yep, he was right—I had to go to work.

As a reminder that one always pays a price for excess, I felt lousy all morning. I feared that if I gave notice early, they would let me go immediately, so I decided to quit on one day's notice. I didn't care if a bad mark went into my file because I didn't intend to work there ever again.

The Wind Down

When I called Gin, we agreed that I'd take her to my grandparents' home on Friday to see Mom, who was arriving on Thursday. I think we both felt relief that a decision had been made and there was nothing left to argue about. Ironically, I wondered if her father would be relieved or disappointed when he learned the truth. Or, would it be a pyrrhic victory for him?

When Mom arrived, she and I had a conversation about her future. She complained that in California, everyone was running around, trying to make more money. She didn't like the rat race. Maybe because of that, she and George weren't getting along and she wanted to get away to think things over. She leaned toward moving back to Ohio permanently. Apparently, it was not possible for Mom or Gin to break out of Beerport

Gin drove out to the house on Sunday. Everyone was there: uncles, aunts, single and married cousins with husbands and wives, and the children that had so far been borne by my generation. Gin was welcomed with open arms. Everyone assumed that I had come back to get married, and questions were asked. Gin fended them off with, "Al has to finish his degree before we can make long-term plans." Everyone seemed to accept this.

When the party broke up, Gin drove home and I stayed. We both needed a good night's sleep. It had been a stressful week. I had a private conversation with Mom and told her the truth about Gin and me. Mom echoed Grandma: "If she doesn't love you enough to give California a try, it makes sense that you go your separate ways." Since she had just left her husband in California, it was an ironic statement, but that didn't occur to her.

The last few days passed quickly. Most of my belongings had been shipped a week earlier, and final arrangements were set with my driver. Gin and I were together every evening. If awards were given for ignoring the elephant in the room, we would have won first prize. We held hands, danced close, had the occasional light kiss, and otherwise looked normal. Inside, I was in turmoil. We were living out the last days of our long love affair, and we were both aware of the finality of it all. It was like a deathwatch.

Marie was the only friend who knew the score. Wendell knew both of us oh so well and he smelled a rat. He said we didn't look at each other or hold hands the same way. He held me to the honesty pledge we'd had since grammar school: "Scheid, don't lie to me; something ain't right here."

I told him what had happened. His comment was, "That f*****g stupid girl ... What the hell is she thinking? She's breaking up with you and staying with that wimpy-ass truck dispatcher? Now that Roy has changed, it would have been clear sailing. She's out of her f*****g mind to break up." He was on my side, as he had always been. It hit me that I would soon miss my old pal again.

The Finale

We had a quiet dinner in Wheeling on my last night in town. Then we went to the Rainbow Room, where we could play the jukebox and dance. I had been handling the situation well all week, but dancing close was having an effect on me. Gin put some more money in the jukebox and picked Nat King Cole's rendition of *Tenderly*. We danced to our song. The last two lines—*Your arms opened wide and closed me inside. You took my lips, you took my love, so tenderly*—was more than I could take.

I walked her back to the table and said, "I have to go outside for a minute. Please don't follow me." Once out the door, I felt the emotions overtaking me, and tears were coming by the time I reached the back of the parking lot, where it was dark.

About ten minutes later, I walked back in. As I approached the table, I saw that she had been crying. I said, "Gin, it's time for me to take you home. I can't deal with this anymore." With no reply, she got up. Not a word was said during the drive to her house.

I parked near her walkway, and I started getting out. She asked me to stay a minute and said, "Alf, I know you're hurt and angry with me. I'm aching inside. I love you and wish there was some way we could be together, but I know in my heart it won't work. If I forced myself to live in California, I'd make you unhappy in a short time."

Her mind was made up that she couldn't live in California, no matter what. She had created a self-fulfilling prophecy. Anger at her was welling up within me. She was taking away the person I loved.

I asked, "Why did you suggest that I skip summer school and come back here? I think I know the answer, but I want to know for sure. Please tell me—you owe me the truth."

She looked down as she said, "All your friends were back from the service, and things were getting back to the way they were before you left. I hoped that after a summer here, you'd change your mind and stay. I realize it was selfish of me to do that, and I'm deeply sorry. Please forgive me. I still love you."

I said, "You got it all wrong, Gin. Your love isn't strong, at least not strong enough for you to take a chance. The truth is that you don't need me. You have good old Jack, waiting like a panting dog, and you'll be shacked up with him, telling him lies about us within a day after I leave. Well, f*****g go do it and have a good time. You got me to come here and miss summer school based on a false hope. You knew this would f**k up my education, and you didn't care. You're not only selfish, Gin; you're a coward. You're afraid to deal with life. Well, I hope you have a happy time here in your shitty little town with your exciting lover."

I was beginning to shake. I got out of the car. She sat in the car sobbing, and that made me feel terrible. I couldn't stand seeing her cry. Finally, I opened her door and helped her out. Neither of us spoke.

We stopped at the beginning of the sidewalk to her house. She was still crying as I held her close for a moment. Without looking up, she turned, and I watched her walk slowly down the walkway, up the stairs, and into the house. It was gut-wrenching torture for me. I got into the car and drove west on Route 40 until I retrieved some self-control. On the way home, I stopped at a roadhouse and had a few shots of scotch as a sleeping potion. I slept on the living room sofa with most of my clothes on and felt crappy when Grandma woke me up at dawn.

After my driver picked up the Metro, Grandpa drove Mom, Grandma, and me to the Pittsburgh airport. We talked about many things on the trip, but not about Mom's George or my Virginia. As we said good-bye, I couldn't resist saying, "Well, what about this bullshit I've always heard that love conquers all?" They saw the humor, and there were smiles ... but no laughter. Grandpa just nodded his head yes.

Grandma said, "We'll see what happens, Alfred. None of us know the future."

The twelve-hour-plus plane trip gave me time to mull things over in maudlin detail. I decided that the thing that would save my sanity was to put Gin out of my mind, not as I had before but completely this time.

One of the things she had said to me during our last few days was, "Alf, you'll find a beautiful, educated California girl and forget about me in no time. I know you will." I couldn't forget her, but I intended to make the rest of her prediction come true. There were millions of girls in California, and I'd make it a point to meet one who was right for me.

Despite evidence to the contrary, I was not a complete fool. I understood that grieving over a loss was a normal first step to healing. I had to buck up and accept what fate had dealt me—and I would recover.

***

The world breaks everyone and afterward
many are strong at the broken places.
But those that will not break it kills.
It kills the very good and the very gentle
and the very brave impartially. If you are
none of these you can be sure it will kill you
too but there will be on special hurry.
—Ernest Hemingway, novelist, Nobel Laureate (1899-1961

CHAPTER 38

A man can be happy with any woman
as long as he does not love her.
—Oscar Wilde, writer, playwright (1854–1900)

All changes, even the most longed for,
have their melancholy
for what we leave behind us is a part of ourselves;
we must die to one life before we can enter another.
—Anatole France, novelist, Nobel laureate (1844–1924)

GETTING ORGANIZED

Things fell into place quickly. Schmidt had found a two-bedroom apartment in Arcadia, and my box of clothes had arrived at Uncle Al's house. My Metropolitan dealer friend gave me a used Ford for $5 a day, solving my transportation problem.

The Citrus student employment office sent me to a nearby liquor store that was looking for someone to stock shelves and do carry-out. It was owned by a Mr. White, a plain-looking chubby man in his fifties. After reviewing my background, he asked, "Since you have cashiering experience, why don't you get a job at a supermarket?"

I said that I had a heavy class schedule and couldn't work the day hours that markets needed. This seemed to satisfy him.

He explained, "On weekdays we close at nine, and on Fridays and Saturdays, we stay open until ten. I need someone reliable to start at four on weekdays and at one on Saturdays and Sundays. Tuesday or Wednesday can be a day off. The pay is one fifty per hour. I'll expect you to show up on time and get all the work done the way I want it. Can you start tomorrow?"

I calculated quickly that the pay would be just over $50 a week and I could just get by on that. I said, "Mr. White, you have quite a few empty spaces on your shelves right now. Would you like me to put in a few hours today and fill those for you?"

He was visibly taken aback and said, "Uh, yeah, great idea. I'll get you an apron and show you around the back room and the beverage cooler." Four hours later, the store and the cooler were fully stocked and the floor swept. I could tell he liked my attitude. Demonstrating a willingness to go to work immediately always pleases employers. Mr. White turned out to be a decent guy, but his wife, unfortunately, was a sourpuss. She neither liked nor trusted anyone. However, we learned to put up with each other.

The next morning, I called Miss Witten. As always, she was receptive and kind. She was pleased that I'd returned as promised. I assured her that I was sticking to my plan to produce the grades needed for CMC.

Two courses I needed conflicted at Citrus. The only option was to sneak it in at another school (no computers in those days, so no cross-checking). I didn't tell Miss Witten that I planned to take Psychology II on Wednesday evenings at Mt. San Antonio Junior College (a.k.a Mt. SAC). I had not yet signed up at Mt. SAC, so technically speaking; I hadn't lied to her—just left out some information. I was certain she would disapprove of my taking twenty-one units.

It was going to be difficult as hell to get the work done, but I had to have the units to graduate in '57. If I got caught, what could the schools do to me besides make me quit the course? That was a risk worth taking—in for a penny, in for a pound.

My Metro driver arrived a day late, but the car was in fine shape. He'd even had it washed. Things were looking up after being back less than a week. I had a place to live, a job, and my trusty Metro. Being back in California felt comfortable, and Bridgeport was receding into the past.

After two weeks, Schmidt told me he had grossly miscalculated the traffic problems to and from UCLA and had to move closer. He volunteered to pay his half of the full month's rent, so I had two weeks to find a new place. This was a problem I didn't need.

Jim and Aline Jackson had bought a house in West Covina, about two miles south of White's liquor store. When I went to see them, they sympathized with my summer debacle in Ohio and did their best to cheer me up. They also said I could use their sofa for a few nights if necessary. I was hoping it wouldn't come to that, but time was flitting by.

A few days later Jim called me. Bill Billsborough, who worked at the same stock brokerage firm as Jim, had an idea for me. His father had bought a small ranch in La Puente and needed a man to live there and take care of a few horses. We arranged for me to meet Mr. Billsborough at the place early the next Saturday morning.

The ranch was on Desire Avenue, just south of La Puente. The referral and the address reminded me of a line from the play, *A Streetcar Named Desire*, when Blanche said she depends "on the kindness of strangers." That's what I often did.

Desire Avenue (pronounced "Des-a-ray") was about ten miles from Citrus and six miles to my night class at Mt. SAC. It was a great location. The area was sprinkled with small parcels of ten acres or less, nearly all devoted to horses. Six-foot-high white board fences separated most of the properties. Desire was a gravel road that became a trail into the hills a quarter mile south of the Billsborough ranch. It was, as they say, "out in the country."

Mr. B, as he was called, had a five-acre parcel that included a ranch house, a freestanding guest room with bath, a two-car garage, a corral, stables, and a few acres of alfalfa.

Mr. B was an overweight man of about sixty-five who smoked large cigars stuck into a plastic holder that he clinched in his teeth. He wore a dark ten-gallon hat, western boots, jeans, and a western shirt that was too tight for his girth. Removing his cigar he said, "Jim Jackson tells me you lived on a farm in the Midwest and did a lot of riding. Now you're going to college and need money and a place to live. Is that about right?"

"Yes, sir, that's my situation, but I'm not an experienced ranch hand. The truth is that I worked on an Ohio farm in the summers, mostly pitching hay, hoeing corn, and driving a tractor. I rode workhorses bareback for fun and one saddle horse to look for lost cows. I also did some English saddle riding at a public park. I'm not afraid of horses or work."

He said, "I'm glad to hear that. Work scares the hell out of most young men nowadays." He went on to explain that he raised only palomino horses and had no interest in thoroughbreds. He told me that a half dozen or so of his horses were in the Rose Parade each New Year's Day and he rented palominos to ride in shows and parades all over the western United States.

He wanted the horses fed each morning and the stalls cleaned at least three times each week. Another of my jobs would be to ride each horse for twenty minutes, at least once a week, so they wouldn't go saddle shy. There was also three acres of alfalfa that had to be irrigated during dry weather. I asked how many horses were involved. He replied, "Well, let's take a walk and I'll show you around."

There were ten horses in the corral, and he said it could go as high as fifteen and as low as six or eight because he was always buying and selling. Desire was sort of his horse storage ranch. He had a larger spread in Chino that was used for breeding and training. I wouldn't have to care for colts or foaling mares. That was a relief.

The stables were first class, painted a soft deep red with cream-colored trim. The stalls had the Dutch doors, typical of horse barns. There was a phone on the wall with a clipboard hung next to it. He explained the phone was so he could reach whoever was working at the barn and the clipboard was for notes. He gave me the number and said he would have an extension put into the guesthouse. He wanted to be able to reach me day and night. He added that I could use the phone, but any charges I accrued would be deducted from my pay.

There was a small barn for storing hay, straw, and feed grain, and a tack room next to that. The so-called guesthouse was really a guest room with a small closet, a shower, a sink, and a toilet. He said I could park my car in the attached garage. The room had no furniture, no kitchen, and no stove or heating system. The only water source was the bathroom sink. There was an old refrigerator, and the two beers inside it were cold. At least that was a good sign.

When I asked about essential items like heat, he said, "You can get one of those electric space heaters with a fan. That should work for a room this size. Also, there's a small table in the house kitchen that you can move in here, if you want it. The rest is your problem." He didn't offer to pay for anything.

If I wanted the job, he would pay me $1.25 an hour for irrigating, riding, stall cleaning, and any odd jobs he assigned. The room would be rent-free.

I said, "I get paid one fifty per hour stocking shelves in a liquor store."

He answered, "Yeah? I'm willing to pay one twenty-five an hour, no more."

Ignoring his statement, I said, "It sounds as if I'll be paid for at least twenty hours each week, depending on the number of horses. Is that about right?"

He thought about it for a minute before saying, "How did you figure that?"

I said, "Well, there are a dozen horses, and at half an hour for saddling and riding each one, that's six hours. There are eight stalls to muck out. I figure that's about ten hours. I'll irrigate the alfalfa on weekend mornings. That's three or four hours to move the irrigation pipe each week.

He looked at the sky, looked back, and said, "Okay, you're a smart kid; you know how to cut a bargain." He nodded, we shook hands, and I had the job.

With this job, I would make about $25 per week. With that plus the $45 to $50 from the liquor store, and my GI Bill of $110 a month; I'd be making about $400 per month with no rent to pay. The open question was; how in the hell I'd handle all this, and still do homework?

With George's help, I was settled in by the middle of the week. At a used furniture store I bought a single bed with open springs, a stuffed cotton mattress, a large electric fan heater, a two burner hot plate and a metal cabinet. All of this, plus an old desk and some utensils raided from Mom's storage garage furnished my new place. I was all set.

That night, I listened to classical music on my old phonograph while heating up canned beef stew spiked with canned peas. Concoctions like this, with variations, became my normal fare for the rest of my stay on the ranch. It was minimal, but I was a minimal guy.

The Ranch Hand

Early on my first Saturday two of Mr. B's Latino ranch hands arrived to give me some training. The leader was an old guy named Pedro, who was friendly and helpful. The other was stable worker who said nothing. Pedro said, "You may have some problems with a couple of these horses. No one's been on 'em for months. Give each one a good ride today, but after that, don't take the boss too seriously. He wants all his horses ridin' ready, but none of his kids ever ride. Every week I'll bring in hay, feed, straw and haul the manure away." When I shook his hand it had the feel of cracked leather.

I outfitted myself for riding with navy marching shoes, fatigue pants tucked into lace-up navy leggings, and a blue denim navy shirt. This stylish outfit was topped off with an old Eagles baseball cap. I found some well-worn leather gloves in the tack room and that completed my ensemble.

Even though I did short, get-acquainted, rides, I was in the saddle for over two hours. My mind had been so filled with optimism and the anticipation of riding that it hadn't occurred to me that I hadn't been on a horse in about five years. I didn't plan on saddle soreness, a.k.a. saddle fever. All night the pain in my inner thighs and my Gluteus Maximus kept waking me up. By Sunday morning, I was in serious pain, but there was no choice but to work through it. I had a legs-spread walking style. The pain lessened day by day and, by the end of the week it was bearable. There was less pain the next Saturday, and by the third week, there was only a little discomfort. From then on, I looked forward to my riding chore as a welcome break in my cloistered life.

My daily drill was to get up at five thirty, feed the horses, muck a couple of stalls, shower, shave, have breakfast, and drive to school. I arrived before eight for work in the library or an early class. At 3:45, I left school for work at the liquor store. If it wasn't a busy evening,

I arranged liquor cases to create a seat and desk for some start and stop reading. I got home about nine thirty, did a quick flashlight check of the horses and then studied as long as I could manage. Sleep came easy because I was tired and it was so deeply quiet. There was no time for anything but classes, studying, and work. The regimen suited me.

On Wednesdays, my liquor store day off, I had some extra time for the library, after which I went home to clean stalls. After one of my concocted dinners and a beer, it was time to drive to Mt. SAC for my three-hour psychology class.

The next morning, it all started over again. It was a grind, but I looked forward to each day as I had rarely done before. A sense of accomplishment fuels optimism as few things do, and I felt accomplishment every day.

Mrs. White was always on the lookout for a dead fly on a shelf or a bottle label that was not exactly facing outward. With a sense of satisfaction, she would point these out to me. Mr. White, on the other hand, became friendlier. He knew about my ranch job and admired my work ethic.

When two more horses were added to my workload, I couldn't finish riding and get to work by one in the afternoon. I got Mr. White alone and explained my dilemma. He kindly changed my start time to two o'clock on weekends. It actually saved him money because I did the same work for less money. But Mrs. White was unhappy. My reading in the back room bugged her, but since she rarely worked evenings, she was spared the pain of seeing this sin actually happening.

Early on my second Saturday, a father and his two sons, neighbors from across the street, came by to say hello. The boys were about ten and twelve. Like most families on the street, they had horses. An idea came to me. I asked the father if his sons wanted to make some money on Saturdays. He had no objections to them helping me, so we struck a deal.

The tack room had several saddles, bridles, and other gear. The system was for me to have the first horse saddled when the brothers arrived. As soon as I rode away, they brought out my next ride and saddled it. Upon my return, I changed horses and rode again. The boys wiped down the first horse, led it back into the corral, and saddled the next one. We repeated this until all the horses had been ridden. It was a sort of a pony express system. The boys had a good time and made some spending money - and I finished riding early.

With their help, my chores could be done by noon. Their father, a nice man named John, came to fetch them for lunch, and they showed him the money they had earned. I had given each of them a $1.50 and he felt it was too much. To me they were worth every penny.

On one ride, I reined in and sat looking north, over La Puente, with the snowcapped San Gabriel Mountains in the background. I could see cars over a mile away, moving silently on Valley Boulevard. The other directions were filled with higher and higher hills stretching to the horizon. The views were serene and beautiful and I felt lucky to be there. Then I wondered what Carl, Wendell, and the other guys would say if they could see me now. How strange it was that the pool-gambling, baseball-playing city boy was riding horses to earn his way through college.

Many years later, a movie character named Forrest Gump covered the situation beautifully when he said, “Life is like a box of chocolates; you never know what you’re gonna get.”

A Pretty Arrival

On my next Saturday as a wannabe wrangler I saw a female rider cantering up the driveway on a handsome mare. She was hatless, wore sunglasses and her bouncing light brown hair glistened in the sun. When she got close, I could see she was wearing expensive boots, a feminine western blouse with pearl buttons, and was sitting on a handmade saddle. She had on tan doeskin gloves, and just the right amount of makeup for a sunny day. The oldest boy said, "That's Sally – isn't she pretty?" He was right as rain.

She reined up, leaned forward, and said, "Hi, I'm Sally Vanwey from across the street. I've seen you riding and thought you might like to meet a neighbor." As I looked into her blue eyes my heart skipped a beat

As I reached up for her gloved hand, I could see she had a beautiful figure and a happy smile. She was young, about eighteen I guessed. Her face was compellingly attractive, though not drop dead beautiful and she had a perfect complexion. I said, "I'm Al, Sally, and I've been wondering when a pretty girl would show up and ride with me. Let's go."

For the first time, I walked a horse for ten minutes as I was supposed to do. Sally was chatty, telling me her parents kept three horses and loved riding, as did her younger brother. She rode when the mood struck her, but she was not in love with it. She was nineteen, worked as a bookkeeper at the Hacienda Country Club, about ten miles to the south, and had graduated from high school the year before.

I thought she liked me because she smiled in the right places in our conversation. I made it a point to listen to her carefully. When we arrived back at the barn, I thanked her for her company, switched horses, and rode off, assuming she'd go home.

When I came back, she was still there, helping to saddle a horse. She offered to ride some of the mounts, and I willingly accepted her generosity. She shortened my workday by an hour.

As we put the last horse in the corral, she said, "Would you like to come over and meet my parents? My father always has a cold beer handy." I told her that the beer and more time with her were both tempting, but I had to go to work.

"You're going to work? What have you been doing all morning?"

I explained my other job.

As I watched her ride down the drive with her perfect bottom bouncing in the saddle, I told myself that I had a mission and didn't need the distraction of a pretty woman-child. Besides, a stylish, good-looking girl like her was certainly noticed by the young men whose fathers belonged to the country club. She was out of my class. I cleaned up, and drove to the liquor store.

CHAPTER 39

Sex is one of the nine reasons for reincarnation.
The other eight are unimportant.
—George Burns, comedian (1896–1996)

Love is like war: easy to begin but very hard to stop.
—H.L. Mencken, journalist, satirist (1880-1956)

There's the thing about girls. Every time they do something pretty, even if they're not much to look at, or even if they're sort of stupid, you fall in love with them and then you never know where the hell you are.
—The Catcher in the Rye, J. D. Salinger, novelist (1919–2010)

A LETTER FROM A FRIEND

When I left Ohio, I didn't have a California address. One time it crossed my mind to send an address to Jake, but I put the thought in my Scarlet O'Hara file and it stayed there. A letter from Jake arrived at the school. I stared at it, like an artifact, before stuffing it in my notebook and rushing to class. It wasn't until I was alone in the rear of the liquor store that night that I remembered it.

It was only November, but it felt to me like the previous summer had happened years before, more like a dream than a real event. I had successfully kept Jake out of my mind most of the time and wasn't sure I wanted to change that. My soft spot, when thoughts of her sneaked in, was just before I went to sleep. After all that cogitating, I went out to the car and got the envelope.

Along with the letter were snapshots taken at the summer picnics. The fun we had on those occasions flipped through my mind. Then the last picnic came on my mental screen and the good memories ended. She started by scolding that I hadn't sent her an address. She wrote, "We've never gone this long without a phone call or a letter. I called your grandmother, and she said your mother hadn't heard from you either. No one has heard from you. If you get this, please call me and reverse the charges. I'm worried about you." Without realizing it, I had gone underground.

She went on to say she hadn't been out with Jack since I left. She wasn't dating and was spending time alone, reading and trying to get her mind straightened out. At the end was another plea to call her and she finished with, "Love, Gin."

In our old days, I would have called her, but now I really didn't want to talk to her. I was curious about her not seeing Jack, but one conversation with her could f**k up everything I was accomplishing. I didn't need complications in my life. I had to keep it simple or fail.

Until then, I hadn't realized how angry I was with her. She had messed me up, and now she wouldn't leave me alone. If I had been eager to hear from her, it would have occurred to me to send an address. It was time to be selfish and think of myself. After all, she had put herself wherever she was emotionally; it wasn't my problem. I put the letter away. One day more or less would make no difference. When I got home, I left the letter in the car so I wouldn't be tempted to read it again. I needed my sleep to keep up with the treadmill I was on.

In the library the next day, I wrote to her and called her Jake. Gin, the girl I had loved, had gone away. I explained the classes I was taking and my two jobs. I said that I didn't want to begin exchanging letters because I had no spare time and there was really nothing left for either of us to say—we'd said it all. I made it clear that I had come to realize she had made the right decision for both of us. At the end, I signed it simply "Al."

As an afterthought, I put the liquor store address on the envelope. It was an impersonal address, but that's the way I felt. Before I had time to change my mind, I put on a stamp and dropped it in the school mailbox.

My reading had taught me a few things. As long as she was in my thoughts, I was not out of love. Anger did no good, and I could never hate her. Besides, hate is not the opposite of love; that is indifference, and I was definitely not indifferent … yet. When pesky thoughts of her wormed their way into my consciousness, I repeated over and over to myself as a mantra, "Time heals all wounds … Time heals all wounds." I believed it and had faith it would work.

School, Work, and Social Life

Of the seven classes I was taking, the one I was most concerned about was physics. I had not taken trigonometry, solid geometry, or even plane geometry in high school. The algebra class at Citrus had been the high point of my math education. However, I found a secret weapon. She was a classmate named Sally Dale.

Sally had graduated from Glendora High School as class valedictorian. We were both library rats and always said hello, but we had never had a conversation. It was known that she spent all her waking hours studying and received an A in every class she took. I never saw her talk to a boy and rarely to anyone except teachers. Based on my meager psychology education, I concluded that Sally was an extreme introvert.

The first day of physics class, the instructor told us that half our grade would be based on laboratory work. He suggested we hook up with another student as a lab partner. As Sally was leaving the classroom, I caught up with her and asked if she would consider me as her lab partner. She looked at her feet for a moment before quietly saying, "Yes, that would be fine, if that's what you want to do." As I walked her to her next class, I assured her that I was handy with tools and we would be a great lab team. She said little but nodded agreement. With her math ability, I felt I had an even chance for a B in the class.

I had bought "cramming" books on physics and trigonometry and had been trying to understand them. I marked the books up with questions and slowly learned the theorems needed for the class, but I was running out of time. The process had to be speeded up.

A few days later, as Sally entered the library, I asked her to step outside. "Sally, I know you do homework between classes every day, and I don't want to take up your time, but could you help me understand a theorem we'll need in physics?"

I half expected her to say something like "Do your own homework and leave me alone." She said, "Yes, I'll help you. Where do you want to do it?" It was late in the school day and there were several empty classrooms, so we went to one and she tutored me until I had to run to work.

From then on, a several times each week, she asked if I needed help, and I always did. She even smiled occasionally. One day she admitted that tutoring instead of studying was a welcome change of pace and helped her understand the material better. She was right. The teacher often learns as much as the student.

I had made a good guess. Sally didn't know how to use a screwdriver, and she was freaked out about lighting a Bunsen burner, let alone using one. She was so much my teacher that I began calling her Miss Dale. She liked it, and it became my pet name for her.

The instructor offered us extra credit for one experiment. The experiment was to prove the speed of light. There was an instruction booklet to guide us. Sally did the math part, and I figured out how to set up the mirrors and instruments. It was a difficult job. When I explained the difficulty to Mr. White, he let me come in late a couple of days. We finally got the experiment set up, and it worked the first time. The teacher was so thrilled that he devoted part of a class session to having us repeat the experiment.

In early November George called me at the ranch. He had received a letter from Mom, and she had decided to return to California—to stay. She would arrive by Greyhound bus in less than a week. Mom didn't do airplanes. Her plan was for them to find a place to live and have a big Thanksgiving dinner for the family. She would have only two weeks to get this all done. But I told George that, Mom being Mom – single minded and indestructible - it was in the bag. Hmmm, who else operated that way? As Grandma said, the fruit falls close to the tree.

Two weeks after my letter was mailed, Jake's reply arrived. It was a friendly message saying she understood my point of view and wished me good luck in all I was trying to accomplish. She apologized for messing up my summer, and said she had a substantial savings if I needed money. There was no rancor. It was written like a letter from a close friend. There was no mention of Jack or what was happening in her life. It sounded a bit like she had concluded, as I had, that we were better off without each other. She called me Alf and signed Gin. I put the letter on my desk and decided to reply in a month. I didn't have a clue what to write anyway.

Thanksgiving Fun

Mom did it. It was crowded, but she had the family group for her turkey dinner on Thanksgiving Day. I was there for only two hours because I had a problem.

My accounting instructor used the traditional work package that required students to do a year's work of debit and credit entries for a fake company and make the books balance at year end. The finished project was due the Monday after Thanksgiving. We had been told it was a thirty to forty hour project, and I was only a third of the way into it. I had been buried by my jobs and other homework.

I decided I had to work on it every spare moment, from Wednesday after school through Thanksgiving and over the weekend. I gave myself the weekend off from horse riding. How could I have been so stupid as to let things get into such a mess?

The Whites went to Iowa and left an ex-employee to open the store and handle the cash register. He was a Spanish Basque from Flagstaff name Joe. We hit it off well immediately. I told Joe about my project problem, and we worked out a solution. Thanksgiving the store was closed. There was no school on Friday, so I would come in early and stock up. During the day, he would keep the shelves stocked well enough to do business, and I would return at four for the busy evening trade. Saturday would be a big day, so I'd work as much as needed, while spending as much time in the back room, on my project. In return for his cooperation, I would pay him for the extra work he had to do.

Except for Thanksgiving dinner and the hours at the liquor store, I worked feverishly at the accounting project. It was not a knowledge problem. The bookkeeping was much the same as I had done at the hospital. It was the sheer volume of entries that had to be done by hand.

By Saturday night, I was confident I'd get it done. Then on Sunday the accounts wouldn't balance. I tried all the tricks: dividing the error by nine, ten, a hundred and a thousand. Nothing worked. I had a careless entry mistake somewhere. Desperate, I called a fellow student who was an accounting major. He gave me the correct balance numbers, so I knew the bottom lines. By then, I was running out of time.

So Sunday night I did what embezzlers and stupid accounting students have done since double entry bookkeeping was invented—I fudged the numbers. That is, I went back into the journals and "plugged" a number, then carried it forward so the accounts would show the correct footings.

My bet was that the instructor, who was a full-time CPA, would not check that deeply. I hated cheating, but I had no choice. If I had worked on it long enough, I would have found the error.

It was once again proven that there is a divine providence for fools, children—and lazy accounting students. I sweated for a week before the instructor gave out grades. Mine was an A. He knew about my bookkeeping job at Huntington Memorial Hospital, and I was a good student of accounting theory. He may have figured that the project was an unnecessary exercise for me anyway so he didn't check my work. Who knows? There's a lesson in everything. That was the last time during my education that I left a project until the last minute.

Christmas Break

By December, rain had come, negating the necessity of irrigating the alfalfa, and Mr. B had taken a couple of horses away. I made a little less money, but the time off was worth it. I bought an old Dumont black-and-white TV (there was no color TV yet). It brought in only two channels, and those were fuzzy, but I could get the news.

Because I had books stacked around the room, I decided to build a wooden bookcase during Christmas vacation. I drew up a plan and had a lumberyard cut the boards to my specifications. I bought sandpaper, stain, varnish, and brushes and put it all in the garage, where I intended to put my rusty carpenter skills to a test. In a few hours I had a tan-colored bookcase with a satin finish and I was rather proud of it. For nearly sixty years, that piece has gone from home to home, office to office, and it is still in use in 2014 at Scheid Vineyards Inc. It was an important accomplishment for me.

After her first visit, Sally came by most Saturday mornings and exercised a few horses with me. She joked about my strange riding garb. She said she had never seen anyone ride in marching boots, canvas lace-up leggings, and a baseball cap. I told her, "This was how I dressed in the navy, and Uncle Sam didn't mind." She was a charming young woman, and I liked having her around.

One Saturday morning there was no riding because of rain. Just after I had applied the last coat of varnish to my new bookcase, Sally drove up to the garage. After dutifully admiring my handiwork, she asked, "Are you ever going to come over and meet my parents? They'd really like to say hello to you."

I wiped my hands, got in her car, and, while smelling of varnish, met Sally's parents, her little brother, Bobby; and Hondo, the short-legged mongrel they all loved. Jim was about fifty, and Helen was in her forties. Jim had been a minor league catcher, and when he failed to make it past the triple-A league, he quit and became a plasterer. Now he was a plastering contractor. He laughed when I told him about my days as an amateur hod carrier, and was sympathetic when I described how I left baseball.

He said, "It's tempting to keep chasing a dream, but reality catches up with everyone. Your manager did you a great favor. I hung in with baseball way too long." He was a nice man, and I liked him from the first moment.

We sipped a beer and talked until I had to leave for work. Helen invited me to stop by anytime, saying, "No one leaves after just one beer." I promised I would come back for the other beer soon.

That night, when I was driving home past their house, I noticed Sally's car parked by the street. On the windshield was a large white paper sign with "Want the other beer?" in red crayon. *Very clever,* I thought as I parked and rang the doorbell.

Sally was there with her brother and Hondo - the parents were out for the evening. As she opened the door, she handed me a cold Bud and said, “I thought you’d see the sign.”

While her brother watched TV, Sally asked questions, and I responded to the quiz. She was a spirited talker and funny, in a cute way. She told me she had been very shy in school. That was hard to believe.

Three beers and about a hundred questions later, her parents came home. It was late, so I politely excused myself. I didn’t want them to think I was hitting on their daughter, so I dropped the fact that I was there by invitation. Helen laughed and said, “Oh, so the sign worked?” It was clear Sally was on a long parental leash. I was curious why she didn’t have a date on a Saturday night but didn’t ask.

From time to time, I had passed different cars with Sally in the front seat and a young man driving, so I surmised she was dating, but it never crossed my mind to ask her out. I hadn’t been on a date since leaving Ohio and, besides, I saw her as too young for me.

Things Get Complicated

On a Friday evening about eleven, I was reading when my doorbell rang. It was a first; I didn’t even know I had a doorbell. Sally said there had been a prowler around her house so she got in the car and drove to my place. She explained that her parents were doing an overnight stay at a square dance party and had taken her brother along. She stayed home because she had to work on Saturday, and besides, she couldn’t stand square dancing. We agreed on that.

She looked around and said, “So this is where you live. Do you like it?” She sat down in my spare chair.

“No, I don’t like it much, but I don’t pay rent so I can’t complain. Let’s go back to your house and I’ll look around. It was probably just the wind.”

“No, it was a person, and I think I know who it was. I was supposed to be at a party with him tonight, but I called it off yesterday.”

"Why did you call the date off?"

"I cancelled when he told me what to wear. F**k him—no guy tells me what to wear. He thinks he's a big shot because he goes to Whittier College, has a new car, and his father belongs to Hacienda. He came to the house to scare me because he couldn't find another date. He's just lucky I didn't shoot him."

Now what do I do? I asked myself silently. I suggested taking her home and sitting with her for a while. If the guy was still there, he'd probably go away when he saw an adult male. Also, if she wanted me to, I'd take one of her father's rifles and walk around outside. That would sure as hell scare him off.

As we stood up to leave, she stepped close to me, and suddenly we were kissing. It had been a long time since I had kissed a girl. It was a long, wet kiss, the kind that made me think that Sally had some kissing experience. After that, one thing led to another.

About two in the morning, I insisted that she drive her car home because the neighbors would see it as soon as it was light. She said, "Okay, I'll go home, but only if you promise to come over and have breakfast with me." That was an easy yes.

I went with her, watched her get into the house, and walked back. All I could think was - *you're screwing yourself up, Scheid – you don't need complications like this.*

I promised myself this was a one-time mistake, not to be repeated. I'd tell her that, and I'd stick to it. I heard a distant echo of Grandma saying, "Alfred, the road to hell is paved with good intentions—be careful."

Sally made a great breakfast. We chatted about their horses, played with Hondo, and behaved as if nothing had happened. Abruptly changing the subject, I said, "Sally, you're only nineteen. I'm too old for you. I should not have let things get out of control last night, and I'm sorry. We can't do that again."

She cut me off. "The age thing is bullshit. My father is nearly ten years older than my mother, and besides, who's asking you to get involved? Have I asked you to do anything?"

I tried to explain that sex led to involvement. She set me straight. "Look, Al, you're in California now. We begin sex education in the seventh grade. To ease your guilt, I stopped being a virgin when I was seventeen, and I don't regret it. It's no big deal. My parents trust me not to get pregnant, and they don't interfere in my personal life. Some of my girlfriends are already married, and I'll be twenty in a few weeks. I'm an adult, so don't try to protect me from myself. I don't need it and I don't want it." I had no questions; the lady had made her position quite clear.

With the situation put on the line like that, I said I'd think things over. "Why don't you stop by and talk to my father. He'll tell you I'm free to do as I like as long as I don't embarrass the family."

Talking to her father didn't appeal to me - not even a little. It occurred to me that I was an old fogy and wasn't quite twenty-four yet. I had to wake up to California culture. The ethos of my hometown had caused me many problems over the years, and here it was again. I was confused, so I took my usual remedy for confusion: I went to work.

A few days later, I called Sally and asked if it would be okay for me to stop by for an hour after work—but not to talk to her father. She said, "Daddy will be asleep by the time you get here. The only rule is that I have to be in bed by eleven so I won't fall asleep at work."

We watched the news while I had a sandwich with a beer. We kissed and hugged, but there was no hanky-panky. As I was leaving, she said, "You don't have to call before stopping in. If my car is in the carport, it will be fine. I always stay up till eleven."

On Fridays and Saturdays, Sally was usually out with girlfriends or on a date, and on weeknights her parents retired early. My promise that our intimacy would be a one-time event was soon broken, but we had an honest relationship. I stopped by or I didn't, and neither of us asked any unnecessary questions.

When her parents took another overnight trip, she called and invited herself over to my place. I set an alarm clock and walked her home well before sunrise. I didn't want to advertise our activities to the neighbors. I was feeling very protective of Sally, and that bothered me. I didn't want complications, but I was creating them.

She continued to help me exercise the horses. She was a skilled equestrian and taught me some things about riding. Our relationship seemed too good to be true, and as Grandma said, "Things that look too good to be true are usually not true and bring regrets." I decided not to think about the consequences. Scarlett's put-it-off attitude was alive and well within me.

For her birthday, I gave Sally the kind of cashmere sweater set that was fashionable at the time; a short-sleeved cashmere sweater with a matching cardigan. It was the same kind of sweater set I had sent to Gin a year before. I had no imagination when it came to gifts for women.

For my birthday, she gave me deerskin riding gloves to replace the ugly ones I'd found in the tack room. I loved the gloves but only wore them when we rode together. Sally was a nice, sincere girl, and she deserved something better than a junior college student with no time or money.

One day, as I drove by, I saw her mother, signaling me to stop. When I opened my window, she said, "Do you have a few minutes to talk?"

When I got out of the car, she began, "Al, I want you to know that Jim and I like you, and we are not naive parents. We were young not so long ago, and we know how boys and girls behave. The only concern we have is that Sally doesn't get pregnant." With that, she waited for me to respond.

"Well, Helen, you don't have to worry about that; it won't happen. I'm on a mission to complete my education, and I don't want complications in my life. Just say the word and I'll stop seeing Sally. Maybe that's the best idea. I'm just not good boyfriend material." I was losing my grip as I implored, "Please think it over and tell me what you want me to do." This conversation was foreign to me, and I didn't know how to deal with it. Embarrassed and confused, I turned toward my car. I just wanted to leave.

She followed me and said, "Sally told me about your breakup with the girl in Ohio. I'm sure you learned from it. I didn't stop you to force anything on you. Jim and I just want you to know we understand things. You're a sincere young man, and we trust Sally to make her own decisions. There's no reason for you to stop seeing each other."

As I was closing the car door, she added, "Al, you have nothing to apologize for. We know you haven't taken advantage of Sally—she told us the story. She's a big girl and she did what she wanted to do." I thanked her and drove away.

On the drive to work, the dumb thought that entered my head was, *how life changing it would have been years ago if Jake's parents had been as clued in and understanding as Sally's?*

The Nurse I Knew

After finishing nurses' training near the top of her class, Alyce accepted a job at Huntington Memorial Hospital. She was sharing an apartment with another nurse and was still unattached. I intended to see her often. The truth was that I never had a weekend evening off, and I had homework every weekday night. After explaining this to her, she said, "I understand. Regular dates were a problem when I was in training. Now you have no free evenings and we live about thirty miles apart."

My only other feminine contact was intellectually rewarding conversations with Lee Chamberlain. She had matured since we met. I had no romantic feelings for her and hoped she didn't end up with some jerk. She still worked for the Glendora paper, and I read her stories. She wrote very well. We were becoming good friends.

The year 1956 was off to a good start. Mom was back, school was going well, I felt my life was under control, and visions of Jake were appearing less often. Some lines of Robert Browning's that I had memorized in high school came back to me:

The lark's on the wing;
The snail's on the thorn;
God's in his heaven -
All's right with the world!

1955 been a very eventful year for the bumpkin from Beerport.

Chapter 40

There is only one good – knowledge;
And only one evil – ignorance.

—Socrates

Men acquire a particular quality by constantly acting a particular way. We become just by performing just actions, temperate by performing temperate actions, brave by performing brave actions.

—Aristotle

New Adventures

December had been wet but moderate. Just after Christmas, cold weather arrived and the temperature at Desire fell below freezing every night. A few mornings I had to break ice on the watering trough. My electric heater fan just didn't do the job, and I was cold no matter how many blankets and jackets I stacked on.

The horses concerned me, so I called Mr. B. He said the horses were fine. They'd crowd together in the stalls and be fine down to much lower temperatures. That was my short lesson in animal husbandry.

When I mentioned how cold my room was, he had the usual "That's your problem" attitude. The incident went into my mental scorecard on Mr. B. On the same call, I reminded him that several horses had loose shoes, and he responded, "You just do your job. You told me about that before, and I'll take care of it. I don't want to hear about it again." I was beginning to dislike the old man.

I bought a large electric space heater and put it in front of the old one so the fans pushed more hot air toward the bed side of the room. It made the air dry so I hung up wet towels for evaporation. The new heater was a power gobbler and Mr. B paid the utilities. I had a hunch I'd hear about the electric bill.

School Marches On

Mr. Bergen, head of the math department, canceled the statistics class for the semester. He said I was the only student signed up for the subject. I explained that I had to have stat to graduate in the spring of '57. He said that if I could round up three more students, he'd teach the class with a floating schedule. After thanking him, I went to the art department, borrowed the right materials, and made a sign for the student bulletin board.

There was a new rule that ex-GIs had to begin taking three hours of physical education (PE) each week and one semester health class. I went to see my new health instructor, a Miss Laura Brathwaite. She offered to be flexible with my class appearances. She asked me to show up as often as possible and take all the tests. She said, "You're also in my PE class, where I can't be quite as flexible; you have to put in the hours. But I don't care what days you show up. Just come to three PE activities I'm teaching each week." I thanked her for being so helpful.

On the good news side, the class at Mt. SAC was over, so my Wednesday nights were free. Some pressure was off, but new pressures were on the way.

Joe Olivo talked to me about competing in a public speaking contest. His attitude was that even if I didn't win, it would be a boost for a scholarship to CMC. I gave in and promised to compete.

In addition, he wanted me to be a speaker for a muscular dystrophy (MD) fund-raising drive. Since all the appearances were at lunchtime and it just meant missing a class here and there, I agreed to do it. I recognized that he was trying to help me, but I had never done any charitable work, never competed in public speaking, had two jobs, and needed a high GPA. But no was not an answer that Joe found acceptable.

Serious Public Speaking

I learned that the head fund-raiser for MD wanted a healthy-looking male college student who was capable of making speeches. Being a navy vet was a plus. Their theory was that contributors would react more positively to someone like me rather than some official-looking middle-aged man with a potbelly.

They gave me a schedule of appearances. Joe worked with me, and we outlined a speech that could be done in five minutes. It all went rapidly and well.

Two little boys in wheelchairs, accompanied by their mother, were always at the same table with me. After introductions, my job was to stand up, introduce the boys and make the plea for money to support research to cure their disease. The physical contrast between the boys and me was stark. Each week we made the same presentation at two or three lunches. The program exceeded its money-raising goals, and everyone was happy. A picture of me presenting a check to two boys appeared in the Glendora paper

Suddenly, I had a few days of minor celebrity status. I was surprised the campaign received so much attention. Mr. White had a copy of the local paper in his hand as he congratulated me. I thanked him for letting me come in late many days. Even Mrs. White offered her congratulations and proved I had been wrong—she actually did know how to smile. It pleased the Whites that their employee was a good citizen and my next check had no deductions for the few work hours I'd missed. Mr. White was a fair and generous man and I thanked him sincerely.

I had done all the appearances, but I had a problem. Toward the end of the campaign, I looked up MD in the library and learned that the disease was not only preventable but predictable. If one parent carried the gene, it was likely that any boy born to that parent would develop MD. Girls were affected only rarely. In addition, a scientific test could determine if a person was a carrier of the gene. This had not been explained to me. They only said that the money would be used to do research for treatment.

I found that the two boys with whom I'd been appearing each had brothers with MD. So why did the parents have another child when they knew that one of them carried the gene? Why would they be that stupid?

It was because they were devout Catholics and could not use birth control. I thought that was crazy. When I asked one of the mothers the obvious question, her reply was classic: "We live our lives in line with the teachings of the Church, and whatever happens we accept as the will of God." I was incredulous at this response. Rather than offend the teachings of the Church, they were willing to take a high risk that another son would be born with the disease and die before the age of twenty.

The kicker to me was that they asked the public to put up the money to treat a preventable disease. Immediately after the picture was taken of me with the two boys, I told the organizers that this was my last appearance. A priest who served on the drive committee asked why. I said, "Father, when you come out and tell potential contributors that MD is an inherited disease that can be stopped by using birth control, I'll reconsider."

Taken aback, he replied, "Well, I'm sure you know the Church doesn't support birth control—what you suggest can't happen."

"Abstinence has worked for you, hasn't it?" I asked.

He looked at me for a few seconds before he turned and walked away. *Maybe it hadn't worked for him,* I thought. When I told this story to Joe and Frank, who had both been raised Catholic, they laughed. They thought my put-down was apropos.

The honor society for the California Junior College system is Alpha Gamma Sigma.[28] Nearly everyone has heard of Phi Beta Kappa, the most prestigious of the honor societies. AGS was not at that level but was respected among junior college faculty and student bodies.

It was difficult for me to imagine being in an honor society; it just didn't fit my self-image. But there it was. I was undoubtedly the most surprised and pleased of the honor students that year. There was a ceremony, and AGS emblems were hung around our necks. Lee Chamberlain and Sally Dale were also selected, of course.

Meanwhile, Back at the Ranch

After the conversation with Helen, a thought hit me. What if Sally got pregnant by one of the guys she dated? I had been careful, but how about them? In those days, blood type comparisons could only prove that a man was not the father. If his blood type was the same as the baby, he could be the father, or it could be a coincidence. Society generally assumed that the father was the man a woman named. The thought frightened me into celibacy in a flash. In the next flash, I decided to discuss it with Sally in the cold light of day.

The next Saturday while we were riding, I dismounted, and asked her to do the same. While walking the horses, I told her of my concern. She said, "What makes you think I let the other guys make love to me? I don't, you know." I didn't expect that response after her lectures on how free she was.

---

28 Alpha stands for Arete, meaning Excellence. Gamma stands for Gnosis, meaning Knowledge. Sigma stands for Sophrosyne, meaning Wisdom. It was just about as snooty as Phi Beta Kappa.

I explained, "Sally, I just can't take the chance. I've bet everything on finishing college, and I may want to go on to graduate school."

"Okay, I can understand why you might think I play around with my dates. So we'll do it your way, no more sex, as long as you tell me you're not just trying to get rid of me."

The truth was that her answer didn't solve the problem for me. As long as I spent time alone with her, even if we did nothing, the same risk would be there. I said, "Let's not see each other for a month and see how we feel then. I'm not comfortable with the way things are." I could tell at once that she didn't buy it.

"That's bullshit, and you know it," was her retort. "Just come out with it. You don't want to see me anymore, isn't that it? Look at me and just say it."

I looked at the sky, then the ground, trying to figure out what to say. Without a word and in one smooth move, she was on her horse and galloping down the trail toward home.

A sincere and lovely young woman had just ridden out of my life—if I wanted to leave it that way. The complication I had tried to avoid had arrived, and it had been foreordained from the first kiss. Was my head f****d up or what?

No Luck with Women or Horses

Mr. B had switched some horses around, and the Desire ranch ended up with a couple of new mares that were nice ladies and a palomino gelding that was crazy.

In Greek mythology, Pegasus is the divine flying white horse that ascended to heaven just after his birth to join Zeus. This Pegasus was too light in color to be a champion palomino and too ornery to be a good riding horse. I asked Pedro why Mr. B kept the horse, and he had no idea. He agreed the gelding was crazy and said the horse had bitten him.

Pegasus was also a cribber. That is, he chewed the boards around the corral for hours each day. I painted the top edges of the boards with creosote, but he seemed to develop a taste for the black goo. He also loved to bite and kick. When I went into the corral, he often ran straight at me, pulling up short and showing his teeth.

By the time this beast arrived, I had accumulated some riding experience. I decided to give a few of the sensible horses a Saturday off and give this bastard a good ride. It was a matter of personal pride—or perhaps I just needed something to work off my frustrations. In any case, there was no way I was going to let him intimidate me.

Pedro had told me he respected a crop (whip), but you had to use it so he'd know you weren't bluffing. My plan was to lasso the horse from outside the corral and pull him out the gate. Pedro also suggested that a hackamore bridle be used. He had gotten one out of the tack room and showed me how it worked. He said, "He'll bite you for sure, if you try to put a bit in his mouth."

Once I had the rope around his neck, I was able to muscle him out of the corral, tie him to a post, and get a saddle on him. He tried to bite, then swung around and tried to kick. I hit him on the nose with the whip just hard enough to get his attention. He settled down.

With my oldest helper holding the crop where the horse could see it, I was able to put the hackamore on. There were several types of hackamore halters and this was the type used on unruly horses.

When I mounted, he sidestepped and moved in circles. When he began to buck a little, I held the crop where he could see it. Finally, I maneuvered him out on to Desire. I used the crop to get him started and then let him run - and he could run. I never pulled him up; he decided when to slow down. It was actually the most fun ride I'd had.

By the time we got back, he was lathered up like a racehorse. When he tried to kick one of the boys I rode him hard for another ten minutes. He was calmer when we returned. We were giving each other lessons.

When I pulled off the saddle I called him el Caballo Loco—the crazy horse. He didn't deserve a name from Greek mythology. From then on he was called El Loco or just Loco. The boys loved the name.

On Sunday, I called Mr. B to talk about El Loco. I told him the horse was dangerous and it took so much of my time to handle him that I couldn't get to all the other horses. "Well, if you can't handle him, just say so," was his reply.

My reply was, "Mr. Billsborough, I'd like to have a face-to-face meeting with you about several things. I can come by your house Wednesday afternoon. It won't take long; I just need to get a better understanding about a few things."

He said, "All right, come to my house about five on Wednesday."

When he opened the door he gave a dead-fish handshake and led me into his den. The phone rang and, as he was going for it, he said, "Help yourself to a drink." I went to the bar and looked around. I spied an eighteen-year-old Glenlivet scotch and poured about three ounces. When he returned I was leaning on the back of a beautiful dark red leather easy chair.

"What are you having?" he asked.

I said, "Glenlivet - I've often put it on shelves at work but never tried it before. It's better than I expected. Thank you for the experience."

"Well, you know how to pick the most expensive stuff. Hope you enjoy it. Now, I have a couple of things to discuss."

Before he could go further, I asked, "Is one of them the electric bill?"

"Yes, it is. Are you leaving the lights on all day and night?"

"No, sir, it's my new space heater. As you suggested, I bought a larger electric heater. It's just barely adequate, but I'm getting by."

"Do you leave it on all day?"

"No sir that would be dangerous. I turn everything off when I leave. If you don't mind, there's something else I'd like to discuss. He nodded as he poured a cheaper scotch for himself.

"It's about my pay. I accepted one twenty-five per hour because I lacked experience and needed to learn the job. I think I've paid my on-the-job dues and would like a raise to one fifty an hour."

His response was, "Before we get to that, what about your horse problem? Now that you're such an experienced horseman, why can't you handle Pegasus?"

"Your ranch hands say that Pegasus is dangerous. As you know, I pay two neighborhood kids to help me on Saturdays so I can get all my work done by noon. I'm afraid he might hurt one of them. Also, the horse has chewed halfway through some of the boards of the corral – creosote doesn't even slow him down. I'm asking you to take him back to your other ranch where you have men who can manage him."

His reply was stupid. "I hired you to take care of the horses; those young boys are your problem. I'm not sure it's a good idea for them to be there anyway. As far as the cribbing goes, I'll send the vet around to look at him. You just keep up with the creosote."

Without responding I finished my drink and moved toward the door. Mr. B said, "That's it? You have nothing more to say?"

I shook my head. "No, that's it. I've said all I came to say." In his eyes, I was a smart-ass kid who didn't know my place, and in my eyes, he was a mean old rich man who got his kicks by pushing people around. I realized it was just a matter of time before I quit or was fired. But I wanted to pick the time, and now was not it.

As I reached the door, he said, "I was thinking about giving you a raise anyway, so you got that, and I'll consider moving Pegasus. In the meantime, you handle him on your own so those boys don't get hurt. How's that for now?"

I thanked him, and he managed a small smile when he gave his dead fish handshake. He had one more thing to say.

"By the way, if you need money so badly, why haven't you cashed all your checks?"

I said, "Mr. Billsborough, I'm busier than a one-legged man in an ass-kicking contest. I have homework, and I work two jobs. I haven't had time to cash your checks, but they'll be cashed eventually."

While driving away, I concluded that he was feeling both magnanimous and victorious. He had given me the paltry raise, and I still had Loco to fight. I had stood up to the man, but there wasn't much satisfaction in that.

The Critical Class

My sign failed to recruit another student for the statistics class. I went to Mr. Bergen's room to tell him. He wasn't surprised and said he was sorry. I thanked him and started to leave.

As I neared the door, he called out, "Can you really graduate next year if you get stat now? Are you sure you can't get it at CMC?"

I said, "I'll be happy to give you the phone number for Miss Witten, the registrar at CMC. She'll verify those facts. She has been guiding me for nearly two years so I can get a scholarship at CMC. If I get stat done, take six units in summer school, and carry a heavy schedule next year, I can get my degree a year from this June."

He said, "Okay, I'll teach a single-student class for you, but here are the conditions. You will come to my classroom and work while I'm grading papers. I'll take the time to get you started on the math, and self-study will be the rest. If you need so much help that you interfere with my other work, I'll stop the course. You will do all the assignments on your own, with no futzing around and no help from friends. All assignments will be in on time and if you miss one, you're out. I want your word that you'll do exactly as I say, and I don't want any begging for more time or missing a scheduled day. Are you sure you want to do this?"

I was seldom at a loss for words. A teacher giving a class for one student was unheard of. I asked, "Will Mr. Eisenbise [the director of the school] approve this for full credit?"

"Merlin Eisenbise is my problem. You'll get full credit. And one more thing: you're not to discuss this arrangement with anyone. I've never done this before, and I don't want to do it again. Understand me?"

I assured him I understood, and in ten minutes, we worked out a schedule that accommodated both of our time commitments. Mr. Bergen knew I worked full-time, and I figured that's why he was doing this for me.

I was deeply flattered that several teachers had gone so far out of their way to help me.

CHAPTER 41

Success is a journey not a destination.
The doing is usually more important than the outcome.
Not everyone can be Number 1.
—Arthur Ashe, tennis champion (1943–1993)

One is happy as a result of one's own efforts
once one knows the necessary ingredients of happiness:
simple tastes, a certain degree of courage, self-denial to a point,
love of work, and above all, a clear conscience.
—George Sand, novelist (1804-1876)

LIVING IN THE PRESENT TENSE

My discretionary time was counted in minutes; picking up laundry, gassing the car, and all the trivial necessities had to be squeezed between deadlines. Even bathroom necessities were done in a rush. I was a prisoner in a cell of my own design. Sleep was my only respite, and that only lasted five or six hours. I was learning one of Ben Franklin's lessons: "You may delay, but time will not, and lost time is never found again."

Driving was my only free-think time. *How long can this last?* I thought. My answer was: *Go one day at a time, until the end is reached.*

There was no thought of being happy or not—it was just "being." Finally, I concluded that I was in a narrow space between the absurd and the painful, and I just had to gut it out. Crazy thinking like that kept me going day after day.

To make matters more challenging, Joe Olivo wouldn't let me out of the public speaking contest I had promised to enter. The first competition was within Citrus, and that round was easy to win. Then there was a sudden death elimination competition among the participating junior colleges until there were three finalists. When the eliminations were completed, I was one of the three.

Joe called a meeting. He began, "Al, you've coasted through this thing. None of your speeches were near your potential. You are technically a very good speaker, but you're not getting your heart into it enough. The final speech will be difficult because the title is 'Americanism—What It Means to Me.' Al, this title is an invitation to emote, to show some fire. That's what you gotta do to win—get 'em on their feet. One of your two opponents is very good, I watched him during the eliminations. He's the one you have to beat."

I said, "I toned myself down so I'd keep a rhythm and enunciate clearly, just as you've been teaching."

"Al, for this contest the judges will react to the emotions of the subject, not technicalities. Think of the theme Americanism. It is loaded with feelings. There will be a five-minute limit, and you gotta have the audience roused up at the end. Many of the men on the judging panel served in the big war or Korea. Just about everyone in the audience will have known a man who was killed or wounded. Give them some raw emotion and they'll be with you."

"Okay, Joe, tell me what to do. Coach the hell out of me. I've come this far, and now I want to win the damned thing."

For the next week, he coached me at least an hour each day. A few times I "emoted" with such vigor that people passing the classroom door looked in to see what was happening. Joe wouldn't let me memorize the words. "I want your delivery to be fresh and free. Feel it and finish strong." Finally, Joe approved some prompt notes on three-by-five cards. I thought the speech was a little corny, but so was the subject.

The Kiwanis Clubs of Glendora, Azusa, and a couple of other local towns were the sponsors, so the speeches were made to an assemblage of members and guests at a luncheon. The prize was $300, and a panel of seven would pick the winner. There was no second place. The day arrived.

I was afraid to eat lunch. I didn't have butterflies in my stomach; I had a flock of crows. It was more like going into a barracks fight than a speaking competition. After what seemed like half a day, the MC started the program.

I had found the time to buy a new blue blazer, gray slacks, shirt, and tie and had put a spit shine on my trusty navy black shoes. My competitors both wore dark suits, and looked great.

Just before the first speaker was introduced, I gave myself a mental lashing. What was I so concerned about? Hell, here I was, the kid from the coal town who made it to the final three. So if I didn't win, so what? I said to myself, *there is nothing to be concerned about. Just give it your best shot and what happens, happens.*

The first man was visibly nervous and stumbled a little, but he did a decent job. He was the youngest, and this might help him in the vote.

The second man was the one that concerned Joe. He was a good-looking ex-marine and Korean vet. He was in control as he walked deliberately to the podium. He began by repeating the title of our talk, "Americanism—What It Means to Me," and began answering the implied questions. He used a few three-by-five cards as prompters, just as I planned, but he barely glanced at them; he was well rehearsed and confident. I would have been more than happy if my effort was as good. When he finished, the applause was loud and long.

Here we were at the bottom of the ninth with two outs and I was at bat. A walk-off home run was the only thing that would win.

It took nearly a minute for the applause to die down and the MC to take over the podium. The previous speaker had taken the crowd to a high level of emotion. If I let them lose that, I'd never get them back, and as Joe had emphasized, I had to close with their emotions at a peak.

The night I took Tex's truck flashed into my mind. As I stood in the dark at the top of the hill, I had hesitated in a moment of doubt. Then it came to me. Just start down the f*****g hill - just let yourself do it because you know you can.

At that instant, I decided to throw caution to the wind and do an impromptu speech. I put my prompting cards face down on the table. It was going to be a walk-off home run or a strikeout. When the MC spoke my name, I took two deep breaths and walked to the podium—deliberately, confidently, with my head up and shoulders back.

The speech began. "As a boy, I was taught that it was not manly to cry, and I seldom do, but today, ladies and gentlemen, may be an exception because talking about Americanism is very emotional for me. When I think of the word 'Americanism,' I see gold stars in the windows of families whose sons will never return, I see rows of white crosses in foreign lands, I see flag-draped coffins, and I hear a bugle playing Taps, the saddest melody ever written. I see young men on crutches and in wheelchairs. I see men with empty sleeves. Beyond all of this, I see the ranks of the next generation of young men in uniform, taking their turns, marching off to war. After victory, I see them coming home, taking jobs, getting married, and sending kids to school. We have all seen these things because we've fought two wars in the past twenty years—and we have prevailed in both."

A clock was prominently displayed so the speakers could time their speeches. I kept up the same pattern of talking about the sacrifices every American had made, mentioning food rationing, war bond drives, and so on. I sensed the audience was coming along with me and warming.

With half a minute remaining, I got back to the word "Americanism." With a raised voice, I said, "To me, true Americanism is the willingness to give it all for our country. We do what is required when it is needed and go wherever we must go. We don't shirk, we don't falter, and we sure as hell don't fail—we win!" I could see anticipation growing.

Then, very deliberately, speaking every word clearly, I said, "The ultimate Americanism statement was made by twenty-one-year-old Lieutenant Nathan Hale in seventeen seventy-six, and he spoke for every generation of Americans since then. A moment before he was executed by the British Army, Lieutenant Hale said, 'I only regret that I have but one life to give for my country.' And then [with emphasis] they hanged him!" With a shaky voice and tears welling up, I added, "Now, will you all please stand, face the flag, and applaud Nathan Hale—the patriot who defined Americanism for all of American history?"

With that, I turned toward the flag, six feet to my right, and began applauding. The audience stood as one, faced the Stars & Stripes, and applauded long and loudly. Tears were running down my cheeks as I took a handkerchief from my pocket and wiped my eyes. The tears were genuine, and I had spoken from the heart, sharing my emotions.

The applause continued as I walked to the speakers' table. Joe looked at me, teary-eyed and shaking his head in disbelief as he took my hand and said, "It was terrific, Al. It was the best you've ever done - but it's a gamble." He knew, as I did, that asking the audience to face the flag and applaud was a bit of showmanship, and it might work against me if the panel saw it that way. But if applause volume mattered, I had that part nailed.

When the applause died, the MC said dessert would be served while the panel did its voting. Seven men arose from seven different tables and left the room. Now I was hungry, and the dessert went down fast.

After a few minutes, the MC asked me to come to the podium to accept the prize. The applause was enthusiastic as I walked to the podium. After a congratulatory handshake, he spoke to the audience. "Well, that was a memorable speech, and I know many of us had tears in our eyes at the end."

He introduced the president of the Kiwanis Club, who congratulated the other two speakers and thanked them for participating. Then he handed me an envelope and shook my hand.

Members of the audience came to our table and congratulated all three of us. A few women were still teary-eyed. I knew that spoken words influence human behavior, but I had never experienced it at this level before. It was heartwarming and gratifying.

The ex-marine congratulated me. He praised my speech and admitted he was wiping his eyes at the end. I liked him, and I wish I had gotten to know him. He was the kind of guy I admired.

On our way to the car, I told Joe, "He's the guy who should have won. He actually fought in Korea. All I ever did in the navy was type and drink beer." I meant what I said. Life is only randomly fair.

When I slumped into the passenger seat of Joe's car, I was emotionally drained and could have gone to sleep in a minute flat. Joe asked, "How do you feel besides tired?"

"Joe, this was the biggest accomplishment of my life and one of my happiest moments. I've never before won anything worth mentioning—and you made it possible. He began to protest, but I waved him down. "Seriously, Joe, I would never have had the guts to go through this without you kicking my ass. I realize you pushed me into that muscular dystrophy thing to build my confidence for this event. You are the reason I competed and won. You told me, "Get 'em on their feet at the end'—and that's what I did."[29]

"But, Al," he said with a laugh, "I meant getting them on their feet metaphorically, not literally."

There were important lessons in this event, not the least of which was how a teacher can inspire a student. I also learned that I had to trust my inner self and that memorizing a speech can kill the emotions.

---

29 The exact text of the speech is lost from memory, but it was close to what is written here, especially the ending of the speech. Going impromptu was an act of desperation, backed up with a conviction that if the crowd rejected my style, I could live with the embarrassment of striking out.

Al giving a check to two boys suffering from muscular dystrophy - money came from fund- raising lunches where Al made short speeches

1955 Nash Metropolitan like the one Al owned while in college

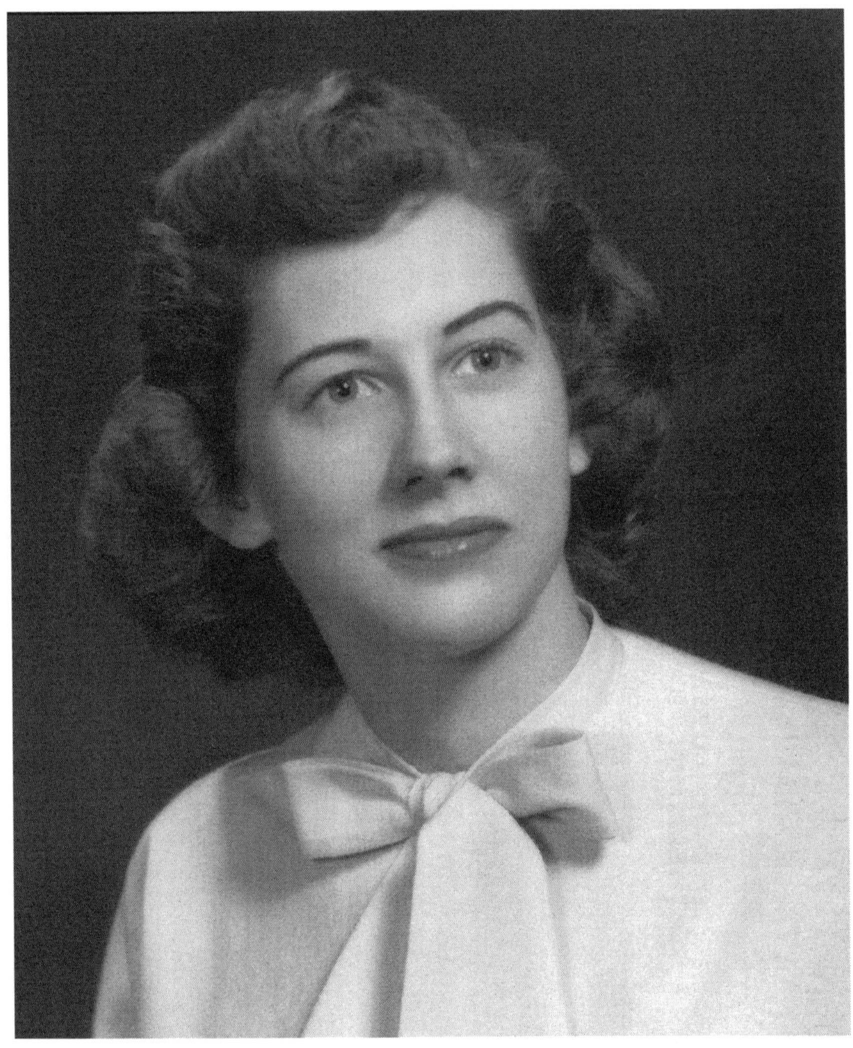

Virginia (Jake, Gin) Davis, picture a gift to Al, summer of 1955

CHAPTER 42

We human beings do have some genuine freedom of choice and therefore some effective control over our own destinies. I am not a determinist. But I also believe that the decisive choice is seldom the latest choice in the series. More often than not, it will turn out to be some choice made relatively far back in the past.

—Arnold Toynbee, historian (1889–1975)

There are lies, damn lies, and statistics.

—Mark Twain, author, humorist (1835–1910)

A MATH EDUCATION

Mr. Bergen said, "Mr. Scheid, if you successfully complete this course, you will perceive the world in a new way and you will automatically analyze things differently." He was absolutely on target. Statistics was one of the most important subjects I ever studied.

Prominently displayed in the front of the room was a plaque that read, "A polygon is not a dead parrot." In Bergen-ese, it meant that words can be misconstrued. He was a stickler for using words correctly. He wanted precise language, precise graphs, precise conclusions - precise everything. He had no patience with nuances. He said, "If you want multiple meanings, go to an art class." This excellent mind training went way beyond statistics.

Homework assignments were mostly reading about statistics and how they could be used and misused. I found the readings fascinating. After each of these assignments, we would spend time at the blackboard reviewing the math.

One day, when he knew it was my day off work, he told me to go borrow a dustpan and broom from janitor. When I returned he took me to a small wooden barrel that was nearly full of steel washers of all sizes. He said, "You'll need the dustpan and broom to gather up the washers when you're finished."

He leaned the barrel over and let about half of the washers fall to the floor; there were hundreds of them. "Mr. Scheid, the assignment is for you to design and execute a statistical analysis of the sizes of the washers on the floor. Here is a caliper; you'll need it for measuring the washers. A team of two can get this done in three or four hours. You're alone, so I suggest you get started."

Measuring a sample of washers was slow and boring. About six o'clock the janitors told me I had to leave. The next morning I was there before eight and finished the project. He accepted my graphs and explanations. That afternoon, he congratulated me on a job well done.

Probability theory was Mr. Bergen's real passion. He admitted that he loved playing bridge and poker because someone who understood probabilities had an advantage. He taught probabilities with a deck of cards, dice, and problems from a textbook.

Mr. Bergen was more a tutor and a coach than a teacher. He told anecdotes, asked rhetorical questions, and made me explain assigned readings, but he never lectured. He also gave no grades, and when I asked how I was doing, his reply was, "Well, I haven't thrown you out yet, have I?"

THE TEST

For admission to CMC, I had to take the Scholastic Aptitude Test; it is now called simply the SAT. Lee Chamberlain and I went together to Pasadena City College for the test. When it was over and we met back at my car, we both felt good about our performance. But I had one question. "What does perry ferry mean?" I asked her. "It was the only word in the vocabulary section that I didn't know."

She asked, "How do you spell it? I don't recall seeing a word like that."

I said, "P-e-r-i-p-h-e-r-y—perry ferry."

Lee laughed aloud and said, "You idiot, that's periphery. You know that word." The second she said it, I got it. What a dumb mistake. We had a good laugh over my stupidity. I have told this story to many people, but no one sees as much humor in it as I did then—and still do.

THE DAWN OF SPRING

Wendell and I liked a stupid rhyme that is often attributed to Ogden Nash: *Spring has sprung, the grass is ris, I wonder where the posies is.* The lines came to mind one dawn while I was walking to the stables. Alfalfa has its own pungently sweet odor and, in the freshness of dawn, a gentle breeze wafted the fragrance over the ranch. It was delightful.

Spring arrives in Southern California about the time of the vernal equinox, and that year it came on like thunder. The winter rains had been generous and the hills had burst into a bright green. Wildflowers were coming up and adding color. The mornings were still chilly, but the sun was bright, and by noon soft warmth took over. Even the horses seemed to know the season had changed. They came to my side of the corral to be petted—all but Loco, that is.

Twice a week, my first class wasn't until nine, so I sometimes got one of my rides done before leaving. Just after sunrise one morning I rode to the top of a hill and looked around—360 degrees. As I sucked in the fresh cool air, something hit me. Here I was working my ass off and didn't have much money, but how many people can go riding before school or work? Was I lucky or what? I marveled at how much fun I was actually having in these strange circumstances. My protean life was full of work and stress but was rich in rewards as well. It was one of those rare moments in life when you suddenly realize you're happy.

Living alone in the quiet atmosphere of the ranch had been good for my introspection. If you can chew gum and walk, you can ride horses or shovel horseshit and think about your life at the same time. Sometimes I got so deeply into daydreaming that I'd ride past my turnaround point or put too much hay into a stall. My thoughts ranged from the previous summer, to homework, to Sally, and on to the hated Loco—all in a few minutes. Psychic healing was happening and my views of Jake had softened.

Also, my self-appraisals were not as harsh as they had once been; a little self-forgiveness had crept in. I knew I was doing well in all my endeavors, but I was keenly aware of the risk of self-delusion. All my life, I had known people who had inaccurate self-images. Self-delusion was a trap I intended to avoid.

Getting away alone and taking stock did not always result in good answers, but it sure helped reject the wrong ones. Setbacks had come my way, and I lectured myself to accept them as just the way life unfolds. The main thing was to keep my goals clearly in mind.

The Albino and the Light Tan Horse

I was getting to know Miss Brathwaite because I showed up in her tennis class as my PE course. She was from Saskatoon, Saskatchewan, and had spent several years skating in a traveling show that was sort of the Canadian answer to the Ice Follies. She was not a beautiful woman, but she had the slim muscular body of a skater, a nice smile, and a pleasant personality.

One day she told me about something strange. Several times a young boy with very white skin had flaunted himself, completely naked, in front of girls on the tennis courts nearest the adjoining orange groves. She said he might be an albino; she had never seen anyone so white. She had called the police, but he was gone by the time they arrived.

I was on a court when I heard Miss Brathwaite call to me. I looked where she was pointing, and there was a stark-naked boy, waving at some girls on the court farthest away from me. He was behind the tall chain-link fence that separated the orange grove from the tennis courts. An idea hit me.

I ran down to the orange grove fence, stuck my shoe toes into the links, climbed up, and jumped over to the orange grove side. By going two rows of trees into the grove, he couldn't see me. I trotted toward him. When I saw a pile of clothes on the ground, I stood behind the trees and waited. In a few minutes he came through the trees. He was the whitest human I had ever seen. I cut him off from his clothes and tried to talk to him. He ran and I followed.

He was running barefoot on muddy ground, covered with dry, brittle twigs. After a minute or so, he stopped. We were both breathing heavily.

I approached him and said, "I'm not going to hurt you. I'm Al. What's your name?" I sensed he was about to run. I walked to him slowly, took his arm, and said quietly, "I'm not going to hurt you, kid. Let's go. Your feet are bleeding." He allowed me lead him to his clothes.

I let him put on his underwear, pants, and socks, but I kept his shoes and shirt. He asked, "May I have my shoes and shirt?"

In a calm voice, I replied, "No, you'll run again—I can see it in your eyes. You're coming with me. I won't hurt you if you come along.

If you run, I'll catch you, and then I'll kick the shit out of you. Do you understand?" He nodded yes and walked ahead of me as I directed.

When we got to the fence, Miss Brathwaite and a male PE teacher were waiting on the other side. I helped the kid over the fence and climbed over after him. We walked him to the PE building.

The kid had deep scratches on his feet and ankles, and he was muddy up to his knees. I was a mess too, muddy and dripping with sweat.

Miss Brathwaite and I went outside for a cigarette. I said, "I don't think he's an albino. His hair is reddish-blond. He must stay inside all the time, so he's super white."

She agreed. Then she said, "Well, thanks for helping me out with this. Your shoes and clothes are ruined."

I lifted up a foot and showed her the bottom of one shoe. There was a hole all the way through it, which I had blocked with cardboard. "They were already ruined." New shoes were not on my list of priority expenditures.

"Well, you ruined them on school business. I know that Mr. Eisenbise will insist that the school buy you a new pair along with new tennis shorts. Those are torn."

"In all honesty, the tear was there before today. These are cutoffs of my navy pants." Our chat ended, as I had to get cleaned up for work.

Stories about the naked boy spread through the school like wildfire. It turned out he was a student at Azusa Pacific University, a Christian college that bordered the opposite side of the orange grove.

The next day, Mr. Eisenbise called me into his office and asked me to describe what had happened. At the end he gave me a chit to take to a nearby sporting goods store. My pay for this adventure was one pair of new Converse tennis shoes, white socks, and tennis shorts with a matching shirt. It was much more than I expected.

I flattered myself that I took unusual events in stride, but I had bad dreams about the naked kid. I was always chasing him in circles around orange trees, and he was crying. I wanted him to leave my dreams; he was too creepy for me.

Pegasus

On a day off, I got back to the ranch in a steady drizzle. As I pulled in, I could see the stall Loco used was wide open, so I went directly there. There was a note on the clipboard from the father of my two Saturday assistants. John's note read, "Four of your horses got out—able to put three back - Loco still out there."

I pulled on a poncho, heaved a saddle onto a horse, and rode over to John's house. He saw me coming and came out. He said, "I'm still saddled up. It'll take both of us to get that horse back in the corral."

His light color helped us spot him grazing in a neighbor's field. We rode in a tightening circle around him until John got a rope around his neck. By the time we led Loco back and put him away, we were both wet and cold. John invited me to dinner.

After a fast shower, I took a bottle of my favorite Vat 69 scotch and walked across the street. After a cocktail, we had a nice family dinner.

The next Saturday morning, I checked out the latch on the stall door. It was a simple eye and hook system. Loco had figured out how to use his teeth to lift the hook out of the eye and then push against the door until it swung open. Loco was a smart horse, maybe that's why he wasn't trainable.

I found a large eyebolt among the junk in the tack room. My plan was to screw it into the bottom stable door and fasten a hasp so it fit over the eye. The eyebolt could then be turned by using a long bolt as a lever. I had found a fifteen-inch-long bolt for the job. I drilled a hole in which to start the eyebolt. This noise got Loco's attention and he came into the stall. I ignored him. I was bent over, using the long bolt to turn the eye. About each half-turn, I had to take the bolt out and put it back in. It was warm, and I was wearing a white navy T-shirt.

As I took out the bolt to get a new purchase on the eye, Loco put his mouth over my left shoulder as far as he could and clamped down. Suddenly, he was lifting me off my feet.

In a flash, with no thought, I swung the long bolt with my right arm as hard as I could. The bolt hit Loco on the head, about halfway between his left eye and ear. When the bolt struck, he let go and I jumped away. As I looked at him, I saw his lower jaw hanging on the door. His eyes were rolling, and his forelegs were collapsing. He was also making gasping sounds. I thought, *Oh my God, I've killed him.* I opened the lower door quickly, and as I did, he rolled onto his side, his head partway out the door. His legs were jerking, and the eye I could see was rolling around.

My first thought was to get the vet as quickly as possible, but I didn't have his number. I called Mr. B, and he answered. I explained what had happened and added, "We need the vet here right away. The horse may be dying." Mr. B began asking dumb questions like, "Why did you have a bolt in your hand?"

I said, "Look, I can explain everything when I see you. That's enough questions. We need the vet here. I'm going back to take care of the horse," and I hung up. By the time I got back to Loco, the phone was ringing. I knew who it was and didn't answer. After about ten rings he gave up. Loco was trying to stand but couldn't get to his feet before rolling down again.

The vet arrived in about twenty minutes. By then, Loco was staggering around in the stall like a drunk. The vet looked into his eyes and walked him around the corral. He said, "Well, he'll be all right. I'll treat the cut on his head. It just needs some antiseptic salve. You're the guy I need to treat. Get that T-shirt off." My tee shirt shoulder was soaked in blood.

My horse boys arrived. I sent them home and said I'd call their father later.

When Mr. B arrived, the vet was just finishing with the bandages on my wound. The skin on the back of my shoulder was abraded and bleeding, while in the front there were teeth marks seeping blood.

Mr. B's first question was, "How's Pegasus? Will he be all right?" I knew then that I didn't want to work for him. This man was worse than a fool; he was just plain ignorant. The damned crazy horse was more important to him than an injured employee.

After receiving assurance that Loco's worst case was a headache for a few days, he turned to me. "Now, tell me, what happened here."

I took him and the vet to the stall door and showed them exactly what had taken place. I told them about the horse getting out of the stall the day before, and my idea to create a system that he couldn't work with his mouth. Mr. B criticized my plan for fixing the latch, "Why didn't you lock him out of the stall while you were working? You brought this on yourself, young man."

That was it. I lost it. I shouted, "That f*****g horse is crazy. He's a menace to anyone who gets around him. He's ugly, he's mean, and he can't breed. Why do you keep him? He's dog food on the hoof!"

"My employees don't talk to me that way," he replied loudly. "Shut up! And you hung up on me. No one hangs up on me! You have no respect, and I wonder if you didn't set this up so you could hit the horse with that bolt. I know you hate him."

The vet interceded, saying, "Mr. Billsborough, the horse is gonna be fine. Your man was hurt worse than the animal. Let's cool down for a minute."

I was more deeply angry than I had been in years. If he had been a young man, I would have hit him. I said, "You say no one hangs up on you? Well, does anyone ever tell you to stick a job up your fat ass? Well, that's what I'm telling you right now!" I walked away quickly, back to my room, undressed, and took a shower. I had to cool down and get control of myself.

As I was dressing, I wondered how I was going to put new bandages on my shoulder when the vet tapped on the door. I opened it, and he came in.

"Here's some dressings and antiseptic for your shoulder," he said. "Horse saliva has a lot of bacteria; you have to clean that wound every day for a few days." Then he added, "Sit down and I'll do it for you again."

As he bandaged me, he said the old man had left. "I've known the Billsborough family for a long time. He's had his share of disappointments and he's a prideful man who has no patience with people. I think that's why he likes horses—they never talk back, and he's in complete control of them. If you want to keep your job, just call him. He knows you're right about the gelding; I told him so and he listens to me about horses. He also understands that it wasn't your fault the crazy horse attacked you."

I thanked him for his help and kindness and told him I couldn't take Mr. B any longer. I had grown to dislike him because of his unfair attitude and his stinginess. I said, "It seems obvious that he doesn't like me and never has. I can't imagine why he hired me."

The vet looked away for a moment. "Maybe you're too close to what he would have liked a son to be. Please don't repeat that. I shouldn't have said it." When we shook hands, I guessed I'd never meet the vet again. I always felt sad about good people disappearing from my life, as so many had.

I did schoolwork for a while and calmed down. On the way to work, all I could think of was what had happened with Loco. My inexperience with horses certainly contributed to the event. The men from the Chino ranch had warned me never to turn my back on the horse. Now I was going to have to move on. And I'd been looking forward to a summer with less school and more time to enjoy country life.

At seven that morning, I was happy, maybe even elated. Things had fallen into place, and graduation was coming up. Then it was all gone and I was depressed.

When I arrived back at Desire that night, the moon was nearly full and I could see the horses well. When I stood by the corral, they came to me, but not Loco. As I rubbed their noses, I realized that my time with them was nearly over. Loco had been my white whale. He had won; I had lost.

My God, I thought, *will I ever stay with anything? I move from job to job, and just as I learn enough to be comfortable with the work, something happens and I'm moving on again.* Then I thought, *Come on, Scheid, get with it. You're not a victim of fate. You're doing what you gotta do. Think about getting your degree in June next year and let nothing stop you. You'll land on your feet. You always do.*

By the time I had a scotch and climbed into bed, I'd made a decision.

Chapter 43

Savor every moment of life and reflect deeply on each experience. Celebrate the peaks and valleys. Become aware off the authentic joy that continually binds moment to moment, year to year and generation to generation.
—Frederick Buechner, novelist, theologian (1926–living)

People of mediocre ability sometimes achieve outstanding success because they don't know when to quit. Most men succeed because they are determined to.
—George Herbert Allen, NFL coach, Hall of Fame (1918–1990)

Everyone Moves on Eventually

As much as I had been looking forward to the summer on the ranch, my pride required that I cut loose from Mr. B. I saw no option but to call him and discuss the terms of my departure. When he answered I began, "Mr. Billsborough, I'd like to discuss when I will move from the Desire ranch. I need a few days to find a new place to live."

His reply was unexpected. "Oh, you really want to leave? I thought that was just a temper tantrum. You can stay if you want to."

"Well, all things considered, I think it best if I go. I can be out by next Saturday, but I'll take care of the horses until then."

"I've thought about it, and if Pegasus is that much of a problem, I could move him back to Chino next week. Your work has been satisfactory, so I'm willing to have you stay. All you need to do is agree to show me some respect in the future. How about it? That's a fair trade, isn't it?"

I couldn't believe it. He was willing to give in on Loco if I agreed to kiss his ass. I said, "I can't imagine you changing how you operate. Your attitude during the Pegasus incident was the crowning blow. I don't want any bad feelings. I'd just like a week to relocate."

Amazingly, he said, "I know I can be abrasive, but I like young men who work hard. We can iron things out, but if your mind is made up, go ahead and leave."

It was tempting, but I didn't trust him. Jackals don't change into puppy dogs. I said, "I've enjoyed many things at the ranch and will remember my time here fondly, but it's time for me to move on."

"Well, our paths will cross again, I'm sure. I'll have a man come over Saturday morning to take over."

I responded, "Just mail my last check to the liquor store as usual."

He said a curt good-bye and hung up.

A sense of relief came over me as I walked outside, took a few deep breaths, and looked around. Yep, I'd miss the horses and being in the country, even the faint smell of manure. As I looked at the mountains in the distance, I'd never felt so far away from Beerport. I never saw Mr. B again.

Time Speeds Up

It had been weeks since Sally and I had spoken and I couldn't just leave without saying good-bye. On my day off, I got home before five, saddled a horse, and rode down Desire so she'd have to drive by me on her way home.

When her car came up the street, I signaled her. She stopped and opened the window. "Are you angry with me?" I asked.

Never at a loss for words, she said, "Hell no. You ignore me completely for weeks and then you stop me in the middle of the road, to ask if I'm angry. I'd be awfully stupid to be angry, wouldn't I?"

"I'm sorry, Sally, and I owe you an explanation. Let me saddle up your horse. We'll go for a ride and I'll explain everything."

"I can saddle my own horse. I'll be at your place in fifteen minutes, and your story better be good." Not waiting for a reply, her tires threw gravel as she sped away.

When she arrived, I was standing by my mount, sipping on a paper cup of scotch. She motioned for the cup, had a swig, and handed it back. We let the horses walk toward the hills. As the scotch soaked in, I felt peacefully romantic. The sun was creating long, soft shadows and it was cooling off—just cool enough to make you want to be close to something warm.

We dismounted in the hills, walked to each other, and kissed for a long time. When we stopped she had tears on her cheeks and I felt like a heel. A sweeter, gentler girl I'd never known.

I told her I'd stayed away because I was confused about us and wanted time to think things over. Wiping her eyes, she said, "So what did you decide?"

"Sally, if I let myself go, I'd fall deeply in love with you, but I can't do that. I've got a lot more college to finish. It just wouldn't work. It's impossible for me to explain how sorry I am."

"So nothing's changed. You still believe I'm a roadblock to your ambitions, right?"

I said, "It's not you personally; it's anyone. You're a wonderful human being. You're smart, funny, kind, and lovely—and I care for you. But I have no space in my life for a relationship."

She walked away a few yards before turning. "Well, I told Mom this was where we'd end up, and since I expected it, I'm not as hurt as I might've been. She and Dad know how I feel, and it really pisses me off that they agree with you. They say you have no time for a woman and they know I want the kind of man who puts me first."

"There's one more thing. Mr. B and I had a fight over that damned crazy horse, and I quit the job. I'm moving out on Saturday."

"Will I ever see you again? Is this it, nothing more? We just ride away?"

"I don't know when I'll be able to visit, but I'll stay in touch. I'm moving in with my mother and stepfather and live there until graduation. After that, I'm going to summer school in Claremont and may move there. Now you see what I mean? I have no time for a personal life."

We rode back to her stable. She said, "Mom and Dad expect me to invite you in for a drink. Will you join us?" I didn't feel comfortable going into the house but saw no alternative. After dealing with the horses, we went in. Her father fixed drinks, and I told about the blowup with Mr. B.

Jim said, "John told me about that horse you call El Loco. It's been lucky that he hasn't hurt someone. The animal sounds too far gone to fix."

Helen insisted I stay for dinner. We laughed and had a good time. *They would be fine in-laws,* I thought. There was an elephant in the room that we didn't discuss. I figured Sally could tell them the story after I left.

She walked with me to my horse, and we wrapped ourselves around each other for a few emotional minutes. God, it was rotten saying good-bye, and it was too reminiscent of the Jake good-byes.

Over my bedtime scotch, I thought about breaking off with Sally. While it didn't feel good, deep in my soul I knew it was best for both of us. I was lonely and on the rebound from Jake. If we kept up any relationship, I'd be hopelessly attached to her in no time. Maybe this was the real reason I refused Mr. B's olive branch. I had to get away from the ranch.

One of the take-home lessons from the Jake breakup was the reality of an educational gap, and the gap was just as real with Sally. The problem was there when we took our first ride together, but I ignored it. Sally would have accepted the problem and tried to work through it, but would we be successful?

That night, I promised myself I wouldn't get into a relationship again until my education was completed. If I met another desirable woman, I'd walk away the moment I looked at her the second time. However, as Grandma said, "Promises are like pie crust; easy to make and easy to break."

There were women, like Wanda, who understood the unspoken rules of having an affair and knew that there is no long term. That's the kind of woman I was going to seek from then on. No more beautiful, soft, cuddly, sexy girls who were looking for marriage and children.

An Unexpected Win

I got word to go see Frank Martinez. He asked if I was aware of the annual Bank of America Award. I was not. He explained that B of A gave annual awards to the outstanding male and female students studying business. He said, "Today the director completed checking grades and talking to the teachers. You've won the award." I was shocked.

He gave me a strong handshake and said, "Just before graduation, you have to attend a banquet in downtown LA. The award is $100, and the president of the bank will personally hand them out." This was exciting news. I'd never won anything like this before, and $100 was real money in 1956.

The next day, the announcement was posted. Every teacher I saw, and quite a few students, congratulated me. A calm happiness came over me because I knew this would look good on my application to CMC.

George arrived early on Saturday morning. As we were loading up, the foreman from the Chino ranch arrived and inspected the horses, tack room, every corner of the storage area, and even my room. Mr. B apparently wanted to make sure I took nothing with me.

An Unexpected Relationship

Since the naked boy incident Miss Braithwaite and I played tennis two or three times each week. She was not a great player, and I was terrible. We became Al and Laura when there were no students around.

She said she was a fan of thoroughbred racing. On my next day off we drove two cars and met at Santa Anita to watch the last few races. We had drinks, laughed constantly and, with the luck of beginners, we won a few bucks. After the last race we went to a nearby bar called the Tack Room. After more drinks we decided to have dinner. She and her roommate lived nearby, so we dropped her car there.

When I took her home, one thing led to another and we had a kissing marathon. That activity was terminated when her roommate arrived. It had been an enjoyable afternoon and evening. She walked me to my car, and we agreed we had to do this again. I said, "Good night, Miss Brathwaite." We thought that was funny and it kept me in the habit of using her school name.

The next day she said it was the most enjoyable time she'd had since arriving from Canada, but she had a concern. "As you probably know, it's considered bad form for teachers to date students. If the school finds out about it, I'll probably lose my job." I pointed out that I was an adult, not an eighteen-year-old boy a teacher might take advantage of. We agreed we'd talk later on the phone.

On my next night off she made dinner at her place. After dinner she set an alarm clock so we'd be up and fully dressed when her roommate came home. We began seeing each other on my nights off work.

One evening we met at the Tack Room. The bar was nearly empty, but we took the last booth in the back, completely out of sight. We sipped beer, ate pretzels, laughed, and snuggled. The evening was off to a fine start.

I leaned out of the booth to hail a waitress just as Frank Martinez, Merlin Eisenbise, and another teacher walked up, on their way to the men's room. She didn't see them and put her arm around my neck as I straightened up. They stopped and everyone sort of froze in place. The men said hello as normally as they could and we answered. They continued on.

We looked at each other, and she said, "Oh, shit, that's it. There's no way to talk my way out of this." She was stating a fact.

When the men came out of the john, they looked straight ahead and walked by to a booth near the door. They left about twenty minutes later.

I went to see Frank the next day to ask about repercussions. He said, "It is my understanding that Laura may not be fired, but Merlin will decide that when he meets with her. The problem is that physical intimacy with a student is a big no-no."

I said, "Frank, she and I are practically the same age, and nothing you saw proves we're having an affair. It was only the second time we'd had a beer together."

He laughed aloud and said, "We saw what we saw, and now it's up to the director. He wants to avoid any embarrassment. As you know, Al, the sophomore class voted on the three candidates the faculty nominated for the Covington Award. The graduation program went to the printer yesterday and your name is in it as the winner. It would be embarrassing if word gets out that the Covington Award winner has been having an affair with a PE teacher. Do you get the picture? You're lucky you weren't caught with Laura before the faculty nominations, and she's lucky you won. It may save her job. You can't tell this to anyone."

"Thanks for telling me and I'll keep the secret. Winning the award is a real honor."

Laura was meeting with Mr. Eisenbise the next day. If she told the truth, he'd have no choice but to fire her, so she lied and repeated what I'd told Frank. It didn't ring completely true, but it gave Mr. Eisenbise a handle.

A deal was made. Laura agreed she wouldn't see me until school was over, and she'd submit a resignation, effective at the end of the term, giving some innocuous reason for resigning. She'd get a good reference and there would be no embarrassment for anyone. It was a sensible solution for all concerned.

Just after the school year ended, Laura applied for an opening as head of the girl's physical education at Pomona High School. She was hired and her salary was higher than it had been at Citrus. All's well that ends well.

The End Arrives

I met with Miss Witten and we finalized my summer school plans at Pomona College and fall courses at CMC. One summer class was Money and Banking, a difficult three-unit course. The second was a social science course. At the end of our meeting, Mr. Frisbee handed me a letter which granted me a full tuition scholarship to CMC. It was an exciting moment, but no surprise; Miss Witten had tipped me off.

With my job at the ranch concluded, I had the most study time available since beginning college. I felt confident I could handle the work. I'd been working two jobs, won $400, and had been frugal, so money was not an issue. I decided to coast through the summer with only the liquor store job. It would be like a vacation.

An Unwanted Gift from Sally

Suddenly I began to have difficulty getting started in the mornings. I ascribed this to sort of a "let go" after so many months of high pressure. But I was drowsy during the day and the boxes of booze and wine were feeling heavier.

A few days later Helen Vanwey called. She said, "Al, I don't want to alarm you, but Sally is sick."

I was alarmed. "What's wrong with her?" I asked.

"She has mononucleosis. It's a virus, and there is no treatment. She just has to get lots of rest and live through it. The doctor says it may be two months or more before she's normal again. I'm contacting you because you may be infected." Sally was sleeping so we didn't talk.

The doctor felt my lymph glands and took blood. He said, "I'll run the test, but I know you have mono. It's been spreading around the local schools." I asked for and he gave me a signed note, which I could give the school in case I was too sick to take my finals exams. This was a major pothole in my road to a high GPA.

My energy dropped like a rock. I could just struggle through the evening, drive home, and go to bed. Finals were starting in days. I decided to take decisive action.

I told Mr. White the truth and said I'd have to stop working. He and Mrs. White were sympathetic. Now I could concentrate on studying for finals and sleeping.

I called Laura with the news. She wasn't surprised. "When you begged off tennis, it crossed my mind that you had mono symptoms. I had mono, and I think that gives me immunity."

CHAPTER 44

There are essentially two things that will make us wiser:
the books we read and the people we meet.
—Charles Jones, car salesman, motivator (1927–2008)

If you don't know where you're going,
any road will get you there.
—Alice's Adventures in Wonderland, Lewis Carroll (1832–1898)

ON TO FINALS

As long as I could stay awake during school hours, I figured I could muddle through. I needed only enough energy to review my notes and marked-up textbooks. I didn't want to ask for special treatment, but I was concerned about staying alert during multiple finals in the same day. I went to see Mr. Eisenbise.

He read the doctor's note, and then handed it back to me. I said, "I was hoping you had experience with mono and you could advise me. I hate the idea of going to teachers and asking for favors, but I'm concerned about grades. I need a high GPA to keep my scholarship at CMC."

He said, "Taking several finals the same day is tiring. Let me check the schedule and see what I can do."

As I was leaving, he said, "If you can't make it to the graduation ceremony, it's important that you tell me in advance. I hope you'll be there." I assured him I'd be there if I had to crawl because my mother was so looking forward to it.

When I arrived for my last class with Mr. Bergen, he said, "Merlin Eisenbise told me about your health problem, and that's a bad break," he said. "Let's talk about your stat final. How do you feel today?"

I said, "Not real great, but I'll be all right. I quit my job so I can go home and sleep."

"What if you started your final today? The second part will require more concentration, but you'll have no problem with the first part. Al, I already know how much you've learned, but I don't want you to go to CMC without taking the final. Work until you finish part one or get tired. You'll take the rest of it in a couple of days, as scheduled. Let's get started."

I focused hard for over an hour and finished part one. The fatigue hit me about halfway home, I kept driving, but it took all my will power to stay awake.

Mr. Eisenbise did his magic, and I had no back-to-back finals. I took the health final alone with Laura as my proctor. The test was a joke and I finished it in twenty minutes. We parted without coming within touching distance.

The last day of finals, I did the second part of the stat exam. It wasn't easy, but there were no surprises. I remembered all the key formulas and did well on the essay questions. I was pleased with my performance but couldn't wait to get home and into bed.

Bank of America

The banquet was held on Friday evening in downtown Los Angeles. Studying and taking finals had taken their toll, and I wondered if I could drag myself to it. I slept all afternoon. After I showered, I felt I could make the scene.

I had never attended an affair like this. A state senator and other official-looking men made speeches extolling the virtues of the Junior college system.[30] Jesse Tapp, president of B of A, made the keynote speech. He was a corpulent man with pasty white skin that looked as if it had never seen the sun, but he was a fine speaker. I admired his delivery and use of language.

As our names were called, we walked up to Mr. Tapp, who shook our hands as he gave us each an envelope and a framed certificate. A few of the winners were older adults who attended mostly evening classes. I admired those people who spent their evenings improving themselves.

The envelope contained a letter and a Bank of America check for $100. The letter congratulated us, then went on to say that if a recipient applied for a job at the bank to tell the interviewer that he or she was an award winner. Our names would be in a permanent file.

GRADUATION

Mom was excited. Neither she nor George had ever set foot on a college campus. We went early, and I gave them a tour.

Mr. Eisenbise began by calling students to the stage to accept honors and prizes.

My friend Lee; my tutor, Sally Dale; a couple others, and I were called to the stage to receive our scholarship letters. Lee and Sally had won full scholarships. It was announced that Sally was first in the class, with a 4.0 grade point average; Lee was second, with 3.9; and I was third, with 3.87.

30 The old Junior College System is now called the California Community Colleges System. As of 2012, there were 112 of these colleges operating. In the 1950s, there were fewer than half that.

The B of A awards were announced and I was recognized as the winner of the Kiwanis public speaking contest.

The last item was the Covington Award, which was a gold Omega wristwatch. Mr. Eisenbise told the audience who Dr. Covington was, and then he recited the inscription on the back of the watch:

Boy most likely to succeed
Alfred G. Scheid
Citrus College – 1956

Mr. Eisenbise gave me a handshake and a smile as he handed me the box. The finale of the evening was when the students walked onto the stage and received their diplomas. After a cheer by the students and applause by the audience, the ceremony was over.

I found Mom and George in the crowd. Mom was crying. This was not like my high school ceremony, where I was recognized for nothing. Her son had actually achieved something. Just seeing her that happy made all the effort seem worthwhile.

Mom admired the watch and said, "Alfred, you never told me about all the things you won. You went up on the stage more than any of the others." Mom and I had traveled a long road since our days of struggling to get by in Bridgeport. Graduation was an accomplishment.

After a quiet dinner, George drove us home and I went to bed. For the next week, all I did was eat, sleep, and take short walks. I had pledged no booze until mononucleosis was in my rearview mirror.

The Struggle

My original plan was to take Money & Banking from nine until eleven, have lunch, and then take my second class from one to three. This regime would last for six weeks. After that it was a month before classes began at CMC.

My energy level was low and I realized there was no way I could handle four hours of classes plus homework every day. One two-hour class and driving would be taxing enough.

I went to see Miss Witten and gave her the doctor's memo. She was nonplussed, "Don't risk your long-term health; take care of yourself." She volunteered to cancel the afternoon class for me.

Fortunately, my friend Ralph Wood had managed to get into the M & B class and Lee was taking a morning class at Pomona. We agreed that I'd arrive at Ralph's home in Glendora every weekday morning at eight. Then we'd pick up Lee, who lived two blocks away, and Ralph would drive us to Claremont. This cut my driving time in half. I brought a pillow and slept during the drive to school.

M & B was taught by Professor Jahangir Amuzegar, a young Iranian PhD.[31] In his first lecture, he made it clear that he expected us to gain a full understanding of the workings of the American banking system, money markets, and the Federal Reserve System. He explained that the final exam would cover the entire course and would count for sixty percent of our grade. Unfortunately, he had an accent that seemed to worsen as the two-hour class progressed each day. Ralph and I decided to go over our notes after class each day. We hoped that what one of us missed, the other would get.

Another student overheard us and introduced himself. He was Les Fiedler, and he was transferring to CMC from the University of Redlands. Within a few minutes, he had insinuated himself into our daily study program. Les said he planned to live off campus and was looking for a roommate. I put this in the back of my mind but wanted to get to know him better before considering sharing quarters.

---

31 6 Some years later, Mr. Amuzegar held a number of positions in the Iranian government under the Shah, and he eventually became chief economist. After the Iranian revolution, he became a board member of the International Monetary Fund and an internationally recognized economist.

I was getting about twelve hours sleep each day and was able to keep up with the required readings. By the fourth week, I wasn't fighting fatigue as much and was no longer sleeping on the way to school.

Les, Ralph, and I decided that for the last two weeks of the class, we'd work two hours after lunch. The textbook was the most difficult I'd ever seen.

About ten days before the final, I began feeling much better. I was wide-awake until evening. My turnaround from near zombie state to a fully functioning human took only a few days once it began. When I went in for a checkup the doc said I was lucky, mono usually lasted longer.

For the final exam Amuzegar took the most obscure parts of the course and focused on those. Even the multiple-choice questions were set up to extract wrong answers. Ralph said he had a tough time with the test; Les felt all right about it and was praying for a C. I genuinely felt that I had a solid B or B plus.

A few hours after the final, the three of us met for beer, followed by dinner and a little barhopping. Les told me that he was being pressured by CMC to live on campus. No one had told me of this requirement.

When we received the grades, we all did better than expected. Les got a B, Ralph a C, and I pulled the A I needed. If I had ever seen Amuzegar again, I would have thanked him for forcing me to learn so much about the financial system.

I let myself think a little about the Harvard Business School. The library yielded a lot of information. Harvard had pioneered the case method of studying business problems, much the same as law schools study court cases. One article stated that Harvard had the best graduate business school in the world which made it hard to get into. Should I daydream about getting into something as exclusive as that? Jerry and Grover had both told me that Harvard was where I should get my master's degree. I decided to talk to Jerry again.

UNFINISHED BUSINESS

It had been my intention to thank Dr. Covington for the award he sponsored, but mono and summer school had gotten in the way. I went to the Citrus administration office to get some information on the good doctor. Mr. Eisenbise saw me and asked, "What can we do for you, Al?" I explained why I was there.

He said, "I'm glad you're taking the initiative to thank Dr. Covington. He's a nice old man and lives alone at the Canyon City Hotel in Azusa. He'll be glad to see you. Please tell him I said hello."

I called the Canyon City Hotel. He came on the line immediately and asked, "What can I do for you?"

"Dr. Covington, my name is Al Scheid—S-c-h-e-i-d. I won the Covington Award this year. I'm calling to find out if I can thank you personally for the award. May I come by and see you?"

Hesitantly he said, "Well, yes, that would be fine. When do you want to do this?"

"Will tomorrow afternoon about two be okay?"

"That's fine. I'll see you then."

When I arrived he was sitting in the lobby, dressed in a suit and tie. He was a trim man with gray hair, in his late sixties, I guessed. After sitting down, I asked some questions about where he had practiced, gone to medical school, and so forth. He answered with as few words as possible. When I asked about the genesis of the Covington Award he said he wanted to encourage some young person that the faculty and students thought would be a success.

He asked where and when I was born. I tried to skate through things quickly, but he bored in with questions. Eventually, he had the whole story. I told him about everything except my love life. He, like everyone, wanted to know about car repossessions. After nearly two hours, he looked at his watch.

As we were saying good-bye, he said, "Al, this has been a wonderful afternoon. This is the tenth year I have given this award and you're the first winner who has ever come to say thanks. I really appreciate it. You're going to be a successful man, even if you don't get into Harvard." With a serious look, he added, "Now, listen to me—and I mean this: if you ever need anything, I want you to call me, even if it's just to ask advice from an old man. I like to help deserving young people."

After the meeting, I thought, *I may need help or advice someday, and I'll bet he has a lot of wisdom inside that old head.* Besides, I wanted to hear how he made so much money; I had some interest in that subject.

I called Sally. She had just gone back to work. She didn't suggest getting together, and I didn't mention it. I had warm feelings for her, and a face-to-face meeting might drag me in again. I couldn't risk it.

Miss Brathwaite called to check on me. I was delighted that she hadn't come down with mono. She had moved to Pomona and was all set for her new job.

An Accomplishment

The previous summer, I was working in an Ohio steel mill and was in deep love with Gin. That summer now seemed as if it had happened to someone else. Now it was time to deal with job hunting. There were challenges ahead, but I was optimistic about the future.

Except for physics and statistics, Citrus had not been academically difficult. Sure, there were some smart students, but it was easy to stand out if you were four or five years older than most of the competition. Most students chewed on pencils or stared out the windows, whereas guys like me made it a point to ask questions or make constructive comments in class.

The teachers were not accustomed to students who read textbooks ahead of assignments, completed their homework, and came to class ready to do battle. In addition, it was well known that I worked long hours, and I felt that teachers had often given me the benefit of a doubt. It is human nature to root for the underdog. And I didn't let pride get in my way; I accepted any and all help gratefully.

It was late July and I had a list of calls to make. I called Pevehouse and learned there had been no news about Jack. Deke's act hadn't changed, and Charlie was chugging along as usual. Wanda had a steady boyfriend and thought she was in love. Leland and I had a nice phone visit. My Long Beach friends were all doing fine, but our common bonds were fading. I realized we'd lose contact and it saddened me.

I had gotten to know Lee better and had visited her home. Her parents were cordial and seemed to like me. I took her to a couple of movies and once to Chinatown for dinner. She was the smartest girl I'd ever met, and I found her interesting. She was naive about boy-girl things, and I didn't want to be her educator. As a precaution against mono, we had not kissed. That rule was soon broken.

My social life was mainly drinking beer and watching TV with Jim and Aline Jackson. Not working for a while gave me the break I needed, but I had to find a job and resolve where I'd live.

I spent a couple of hours on my old Smith Corona, creating a new résumé. With the original and two carbon copies in hand, I felt prepared to go out job hunting.

CHAPTER 45

The secret of making something work in your life is,
first of all, the deep desire to make it work; then the faith and belief
that it can work; then to hold that clear definite vision in your
consciousness and see it working out step by step
without one thought of doubt or disbelief.

—Eileen Caddy, founder of Findhorn Foundation (1917–2006)

The elevator to success is out of order.
You'll have to use the stairs … one step at a time.

—Joe Girard, master car salesman (1928–living)

A NEW JOB

Frank made it possible for me to use the Citrus student employment service. They had a possible job at a Riviera sofa bed store in Azusa. The manager wanted someone to do his bookkeeping and sales records. He'd pay $1.50 an hour, and he had indicated that he would teach the right man how to sell sofa beds.

The store was large, about forty-five feet wide and nearly seventy feet deep, and filled with a sea of sofas, wood tables and comfort chairs. It was a well-stocked store.

Jerry Fletcher, the manager, looked at my résumé for a long time before he asked, "Did it bother you to take a man's car?" I gave my stock answer that the goal is to get the late payments and repossess only as a last resort.

After asking about my selling experience he said, "Okay, I'll give you a tryout if you want the job."

I replied, "I'll take the job, but can we begin today?" Employers like people who are eager to start work. Moreover, if I didn't like the job, I could quit and not waste another day.

Jerry said, "Let's go back to the office and I'll explain my problems."

Jerry tried to show me how orders had to be filled out, a ledger kept, deliveries scheduled, and many other details. He said the forms were complicated, but he exaggerated the difficulty. He was simply hopeless at dealing with paperwork. For two hours, I did my best to organize things, but I needed to know more about some of the forms.

The next morning, at my suggestion, Jerry introduced me by phone to a cooperative Riviera bookkeeper. During several calls, she taught me about the sales number system, order forms, and how commissions were calculated. She also gave me the scoop on Jerry. He had been the top salesman in the Hollywood store and had been promoted to manager of the Azusa store about six weeks earlier. Managers normally did the paper work, but Jerry couldn't handle it. Someone had to come out every week and fix mistakes. He was told to hire help, at his expense, or go back to being a salesman.

Because of manufacturing schedules, the information had to be accurate and mailed in every day. I figured I could keep the paperwork running smoothly in two or three hours each day. But, I wanted to be a salesman, because that's where the real money was.

On or Off Campus

Miss Witten said, "Al, I'm terribly sorry we never discussed living arrangements. It never occurred to me that staying on campus would be a problem for you. With a few exceptions for medical reasons, all students are expected to live on campus. Dr. Benson has known about you for over a year and I told him you were coming in today. He wants to meet you. Rather than submitting an appeal to the housing dean for off campus living, I suggest you appeal to Dr. Benson."

I had read about Dr. George C. S. Benson, the founder of the college. He had a PhD from Harvard, had been an army officer during WWII, taught economics at Harvard, and worked in the federal government.

Dr. Benson came around his desk and shook hands as he motioned me into a chair by a coffee table. He offered me coffee. I said, "Yes, thank you. That would be nice. Black, please." He opened the door and ordered it.

"Well, I've read your file, and you have an interesting story. I don't think we've ever had a student who made a living working in tire factories, repossessing cars, and riding horses. Miss Witten is certainly a supporter of yours. She tells me you want to get your degree next June, and that will require carrying more units than we usually permit students to carry." He looked at me questioningly.

"Dr. Benson, CMC has high academic standards, but I've proven I can carry heavy workloads and still produce good grades. I hope you'll give me a chance to reach my goal."

"She also tells me that you hope to go to Harvard Business School," he continued.

"Well, I think that depends on how well I do this semester. I'd like to go to Harvard, but I know it's hard to get in. It's probably just a dream."

"Dreams are good. Don't give up on them. I taught at Harvard, as have several other professors here. If we think you have the right stuff, we might be of some help to you. I'm here to help students, so don't be afraid to come and see me."

"Dr. Benson, I hesitate to bring this up, as I know it's not something the president of the college normally deals with, but I really need to resolve my living arrangement."

He replied, "Yes, Miss Witten mentioned there was a problem about living on campus."

I said, "Dr. Benson, I work weekday evenings until nine and all day and into the evening on Saturdays and Sundays. I've been working full time since I started college, and I've learned to organize my time to get my schoolwork done. I know living on campus isn't going to work for me. I'm way past throwing cherry bombs under windows. I'll have homework to do every night."

He looked at me sympathetically and answered, "I understand what you're saying, but we have a pretty firm rule about the entire student body living on campus. We think it adds to the college experience. You'll miss a lot of good things if you don't live here."

I replied, "Dr. Benson, I'll miss the college social life anyway because I'll be at work or studying. The past two years, I have never attended a school function—not a dance, not a football game, nothing. I hadn't seen a movie during that time until a week ago. But I participated in debate, was spokesman for a muscular dystrophy drive, and won a public speaking contest. I was able to make time for educational things. I did my share of beer drinking years ago. Most of the men graduating next June will be twenty-one, and I'll be twenty-five. We don't have much in common. I just need my privacy to study. And with my schedule, I'd be a lousy roommate for anyone."

"Where are you working?" he asked.

"I have a job in a Riviera Sofa Bed store in Azusa, and my boss lets me do homework when business is slow."

"You make your points well. Let's do this: you write a letter to me, laying out your reasons for living off campus. This is not something I want to deal with on my own. We have a faculty committee that makes decisions about off-campus living."

I thanked him, promised to hand deliver the letter, and took my leave. Dr. Benson seemed to have the best interests of his students at heart and I felt I could depend on him to be fair. But I really didn't intend to live on campus.

On the way out, I filled Miss Witten in. She said, "Write the best letter you've ever written but keep it short. If Dr. Benson likes your letter, the committee will go along. He just needs something to put in the file." I delivered the letter the next morning. If CMC insisted I live on campus I intended to make a last-minute application to UCLA.

Late in the day, Miss Witten called and told me my request for off-campus residency had been granted. I called Les Fiedler's house and left a message. He called back and said he had also received permission to live off campus. I asked how and he said, "My dad wrote a letter saying I'm being groomed to take over his manufacturing business, so it's important that I spend as much time there as possible." Because Les hadn't worked during summer school, it was obviously a con job by father and son.

Les had located an apartment not far off campus. The place was the upstairs of a small furnished duplex, with a serviceable bathroom and a small kitchen. The apartment was on a month-to-month rental, so I could always move out if I didn't like his behavior.

"Enjoy Life on the Riviera—Sofa Bed, That Is" (company slogan) The Riviera Sofa Bed Company was well known because it had about thirty stores in California and advertised heavily. In the 1950s, thousands of small new homes were being built. The founders of Riviera had realized that there was a need for extra beds as families grew and visitors arrived. The sofa bed was created and the public responded favorably.

Riviera used TV, radio, and print advertising to draw customers into the stores. Salesmen demonstrated the most efficient way to remove the sofa seats and flip open the bed. The sheets and blankets could be left in place. Ninety percent of the sofas were made to order and the rest were sold from showroom inventory. With guidance from a salesman, the customer selected the style, size, and the fabric to cover the sofa. Delivery was in three weeks, directly to the buyer's home. With a twenty-five percent down payment, monthly payments were offered.

Jerry Fletcher was a small man, about fifty, with a Brooklyn/Jewish accent which included a heavy sprinkling of Yiddish words. He had a stomach paunch and wore a hairpiece that was never perfectly in place. Jerry was a journeyman pitchman, who had sold mink coats and other furs in New York.

Because Jerry was an accomplished sales coach, the Azusa store was used for training salesmen. Customers rarely showed up before noon, so trainees arrived at nine in the morning and were schooled until lunchtime. He received compensation for this chore.

Jerry's attitude was that a chimp could learn product information, but learning to close a sale took skill. Even with serious training, only a few new men ever became accomplished pitchmen. Riviera's most successful salesmen had pitched other things before sofas, including aluminum siding, Fuller Brush merchandise, household appliances, and used cars.

Most of the trainees used poor English, some had accents, and nearly all wore wrinkled not-quite-white shirts with ugly ties. Mostly they were men who wanted jobs that required minimum physical exertion.

Jerry explained that the Siegel family often gave jobs to extended family members whom he called *mischpoche* (family). Some of them were recent immigrants from Israel or Europe and had thick accents. Those who failed at sales went to work in the sofa factory or made deliveries. [32]

I approached him, "Jerry, I have another job I can go to next week if you aren't going to give me a chance to sell." It was a lie and a gamble, but I knew that the accounting people were pleased with my work, and that had put him in seventh heaven. He needed me.

Finally he said, "Okay, Al, you wanna be a pitchman so give me a pitch. Sell me a sofa."

This was hardly fair, but I gave it a try. He pretended to be a typical housewife, asking dumb questions in an obvious attempt to confuse me. His tactic didn't work. He wasn't aware that I had studied the product manuals and the sales literature stacked in his office. I understood the product better than most of his trainees. I had also opened and closed sofa beds many times, imitating his style as best I could and I had watched him give his pitch to real customers.

After game playing my pitch for a while, he broke it off and grudgingly said, "Okay, so you know quite a bit and you've memorized my pitch, but I can't make you a sales trainee. Only Eddy Siegel can do that."

I responded, "Jerry, we made a deal. Set up a meeting and I'll go see Mr. Siegel. If he doesn't hire me, you're off the hook." He said he'd think about it.

It made sense for me to keep this low-paying job while I looked elsewhere, but I had to make more money. Then something occurred to me. Riviera had a big Labor Day weekend sale coming up. I went to him and said, "Jerry, I know my bookkeeping pay is taken out of your pocket. How would you like to save that money?" His ears perked up on that one.

"How can that happen?" he asked.

32 *Mischpoche* (family) was the first of many Yiddish words I learned. They will appear in the text from time to time.

I said, "It's simple. You let me sell sofa beds and we subtract every dollar I make in commissions from the money you owe me for bookkeeping. If I make one good sale a week, bookkeeping won't cost you a dime. What do you have to lose?"

He said, "Well, the other guys won't like it if you get as many ups as they do, and I don't know what Eddy Siegel would think of the idea. Let me think about it." [33]

I said, "Jerry, you're going to have only one senior salesman and two trainees working with you on the Labor Day weekend. I'll take an up only when everyone else is working a customer. The guys won't be losing anything. If I get lucky, you'll have a great deal. Come on, Jerry, let's give it a try. If I make a sale, you can say that your bookkeeper just talked to overflow customers and got lucky."

If Jerry was anything, he was cheap. It hurt him to hand over my meager check every week. Greed overcame fear and he agreed to my idea.

Jerry wasn't a bad guy; he was just insecure.

Like most salesmen, he liked to show off his knowledge, so I asked questions and flattered him. As he pontificated about his sales theories, I learned more. I watched him work customers into a sale when they had no intention of buying during their visit. He was damned good.

THE SYSTEM

In the Riviera system, maximizing the sales price was the goal for salesmen. Every item in the store had three prices. The standard price was the "emes" (true) price and the lowest price was the "schlock" (junk) price. The highest price was the PM (premium money).

33 You were "up" when it was your turn to take the next customer that walked in. The more ups a man could get, the more chances he had to make a sale, hence ups were bartered, sometimes sold, and frequently bet on, as in, "I've got two dollars that says I sell my next up."

A salesman quoted the PM to the customer and then discounted as needed to make the sale. A few customers accepted the quoted price, but most needed the incentive of a discount. It was important to make the sale while the customer was there, because once they left the store there was only a slim chance they'd return. The saying was, "You'll starve to death while waiting for "be backs."

A salesperson's commissions ranged from a low of seven percent to as much as twenty percent during sales and special events. Some men thought they could predict which customer could afford the higher price. In fact, the way people dressed or spoke was not a reliable predictor of what they would buy. Jerry's theory, which I adopted, was that if a customer paid attention for the entire pitch, they could afford the product—*if* they wanted it. Our job was to help them come around to wanting it.

Some salesmen would beg the manager to let them drop below the schlock price. These were weak salesmen, and they usually went into some other line of work.

One clever way to discount a sofa was to throw in accessories at ridiculously low prices. We could say to a customer, "I can't give you a deep discount, but I can add in those two end tables for ten dollars each if you'll buy your sofa tonight." This often closed a sale if you had learned that she wanted new end tables. It paid to listen to customers.

It became obvious to me that selling sofa beds was not much different from selling an RCA TV service contract or persuading someone to make a payment on a delinquent car loan. The real trick was to read people well and gain their confidence. As Duke had taught me, reading people gives you a distinct advantage in all human interactions.

Successful salesmen read body language, were students of facial expressions and listened to what the customer said. It's not difficult to discern when a person is getting bored and it is the same with interest and pleasure. They smile, they look directly at you, they lean forward, and they touch the merchandise. The signals are always there.

The Opportunity

Riviera TV ads ran on several TV channels starting on the Wednesday evening before Labor Day. The company had projected that it was going to be a big weekend. My hopes were high, and I wanted to be prepared.

A senior salesman named Benno Eisenberg was assigned to our store for the weekend. Benno was about sixty-five, overweight, and polite. He wore a suit and tie when he worked. The women respected him like a grandfather, and he played the part of a senior advisor. When he spoke to customers, his English was good, but the rest of the time, he used Yiddish and Hebrew words extensively.

The day of his arrival, I admitted to Benno that I had never made a sale and asked him to critique my pitch. He said, "It's good you should ask for help. Most young men think they know it all. Give me your pitch, kid, but don't spiel [drag it out]."

When I finished, he said, "That's great. Why haven't you made any sales?"

"Well, Benno, I've never pitched a customer. This weekend I'm allowed to take an up only if everyone else is busy, so I want to do the best I can."

He was disbelieving. "You gotta be kidding, Kid. You got a better shtick [act] than most of the schmucks in the Hollywood store. You're gonna do fine, but if you get in trouble, T-O to me and we'll split." [34]

---

34 T-O (tee oh) is a "turnover." If things are not doing well with a customer we often turned them over to another salesman, introducing the new man as the manager, a factory rep or whatever title we thought would help make a sale. The T-O was ingrained at Riviera to the point that split commissions were nearly as common as individual ones.

When I said I didn't know if Jerry would like that, he said, "Well, f**k Jerry. Sanford Siegel and I are mischpoche." I decided to use Benno if the need arose and worry about Jerry if necessary. I understood that being mischpoche with the Siegel family meant Benno had influence.

When I asked Benno to teach me something about fabric selection, he took me through an hour of what to say about certain sofa coverings. He knew the sample book by heart. Benno became my fabric guru.

The first customers arrived on Thursday evening, even though the ads stated that the Labor Day Sale prices started on Friday. Jerry said they were "gun jumpers" and usually easy sales. He and the three others were all busy, and I took my first up. I missed that one, but later I wrote up a sale of nearly $400. On Friday, we had a steady flow of customers but no ups for me until late afternoon. I closed one that evening for about $350.

Saturday was a busy day, and I sold two more sofas. And on Sunday I closed a couple more. Jerry called total sales in to the home office every morning and he told us Azusa was beating some other stores.

On Monday evening, a dapper-looking man in suit and tie walked in. Since everyone else had a customer, I welcomed him to the store, gave my name, and shook his hand before I said, "May I know your name?"

He replied, "I'm Eddy Siegel. What's your name again?" I had met the Riviera VP of sales, but not in the right way. I explained that I was the man Jerry hired to do bookkeeping, and he said, "Yeah, I heard about you. The office says your work is good. Are you pitching customers?" I explained that I was only talking to customers when all the salesmen were busy; he said nothing.

As quickly as he could get free, Jerry rushed over and said, "Eddy, what a great surprise to see you. We've had a great weekend. I've never seen so much traffic on a Labor Day sale. What can I do for you?"

Eddy said, "You can begin by telling me why Al here is selling. You know every salesman needs my approval before he can pitch a customer."

I saw what was coming and decided to cover Jerry's ass if I could. I slipped away from the conversation, rushed to the office, and grabbed my sales contracts and my résumé.

When I rejoined the two men, Jerry was explaining that I was talking to customers to keep them busy until a salesman could get to them. He was sorry. He didn't mean to hire a salesman without Eddy's approval. He was scared silly, and Eddy was letting him sweat.

I figured there was nothing to lose. If I got fired, I got fired. But it made no sense for Jerry to get beat up like this. I said, "Mr. Siegel, I'm sorry there's been a misunderstanding. I begged Jerry to let me speak with customers. Here are the deals I wrote and my résumé. I'd like to be interviewed for a job as a Riviera salesman as soon as possible."

He sorted through the six contracts. He looked at me and asked, "Did you actually make these sales yourself? Who helped you?"

At that point, Benno walked up and said, "Eddy, great to see you. Hey, Al here is going to be a fine salesman for us. He knows the product, he knows how to make a pitch, and he closes deals." Eddy respectfully greeted him as "Uncle Benno" before he walked away to the office.

Jerry said to me, "Well, I did you a favor, and now I'm in deep shit. Eddy's pissed off at me, and I don't need that. I've got enough problems." He was hand-wringing by then.

After a couple of minutes, Eddy stepped out of the office and said, "Al, please come here."

He offered me a seat, pointed to my résumé, and asked, "Hey, did you actually repossess cars?" It never failed. Repossessing fascinated everyone. I was well practiced at answering the question.

When Eddy and I came out of the office, it was closing time and only Jerry was there. He stood up with a nervous smile, reminiscent of a panting young dog, hoping to get petted, not kicked.

Eddy said, "Jerry, I've interviewed Al, and I'm going to make an exception to our rule about part-time salesmen. Here's the deal. He'll come into the store about four on weekdays and noon on the weekends. He'll do your office work just as he has been. When he's done with that, he can take his turn with ups, but—and this is important—every salesman on the floor has to get at least one up before Al gets his first one. He'll make certain all orders are checked and mailed before he leaves at night. The two of you work out his days off. He'll be on our standard commission schedule, and you don't have to pay him for the office work. Are there any questions?"

Jerry, who would risk death rather than disagree with a Siegel, said, "That's fine with me, Eddy. I'll keep training him, as I've been doing. He did really good, didn't he?"

Eddy said, "Yes, he did fine. That's why he's got a job. Now, I want this deal to stay quiet. I don't want a barrage of mischpoche hitting me up for part-time jobs for their college kids. If this gets out, Al will lose his job and you'll have to pay a bookkeeper. Both of you understand?" We assured him that we both got it. I thanked him for giving me a break.

After Eddy left, I said, "Jerry, you won't regret this. I'll do a good job for you. Now, I have an idea. Give me a key so I can come in early tomorrow morning and check all the contracts when I'm rested. Then I'll drive them to the factory and turn them in. We gotta make sure there are no mistakes."

He handed me the key and said, "You lock up. I'm beat, and I'm leaving." The scene with Eddy had stressed him out. On my way home, I decided that Jerry must have been treated badly as a puppy because he was such a frightened dog.

Another thing occurred to me. I had never met a Riviera salesman or trainee who wasn't Jewish. When Eddy interviewed me the issue never came up. I decided to let that sleeping dog lie. Now, the question was, could I sell sofa beds or had the weekend just been beginner's luck?

The next morning, I was at the store at seven, reviewed every deal and corrected mistakes. At nine I turned the papers in at the factory with a covering memo from me. I wanted them to know that I had delivered the orders in person.

Most sofa beds sold for between $300 and $400, with commissions from $25 to $40 each. The weekend was a bonanza for me. Truth be known, a cigar store Indian could have made a couple of my sales. They were people who had decided to buy a sofa bed. All they needed was help in fabric selection and the order written up.

CHAPTER 46

One of the greatest discoveries a man makes,
one of his great surprises,
is to find he can do
what he was afraid he couldn't do.
—Henry Ford, industrialist (1863–1947)

Solitary trees, if they grow at all, they grow strong.
—Sir Winston Churchill (1874–1965)

10% of life is what happens to you,
90% of life is decided by how you react to the 10%
—Charles Swindoll, pastor, writer (1934-living)

CMC AT LAST

Claremont Men's College had welcomed its first students in 1946. George C. S. Benson, the founding president, worked hard and led well, and success came. He recruited respected professors who were retiring, mostly from Ivy League colleges. The plan was for great teachers to teach small classes, which would attract better students. The professors could live their last active years in the quaint village of Claremont with no obligation to write books. The concept worked exceedingly well. Within its first decade, the school was building a reputation for having a highly qualified teaching staff and a challenging academic atmosphere. The number of applicants increased each year, and only the best were admitted. By the time I arrived in the autumn of 1956, the school's reputation had improved dramatically. [35]

My favorite class was labor economics, taught by Professor Orme Phelps. He was the most interesting teacher I had ever met. During a class discussion, he learned that I had belonged to several unions. After class he said, "Come by my office this afternoon and we'll talk about unions."

After relating my experiences with the United Steel Workers, a carpenters' union, the United Rubber Workers, the painters union, and the Retail Clerks Union, he had no doubt that I was not a union lover. We discussed the history of unionism. His knowledge was wide and deep.

He asked how many hours I worked, and when I said, "About forty per week," he was surprised.

"Do you think you can make high grades at CMC with that schedule?" I explained how I was able to study at work. As I was leaving he said, "Well, Al, you may be able to handle the schoolwork, but remember that you have your senior thesis to write and that may overload you." I thanked him and left. I liked Dr. Phelps; he was a gentleman and a fine teacher.

As I went from class to class, I discovered that each of the professors found an excuse to invite me to their office for a chat. Miss Witten had told me I'd get to know the professors. I saw a plan at work. They were going out of their way to meet me on a personal level.

---

35 In 2012, *Newsweek* magazine listed CMC as one of the ten best colleges in the United States. In 2011, admission was granted to slightly over 12 percent of the applicants. CMC became coeducational in 1976, and its name was changed to Claremont McKenna College in 1981, keeping the initials CMC.

Since Laura lived in Pomona and we began to see each other more often. One evening in a pensive moment, she said, "You know, Al, you've become a professional student." When I asked what she meant, she said, "You go to school like most people go to a job—you're methodical. You don't mix with other students, you don't go to school functions, and you make homework and study the priority of your life. But I gotta tell you, you're missing a lot. You know, there's more to college than just getting grades. You ought to get involved with social things at CMC; meet other students and enjoy college." In my defense, I pointed out that I had gotten to know some of my teachers, one of them quite intimately. She acknowledged the remark with a laugh.

Cute remarks aside, she was right. I had become the polar opposite of what I had been in high school. But there was no way I could get inside the student culture at CMC. I arrived too late in my college career. Most of the seniors had been together for three years and their cliques had been formed. Getting to know a transfer student was not in their game plan. I would remain an outsider.

Another way I didn't fit into the CMC was a matter of wealth. This was primarily a rich boy's school. The tuition was as expensive as the Ivy League and most of the students had nice, mostly new, cars. My little Metropolitan attracted some attention because it stood out among the large cars on campus.

I was also different from many students in my commitment to studies. Immodest as it may sound; my classroom participation was damned good. The professors recognized that I arrived prepared and took notes. There's no better way to please a professor than to quote back to him his words from a previous lecture. When the first grades came out, I was A across the board.

Our Apartment

When I arrived home on a Saturday night, there was a crowd on the lawn in front and all the lights were on. Les was having a party and it had turned into a mob scene. A neighbor had called the landlord who showed up and gave us two days to move out.

Fortunately, Les got off his ass, and found a two-bedroom guest-house behind a large house on Foothill Boulevard, not far from the CMC campus. It was a much better place, private and secluded, with a food market next door. Because he promised not to screw up again, I decided to move into the new place with him.

Dynamite Les

Les was a bright guy who found many ways to waste time. One of his favorite pursuits was to go out into the desert with some likeminded friends and ignite dynamite just to hear the boom and see the dirt fly. I thought it was a dangerous hobby and passed on all invitations to join in the fun.

One day I saw something in the back of our garage that I hadn't noticed before. It appeared to be three file boxes covered with a blanket. I looked inside one box. It contained dynamite and fuses in clearly marked wrappers. I was instantly angry. My bed was on the opposite side of the wall against which the boxes were stored. All I knew about dynamite was that it could blow you to kingdom come.

I took the boxes out of the garage and put them near the front door with a note telling Les to get them the hell away from the house. When I returned after work, the boxes were back in the garage. I was in a rage when I entered the house.

He told me the stuff was safe; he wasn't worried about it. He just didn't get the picture. The argument escalated, and he flatly refused to move the boxes. I gave him a count of ten to get on his way to the garage. He could see that I was genuinely angry but stood his ground. When I reached ten, I grabbed him in a headlock and dragged him through the front door to the garage.

At that point, he managed to hit me in the face as he broke free. It was a two-punch fight after that. Les was no fighter. I helped him up and offered to help him put the boxes in his car. He yelled, "Well, smart-ass, what happens after they're in the car?"

I said, "Les, that's your problem; you deal with it. Take them to your Dad's factory, where you're supposed to go every day, or home—anywhere but here." We put the boxes in his car trunk, and he drove away.

I figured that was the end of the roommate situation and started to think about where I could move. In less than an hour, Les was back. I asked, "Where did you take that stuff so fast?"

"What do you care? It's gone from here. Isn't that what you wanted?"

I pushed for an answer, and he said, "It's in my car about eight blocks from here. I'll take it to a better place tomorrow. Now I have to put some ice on my jaw where you hit me. Don't talk to me anymore."

I didn't like the fact that he had parked lethal explosives near some unsuspecting neighbor's home but decided to let it go. He never told me what he did with the stuff.

The next morning, we didn't speak as we had breakfast. When our paths finally crossed, he asked some question about the corporate finance class we were both taking and the dynamite never came up again. Les was like that. I never knew what dumb thing he'd come up with next, but I liked him nonetheless. I seemed to have a weakness for f****d-up friends.

Time Flies

Oddly, after the explosives incident, Les and I got along just fine. We often made pancakes in the morning while listening to *La Bohème* and other Puccini operas, which we both loved. We talked about politics, upon which we were in close agreement. When his adult side was working, Les was an interesting fellow.

He had a pilot's license. On one of my days off, he rented a small single-engine plane and took me flying. It was exciting. The next time we did this, he allowed me to take the controls during takeoff. After flying around for a while, he let me bring it around into the landing approach before he took over. I liked flying, but I lacked the time and money for lessons.

Changes at Riviera

One day in December, with no warning, Jerry Fletcher was gone and a man named Eddy Singer was the manager of the Azusa Store. It only took one conversation for me to realize that Eddy was a much more competent manager than Jerry. He was accustomed to doing his own paperwork and said he would relieve me of that responsibility. My concern, which I didn't hide, was where this change put me in the scheme of things. Eddy said, "Eddy Siegel and I talked things over. Your arrangement has worked fine, and he likes you. You have a job whether you do any paperwork or not. My wife comes in when we have sales events and she knows the work backward and forward. We'll get along just fine."

Eddy told jokes better than anyone I'd ever met. He was an accomplished salesman and, unlike Jerry, he dealt with problems easily. Eddy also had a New York Jewish accent. He delighted in teaching me Yiddish words, often making me repeat them back to him until I got the accent right. His wife was a warm, sweet Jewish mother, and in a short time, they became my friends.

One evening Eddy told me that he, a man named Danny Kaiserman, and Danny's father, Joe, were buying the Azusa and Pomona stores along with opening a new one in San Bernardino and another one in Phoenix. Riviera had decided to begin franchising their stores to salesmen who had the cash to buy and operate them.

I met Eddy's partners, Danny and Joe, a few days later. Danny had me do a complete pitch while he playacted the mythical Mrs. Smith. At the end he said, "You're damned good for a goy [gentile]. Jerry told me you were a *Yiddisher* kopf [head like a Jew]. You'll do fine as soon as Eddy and I teach you some tricks you haven't learned yet."

I said, "By the way, I'd like to transfer to the Pomona store. It's closer to my school." The next day, Eddy told me I could transfer to Pomona after they took ownership.

Gotta Move

Les didn't make a B average and was ordered to move into a dorm. The little house was cozy and convenient, but the rent was too high for me alone and I couldn't bear the idea of looking for a new roommate.

I found an unfurnished place across a residential street from the Pomona High School, about a mile from the Riviera store. The apartment was literally a small lean-to that had been grafted on to the back of a house. It had its own outside entrance with a tiny bathroom and shower just inside the door.

The five-foot-wide bedroom had just enough space to put in a single bed and walk past it. It was necessary to shuffle sideways by a small table to access a two-burner stove and an apartment-size refrigerator in the kitchen. The place was tiny but had everything I needed.

My share of the guesthouse had been nearly $60 per month. This place was $22 per month, and they paid the utilities. I looked forward to a shorter drive to school and work and not being bothered with a roommate.

Graduate School and Thesis

After two years on the work-study grind, my urge to live a normal life was growing. Two more years in graduate school was not inviting either. Selling sofa beds was not what I wanted as a career, but most of my classmates would earn less than $300 per month in their first jobs, whereas my commissions were well in excess of that.

Dr. Phelps advised me to take the Graduate Management Admissions Test (GMAT) and see how well I did. If I didn't do well on the GMAT, maybe an MBA degree wasn't for me anyway. He also urged me to write to Harvard, Stanford, and Wharton to get their admission forms.

CMC was one of the few colleges then that required a senior thesis. The thesis had to be written for a professor who had agreed to be your reader and grader. Dr. Phelps required a couple of papers for his labor econ class. He graded down for everything. The best I had done on a paper for him was a B+.

The thesis subject I had picked was "John L. Lewis, His Importance to the U.S. Labor Movement." Lewis was the founder of the United Mine Workers. I had heard and read much about him while growing up in coal country and I had done a cursory research on him. Phelps was the perfect reader for this subject.

As Dr. Phelps and I finished a chat one day, I impulsively asked if I could write my thesis for him. He smiled as he said, "Mr. Scheid, you're new here. I suggest you ask around about me. I have a bad reputation as a thesis reader."

"Why is that?" I asked.

As he turned to walk away, he said, "Ask around and you'll find out."

"Are you saying you don't want to be my thesis reader?"

"No, that's not what I said. I meant that after you talk to students who have been here for three years, you won't want me as a reader."

"Frankly, I'd rather you tell me why I shouldn't want you to be my reader," I probed.

"Look, I think the senior thesis is great. It is the best course we offer, and every man learns from it. But it's not worth my time to read a thesis that is typically poorly done and deserves, at best, a D, which on one wants."

My usual stubbornness surfaced. Taking no for an answer was not the way I made a living. "Dr. Phelps, I am formally asking you to be the reader for my senior thesis."

Taking his pipe out of his mouth, he said, "Okay, goddammit, I'll read your thesis. But don't say later that you weren't warned. Have you started yet?"

I opened my briefcase, took out the typed outline, and handed it to him. He looked through it and said, "This is a great subject, and I'm probably the right reader for you. Let's meet again after you've put more detail into your outline. At that meeting, I'll enlighten you about my demands regarding punctuation, syntax, paragraphing, and so on. You'll need to work hard to get a good grade." He reset his pipe and walked away. I stood there for a while, wondering what I had just done to myself.

I took the GMAT with only a little preparation. It was the most difficult test I'd ever taken. It lasted four hours and had four sections, two of which were in essay form. I felt I did well on them, but the math was more questionable. In two weeks, my score came back; it was in the ninety-fifth percentile. According to Dr. Phelps, it was high enough to get into the Harvard, Stanford, or Wharton.

A New Friend

On my way home after work, I frequently stopped at a German beer garden on Foothill Boulevard. Early in the school year I had met Professor Proctor Thompson there. I knew he was a much-admired assistant professor of economics, though I didn't take his course. We just happened to sit next to each other at the bar, and I introduced myself. We discussed economics, and I found he was a staunch economic conservative - my kind of guy. By the end of the evening we were addressing each other as Al and Proctor. After economics and politics, a love of beer drinking was our bond, and we matched stein for stein.

When I told him my GMAT score, he said, "That's high enough for Harvard, but the grad schools are more impressed with the essay parts of their applications than they are with GMAT scores. Work your ass off on the application, then ask Professor Gibbs, Orme Phelps, and me to review it."

On my first day off after the applications arrived, I went to the quietest part of Honnold Library and worked on the one from Harvard. In a few hours, I had a first draft for every part of the application. After typing them, I decided to get help.

Proctor liked all my essays but one, which he asked questions about. He refused to suggest specific changes, saying, "Harvard wants to judge your ability at self-expression, not mine." After I rewrote the essay and he read it, he said, "Take the essays to Gibbs and Phelps and see what they think of them. What about the applications to the other schools?"

I said, "Proctor, I know you'll think this is crazy, but if I can't get into Harvard, I'm not going to graduate school. I'm tired of studying. I want a life. I'm willing to suffer through two more years at the best business school in the world, but not for anything less than that."

"Well, Al, it's your life, but that's crazy thinking. You stand a much better chance of getting into Stanford or Wharton than Harvard. Think that over. It's only two years, and it will go by quickly."

I replied, "Thanks, Proctor, but my mind is made up. It's Harvard or I go to work as a CMC grad."

Both Gibbs and Phelps liked my work and made only a few comments. None of the professors suggested a specific word or sentence. All they did was say something like, "Hmm, that's good" or "You should rethink that third paragraph." Both of them brought up the other schools, and I gave the same answer. Neither of them agreed with my decision.

After those meetings, the application was done. I rolled the original forms into my new Olympia typewriter and carefully prepared the application. It was finished by Sunday night and sent by registered mail on Monday. Now it was a waiting game. I'd done all I could—or so I thought.

A couple of weeks later, I was walking across campus and, as I passed Professor Gibbs, he asked, "How did your interview go?"

"What interview?"

He looked at me with astonishment as he said, "Harvard Business School applicants' interviews are today. Didn't you sign up for an appointment? It's been on the bulletin board for weeks." Since I was totally out of campus life, I hardly ever looked at the postings, so I'd missed it.

I thanked him and ran to the bulletin board. There was a notice to call a number at Pomona College to make an appointment with Mr. James Borreson, an assistant dean at Harvard Business School.

I called the number and asked if there were any appointment times left. A female voice told me the interviewer was fully booked. I asked what the time of his last appointment was, and she said it was at four; it was after three. I called the store and told Eddy I had an emergency and would be late.

When I walked into the reception area, there was one student there and he confirmed that he was waiting for Mr. Borreson. I sat down and began reading. I intended to beg for five minutes with Mr. Borreson to show I had made an effort. It was a long shot, but what did I have to lose? If he refused, he probably wouldn't remember my name anyway, so no harm done. Besides, I had made circus catches before and maybe I had one more coming.

At four sharp, a student walked out of the interview office and a man in a dark suit motioned the guy who had been waiting to come in. He looked at me but said nothing as he closed the door. At four thirty, the student came out, closing the door behind him.

I rushed to the door and gave a light knock. A voice inside said, "Yes?"

I opened the door and leaned in, saying, "I know you have no more appointment times, Mr. Borreson, but will you please give me five minutes before you leave? My application and GMAT scores were sent in. I just want to show you my résumé."

He thought for a moment and said, "Well, okay, but five minutes is it, and then I have to leave." He took my résumé, motioned me to a seat, and sat back down. After a few minutes of silence, he asked, "So you repossessed cars?" I gave my standard description about GMAC, speaking slowly and carefully. He took a few notes, and then asked more questions.

Over half an hour later, he said, "Al, I'm glad you took the initiative to show up without an appointment. You've had an interesting struggle to get an education, and you are not the typical applicant. My interview notes are only one of many factors the admissions committee considers. But I will say that what I intend to write about you won't hurt your chances."

The sale had been made - he liked me. I walked with him to the outside door. As we shook hands, he said, "Here's my card. Look me up if you make it to the B School." I promised I'd do that.

That night I had a beer with Proctor and told him about my interview. He broke up laughing. "You are one lucky asshole. You had the best interview time of the day. Being the last man, he had to be comparing you to the boring young students he'd been with all day. Al, you have some rough edges, but you're not boring." My hope for admission had gotten a big boost. But I had been disappointed before and knew that the higher the hope, the bigger the fall if things didn't work out.

Dr. Phelps had liked my new detailed senior thesis outline and the list of reference books I had compiled. The tough thing now was to find the time to hole up in the library and do the research. From that day until it was finished, I devoted every spare hour to my thesis.

CHAPTER 47

In a library we are surrounded
by many hundreds of dear friends
imprisoned by an enchanter
in paper and leathern boxes.
—Ralph Waldo Emerson, writer, poet (1803–1882)

Every saint has a past
and every sinner a future.
—Oscar Wilde, writer (1854–1900)

UNEXPECTED MONEY

Eddy picked me to be one of the salesmen to work the grand opening sale at the new San Bernardino store. Benno called and said, "Al, I saw your name on the list for the San Berdoo opening. You can make a lot of money that weekend. Don't let the old shmucks [pricks] push you around." Benno had become like a grandfather to me.

The sale covered a Friday, Saturday, and Sunday. Riviera loaned a group of salesmen for the event. To encourage men to travel to San Berdoo, there would be various prizes and a higher commission schedule. Eddy said to me, "If we get the crowd we're expecting, there won't be much time for a T-O, and we don't want to give big discounts. We're going for PM prices. I'm giving you a break here *sheygets* [non-Jewish boy]. Don't let me down!"

The Jews I knew didn't drink much, but the guys had a weekend away from the wives in a male environment. Most of them hit the bar on Thursday night. For once, I took it easy, had only a couple of beers, and was in bed by ten. After an early breakfast with Eddy and Danny, I helped them open the store.

When we opened, it was a chaotic situation. It was one customer after another. You did the pitch, showed the fabrics, qualified the customer, and wrote the order—or moved on to the next one. If the customer was undecided, the efficient thing was to make one last effort with something like, "Mrs. Jones, this is Riviera's biggest sale ever, and you'll never see these prices again. But if you'll sign the order and give me a check, I'll knock off fifty dollars. It cuts into my commission, but I'm willing to do it." A sense of urgency was already in the air, and the pitch fed off of it.

Riviera salesmen were not hardworking men. Their normal day was to sit around the store smoking, drinking coffee, swapping small talk, and waiting for customers to walk in. Most of them didn't get much exercise, so they had no endurance. The Boys (my name for the Danny and Eddy team) intended to keep the store open as long as customers were walking in. After being on their feet for only five hours most men began asking for a break.

The Boys had asked everyone to wear suits, but most of them wore the usual wrinkled sport coats and ugly ties. They also took off their jackets. I kept my suit coat on all weekend. I was there to make money.

Food breaks were staggered, and many of the men overstayed their time. A few of us went to a nearby diner and brought sandwiches into the back room. I lost less than two hours of floor time all weekend on food and toilet breaks. I wanted to maximize my commissions, and that required floor time, not eating and peeing time.

Eddy Siegel had sent average of below salesmen. Even at that, by Saturday night closing, some men had earned a month's normal commissions. By then, their legs and backs were hurting and a few were in need of a drink. Pitching customers on your feet for twenty hours over two days was tiring. When we closed at ten, I was mentally tired, but my legs and body were still ready to go.

TV ads were running on a local station on Saturday night, and The Boys expected action on Sunday morning. The salesmen were encouraged to come in early. As Eddy and I were opening the store, a middle-aged couple parked a new Cadillac in front and walked in. Because I was the first salesman there, they were my first up.

The Cadillac was an indication that they could afford the best, and I went all out. The lady said they were refurnishing their large family room. I showed them only the most expensive fabrics and she picked the best of those. They bought two king size sofas, end tables, coffee tables, and the best lounger chair we carried. They never even hinted at wanting a discount and they paid cash.

After they left, I looked at Danny, smiled and said, "The early bird got the worm."

He took my clipboard and looked at the order. It came to nearly $1,500. He said, "Al, I think you'll win the prize for largest single order. Are you aware that just a few Riviera men have ever written an order over a thousand dollars? I've done it only a few times. You harpooned a whale." It was about ten, and I had another up waiting.

By Sunday afternoon, half the salesmen were gone, but the customers kept coming. The TV commercials had worked wonderfully. For the few guys still able to make a decent pitch, the good times were still rolling.

We closed up about nine Sunday evening. Only Eddy, his wife, Danny, and I were left. Mrs. Singer had been keeping the records, and she had a tally. The highest single sale prize was mine, and I won the most orders-written prize by one sale. The overall total-dollar-sales prize was mine as well. I had won three of a possible five prizes.

It was a $1,000 plus commission weekend for me. It would be a few years before I'd make that much money again for three days of work.

Pomona was a good store. My commission income became consistent, and I no longer worried about money. It wasn't that I took making sales for granted, but the panic, after going dry for a day or two, was gone. The days averaged out. I had the largest savings account I'd ever had. It was ironic that the first financial security of my life came while I was a senior in college. What were the odds of that happening?

The Boys told me to take a long weekend off if I wanted it—and I took it. It was a great reward and the first weekend I hadn't worked since the previous summer. Saturday night I had a long awaited date with Alyce. I left Mom's house for Pasadena in a heavy rainstorm. As I was making a left turn off Rosemead Boulevard, a speeding car came down the outside lane toward me. My little Metro was T-boned at the passenger door. Seat belts were unknown then, and I was thrown headfirst across the car and into the passenger side window. Both cars ended up on the median. I was unconscious for a minute until a policeman opened the driver's door.

He helped me out, and I was soaked in seconds. Traffic was tied up, and a man came to me asking if I needed an ambulance. I said I didn't think so and asked if he had seen the accident. He had been directly behind me and had seen it all. He gave me his business card and said, "That kid was going about fifty through an intersection in the rain. He should be arrested." It turned out that the driver was a sixteen-year-old boy who had just gotten his driver's license the day before and was joyriding with three friends. None of them were hurt.

I found a phone booth and called my stepfather, George. He picked me up and I called Alyce from home. The next day she came to visit. She wanted to take me to her hospital for an examination, but my body hurt too much to move. Because she was a nurse, Mom liked her, even though she was a sexy-looking girl.

When George and I went to see the Metropolitan, I marveled that I had survived with no injuries other than many bruises and a lump on my head. The passenger door was pushed halfway to the steering wheel, the hood was off, and the wheels were turned under the car. My old Metro was a total loss, and I hated to see it go. It had served me well. A used Chevy was in my life by Monday evening.

The Auto Club of Southern California insurance adjuster took a statement from the witness who had given me his card, and they paid off with no fuss.

A Tragedy

I visited with Ruth Witten to get my courses approved and ask for help. To graduate in the spring, I needed to carry an extra class which required permission from some higher authority. When I told her I was writing my thesis for Dr. Phelps, she didn't smile. "I had hoped you'd keep your GPA up. Writing for Orme Phelps and taking extra subjects will make that quite difficult. Can't you get a leave from your job? The school will loan you some money if you need it."

I said, "Miss Witten, I've got a good job and it pays well. I can't walk away from it. If I get accepted to Harvard, I'll need every dime I can save." She was my cheerleader, so she gave in easily.

Then she told me she was going into the hospital for a major surgery. If it was successful, she would be on her way to walking without a crutch, and she was excited about it. She would be on medical leave for a month or more, and Professor Povlovich, whom I had never met, would take over her duties. She said before she left she'd make certain I had clearance for the extra course and she'd write a memo to Povlovich explaining my case. It was a warm good-bye, and I sincerely hoped the surgery would be a success.

About a month later I walked through the lobby toward the campus, and the receptionist didn't say hello and looked like she'd been crying. I walked on through the building and went to the dining hall. I sat with a couple of guys I knew, and one asked, "Have you heard about Ruth Witten?"

I said, "No, what happened?"

He had watery eyes as he said, "She's dead."

I was immediately in a state of shock. "What happened to her?"

"There are rumors that she shot herself because her surgery was a failure, but no one has heard anything official." There were official and unofficial details that I heard later. As I sifted through them, it appeared the short answer the student had given was accurate.

Ruth had taken an interest in my problems way beyond the call of duty. She was as responsible for my academic success as anyone who helped me—and many did. She was on my mind frequently for a long time afterward.

It Actually Happened

One evening Mom called and said a letter from Harvard University had arrived. I drove to her place after work and opened it. I had been accepted! Rather than feeling joyous, I was stunned. Could this be true? I went over it several times to make certain I hadn't read it wrong. Then it sunk in. I had been invited into the best graduate business school in the world. Sleep was spotty that night. Each time I woke up, I had to tell myself it was not just a dream.

The German beer garden was miles out of my way now that I was living in Pomona, but I wanted to show Proctor the letter. I stopped by his classroom and verified that he'd be on his usual stool that evening, but I said nothing about the letter. This was a victory lap I wanted to savor.

He didn't disappoint me. He showered me with congratulations and paid for all the beer. He was an unusually caring professor and a fine man.

The next morning, I saw Dr. Phelps between classes and handed him the letter. He congratulated me in his usual calm way, then added, "This makes your thesis all the more important, you know. Where you're going, you'll be writing papers and analyses constantly." As I walked away I wondered, once again, why the hell I'd let my ego push me into writing for him. I wanted a high grade, and he might not give it to me.

I left the letter with Dr. Benson's secretary and said I'd pick it up later in the day. When I returned, she sent me into his office. He was smiling and happy as he shook my hand and pointed to a chair. "Well, how do you feel about this?" he asked.

"Just numb, sir," was my reply. "I really didn't believe it would happen. Harvard was the only grad school I applied to. It was Harvard or nothing."

He looked astounded. "You mean you put all your eggs in one basket?"

"Dr. Benson, I have some concerns about two more years of college. I've had practically no personal life for nearly three years, and I'm tired of studying. I don't know if I can handle two more years as a student."

He said, "Al, you're the second CMC man to be accepted to Harvard Business School and the first man didn't finish. I'm anxious to see you go there. We're still a young school and we need our men to go to graduate schools like Harvard. You'll have all summer to rest up and get mentally ready. If you continue to have doubts, call me and we'll talk about it. I think I can be helpful. This is the chance of a lifetime for you and the time will go by quickly."

Winding Down

After hours of research and many rewrites, my thesis was finally as done as it would ever be. I met with Dr. Phelps and went over a couple of things concerning layout and presentation. When he held the file for a moment, he volunteered, "This may be the heaviest thesis I've seen. I hope it doesn't have a lot of redundant information." That remark made me read it again cover to cover and cut out some extraneous language.

A week later, I gave the finished thesis to Dr. Phelps. He said, "Since you're the only man writing for me, I'll read it and have your grade available a week from today. Come and see me that afternoon."

I arrived in his office a week later to the hour. He gave me back the same large manila envelope I'd handed him. I took it and paused. He said, "Well, aren't you going to look at it?" It sounded like he'd given a present to a child who needed prodding to open it.

I opened the envelope and took it out. At the top of the first page, in red pencil, he had written A+, followed by his signature. I stood there staring at it for a while before I said, "This is too much; I've been accepted to Harvard and gotten an A plus on my thesis. I'm too weak-kneed to jump with joy and too old to cry. What should I do?" My remark was so bizarre that he broke into laughter.

Typical of Dr. Phelps, he went over my writing style, pointing out some small things that could have improved the presentation. As I was leaving he said, "Now don't let this go to your head, Mr. Scheid, but that work is as good as I've seen from a CMC student. The footnotes were well done, and your writing ability is above average. You'll need those skills when you get to Harvard." This victory was an immensely satisfying. But, there was a long grind ahead of me

The Great Surprise

A couple of days before finals were to begin; I received a note directing me to see Dr. Povlovich, the acting registrar. He was not well liked by the students, and I'd heard disparaging remarks about him from time to time, but that was all I knew. He was in what had been Ruth Witten's office.

He began by saying, "Mr. Scheid, I've reviewed your credits, and you don't qualify for graduation. You'll have to come back in the fall to take the prerequisite courses you've managed to skip."

I said, "Miss Witten cleared me for graduation weeks ago and I've been accepted to the Harvard Business School. I have to graduate."

His haughty reply was, "I'm the registrar now, and I say you are not qualified to receive a degree. As far as Harvard is concerned, they'll let you enroll next year. Your timetable has just been moved back a year; that's all. Now, if you don't mind, I've got a lot of work to do."

I tried to talk, but he waved me away, saying, "There's nothing more for us to discuss, and I'm busy."

I was insistent and pressed my case. He raised his voice and said, "As long as I'm registrar, no one is going to get a degree from CMC after only two semesters. You got your grades in junior college where they come easy. This school is not going to give you a cheap degree. Now please leave." This was getting personal.

My anger welled up, but I stayed in control and walked out. I had to figure out what to do. This was a disaster. A year of my life had just been taken away from me.

That evening I came up with an idea. I still had Mr. Borreson's card. I decided to call him and make certain I could get into the B school a year later. That is, if I decided to go at all.

At ten the next morning, Boston time, I identified myself to Mr. Borreson and thanked him for what must have been a good report about my interview. Then I said I had a problem. "Tell me what it is," he encouraged.

I said, "CMC has a new registrar, and he found a technical problem in my course credits. He refuses to certify me for graduation, so

I won't get a diploma this year. I called to find out what I have to do to keep my acceptance alive and start the business school next year.

He replied, "Al, there's no reason to do that. We don't care if you have a degree; it's not a requirement for acceptance."

I stammered, "You mean I can start in September, this year, without actually getting my degree from CMC?"

"Yes, that's what I said. You've been accepted. We will welcome you in September. Do you have any more questions?"

I thanked him, hung up, and leaned back laughing. The last laugh was on that schmuck Povlovich. Fittingly, he was also known as sunuvavich. He could stick that diploma up his egomaniac registrar's ass.

I stopped by Dr. Phelp's office and told him the story, I thought he'd see the humor. He said, "You mean you're going to the Harvard Business School and you won't be a CMC graduate? Have you told George Benson about this?"

I said, "I assume he knows I'm not getting a degree. I just learned this morning that I can go to Harvard without a degree, so he doesn't know that part."

"Holy shit," he replied. "I'll call George. We gotta do something about this."

A note was handed to me when I arrived at the cafeteria for lunch. George Benson wanted to see me—now or sooner. I choked down some chow and went to his office. He said, "Orme Phelps filled me in a little about what Dr. Povlovich told you, but I want a careful recitation of the facts from you."

I began at the beginning, and went all the way to my phone call that morning to Mr. Borreson. He let me finish before he said, "Well, this is not an acceptable situation. I have to talk to Dr. Povlovich and hear his side of the story. You can go now but please come back here before you leave campus today."

Upon my return I was ushered into his office. He said, "I've spoken to Dr. Povlovich, and he insists you haven't qualified for a degree. So we have to qualify you."

"What does that mean, sir?" I asked.

"Beginning tomorrow, you will have to go to certain professors' offices and discuss the subjects you apparently didn't take—trigonometry, for instance. If that professor is satisfied you could be tested on the course and pass it, he'll give you credit."

I thought this was a bit bizarre. I was going to get credits for courses I'd never taken. But should I care? All things being equal, I'd rather have the degree than not have it.

As I got up to leave, he said, "We have to get this all sewn up in time for graduation, you know."

"I hadn't thought of graduation," I replied. "Apparently, Dr. Povlovich took me off the cap and gown list, so I don't have one."

Dr. Benson's irritation showed through his usually calm persona. "Oh my God, another problem, but we'll solve it. Come to see me the first break you have tomorrow."

When I showed up the next day, his secretary handed me an address in Los Angeles and told me to go there and ask for a certain lady, who would give me a cap and gown. She also gave me the names of different professors I had to visit.

For the next three days, sandwiched between final exams, I went to professors' offices and was quizzed about several subjects, mostly math. I suspect an objective listener would not have judged me qualified in some of the subjects. I was okay with geometry because of my cribbing through physics, but my algebra was rusty at best. The Spanish teacher and I carried on a five-minute conversation in simple, everyday Spanish. If I had been asked to conjugate an irregular verb, I would have failed. All of these "tests" were window dressing to justify my degree. I was not the least bit embarrassed by this charade. Povlovich was the villain, not me.

Graduation day arrived. Counting me, there were seventy-six men for the ceremony. I hadn't been invited to the rehearsals, so Jack Stark, class president, gave me some instructions. As we were waiting to march in, a couple of guys asked why my gown was a darker blue. I said it was too complicated to explain. Soon a recording of *Pomp and Circumstance* began and the entourage marched in. During the ceremony Dr. Benson announced that I had been accepted by the Harvard Business School. It felt great to hear that.

I found Mom and George in the crowd after the ceremony. Mom was crying, and I did a little tearing too. We stood around in the crowd, and I exchanged congratulations with the few guys I knew. Among them was Jack Stark, one of only a few classmates I had gotten to know. Not many years later, Jack succeeded George Benson as the president of CMC and retired from that post.

I excused myself from Mom and George and walked over to Dr. Benson. As he held my hand, he said, "Well, Al, it wasn't easy, but you got your degree. And I know you're going to do well at Harvard. Remember, if you develop some doubts about this, call me."

I said, "All I can think of is Ruth Witten. For me the ceremony wasn't complete without her." He understood how important her help had been to me.

After lunch, Mom and I went to work. Saturday was a big day in the jewelry business and at Riviera. We were back to our everyday lives by midafternoon.

Except for the two courses at Long Beach City College, my college career began in September of '54. It was now thirty-three months later, and even though I spent the summer of '55 in Ohio, I had my bachelor's degree. It was hard for me to believe it had happened. It had a feeling of unreality.

Throughout this ordeal, The Boys had been generous with my time off. Since the opening of the San Bernardino store, their attitude toward me had changed. In their eyes I had achieved full-fledged pitchman status. Both of them told salesmen that the training they gave me was what led to my success. There was some truth to that, but old Jerry Fletcher deserved some credit as well.

My second semester at CMC had been a busy, stressful time in both school and business. Now I needed a vacation, which Eddy encouraged me to take.

CHAPTER 48

As youth lives in the future, so the adult lives in the past:
No one rightly knows how to live in the present.
—Franz Grillparzer, Austrian poet (1791–1872)

Love makes the time pass. Time makes love pass.
—Euripides, Greek Playwright (circa 480–406 BC)

VACATION

Jerry Cassaday was working at Standard Oil in San Francisco, and Grover was attending Hastings Law School in the same city. There was no doubt where I was going for the week. Laura wanted to go along, but she'd been getting possessive and was making me uncomfortable. She was also unhappy that she hadn't been invited to my graduation. She was not a girl I wanted Mom to meet. It was time to cool off that situation.

My two mentors and I had a great reunion. It was another victory lap for me. They were delighted that I had followed their advice all the way to HBS. Friday through Sunday, we ate too much and drank way too much. On Monday, Grover and Jerry had to go to school and work, and I was on my own to roam the city. I spent time revisiting places I'd been with Jake and on two visits with my pal Ray Helstrom.

By Wednesday evening, I was bored with my own company and decided to work the weekend. My last night, Jerry and I had dinner and then listened to folk singer Odette at the old Tin Angel nightclub. It was a delightful end to a great trip.

While driving to LA, I began getting twinges in my stomach. By the time I got to Mom's house, I was almost doubled over with a cramping pain. The previous summer it was mononucleosis, what was it going to be this year?

After a gastrointestinal X-ray procedure, a doctor diagnosed early stage stomach ulcers. He put me on a soft food diet, plus half pints of cream at midmorning, midafternoon, and an hour before going to bed. I was to have absolutely no alcohol and had to quit smoking. His description of stomach surgery motivated me to stay on the regimen. The stomach pain went away in a week, but I began to gain weight.

Another Work Summer

During the summer between CMC and Harvard, I had time to think deeply about life and what I wanted from it. Walking around the quiet streets of Claremont was my substitute for the Ohio woods and I wondered about Sally Vanwey. She'd said she'd call me the last time we talked, but she didn't. Alyce came to mind, but she worked weekdays, I worked weekends, and we were thirty miles apart. It was hopeless. I enjoyed being with Lee, but she was young and fragile, and I feared hurting her. Laura crowded me, and I had lost interest in her. Now that studying wasn't necessary I had time for a love life, but I had none. It was ironic.

Female diversions and school had kept Jake nearly out of my conscious mind for many months, but her specter was always there. A long letter from her congratulating me on graduating didn't help. I decided not to tell her about my acceptance to Harvard because it would be all over Bridgeport in a few days. If I stopped there on my way to Boston, I didn't want the news preceding me. But, should I stop? It was time to wrestle with my feelings.

I wondered if every man went through this rehashing of the past. Was I normal? Or was I an incurable romantic who couldn't let go and move on? For the first time ever, it didn't feel good to be alone, walking, reading, or just thinking. The wrong thoughts kept coming up. It had been nearly two years since I had watched Jake walk away for the last time. It was over then. Why was she back in my head now? Maybe I needed the diversion of homework for mental health.

My mental meanderings began to make some things coalesce in my mind. Jake had admired and encouraged my early ambitions, but after the navy, nearly everything I accomplished drove us apart. I had dreamed of us escaping from Bridgeport together. But the closer I came to making that goal a reality, the more frightened she became—while still professing love. It made no sense.

Then an epiphany landed on me. Love for Jake had been my main motivator to grow up and deal with life while my friends were still behaving like pubescent boys. But the motivation led me to do the very things that tore us apart. A tipping point was reached when she realized I was actually going to make it through college and would never move back to her. That's when she gave up, and it all went downhill from there. It was all so clear and obvious to me now. Her fear of the world overcame her love for me.

Indecision and Money

To go to Harvard or not to go, that was the question. A part of me felt I had an inferior education and wouldn't be able to compete successfully. Povlovich had been correct; I had gamed the system by using math crib books and had gotten high grades because junior college was easier. In my defense, I had competed well at CMC. Maybe I was just being a coward, fearful of flunking out of Harvard and having to sneak back as a loser?

If I didn't give it a try, I was going to disappoint some people. Mom wanted me to go, and I was sure that if I called Dr. Benson, he'd talk me into going. If I flunked out, it would be no worse than failing at two sports, and I had survived those traumas. The decision made itself based on these considerations. I had to go.

Money was another problem. I had filled out the papers, and Harvard had come up with a financial package that included a scholarship, a grant in aid, and a loan. They had calculated that these amounts were enough. I did projections on my own and found that with my savings and a good job the next summer, I could just barely make it. This didn't thrill me. At twenty-five, I was tired of being poor. I wanted to dress well and have some money to spend on dates and do a little partying. I figured I needed another $1,500. With that amount added to what I had and what Harvard promised, I could be a worry-free student.

Then Dr. Covington's last words came to me. Well, I needed help, so I called him. With no hesitation, he invited me to visit.

After pleasantries, I gave him my Harvard acceptance letter and my updated résumé. He congratulated me, read the résumé, and then said, "I suspect you're here because you need money. Am I correct?"

I opened up and told him I needed a $1,500 loan. He said, "I think I can help you out, but first I have to make a phone call." When he returned from the call, he said, "Drive me to a place not far from here. I want you to meet my friend Penn Phillips." He went on to explain that Mr. Phillips was a successful businessman with whom he invested money.

The M. Penn Phillips Company was a couple of miles west of Azusa. Dr. Covington took my acceptance letter and résumé into Mr. Phillip's office. In ten minutes, Dr. Covington called me in and introduced me to Mr. Phillips. Dr. Covington then said, "Now that you've met, you don't need me. I can get a ride back to the hotel." He left immediately.

Mr. Phillips was a short roly-poly man about seventy years old. He smoked cigars in a holder just as my horse breeder boss had. They were of the same generation, and I hoped they didn't know each other. He asked why I wanted to get an MBA degree, and after I explained, his next question was no surprise: "Tell me about the repossessing cars thing you did." It simply never failed.

After about half an hour of his questions, he looked at his watch and said, "I understand you need fifteen hundred dollars to go to Harvard. Is that right?"

I said, "Yes, sir, and I'll repay the loan after I finish school."

He pushed a button on an intercom and said, "John, come in here and bring a checkbook." John's left arm was missing nearly up to the elbow, but it held a ledger-sized checkbook against his body.

Mr. Phillips said, "Give Al a check for fifteen hundred dollars. Al, spell your last name for him." He handed the check to me as Mr. Phillips stood up. Our meeting was ending.

I said, "Mr. Phillips, I am asking for a loan, not a gift. I intend to pay this back as soon as I finish school and get a job."

He replied, "Okay, you can pay it back someday. I'll trust you for it."

I said, "I'd like to sign a note with an interest rate on it."

"I'd just as soon trust you for it, but we'll do it your way. John, give him a promissory note to sign. We shook hands, and I followed John to his office, where I signed a $1,500 note bearing 4 percent interest, due and payable twenty-seven months later.

Mr. Phillips peeked into John's office and said, "By the way, if you need a job next summer, call me. We might have something for you." I thanked him, and he went on his way.

I borrowed a phone at the Phillips reception desk and reported in to Dr. Covington. His response was, "Now make good grades and stay in touch." It had been a successful visit. Now I could live a full life without worrying about running out of money.

Harvard sent a form to fill out, for matching up roommates. They asked questions about religion, sleeping habits, alcohol consumption, and so on. This questionnaire was a great idea and I answered it truthfully. For religion, I put down "none"; for sleeping, "windows open"; for drinking, "quite a bit"; for smoking, "don't care"; and for sexual mores, I wrote, "very liberal—I like girls." It was difficult to be so honest, but I wanted to avoid a roommate who didn't drink, liked hot rooms, or didn't like girls.

Woman Problems

The arrangement with Laura had always been one of mutual convenience. We'd get together for a night and not see each other for a week. Our pattern was to see a movie or have dinner, go to my lean-to apartment, have a couple of drinks and she would leave about midnight. My bed was too narrow for two people to sleep comfortably. She had the summer off and had become bored and I assumed I was just a diversion.

I came to realize that she had more ambitious plans for us. Finally, one evening I told her I had been seeing Lee, whom she knew from Citrus days. I explained that we had to stop seeing each other, implying that Lee and I were serious. Laura didn't take this well, but I stood my ground. After an hour or so, she left. I breathed a sigh of relief, naively believing it was over.

A couple of nights later, I was reading in bed when she knocked on the door. She had been drinking and refused to leave. I was afraid to make her drive, so I let her sleep in my bed while I slept on the floor. In the morning, I was angry and told her to leave and never call me again. She left but continued to stop by my lean-to and look in my window if my lights were on. One night she showed up when Lee was there. I refused to open the door and threatened to call the police.

The next day, Laura called me at the store, apologized, and said she was going to Canada for a while. I never heard from her again.

I would like to say this ugly breakup taught me some lifelong lessons, but it didn't. Men, especially this one, learned about women slowly—if at all.

In August, I gave in to an impulse and called Jake one weekend morning. I swore her to secrecy and then told her about being accepted to Harvard. She had not known I had applied to grad school. "You mean you're going to Harvard. Oh my God, I'm so happy for you and I know you'll do well there. Why do you want it kept secret?"

I explained, "Jake, I may stop in Bridgeport on my way to Boston, and I don't want it to look like I'm there to show off. You know how the people in that town react."

She said, "You're absolutely right. It's better if no one knows, and I won't tell anyone."

I added that I would stop in Bridgeport only if we could spend time together. Without hesitation, she said that she would make the usual arrangement with Jack and we'd be together while I was there. I asked, "Are you sure you want to do that? Isn't there some limit to what Jack will agree to?"

She replied, "He'll go along with it because he knows I'll do it whether he agrees or not."

It all went so easily, and she was so cheerful. Had there been a change in her thinking? Or was she simply giving in to an impulse as I was? Was I aiming myself down yet another path that could lead only to frustration? But there was only one way to find out. I wanted to see her, no matter what happened after that.

The Boys and Good-byes

During downtime between customers and carry-in lunches in the back room, Danny, Eddy, and I exchanged thoughts, told jokes and talked politics. They were my sales mavens (experts), and I was the top-producing salesman within the three stores they owned. I understood the good fortune of working with such men.

When my acceptance to Harvard arrived, I couldn't bring myself to tell them I'd be leaving in late August. My Scarlett complex lived on. The week after graduation, they told me that Eddy was going to spend more of his time training salesmen and Danny was going to handle the opening of a new store in Phoenix. Then they appointed me manager of the Pomona store. This shocked me beyond words, and I was sincerely grateful. As manager, I'd receive 2 percent of the store's gross sales above a minimum level. Now I was in a pickle. I had to tell them about Harvard immediately and pretend it had just happened.

I said, "There's something I should have told you earlier. I've been accepted to Harvard Business School, and I'll be leaving for Boston at the end of August."

Eddy said, "Why do you need another college degree? You just got one?" The business school meant nothing to him, but Danny was aware of the school. After a few minutes of explanation, they congratulated me. As Danny held my hand, he said repeatedly, "So you're going to Harvard. Who would have thought? Who would have thought?" I suggested they appoint someone else manager and let me stay a salesman, but they wouldn't even discuss the subject.

Shortly before my departure, Eddy told me that he, Danny, and their wives wanted to have a little dinner for me as a send-off. No girl I knew would be a good fit with this group, so I went to the dinner alone. When I arrived at the restaurant, I found that some of the salesmen and their wives had been invited and there were about twenty people in a private room.

There was a special cake with an inscription on it, something like "Good luck at Harvard, Sheygets (gentile boy)." In their speeches, they joked about how much Yiddish I'd learned and made me sound like the best salesman and most loyal employee who ever lived. They told about how I studied in the office between customers and how I won the most prize money when they opened the San Berdoo store.

I managed to avoid tears when I thanked them. I spoke about how their understanding and cooperation helped me through college. Then I showed off some of the Yiddish words and accent I had been learning, finishing with something like, "I peddled your *fercockta* [crazy] dreck [trash] because I needed the gelt [money]. Only a schlemiel [retarded] goy [gentile] like me would work for such grifters [con men]." Since I was the only gentile and I was messing up so many Yiddish words, everyone laughed hard. Then I said, "Seriously, I will miss working with *meshuganas* [crazy people] who made me feel like mischpoche, not a mamzer [outsider]. Eddy even tried a couple of times to drag me off to the moyel [circumcision man]." More laughs.

"How can I tell you how much I appreciate the break you guys gave a young goy? That's the megillah [whole story] for me. Thanks for being my mavens [instructors] and teaching me how to be a real pitchman. I'll never forget you!" I sat down and wiped my eyes.

Danny told me to stand up, and he and Eddy jointly handed me a small box and urged me to open it. In it was a check for $500, a very large gift for those days. I would have been pleased and surprised with a small remembrance, but $500? Wow! That was enough to buy the winter clothes I needed for New England weather. I choked up when I hugged and thanked them and their wives.

The Boys were experienced, hardened pitchmen and sometimes their ethics were questionable, but there was no doubt they had great hearts. I assumed I'd be asking them for a summer job between years at Harvard

To Harvard I Go

The cheap way to get to Ohio was to get a ride with someone. I searched the classified ads. On the first call, the one-in-a-million chance happened: I found Harry Gelles. He was driving to Boston to complete his second year at the Harvard Business School. Unbelievable! He had just gotten married, so he was going early to find an apartment. He was disappointed that I'd leave him in Bridgeport but decided that having a compatible partner for the first 2,500 miles made up for going the last 600 miles on his own.

I did my good-byes with Lee and Alyce. Sally was friendly on the phone, and I was pleased to hear she was dating a guy she liked. When I called Jake, she reassured me that she had told no one about Harvard. I just wanted a quiet visit with Jake, a few beers with friends, a visit with Dad and my grandparents, and then to slide out quietly. I planned to be there for six days.

Harry was on time, and our trip to Boston began in the new bright red Ford his father-in-law had given the newlyweds. I hoped this trip would be much less eventful than previous ones.

Harry planned to use the backseat for one of us to sleep while the other drove. As a result, the trunk of the Ford was overloaded with dishes and other heavy wedding presents. The rear tires were bulging noticeably, and the car was almost down on its axle. I observed that this was a dangerous and that some load should be shifted forward. Harry didn't agree, and we left things as they were. Harry didn't know much about cars.

When he turned east on Garvey (Route 66), he had a near miss with a curb as the heavy rear end tried to pull the car into a skid.

After some discussion, he agreed to stop at a gas station and get a second opinion. The mechanic on duty confirmed my concerns, so we switched some heavy stuff into the backseat; sleeping would be done in the front passenger seat. Harry was an inexperienced driver, but not being aware of this, he liked to drive fast. The second scare happened when he almost rear-ended a truck. After that, he agreed that the brakes couldn't handle the weight for a fast stop and slowed down considerably. Sixty was our top speed from then on, and even that was pushing it. The rear tires had to be replaced in St. Louis.

We did the usual life history swapping conversation. Harry was Jewish and had gotten high grades during four years as a Harvard undergrad. After hearing my story, he was amazed that I had gotten into the B school. He described the competitive environment, the high quality of the students, and the need for math expertise. He opined that I'd be lucky to make it through the first year.

It was déjà vu – just like Buck Gaouette. It made both of them feel good to tell a *schlepper* (incompetent) like me that I was unworthy to be at their level. Harry also didn't like me using Yiddish words.

We had nothing in common and conversation dried up. We arrived in Bridgeport nearly sixty hours after we left El Monte. I unloaded my stuff on a curb and made polite good-byes, and Harry headed for a motel in Wheeling. We saw each other many times during the ensuing school year, and we were polite, but we made no attempt to be friendly. Well, at least the weather for the trip had been good.

It was a balmy evening, and I was genuinely happy to be in Bridgeport. I called Jim Reddy, and he came to pick me up. Eleanor had the sofa all set, and I needed sleep. I told them about Harvard and they promised to keep my secret. Jim took the bus to work in the morning, leaving his car for me. That was the kind of friend he was.

The Visit

It was late when I got up. When I called Jake, we agreed to meet when she got off work. She sounded excited about getting together.

I drove to the Pastime to learn the latest gossip and news. The George brothers and other guys were all smiles, handshakes, and questions like, "How the hell did you get into Harvard?" It was embarrassing, but nice in a way. I asked how they found out about Harvard, and Manuel handed me a copy of the Sunday newspaper.

It was obvious that Lee had used her position at the *Glendora Press* to send a "local man does well" story to the Martins Ferry and

Wheeling newspapers. She had sent the same headshot of me that had been in the Glendora paper. The article enumerated my school accomplishments and gave some background on the B School. This was not what I had wanted.

For the rest of my stay, I kept running into people who had read the story or knew about it. Most people were congratulatory, but as I knew would be the case, a few were contemptuous and didn't hide it. This attitude surfaced when I ran into a drunken high school classmate in the men's room of Melody Manner. He accused me of coming to Bridgeport to show off about Harvard. Wendell and Jim stepped in and stopped a potential fight, much to my relief. I didn't want to arrive at Harvard covered with fight marks. Unfortunately, he was not the only guy around with that attitude, but there were no other confrontations with envious idiots.

I returned Jim's car to his office, and Jake met me there. As always, she was dressed impeccably and looked terrific. She drove us to Ogleby Park. I had suggested this place because I couldn't bear visiting our old site overlooking the river. We walked down a woodsy path and found a bench. The glow of being together again made us ignore our problems. It was almost as if we had never been apart—almost. Her first words were, "Well, I notice I'm Jake again. Have I been demoted from Gin the lover to Jake the friend?"

My response was, "It's no demotion. We haven't been Gin and Alf for two years." We hugged and kissed, enjoying the contact and said nothing. Later some issues crept into our conversation, but we agreed to leave the problems alone and enjoy our time together more physically.

She took the next day off work. My grandparents were living in a rented house near the river in Tiltonsville. When I called, Grandma's first question was, "Will you bring Virginia with you?" In Grandmaese, that meant "bring Virginia."

When we got there, Grandpa dragged me out of the house for a walk by the river on the pretext that he wanted to hear about Harvard. I wasn't fooled and told him so. He smiled and said, "Well, you know your grandmother."

After the visit, Jake told me that Grandma had told her; straight out, that we were both fools. Jake had admitted that she was afraid of the bigness of California. She said Grandma lectured her on having the courage to follow her heart and the man she loved.

Obviously, this put the issue on the table, and we had a long—sometimes emotional - but civil, discussion. A lot came out that hadn't before. Jake had it in her head that I couldn't really be in love with her. After all, in the two years we had been apart, there had been other women in my life. I had gotten a college degree and was now going for more education. She believed I could never be happily married to a small-town girl like her. She had a point.

She had met with her pastor, and he had advised her to follow her heart. Her best friend, Marie, had told her the same thing, as had Wendell's mother, Kitty. None of this seemed to influence her.

She insisted that she didn't intend to marry Jack, and I believed her. I flattered myself that after all these years; I could tell when she was sincere. She made it clear that she was as eager as I was to be intimate. There had never been any hesitation on her part. But nothing happened.

After a couple hours of walking, sitting in the car, hugging, kissing, and even laughing, we were both tired. We had a quiet dinner, and she dropped me in Bridgeport on her way home. I met up with some guys at the Lincoln, called Reddy's house and persuaded Eleanor to let Jim come out, and—surprise —we drank too much.

When Dad and I met at the Eagles, he had a copy of the newspaper story and asked questions about the awards I'd received. He showed the paper around and introduced me to men I had known since childhood. He was a proud father, and that made me feel good.

For the rest of my visit, Jake and I tried to be normal with each other, but I wasn't good at it. I was becoming convinced that she was right about the educational gap. When I exposed a little about what I had been studying, she had limited interest. I had talked myself into another pointless visit. Nothing had changed since I left in August of '55.

She drove me to Pittsburgh to catch the train. We agreed that we still loved each other. She repeated that she didn't intend to marry Jack and had told him so many times. She kept seeing him because there was no one else she wanted to date and she got lonely.

We had a sad parting, more like a wake than two lovers tearing themselves apart. This wasn't the way I wanted to go to the important challenge of my life, but I had learned that you have to take the pitches as they're thrown.

CHAPTER 49

The desire of knowledge, like the thirst of riches, increases ever with the acquisition of it.
—Laurence Sterne, novelist and clergyman (1713–1768)

A person who doubts himself is like a man who would enlist in the ranks of his enemies and bear arms against himself. He makes his failure certain by himself being the first person to be convinced of it.
—Alexandre Dumas, playwright, novelist (1802-1870)

ARRIVAL AT HBS

It was pleasantly warm and sunny when I stood for the first time at the corner of North Harvard Street and the tree lined Harvard Way that is the entrance to the school. The full name of the place is the Graduate School of Business at Harvard University. It is also known, somewhat egocentrically, as HBS or The B School (as though it was the only one). [36]

---

36 The school was founded in 1908 with fifty-nine students. It began using the case method of teaching (analyzing a business situation—a case) in 1920, which revolutionized the teaching of business. The use of "the B School" irritates many people who have earned their MBA degrees at other fine graduate schools of business. The usage dates back to when it was one of only a few graduate schools of business and was widely considered the best.

It seems melodramatic now, but as I stood at that corner, my heart rate increased perceptibly. I put down my bag, stared down Harvard Way, and said to myself, perhaps out loud, "You're here, dammit. You made it to the big leagues. You had to hit four hundred and win a golden glove—and you did it. Now just don't f**k it up." I didn't move for a full minute of enjoying the pleasant spell.

It was a short walk to the entrance to Gallatin Hall, where I had been assigned to a suite. [37] Built of reddish-brown brick covered with ivy, with a series of gables jutting from the roof, it looked staid and strong. It was exactly what I had imagined an Ivy League building would look like. Harvard made the stucco and wood frame buildings of Citrus and CMC look like public housing projects.

There were handwritten signs directing new arrivals to the basement. There I found a friendly custodian who gave me my suite key and then helped me wrestle the trunk I had shipped earlier up the narrow stairs.

I let myself into a comfortable-looking study room with two desks, a sofa, a fireplace with mantel, and two windows overlooking the courtyard. The small adjoining bedroom had twin beds separated by a window. The head (bathroom) was shared with two other rooms housing two men each. Given the size of the head, one inevitably got to know his head mates quite well.

While I was unpacking my new roommate arrived. Jim Rohleen was blond, athletic looking, over six feet tall, and had a confident smile. He walked in briskly with his hand extended.

Jim had a degree in nautical engineering from the U.S. Merchant Marine Academy at Kings Point, Long Island. As a part time job he had modeled men's clothing in New York. After graduation, Jim spent two years as a merchant ship officer and had been all over the

---

37 The building was named for Albert Gallatin, secretary of the treasury under presidents Jefferson and Madison from 1801 to 1814. He was also a founder of New York University.

world. His education and travel impressed me tremendously. I had traveled nowhere, seen nothing and had a questionable college degree. I thought; H*ow will I keep up with guys like Jim?*

After our first lunch in Kresge Hall, we stood on the steps of Baker Library and gazed across the Charles River at the picturesque Weld Boathouse with the buildings of Cambridge behind it. It was an awesome scene. We agreed that we were damned lucky to be there. Jim had grown up on the bottom of the economic ladder in Seattle and never expected to do what he'd done. We had a lot in common.

After dinner, we walked across the Harvard Street Bridge into Cambridge with a group of classmates and embarked on an impromptu barhopping evening. As we progressed the crowd thinned out until it was just Jim and me. As we staggered back to Gallatin, we agreed that sailors and coal town kids could drink the Ivy League wimps under the table. A hurdle had been jumped. I had a great roommate.

On our guided tour the next day, we learned that one could walk through tunnels from our building to most other buildings on campus. These tunnels also accommodated the central steam heating system for the school, and there were Ping-Pong tables in small rooms. In the basements of different buildings, there was a barber shop, a dry cleaning and laundry drop-off, and a small store that sold snacks, soft drinks, razor blades, and other small items.

We were given a handbook that explained the rules of behavior. The parietal rules (behavior between the sexes) were of particular interest. It was made clear that under no circumstances was a female to be in a room after ten or anywhere on campus after eleven unless attending a planned event.

The honor code was easy. Anyone caught cheating in any way was subject to immediate dismissal.

In that era, each class at HBS started with 630 students, broken into seven sections, A through G, of ninety men each. Jim and I were in section B. Your section was like a tribe. We attended all the same classes, ate together, studied together, and partied together. Section parties were a major part of our limited social lives.

During the all-day orientation, several professors spoke. One said, "We're here to guide you. The cases and your class discussions are where you learn. Professors are more choreographers than teachers. That's what the case method is all about."

Another said, "We expect you to be prepared for every class. When your ideas are challenged, defend them. We simulate business conditions as close to reality as possible, and there will always be more work than you can complete. You must make choices about using your time." They said we would have to make at least a thousand business decisions over the two school years. The grading system was no pass, low pass, pass, high pass, and distinction. Class participation would account for half of our total grade.

We were expected to form our own study groups, or we could work alone. The choice was up to each man. Studying alone sounded to me like one sheep surrounded by wolf packs.

Professor Christensen gave the talk that got the most attention. Among other things, he said, "When you leave this school you will be a different person than you are today. You are all intelligent men and the school won't change that, but when you complete these two years you will see the world differently. Hopefully, you will be problem solvers and planners. As you progress you will realize this is happening. I hope you enjoy the experience."

His last words left an indelible impression. He said, "Gentlemen, look across the room and pick out a man, then count nine men in any direction, and take a hard look at that ninth man." He paused about ten seconds and then continued, "There's a high probability that man won't be here for the second year." He stood quietly as we chuckled nervously. Then he said, "Best of luck to all of you and be prepared to go to work on Monday."

His message was clear: they expected about 10 percent of us to flunk out or leave for some other reason before the first year was completed.

Students and professors wore coats and ties to class. I did my shopping at the Harvard Coop. [38] I spent much more than the $500 The Boys had given me. I figured I might flunk out, but I'd do it as a well-dressed failure.

We picked up our first three cases in the basement of Baker Library and rushed to our suite to read them. Later we discussed them with some other men and read them again. By Sunday, we felt there was nothing left to discuss, so we took the subway to Boston and saw the hit movie of the year, *Around the World in Eighty Days.* It was the last movie either of us would see until the following summer.

Classes Begin

A few men had been accepted straight from college, but about eighty percent had worked, done military service, or both. We had a number of men who had master's degrees in engineering or other fields or had been to law school. About a quarter of our class was married and lived off campus. There was a complement of foreign students from England, Australia, Switzerland, Turkey, Japan, Netherlands, France, South Africa, Canada, and other places. Sliced and diced, the class was the most diverse group one can imagine.

Every man had achieved some sort of success, everyone had a large vocabulary, and everyone had a high score on his GMAT. Last, and most importantly, everyone was intelligent. But, as I discovered, there were weaknesses. A few didn't have strong skills in verbal and/ or written expression. It is possible to get a master's degree in some

38 The Harvard Coop was founded as the Harvard Cooperative Society in 1882 to supply books and coal to students and employees of Harvard University and the Massachusetts Institute of Technology (MIT). By 1957, it carried everything a department store normally carries and at lower prices than free market stores.

disciplines without being a competent writer and speaker, but the Harvard MBA program was not one of them. Communicating was to be the Achilles' heel for many of my otherwise brilliant classmates. Poor class participation and below average writing were the primary reasons students flunked out.

In our first class, Jim and I were both as nervous as whores in church. We thought we understood the case, but during discussions, we learned things that had not crossed our minds. The second class was the same. By the end of the day, I was stomach-fluttering insecure. In college, I had become accustomed to being one of the best students in the room. But there were eighty-nine guys in section B that were at least as bright as the Beerport kid and probably all of them were better educated.

Back at the room, I lay down and stared at the ceiling. My confidence, already a little shaky, was shattering. And, dear reader, this is not just melodrama to make the story more interesting; I was scared! My mind was turning to exit strategies when Jim kicked my bed and said, "Come on, it's time to start reading the cases for tomorrow." That old bromide (truism?), "*When the goin' gets tough, the tough get goin'*" popped into my head. It was time for me get off my ass and go to work.

After several semi-successful attempts to get my brain around the first case, we went to dinner with our head mates. After some open talk, I learned that some others shared my fears and doubts.[39] We worked late.

On the way to breakfast, I told Jim we had to run or fight. He looked at me, smiled, and said something like, "Does a kid from a coal mining town or a professional sailor run? If we get thrown out, life will go on." His what-the-hell attitude made me feel better. He

39 Jim Ullman's father was the then-famous novelist James Ramsey Ullman. He had majored in English but had no flair for writing like his father. Unfortunately, his classroom participation was found wanting and he left the school before the end of the school year.

was right. If I flunked out, my life wouldn't end. My worst-case scenario was to go back to California and sell something. The one thing I knew for sure was that I could sell, face-to-face or on the phone.

The Case Method—A Digression

The case method was still a somewhat controversial teaching system because it assumed that a classroom full of students could reach logical conclusions through discussions and debate. It was assumed that analyzing the problems in a case put students' minds into a business situation, close to real life. In the crucible of vigorous discussion, students learned to present ideas, defend them, and if proven wrong, accept the result, learn from it, and move on. A class at the B School is no place for those sensitive to having their ideas taken apart and critically discussed in their presence. It was assumed that if a student lacked the courage or ability to participate in this competition, he shouldn't be there. If this open conflict led to a personality clash, so be it. That's what life is like in the real world of business.

The shape of the classroom invited debate. It was a horseshoe shape with seats rising up about seven rows from floor level. The professor stood on the floor in the "pit." Built into the wall behind the professor were multiple layers of green chalkboards that could be moved up and down as desired. As students made points, the professor used white chalk to make notes. It was his job to guide the class through the case by calling on raised hands or posing questions. He supplied no answers and no facts, but he sometimes referred to parts of the case or pointed out notes he'd made on the chalkboards.

The professors had studied the analysis the case writer had prepared for them, so they had a complete understanding of the case. Controlling the discussion among ninety intelligent, motivated men for an hour and a half, and sometimes longer, was a daunting task. One professor told me he was completely worn out after teaching two cases in one day.

Vigorous class discussions can be ego threatening. Some erudite students have an advantage over less gifted colleagues, so this criticism has some marginal validity. The counterargument is that if you don't have the "right stuff" to compete, you're better off finding out in class and correcting it - or finding some other educational experience.

Students were expected to be civil and not speak until recognized by the professor. Ad hominem attacks and profanity were considered bad form and not tolerated. Good humor and some sarcasm were expected and sometimes men got a bit testy - C'est la vie. The case method, properly done, is highly charged, competitive, and engaging. Fortunately for me the method played into my strengths.

During orientation an essay was passed out that gave a rationale for the case method. It was written by HBS Professor Charles Gragg in 1951 and the title is *Because Wisdom Cannot be Told.* The following quote from the writings of Honore de Balzac appeared just below the title.

So he had grown rich at last and thought to transmit to his only son all the cut and dried experience which he himself had purchased at the price of his lost illusions; a noble last illusion of age.

The meaning is clear – it is difficult to pass on wisdom. We can hear wisdom all day, for years, and it will not have nearly the impact of one experience. I repeat this quote here because it had such a huge influence on me.

Study Group

After lunch and dinner, first year students milled around Kresge Lounge meeting classmates. It reminded me of a group of dogs smelling each other, becoming friends, or moving on. This was the primary way study groups were formed. Second-year men advised us a group of four, with varied backgrounds was optimum.

Jim and I decided to be in different groups so we could share more points of view. We thought this was clever but soon found out that nearly every pair of roomies did the same thing.

My first group was a flop. By the third day of classes, I was concerned about ending up with a group of outcasts.

Demolishing the conclusions presented by a classmate, factually, logically, and with verbal precision, made a positive impression on professors. Letting several students go down the path of reinforcing each other's points, then taking apart their arguments with a deft, rapier-style speech was the greatest.

Eventually, most of us learned the fine art of using an ambush technique. The method was to hang back and let a speaker go on until he made a questionable assumption or statement – then pouncing on him and correcting his errors. We learned to avoid going out on a limb too far and becoming an ambush victim. This methodology suited my nature, but sarcasm, both gentle and strong, came easily to me - frequently to my later regret.

We had a case that seemed to be about using sales administration techniques to increase profits. The street smarts I had picked up about the gritty problems of handling commission salespeople gave me some insight. I had only spoken in class a couple of times and then only with weak comments. This could be my chance.

Several of us raised our hands to start the case, but I was not selected. The man the professor picked launched into a well prepared presentation which he finished by stating that his conclusions resolved the issues in the case. The professor had let him go on for over five minutes, writing down his points on the blackboards. Then a few hands went up and each speaker supported the first presenter. I guessed they were all from the same study group. Supporting your study group mates was a common practice.

In my opinion, they had missed the essence of the case. They had done extensive analysis as to how various changes to marketing costs and salesmen's compensation would mean more profit. Buried in the case was a short paragraph that described the business as being in a price competitive market with little product differentiation and limited brand loyalty. This meant to me that the salesmen's relationship with the customer was extremely important to retain the customer. If the salespeople didn't embrace the suggested changes, wouldn't there be morale problems—or worse?

My hand went up, and I was called on. In that moment, I decided to go all out. I said, "If the plan being discussed is adopted, the company will quickly be in disaster mode."

My opening sentence had put me on a collision course with the presenter and the only way out was forward. I followed my notes and explained why the most productive salesmen would likely jump ship to a competitor and take their client relationships with them. I explained that in nearly all fields of commission sales, something like ten to twenty percent of the salespeople produce about eighty percent of the sales. A loss of just a few of the most productive salesmen could wreak havoc on the company's sales and profits.

My presentation was over in less than five minutes of steady talking. Jim sat next to me in all our classes. As I finished he passed me a note that read, "You got 'em."

Tom King sat across the pit from me in a front row seat. As I finished, his hand went up. He supported my position eloquently. The presenter and his pals gave it a valiant effort, but it was in vain. One of them said that if a top salesman left, the company could simply assign his accounts to the next best man and so on. Another man added that the sales staff was overpaid and the company had to bring them into line with other employees. I jumped on that by pointing out that he was betting the company's market position on an unproven, untested theory that defied common sense. A real donnybrook began as hands went up. Many men now saw where the case was going, and toward the end of period, the discussion had progressed to looking for ways to save money rather than fiddling with the sales force. It was a clear-cut victory for our side.

My time at RCA Service and Riviera Sofa Bed had taught me that salespeople are suspicious of any change in their commission structure or territories and distrustful of anyone who suggests such changes. The other guys were correct in their mathematical conclusions, but they had missed the core issue. The best way for this company to make more money was to make a better product, widen the product line, or manufacture more efficiently. Chiseling on commissions would be counterproductive.

After the class Tom King congratulated me and I thanked him for coming to my aid. He said, "Forget it. You were doing great without me." Then he asked if I would have lunch with him and another man - just the three of us.

Lunch with Tom and Barry Merkin was really an interview for me to be invited into their study group. Tom said he was impressed with my performance, but they wanted to know more about me. When they learned I had done that morning's case alone they were impressed. They had followed the same logic as the student who started the case. They hadn't realized the numbers in the case were a trap; the real point was how to manage a sales force. Like most intelligent people, Tom had no problem changing his mind quickly.

Barry Merkin was a short, feisty Jewish guy who went to Brown and majored in engineering. After graduating from Harvard undergrad with honors, Tom had been an officer in the navy and then attended the Harvard Law School for two years. I was the only one with down-in-the-dirt work experience. We were three men with very different backgrounds, which made us a productive study group.

They asked me to attend two study sessions with them to see if we clicked. If we did, we would recruit our fourth man. After a few sessions, we invited Charlie Connolly to join us. He was a pleasant fellow, married with an eighteen-month-old child. At thirty-four, he had over a decade of sales experience. We read the cases on time, argued with each, and came to the rescue if one of us needed help in class. In the process of studying together, we became close friends and an inseparable team.

After going all summer without one, my headaches returned. When I went to the Harvard infirmary, the doctor explained a method of relaxing the mind. After some coaching sessions, the system was working and the headaches tapered off. By Christmas break, they had stopped, and I never had the problem again—ever. After suffering headaches all my life, it was strange that they stopped while I was under the most pressure I had ever experienced. No doctor has ever been able to give me even a theory of why this happened. This comes under the heading "Never look a gift horse in the mouth." Just accept a fortuitous event and don't question it.

The Historic Sputnik Event

On October 4, 1957 the Russians put the first satellite into Earth orbit. The success of Sputnik was a disturbing event for Americans and a psychological victory for the Ruskies. Someone figured out when to watch for Sputnik to go overhead, and the word got around quickly. That evening several hundred HBS men stared into space while lying in the grassy field in front of Baker Library. Right on schedule, someone shouted, "There it is!" and we saw the satellite pass overhead. It was only two feet in diameter, but was covered in gold and reflected sunlight so brightly that it was easy to see with the naked eye. It fell out of orbit after about three months, but Sputnik marked the beginning of the Space Race.

Autumn colors arrived. The school and all of Cambridge brightened up – it was beautiful. By mid-November I experienced the first cold weather I had seen in six years. I never suffered from homesickness, but I missed the mild autumns of California with cool mornings and gentle warmth by early afternoon. But, I was too busy to dwell on the weather for long.

WAC

WAC stands for Written Analysis of a Case. It was the most feared course for first-year students. WAC cases were not released until Friday afternoon and they had to be turned in on Saturday evening before nine. This was in addition to studying new cases for the next week. These were not relaxing weekends.

The point of the WAC was to make students reach logical conclusions, with a limited number of words, be very precise about details, and meet a difficult deadline.

The WAC was always a difficult case, but you were permitted to discuss it with other students. But it was a competitive environment, and most men would share their thoughts or research only with their roommate or study group.

The WAC had to be typed on a special light green paper, size 8½ by 11, with red lines on all four sides, about half an inch from the edges. Only a designated typeface could be used, and not one letter, or a period, could touch a red line. In addition to all of that, there was a strict word limit for each WAC. One word over was an automatic penalty. Content was most important, of course, but grammar, spelling, and syntax were graded as well. It was possible to write a great WAC with persuasive arguments and a logical conclusion but have it downgraded dramatically for English usage or typing errors. It all had to be perfect and turned in on time. There were no exceptions.

WACs had to be put in a special envelope, properly labeled and "down the chute" by nine o'clock sharp. The chute, on the side of Baker Library, went down about seven feet, ending just above a large canvas mail container on wheels. A guard pushed the container aside at exactly nine. There were horror stories of envelopes hitting the side of the container just as it was being rolled away and the guard refusing to pick it up and put it in. Trying to bribe a guard was a violation of the honor code.

In decent weather a few enterprising souls set up a card table near the chute and served hard liquor drinks to the late arrivals (donations were expected). They set a good example by imbibing themselves. Every WAC week, a few men, for one reason or another, didn't make the deadline. No mercy was shown, and they received a "no pass," which was the equivalent of an F. This put a serious hole in their grade record.

Finding a reliable, competent typist was difficult, even though the word was out among the local females that typing papers was an easy way to meet an eligible HBS man. There was humorous speculation that many of the married men picked their wives primarily because of their typing ability and planned to divorce them when they started making the big bucks. It was just a joke, but we wondered about a few of the couples.

The Olivier WAC Caper

Olivier Martin - pronounced Oliv-e-ay Mart-an became a close friend. He had been in the French army, liked to drink, and loved women. He was adept at finding girls who had a girlfriend in need of a date, and I was frequently the fill-in guy.

Jim and I always kept a bottle of Vat 69 scotch and four small glasses on our fireplace mantel. Because of our friendship, Olivier felt licensed to wander in and help himself to a snort when the mood struck him.

One WAC Saturday, Olivier had arranged a double date for us after WAC turn in. We agreed to be finished early. I had worked conscientiously all day and was nearly finished before seven. In his usual suave manner, wearing suit and tie, with several envelopes in his hand, Olivier came through one of our head mate's rooms and sauntered in. I was just finishing the last careful check of my WAC, so without looking up, I said, "Olivier, have some scotch but don't talk to me."

Olivier downed his scotch and then said in his soothing French accent, "Since you are late and not being friendly, I will go mail my letters and turn in my WAC. I shall wait for you at the WAC bar. Please arrive soon; we mustn't keep the ladies waiting."

About three minutes later, I ran down the stairs and across the street to drop in my WAC. On the street corner, near the chute, there was a large dark green U.S. mailbox. As I approached, I heard Olivier's voice, loud and cursing in French. The mailbox had been pushed over on to its side, and Oliver was jumping up and down on it.

After talking him down from the mailbox, I began asking questions. There were tears in his eyes, and he was deeply disturbed, but he was soon able to tell me what happened.

As he was walking past the mailbox he had decided to drop in his letters. In his slightly intoxicated state, he became confused and dropped the WAC envelope into the mailbox. Then he went to the chute and had almost dropped in his outgoing mail when he discovered his mistake. That was when he went berserk.

A couple of the men tried to get one of the guards to come out so he could bear witness that Olivier's WAC had been there on time. No luck with that; the guards saw the humor of the event and laughed aloud.

First we put the mailbox upright; we didn't need a federal charge of damaging post office property. I borrowed a notebook and wrote, "The HBS students signing this document swear that they were present when Olivier Martin mistakenly dropped his WAC into the mailbox at 7 p.m. on Saturday." I circulated the paper, and ten men signed it. It was not likely to work, but it was worth a try.

The notice on the mailbox stated that the next mail pickup was at eight on Monday morning, so the WAC would be there until then.

Olivier, Jim, and I went back to the scotch on the mantel. We decided to go to the main post office in Boston.

Olivier called the girls and charmed them. As he saw it, "Why turn a terrible situation into a worse one by being without a girl for the night?" With the optimism and egos of privileged youth, we set off to pick up the girls and rescue Olivier's WAC.

With the girls in the car we went to the main post office. Since we were wearing coats and ties, we looked a bit official and were able to get into the building through the loading dock. We found an older, official looking employee. He advised us to come back very early on Monday morning, talk to an assistant postmaster, and try to get the envelope that way. Since nothing could be done until Monday, we did the obvious thing. We took the girls to a restaurant, drank large amounts of wine, and didn't make it back to the school until Sunday morning.

On Monday, Olivier arrived at the main post office when it opened and spoke to the postmaster. He arrived in the middle of the first class, gave me a thumbs-up, and smiled. His French charm had worked. The postmaster agreed to address and mail the envelope to the WAC director, with a note as to his part in the plan. Olivier took the petition to the WAC director, who said he would accept the envelope when it arrived. However, he said there was nothing he could do. There were no exceptions to the deadline for WACs.

We went to see John Jeuck, the professor with whom Jim and I had become friendly. He couldn't help laughing as we told the story, but he was sympathetic and said he would visit with the WAC department. The result was that a few of the men who had signed the petition were questioned. Olivier was then told that no matter how good his WAC was he would get a low pass grade. Word came out that this was the first exception ever made on a WAC deadline. A low pass was bad, but not filing a WAC was a train wreck.

MAKING THE CUT

Men who were getting mostly low pass grades were called in for a conference in early December. Some were encouraged to leave, and some were put on probation until mid-January. If a man's performance hadn't improved by the January review, he might be allowed to take remedial classes somewhere and start over in the fall. A few borderline cases were allowed to continue on probation. If he was called in again, it was all over. Some took the leave option, and some gambled that they could make it. Two married men in my section had what amounted to nervous breakdowns and had to leave the school. A number of others were gone in January and more left a month or so later.

The shocker was when our head mate, Jim Ullman, was called in. We all knew he was a dilettante, but he was so glib and had such good grades as a Harvard undergrad that everyone assumed he was doing well. His problem was that he spent a too much time trading stocks. We assumed he'd turn things around.

My roommate was called to a conference. He was told he had to buck up his class participation and WAC writing. Jim was bright, but spending years at sea talking to sailors doesn't develop verbal dexterity or creative writing skills.

We worked together on his writing, and it improved. It was against the rules to do another man's writing, but I read his WACs made specific suggestions about grammar and syntax. It was shaving the rules close, but other men we knew did the same thing.

Second-year students told us that no matter how difficult the first semester had been, the second semester was worse. Jim feared being called in for another conference. The HBS system was not a game for sissies.

Just before Christmas break, I estimated my grades and decided I was averaging just under high pass, assuming I was getting a pass in class participation. Our study group was functioning well, and I had every reason to feel good about school.

Pressure Relief

After a month of school, a self-appointed committee decided section B needed a party. Arrangements were made to take over the main lobby room of Gallatin on a Saturday night. A bartender and well-stocked bar were planned. It was our first bash, and everyone wanted it to be a good one. Word was put out to Smith, Radcliffe, and Wellesley (local girls' colleges) to call in. More girls called in and registered than could be accommodated.

It was a hell of a party. I spent most of it with a good looking Wellesley girl I never saw again. Wellesley girls were known to be a bit straight laced. But, just kissing a girl was a pressure reliever. It seemed to me she thought I drank too much and she was correct.

Some nostalgia for Christmas in Bridgeport was building in me. Having missed the previous four Christmases there, it would be fun to see old friends. But there was Jake to consider. If I went, should I see her or not? Despite all that had transpired, deep inside I didn't feel we had reached complete closure.

CHAPTER 50

Life belongs to the living,
and he who lives must be prepared for changes.
—Johann Von Goethe, novelist, philosopher (1749–1832)

Never allow someone to be a priority
while allowing yourself to be their option..
—Mark Train, novelist (1835–1910)

CHRISTMAS VACATION '57

Since school began, I had studied every day, including Thanksgiving weekend. Over the Christmas holiday, Jim planned to visit friends in New York and Olivier was heading for the ski slopes. They'd heard my messed-up love story, and both told me that I should make a clear-cut, unequivocal break rather than continue the lingering feelings. They were right; being in love limbo was not conducive to handling the pressure of HBS. Olivier, with his French attitude about women, posed another question: "Al, why do you want a woman who's afraid to come to the man she says she loves? A French girl would have come to her man in California years ago." He was right. I wanted my woman or the emotional freedom to move on. It was hard to admit defeat, but I had lost.

I wrote to Grandma and invited myself as a houseguest. I told her not to tell anyone I was coming - I wanted to sneak into town. Grandpa met my train and drove me to their cottage in Tiltonsville. Grandma cooked a fine meal, and we had a quiet evening just sitting and talking. I told them I intended to buy a used car and drive it back to Boston. Cars were cheap in the farm country, especially in winter.

My plan was to call Jake the next day and meet with her in the cold light of day, not at a romantic dinner. If things went the most likely way between us, I would leave the day after Christmas. A classmate had invited me to a New Year's Eve party, and I could use a few days of library time.

My train arrived in Wheeling at night. The next morning I was having coffee in my grandparents' living room when Jake's car came down the lane. I walked out to meet her. She wasn't smiling as I opened the passenger door. Her greeting was, "Did you intend to see me or were you going to ignore me while you're here?" It wasn't a good start.

"Sorry, Jake, I intended to call you today," I said. "I'm here for a purpose, and I suspect you know what it is." I knew if the kissing began, I'd go soft and never get to the things I had to say, so I began, "Darling, I'm here to get a final, final decision from you. I'm not going to stay in this game any longer. You have to decide to leave Bridgeport and come to me or stay here. If you stay, we're finished. We won't write and we won't talk on the phone. I love you, I want you with me, but the game is over for me. Do you understand what I'm saying?"

When she began sobbing I relented and held her close. At that moment, I knew what people meant when they said, "*my heart is breaking*." It was agony for me because I understood why she was crying so hard. Our love affair was finally over. I felt cold all over and had a knot in my belly, but I didn't cry. I had rehearsed the scene so many times in my mind that there was no shock. What I had believed in August was confirmed.

After a while, she pulled herself together and we sat silently. She said she knew I had arrived because a girlfriend of hers had run into one of my cousins. It really didn't matter. It was actually better that we were meeting in a car on a cold and cloudy morning.

She said, "If only you'd told me you were coming, I would've worked out some times for us to see each other."

I said, "Jake, you don't understand. This is it. You just gave me your decision. If you wanted to be with me, we wouldn't be sitting here like this; we'd be making plans. I traveled a long way to get a final decision. You owe it to me, yourself, and Jack to bring things to a conclusion. You've been messing up three lives for years because you won't face life. Now that it's over, there's no reason for us to see each other again."

"What if I haven't fully decided—what then?" she asked.

I said, "You weren't crying a few minutes ago because you're undecided, were you? You were crying because you have decided. You won't leave this place. And, you know how much you've hurt me over the years. Those are the things you were crying about. You've decided."

She broke into sobbing again, saying, "I love you, I've always loved you, and I'll never stop loving you. I can't live without ever seeing you again, but I can't come to you. I can't leave here - I can't - I can't - I can't!" Her shoulders were shaking.

We were both out of words. But I had the finality I sought. The answer had been obvious for years, but my heart hadn't accepted it. Now I had to move on with my life.

She put her arms around my neck and we had one last long kiss. Not a word was said when I got out of the car. As I walked to the house, without looking back, I heard the car start and drive away. Strangely, my first thought was how happy Jack would be.

My grandparents knew what had happened. Grandma hugged me and said, "Alfred, you'll be just fine. Some things we want are just not meant to be. You'll meet another girl and fall in love. That's the way life works."

Not wanting to cry, I broke loose from Grandma and said, "Hey, Grandpa, let's go buy a car." We were at a country used-car lot in half an hour.

For $300 I bought a 1948 black Ford with new tires and an engine that didn't spew out a lot of blue exhaust. It would work until I graduated.

The Bridgeport Scene

When I walked into the Eagles, Dad was overjoyed to see me. He asked questions about school as we drank the usual whiskey shot with a beer chaser. After two of those, I suggested we go to the local diner. While we ate, he told me that he and Blanche had gotten married and I congratulated him. I liked Blanche and made a time for the three of us to have a beer together before I left. Our conversation wound down and I was having a beer in the Lincoln before eight.

Wendell and Jim met me. I told them the truth about finally calling it quits with Jake - for sure this time. They weren't surprised. They couldn't fathom what she saw in Jack. He didn't shoot pool, didn't hang out in the downtown bars, and didn't watch high school sports. In short, he was not one of the local guys. I pointed out that that was probably what Jake liked about him.

We wanted to throw a Christmas party at Reddy's house. When Jim called Eleanor, she vetoed the idea but agreed to a party the Saturday after Christmas. Over the next few days, we invited as many of our old crowd as we could find. Each of us put up some money, and we'd charge $5 a person at the door, which was an accepted practice in our society.

Wendell's uncle on his mother's side had a Christmas Eve celebration and I was invited. It was a boozy party and Wendell and I led the group in singing Christmas carols and popular songs for a while.

Betty Orloff, an old friend of Jake's and mine was there. We hadn't seen each other for several years. She wasn't shy about telling me that she and Marie thought Jake was crazy for staying in Bridgeport.

Betty had recently terminated a painful affair and needed cheering up. We ended up drinking in a quiet corner with her relating things that surprised me. She said Jake had broken up with Jack at least twice during the two years I hadn't seen her. The Christmas after my 1955 summer in Ohio, he had bought her a ring. She wouldn't accept it. He accused her of stringing him along until I came back, and walked away. In a month, he begged his way back. A breakup the next year was because she still wouldn't accept the ring. Jake had told me none of this.

She said that Jake liked being in the same routine, doing the same things, month after month. Betty explained that one summer she and two other girls asked Jake to join them for a short shopping trip to New York. Jake wouldn't even consider it. She said Jake feared the world outside her area. She added, "If you moved back here, Jake would marry you. But she knows you wouldn't be happy here. After all, you never were."

The things Betty said convinced me that Jake had been telling the truth all the years before. But I hadn't wanted those things to be true and had refused to believe them.

While driving alone the next day, something I had read in a psychology textbook came to me. It was an epiphany if I ever had one. If what Betty said was true, it was irrational fear that stopped Jake from leaving Bridgeport. Was it possible that she had agoraphobia and that was what had been messing up our lives? [40] It made sense, but if that was true, how could I have missed it for so long?

Now that the idea was in my head, it seemed obvious—but what could I do about it? I doubted Jake would ever submit to therapy, even if it were available. It all added up. This phobia prevented her from leaving, and it had gotten worse after her visit to California in '54. The conclusion was inescapable and it explained everything. I had read that people with extreme agoraphobia sometimes became afraid to leave their home. It was the diagnoses of an amateur, but still convincing.

But did a phobia really matter to us anymore? We had other compelling reasons to give up on each other. We were now from different planets - whatever commonality had kept us together had slipped away. My education and experiences had created a canyon between us. We both had to move on with our lives.

Wendell

While under the influence of our favorite beverages, Wendell decided it would be a great idea if he went with me to Boston. He'd sleep on the sofa in our suite and observe some classes.[41] Carl was in on the conversation and encouraged us to do it; we'd have a great time. For many reasons that came to me the next morning, this was not a good idea. But we had shaken hands and it was a plan unless he backed out. We decided to leave Bridgeport at five in the morning on January 2 and drive straight through to Boston. It was over

40 Agoraphobia is the abnormal fear of being helpless in an embarrassing or inescapable situation and is often characterized by the avoidance of open or public places. California was just too big and scary for Jake. I had learned about agoraphobia in psychology classes but never put two and two together before this time.

41 HBS permitted a couple of guests in each class. They had to dress appropriately and sit quietly on the top row, but that was the only rule. Meals could be bought in Kresge by anyone accompanied by a student or professor.

600 miles, but if the weather was good, we could make it in about fifteen hours.

The party at Reddy's house was a big success. Betty was my date. We had all the traditional Beerport delicacies: beer, salami, cheese, bologna, white bread, potato chips, beer nuts, popcorn, and, last but not least, more beer. Popular records were played loudly. The dancing and singing never stopped, and we all had a great time. The neighbors were all invited, so there were no complaints.

About eleven, we put Wendell in the bathtub in case he got sick or urinated. I put a pillow under his head and threw a blanket over him. It was likely someone would turn on the tub water taps, so we turned off the valves. I sent Betty home in a cab, and I slept on the Reddy's sofa. There was no way either of us could drive. Eleanor wasn't happy with the mess the next morning, but they had thrown the best party of the season.

New Year's Eve was quiet. Wendell, Betty, and I barhopped all evening, ending up at the Lincoln for the midnight celebration. I left my car parked downtown, took a cab to Betty's place and slept on her sofa.

Wendell and I left as planned and the weather cooperated. We arrived tired but excited to be there. After Jim, Wendell and I bottomed out the Vat 69 on the mantel we all slept well.

For the next few days, Wendell and I had a good time. We relived our years together as best friends and exchanged stories of our military lives. We told each other things we had never shared before. One evening I did our old swear-to-secrecy pledge and I shared my deepest secret with him. I said, "Wendell, I have a goal. I intend to be a millionaire by the time I'm thirty-five. I don't know how I'm gonna do it, but I intend to find a way." I waited for him to tell me I was a dreamer and a fool.

He said, "Shit, Al, I think you'll make it before you're thirty-five. This is no shocker. I expect you to be a multimillionaire. When I found out you got into Harvard, I told Jake you were on your way to being rich as hell and that she'd better marry you while you still wanted her." That was interesting.

Of all the times Wendell and I had spent together, this was the best. He had no envy and no jealousy - only admiration for what I had done. He was truly like a brother and I was glad he had come to Harvard with me. I determined to find a way to get him out of Bridgeport and into a better life. I didn't have a clue how to do it, but it was a priority for me.

He had the native intelligence to handle college. The air force hadn't told him his IQ, but he was way above average intelligence. At the end of basic training, he had been selected to go to a communications school. He hadn't studied hard, but he'd graduated and worked in telecommunications for the rest of his four years. It was such a pity he was wasting his life as a drunken carpenter.

Wendell read our cases and, considering his lack of education, he had a good understanding of the issues. He promised to sit quietly and listen, so I took him to my study group.

Jim didn't mind Wendell sleeping on the sofa, but I had to get back to serious work. On his last evening, we agreed that he'd save money and come to California when I got back there in June. I knew he'd get a carpenter job easily, and we'd wing it from there. I had visions of him attending Citrus JC. The next day he left for Ohio.

I called the Harvard infirmary and made an appointment to see a psychologist. He listened patiently while I explained Jake's situation. He asked a few questions before he said, "You must understand that without seeing the patient, I can't do a reliable diagnosis. But with the information you've given me, I can tell you that your friend has the classic symptoms of agoraphobia. It sounds as if she has had this problem most of her life. Your love affair supplied considerable motivation to deal with it, but she didn't. Time with a psychologist might help her overcome the phobia, but it would probably be a long road. I can answer some questions, but there is little to add to what I just said."

He had been generous with his time, and the only question I had was, "Is it possible that the passage of time will resolve this problem?"

He replied, "My studies and experience tell me that's a long shot. To change she needs professional help, most true agoraphobics do."

I thanked him and left. I felt better knowing that my amateur diagnosis was probably accurate. Jake's symptoms were, as he said, classic. Now, should I share this information with her?

When I told Olivier about my last scene with Jake he said, "What you have to do now is pretend the girl in Ohio is dead. As far as your life is concerned, she is buried and gone. To make it official, we'll have an Irish wake for her if you wish." That idea, as macabre as it may sound, made perfectly good sense to me – we could drink her gone.

The Grind Begins

With my confidence growing, I lusted for a distinction on a WAC. So far, I had gotten one high pass and the rest were only pass. Distinction was the highest grade possible, and competition was stiff. The men who were aiming to be Baker Scholars knew they had to pull distinctions to stand a chance for the honor. There was no limit to the number of distinctions that could be given on any one WAC, but the grade curve is always in play, if only subconsciously.

I wasn't self-delusional enough to think I could be a Baker Scholar. This is not false modesty; it was just beyond my capabilities to be in the top 10%. Many of the men competing at that level had advanced degrees from fine schools and their math skills were off the charts. Nonetheless, I wanted a distinction just to prove that I could do it.

My modus operandi was to read, reread, analyze, and then have a draft of my WAC by midnight Friday. Our study group met after early breakfast on Saturday to compare conclusions. The rest of the day I wrote and rewrote, counting the words carefully. It took all my willpower to grind away like this. I had just about given up when it happened – a distinction.

Perhaps emboldened by my first, I received another distinction on the next WAC. The word got around about a second distinction by a guy who was definitely not Baker Scholar material. The second was to be my last, but since only few students got even one, it made me feel I had proven something. I could compete with these Ivy Leaguers.

Once I had reached a comfort level in class, I began to participate in more of the humor that took place in and out of the classroom. The professors rarely participated, but accepted it as a good tension reliever. Most of the quips were of a sarcastic nature. Once I said, "Your presentation was artful and well done – it's a pity it reached the wrong conclusion." Tom once told a speaker, "I marvel at the way you missed nearly every salient point." My best contribution was to use my old, not very good, cartooning skills. I did cartoons overnight, then got to the classroom ahead of the crowd and taped them to the chalk board. I usually didn't retrieve them but everyone knew who the author was. Two of these attempts at humor are at the end of this chapter. Everyone knew these were self-deprecating because, after being shot down in a debate the day before, I had said, out loud, "I made a few dumb ass assumptions – didn't I?"

A Chance Meeting

Jim Ullman got word that he could use his father's apartment in New York for a weekend. He invited Jim and me meet him there. We couldn't pass up a weekend in the luxury apartment of the famous author, James Ramsey Ullman.

Jim got lucky and found a round-trip ride with a classmate. I found one on the bulletin board. There were three girls, the driver and me. I sat behind an attractive blonde in the front passenger seat. Her name was Virginia Johnson, and she had completed her MBA at Radcliffe a year earlier. She was vivacious, friendly, and had all of us singing by the time we were out of Boston. She and I knew the words to just about everything. Halfway to New York, the girls in the back seat were asleep and Virginia was turned around facing me and talking.

The man she was visiting had graduated from HBS the year before, and was from Wheeling. His last name was Wheeler and I had never heard of his family. We talked about her job with Prudential Insurance and my experiences in California. The trip was over before I knew it. We were dropped at the Plaza Hotel and agreed to meet in the same place on Sunday afternoon.

The Ullman apartment was in the seventies at Fifth Avenue. It had a view of Central Park, was luxuriously furnished, and the guest beds were wonderful. It began snowing, but we went sightseeing all day on Saturday. Ullman shepherded us to dinner and several nightclubs on Saturday night, and we all got sensibly drunk. We got home about two in the morning, quite early for the city according to Ullman. Sunday morning Central Park was gorgeously shrouded in white as we went walking. It was a winter wonderland. After lunch it was time to meet rides and start back to Boston.

Virginia volunteered to sit in the back next to me. I liked that. She said she was glad the weekend was over but gave no details. Again the two girls slept while Virginia and I talked. By the time we were entering Boston, we were holding hands and she was leaning against me. I really liked her. She took a pencil and paper from her purse and wrote something.

I got out with her to say good-bye, and as we hugged, she slipped the paper into my hand. She had given me both her office and home numbers. I was elated. I called her at home the minute I got into my suite. We made a date for lunch the following Sunday.

Monday came, and it was back to the routine. The work poured in over us like a tidal wave. Life was a blur of case reading, research, study group meetings and classes.

The mid-semester exam cases were handed out by a proctor. Once everyone was settled in, the proctor said, "Gentlemen, you have four hours beginning now, and he started a timer on his desk. It was four hours of intensive work, but I was on a good track that day. I got a distinction on the exam

This distinction was a victory equal to a WAC distinction, and it was the only one I got on an exam. On the next round of exams, I missed a subtle point in a case and got only a pass, but by then it was March and the heat was off.

A Pleasant Surprise

Near the end of each school year, the faculty members who had been teaching first year classes selected a student for an award. They based their selection on classroom contributions concerning the interplay of business and politics. The award was $2,000 in the form of a credit against school expenses. The reason for the award was to encourage the students to become more aware of how political considerations can influence business decisions and vice versa. The faculty had a tie vote between two men, Fred Braun in section D and me in Section B. We each got a $1,000 contribution to our expenses.

Like most students I was not aware the award even existed. The winners were posted on the bulletin board. There wasn't much recognition given, but I'd never won anything this large before. My best buddies and I guessed that I was a winner because I had expressed strong opinions regarding collective bargaining, labor law and historical labor events when we had a series of cases involving unions and business. These cases had played straight into my senior thesis at CMC and other papers I had written for Dr. Phelps. That was a bit of luck.

As a result of the prize, Fred and I got to know each other and often discussed cases from a political point of view. He was far more sophisticated about politics than I was and I learned from him.

A Casualty and a Romance

We got a shocker when Jim Ullman announced that he was leaving HBS. His heart wasn't in the program. He did well in the stock market, but not well analyzing cases. Jim and I had become good friends with Ullman and we were truly sorry to see him go.

Not long after our first date, Virginia and I were getting close. She sometimes drove out to the school for dinner after my study group meeting. When the WAC program was completed in the spring, we played tennis on weekend mornings and partied on Saturday nights. I did some Saturday overnights in the two-bedroom, one bath apartment she shared with another girl. They were open minded girls. If one of them wanted a man to stay overnight, the other put up with the inconvenience.

It was predictable that I'd slip and call her Gin one day. I did it in a sleepy moment one evening, and she picked up on it. "Why did you call me Gin?" I said I just thought it was a cute name. Her response: "I don't care for Gin. If you must shorten my name, make it Virgin." She had a great sense of humor. I made a mental note that someday I'd have to tell her the truth.

Summer Problems

My feelings for Virginia were deepening, so I decided to find a summer job in Boston. The newspaper want ads were sparse and I didn't have time to search the job market. I went to see Professor John Jeuck and told him I wanted a summer job in Boston and why. He was a consultant for Jordan Marsh, the largest Boston department store, and he knew executives at Filene's, the other large department store. He promised to make job inquiries for me.

Virginia was excited about me staying in Boston and tried to help my job search. But nothing worked. Professor Jeuck called and said he had no ideas for me. In LA, I would have had a job in a week, but in Boston I couldn't even get an interview. There were just too many students. Staying in Boston wasn't going to work.

When I called Eddy to ask if I could work at one of their stores, he gave me a shocker. The demands of school had left no time for keeping up so I wasn't tuned into what was happening in California. A recession had begun in the fall of '57, and sofa bed sales had plummeted. The winter was bad and spring did not rebound. By April, they had decided they were throwing good money after bad, so they arranged to give the stores back to Riviera. Sanford Siegel was pissed off about this and wouldn't let them stay on as store managers or even as salesmen. The Boys were out looking for something new.

In about eight months, The Boys had gone from prosperous and optimistic business owners to unemployed pessimists. I promised I'd call when I got back.

I typed a neat letter to Mr. Phillips and asked if his offer of a summer job was still open. A few days later, Carlo Giuntini, Mr. Phillips's son-in-law, called. Skipping polite chitchat he said, "Mr. Phillips asked me to call and ask what kind of job you're looking for this summer."

My answer was direct. "Mr. Giuntini, I'll do anything you need done. Mr. Phillips has my résumé. If you look at it, you'll see that I've worked in factories, as a carpenter, sold TV repair contracts, repossessed cars and ridden horses for pay. The navy put me through a school for office work and that's what I did during my enlistment. My last job was as a successful salesman and store manager for the Riviera Sofa Bed Company. You name it - I'll do anything that's legal."

After a pause, he said, "I'm glad you don't want an easy office job, because we don't have any. I like your sales background. How would you like to try being the assistant to our new sales manager?"

"That sounds great to me. For what it's worth, I was making about six hundred and fifty per month selling sofa beds. I can give you my old boss's phone number so you can verify my record."

Ignoring me, he said, "When will you be able to start work?" I gave him the date I expected to be back, and he replied, "We'll expect you at nine in the morning the first Monday after you arrive." I assured him I'd be there, and the call ended. Pay was not discussed, but I had floated the $650 per month figure. In fact, I would have to accept whatever they offered.

I hated leaving Virginia. I was depressed, and it showed. Her usual upbeat attitude asserted itself, and she said we'd write many letters and talk on the phone. "You'll be back in three months and the time will pass quickly." The constant optimist, Virginia's glass was always full.

Our relationship had developed fast - maybe too fast. Beginning with our first date, our feelings had been intense. Olivier reminded me that I was on the rebound from a painful breakup and it was easy to transfer feelings to someone new. Beyond a doubt, he was right. Also, Virginia had just terminated whatever she had going on with the man in New York. Maybe she was rebounding too, but I hoped not. Perhaps it was a good idea for us to have some time apart; at least that's what my French love advisor told me.

Time to Leave

There was one last drunken section B party where Jim, Olivier, and other friends danced with Virginia. She fit into my group perfectly. We left before the party ended and went to her place for some alone time. Promises were made, and I was somewhat at ease about a three-month separation. It would be another long summer.

In those days, the cheapest flying was on nonscheduled chartered flights between big cities. Their departure times were not firm until the day before departure and there were loose connection times. My flight was Boston to La Guardia, by bus to Idyllwild (now called Kennedy), then to Chicago and a plane change – and then on to LA. Lift-off to touch-down was about twenty hours. Just a few years later this distance took five hours on a non-stop jet.

One of Al's HBS cartoons. Badge says "Alpha Gamma Sigma" (junior college honor society). Caption said, "HBS student as he sees himself"

Self-critical cartoon with caption: "HBS student as classmates see him." Badge says, "Ass of the Week," which described the Al's performance in class the previous day.

James Rohleen, Al's HBS roommate.

Chapter 51

To get it right, be born with luck or else make it.
Never give up.
Get the knack of getting people to help you
and also pitch in yourself. A little money helps,
but what really gets it right is never,
I repeat, never under any conditions face the facts.
—Ruth Gordon, actress, writer (1896–1985)

There is something beautiful about scars,
of whatever nature. A scar means the hurt is over,
the wound is closed and healed, done with.
—Harry Crews, novelist, playwright (1935–2012)

Home Again

It was great to be back. I hadn't realized how much I'd missed living in California. Mom and George had moved again, but everything else was the same.

Lee was graduating from Pomona. We had exchanged several letters, but contact had been limited. When I approached her family after the ceremony, they were friendly but cool. I wandered a few yards away until Lee appeared. She was smiling and happy and gave me a brotherly hug. Then I knew things had changed. Before I could say much beyond "congratulations," she said she had to get back to her family and boyfriend. I took her hand for a brief moment and wished her good luck. There was nothing more to say. I was sorry to lose her as an intimate friend, but I had a new love interest in Boston and a new job to attack. My plate was full.

For months, I had suffered a guilty conscience about not telling Jake about agoraphobia. The things the Harvard doctor had told me were convincing, but I had to get some deeper knowledge. A day later, I went to the stacks at Honnold Library. I learned that the condition was twice as likely to affect woman as men and that it was difficult to cure. The treatment was to do things that brought on the phobia and exert the willpower and discipline to overcome the fear. It was a matter of facing down deep-seated fear and, occasionally, getting through panic attacks. Even if the phobia was overcome, it was likely to surface again in stressful situations. After this research, I was convinced the Harvard doctor had called it correctly. Now the question was how to handle this information.

It didn't seem fair to keep all of this away from her. How could I not tell her? I decided to type a carefully crafted letter. The letter might make her angry, but what difference could that make? It took hours to compose something that satisfied me. It was a weight off my mind once it was in the mail.

M. Penn Phillips Company

Mr. Phillips welcomed me with a hearty handshake and smile. After pleasantries, he launched into explaining his company to me. The company's business was developing outlying land into lots which they sold to the public. He was seventy-two and had been selling speculative land since he was in his early twenties. He'd been one of the early developers of Compton and other towns surrounding LA. As population grew, he went further away from LA to find cheaper land to subdivide. By '58, the company was subdividing a large parcel in the high desert at a town called Hesperia. This small village was surrounded by nothing but desert, but there was water under the ground, and the development had been approved by the state. He planned to sell hundreds of Hesperia lots over the next year. [42]

Using existing real estate brokers and their salespeople hadn't worked well. Conventional real estate people worked in the cities, and Hesperia was in the high desert about 80 miles from downtown LA. Sales people didn't want to drive that far.

In an attempt to overcome these problems, Mr. Phillips had hired a new vice president of sales whom he believed had a knack for persuading the public to buy whatever he was selling. My summer job was to work as this man's assistant, doing whatever he wanted me to do. It was kind of a made-up job, but my plan was to make myself valuable in any way I could.

Mr. Phillips called Carlo Giuntini, into the office and asked him to introduce me to my new boss. Carlo said, "Call me Carlo" as we shook hands. The man I was to assist was named Joe Karbo. I didn't recognize the name, but when we met, I knew the face immediately. I had seen him on TV many times as a pitchman for the Maywood-Bell Ford dealership. He stood on hoods, dared the public to come in and make low offers, and did other things to attract car customers. Joe shook hands and offered me a seat as Carlo excused himself.

Joe was about my height, mid-forties, carried a spare tire around his middle, had jowly cheeks, and smoked a pipe. He began, "I reviewed your résumé, Al. You've packed a lot of experiences into your life and managed to get a great education to boot. I never got beyond high school, but I don't brag about it. You were smart to go to college. My family pushed me to find a job and get married; Jewish

42 Hesperia was considered by many to be a lot sale scam in the 1950s and 1960s, but the population grew - slowly at first, then faster. By 2010, the population was approximately ninety thousand.

mothers do that to smart-ass sons. Now, tell me about selling sofa beds."

We discussed my selling experience, and he seemed pleased. He understood the Riviera T-O system and he used Yiddish words much like the Riviera guys. Then, as it always happened, he said, "Tell me about repossessing cars and skip tracing."

He listened attentively as I gave my well-practiced explanation. I knew car dealers hated getting a repo, so I asked how he felt about guys like me. He said, "I have no preconceived notions about any job. I suspect you did what you were paid to do."

Then he said, "Since you're an LA guy, you have probably seen me on TV, pitching for Maywood-Bell Ford." I nodded affirmatively. "Al, I'm straight with people I work with, so here it is. I've seen every con scheme and racket there is. I started out doing shitty jobs for a few bucks. Then I got into a small advertising agency and had a boss who taught me a lot and let me use my imagination. In a few years, I was writing scripts for TV advertising and ads for print media. I met a used-car dealer who couldn't afford a pitchman, and I agreed to work free if he'd pay for the TV spots. I worked out a shtick, which you've seen, and started pitching his dealership. Every time I was on TV, his sales increased and I began developing a reputation as an effective marketing guy."

When he paused, I asked, "How did you go from pitching used cars to head of sales for M. Penn Phillips?"

"One day the owner of Maywood-Bell Ford called and offered me a salaried deal. I took it, and in less than three years, I became the best-known TV pitchman in the LA market. When I asked for a piece of the action, he turned me down and I quit. In no time, he was kissing my ass to come back. I told him to go f**k himself. I never really liked the car business anyway. By that time, I'd met Mr. Phillips. He offered me an incentive deal. I get a salary plus an override on gross sales. I've been in the job a little more than three weeks, and I intend to make the company and me a pile of money."

That was Joe. I was to learn that you were never starved for information when you asked him a question. I liked that style and we hit it off from the start.

He explained that licensed real estate salesmen were a joke; they sat in an office and waited for the phone to ring. We agreed that selling could be taught, but that took time we didn't have. The company needed people who already knew how to sell.

The ads Joe had written for print media had been productive. They had produced lot sales leads that the real estate agents didn't know how to handle. Lot sales were stalled. Joe was wrestling with overcoming the inertia of a poorly conceived sales program.

Joe had meetings waiting, so he showed me into a small office and said, "This is yours. When I come back at four, tell me how we're going to come up with a hundred salesmen who know how to close a deal."

It was a fascinating real-life case study. I read every scrap of information Joe's secretary gave me. By four, I had a long list of questions, most of which were to educate me. More importantly, the seed of an idea was germinating in my brain.

When we reconvened I asked: How many competent salesmen do we have? Where do they live? How much are they selling? Who passes out leads? Who organizes their sales pitches? Who trains them? Who holds sales meetings? And so on.

At six, I was still asking questions when Joe said, "As soon as I call my wife, let's get some dinner and continue this. It's constructive."

At the end of dinner, he agreed to meet with me the next morning to consider an idea I had in the back of my head. He'd wanted to know the idea. I said, "Joe, trust me. I need twelve hours on this one. I'll be ready in the morning to share the concept and sell you on it—or tell you it was a shitty idea."

He laughed. "Okay, make it, bake it, and bring it in."

First thing the next morning, I called Eddy Singer and told him about the Hesperia lot sale program and sprung my idea of his coming to work with Phillips and selling Hesperia lots for a living. He was not enthusiastic, "So what do I know about real estate?"

"At least as much as you knew about sofa beds the first time you saw one," I responded. "And that goes for everything else you've ever sold. Am I right?" He agreed, and we made a date to meet in my office at noon. My last words were, "Eddy, remember that I'm the sheygets you said was a *Yiddisher* kopf." He promised to keep an open mind.

When I met Joe, my first words were, "There's one question I forgot to ask last night. What am I being paid for this gig?"

He said, "I thought that was worked out, and Carlo never mentioned it. What were you making at Riviera?"

I replied, "I averaged about six-fifty a month for the last few months I worked there." He gave me a funny look. Anticipating some doubt, I added, "You can verify that with my old boss, and he'll be here at noon."

Joe said, "I'm going to trust you unless I find I can't. If you tell me it was six-fifty a month, that's what it was. Are Mr. Phillips and Carlo aware of that number?"

"I told Carlo, but he may not remember it. By the way, Joe, I'm working for you, not Carlo. I don't think he likes me very much and I'd rather not deal with him."

He thought a moment before he said, "As far as Carlo is concerned, you're right on both counts. You don't work for him, and he thinks you and Doc Covington conned Mr. Phillips into giving you a summer job and loaning you money. Don't take it personally. Carlo doesn't like college boys, and going to Harvard only makes it worse.

I'll tell you more about him another time. Tell you what: I'll put you on the payroll at six hundred a month and we'll see if you can justify it. Is that fair enough?"

It was more than I had expected, but I managed to hide my surprise as I asked, "Any chance I could get a three-hundred dollar advance? My plane flight from Boston tapped me out, so I'm flat-broke."

He laughed as he said, "Oy vey, you've got chutzpah. Do you want anything else before I hear your great idea?"

I thanked him, but I couldn't resist adding, "My old bosses at Riviera called me *Yiddisher kopf*." He laughed and said I'd have to prove it.

The Concept

"Joe, we have to recruit successful salesmen, and we both know the best guys are hardly ever looking for work," I began. "The recession hit Riviera sales hard, and some of the salesmen are looking for a new deal. Most of them are *shmendrik* [stupid], but a few are damned good. I'm meeting my ex-boss, Eddy Singer, at noon; he's a pitch maven [teacher]. My plan is to get him to come to work for us. If we can get him his partner, Danny Kaiserman, will come too. Trust me, these guys are pros, they can sell snow to Eskimos – if the deal is right."

Joe was listening closely as I added, "Eddy and Danny know the best men. If we can get them on board, they'll attract others. I'd like to convince them to take the real estate exam as soon as possible, but I know they won't hang around for a month on faith alone. We'll have to offer them some compensation during the four-weeks before their licenses are issued and a recruiting deal afterward."

Joe was clearly interested and asked, "You mean they'll expect a finder's fee or an override on the sales of guys they bring in?"

"Yep, that's what I mean. But one of these men will sell more than thirty guys in a Coxy operation, and [43] it seems to me we're going to be a Coxy operation if we continue on our present path."

"How the hell do you know about Coxy operations? They don't teach that stuff at Harvard—do they?"

"Joe, I sold sofa beds, but I learned much more by listening to old dogs who'd sold aluminum siding, furs, vacuum cleaners, and everything imaginable. One maven explained a Coxy operation to me in detail. Also, I've read in American history about Cox's and Coxey's armies. If you want to know about them, ask me."

He shook his head and asked, "Do you really fit in at Harvard? Okay, I agree the old pros are the way to go, but I don't know if they'll buy into a desert lot sale program. If things with Eddy go well, I want to meet him."

He laughed, "*Farshteyn* [understand]?" He had begun to assume I had learned enough Yiddish for him to let loose with it.

Eddy arrived on time and surprised me by bringing Danny along. It was great to see The Boys again. I thanked them for all they'd done for me. They were still shaken about losing their business and a bunch of money. Over lunch, they told me in detail what had happened. It was a sad story, and I commiserated with them.

I gave them as much as I knew about Hesperia and the lot sale program. They knew who Joe Karbo was and had mixed feelings about working with a used-car pitchman, calling him a ganef (thief).

---

43 A Coxy operation is one that recruits many people, but gives them limited training. After they've sold the product to a close friends and relatives, it is expected most of them will drop out of the business. The origin of the term can be disputed. One theory is Coxey's Army of unemployed in 1894; the other possible origin is a similar march on Washington led by Father James Cox in 1932. In either case, the analogy is obvious—an uncompensated army of naive people temporarily drawn together under a leader who has a goal. The spelling of Coxy is arbitrary.

But they agreed to reserve judgment until they met him. When I told them the commission structure, their interest rose. They could make 20 percent on sales, with the percentage rising in steps up to 35 percent on large lots. A man could salt away some real cash if he got hot.

I reminded them that it had been my idea to bring them in, not Joe's. We had to play our cards carefully. I wanted Joe to buy into making a deal with them that was mostly his, not mine. This bit of intrigue pleased them, and they agreed to follow my lead.

I shouldn't have worried. When the three of them met, they joked about the college goy who brought them together. The Boys told Joe what a great sofa bed salesman I was and how I had won the San Berdoo sales contest. Joe seemed to enjoy the chitchat. Fifteen minutes into the meeting, it was obvious that he, Eddy and Danny had a bond beyond being Jewish. They had grown up tough, worked from a tender age, and were accomplished pitchmen. Men who have experienced the same hardships tend to understand each other.

We got into the brass tacks of the situation when I said, "You'll make a lot of money. Joe's ads bring in the leads; you'll have plenty of them. The system will be to get on the phone, make appointments, and then sell the idea of owning a lot in Hesperia. I know you guys can do it, and so do you.

Danny said, "We need to get by ourselves and discuss this. We've been partners a long time, and we don't make decisions until we talk it through. How late will you and Joe be here today?"

Joe jumped in and said, "Of course you have to think it through. I'd like to have you on board, and I know you'll do well. Just be realistic about what you ask for." After everyone shook hands, The Boys left.

Joe said, "Al, I think you've came up with a great idea. I liked them. What do you think they'll do?"

"I think they'll come back with a proposal that we pay each of them at least two hundred dollars a week while they learn the product and pass the exam. That'll cost us about sixteen hundred for the four weeks. You already have a guy to teach them how to pass the exam, so that part is easy. If they sell four lots each the first month after they're licensed, we'll have a great return on our investment."

The four of us met at five. They asked for $250 per week and we settled at $150 and expenses. The Boys were on board, and it felt great to repay them for the help they had given me.

We didn't discuss having The Boys bring in more salesmen. My suggestion had been that we get The Boys acclimated before widening the deal. Accomplished pitchmen like action and I was concerned they'd get bored. We had to keep them busy. We reserved a conference room three afternoons each week for Eddy, Danny, and me to be taught how to pass the California real estate exam. We took them to Hesperia multiple times for onsite education.

Joe took me to his meetings with the independent brokers. The largest and most successful was Dick Thayer, who had the same pedigree as Carlo, i.e., he was also Mr. Phillip's son-in-law. Joe wanted to pick Dick's brain about training and motivating lot salesmen. Joe cautioned me to handle Dick and Carlo with kid gloves. He said these men didn't care much for each other, but they kept an uneasy peace. This added an interesting dynamic.

During our almost daily in-office lunches, Joe lectured me on many things and gave me multiple assignments. He did little explaining. It was up to me to figure out how to do whatever task he assigned and he never tired of teaching.

My summer had gotten off to a fantastic start. After only a few days on the job, I had made a meaningful contribution. Moreover, I was learning new things daily. But I needed some recreation time, and Joe encouraged me to take one or two weekends off before the new sales programs took off.

Recreational Life

People from the nearby Aerojet General plant hung out at a local bar after work. One afternoon, I spent some time with a cute, well-built Aerojet secretary named Sharon. We ran into each other again a few days later and she suggested we meet at Little Corona Beach on Saturday for a picnic lunch. After apologizing that I'd look like an albino, I agreed to meet her. It sounded exciting.

When I found her at the beach, she was sitting with a girl she introduced as Sue Biely. Sue was more attractive and sophisticated than Sharon. Sue said her visit was a last-minute thing and she had no date. Sharon wandered off into a nearby group and left us alone. I wasn't very comfortable with this, so I slathered on sunscreen and went bodysurfing. After a while, hunger drove me out of the water. Sue was still there, sitting next to the picnic basket.

As I was toweling off, Sharon came back and pointed out a keg buried in the sand with towels on the tap so the cops wouldn't see it. She said we could help ourselves to the beer. After a few minutes she left again. It occurred to me that I had been dropped. So be it. I said, "Sue, I'm going up to the Hurley Bell [a nearby restaurant] to have lunch. Would you like to join me?"

She pointed to the basket, saying, "When Sharon invited me, I volunteered to bring lunch for the three of us. I'm hungry. Let's eat." It sounded like a good plan. I fetched two cups of beer, and we dined. It was an elaborate picnic lunch and complimented her. After lunch I escaped into a book and she went for a walk.

The afternoon wore on. I was thinking of going to the Hurley Bell for some live music and invited Sue to join me. She said, "Fine, let's go. Sharon and I are old girlfriends, and she'll understand." So the dateless pretty girl and the abandoned guy with sunburn went music listening. When we left for home over two hours later, I had her phone number and a date for the next Saturday night.

We met for dinner and a movie. She asked many questions about Harvard. She didn't tell me much about herself, other than she was divorced and had a three-year-old son named Richy. After the movie, we had one light kiss next to her car. She said, "I had a great time, Al. Please call me again." The lack of physical contact was fine with me. I would have felt guilty about Virginia if more had happened.

Letters from my Virginias

A letter from Jake arrived. She was not angry—quite the contrary. She had been aware for a long time that she had a problem, but she never had a name for it. She had simply accepted her fears of large places. My letter had motivated her to speak to her pastor and family doctor. Her pastor told her to pray for help and use willpower. The doctor's advice was to face the problem. He prescribed short trips to places like Pittsburgh and Cleveland. He said she had to use willpower. She intended to do nothing. She had decided that agoraphobia was something she had to live with.

After rereading her letter, I decided she'd probably reached the right conclusion. Her style was not to resolve problems but to accommodate them. She had accommodated the problem with her father by putting me aside at first, then by going behind his back. Never in her life had she faced a tough situation and made a firm decision.

I decided to leave well enough alone. We were irretrievably broken up, and I had no right or reason to make her more uncomfortable than she was already.

In my reply, I agreed that the easy thing was to live as she had been. After all, she'd gotten along with agoraphobia so far. I wished her luck and said nothing to encourage her to answer.

A few days later a letter from Boston Virginia arrived. If a man must receive a Dear John letter,[44] it should be like this one. She was kind and complimentary, saying nice things about me. Her message was that I was the second-best man she'd ever known and that this was the most difficult decision of her life. The bottom line was that Wheeler had come to Boston, presented a ring, and begged her to marry him. Prudential had agreed to transfer her to New York. Though it wasn't mentioned, it seemed obvious that she intended to get married.

I was becoming the strikeout king of romance. The question was should I answer the letter? I was angry with her for stringing me along. She wasn't over Wheeler as she'd told me or this wouldn't have happened only a month after I left. After some thought, I decided it would be unfair not to acknowledge her letter.

I addressed her as "Dear Virgin" as she had once suggested – I loved the irony. I said I'd miss her for a long time, wished her good luck, and added that I sincerely hoped she'd end up living in Wheeling because she deserved it. Since I had described the town the humor was obvious. I sincerely wished I felt as blasé about losing her as I hoped the words sounded. Actually, I was hurt and in pain. It was not nearly as bad as losing Jake had been, but it hurt.

Getting Back into the Game

I invited Sue to a Hollywood Bowl concert and bought the best seats a ticket agent had. Sue's house was in Sierra Madre, on the edge of a large property that was covered by the oldest and largest wisteria vine in the country. When I knocked, she was ready to leave. We had

44 A Dear John letter is one in which a sweetheart or wife breaks up with a man. The expression dates back to at least WWII, when soldiers often lost sweethearts while they were off to war. It might have originated with a song in which a girl says, "... Dear John, I've sent your saddle home ..." implying she had been keeping it for his return and doesn't want to see him again. Hank Williams recorded the song, but his was not the original.

an early dinner before the concert. I brought a bag with paper cups and a bottle of premixed screwdrivers to sip during the concert. It turned out to be a perfect evening.

After the concert, we went to her house for a drink and I noted that her little house was beautifully decorated, with upholstered furniture and a maple dining table and chairs. It reminded me of the Cassaday home and the Ullman apartment in New York.

Once we were sitting with drinks in hand, she opened up about her life. Her mother had started her modeling children's clothes when she was ten. By the time she was in high school, she had been the cover girl on a number of issues of *Seventeen Magazine* and done other modeling. Her career had ended when she became pregnant just before graduating from the Anoakia School, a nearby private school for girls.

The boy didn't have a job and lived with his parents in a rented house. At their first meeting, his father suggested to Sue's father that he take his son into the family business. This convinced her father that the boy had intended to get her pregnant.

There was a quick marriage to "give the baby a name" and the couple never spent a night together. After Richy was born, there was an uncontested divorce.

It was getting late, so I thanked her for sharing her story and began leaving. When we were at the door kissing good night, she said she wasn't picking up her son until late the next morning. "If you'd like to, you can stay here tonight." I woke Mom up to tell her I'd be home in the morning. It was no problem; she was accustomed to my lifestyle.

The Plan in Action

Our plan was to recruit dozens of salespeople, help them get their real estate licenses and use them for bird dogs to find prospects for lot sales. Girls took calls from newspaper ads and meetings were set.

We rented a meeting room in a downtown hotel. I did the warm-up talk with the attendees. I gave Joe a big buildup without using his name. When they were sufficiently curious, I pointed to the door and said, "Ladies and gentlemen, I introduce a man you already know from television—Joe Karbo." There was big applause.

Joe was a natural at persuasion. By the end of the evening, nearly all of the people had filled out applications. The first recruiting effort for our Coxy operation was a smashing success.

We reviewed the applications, and I called the best ones back for one-on-one interviews so we could qualify them. The main thing was that they had to be willing to hang on for a month to take the real exam. Within that month, we planned to teach them about the product and take them on at least one bus trip to Hesperia for on-site training. It was a large energy-consuming project and would take most of my waking hours.

Eddy and Danny stuck to their agreement, and the three of us passed the real estate exam easily. We made trips to Hesperia and soaked up all the background information we could from the on-site manager. The Hesperia Hotel and the Hesperia Golf Course and clubhouse, were already built and operating. The small village had a small market, a gas station, a post office, and a row of shops. Things were moving fast, and The Boys were eager to get started.

One day Carlo stopped by my office. He was uncharacteristically friendly and complimentary, saying that he and Mr. Phillips were impressed with the work I had done. He said he liked my idea of bringing in Danny and Eddy. He said, "If these two old pros succeed, we'll have to find more like them. Please keep me informed as we go along."

At lunch, I told Joe about the visit and thanked him for the good publicity he'd given me with the boss. He said, "That reminds me. In my meeting with the old man this morning, he asked me to tell you to come and see him after his afternoon nap."

I had no idea why he wanted to see me. He began by saying, "I hear you work twelve hours a day and most weekends. I'm glad you're trying hard, but you do need a personal life. Do you have a girlfriend?"

I said, "Well, sort of. I met a really nice girl and I like her, but there hasn't been much time to see her. I'll be going back to Boston at the end of August, so this isn't a good time to start a romance anyway."

He said, "Well, you should take these things as they come. When you meet the right girl, grab her and keep her. The good ones are scarce. Is she pretty?"

She's so pretty it almost scared me away. I expect she gets a lot of calls, but I have another date with her this Friday. The weekend is out because I'm meeting trainees at Hesperia. Maybe I'll see you there."

He said, "Yes, I'll be there. If it isn't too hot, I'm playing golf with Carlo. Maybe our paths will cross." I stood up and eased out the door.

When I arrived on Friday, Sue said, "I got some steaks for dinner and we can watch TV afterward; there are some good things on tonight."

It was a pleasant surprise; I was tired of eating out. She suggested I fix drinks and we'd sit in the living room for a while. She sat on an ottoman facing me and said, "I have something to tell you. It's something I'm ashamed of, but you need to know about it. You'll be angry with me, but I must tell you the truth." She paused, awaiting some assurance.

I said, "Now you've made me damned curious. But I warn you, it's hard to shock me. And I won't be angry—I promise. What is it?"

She said quickly, "Penn Phillips is my grandfather, Carlo is my uncle, and Dick Thayer is my father." She paused to let that sink in and then said rapidly, "I've hidden all of this from you, and I feel awful about it. Please forgive me. I didn't have the courage to tell you these things, but my father said if I didn't tell you, he would. That's it. That's all there is." She looked at me expectantly.

I sat there for a moment, trying to process the information. "Are you telling me you found out where I worked when we met at the beach but decided not to tell me your connection?" I asked.

"No," she said, "it's worse than that - much worse. Sharon told me about your job and then we cooked up the idea that I'd meet you on the beach and we'd make it look accidental. I didn't want to tell you the truth until we'd had a chance to know each other a little. I've meant to tell you every time we've been together, but I always lost my nerve."

"So Sharon passed me on to you like a stray dog? That's why she invited me to the beach? She had a boyfriend in the group with the beer keg, didn't she?"

Sue said, "You were hardly a stray dog, and yes, her steady guy was there. That's why she disappeared. A few days after you started work, my grandfather told me about you. He told me your name and said I had to meet you. So when Sharon met you in the bar she knew your name. That evening she called me and said the situation was too good to pass up. I could find out if I liked you before you knew who I was. If we didn't get along, there'd be no harm done. And if it went well between us, we could straighten things out later.

Then, my Mom told Daddy about the scheme. The whole thing is indirectly his fault anyway."

"Why is a scheme you and Sharon cooked up your father's fault? I don't get it."

"It's because he believes every man I meet is after me because of our money. Richy's father was a gold digger. A year after Richy was born I met a guy in the real estate business and he was nice, but he asked Daddy for a job. He hated the guy after that. He thinks every man is after the family money. That's why I wanted you to know me as me as Sue Biely, the divorcee with a son, not the granddaughter of Penn Phillips. I wanted to find out if you were like the rest of them."

Tears were now running down her cheeks as she said, "Now that I know you, I understand you're not the type to chase the boss's daughter. Besides, you already have the job. Grandpa says you don't need his money or mine; you'll make plenty on your own. Now I've made a mess of things. Will you ever forgive me?"

I said, "Godammit, Sue, you're absolutely right. Plain girls like you attract only gold diggers - right? You're as plain as a barn door. By the way, what are these?" I held up several copies of *Seventeen Magazine.* "No man in his right mind would want you if it weren't for all that money." She laughed through her tears.

"I was wrong about one thing," I continued. "You sure as hell did shock me, and I'm at a loss to know how to respond. I'm half-angry and half-confused. I need some time to think. Why don't you go into the kitchen and start dinner? I want to sit here quietly, mull things over, and finish my drink." She kissed me on the forehead, put on a classical record, and went into the kitchen.

As I was finishing my second scotch, she walked back in and sat down. I said, "I think I've figured it out. Everyone—Mr. Phillips, Carlo, and your father—knew about the charade you were putting on. That's why Carlo has been friendlier and why Mr. Phillips asked me if I had a pretty girlfriend. Everyone was enjoying my being put through your tests. Am I right?"

She replied, "I sneaked into grandfather's office the week after we met. I told him everything and asked for his advice. He said he'd been trying to figure out a way for us to meet and he was pleased it had happened. He didn't consider your feelings because he assumes any young man would want his granddaughter. Then he told Uncle Carlo and my Daddy what was going on. Daddy didn't like the whole thing, and he's been after me to tell you the truth. He said that you'd worked for everything you've achieved and he had no doubt about your sincerity. He saw your car when you spent the night here. He called that morning and yelled at me that it wasn't fair to you to keep up the lie."

Because she was young and inexperienced, she made a major mistake getting pregnant. Now she had a hard time trusting men. She wanted to be loved for herself, not for her family's money. And, her father and uncle had both married into the Phillips family. Were those marriages for love – or money? It was all understandable.

The odds against us meeting the way we did were astronomically high. If her grandfather had introduced us, I'd never have asked her for a date. I couldn't bear being seen as a gold digger. Now I was beyond that accusation. In hindsight, Sue and Sharon had actually come up with a good idea.

I said, "Sue, I don't know how I'll feel about this tomorrow, but for now I understand why you played the game and I'm not angry. I just have to figure out if I can justify sleeping with the boss's granddaughter. And I'm concerned that company people assume I got my job because of you. I need to think this through."

Over dinner, she explained that her parents lived in a large house up a path under the vine. That explained how she was able to leave Richy with her mother so easily. Mysteries were clearing up one by one.

She said her parents didn't care if I stayed over. They looked upon her as an adult who could run her own life. Despite that, I moved my car as out of sight as far as possible and left early in the morning.

The next day I asked Joe if he knew anything about Mr. Phillip's granddaughter. He said that he'd met her once and she was a beautiful girl with a young son. When he asked why I needed that information, I told him the whole story, leaving out my overnight stays. He laughed aloud.

When I asked why it was funny he said, "First of all, the way the two girls conned you is a cute story." Then he said, "Carlo and the old man have been asking me questions about your performance and abilities, and now I know why.

He added, "You should get to know Dick Thayer. He knows how to run a sales business. Even though he has an alcohol problem, I have a lot of respect for Dick." Sue's father sounded better all the time. Being an alcoholic was practically a normal condition where I came from.

I wasn't comfortable going to see Mr. Philips. He said, "Al, I'd go see him, and tell him that while the joke was on you, it was a good idea. Then, never discuss it again. Just do what you've been doing."

It was sound advice, and I took it. At five, Mr. Phillips and I had a laugh over con job Sue had done on me. He was pleased that we'd met and said he wouldn't interfere in any way. Whatever happened between us would be fine with him. Mr. Phillips was a smart and perceptive man.

CHAPTER 52

Kindness and intelligence don't always deliver us from the pitfalls and traps: there are always failures of love, of will, of imagination. There is no way to take the danger out of human relationships.
—Barbara G. Harrison, avant-garde writer (1934–2002)

It is not easy to find happiness in ourselves, and it not possible to find it elsewhere.
—Agnes Repplier, essayist (1855–1950)

A GOOD DEED GOES UNPUNISHED

Wendell and I had agreed that he should come to California and start over, but I didn't expect he'd do it. He wrote and asked if he was still invited. I called him and we agreed on a plan.

In July, I picked him up at the Greyhound terminal. In addition to personal stuff, he had a large heavy bag of tools. I took him to Mom's house and the three of us had a great evening reminiscing about our Bridgeport days.

He was on a two-beer limit and he was determined to do well at the interview I had arranged. After the interview, the Phillips VP of Construction called and reported that Wendell was starting work the next morning. One of his foremen would pick him up at six in the morning and drop him on his way home until he was able to find other transportation. We were excited that he would have a paycheck in two weeks. In the meantime, he had enough cash and didn't need the loan I offered.

It was a load off my mind to have Wendell working. I ran into the VP and asked about my pal. His report was glowing. "Al, your friend has talent. Starting next week, I'm putting him inside hanging doors and windows. His pay will go up. By the way, did you know he doesn't like unions?" I admitted I was aware of Wendell's political leanings. It was the only thing he and his father ever agreed on.

The Plan Works

The Boys closed sales their first week after getting licensed. We made a deal with them to run an elite group and they brought in two ex-Riviera men. Joe was ginning up advertising and that produced plenty of sales leads.

Joe and I worked long hours. We held recruiting meetings at hotels in LA, Whittier, and other cities three evenings each week. The Coxy Army was building rapidly, and the earliest recruits began passing the real estate exam. Everything was coming together.

Hesperia is about three thousand feet above sea level and not as hot as the Low Desert cities like Palm Springs. It was essential that prospects come to the project to experience the climate for themselves.

We loaded buses at the Hollywood Roosevelt Hotel and other locations. Our concept was for the Coxy people to bring their prospects to Hesperia and go with them on a tour of the properties. After that, they were supposed to introduce them to one of the elite pitchmen led by The Boys. We had several desks set up in the Hesperia Hotel lobby. The plan was for the pitchmen to close sales and split the commissions with the Coxy people. Some of the Coxy people wanted to sell their clients on their own and keep all of the commission. They had a point, but it was more likely that they would never close a sale. Getting the order is what successful selling is all about, and it takes experience.

We often had more potential buyers than elite salesmen, so I became an ad hoc member of The Boys' team. Consequently, my name was on a number of lot sales.

It was difficult for me to have a social life. Sue came up with a simple idea. She said, "Why don't I go up to Hesperia with you on some Fridays. We'll have dinner and watch the floor show at the hotel. On Saturday and Sunday, I'll amuse myself until we meet for dinner and then we'll drive back. Grandpa said I could have a free room at the hotel anytime. Mom will watch Richy, and if she wants to come with Dad for the weekend, she'll have Richy and me for company."

I had some doubts about this plan. Her dad and I had never spoken about Sue. I was hesitant, but agreed to give it a try. I shouldn't have worried. When we checked in, the clerk gave us two rooms. When I went into my room later, there was a note under the door: "Call me." When she answered, she said, "Open the sliding door, then step outside and look to your right." I did as she directed. She was standing halfway out of the sliding door of the room next door.

As we strolled to the hotel for cocktails, I asked if she had arranged the room proximity. She answered, "Nope, it wasn't me, but I never ask questions when I get what I want. You can jump back into your room early in the morning. Then I'll go to Mom's room for breakfast with her and Richy." Sue was in control of this scene.

With my permission, Joe had told The Boys the story how Sue and I met. Joe said they had a good laugh about the two girls conning me. It was undeniably a cute story.

Having been around real estate sales people all her life, Sue was expecting a rougher crowd. She didn't realize that The Boys and their associates were social chameleons. At the drop of a phrase, they could change their body language, facial expressions, and accents to fit the audience. They made their livings by being charming and persuasive.

On Saturday night, we had dinner with her family and I was seated across from her father. Dick was friendly and complimented me on the elite salesman system. "Al, you got it right. It's perfect for a bird dog to turn prospects over to an experienced man to close the sale. You learned a lot selling those sofa beds." Dick wasn't as gruff and tough as he appeared to be.

After the floor show ended Sue and I danced a while; then Sue and her family retired. I went to the bar and had a nightcap with The Boys and their crowd. They couldn't resist making comments about Sue. Danny wanted to know when the wedding would be. I told him it didn't matter to him because no ganefs (thieves) would be invited. Eddy said, "Danny Boy, you asked for that one."

Life was continuing to progress well with Wendell. I worked it out for him to come with me to Hesperia on a weekend Sue couldn't make it. We pretended he was a potential lot buyer and had him shown around with a group of prospects. We had meals together and spent time drinking with the salesmen. He was thinking of finding a job in the Low Desert when the weather was cooler. Palm Springs appealed to him because he had taken up golf while in the air force.

Time to Go

Working day and night, I learned one hell of a lot about more things than I could count. I hadn't dreamed I'd get this level of responsibility on a summer job. Our modus operandi was that Joe and I decided what needed to happen and I got the job done. If the project needed money, he signed the requisitions without questions. We had a budget, but we spent money in so many ways that the budget was quickly exceeded. We generated the excitement that had been missing when Joe had arrived on the job and sales followed.

Joe felt it was important to keep a western motif. Small western bands played the music that greeted arriving buses of prospects. I made a deal with the western clothing store in Hesperia for discounts. The company paid for one western outfit for each man in The Boys' group and for boots and clothes for Joe and me.

We spent a lot of money, but it paid off. Lot sales already totaled over a hundred percent of what had been projected for the whole year, and it was only August. By the time I had to leave for Boston we had a successful sales machine operating.

An advantage to no free time is that not much money is spent, and the company paid for most of my meals. I decided to fly back to Boston on a scheduled airline, with served meals and booze. I'd earned it, and I was damn well going to enjoy it.

The Boys had a dinner for me, which I had truly not expected. The difference from the year before was that, with no women present, the jokes were raunchier. They gave me a blue blazer, shirt, and tie from a store in Beverly Hills that sold Ivy League–style clothes. That was a great addition to my wardrobe.

The most important gift they gave me was one that is so seldom given: gratitude. They told the story about losing their stores and being out looking for a new deal when I called and practically dragged them into my office. Joe was there and gave me full credit for conceiving the idea of a group of experienced pitchmen. It was a wonderful evening and a great memory to take back to school.

My last day at work, I went in to say good-bye to Mr. Phillips. He asked if there was anything I needed. I said, "Mr. Phillips, would you be willing to loan me another fifteen hundred dollars? I may be able to get by without spending it and pay it back next spring, but if I need some money, I don't want to beg Harvard for it."

He pushed his magic button, and the one-armed controller walked in. Mr. Philips said, "Give Al what he wants, same as last year." After I thanked him he said, "I expect you'll have job offers on Wall Street when you graduate, but I'd be pleased if you want to come back here." We shook hands and I left. The controller made out the note, and handed me the check plus an envelope. He said, "That's your last paycheck, Al." I thanked him and went to say more good-byes.

When I went to see Joe, his first words were, "Do you really want to go back to Boston and freeze your ass off for another winter? Why don't you graduate in nineteen sixty instead of fifty-nine? I'll arrange for you to make some big money. You'll finish Harvard in style and Sue will be with you. What say?" It was a big surprise, and very flattering.

"Joe, the truth is that I'm afraid that if I don't finish now, I never will. I've told you a lot, but only I truly understand what a mountain I've climbed to get this far. I can't stop now. But I sincerely appreciate the offer."

He laughed a little and said, "I told him it wouldn't work."

Then it dawned on me. "Did Mr. Phillips tell you to make that offer?"

"Yes, and I told him you'd say no. I agree with you. You gotta finish Harvard. No damned job here is worth that diploma. As for Sue, maybe it's better if you get away from each other for a while. God knows she can afford to come and see you if she wants to."

I stopped at the bank to make a deposit and arrange transfer of funds to my Boston bank. As I opened the envelope, I saw a check and a piece of paper. The check was for two weeks' pay, not the one week I had coming and the paper was the note for $1,500 that I had signed the previous year. On the face of it was written, "Paid in full – great job, M. Penn Phillips."

I wrote Mr. Phillips a long thank-you letter on the plane. He had been quite generous and I was embarrassed to have borrowed more money. Now I had a real financial cushion.

My last evening at home, I took Mom, George, and Wendell out to a nice but early dinner. After dinner, Wendell and I went to a local bar and he broke his two-beer limit - again. I apologized for not spending more time with him. He said, "Hell, Al, you've done plenty for me, and you've only got about nine years to make that first million. And by the way, I've never told anyone about your goal - and I won't."

Then he added, "I interviewed for a job in Palm Springs, and I'm going down there next weekend to meet the boss. If I get the job, I'll move there after Labor Day. I appreciate the job you arranged, but I can't keep living with Isabelle and George. I think I'll like Palm Springs, there's plenty of golf there." I was glad Wendell was trying to find his way in life. Maybe he'd become a successful building contractor. He was certainly smart enough to do it.

When I got to Sue's place I wondered what to say about how we'd relate for the next nine months. We'd had a great summer and I liked her a lot, but I'd been in a deep love and this wasn't the same. We agreed to write. I said, "Sue, I don't expect you to sit at home waiting for me to come back. Things will happen as they happen. I'm not asking for any promises and not offering any."

She said, "Al, I respect your honesty. We've had a good time, and I'll miss you."

"Sue, I'll be thinking fond thoughts of you too."

The cheapest scheduled flight left in the afternoon, and after a plane change in Chicago, I arrived in Boston the next morning. Fortunately, I could sleep anywhere, including the noisy prop planes that didn't fly high enough to avoid bad weather.

Chapter 53

I would be married,
but I'd have no wife,
I would be married to a single life.
—Richard Crashaw, English poet (1612–1649)

When I was in my twenties, a friend whose opinions I respected told me his theory about why men get married. It goes like this: One day—God knows why—a man decides he should be married. The next woman he meets who fits most of his perceived criteria for a wife is the one. If that woman finds him acceptable and offers reasonable encouragement, the deed will be done. Within a few years, I began to believe this rather cynical view of marriage. I came to this belief because I observed it happening to men I knew. But I knew it would never happen to me—an illusion I lost.
—A. Scheid, entrepreneur, amateur writer (1932–living)

Getting Organized

Jim met my plane with a used car he'd bought. My old Ford had summered at a head mate's country home. Remarkably, it started with the use of jumper cables.

We had decided to live off campus. We figured that with our own kitchen and lower rent, our overall living costs for the second year would be reduced by about thirty percent. An added bonus was an escape from the Harvard parietal rules.

By late afternoon, we had rented a furnished apartment in the Copley Arms, just across a bridge from the Public Library in Copley Square. The apartment was on the third floor. An old elevator was stuck just above the first floor. The landlord said his father had welded it in place when it broke down during the Depression. We had over forty stairs to climb.

There was one bedroom with twin beds, a small kitchen, a living room with a working fireplace, and a barely acceptable bathroom. The main negative about the apartment was that it overlooked the multiple tracks going into the nearby Back Bay Train Station. We had to learn to live with train noises, but it was much cheaper than the Harvard suite. We agreed we could handle the problems for nine months. It was summer, so we didn't get the picture about the heating system's deficiencies—that came later.

The second year at HBS was not like the stressful near-panic mode of the first year. We could select the subjects we wanted to study. I had picked finance, marketing, and general management as my courses. Jim was more interested in production and manufacturing, so we shared only a finance class.

We agreed that this year there would be some party time. We could go to some of the good restaurants in Boston, drink with our friends and even go to a movie now and then. We were looking forward to some happy times.

We had cases to prepare, debates in class, study groups, and exams, but the main thrust was on writing analyses (called papers). The honor system was just as strict, but sharing of information and collaboration on papers was encouraged, just as it was in the business world.

Unexpectedly our old head mate, Jim Ullman, invited us to his wedding, which was being held in the posh Copley Plaza Hotel, only three blocks from our apartment.

After Ullman had left HBS, he'd taken a job with a mutual fund in Boston and gotten serious about settling down. His fiancée was from a wealthy Jewish family and it was to be a traditional Jewish wedding. Formal attire was required. We didn't fit into that crowd even a wee bit, but it would be an interesting experience. When we called to accept, Ullman said there would be four hundred guests.

I had no one to ask as a date, but Jim invited a girl he'd met in New York. She accepted his invitation to sleep on the sofa bed in our living room. Sleeping in the same apartment with two men was quite adventurous for girls of the fifties.

We rented tuxedos; a first for me. Jim's date wore a beautiful ball gown, and we looked the parts we were about to play. The wedding was the most elaborate I've ever attended, before or since.

We entered a large room lighted by crystal chandeliers. In the middle of the room were several long tables filled with food of all kinds. Dom Pérignon Champagne, which was new to me, was passed by waiters. This was the beginning of my lifelong affection for this fine champagne.

A traditional Jewish wedding is not a short affair, but eventually Jim stomped the wine glass and the crowd applauded. A band commenced playing, and we moved through sliding walls into a large ballroom surrounded by dinner tables, each with a floral centerpiece. It was like nothing I had seen before.

The music played, the champagne flowed, and there was dancing. Then the MC announced the bride and groom as they arrived at the head table. Ullman had told us she was a trained concert pianist, and she proved it when she played Chopin and Mozart. Since I loved both composers, this was the top of the evening for me.

After the performance, the party got going with dancing to peppy rhythms as an elaborate dinner was served. After the meal, the men did the traditional dance in a circle with arms locked. Then they put Ullman on a chair, lifted him over their heads, and danced in a circle.

Ullman brought his bride to meet us; she was quite attractive. They were leaving the next day for a month-long honeymoon. I couldn't help but whisper to Jim, "What are the odds that the marriage can live up to this wedding?"

Jim whispered back, "Not a chance."

It was an uncalled for cynical comment, typical of us.

Before long, a line of waiters carried in silver trays with large baked Alaska desserts on them. I'd read about this dessert but never seen it. It was wonderful, and I loved it.

After midnight, we decided to walk home. The fresh air was badly needed after all the champagne. Hiking up the long flights of stairs was a problem for Jim's date, but with our staggering help, she made it. She crashed on the sofa bed in her clothes and we were too tired and drunk to help her undress.

The next morning, in an attempt to alleviate our gigantic hangovers, we treated ourselves to brunch at the Copley Plaza. After getting Jim's date on a train, Jim and I went for a two-hour head-clearing walk around Boston. We had a beer on the way home, over which Jim told me a mutual friend of ours had a serious financial problem and that we should try to help him.

Harvard Square Camera Store

Jim had become friendly with Dino Leone, the barber we both used in Cambridge. Dino and his brother Leo owned the largest camera store in the town, and it consistently lost money. The bank intended to call their loan and put them out of business unless a substantial payment was made. We thought it strange that they couldn't make a profit in the store's prime location, a block from Harvard Square. Jim volunteered us to look at their books and see if we could give them any useful advice. They were desperate and accepted the offer.

We asked Dino why they had bought the store about six years earlier. He said that photography was his brother's hobby. He had quit his job as a laborer and gone to work as a clerk in a Boston camera store where he learned a lot about photography and equipment. After a couple of years the two brothers pooled their savings and bought the store.

We spent an afternoon in the store's basement office reviewing the papers their accountant had delivered. As I glanced around the room, I saw that the basement was piled high with camera equipment and opened boxes. I asked Leo why. He said it was stuff that hadn't sold so he stored it there. There were items that had been there since they bought the store.

We spent a few hours listing the old inventory in the basement. There were hundreds of items. We believed Leo could have a big sale and dispose of most of the stuff for enough cash to make a large payment to the bank.

Leo wasn't the sharpest knife in the drawer. He felt that a sale of old inventory would detract from his regular sales. After a long discussion he finally agreed to consider a big sale in late November. My concept was to mix in some new inventory and try to pick up some Christmas sales early.

A Major Paper

We had to write papers for each class and have our names on at least two major papers for the year. I got the idea that the camera store could be a fine subject for a major paper for our finance class. Jim said he'd do the research. He needed to get his name on major papers without being the lead writer. We invited a classmate named

Bill to be a participant, in return for which he'd put Jim on a major paper he was writing in their production class.

The plan was to display some of the merchandise upstairs at rock bottom prices. The rest would stay in the basement and customers would be herded down there to see the bargains.

I also wanted some of the suppliers to give us additional equipment on consignment. As long as we were going to gamble what little cash they had on advertising, we might as well sell all we could—all at discounted prices. Leo said he already owed all his suppliers and they would never cooperate. We pointed out that this was the way for them to get payment. He set up some meetings and the major suppliers agreed to the plan to various degrees. As I had suspected, they'd done this before.

The bank officer was cooperative. He had no desire to put them out of business. If he got a reasonable pay down, he would rewrite the loan so they could stay in business.

Leo had become a camera expert, but he had no idea how to give a discount to close a sale … Riviera style. He also bought small ads in the papers frequently. My experience was that big ads and big sales were more effective. What he needed was an operating plan to follow after the current bank problem was resolved.

We had a couple of weeks before the sale, so I spent time teaching Leo and his clerks what I had learned about closing sales. Leo felt it cheapened his store to bargain prices. His idea was to reduce the prices for every customer or not at all. Leo had quite a few gut reactions that were pure nonsense. By the time the big sale started, Leo and the clerks knew how to give a discount to close a sale.

During all of this, I approached Professor Paul Cherington about writing a major paper for him. The camera store debacle would be the subject. It was unique in that it was an actual business experience, not an academic exercise. I went to see him alone because I wanted to give the pitch my way.

The prof tut-tutted a bit because it was just a camera store. Most major papers were written about an industry or a large company where executives were interviewed before the analyses were written. I explained that not only were we fighting to save the business, but we were also creating a long term business plan. He liked that part.

After nearly an hour of explaining and persuasion, he gave in. "Okay, the risk is yours. If this turns out to be a thin, watery paper, I'll reject it and you'll be stuck finding another major project." I thanked him and got out the door before he had a chance to change his mind. Eddy's lesson about "drop into the floor when the sale is made" guided me.

There were two attractive young women at desks in his front office. One had black hair and a sunny smile; the other had a more demure look and well-coifed light brown hair. While waiting, I had begun a conversation with the one with dark hair and learned her name was Joyce Pfeiffer. She was friendly and introduced me to Marna Taitel, the other girl. I noted they both had bare ring fingers.

I told them I was hoping Professor Cherington would let my group write a major paper for him and used the quote "Hope springs eternal in the human breast." Marna asked who I was quoting, and I drew a blank. Joyce said, "Oh that was Alexander Pope." At that point, the prof had called me into his office.

After my meeting, I said, "Joyce, I don't think it was Pope who wrote that quote. In fact, I'll bet you a cocktail it wasn't him."

She said, "Okay, it's a bet. Loser buys." I didn't care who was right; I just wanted to have a drink with her—I couldn't lose.

I went directly to the library to check the quote, and sure enough, she was correct. I called her, and we agreed to meet at a bar on Harvard Square.

When I told my partners we had the major paper deal with our finance prof, Jim was elated. Bill was concerned that a camera store was too simple to support a major paper. He said, "It's your idea, Al, and I'm going along with it, but if he doesn't like the paper, it's your job to find us another major subject."

My reply was, "First, I feel confident this case will work as an academic paper; and second, if Cherington turns it down, I'll use it in my management class. And I promise I'll find another subject for us." I sounded convincing, but I was worried. A lot depended on how well the paper was written.

To pay my bet with Joyce, I made certain I got to Cronin's bar first. I had only seen her briefly and sitting behind a desk, so I was pleasantly surprised as I watched her enter. She was well dressed but not showy and had a great figure topped off by a cute pageboy hairstyle. She walked with perfect posture and her smile lit up the room. Many women wear a smile like they wear makeup, but Joyce had the kind of smile that looked like it was just for you. Every man stared as she passed by. I didn't believe in love at first sight, but I knew at once that I wanted to get to know her—and soon. Attractive self-confident women always diminished my confidence, but I stood up and took her hand as she sat down.

In a few minutes I learned a lot. She was born and raised in Rio de Janeiro and had attended the private American School, where teaching was done in English. She had the slightest hint of an accent, just enough to be charming. She was also fluent in French and Portuguese. She had graduated from Penn State with a degree in business administration. I was totally impressed. When I asked if she liked to dance, she laughed and said, "Al, I'm a Brazilian—everybody in Brazil dances."

I passed over my background as quickly as possible. She had never heard of CMC, and somehow I didn't think she'd find stories about Bridgeport enthralling. I did tell her I worked my way through college but didn't mention that most of it was in a two-year junior college.

Exactly an hour after her arrival, Joyce tactfully said she had to take a train to the Boston apartment she shared with a sorority sister. I walked her to the subway station. I wanted to see her again and began thinking about what we could do on a date.

The first ad ran in the Sunday paper. Until the cops stopped us, we put handbills on car windows and paid a couple of students to post them on Harvard bulletin boards. We posted them at the B School. The flyer announced it as "The Pre-Christmas Cellar Sale at Harvard Square Camera," where cameras and equipment are at bargain-basement prices. Open until midnight Monday through Saturday (Sunday selling was not legal).

Foot traffic was steady all day and into the evening. Not only students showed up; there were camera buffs that lived in surrounding communities all the way to Boston. We were delighted.

The sale was going so well that by Thursday we convinced Leo to give the distributors some money and ask for more merchandise. Jim drove to Boston and stuffed his car full of stuff.

We got an ad in the following Sunday paper saying that the sale had been so successful that it had been extended through the Saturday after Thanksgiving. Customers seemed to feel they got the best buys in a damp, cold basement, so we moved more stuff down there. By the end of the second week, Leo had an entirely new view of how to price and sell cameras and equipment.

The brothers paid down the bank and got a new loan agreement. Leo followed up with a smaller pre-Christmas sale; he had learned the system. By the end of the year, Leo was planning a spring sale. They swore they'd have at least three massive promotions each year and always be willing to cut a price to make a sale.

Within a week or so after the sale ended, Jim and Bill had assembled the data I needed and I had completed a rough outline of the paper. We were in good shape. All I had to do was put the pieces together, write the text, get it typed, and turn it in before the middle of January.

Dr. Cherington's Assistants

Dr. Cherington wanted to meet my partners, so the three of us stopped by his office. After the meeting I introduced Jim to Joyce and Marna. After we left, Jim reminded me that we needed dates for the upcoming section B Christmas party. We both had it in mind to ask Joyce. Since I had already had a cocktail date with her, I claimed priority. Jim disagreed. He argued that a one-hour cocktail didn't count. It was an impasse between buddies; lady luck would decide. Jim lost the coin flip.

When I called, Joyce said she would be delighted to go to the party and Marna said yes to Jim. Since Jim was such a handsome guy, I wondered how Joyce would feel if she knew she'd lost the coin toss. Jim and I agreed the girls didn't need that information.

Section parties were always fun, and this one was especially so. Some of us had hardly seen each other since spring because we were scattered around in so many classes.

Shortly after we arrived, I found out that Joyce could dance to everything the band could play. She was also a party leader. By the middle of the evening, she was using me as her demonstration guinea pig to get everyone on the floor to do the samba. We had quite a few staid New England types, whose dancing was limited to a foot shuffling slow dance. Soon she had most of them trying the samba.

In the few days I had known Joyce, I had enjoyed every minute I'd been with her.

We had a dinner date less than a week later, and she invited me to the apartment she shared with her friend Carol. We talked and laughed; she was great company. When I left, we kissed good night rather properly but with some feeling. I thought a message had been sent that she liked me.

After that night, we fell into a pattern in a natural way, without ever discussing it. We got together every weekend evening and twice or more during the week. We went to movies, had dinners, walked around Boston, or just hung out around one of our apartments. We never ran out of things to talk about. When Thanksgiving arrived, she went to visit her aunt and uncle in Bronxville, New York, and I missed her.

Christmas Work

We learned that Jordan Marsh, the largest department store in Boston, was going to hire a few HBS men for Christmas work. Jim and I hustled to the store. They were looking for business students with some interest in the retail business. We had to fib a little for that one.

Jim was put into men's jewelry and accessories and I was assigned to work on an upper floor where a massive sweater sale was scheduled. We were told to wear coats and ties. My first job was helping the female clerks open hundreds of boxes of sweaters. When I pitched in and actually worked, the ladies became friendly. They said there would be a huge crowd and it would tend to be unruly. They told me a few snippets of past events that I thought were exaggerated. They weren't.

The sale began at eight thirty in the morning, and we had to be at our battle stations by eight. When Jim and I arrived, the street in front of the building was swarming with women. It was a little scary.

Stock boys were posted at the stock room doors to prevent customers from entering. The sales clerks were at the cash registers, and I was trying to look like I knew what I was doing. When the doors were flung open, there was a rumble as the more energetic women ran up the escalators and others poured out of the elevators. I was supposed to help customers find what they were looking for and bring more merchandise from the back room as it was needed. When I offered help, I was ignored; these women knew what they wanted. My main role became that of a referee in disputes.

Arguments often began when two women grabbed the same sweater at the same time. In one case, I intervened and promised to go into the back room and return with an exact duplicate if they'd just stand quietly for two minutes. When I returned with the same style and size sweater, one thanked me; the other grabbed the sweater and moved on. If I had ever had any interest in the retail clothing business, it would have evaporated that day. Nearly every day, there was a special sale somewhere in the store and I was assigned to it.

Christmas fell on a Thursday, and Joyce was going to Bronxville to spend the long weekend with her family. Her parents were visiting from Rio, and her sister, Jackie, would be there. I was invited come to Bronxville on Friday to meet her family. On Saturday, the two of us would go into Manhattan for sightseeing, dinner, and a show. Then, on Sunday, we'd take the train to Boston so she could work on Monday. It took all of ten seconds for me to say yes.

Her father, Herman Pfeiffer, was a friendly man with an accent that sounded German. Rita, Joyce's mom, her aunt Sid, her uncle Eddy, and Jackie were all friendly and welcoming. Jackie was a cute blond, a couple of years younger than Joyce, and a student at the University of Connecticut. They didn't resemble each other, but they had similar happy personalities.

Joyce had told me that Herman was Swiss by birth; spoke Portuguese, German, English, Italian and Romansh; and was an executive with an American coffee company. He liked an afternoon Manhattan cocktail and invited me to join him. I happened to like this drink, and I recited the recipe. He said, "Al, you make the Manhattans. I'll give you a try."

"Do you like whiskey, scotch, or brandy," I asked, adding, "I prefer scotch."

He said, "Yes, scotch is my preference too. You're an exception, most Americans prefer whiskey Manhattans." I mixed the scotch, sweet vermouth, Angostura bitters over ice, stirred, poured, dropped in a Maraschino cherry, and handed him the drink. He took a long sip, savored it, and said, "Al, you can mix my Manhattans from now on." I had scored a goal with Herman. He had me mix us another round before sitting down to a great dinner.

The next morning, Joyce and I took a train into Manhattan. It was cold, but our first time in New York together was romantic. We walked in Central Park and inside the Plaza and Sherry Netherlands Hotels. After lunch, we watched the skaters at the General Motors Building and window-shopped down Fifth Avenue. Finally, we had an early dinner and went to a play. On Sunday, we took an express train to Boston, holding hands and talking all the way. When we arrived, the temperature was in the low twenties and the forecast was for lower.

Rescue of the Andrea Doria Camera Company

We had promised the Leone boys that we would not use real names in the paper, so I had to dream up a bunch of pseudonyms. On the train to New York, I read an article reviewing a famous disaster that had happened over a year earlier. It was the collision of the *Andrea Doria* and the *Stockholm*, near New York Harbor. The *Andrea Doria* was Italian, as were the Leones, and it occurred to me that I could use the names of the ship's crew as pseudonyms. Then, I had a thought. The Greek philosopher Thucydides wrote, "A collision at sea will ruin your entire day."

A collision with a bank was what had ruined the Leones's day. Since I had to disguise the names anyway, perhaps I could make the camera store saga into an allegory of this famous ship collision.

First thing on Monday morning, I went to the library to get the facts. On the evening of July 25, 1956, the *Andrea Doria*, carrying 1,700 passengers, was approaching New York Harbor in a dense fog. The *Stockholm* was headed out of the harbor. Due to miscalculations by the crews of both ships, the *Stockholm* rammed the *Andrea Doria* amidships. The bow of the *Stockholm* was crushed, but it was never in danger. The *Andrea Doria* immediately listed to starboard, putting half its lifeboats below water. Nearby ships answered pleas for help, and the rescue attempt was mostly successful. Fifty-one people died, forty-six from the *Andrea Doria* and five from the *Stockholm.*

My idea was to call the camera business the Andrea Doria Camera Store and Leo would become Piero Calamai, the ship's captain. The bank would be the Bank of Stockholm, and the bank officer would be Henry Nordenson, the captain of the *Stockholm.* Others would be named for more junior officers, and the names of the captains of the rescuing ships were used for Jim, Bill, and me. Carrying the allegory to its reductio ad absurdum, the names of rescuing ships would be used in place of the suppliers that supplied consignment merchandise. The paper would be titled "The Rescue of the Andrea Doria Camera Company."

After drafting the introduction, I was convinced this approach would make the paper into a business novella. It all made sense to me, but would it offend a conservative professor? I knew a way to get a valid opinion—I talked to Joyce.

When I described the concept, Joyce thought it was a great idea. She said her boss had a fine sense of humor and had said that the papers he read were dull and dry. I began writing in earnest the next morning.

There was an unexpected impediment. The apartment was freezing. The landlord said the problem was that the apartment below ours had their heat on full so there was not enough hot steam to make it to the third floor. He insisted there was nothing he could do.

When I went out for lunch, I learned that the overnight temperature was forecast at near zero and the daytime was to be in the low teens for days. This was a major obstacle for my writing plan.

For the next few days, I typed in the kitchen with the oven doors open and the thermostat set on high. In addition, I turned on the stovetop burners. This brought the temperature up to about fifty degrees. I wore wool socks under an old pair of ski boots and put on two pairs of wool pants and two sweaters. To keep my hands warm for typing, I wore my rabbit fur–lined gloves while reading or making notes. When my hands were warmed up, I pulled the gloves off by putting them in my crotch and pulling my hands out. Progress was steady, and I finished the first draft.

During this ordeal, Joyce called a couple of times each day to cheer me on and I went to her place every night to warm up before we went to a local joint for dinner. It was risky, but I left two stove burners on all night. Everything was on my bed—topcoat, jackets - everything. I had a generous helping of Vat 69 before lights out and slept relatively well. Ironically, the weather warmed up the day I finished the paper.

Joyce volunteered to type a clean draft. She liked the paper and thought the names of the characters would catch the professor's fancy.

Jim returned from skiing in time for New Year's Eve so he could take Joyce's roommate to a party at HBS. Jim and I began the celebration in the afternoon at a pub, where we got the sophomoric idea of showing up dressed up as bums. The girls were both beautifully dressed and were shocked. We were two beauties and two beasts. But the ladies were good sports, and we all had a great, late night.

A couple of days later, Jim and Bill passed pages between them as they read the paper. After about fifteen pages Bill opened up.

"Al, fun to read, but I don't think Cherington will like the *Andrea Doria* allegory approach. I think you should rewrite the paper and play it straight. Jim, what do you think?"

He said, "I agree that Cherington probably won't be amused. In my opinion, he's not a humorous man."

I wasn't pleased that a rewrite had even been suggested. "Well, boys, you went on vacations while I froze my ass off writing this thing," I said. "If you wanted to be involved in the writing, you should have stayed in town. This is a damned good, well-organized analysis of a real-life business situation, and it will stand on its own as a major paper. The allegory gives it a piquant uniqueness that other papers won't have. You guys did great research and stat work, and that's what the professor will focus on. I'm not rewriting it, and my promise keeps—if he rejects the paper, I'll find another subject and do the writing."

A rejection would be embarrassing, but Joyce thought it was well done and the allegory just made it more interesting to read. After a couple of revisions, I turned it in.

The fateful day arrived when Joyce called and said that Dr. Cherington was ready to meet with us. The next day three nervous students sat in front of his desk. He began by saying, "Well, this is the most unusual paper I've ever read. It plows new ground. You guys saved a business and created a modus operandi for the future. I haven't seen that before and I like it. In addition, this is the first paper that made me laugh out loud a number of times. It was a great mix of near tragedy, planning, risk taking, imaginative execution, and humor. Playing off the Thucydides quote was a nice touch. I'd like to keep the paper a few days and let one of my colleagues read it."

The review was over in fifteen minutes. He awarded us a distinction.

As we left, I reveled in the plaudits of my partners. It was a big victory, right up there with my first WAC distinction. Joyce and Marna congratulated us. My partners paid for the beer we drank later. After an hour, Bill left and Jim and I opted for another beer.

Jim asked, "As painful as some it has been, will you miss the school? My reply was quick. "Jim, do you realize that, it is highly unlikely that we'll ever be in a room full of men at this intelligence level?

As I think back from this time distance, I know it did happen to me several times ... at reunions.

An Unexpected Visitor

In January Sue called from New York, where she was with her father. She wanted to fly to Boston for a visit the next morning. I pointed out that I had classes. She was fine with taking an airport cab. She asked if she could stay at the apartment, and I explained that the place was small and grungy—she wouldn't like it. I volunteered to make reservations for her at the Vendome, a fine old hotel about six blocks from the apartment.

I decided to tell Joyce about Sue. She was aware that I had dated someone the previous summer, but she knew no details. I explained that I had never been in love with Sue, that she'd stay only a couple of days and that there would be no intimacy between us. I'd have to play host, but she would stay at the Vendome. Though not happy with the situation, Joyce essentially said, "Do what you must. I trust you to be honest with me." I promised to call every evening.

After classes the next day, I picked Sue up and drove her around Boston for a while. I could tell that she was a little shocked at my dirty old black Ford, but she made no comment.

She said she had invited herself along on her father's business trip just to get away for a week and to see me. She said she'd missed me, but back in November, she had begun dating a man she'd known for years. I asked no questions, and she volunteered nothing.

While we had dinner, I watched her closely. She was a lovely girl, and memories of the previous summer floated through my mind. Our conversation was limited to her catching me up on her family and her latest experiences with Richy. She reminded me that I'd told her that guests could attend HBS classes as observers.

After dinner, I took her to the hotel, and she didn't invite me to her room, which was a blessing. I would probably have accepted the invitation, and that would have been a mistake. It had been my experience that intimate contact only compounded problems in a relationship.

The next morning, we went to my first class. She was wearing medium high heels, and when she took off her coat, she looked terrific. She was wearing a navy skirt and red blouse—both emphasized every curve, and she knew how to walk. When we strolled in, every man looked up. Visitors were not unusual, but they didn't usually look like Sue. She smiled confidently as she sat down in the top row. I had purposely seated her where I could see her reactions to the class.

At lunch, she was bombarded with questions. As attractive women are, she was accustomed to being the center of attention when with multiple men. She handled everything in a sophisticated and friendly manner. After the next class I took her on a tour of the campus.

As we walked around campus, Sue said, "I guess I'd better tell you why I'm here. I mentioned that I began seeing a man I knew before I met you. We dated a few times when Richy was about a year old, but I wasn't ready yet. About eighteen months ago he was going to get married, but that blew up. Then he called last fall and we started a dating relationship that has grown close. He's older and more settled than you and he and Richy get along really well. He's considering a new job in Florida. If he accepts it, he'd like Richy and us to go there with him … as his wife and son."

I responded, "I don't know what to say, Sue. If you're getting married, you could have told me that in a letter or on a phone call."

She said, "I wanted to see, face to face how you'd react to the story I just told you. I don't think you care if I'm engaged when you come back. If that is correct, I'm going to accept the ring and see where it leads."

I answered the only way I could. "Sue, you should do what you think is best for you and Richy. I don't know how I'll feel when school is over. My life the last three years has been like being in a prison. I have to finish school and get my feet on the ground before I can trust my emotions."

"Well," she said, "please answer this question: did you love me last summer? I need to know."

I said, "The only answer I can give you is that I thought I loved you toward the end of the summer but I wasn't sure. We just didn't have a normal relationship – everything was always so rushed. Once I got back here, last summer seemed so long ago. Also, I've been dating someone here, which adds to my confusion. I'm not ready to make a commitment to anyone. My only focus is on finishing school and I'm in the home stretch."

She was dabbing her eyes by then and said, "That's the answer I expected. Mom told me that if you loved me, you would've told me before you left. And, another woman in your life makes things even more complicated. I'll be on the first plane to New York in the morning." She insisted on taking a cab to the hotel. "You go do your study group. I'd feel guilty making you miss that. Just pick me up for dinner."

We had a quiet dinner with conversation limited to her impression of the classes she observed and questions about Harvard. We kissed goodbye when I dropped her at the hotel. She left the next morning without calling to say goodbye.

I didn't feel good about what had happened with Sue. She was a first-class human being. We just hadn't had enough quiet time together to get past lust and into more serious feelings. I realized I might regret what had just happened. I didn't know how Joyce and I would feel about each other in a month or two. The human heart is unpredictable. Thoughts like these ran through my brain for days after Sue left, but I was never tempted to call her and change anything.

Another close relationship had ended. Was it me or was this just the order of things?

I had read G. B. Shaw's *Man and Superman*, and though I abhorred Shaw's political beliefs, I felt I had an understanding of what he meant by the "life force" that inevitably pushes human beings in nature's intended directions. Perhaps my problem was that I ignored the natural order of things and swam against the tide of human nature. I knew that one day I'd get married, but I feared being totally committed to one person. My love had been committed for years, and I'd suffered for it. Maybe this was why my feelings were so elusive.

In addition, Jake had put the educational gap concept into my head, and I couldn't shake it. That problem also existed with Sue. I knew that Jake's phobia had been her big problem, but the education gap was still there. And, the same virus had infected my feelings for Sally. And I had thrown myself headlong into a love affair with Boston Virginia, with whom there was no education gap. That infatuation had been a losing game from the beginning, and I should have known it.

My pattern of failures in love was unmistakable. My only solace was that I had been lucky in being with such nice, attractive women. Maybe they liked me because they sensed that I honestly felt honored to be close to them. I had made so many mistakes with women that there was no rational reason to have faith in my judgment. I thought that perhaps, once I was out of school and had a regular job, my thoughts would be more settled - perhaps … or perhaps not. Scarlett and I would think about it more tomorrow.

CHAPTER 54

The reasonable man adapts himself to the world: The unreasonable one persists in trying to adapt the world to himself. Therefore, all progress depends on the unreasonable man.
—George Bernard Shaw, playwright (1856–1950)

It is well to be happy and wise
and well to be honest and true;
it is well to be off with the old love,
before you are on with the new.
—Source Unknown

A ROMANCE BLOOMS

Maybe Sue's visit was the medicine I needed. In a matter of days, Joyce and I became much closer, and the contrast became obvious. Sue had been an exciting affair, but with Joyce it was more like love. This conclusion came to me by surprise—one of my epiphanies. But what should I do about it?

Joyce's parents decided to visit Boston. I figured they wanted to eyeball me for a longer time than our short Christmas visit. I left everything in Joyce's hands. I said I'd do whatever she asked and would try not to make a social faux pas. Her father was a successful and sophisticated businessman, and I was a somewhat educated pitchman. I was in awe of him and wanted to make the best impression I could manage.

Both parents were gracious, and her father refused to let me pay for anything. I assumed Joyce had clued them that I was a poor boy and not eager to talk about my background. They asked none of the usual questions about my father and what he did for a living. They stayed with questions about Harvard and my future plans. They understood that Joyce and I were in much more than a dating relationship. It appeared to me that they wanted whatever was best for Joyce and intended to stay out of her personal life.

Joyce arranged an evening at a nightclub in a well-known place called Blinstrub's Village. We ate, drank, and danced. I was easily infected by the Brazilian penchant for singing and dancing. These people loved to have fun, and I liked their spirit. Brazil must have been a great place to grow up.

Her parents had come to see how Joyce lived and to size up the man in her life. When those missions were accomplished, they went home to Rio. Joyce gave me a Distinction for my performance during their visit.

The school year moved quickly, as did the relationship with Joyce. By the time of my birthday in early February, we were becoming cozily comfortable with each other. Ours was not a relationship of mutual sexual convenience, as some others had been. This was a steadily growing, mature relationship. Joyce had both feet on the ground. She was sure of herself, feminine and sexy. She was on my mind all day. Sometimes I called her Judji, her nickname, or Judjica (Portuguese diminutive for Judji), as her family did. It felt natural and loving.

Locke-Ober was the third oldest restaurant in Boston, very upscale and one of my favorites. Joyce said she was taking me to dinner for my birthday to a new place called Oberlocks—the word reversal went over my head. She went to Locke-Ober a day in advance and paid for dinner. I discovered the real name at the front door, and it was a fine surprise. A perfect evening was topped off by a perfect baked Alaska. I had told her about loving the dessert at Jim Ullman's wedding. It was as fine an evening as I had ever experienced.

Jim, Olivier, and other friends loved Joyce and told me repeatedly not to let this one get away— she had it all. I agreed with them, but the thought of marriage still scared the hell out of me. We spent some evenings with my study group pal Charlie Connolly, his wife, and child. We brought food and wine to their apartment, and Charlie and I cooked. I saw how happy Charlie was with his family life, and I envied him. I knew I should ask Joyce to marry me, but was I really up to the responsibility?

By late March, we were either in love or living an excellent imitation. My schoolwork was going well, and classes would be over before the end of May. Then what? One evening we spontaneously began talking about our future. She knew I was set on going back to California. She had no interest in returning to Brazil, and with her parents' blessing, she planned to become an American citizen.

I had learned some things about relationships, and I was concerned about our long-term compatibility. She was accustomed to a nice home on a hill near Ipanema Beach, complete with servants. She had never cooked or done household chores. Her big culinary accomplishment was to put frozen waffles in a toaster and serve them with warmed-up syrup. She was relaxed about this, saying she'd learn cooking and all that stuff when the need arrived.

I had little money, owed some and wouldn't have a high-paying job. She was the kind of girl a successful New York executive or professional man would want as a wife. He'd have everything to offer her: a house, servants, money, and private schools for kids. If she moved to Manhattan and went to work there, she'd meet men like that the first week. Marrying me was a bet on a blind horse in a tough race. It might be a romantic ideal to marry a guy who would be struggling to start a career, but would it last when reality set in?

We had long talks about the differences in our backgrounds. She took my concerns seriously but minimized them, saying she wanted love, not possessions or position. She realized that an MBA from Harvard was no guarantee of financial success, but it was a big step in that direction. We talked a lot but resolved nothing. It made my head hurt. As my muse Scarlett said, "After all…tomorrow is another day."

A Job after Graduation [45]

Many companies sent recruiters to HBS and we could sign up for interviews. About a week before this process began, Carlo called me. He said Mr. Phillips wanted to know if I was coming back to work. I said I hadn't made up my mind and engaged him in conversation, hoping he'd say something about Sue. He didn't take the bait. I promised I'd make a final decision in two weeks and call him back. He said, "Call Mr. Phillips tomorrow. He wants to hear from you."

The next morning, Mr. Phillips said, "I liked what you did last summer, and I think you have a bright future with us. You'll get a nice raise and we'll work out some incentives for you. We have a lot of land to sell." I replied that I was in the process of deciding what to do after graduation and needed some time before I made a commitment. He said, "Al, that's fine. Call me when you decide; the door will be open." It seemed to me that they were trying awfully hard to smoke me out. Why?

I called Sue and asked what she'd told her family about us. She replied, "Daddy and I agreed not to tell the rest of the family that

---

45 The HBS class of 1959 began with 630 students and 81 did not get their MBA – a loss of 12.8%. Most flunked out, but some left for other reasons. Nowadays students are tutored as necessary to get them through the program and few students don't complete the two years and get their MBA.

you and I met in Boston. He doesn't think things between us matter to my grandfather or Carlo. Because you did so well last summer they want you back, regardless of me. My father's not angry with you and neither am I. None of us can control our feelings of love. Also, I'm going to accept that engagement ring, and my grandfather will know about that in a matter of days."

I said, "Thanks for being so understanding and honest, Sue, and I sincerely hope you'll be happy." It was a pleasant conversation, and everything she said was comforting. When she announced her engagement, they'd believe she dumped me, so I wouldn't be the villain.

The Phillips job opportunity was now in play, but I decided I owed it to myself to meet a few recruiters. I looked at the company names and none were LA headquartered. Some companies were proactive and had developed relationships with certain professors who would tip them off that they should take a hard look at particular students.

I received a call from a Goldman Sachs man. He said Dr. Jeuck had recommended me. An appointment was set. The Goldman man read my résumé carefully and then asked how I liked collecting bills and repossessing cars. It just never failed. After a few more questions, he told me about the opportunities at Goldman. It sounded like a great place to build a career. He said that after two years of Goldman training, a man was assured of a successful career on Wall Street. Goldman sounded like a fine opportunity.

I asked if there was any chance of working in California. He said that someday the firm would have an office in San Francisco, which he saw as the key city in the state. He didn't understand how California was developing. I promised I'd get in touch if I wanted more information.

That afternoon, he called and invited me to join him and two other HBS men for dinner at Durgin Park, Boston's most famous restaurant. It was tempting to get a fine free dinner, but I said, "I appreciate the invitation, but I want to live on the West Coast. I'm going back to California." He thanked me for my honesty.

More as a matter of gaining experience rather than job hunting, I interviewed with several other companies, most notably Procter & Gamble, which hired four or more HBS grads each year. None of the companies interested me. M. Penn Phillips had to be my choice unless I was willing to live on the East Coast.

Joyce and I had admitted our love for each other, and we got along perfectly. Without either of us making a formal proposal, we had spontaneously begun to talk about marriage. If marriage was in our future, it was best if we talked about job offers. I told her about Goldman and said, "Honey, it would be fun living in New York for a while. Assuming I'm successful, I'd be making decent money in a few years and we may have children. Suddenly, we'd be locked in because it would be difficult to start over in California. Long term, I don't want to live in New York or any eastern city; they're old, dirty, and cold. I'm a Californian now; I like the sun, the beach, and the style of living. I'd die a slow death in New York."

Joyce had left Rio, spent five consecutive winters in United States and had adjusted well. Her attitude was that she'd go wherever I wanted to build a career and we'd make a life together. How could I ask for more from a wife? Joyce had no phobias about travel and geography.

The difference in our backgrounds still concerned me, but she was convinced that she could adjust to living in California. I suggested we both move to LA. I'd take the job at the Phillips Company, and we would live separately. In about six months if she didn't like LA or decided I was not the man for her, she could move back to the East Coast. If we continued to love each other and she liked LA, we could set a date and get married. That made sense to me - but not to her.

She was emphatic when she said, "Darling, I love you and I'm ready to marry you. But, my family would never understand if I moved across the country with you. I can't live like that for even a little while. In our culture, a girl who becomes a mistress has given up ever marrying a good husband. There are names for women like that, and I just can't do it." This was not a phobia; it was a matter of morality and her cultural background.

I wanted to marry Joyce, but I wanted to know that she'd be happy in LA. What if she didn't like my friends? LA is a big sprawling city, and she didn't even have a driver's license. I realized my concerns sounded like those Jake had, and perhaps that's what brought those thoughts to mind.

Joyce wouldn't move to LA until a wedding date was set. And even then, she would move there for only a short time before the ceremony. This conversation was repeated a number of times over a week or two. We were at an impasse, and I was faced with what was - in essence - an ultimatum.

Joyce felt the job decision was mine to make. I told her about the Phillips Company and what I'd done there. She thought it sounded as if I would do well there. Better yet, she was not concerned about the family connection with Sue. She understood that relationship was over.

It was time to call Mr. Phillips and accept the job offer. He was cordial and asked when I wanted to start. I picked a date about three weeks after my last day at school, and he said that was fine with him. It was a short, friendly conversation. When I hung up, I breathed a sigh of relief. I had committed to a job. Now was I getting married or not?

The Big Decision

During a few wakeful nights, I gave myself several lectures. Finally, I knew I'd regret losing her, so the decision made itself. When I saw her I said, "When would you like to get married, Darling?" We had a celebration dinner. It was late April, and we decided to tell our friends and families in mid-May. August was picked as the best time for a wedding.

We made other plans. The day after school was over, we'd drive to Bronxville, stay overnight with her aunt and uncle, and then drive the five hundred miles to Ohio the next day. She would stay with my grandparents for a few days and I'd bunk on the Reddy's sofa. I wanted her to see where I came from because I feared she didn't understand what poor really looked like.

After her Ohio visit, Joyce would go back to New York. I'd sell the car and fly to LA. She would come to LA in July to stay with Mom, and I would live elsewhere. Everything had to be on the up-and-up. Her mother would arrive about two weeks before an August wedding to help her settle all the details. The exact wedding date would depend on availability of an acceptable venue.

Announcement of our wedding plans was done by phone and personal letters. No one in her family was surprised. I wrote to Mom and enclosed a picture of Joyce. She was not surprised either.

A Big Surprise

Just before finals started, Joe Karbo woke me up one morning. After a few pleasantries he said he was leaving the Phillips Company. It hit me like a ton of bricks. He was my mentor and guiding light at the company. Did I want to work there if he was leaving?

Joe said, "Carlo wasn't thrilled about me coming in here to begin with; that was the old man's idea. He's been on a campaign to convince the Old Man that I'm no longer needed, and he finally succeeded after we had a serious argument over a trivial matter. The sales force is running fine, and Carlo thinks he can use an advertising agency instead of me to produce leads for the salesmen. He also wants to get a piece of my override on sales for himself. And you can throw a little anti-Semitism into the mix; Carlo is not a Jew lover."

"In other words," I said, "Now that the plane is built and it flies Carlo thinks he can be the pilot and avoid paying you. What a dirty deal. I assume you're going to sue them."

Joe replied, "No need to sue them. The old man and I agreed to a cash settlement of my contract. You know, he has more common sense and integrity in his little finger than that mouth-breathing Italian sewing machine salesman has in his entire body. The lawyers are drafting the agreement as we speak. Well, old buddy, I'll be gone before you get here. I hope it all works out for you. Just be careful of Carlo if you marry Sue. He hates competition."

I was concerned that Carlo probably saw me as Joe's protégé. Joe felt I was safe because Mr. Phillips liked me. I wasn't so sure.

I said, "Joe, I'm going to tell you a secret. The summer romance didn't work out. Sue is about to announce her engagement to a guy in Arcadia, and I'm getting married in August. That might change the cards for the game with Carlo. What do you think?"

After congratulating me, he thought for a moment before saying, "I think you and Sue not marrying will make Carlo happier than if you did. He's not *meshugganeh* [crazy]. He doesn't want a bright, aggressive guy like you around as *mishpocheh* [family member]. He knows where you stand with the boss, and as I said, he's afraid of competition. You can become a major player here, but you'll have to get along with Carlo. He's walking into water way over his head and he'll realize it in a few weeks. The company is gonna need a lot of imagination, management skills, and chutzpah [guts] that he doesn't have. Carlo is a *klutz* (dumb person), but he'll love you if you can keep things going for him. He really doesn't understand what we've put together here or how to run it. He also doesn't know how to relate to Danny, Eddy and their group and he can't afford to lose them. Did you know that the pitch man crew you created is producing over half our sales volume? They owe you in a big way, buddy; they've never made money like this before. So come on back and jump in."

I could see Joe's point, and I really didn't fear Carlo; I had my share of intellectual arrogance when it came to people like him. It now made sense to me why Carlo had called me about coming back to work. He was counting the soldiers before the final battle with Joe. I was hearing only Joe's side, and I knew him well. It was quite likely that he caused about half of the friction with Carlo. Joe was quick-witted and sharp-tongued and, in a spirited discussion, Carlo was no match for him. It would have taken only one or two exchanges with Joe putting Carlo down hard for a feud to erupt. Before the conversation ended, I had to know something. I asked, "What are you going to do, Joe?"

He laughed. "Al, I have a bundle of cash now, and I have a thousand ideas. Let's get together when you get back and I'll tell you some of the things I'm considering." That was the end; I had to go to school.

After thinking about it, I decided that Joe's departure might make things better for me. I'd been there when Joe was on a honeymoon with the company. Things had gone better than expected and I'd been in the thick of the battle. It was well known that I dreamed up the idea of bringing in pitchmen and that I'd rounded them up. The people that counted would remember me as the guy associated with success, not the later friction between Joe and Carlo. I had no idea what Mr. Phillips would want me to do, but I had confidence that I could do just about anything he needed.

Leaving Boston

On my last day on campus I walked the length of Harvard Way, past Gallatin Hall, and to the corner of N. Harvard Street. I stood exactly where I had stood when I arrived twenty-one months earlier. I took deep breaths as recalled my feelings the last time I stood there. I felt like jumping up and down as I said, quietly, "You made it – Goddam it, you made it. The work horse ran with the thoroughbreds and didn't get left behind." As I walked back, I stopped in front of Baker Library and stood where Jim and I had stood our first day and looked across the Charles River. I was happy it was over, but sad to leave the scene of the greatest accomplishment of my life. There were no tears, only a small regret that Joyce was not there with me at that moment.

Attending the graduation ceremony meant sticking around for a week after the last exam. The only reason to go through it was for a family in the grandstand, and mine wouldn't be there. Nearly all of my closest buddies decided to skip *Pomp and Circumstance* and get on with the rest of life. My walk down Harvard Way was my graduation ceremony.

Jim and I had shipped our steamer trunks several days earlier and had kept only a duffel bag of stuff. The last night before leaving Boston a few of us had a boozy get-together at Charlie Connolly's apartment. We got home late.

About two in the morning, pounding on the door awakened us. Someone yelled, "Evacuate your apartment! There's a fire in the building!"

We were groggy, so it took a while for the message to sink in. We looked out the kitchen windows and saw a fire engine below. Jim opened the window and yelled down, "Is it serious?" There was no reply. He yelled louder, "Is the building burning down?"

A fireman with a bullhorn answered, "Get down here right away; the fire is spreading on the second floor!" When I opened the door the hall was full of smoke and I could feel heat swooping up the stairwell. I ran back and told Jim that I had a hunch it was serious—we had to go.

One of us pointed out that our duffel bags would be a hindrance if we had to run past the fire on the second floor. Jim said, "Hey, let's dump the duffels out the window and pick them up when we get down there. We hoisted them up and chucked them out the window.

Then we ran out the front door and down the stairs, each draped in a wet blanket to block the heat we expected.

On the second floor hoses covered the stairs like a nest of snakes and the firemen were doing the things firefighters do. Smoke was billowing, and a man with a bullhorn was shouting directions. It was complete chaos. We picked our way through the hoses, down the stairs, and out the front door. The chief in charge yelled at us, "What the hell were you guys doing up there so long? And you damn near hit some of my men with those bags you dumped out. Go pick 'em up!"

We retrieved the duffels and loaded them into our cars. The excitement was over in an hour. After a while we were permitted to return to a smoky, smelly apartment. We both conked out immediately. In the morning we agreed that it was a fitting end to our stay in the Copley Arms. It had been a miserable place to live for nine months, and it had now given us an insulting good-bye.

The Drive and Visit

Joyce and I had an easy drive to Bronxville where I was treated like a member of the Sid and Eddy family. We left early the next morning and drove straight through to my grandparents' cottage in Tiltonsville and then I checked into my usual hotel—Jim and Eleanor's sofa. The next morning, we went to Piedmont Lake for fishing and a picnic lunch. Joyce and Grandma became close friends after an hour of chatting while Grandpa and I caught a few small fish. We had a nice day and evening.

The next day, I gave Joyce the grand tour. I took her into the Eagles Club and the Lincoln, toured the high school, visited the athletic field and drove past most of the places I'd lived. I drove us through a few small mining villages where the poverty was stark and I could see she was shocked. I asked if it reminded her of the favelas (poor slums) of Rio. She admitted that she'd never been in the favelas, but what she was seeing looked like pictures from certain parts of Rio. I was once again reminded that we came from widely separated socioeconomic backgrounds. She was convinced that she could and would adjust to a different life with me and her confidence buoyed mine. I reminded myself that my bad experience with Jake shouldn't color my thinking about Joyce's adaptability. She was an unusually determined girl, and I loved her for that—and many other reasons.

When we stopped in the Lincoln to see Carl he charmed Joyce by telling her how proud he was of me. We had drinks with Dad and Blanche who, thankfully, were relatively sober. Blanche carried the conversation, asking all the appropriate questions about wedding plans. The best Dad could do was tell me how lucky I was to be marrying such a pretty girl. Joyce said later that she liked Blanche's down-to-earth demeanor. Finally, my old friends Jim and Eleanor joined us for dinner.

The next day, I drove Joyce to Pittsburgh to catch an overnight train to New York. Seeing the station reminded me of all the anguished good-byes I'd been through there. This one was different—I felt secure. It had been a short but successful and necessary visit. For my peace of mind, Joyce had to meet the culture and see the truth of my upbringing.

The Cheshire Cat reappears

Jake called me at Grandma's house. I had written a short note to her, so she was aware of my wedding plans. We agreed to meet at Ogleby Park for lunch. We hadn't seen each other since Christmas of '58, about sixteen months earlier.

Simultaneously I wanted to see her and didn't want to see her. How should I act? What should I say? I was in love with someone else, which I had once believed was impossible.

I was seated at a table when she walked in. She looked as lovely as always and was, as usual, well dressed. There was an involuntary flutter in my chest. She said she had the rest of the day off and wanted to hear about my life since we'd last seen each other. She asked how my second school year had gone, how my grades came out, what kind of a job I had taken, and much more. I answered methodically and slowly. In a while I became comfortable talking to her as an old friend. I asked about her job, her parents, and Wendell. It took a while to cover Wendell. He had managed to get back into the air force, where he'd be taken care of for the next two decades or more.

She thanked me for my letter on agoraphobia. She said, "I'm not the type to go traveling to strange big places just to overcome a problem I've lived with all my life." I agreed with her and said she'd live a long, happy life with the problem, as many people did.

For an hour, we danced around the elephant in the room. When we finished lunch, she said, "Do you mind going for a walk down by the little lake?" She drove us there, and we walked the circular path around the lake. She sat down on the first bench in the shade. I could see that she had decided to open the conversation she really wanted.

She asked, "Alf, are you certain you're in love with Joyce and want to marry her?"

I said, "Yes, I am. I crossed that bridge many months ago."

She said, "I've been such a fool for all these years. I know that now. I ruined everything because I didn't have the courage or determination to overcome a psychological problem. That's what I've always loved and admired about you. You set your sights on something and go for it, all out. You let nothing stop you. I wish you'd have given me a blood transfusion so I'd have some of whatever it is that you have."

I said, "Gin, we've traveled a long road together and now we have separate paths to take. We've both made mistakes, but I think it's ending where it should. You have Jack, and he's devoted to you. Marry him and live here. There are many places worse than the

Ohio Valley—you'll be happy here. I'm just a shadow from your past, and I'll be out of your mind after some time passes."

"But what if I had moved to California?

"Well, you could've done that, but you didn't, and that's a fact. And what if I'd moved back here? Well, I didn't, and that's also a fact. There's no point in rehashing the past. We're where we are because we put us here."

She said, "Last night I decided to ask you to call off the wedding and give us another chance, but I know you'd never do that. Even if you did, I'm not sure I could follow through. Even when we broke up, I could still love you … knowing I'd see you again. Now you're not going to be there anymore, waiting and free. You belong to another woman now … and I don't like it." She dabbed a tear, and I hoped she wouldn't cry and make me do the same thing.

The conversation was getting maudlin and uncomfortable. I could have gotten angry if I'd let myself go. Then I would have said things like, "You and only you f****d up our lives for years. You never gave an inch; you never really tried. And now you're grieving for our lost love and the years that were wasted. It's over. Get it through your head—it is o-v-e-r. Face our situation like you've never faced one before."

It was good that I took time to think through these thoughts because it made me realize that I couldn't say them to her. I had loved her like life itself from age seventeen. Now I couldn't do or say anything to hurt the object of that love. The romantic love was gone, but I still cared for her and wanted her to be content. But her happiness wasn't something I could bestow. She was the secret to her happiness—and had always been. She had to let go as I had let go. My internal conversation went on and on.

Suddenly, I realized we hadn't exchanged a word for fifteen minutes. We'd just sat there, looking at the ducks on the lake and thinking our own thoughts. Someone had to break the ice. I said, "Gin, we have to go. We're doing nothing here but feeling horrible about things we can't change. I'm going to marry Joyce in August. You have Jack and you should marry him. Neither of them would be pleased if they knew we were doing this. I think it was necessary for us to clear the air between us and we've done that. Now it's time to go."

She stood up, and we walked to her car. When she parked next to my old Ford, she said, "You will always be my first and deepest love. I'll pray for your success in your marriage and your career. I wish I could meet Joyce and tell her how I've loved you and ask her to love you as much."

"Gin, we both have regrets, but life usually works out because people make it work. The best thing we can do now for the people that matter to us is to move on and build our futures. When I visit here again, I'll call and invite you to lunch. We can't live the rest of our lives with no contact—too much has happened between us. Once in a while I'll need to know you're okay."

She said softly, "Yes, please call me before you visit—I'll want to see you." I opened the door and got out. As she drove slowly away I waved goodbye with one hand and dabbed the tears running down my cheeks with the other. It was one of the saddest moments of my life.

Grandpa and Grandma Jonard, at picnic when Al brought Joyce to visit, May, 1959

Joyce Catherine Pfeiffer who married Al in August, 1959

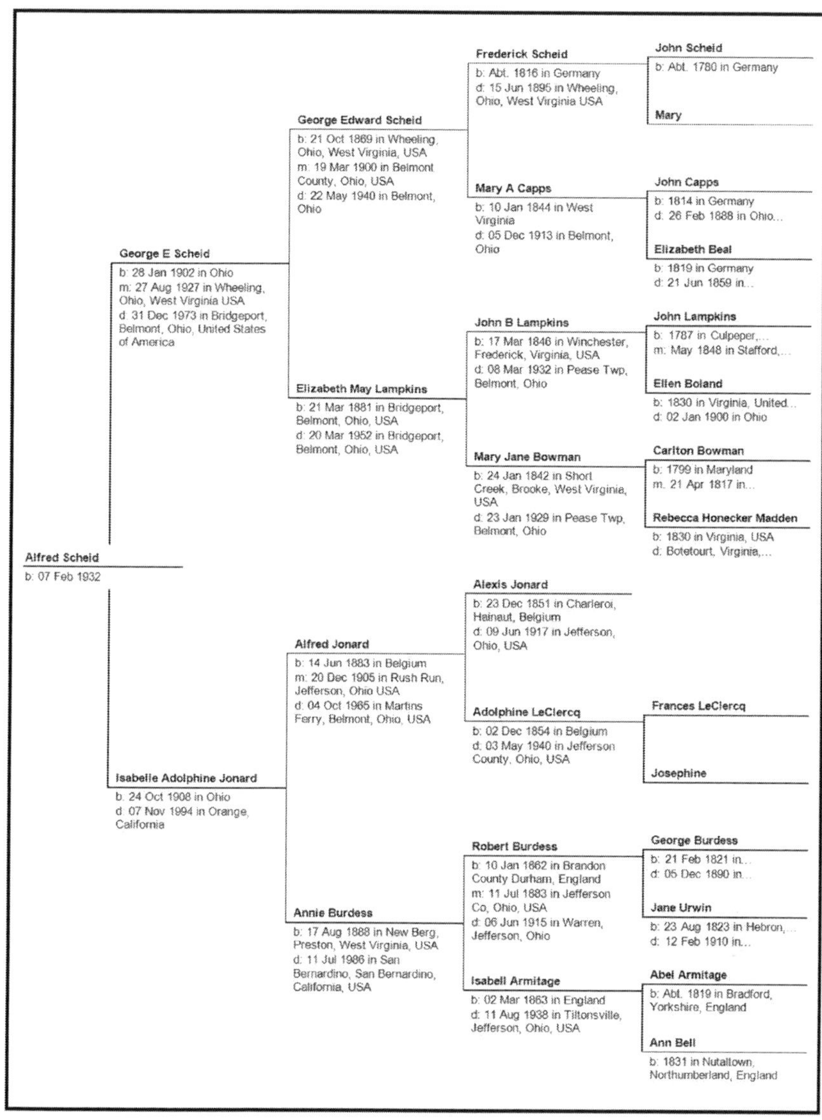

Five generation family tree of Scheid and Jonard families

CHAPTER 55

Your hometown is not where you're from.
It's who you are.
—Arnold Palmer, professional golfer (1929–living)

It is difficult to say what is truly impossible,
for the dream of yesterday is the hope of today
and the reality of tomorrow.
—Robert H. Goddard, physicist, inventor (1882–1945)

THE LAST GOOD-BYE

I was packed and ready to leave as we stood in the front room waiting for Jim Reddy to pick me up for the drive to the Pittsburgh airport.

Grandpa had mellowed over the years, but he was alert and aware; his coal miner core was still tough. The implications of my education escaped him, but he understood that his grandson had gotten a master's degree from the most renowned college in the country. That was enough for him. During our picnic at the lake, he had asked me to describe Harvard, and I had shown him a few snapshots. He had stared at them a long time. To him, Harvard was the palace on the hill, where the likes of us didn't venture. He was all at once pleased, proud, and in a state of wonderment. I understood this because inside I was still a coal town kid.

Grandma was dabbing tears from her eyes as she said, "Alfred, Joyce is a wonderful girl. Thank you for bringing her to see us. I loved Virginia, but it was just not meant to be. But listen to me—if there is any doubt in your mind, wait a while before you get married." As she said this, she had an open hand on each side of my face, staring into my eyes, just as she had done when I was ten years old. She wanted to drive her point home.

"Grandma, I'm committed to Joyce, and we'll be married in August, as planned. All I can think of now is getting back to work. School is over, and I need to build a career. I'm tired of being poor." She hugged me, and kept her peace.

Now it was Grandpa's turn, and he put his hand on my shoulder as he said, "Alfred, do you remember when I told you that giving up your job at General Motors to go to college was a mistake?"

"Yes, of course," I said, "It was in El Monte in nineteen fifty-four."

He said, "I just want to say how happy I am that you didn't take my advice." His good eye was twinkling as he said the words. He clearly recalled the argument we had, and he now saw it as humorous.

Then he hugged me. As he released me, he said, "Tell me. I want to know. How did you manage to get from Bridgeport to Harvard?"

I thought about it a moment. "Grandpa, I'm being honest when I say I haven't figured all that out yet. All I know for sure is that many people helped me and I had a bunch of lucky breaks."

"And you worked very hard," Grandma chimed in.

"Yes, that's true. I worked hard."

As if on cue, Jimmy pulled up in front and gently beeped the horn. There was nothing left to say—my life in eastern Ohio was truly over. My wonderful old grandparents stood on the porch waving as we drove away.

When we turned north on Route 7, tears were running down my cheeks. We talked very little during the trip. At the airport curb, we did the usual firm handshake and manly hug. He said, "I know you won't forget where you came from because you never have. Stay in touch and send us a wedding invitation." I promised both, turned quickly, and walked into the terminal. The old DC-3 left on schedule.

I had selected a seat on the left side of the plane so I could see the valley as the plane climbed out to the west. The Island was easy to spot, and across the west channel was Bridgeport. I imagined myself standing in front of Mom's store, looking at the old City Building and then up Main Street at the library. In a few seconds, my view of the valley disappeared. It came to me that I had broken out of Beerport, but it was still part of me. I wiped some tears, keeping my head turned so my seatmate wouldn't notice.

I didn't know this then, but do now: it takes only a few minutes to like someone; you can have a crush on them in an hour or two; and in a few days, you can love them deeply. And in a lifetime, you can't forget someone who loved you the same way for even for a little while. Jake was in a sad corner of my past. I was no longer in love with her, but I couldn't forget her either.

As we passed through the clouds toward cruising altitude, I thought, *how the hell did all of this happen to me? What did I do to deserve all the breaks? Maybe someday I'd figure it out—then again, maybe I wouldn't.*

I dug a book out of my briefcase, opened it and cozied down, preparing to escape reality—again. Hemingway once wrote, "There is no friend as loyal as a book." I liked Hemingway a lot.

All, everything I understand, I understand because I love.
—Leo Tolstoy, Russian writer (1828–1910)

The End

EPILOGUE

The bitterest tears shed over graves
are for words left unsaid and deeds left undone.
—Harriet Beecher Stowe, abolitionist and novelist
(1811–1896)

Beerport ends in 1959, but the characters lived on. They remain in my memory, and I wish I could thank each of them for the help and support they gave me. I was particularly blessed to know and love several fine women in my early life. Even in short romances, men are changed (matured?) by the females with whom they get close. Each leaves an imprint. As *Beerport* came through my head and onto the pages, I had begun to appreciate the influences these women had on me.

And now, the rest of the story…

JOYCE CATHERINE PFEIFFER

Joyce and I were married in Claremont, California, on August 22, 1959. We lived in Claremont for a few months before moving to Hollywood to be closer to my new job in downtown LA. Our first child, Scott Douglas, was born on May 5, 1960. In 1961, we rented a house in Pasadena on Holliston Avenue for a year and then moved to a nearby rental house on Estado Street. Heidi Menga was born on May 17, 1963. Later that year we bought a house on Greenhill Road in Pasadena.

We separated in early 1966 and were divorced about a year later. The divorce and settlement were amicable, and we agreed to joint custody of Scott and Heidi.

Joyce and the children moved to Costa Mesa, California, where she pursued a career as a high school language teacher. Sharing the children developed into a friendly, cooperative relationship, and I saw Joyce and the children often.

In 1985, Joyce married Tom Perry, who is now deceased. Joyce retired from teaching in 2000 and lives comfortably in Emerald Bay, California. We have frequent and friendly contact.

My Next Few Decades

The M. Penn Phillips Company was not the same after Joe Karbo left and I didn't see a future there. After only a few months, I joined E. F. Hutton & Company, which was then the second largest stock brokerage firm in the country. The job was as the executive assistant to the managing partner of the western region of Hutton.

The job went well but had some limitations for advancement and I switched to being a stock broker. Eventually, I left Hutton and moved into investment banking and entrepreneurial activities.

Soon I began dating Angela Mary Edge, an English citizen, whom I met through work. We were married in London on June 29, 1968. That autumn we moved into a new home on Sunset Boulevard in Pacific Palisades, California. Emily Kate was born on May 17, 1970, and Tyler Patrick came along on June 7, 1974. Angela and I separated in 1979, and our divorce was final in 1982. We agreed to joint custody of the children, which went smoothly as the children grew up. We have maintained a friendly relationship over the years.

Beginning in 1968, I worked at several different firms and was well rewarded financially. By age thirty-six, a year later than my goal, my net worth exceeded $1 million - a handsome sum in 1968. Due to stock market events in 1969 and 1970, half of that value was lost, and it took another four years to earn it back. So my goal was really not met as intended.

In 1970, I founded A. G. Scheid Inc. as a small investment banking and venture capital operation. Within the first year, half a dozen associates joined the firm and the business prospered. Soon I took in a non-working financial partner for $1 million in cash and the company name was changed to Winkler/Scheid Corp. The firm's business was creating and negotiating business combinations for corporate clients and raising money for medium-sized companies. Fee and commission income exceeded expectations.

In 1972, in partnership with E. F. Hutton, we created a series of limited partnerships for developing wine grape vineyards. Over the next few years, we planted over five thousand acres of vineyards in Monterey County. This became a profitable business for all concerned. The same year, we took ownership of a graphic arts business, which soon became a profitable operation.

About 1979, my money partner had business reversals. E. F. Hutton bought his interests in Winkler/Scheid Corp. and the name of the company was changed to Hutton-Scheid (soon changed to H-S Group). This combination further solidified my close personal relationships with key executives at Hutton.

In February, 1982, E. F. Hutton, two scientists, and I founded California Biotechnology Inc. (CBI). Its purpose was to do research and product development in the then new field of genetic engineering. My job as CEO was to get the company funded and organized before bringing in an experienced drug executive as my replacement. Over $32 million was raised before the company did its $15 million initial public offering in June 1983. At the end of 1985, I left CBI and devoted my time to H-S Group's businesses.

In early 1986, two scientists, two venture capital companies, the Baylor College of Medicine and I became the founders of Houston Biotechnology Inc. in Houston. The game plan was much the same as for CBI. E. F. Hutton helped raise the $31 million needed to finance the company. As part of our business plan, a new CEO was hired in late 1988, permitting me to return full time to H-S Group.

In 1988, E. F. Hutton merged with another stock brokerage firm and I bought their stock in H-S Group, which gave me sole ownership.

By this time, most of the original investors in the vineyard limited partnerships had retired and wanted to liquidate their interests. A program was agreed upon for H-S Group to buy the partnerships one at a time. By 1996 H-S Group had bought out all of the partners' interests and had become sole owner of the 5,000 acres of vineyards planted in Monterey County. The company's name was then changed to Scheid Vineyards Inc. (SVI) and remains so today.

Over time, SVI became a wine producer and now operates both a boutique and a large winery making wine from the grapes grown on the company's vineyards. Three of my four children work in the business, and it operates profitably.

These various ventures were not part of a plan, but I did my best to follow common sense and take advantage of opportunities as they came to hand. It has been an interesting adventure, not yet completed.

Shirley Gladden and I met in December 1988 in Pacific Palisades, where we still reside. We were married in February 1995. Shirley had two children from a previous marriage, and between us, we have fourteen grandchildren. We are fortunate that all of our children and grandchildren are friends and are frequently together at family gatherings.

I feel fortunate that Shirley and my ex-wives, Joyce and Angela, are all friendly, occasionally seeing each other at christenings, birthdays, and other family events.

THE CHARACTERS

Below, roughly in order of appearance in the book, are short after-stories of the village and a few of the people who shared my adventure.

BRIDGEPORT, OHIO—"BEERPORT"

Simultaneously with the decline of the steel and coal industries in the 1960s and 1970s, Bridgeport underwent dramatic physical changes. The I-70 superhighway was built directly through the town. Route 7 was widened, crossing under I-70 in the middle of what had been the business district. These changes literally destroyed the town. Sadly, the old Pastime poolroom, the A&P market, and most other businesses were torn down. The downtown business evaporated.

More buildings were razed to rebuild Main Street into a nearly straight road, eliminating the two ninety-degree turns that the Carlton Bar drunks found so amusing.

In the 1960s, West Virginia dramatically loosened its anti-alcohol laws, which took away the incentives for the people of greater Wheeling to come across the river to imbibe in Bridgeport. At the same time, vigorous enforcement of state antigambling laws killed illegal gambling in Ohio. After these changes, the Fraternal Order of Eagles, Aerie #995, no longer attracted new members and patronage dropped. It struggled on through the 1980s and into the 1990s, but the end was inevitable. It finally closed its doors; the club building was abandoned and became dilapidated. Downtown Bridgeport has ceased to exist in any meaningful way. Only a few bars and stores and the City Building/jail are still in operation.

The village had a nearly two-hundred-year run—from a river bank encampment to an organized, buzzing sin town, to a derelict village. Nothing lasts forever. Only the most senior residents still recall the old nickname of "Beerport."

Wheeling, West Virginia

By the 1970s, downtown Wheeling had also fallen on hard times because of the decline of the steel industry. And, with the development of the enormous Ohio Valley Mall, on I-70, nine miles west of Bridgeport, the bulk of the retail businesses moved there or closed. Downtown Wheeling was largely abandoned, with only a few buildings operating as office rentals. In 2014, there is still very little industrial recovery, although the discovery of shale oil in the area has brought in some new investment.

Virginia (Jake - Gin) Davis – The Long Love Affair

Jake married her longtime lover, Jack Donahie, in 1961 and lived the rest of her life within a few miles of Bridgeport. She and Jack had three children, whom I never met. Jake and I met for lunch (always lunch) whenever I visited the Bridgeport area. We also spoke on the phone nearly every year about the time of our birthdays (ten days apart). By agreement, we never spoke of our love relationship—only about our current lives and children. Passion had died, and we had become old friends. Sadly, after a long illness, she died of cancer on June 28, 1982. She was only fifty-one years old.

Isabelle Adolphine Jonard Scheid Pearce – My Mother

Mom made her home in Southern California and continued to work at various retail jobs until she was about seventy. She finally retired and agreed to accept a home and a monthly stipend from me so she could care for her ailing husband, George, and her elderly mother, Annie Jonard. George preceded her in death about 1982, and Mom developed cancer and passed away at age eighty-six on November 7, 1994.

GEORGE EDWARD SCHEID, JR. – MY FATHER

Dad lived out his life in Bridgeport working at various jobs, finally as a janitor at the Eagles Club, where he had once been president. He had a set routine. After work each day, he had beer and whiskey with a few of his Eagle friends, followed by dinner at a local diner. This routine was usually followed by a few more beers and shuffleboard games at the club or some other bar.

When he was in his sixties, I offered to pay for him to visit my family in Los Angeles. He declined the trip, and it was probably just as well. It was quite likely that he would not have enjoyed being in a strange place, with new people, doing things he'd never done before. He liked his beaten path. Most of our regrets are those of omission, not commission, and I later regretted not pressing him to make the trip and meet his grandchildren.

After working a full day and having his usual drinks, he was taken to the hospital, where he died early in the morning of December 31, 1973. The cause of death was listed as cirrhosis of the liver. He would have been seventy-two in less than a month. Considering his lifestyle, it was a tribute to the Scheid genes that he lived so long.

His funeral was attended by well over a hundred friends, mostly Eagles members. I arranged an open bar at the club after the graveside ceremony, and they all showed up. I knew Dad would have liked this kind of send-off. All attendees got suitably drunk, stories were told, and songs were sung. Young George was well remembered. He had become a town character.

Alfred Jonard – My Grandfather

On October 4, 1965, Grandpa passed away in Adena, Ohio, at age eighty-two. He lived a long life for a man who worked in coal mines from age eight until eighteen and smoked strong cigars all his life. I never really satisfactorily answered his question about how I got from Bridgeport to Harvard—another regret to remember.

Annie Burdess Jonard – My Grandmother

After the death of her husband, Annie lived with my mother in California until passing away at age ninety-eight on July 11, 1986. Annie was still an interesting philosopher and storyteller until her mind began fading at age ninety-five. Her body was taken to Ohio, and she was laid to rest next to her husband.

Wendell Lyle – Best Childhood Friend

Wendell rejoined the US Air Force and remained in it until he retired in the late 1980s. We lost contact but met at a class reunion in 2000, where we reunited like long-lost brothers. We had not seen each other for sixteen years.

Predictably, Wendell was late for the reunion picnic. I tried to bet several classmates that within fifteen minutes of his arrival, he would mention his no-hit game that I threw away. There were no takers; they all knew him too well. He recounted the story almost immediately after arrival, and I agreed with every detail as he told the story. Unfortunately, we never saw each other again.

All those years of cigarettes and booze caught up with Wendell in 2001, at age sixty-nine. He holds a special place in my memories.

Marie Gansler – Jake's best friend

As of 2014, Marie is eighty-three and lives near Wheeling. She and I have stayed in touch and used to meet for lunch when I visit. Unfortunately she now suffers from Alzheimer's disease.

Carl Duncan – bartender, philosopher, and mentor

I had not seen Carl for years when he rode in the limo with me to my father's burial in January 1974. He was the same old Carl. After the ceremony, we talked and had too much to drink at the Eagles Club. We lost touch after that. Carl would be over a hundred if still alive.

Jim Reddy – longtime loyal friend

Jim and his wife Eleanor had a girl and a boy. Jim was employed by the same company his entire working life. I saw the Reddys often during my frequent visits and we remained close friends. Jim died from complications of lung cancer in 2010. Eleanor still lives in Wheeling.

Paul Florence – classmate and Mansfield roommate

Paul met a girl in Mansfield, Ohio, married, and had two children. He remained a carpenter in Mansfield the rest of his life. We kept in touch until he died of cancer about 1995.

Delfred Oliver – Mansfield roommate, close friend, and mentor

After I moved to California, Ollie and I lost contact. By 2014, he would be eighty-three or four. Ollie, if you're out there and you read this, call me—I'm in the phone book.

Les Fiedler – Claremont Men's College roommate

Les graduated from CMC and went to work with his father. The business did not prosper and he became a struggling entrepreneur who never hit it big. Les died of a heart attack about 2002.

James Rohleen – Harvard roommate

Jim moved to California after Harvard, but we didn't stay in touch except for an occasional phone chat. He had a number of jobs in technical sales and marketing. He eventually married and had children. I never met his family. He was struck by a sudden heart attack and died about 1986, at age fifty-three. His father had died at the same age and from the same cause.

James Jackson – closest friend in Navy and for years after

Jim had a successful career as a stockbroker and investor. He is eighty-five, a widower and lives in Colorado and Hawaii. We speak on the phone a few times each year.

Grover Simmons – Navy friend and mentor

Grover married and had two children. He is about eighty-four, in good health, and runs his own political lobbying organization in Portland, Oregon. I am still grateful for the help and advice he gave me when I sorely needed guidance - not to mention party crashing lessons.

Jerry Cassaday – Navy friend and mentor

After some years in the oil business, Jerry became a professional investor. He is married, retired, lives in Long Beach, California, and manages his own investments. He is about eighty-five and, I'm happy to say, in good health. We speak often and have lunch occasionally.

LELAND LEWIS – FRIEND AND JOB FINDER WHEN I NEEDED HIM

Leland and I lost contact while I was in college. After graduating from Harvard, I attempted to locate him but was not successful in that effort.

BILL GLITCH – OLD FRIEND AND MY BUDDY ON THE CROSS-COUNTRY-TRIP-FROM-HELL.

Bill's life is explained at the end of chapter 33.

GENERAL MOTORS ACCEPTANCE CORPORATION – STILL IN BUSINESS

After about ten years, I lost contact with Don Pevehouse, Mr. Chill, and others at the company as they moved on or retired.

WANDA GEPHARDT – GMAC GIRLFRIEND AND ADVISOR

Wanda remarried in the late 1950s, and the last I heard, she was still working at GMAC. If alive, she is now nearly ninety.

JACK CRONKITE – LONG BEACH ROOMMATE AND GMAC BUDDY

Jack was declared dead in 1961, seven years after his disappearance in October 1954. No trace of him or his car was ever found.

SALLY VANWEY – GIRLFRIEND FROM THE DESIRE RANCH DAYS

Sally married, moved to Long Beach, California, and had at least two children. After a few phone conversations, we lost contact in the 1960s.

Riviera Sofa Bed Company – Sofa Bed Manufacturer and Retailer

The company prospered for many years, but changes in the furniture market and competition eventually led to the closing of the retail operation. The name is still in use by a company that repairs and refurbishes overstuffed furniture. It is not known if the Siegel family is still involved.

Claremont Men's College – Now Claremont McKenna College

The college prospered under George Benson's leadership. He was replaced by my classmate Jack Stark, who led the school to even greater success until his retirement. In 2012, *Newsweek* magazine rated CMC as one of the ten best colleges in the United States.

Lee Chamberlain Hanson – College Girlfriend

Lee was married in 1959, divorced, remarried in 1963, and divorced again in 1975. She has an adopted daughter. She completed a PhD in art and taught in the California State University system. She is now retired and lives in Culver City, California. We have remained friends and are in frequent contact.

Laura Braithwaite – Citrus College Teacher and Girlfriend

Laura moved back to Canada around 1958, and I never heard from her again.

M. Penn Phillips – Developer of Speculative Land

By the 2010 census, Hesperia had a population of over ninety thousand. Over fifty years had passed since the successful lot sale programs of the late 1950s and early 1960s. This proved that selling High Desert lots was not purely a land speculation scheme as many people believed. Mr. Phillips and I spoke on the phone a number of times in the 1960s. He became a major contributor to CMC in the 1960s and a building bears his name. He passed away in 1979 at about age ninety-two.

Sue Biely – Girlfriend and M. Penn Phillips's Granddaughter

Sue married and moved with her husband to Florida about late 1959. We didn't stay in touch after I moved back to California.

Joe Karbo – Entrepreneur and Mentor

After leaving M. Penn Phillips, Joe conceived the format of late night TV movies with celebrity interviews and ran his program on a Los Angeles channel for nearly a decade. That led him into a career as a TV commercial personality and pundit. Simultaneously with his TV career, he developed a successful mail order business, primarily selling self-improvement books. Joe and I remained close friends and were in frequent contact until he suffered a fatal heart attack about 1984.

The Boys, Eddy Singer and Danny Kaiserman – Pitchmen, Mentors, and Friends

The Boys continued selling speculative real estate after I left the M. Penn Phillips Company in late 1959. A few years later, Eddy moved to Las Vegas to sell real estate there and we lost contact.

Danny divorced, moved to Orange County, and became a developer of residential property. We didn't stay in touch.

Charlie Wilson – close Bridgeport friend, State Senator and U.S. Congressman

Charlie lost his seat in Congress in 2010 and failed to regain it in 2012. He returned to the furniture and mortuary businesses that had been in his family for four generations. Unfortunately, he suffered a brain hemorrhage and passed away in April of 2013. I was honored to be asked by his family to give the eulogy at his funeral.

Closing

The original title for this book was *Life Is Just an Adventure.* The title *Breaking out of Beerport* came later. The working title was selected because it conveys my belief about mortality. I subscribe to no religion and believe that when a life is over, it's over. Therefore, I don't expect to meet in an afterlife any of the people I have known. In all honesty, however, I would be delighted to discover that I am wrong about this important assumption. Soon I will know the truth—or not.

The End

Made in the USA
Middletown, DE
28 November 2014